OXFORD STUDIES IN CLASSICAL LITERATURE AND GENDER THEORY

General Editors
DAVID KONSTAN   ALISON SHARROCK

Oxford Studies in Classical Literature and Gender Theory publishes substantial scholarly works of feminist literary research, which offer a gender-sensitive perspective across the whole range of Greek and Roman literature, from Homer and Augustine. The series welcomes studies of any genre, whether verse or prose, whether approached thematically or by author. The Editors are particularly keen to encourage feminist readings of texts which have not in the past received much attention from a gender-sensitive perspective. It is expected that contributors to the series will express the theoretical principles that inform their approach, but the series does not impose a single line or monolithic viewpoint. Feminist criticism is understood minimally as presupposing that the mental and moral capacities of women and men are not significantly different, and as recognizing that the explicit or implicit denial of gender equality, including equality of attention, is always a form of 'epistemic violence'. Feminist criticism seeks to redress these imbalances by exposing their operation in patriarchal texts and by illuminating counter-tendencies that affirm women's identities in Classical literature.

Gender, Domesticity, and the Age of Augustus,

Inventing Private Life

KRISTINA MILNOR

OXFORD
UNIVERSITY PRESS

OXFORD
UNIVERSITY PRESS

Great Clarendon Street, Oxford OX2 6DP

Oxford University Press is a department of the University of Oxford.
It furthers the University's objective of excellence in research, scholarship,
and education by publishing worldwide in

Oxford New York

Auckland Cape Town Dar es Salaam Hong Kong Karachi
Kuala Lumpur Madrid Melbourne Mexico City Nairobi
New Delhi Shanghai Taipei Toronto

With offices in

Argentina Austria Brazil Chile Czech Republic France Greece
Guatemala Hungary Italy Japan Poland Portugal Singapore
South Korea Switzerland Thailand Turkey Ukraine Vietnam

Oxford is a registered trade mark of Oxford University Press
in the UK and in certain other countries

Published in the United States
by Oxford University Press Inc., New York

© Kristina Milnor 2005

The moral rights of the author have been asserted

Database right Oxford University Press (maker)

First published 2005

British Library Cataloguing in Publication Data

Data available

Library of Congress Cataloging in Publication Data

Data available

Typeset by SPI Publishers Services, Pondicherry, India
Printed in Great Britain
on acid-free paper by
Biddles, King's Lynn, Norfolk.

0-19-928082-7   978-0-19-928082-7

1 3 5 7 9 10 8 6 4 2

For my father, who taught me to seek knowledge,
and my mother, who showed me what it was for

Preface

THESE days, in Europe and America of the early twenty-first century, we tend to take the language of private morality as a natural, normal aspect of political discourse; we now expect our civic leaders to make repeated reference to the virtues of 'traditional' homes and families—even while they take action in their public and private lives which undermines the very values they espouse. It was this, in part, which led me to this project: I was struck by the eerie coincidence between the terms in which I had been taught to understand the moral restoration of Roman society under Augustus and those which I was reading in the newspaper every day. I had long believed one of the great credos of the feminist movement, that attention needs to be paid to the private sphere and the work, primarily done by women, which allows it to function. The attention which it was receiving from both right and left as 'family values', however, was not what I had had in mind. The family, I knew, was an institution, and thus had all of the merits and difficulties of other institutions. Yet as far as I could tell, the family being described by politicians—in its perfect selflessness, absolute acceptance, and unbreakable bonds of loyalty and love—did not describe the familial experience of anyone I knew, or anyone I had ever met. This in turn led me to wonder, not just what politics lay behind the invocation of domestic values as a civic concern in the modern day, but what lay behind it in the age of Augustus. As a historian, I had long been unsatisfied with the explanations which are traditionally offered for the loud trumpeting of traditional values in early imperial ideology; as a feminist, I distrusted the motives of Roman patriarchy in celebrating women's roles within the home; as a feminist historian, I wanted to know more about the conditions under which ancient Roman women were living and what changes, if any, had accompanied the shift from republican to imperial governance. And as a citizen of modern western civil society, I saw in an investigation of the Augustan period the chance to question, from a historical distance, how and why a culture goes about constructing an idea of the family which is profoundly different from the reality of the family, and how and why that construct may be used to support actions which fly in the face of the genuinely productive values (selflessness, acceptance, loyalty, and love) which it is supposed to represent. It was from these different perspectives, and in furtherance of these different interests, that the following study of gender and private life was produced.

I also wrote this book in a deliberate attempt to engage several different conversations which are already happening within classical studies and in the academy generally: between literary scholars and historians, between philologists and archaeologists, between feminist scholars in other disciplines and those who study the ancient world. My hope was to suggest some different and potentially useful avenues of approach to these conversations, although I also hope that I have made it clear how much I owe to the scholars and scholarship that preceded me. It has always seemed to me, however, that the great power of 'marginal' studies—the study of social identities, texts, and materials which lie outside what has been constituted as the norm—is to challenge not just the content of that norm but its epistemology, that is, not just what we know to be canonical but how we know it. Studies of women and gender in the ancient world have made great strides over the past few decades and have come to be seen by many as a central part of the discipline of classics; this is a great blessing, but I think that it may also have caused us to forget how radical such studies can and perhaps should be. It is actually quite difficult to study the lives of ancient women, who on the one hand left behind so few real traces of themselves, and on the other were the subject of fantasy, speculation, and representation by the men around them. It behoves us, then, to be methodologically creative as we attempt to write ancient women's history—a creativity which, I would argue, may then cause us to look back at 'traditional' methodologies and histories to see them in a different light.

The ideas in this book took their first, hesitant steps in my dissertation, completed at the University of Michigan in 1998. First thanks, therefore, must go to my long-suffering Ph.D. committee, who cajoled, comforted, and counselled me to completion of that version of the project: Sara Myers, David Potter, Susan Alcock, Ann Hanson, and Yopie Prins. I was also blessed at Michigan with some exceptionally fine student-colleagues, especially Molly Pasco-Pranger and John Muccigrosso, whose good influence I hope may still be felt even on this, much later and greatly changed, version of the study. In the intervening years, I have accrued even more debts: to James O'Hara for always sensible advice and insight; to my Columbia colleagues James Zetzel, Gareth Williams, and Alan Cameron, who have all given me the benefit of their vast knowledge of Latin literature; to audiences at New York University, the University of Southern California, and Wesleyan University, who listened with great patience and understanding to early attempts at articulating my ideas. Courtesy of a sabbatical leave from Barnard College, a grant from the American Council of Learned Societies, and the exceptional kindness of Simon Goldhill, I spent the spring and summer of 2002 in residence at King's College, Cambridge, where I completed most of the manuscript's first draft; I cannot sufficiently express my thanks to the students and staff of the classics faculty there, especially Simon Goldhill, Helen Morales, John Henderson, Mary Beard, the late Keith Hopkins, Paul Cartledge, Katie Fleming, Aude Doody, Miriam Leonard, and Richard Fletcher. Due to the vagaries of the publishing process, the final edition of the manuscript was produced while I was a Rome Prize fellow at the American Academy in Rome, researching an entirely different project; thanks are most certainly due to my fellow fellows in 2003–4, especially Elizabeth Marlowe, Mary Doyno, Emma Scioli, Catherine Chin, and Jonah Siegel, for their assistance and support during those last stages of revision. I would also like to express my warmest thanks to Alison Sharrock and David Konstan, editors of this series, and to Hilary O'Shea, Jenny Wagstaffe, and Enid Barker at Oxford University Press, for their advice and guidance through the publishing process; the copyeditor Julian Ward and my indexer Marta Steele have also rendered valuable assistance in the production of this volume.

In addition, my life has been immeasurably enriched both personally and professionally by my colleagues at Barnard College in New York City: Natalie Kampen, Elizabeth Castelli, Nancy Worman, and most especially Helene Foley. I knew what feminism was before I met these women, but I had never before appreciated its full power: they have given me more than they will ever know, and more than I can ever repay. In a similar vein, I would also like to thank Mary Poovey for gifts too numerous to mention, except to say that both her keen intellect and her generous spirit were enormously influential on the later stages of this project. Eric Leach and Bryan Burns, each in his own way, were the *sine quibus non* of these pages. Finally, the critique of 'family values' which appears here should not be taken as evidence that my own familial experience has been a negative one. Far from it: it was my firsthand knowledge that families—and women in them—could be and do far more than they are credited with that gave me the will to write this book. For all they have been, are, and will continue to be, then, I would like to thank my mother, Catherine Milnor; my father, Andrew Milnor; my aunt, Lynn Gioiella; and my sister, brother-in-law, niece, and nephew, Erika, Steve, Phoebe, and Owen Hale.

K.L.M.

Barnard College, New York
February 2005

Contents

Abbreviations

Most of the abbreviations used for the names of ancient authors and their works can be found in the abbreviations list of the *Oxford Classical Dictionary*, 3rd edn. (1996), pp. xxix–liv. The following abbreviations for modern works and journals occur in the main text, footnotes, and References.

AJA	*American Journal of Archaeology*
AJP	*American Journal of Philology*
ANRW	*Aufstieg und Niedergang der römischen Welt*, ed. H. Temporini and W. Haase (Berlin and New York, 1972–)
CIL	*Corpus Inscriptionum Latinarum* (Berlin, 1863–)
CJ	*Classical Journal*
CP	*Classical Philology*
CQ	*Classical Quarterly*
CW	*Classical World*
G&R	*Greece and Rome*
HSCP	*Harvard Studies in Classical Philology*
ILS	*Inscriptiones Latinae Selectae*, ed. H. Dessau, 3 vols. (Berlin, 1892–1916)
JRA	*Journal of Roman Archaeology*
JRS	*Journal of Roman Studies*
LIMC	*Lexicon Iconographicum Mythologiae Classicae*, ed. H. C. Ackermann, J.-R. Gisler, *et al.* (Zurich, 1981–)
MD	*Materiali e discussioni per l'analisi dei testi classici*
OLD	*Oxford Latin Dictionary*, ed. P. G. W. Glare (Oxford, 1982)
PCPS	*Proceedings of the Cambridge Philological Society*
*RIC*²	*Roman Imperial Coinage*, 2nd edn., ed. C. H. V. Sutherland and R. A. G. Carson (London, 1984–)
TAPA	*Transactions of the American Philological Association*
WS	*Wiener Studien*

Introduction

There is a paradox evident in the ideals and ideologies of gender which prevailed in early imperial Rome. On the one hand, Roman society (like many ancient societies) had long believed that women belonged to the domestic sphere, that their highest tasks lay within the household, and that their most praiseworthy roles were those of wife and mother. Yet it is also clear that, building on the social and political prominence which certain elite women had achieved during the final decades of the Roman Republic, early imperial culture opened up new spaces for femininity: women emerge into public discourse as builders and benefactors, patrons and property-owners, authors and important actors on the stage of history. In the Augustan period, we find women—far from being invisible and silent, locked behind the doors of their houses—who are able to take on real and important roles in the civic sphere, without compromising their perceived performance of 'traditional' domestic virtues. This book is about the creation and consequences of this paradox, about how and why the early Empire developed new ways of articulating 'correct' female behaviour, and what those new articulations had to do with the larger cultural transformations of the early Empire.

This study is by no means the first to identify the conflicts and contradictions which adhere to the position of elite Roman women during the first years of Julio-Claudian rule. The question has been approached from two different, and equally productive, angles: first, as an historical issue, pursued through a discussion of individual women whose names survive to us—Livia, Octavia, Plancina,

Julia—and whose activities can be reconstructed from a careful analysis of the textual and archaeological records.[1] These studies have given us important insight into the real, material possibilities which existed for certain women, particularly those of the imperial house, to create a place for themselves within Roman political culture. On the other side, literary scholars have focused on the issue as one of representation, and have therefore looked closely at the powerful images of women found in what might be called 'high' literary texts of the early imperial period: Roman elegy, epic, lyric, narrative history. This kind of scholarship has underscored the fact that it is not just women who were affected by the social and political changes of the period, but also 'women'; not just the actual people, but also the representational category. Thus, although Cynthia, Dido, or even 'Livia' in Ovid's exile poetry, should not be construed as actual historical personages who really did what they are described as doing, nevertheless the female figures found in early imperial texts must be understood as inseparable from the historical moment in which they were born.[2]

It will be seen that I am deeply indebted to both of these schools of scholarly thought. At the same time, however, I would argue that we have not gone far enough in considering how femininity functions as a cultural construct, which both creates and is created by a particular historical context. Joan Scott has long insisted that gender must be understood as no more or less than a category of knowledge, 'a way of organizing the world', which is manifested equally in the factual and imaginative products of a period: 'history and literature are . . .

---

[1] A recent, fine example of this kind of scholarship is Severy (2003); also noteworthy are Dixon (1983) and (2001*a*), esp. 89–112; Hallett (1984*a*), esp. 3–34 and (1989); Purcell (1986); Kampen (1991); the articles of Flory, esp. (1996); and Barrett (1996) and (2002).

[2] The representation of women in Augustan literature has been the subject of a vast quantity of scholarship, such that it is impossible to cite every example. Some noteworthy contributions, however, include: Richlin (1983), esp. 44–56 and 109–16; Hallett (1984*b*); Henderson (1989); Sharrock (1991); Joshel (1992*b*); Gold (1993); Keith (2000); and the essays collected in Wyke (2002).

forms of knowledge, whether we take them as disciplines or as bodies of cultural information.... [When] we take the disciplines as analysts and producers of cultural knowledge, we find that what is at stake is not simply a literary technique for reading but an epistemological theory that offers a method for analyzing the processes by which meanings are made, by which we make meanings.'[3] If we accept this theoretical position, it makes sense to seek the traces of gender ideologies not just in representations of men and women, historical or otherwise, but also in larger social structures, and it is similarly logical to think that changes in one would have causes and effects in the other. My argument here, then, is that, by looking at a set of representations which fall in between the spheres of strict social history and high literary culture, we may identify a particular strand of what we might call 'gendered Augustanism': a set of ideals and ideologies which on the one hand imagined themselves to be beyond the petty rise and fall of political systems, and on the other served as one of the fundamental building blocks of the new imperial state.

In the Augustan vision of the new Roman Republic, the family (especially the emperor's own) and domestic life constituted the central space around which the rest of civic life might be built. It is, of course, a fundamentally paradoxical position, but one which was an inseparable part of the project on which the princeps had embarked: transforming what it meant to participate in the functioning of the Roman state, building a new definition of the *res publica*, making the social and political institutions of a Republic appear to support the idea of one-man rule. That the domestic world of women could be and should be a site of politics, I argue here, was an idea which developed in the course of this redefinition of public and private life, as the state became centred on a single man and a single family. Women as the focal point of the domestic sphere had an important role to play in the new vision of Roman society, as representatives of what the imperial regime had to offer—both an

[3] Scott (1999) 8–9.

imagined return to the unproblematic and virtuous past, and a fresh way of understanding what it meant to participate in Roman public life. The result was an overriding concern with feminine virtue and its locations, an extremely public discussion of the private sphere, a discourse which brought women out into public view even as it described how little they belonged there. It is this discourse, and its ironic consequences, which are described and discussed in the following chapters.

One of the fundamental premises on which this study rests, however, is that Augustus and the political system he created were not just historical facts, but also ideas, which came into being gradually, communally, and with some difficulty. The Augustan age, after all, marked just the beginning of a great cultural experiment, whose outcome was by no means certain and whose success depended on its ability to capture the minds, hearts, and imaginations of a significant portion of the Roman populace. It is no longer necessary to think of the early Empire as a time of totalitarian oppression, when Rome suffered under the imposition of a unitary and uncompromising ideology; rather, we now may understand it as a concept, whose power lay in its ability to set the terms which framed any discussion of politics, society, and culture. That concept, however, did not spring fully-formed onto the Roman political scene when Augustus assumed 'office' in 27 BCE, nor did it cease to be refined when he died forty-one years later. Although, as we will see, some aspects of what would become 'Augustan culture' were already in place by the late 20s BCE, others did not arrive until much later in the princeps' rule. In many ways, in fact, the reification of Augustus and Augustanism as symbols took on greater urgency after they were no longer (strictly speaking) living entities. The reason that the title of this study reads 'Gender, Domesticity, and'—rather than *in*—'the Age of Augustus' is that I wish to treat the last as an idea rather than a chronological moment, so that we may consider its creation as a process, and its historical role as a gradually imagined 'fact' which transformed how Roman politics and society would be understood.

PUBLIC VALUES AND DOMESTIC POLITICS: *AENEID* 8

Although this book focuses on works which have by and large escaped the notice of literary critics, I would like to begin by looking at an illustrative moment in one of the 'highest' of high literary texts. In book 8 of Virgil's *Aeneid*, the poet offers an image which has been called one of the most memorable in the entire work.[4] The smith-god Vulcan has been persuaded by his wife, the goddess Venus, to construct a set of armour for her son Aeneas, armour which the hero will then wear through the final triumphant battle which brings both war and poem to an end. Vulcan, we are told, rises from his bed to set about his work in the small hours of the morning (8. 407–15):

inde ubi prima quies medio iam noctis abactae
curriculo expulerat somnum, cum femina primum,
cui tolerare colo vitam tenuique Minerva
impositum, cinerem et sopitos suscitat ignis
noctem addens operi, famulasque ad lumina longo
exercet penso, castum ut servare cubile
coniugis et possit parvos educere natos:
haud secus ignipotens nec tempore segnior illo
mollibus e stratis opera ad fabrilia surgit.

Then, when the first portion of rest has driven away sleep,
 and the course of
night, pressed on, is halfway done, just at the time when
 first a woman,
to whom the task has been given to support life with distaff and
simple handiwork, stirs up the ashes and sleeping fire,
adding night to her time of work, and she presses
 her serving-women
by firelight to their long daily labour, in order that
 she might be able to preserve

---

[4] R. D. Williams (1973) 255. The translation given below is my own, as are the translations of all other passages quoted, except where otherwise stated.

the chaste bed of her spouse, and bring up her little children:
in the same way and no slower in regard to the time
     did the fire-king
rise from his soft bed and go about his craftsman's tasks.

Although the image has clearly been influenced by similar passages in
Homer and Apollonius of Rhodes,[5] Virgil's use of it has been
understood as a manifestation of his unique poetic vision: 'neither
Homer, nor any known author before Virgil, nor perhaps any since,
would have put it here, or could have touched it to so tender an
issue.'[6] R. D. Williams speaks of its 'sympathy and pathos' and notes
that 'its impact [extends] far beyond its immediate point of comparison';[7] K. W. Gransden, following Pöschl, calls this the 'still
center' of book 8, and notes that, despite the simile's Homeric
pedigree, 'nothing could be more Roman than Virgil's picture of
the chaste Roman matron or widow'.[8] In a similar vein, Susan Ford
Wiltshire sees in the passage a prime example of the conflict between
public and private values which she argues is one of the *Aeneid*'s
primary themes: 'Vulcan's piety will result in the production of
weaponry for war for Aeneas, but the process of its preparation is
compared with the domestic tasks required daily of mothers in order
to raise their young... with this collocation Vergil once again inserts
directly into war and the preparation for war a poignant reminder of
responsibilities to care for the next generation.'[9]

---

[5] Homer, *Iliad* 12. 433 f.; Ap. Rhod. *Argon.* 4. 1062 f. and 3. 291 f. Of course, as
always in the *Aeneid*, there are many ways of interpreting this passage, and its quotation
of the earlier epic models is an important aspect of its meaning: Damien Nelis (2001:
341–5) argues that the simile is part of an attempt by Virgil to link Aeneas' shield to the
Golden Fleece. Nevertheless, I would argue that the simile's appearance here—at the
centre of a book so deeply concerned with the material landscape (on the one hand) and
Roman identity (on the other)—is not accidental, and should not be attributed solely to
Virgil's interest in rewriting his predecessors.

[6] Dr Verrall, in *The National Home-Reading Union*, no. 65, 24 ff., quoted in Fowler
(1917) 4.

[7] R. D. Williams (1973) 255.   [8] Gransden (1976) 138; Pöschl (1962) 170.

[9] Wiltshire (1989) 42–3.

In other words, the image of the hard-working mother and wife in *Aeneid* 8 has been frequently understood in terms of a kind of nostalgic domesticity, as Virgil's tribute to the simple virtues of home and family not terribly well represented in the poem as a whole.[10] Aeneas, after all, has by this point left not one but two wives, or potential wives, dead in his wake, women whose only crime was to impede his progress to Italy and his destined bride Lavinia—who, incidentally, has never met him and may be engaged to someone else. Aeneas' particular domestic difficulties aside, we may also note that the marriage bed more proximate to the passage above is hardly a happy, peaceful, or virtuous one: Venus (called 'a wife . . . pleased with her tricks' at 8. 393) has just manipulated her husband with feminine wiles in order to get the armour she needs for her son, the illegitimate offspring of an extra-marital affair. The only other 'wife' in book 8, moreover, is Cleopatra (*Aegyptia coniunx* at 688), who, along with her monstrous army and illicit paramour Antony, threatens Octavian in the depiction of the battle of Actium which decorates the shield. Indeed, what makes the comparison quoted above stand out so prominently is how inappropriate it is to its context, thematically, stylistically, and narratologically: while it may be true that both Vulcan and the hard-working wife display 'chastity and sacrificial devotion to the well-being of others',[11] we are nevertheless forced to confront and question the connection between the pursuit of humble household tasks in a world of women and the creation of divine weaponry in a forge staffed by monsters. Despite the sentimental appeal of the image in *Aeneid* 8. 407–15, therefore, we must avoid being distracted, and ask instead what connection there is between the simile and its surrounding frame. Why does Virgil choose this moment, in this book, to draw so powerfully on the language of virtuous femininity, household work, and the idea of home?

---

[10] More recently, however, some scholars have called attention to the ironies embedded in the simile here, e.g. Oliensis (1997) 299.

[11] Wiltshire (1989) 113.

Aeneid 8 has been called 'the most Roman of all the books',[12] at least in part because it is the only one which takes place at the (future) site of the actual city. As we are often reminded, Aeneas goes to Italy to found the Roman *people*, not Rome itself, a task which lies many generations in the future with his descendant Romulus. In book 8, however, Aeneas finds himself, through a series of prophecies and coincidences, soliciting the aid of the Arcadian Evander, who has founded a rustic community on the very hills which will someday support the city of Rome. Virgil famously steps back from the narrative moment during his hero's tour of the city to offer a simultaneous view of what the landscape looks like to Aeneas and how it would appear in the future: *hinc lucum ingentem, quem Romulus acer asylum / rettulit ... hinc ad Tarpeiam sedem et Capitolia ducit / aurea nunc, olim silvestribus horrida dumis ... passimque armenta videbant / Romanoque foro et lautis mugire Carinis* ('here [he displays] a huge wood, which fierce Romulus restored as a refuge ... here he leads on to the Tarpeian rock and the Capitolium, now golden, but once bristling with woodland thorns ... and here and there they saw herds of cattle, lowing in the Roman Forum and on the luxurious Carinae': 8. 342–3, 347–8, 360–1). While, therefore, the entire *Aeneid* may be said to be 'about' Roman identity, book 8 is the one most concerned with grounding that identity in the material landscape of the city, as it at once evokes the pastoral countryside that the area was when Aeneas visited, and the imposing urban environment it had become by the time Virgil wrote. The simile of the good housewife, then, would seem to spring naturally from the same concern with space and place which book 8 displays elsewhere; in the same way that the Capitoline hill and the Forum speak forcefully to the civic values of the Roman state, so too does the good home described in the simile underscore the domestic integrity which it prized in private life.

---

[12] Fowler (1917) 2; cf. Putnam (1965: 105–50), and, on the ways in which the book may be seen as a microcosm of some of the poem's larger themes, Zetzel (1997).

Book 8's concern with the meaning of the urban landscape, however, not only marks it as one of the most Roman books in the *Aeneid*, but also one of the most Augustan.[13] Recent critical work has underscored the extent to which, like Virgil in *Aeneid* 8, Augustus understood the material fabric of the city not just in terms of its aesthetic beauty, but as a repository of religious, civic, and moral meaning; hence, his transformation of that environment—the eighty-two temples he restored, the majestic space of the Forum Augustum, the Greek and Latin libraries, the porticoes and their art collections—contributed not just to the beautification of the city, but to the reification of what it meant to be Roman.[14] The connection with Augustus in *Aeneid* 8 is reinforced, moreover, when Aeneas and Evander's tour comes to an end at the rustic hut which the former calls home, located on the Palatine hill and looking out on both the Forum Romanum and the Carinae (the south-west slope of the Esquiline). Scholarly consensus thus places Evander's simple house very close to the same spot later occupied by Augustus himself.[15] Since that later house seems, like its predecessor, to have eschewed luxury in favour of simplicity and a certain archaic plainness, the two are linked in spirit as well as location: Augustus also occupied a modest and unpretentious house on the Palatine, apparently deliberately designed to contrast with the wealth of the public spaces which surrounded it. Evander's words as his guest enters the house, then, serve not just to deliver the message of the tour as a whole, but to interpret the meaning of the simple dwelling on the same site in the age of Augustus: *aude, hospes, contemnere opes et te quoque dignum / finge deo, rebusque veni non asper egenis* ('Dare to look down on wealth, my guest, and consider that you too are equal to a god, and come in not scornful of poor circumstances': 8. 364–5). The poverty of Evander's house is thus given a moral dimension, made to articulate not so much how he must live, but

---

[13] Gransden (1976) 36–7; Boyle (1999) 149.
[14] Zanker (1988), esp. 104–56; Gros (1976) 24–30, 41–4; Nicolet (1991) 41–7; Favro (1996) 79–142, 217–50.
[15] Gransden (1976) 30.

how he chooses to live, and to translate that message of simplicity
and moral rectitude to the world beyond its walls.[16]

This idea, then, that the domestic may 'speak' authoritatively in its
own language of virtue and value is picked up later in the simile of
the good housewife. In the same way that Evander's house—and by
extension, Augustus'—serves a critical role in mapping both moral
and material landscapes of the future city of Rome, so does the image
of the hard-working woman serve as a kind of moral underpinning
for the task which Vulcan is about to undertake. After all, it cannot
be forgotten that the armour which the god creates is not simply a
defence against the coming battle, but serves a grander narrative and
thematic purpose: the shield of Aeneas, the subject of the great
ecphrasis at the end of the book, is the vehicle for Virgil's most
specific and detailed representation of the future of Rome, from
Romulus and Remus to the battle of Actium. In this sense, the work
which Vulcan sets out to do is to 'create' Roman history; as the shield
represents the labours of Aeneas' descendants which drive inexorably
toward the triumph of Augustus, Vulcan's work in constructing the
shield is made parallel to the work which it will take to construct
imperial Rome.[17] If, then, the focus of the earlier part of the book is
on what the material landscape means to Rome, the focus of the
shield is on the men whose deeds will give it meaning.[18] The parallel
between the two sections is reinforced when we note that, like
Aeneas' tour of Rome, the description of the shield ends on the
Palatine: seated in front of the temple of Actian Apollo, Augustus
looks out on the vastness and wealth of the Empire from the same
place where Aeneas turned inward to the simple humility of Evander's house (8. 720–8).[19] Yet the implicit earlier reference to the
princeps' own humble abode in the same place pushes us to remem-

---

[16] On the ideological implications of the passage, see Feeney (1992) 2.

[17] The symbolism of the shield is made explicit by Virgil himself in the final line of
the book, as Aeneas, taking up the shield, is described as *attollens umero famamque et fata
nepotum* ('lifting to his shoulder the story and fates of his descendants': 8. 731). For a
detailed and systematic analysis of the shield as both 'cosmic allegory and political
ideology', see Hardie (1986) 336–75; McKay (1998).

[18] Otis (1963) 332–45.   [19] Binder (1971) 266–7; Hardie (1986) 355–8.

ber that simple domesticity and imperial glory exist side-by-side on the Palatine hill in the age of Augustus, as the two halves of the great complex which was among the first of the new ruler's building projects to be completed.[20] Situated as it is between the tour and the shield, the simile of the good housewife acts as a similar point of connection, weaving together the image of the good home and the work which must be done to make it, looking backward to the material and experiential space outlined in the tour, and forward to the triumphs and sacrifices which will be required to make that space into the city of Rome.

Thus, the simile quoted above, I would argue, does not only imply a contrast or conflict between the labour of women on behalf of the household and that of men on behalf of the state, it also underscores the inextricable connection between the two—between, one might say, the work of social reproduction and that of producing the imperial state. Throughout *Aeneid* 8 we are shown the household as the moral touchstone to which more 'public' discourses about Rome return; at the heart of this most Augustan of Augustan texts, we find not war, or politics, or the public institutions so prized by Roman men, but the world of the household traditionally associated with women, and thus traditionally invisible to the public eye.[21] In many ways, of course, this is completely in keeping with the 'Augustan' nature of the text. The first emperor is famous for having continuously and deliberately focused public attention on what might be called traditional Roman domestic values: the sanctity of marriage, the joy of child-rearing, the importance of women's household tasks. This may be seen not just in his programme of social legislation, which sought to preserve the aristocratic household by means of inducements for those who conformed and punishments for those who did not, but in more personal statements as well. We are told that he read to the Assembly a famous speech by Metellus

---

[20] For a further discussion of the Palatine complex, see Ch. 1, pp. 47–93 below.

[21] On the invisibility of ancient women's work and its significance, see Peskowitz (1997) 62–6.

Numidicus, in which the orator urges marriage and remarks on the necessity of living together with women for the purposes of procreation;[22] on the same subject in a different vein, Cassius Dio has him exclaim to a group of senators during an attempt to repeal his law concerning marriage, 'Is it not the best thing in the world to have a wife who is chaste, domestic, a housekeeper, and a mother of children?...'[23] The most public and ideologically invested artistic products of his reign often contain similar sentiments, from the friezes of the Ara Pacis to Horace's *Carmen Saeculare*, both of which seek to link the success of the new regime with the traditional family structure and the female roles associated with it. The good housewife at the centre of *Aeneid* 8, therefore, is an image very much associated with the princeps and his reign, and the idea of virtuous domesticity which it 'publicizes' circulated in many other places as part of Augustan discourse.

It is now a well accepted scholarly tenet that the period of Augustus' rule encompassed not just a transformation in Rome's political system, but a new and differently constituted emphasis on 'ideas, ideals, and values'.[24] Of course, the old Republic was no stranger to moral language in the public sphere: this was a political system, after all, which both spawned and celebrated Cato the Elder, and quite frequently, especially after the end of the second Punic war in 203 BCE, attempted to regulate such 'moral' social problems as private consumption and luxurious displays of wealth.[25] On the other hand, the extent to which Roman mores came to dominate political, social, and artistic conversations under Augustus is unprecedented, and has become an important topic of debate among those scholars who seek to analyse the period in more than purely constitutional terms—as a shift not just in governmental structure, but in

---

[22] Aulus Gellius provides the fragment, 1. 6. 2; the story that Augustus read the speech to the people is reported in Suetonius (*Div. Aug.* 89. 2) and Livy (*Per.* 59).

[23] πῶς μὲν γὰρ οὐκ ἄριστον γυνὴ σώφρων οἰκουρὸς οἰκονόμος παιδοτρόφος;... (Cass. Dio 56. 3. 3).

[24] Galinsky (1996) 8.

[25] On moral regulation in the Republic, see Baltrusch (1989), esp. 5–30.

the way that Romans perceived themselves and the world around them. Roman historians themselves almost universally understood the chaos at the end of the Republic as having been brought about by a decline in traditional values, which does not make it true but does mean that there was a certain urgency at the time to see them restored. But both the univocality of the writers of the time, and our own different understanding of historical causality, have made modern scholars suspicious of the moral explanation of the rise of the imperial state. Andrew Wallace-Hadrill has observed that the very universality of moralizing language in all aspects of the Augustan age ought to make us wary: 'We may take some comfort in being offered by the Romans a conceptual structure that allows itself to be employed so holistically, and which encourages the idea that politics, religion, family life, public and private morality, rhetoric and literary activity and the visual arts might all move together under some common transforming impulse. But it would make a poor basis for our own analysis.'[26]

Wallace-Hadrill is certainly right to insist that we should not take the Romans at their word, and that we must look deeper into the various discourses which made up Augustan culture to discover what larger political purposes they served. We are also, I hope, past the point where we think that we can, or should, look for a single explanation of what happened—ideologically, socially, culturally—to the Roman state under Augustus. On the other hand, I do not think that we have yet fully come to terms with the representation of the first emperor as moral reformer, a representation whose power is attested by its persistence, from antiquity to the twentieth century. It is only in recent years that we have begun to consider the ways in which morality and immorality are not absolutes but constructs, built to serve the particular ideological needs of particular social systems operating at particular moments in time.[27] Scholars have

[26] Wallace-Hadrill (1997) 11.
[27] A central theoretical text in this area is M. Foucault's *History of Sexuality* (1978–86), whose later volumes owe much to earlier work in classics such as Kenneth Dover's *Greek Homosexuality* (1978). For the early Roman Empire particularly, see Earl (1967), esp. 59–79; Edwards (1993) 34–62; Roller (2001) 17–126.

thus become quite rightly suspicious of the 'traditional values' which Augustus sought to promote, as well as his interest in promoting them. We have perhaps been influenced (as were some of the most famous Roman historians of the twentieth century) by our own recent history, and the vision of states whose focus on private virtue goes hand in hand with their performance of public atrocities.[28] This is not to say that I subscribe to the image of Augustus as Hitler, or even to the idea of imperial Rome as a totalitarian state; rather it is to emphasize that most statements on the part of governmental systems are highly self-interested—even, or perhaps especially, when they draw on the language of a transcendent, timeless, and supposedly *dis*interested moral system. But although we have begun to see the rebirth of traditional values under Augustus as something more than a real response to a real social problem, we have not yet fully explained how and why that rebirth was so tightly bound up with the idea of the first emperor, and with the social, political, and cultural changes which he brought to the Roman state.

It is here, I think, that a feminist reading of Augustan culture may help us. There have been a number of cogent and compelling arguments put forward in recent years which attempt to explain the importance of 'values discourse' to the early Empire. Some scholars have argued that the supposed moral rehabilitation under Augustus was part of legitimating him as the best, most virtuous, ruler of Rome, and Rome (correspondingly) as the most virtuous ruler of the Empire—an idea which certainly conforms to what we know of imperial ideology generally.[29] Yet, as Catherine Edwards has pointed out, certain elements in the Augustan programme of moral rebirth would seem to work against this message as much as for it: on the *lex Iulia de adulteriis*, she asks, 'how could a state be thought virtuous where adultery, to be controlled, had to be made a criminal offense? How could husbands be imagined strong and vigilant, if the

---

threat of punishment was necessary to make them exercise proper control over their own households?'[30] Aware of such contradictions, other critics have turned to the more subtle effects of an ideology which effectively focuses the public's attention on an inner, private world of personal morality rather than the external world of civic participation—a means, as they would have it, of transforming what it meant to be a 'good' Roman citizen in an age where the emperor's power had made traditional republican virtues obsolete.[31] Thus, many scholars see the Augustan reform of private values, best expressed in the legislation governing marriage and childbearing in 18–17 BCE, as a means of breaking the will and power of the Roman aristocracy, a sinister and cynical appropriation for the state of the last bastion of individual self-determination.[32] Again, such explanations have a certain amount to recommend them, especially since they help us to understand not just why Augustus did what he did, but why the Roman aristocracy let him get away with it.

What such analyses fail to explicate, however, is the prominence of virtuous femininity in Augustan moral discourse. If the fundamental idea behind early imperial ideology was a redescription of the role of the citizen, why did so much of it focus on those who had no formal role in public life? Why was it the virtue of daughters, wives, mothers, and sisters, rather than that of sons, husbands, fathers, and brothers, that became the focus of public attention? It will be, indeed has been, argued that we find here femininity used as a metaphor for private life, so that, by turning attention to women, Augustus was actually asking Romans to contemplate the part of their lives which lay outside politics as a matter of public concern. Part of the problem with this view is its dependence on a post-enlightenment romance with 'the private individual' and his (emphatically his) right to have a realm unburdened by the demands of the public sphere—a model which has seen a great deal of criticism,

[30] Edwards (1993) 61.
[31] Which is the argument of Raditsa (1980) 281–3, 330–9; see also Habinek (1998) 137–50; Foucault (1986) 69–96; Roller (2001) 124–6.
[32] See, for instance, Dettenhofer (2000) 133–44.

especially from feminist theorists. But more critical for our purposes is the fact that the idea of the home as a sanctuary generally flies in the face of what we know about republican civic life, a great deal of which was conducted within the 'private' space of the house and through such 'private' relationships as that between patron and client. The view, therefore, that representations of feminine virtue in early imperial ideology are merely a back way into the private lives of Roman citizens needs to be re-examined and refined; we need, in short, to be more precise about what we mean when we speak of 'private life', and how we understand the relationship between that construct and the domestic virtues with which it may or may not be synonymous.

PUBLIC, PRIVATE, AND THE ROMAN EMPIRE

It is only recently that the construction of private life in antiquity has been understood as a distinct scholarly problem. Certainly, it has long been clear that, like the modern West, the ancient Greeks and Romans understood the public/private dichotomy to be a fundamental concept for thinking about the structure of society: from Plato's *Republic* to Augustine's *City of God*, we possess a wide array of ancient texts which attempt to explore, comprehend or delineate the proper relationship between the home and the city, between the world of the individual household and that of the wider community. Correspondingly, the 'private lives' of the ancients have been a popular subject of scholarly investigation since the eighteenth century.[33] But historically scholars have taken the constitution of the private sphere as a given, no different in antiquity than it is in the present moment. The last decades of the twentieth century, however, saw increasing interest in, and criticism of, current western understandings of privacy and their origins in modern capitalism, industrialization, and contemporary ideas of citizenship and good

---

[33] On the changing models which classical scholars have employed to discuss ancient private life, see Nippel (1998); Wagner (1998); Katz (1995) and (1998).

government. Using the theoretical models developed principally by Hannah Arendt and Jürgen Habermas, scholars have argued that the public and private spheres as they are currently understood in Europe and America are the product of the eighteenth and nineteenth centuries, the rise of republicanism, and the development of the market economy.[34] Privacy, moreover, has in recent decades become a hot subject of popular debate: in the United States the 'right to privacy' has been brought to bear on everything from reproductive rights to wage controls.[35] In the US and Europe, the 1980s and 1990s saw some rather explosive debates over whether a politician's 'private' life should have meaning for his 'public' career, debates which in turn engendered discussion about what these two terms actually mean in contemporary civil society.[36] In short, modern privacy is the subject of much discussion, but emphatically within a modern conceptual frame; it is generally agreed that what makes the public/private dichotomy meaningful in our own day are our own civic, economic, and social structures.

These facts have not gone unnoticed by scholars of classical antiquity. The last few decades have seen the rise of a lively debate, particularly among French and Italian scholars, about how, why, and where we should use the words 'public' and 'private' to describe the ancient world.[37] The work of J.-P. Vernant on the relationship

---

[34] The two central theoretical texts are Arendt's *The Human Condition* and Habermas's *The Structural Transformation of the Public Sphere*. In their brief histories of the public/private dichotomy in the West, both make reference to the ancient world, but pass quickly from 'the Greeks' to the rise of feudalism. For some feminist responses to the two, see Benhabib (1998) and Honig (1998).

[35] Struening (2002: 36–42) identifies three kinds of privacy which have currency in modern US law: privacy as economic freedom, which governs the right of individuals and corporations to conduct business free of government interference; privacy as family autonomy, which defends the right of the head of a household to conduct matters within the family as he or she chooses; and privacy as personal liberty, which guarantees the individual the ability to make autonomous decisions about his/her own life.

[36] Thus, for instance, many of the papers published in Abe *et al.* (1999) make reference to the Bill Clinton–Monica Lewinsky scandal which was occupying the American media at the time.

[37] See, for instance, the articles published in *Ktema* 23 (1998), a special issue on 'Public et Privé en Grèce Ancienne'.

between individual and community in the Greek world—from Homer to the classical *polis*—has been particularly provocative,[38] as has that of Michel Foucault on the development of 'private life' as an alternative to traditional public roles under the Roman Empire.[39] We are fortunate, as always, to possess the work of the great political theorists from ancient Athens, whose analyses may be seen to speak directly to the question.[40] The archaeology and material details of 'private life' in ancient Greece have not historically been as accessible, although there have been some recent contributions using material from sites such as Olynthos and Delos.[41] The Romans, correspondingly, left us with less theory but more details, present particularly in the sites around the bay of Naples buried so catastrophically in 79 CE. Thus, the discussion of 'private life' in ancient Italy has generally been dominated by social history and archaeology. Andrew Wallace-Hadrill's work on Pompeian houses has been remarkably influential, and has led to a serious re-evaluation of how we assign words like 'private' to the spaces of the *domus*.[42] Annapaola Zaccaria Ruggiu's exhaustive *Spazio Privato e Spazio Pubblico nella Città Romana* laudably attempts a multi-disciplinary approach to the question, using everything from legal texts to architectural theory to material remains in an effort to 'map' the ancient Roman city.[43]

The range of methodological approaches which have been brought to bear on investigating the construction of private life in antiquity is testimony to the breadth, importance, and difficulty of the topic. Part of the problem is that 'private' is a term which had in antiquity, and still has today, a wide semantic range: it means one thing on a material and experiential level—'this is a private office' means that physical access is denied to the general public; something slightly different when applied to social structures—the right to privacy is the right to be free from governmental interference; and

---

[38] e.g. Vernant (1989).   [39] Foucault (1986).
[40] On which, see Swanson (1992).
[41] For example, Nevett (1999) and Siebert (1998).
[42] Wallace-Hadrill (1994*b*).
[43] Ruggiu (1995); cf. the comments of Riggsby (1999).

something different again when it describes an individual—my 'private feelings' are not necessarily feelings which I do not share with anyone else but emotions which are particular and personal to me. The difficulties which this creates are bad enough when we are dealing with our own culture and our own language; in the case of antiquity we are hampered both by facts which are not available and by our inability to understand the ones which are. In the case of Greek texts, a great deal of interesting and productive work has been done simply to determine which words we should be translating as 'public' and 'private', as well as what (if anything) the absence of such terms might mean.[44] In Latin, we are blessed, or cursed, by etymology, as both words have specific cognates which seem, at least on the surface, to overlap neatly with our own use of the corresponding terms. The adjective *publicus* and its linguistic relatives appear to be derived from *populus* ('the people')[45] and thus may mean both 'of the people' generally or 'of the people's government' specifically. The *res publica* is, of course, 'public business' which comes to signify 'the state'; this is why (a fact confusing to students) the government in Rome is still called *res publica* in Latin even when it is no longer in English a republic.

The case of *privatus* is more convoluted. The Romans employed a nexus of different words derived from the root *privo*, 'to cause to be parted (from), deprive or rob (of)': the adjective *privatus, -a, -um*, meaning 'private' as in private or personal property; the noun *privatus, -i*, m., meaning 'a private person' as opposed to a magistrate or official; the adverb *privatim* meaning 'privately' or 'individually'. As I said, there is a general correspondence between the Latin words and our own use of their cognates, but it is worth noting the original Latin derivation. Whereas we in the modern world think of the public and private spheres as coordinated halves of a single whole, *privatus* in the first instance only held meaning in opposition to the

---

[44] Casevitz (1998).

[45] The *OLD* cites a number of early forms, such as *poblicai* in *CIL* i. 397 and *poplicod* in 1. 581.15 which make the evolution of the word clear.

sphere of politics—it meant, literally, to be deprived of it. For the Romans, at least originally, to be private was to be 'apart from' the community, the affairs of the state, the spaces of civic life. As Isidorus says, *dicti privati quod sint ab officiis curiae absoluti* ('people are called *privati* because they have been released from the duties of senate service').[46] *Privatus*, then, even though it would go on to have more, and more nuanced, meanings, began life as a political term, and would continue to have real and powerful significance when used in the context of public life.

I do not intend to offer here a survey of the uses of *privatus* and its cognates in Roman literature or history. As I noted, it is a complicated term and, at least by the time the majority of our texts were written, encompasses a wide range of meanings. On the other hand, I would like to point out one usage which creeps into its semantic sphere during the first centuries CE and which, I would argue, suggests a real shift in at least one of its modes of meaning. Under the Republic, as I said, a *privatus* was defined as a man without a political or military position; thus, a character in Plautus' *Captivi* might sigh, *hic qualis imperator nunc privatus est* ('this man, who was once such a triumphant general, now is a private citizen': 166). Under the high Empire, however, we find that it came to be used of anyone, regardless of political or military position, who did not hold the ultimate 'public' role of emperor. Thus, for instance, Tacitus represents Domitian as jealous of the general Agricola's successes in Britain, *id sibi maxime formidolosum, privati hominis nomen supra principem adtolli* ('this was especially irksome to him, that the name of a private individual was raised above that of the emperor': *Agric.* 39.2).[47] Pliny the Younger writes of his contemporary Verginius Rufus, *perfunctus est tertio consulatu, ut summum fastigium privati*

---

[46] Isidorus, *Origines* 9. 4. 30. Maltby (1991) 496.

[47] Again, in the *Histories*, he sums up the difference between Galba's successes holding office in the provinces with his failures as emperor, *maior privato visus dum privatus fuit, et omnium consensu capax imperii nisi imperasset* ('while a *privatus* he seemed greater than a *privatus*, and everyone would have agreed that he was capable of holding imperial power had he not assumed it': *Hist.* 1. 49).

hominis impleret, cum principis noluisset ('He completed a third consulship, so that he achieved the highest rank of a private individual, since he did not wish to hold that of princeps': *Ep.* 2. 1. 2). He later defends the fact that he himself has composed and performed some humorous poetry—an act which has apparently been criticized as unworthy of his position—by reference to some famous predecessors (*Ep.* 5. 3. 5):

ego verear ne me non satis deceat, quod decuit M. Tullium, C. Calvum, Asinium Pollionem, M. Messalam, Q. Hortensium, M. Brutum, L. Sullam, Q. Catulum, Q. Scaevolam, Servium Sulpicium, Varronem, Torquatum, immo Torquatos, C. Memmium, Lentulum Gaetulicum, Anneaum Senecam, et proxime Verginium Rufum et, *si non sufficiunt exempla privata*, divum Iulium, divum Augustum, divum Nervam, Tiberium Caesarem?

Shall I then fear that this does not befit me, this thing that was fitting for Cicero, C. Calvus, Asinius Pollio, M. Messala, Q. Hortensius, M. Brutus, L. Sulla, Q. Catulus, Q. Scaevola, Servius Sulpicius, Varro, Torquatus, in fact all of the Torquati, C. Memmius, Lentulus Gaetulicus, Annaeus Seneca, and recently Verginius Rufus, and—*if these private examples are not sufficient*—the deified Julius, deified Augustus, deified Nerva, and Tiberius Caesar?

The catalogue begins with some of the great public figures of the late Republic, from Cicero to Hortensius to Sulla, and continues up to some of those in Pliny's own day, including the three-times consul Verginius Rufus mentioned earlier. Indeed, he makes a comment a few sentences later in the letter which makes it clear that he has chosen them specifically because all were senators, unlike Virgil, Cornelius Nepos, Accius, and Ennius (5. 3. 6). Yet all of them are grouped together under the description *privata exempla*, in explicit contrast with the imperial figures who comprise the end of the list. Despite all of their civic, military, and political accomplishments, these men who were not sole rulers of Rome have not, for Pliny, transcended the designation 'private citizen'; only dictators and emperors, it appears, are fully public figures.

The idea that the advent of imperial rule occasioned the rise of a new vocabulary of public life is not an especially new one, nor is it especially surprising. It is curious, however, to see how broad the use of the term *privatus* has become, as it encompasses meanings which would have been literally incomprehensible two centuries earlier. It is also curious (and not, I think, coincidental) that this phenomenon is in a very real sense the legacy of one of the great *privati* in Roman history, namely the young man who was to become the emperor Augustus. In contrast with his adopted father Julius Caesar, Octavian was catapulted by circumstances and (perhaps) native ability onto the public stage at the age of 19, before he had had the chance really to begin the traditional *cursus honorum* of appointed or elected posts; a true *privatus*, he held no official position when he led his army against the tyrannicides. This does not seem to have concerned him—indeed, it is clear that, at a certain point, Augustus put a fair amount of effort into claiming the term *privatus* for his own use.[48] This can be seen in the first sentence of the *Res Gestae*, the princeps' own description of his public career and one of the most carefully crafted pieces of Augustan propaganda: *annos undeviginti natus exercitum* privato consilio et privata impensa *comparavi, per quem rem publicam a dominatione factionis oppressam in libertatem vindicavi* ('At the age of 19, I put together an army, *by my private initiative and at my private expense*, by means of which I freed the Roman state which had been subjugated by the tyranny of a small group': *RG* 1. 1). Strictly speaking, of course, Augustus is here confessing to a crime: as a *privatus*, he had no standing or power to raise an army and lead it against the tyrannicides. But the point is in the very contrast between the unauthorized but outraged young man and the powerful political 'faction' against which he moved. Octavian may have held no civic or military position, but he followed a higher law, in which he found the strength to work for the state against more official, but less legitimate, public authorities.

Indeed, the fact that Octavian took his first, dramatic, political steps as a *privatus* seems to have occasioned some anxiety in Cicero,

---

[48] Béranger (1958); Yavetz (1984) 8.

who spends much of the Philippics generally, and especially *Philippic* 3, urging the senate to legitimate the youth's actions against Antony by conferring its authority. Thus, he asks at 3. 3, *quo enim usque tantum bellum, tam crudele, tam nefarium privatis consiliis propulsabitur? cur non quam primum publica accedit auctoritas?* ('For how long will so great a war, so cruel and so criminal, be averted by private means? Why is public authority not added to them as soon as possible?'). He goes on to remark, in a passage which may in fact be echoed in the *Res Gestae: qua peste privato consilio rem publicam (neque enim fieri potuit aliter) Caesar liberavit . . . cui quidem hodierno die, patres conscripti . . . tribuenda est auctoritas, ut rem publicam non modo a se susceptam, sed etiam a nobis commendatam possit defendere* ('From such a plague Octavian freed the Republic, by private initiative (for it could not have been done otherwise) . . . thus surely today, senators, . . . authority must be given to him, so that he should be able to defend the Republic not just as a task taken on by himself, but as one entrusted to him by us': 3. 5). In other words, the senate is behind the times. Having neglected its job in the first instance, it lost the role of defending the state to the vast private resources of Octavian; now it must quickly put the boy under its own flag, lest public authority lose its standing altogether. In hindsight, we may see that it was already too late, for both Cicero and the senate, and that Octavian was already well on his way to becoming princeps; but the great orator nevertheless deserves some credit for recognizing the terms in which the battle would ultimately be fought.

Ironically, Cicero himself had earlier sketched in theoretical outline the principle later concretely followed by Octavian. Repeatedly in his extant speeches and philosophical texts he speaks with admiration of Scipio Nasica, who took it upon himself as a *privatus* to assassinate Tiberius Gracchus, a public menace; it is a neat historical irony that his earliest use of the example is in the first Catilinarian, to underscore how much greater is his own authority to execute Catiline.[49] In fact, before the death of Caesar and the rise of Octavian,

---

[49] *Cat.* 1. 3; cf. *Planc.* 88, *Brut.* 212, *Tusc.* 4. 51, *Off.* 1. 76. Zetzel (1995) 201–2.

Cicero made it rather brashly clear in the *de Re Publica* that some-times even a *privatus* can, or must, serve a public function. Praising the actions of Brutus the regicide, he remarks (*Rep.* 2. 46):

tum vir ingenio et virtute praestans, L. Brutus, depulit a civibus suis iniustum illud durae servitutis iugum. qui cum privatus esset, totam rem publicam sustinuit primusque in hac civitate docuit in conservanda civium libertate esse privatum neminem.

then a man outstanding in intelligence and virtue, Lucius Brutus, took from his fellow citizens the unjust yoke of harsh slavery. Although he was a private citizen, he bore the burden of the whole state, and was the first in this nation to teach that, in regard to preserving the liberty of citizens, no one is a *privatus*.

The point is that all good men, in or out of office, are responsible for the functioning of the state and the safety of their fellow citizens,[50] a staunch and unobjectionable republican sentiment. It is sobering, therefore, to see how neatly and easily Octavian might turn the same idea—that in the service of a higher good a private individual may transcend the strictures of public life—into the basis of his rise to supreme power. I am by no means arguing that Octavian modelled his career, or even his description of his career, on Cicero's words in the *de Re Publica*; rather, I would say that Cicero represents the extent to which the role of the *privatus* was already in question even before the unknown 19-year-old arrived on the political scene, as well as the extent to which Octavian's pursuit of his *privatum consilium* could be made to fit established republican ideology.

Octavian, of course, did not stay a *privatus* for long, either actually or textually. Historically, the senate did indeed throw its weight behind him, and, following his victory over Antony at Mutina, the young man was made consul. Reflecting this swift metamorphosis, the word also disappears from the *Res Gestae* after the first sentence, returning only as an economic term, to emphasize the personal expenditures of the princeps on building the temple of Mars Ultor

---

[50] Cf. *Rep.* 1. 7–8, 1. 12.

and the theatre of Marcellus (*in privato solo... in solo magna ex parte a privatis empto*; 'on private ground... on ground for the most part purchased from private individuals': *RG* 21). Of course, the use of the word here may serve to remind the reader of its earlier appearance, and to underscore the fact that the temple (at any rate) was built to celebrate the successful completion of the personal vendetta which had brought the *privatus* Octavian to prominence in the first place: vengeance against the murderers of his adopted father, Julius Caesar.[51] But the 76-year-old Augustus who authored the text (thirteen times consul, awarded tribunician power, designated *pater patriae* or 'father of the country' by universal acclaim) is a long way from that young man. Indeed, as we have seen, the position of emperor which Augustus cobbled together in 27 BCE would become incorporated into the Roman system as the ultimate 'public' one—so public, in fact, that it came to trump all others. Yet the appearance of the adjective *privatus* so prominently at the beginning of the *Res Gestae* indicates the extent to which this process began with a thematization, not of politics, but of private life; Augustus would not allow anyone to forget that he started off outside the system, as a young man whose actions were motivated by personal grief rather than political ambition.

In sum, then, apart from whatever other difficulties we may see in attempting to define 'private' in the early imperial state, we are also faced with the fact that at least one aspect of the term was undergoing a transformation, under the pressure of imperial ideology.[52] Octavian *privatus* was to become Augustus *imperator*, a journey which is mapped in the *Res Gestae*. Indeed, it has been noted that the double use of *privatus* in the opening sentence of the text is meant to contrast with its closing paragraph, where the hero is awarded the title *pater patriae* and other unprecedented honours by the senate; thus, the text traces his career from untried boy to

---

[51] Ramage (1987) 93.

[52] Wallace-Hadrill (1982*b*) outlines some of the ways in which, throughout the first century of the imperial period, there continued to be a certain representational tension between the emperor as private citizen and as ultimate public figure.

transcendent public figure.[53] The very terms of that transcendence, however, offer some insight into the ideological processes which made it possible. Even though the appellation 'parent of the nation' had been both formally and informally awarded before,[54] the *Res Gestae* underscores its meaning by associating it with particular places: the text notes that the senate, the equestrian order, and the people of Rome not only awarded the title, but caused it to be inscribed three times, in the Curia Julia, in the Forum Augustum beneath the triumphal chariot which anchored the space, and in the vestibule of Augustus' house (*RG* 35. 1). The places correspond to the different aspects of Roman society on which the title touches, the civic in the Curia Julia where the senate met, the military in the representation of Augustus *triumphator*, and the private or domestic in the reference to Augustus' house.[55] Indeed, the house appears twice in the final paragraphs of the *Res Gestae*, as the site for the display of laurel wreaths and the *corona civica* (awarded for having saved the life of a Roman citizen) in 34. 2, and as the place for the *pater patriae* inscription in 35. 1. The house is also closely associated with the *clupeus virtutis* (whose dedication in the Curia Julia is also recorded in 34. 2)—and especially the last of its four major virtues, *pietas*. If the point, therefore, of the opening of the *Res Gestae* is that a private individual may have a role in defending the public good, the closing of the text makes the same point in reverse: here we see the private space of the *domus* as the appropriate medium to display public honours. Octavian the good son to Julius Caesar, moreover,

---

[53] Ramage (1987) 20.

[54] For an exhaustive anaylsis of the history and significance of the term, see Alföldi (1971).

[55] This point is made by Ramage (1987: 84–5), although he would make *in vestibulo aedium mearum* into a religious reference, due to Augustus' dedication of part of his house to Vesta in 12 BCE. This seems a little tenuous to me. Especially given the connection which Augustus sought to draw between *pater patriae* and *paterfamilias* (see Strothmann (2000: 73–80) for a discussion), as well as the importance of the domestic in Augustan ideology generally, the house here seems more likely to be evoking the familial structures which the princeps both sought to defend and to use as the basis of his authority. Of course, there was certainly a religious element to the role of *paterfamilias*, which is no doubt also evoked here. Cf. Severy (2003) 208.

has been transformed into Augustus the good father of the Roman nation. What I described earlier as the thematization of private life is no longer simply a matter of redefining the word *privatus*, but has broadened within the text of the *Res Gestae*, so that both the space and the language of domestic relationships are included as a part of the emperor's public persona.

FROM PRIVATE TO DOMESTIC: ENGENDERING THE AUGUSTAN AGE

On this level, then, the story which the *Res Gestae* tells depends on the separation of 'private' from 'domestic'; Augustus as the representative of household virtue is still very much alive at the text's conclusion even though Octavian the private citizen has long since perished. This division is possible at least in part because of the different semantic fields of the two terms: whereas *privatus* is necessarily a political word, having meaning only in contrast with the public sphere, the domestic is much broader, and comes associated with a particular set of values which may be brought forward as one aspect of a public identity. The domestic thus functions as a kind of moralized privacy, a concept whose strength lies in its allegiance to supposedly transcendent and apolitical ethical truths. If one of the tasks of the new imperial government was to find a way for Rome, in the aftermath of civil war, to imagine herself once again as a community of shared values, the domestic sphere offered an uncontroversial place to focus public attention—a place where tradition, virtue, and the nostalgic comforts of home might be invoked as the basis of a renewed sense of national purpose.[56] After a hundred

[56] The phrase 'imagined communities' is the title of a famous book by Benedict Anderson (1991), on the development of the discourse of nationalism in the 18th and 19th cents. Although Anderson does not discuss either gender or morality as technologies through which an idea of nationhood may be constructed, he does underscore the importance of 'disinterestedness' as an attribute of an imagined community ('for most ordinary people of whatever class the whole point of the nation is that it is interestless. Just for that reason, it can ask for sacrifices': p. 144).

years of struggle between political factions, during which time the
streets of Rome sometimes literally ran with blood, Rome was ready
to believe in a representative of more universal principles: kindness,
generosity, loyalty to an ideal of family which everyone might share,
rather than to a conflictual world of politics predicated on the
triumph of one group over another.[57]

In some senses, this is not entirely dissimilar to the argument
which has been made about the rise of domesticity and the ideology
of separate spheres in Europe and America during the nineteenth
century. Mary Poovey has described the process by which, during
this period, 'virtue was depoliticized, moralized, and associated with
the domestic sphere, which was abstracted at the same time—both
rhetorically and, to a certain extent, materially—from the so-called
public sphere of competition, self-interest, and economic aggression.'[58] In other words, the rise of modern capitalism in its ugliest
forms entailed the creation of a different space where the work of
emotion, nurturing, and spiritual guidance might be done; the
middle-class domestic ideal thus came into being as a way of absolv-
ing the bourgeoisie of responsibility for moral behaviour in the
worlds of work and politics. Ancient Rome, of course, was built on
a different economic and political system from that of Victorian
England, but nevertheless such analyses of more recent history may
help us to think about the different ways in which social values may
be organized, and what changes in that organization, or in descriptions of that organization, may tell us about the 'ideological work'
done by constructions of the public and private spheres. Similarly,
discussions of the nineteenth century may also serve to alert us to the
conflicts and complications built into a domestic discourse which is
developed in the public arena: along with the Victorian period, the
Augustan age also saw a 'thrusting outward of an inward turning,
the eruption of family life into the light of unrelenting public

---

[57] Yavetz (1984: 4–5) comments on the ways in which Augustus' *Res Gestae* offers a
vision of the princeps as moral exemplar calculated to reassure war-weary Romans.
[58] Poovey (1988) 10. See also Armstrong (1987) 40–1, and Davidoff (1998).

discussion',[59] a process whose very contradictions should alert us to its significance. Rather than seeing an obsessive rhetorical return to 'correct' domestic virtue as, in any sense, a natural concern of government, we must recognize this move in its sinister strangeness, and see its connection to shifts in other political, social, and cultural formations.

The other contribution which scholarship on the nineteenth century may make to an analysis of the early Roman Empire is to focus our attention on questions of gender. The Victorian period left us innumerable images of virtuous femininity, including the famous 'angel in the house', the spiritual guardian and emotional touchstone of nineteenth century civil society. The Romans shared with the Victorians, as well as many other ancient Mediterranean societies, a tradition of dividing gender roles along the line between the public and private spheres. While men were trained for and expected to participate in civic and military life, ideals of correct womanhood emphasized domesticity, and the skills needed to run an efficient household. Lactantius provides an epitome of Cicero's *de Re Publica* 3, where the orator-turned-philosopher criticizes Plato's vision of a communal society, in which everything is shared by everyone: 'indeed, he does not even debar women from the Senate House, and allows them to be in the military, and in the magistracies, and in supreme command. How great will be the misfortune of that city, in which women assume the offices of men!'[60] Scholars frequently cite the evidence of funerary inscriptions, which praise, along with modesty and obedience, wives' skill in tending children and working with wool.[61] The epitaph of Claudia, dating from the second century BCE, is typical: it lists the dead woman's affection for her husband, her two sons, her grace in movement, and her gentle speech, concluding *domum servavit, lanam fecit* ('she kept her house,

[59] Chase and Levenson (2000) 12.

[60] *quin etiam feminis curiam reservavit, militiam et magistratus et imperia permisit. quanta erit infelicitas urbis illius, in qua virorum officia mulieres occupabunt!* (Lactant. *Epit.* 33. 4–5).

[61] e.g. Lefkowitz (1983).

she worked with wool': *CIL* vi. 15346).[62] Richmond Lattimore's study of Roman epitaphs yields many similar examples, including that of a wife who is praised for being *lanifica pia pudica frugi casta domiseda* ('a woolworker, respectful, modest, temperate, chaste, and one who stays at home': *CIL* vi. 11602), and one for a woman who *nihil potius cupiens quam ut sua gauderet domus* ('desired nothing more than that her home should rejoice': *CIL* viii. 647).[63] The qualities of a good woman, measured against those of bad ones, are again illustrated in Livy's famous story of Lucretia at the end of *Ab Urbe Condita* book 1, in which her husband wins his bet with the Tarquins by finding her in her home, surrounded by her maids, and working at her loom.[64] Her position in the home is emphasized (*in medio aedium*) and contrasts with that of the losers' wives, who were discovered out at a dinner party.

Whether the association of woman with the home is an inevitable consequence of the way civilizations understand the relationship between nature and culture is the subject of some debate, although Sherry Ortner and Michelle Zimbalist Rosaldo have famously made arguments to that effect.[65] But it is clear, at any rate, that the Romans, like the Greeks before them, had a clear sense of the different kinds of 'work' needing to be done in the household and in the forum—whether that work be described in practical terms (e.g. child-rearing as opposed to the passage of laws) or more theoretical (social reproduction as opposed to the pursuit of just-ice)—and associated those different kinds of work with the social roles of women and men. In this sense, then, the 'invention' of my title is misleading: it is abundantly clear that the Augustan age did not give birth to the distinction between politics and the home,

[62] On the significance of woolworking, one of the paradigmatic female virtues, see D'Ambra (1993) 104–8.

[63] Lattimore (1942) 295–300.

[64] *sed nocte sera deditam lanae inter lucubrantes ancillas in medio aedium sedentem inveniunt* ('but they found her late at night devoted to her weaving, sitting in the middle of the house among her toiling maidservants': 1. 57. 9).

[65] Rosaldo (1974); Ortner (1998). For an overview of different feminist approaches to the question, see Landes (1998*a*).

between certain models of public and private life. On the contrary, Roman society had long been structured by that very dichotomy. What I mean by 'inventing', then, is not by any means the creation of something out of nothing, but rather, looking back to the word's original Latin root *in-venire*, the process of 'coming upon' and recognizing that which had been present all along. It is not so much the fact of a gendered divide between public and private life which I argue was born under Augustus, but rather the celebration, negotiation, and continuous anxious return to that fact as a significant aspect of Roman culture. What was created in the age of Augustus, then, was not so much a particular experiential distinction between the home and the forum, but rather a new language used to debate, delineate, and defend the correct relationship between the two.

In this sense, there is perhaps no more 'Augustan' document to have survived to us than the epitaph of a certain Murdia, a *laudatio* by a son from her first marriage which was erected at some time during the reign of the first emperor.[66] The good qualities which it praises in the dead woman are familiar from epitaphs both before and after it; 'modesty, purity, chastity, obedience, woolworking, diligence, and loyalty.'[67] What is more interesting, however, is the section which precedes the list, in which the son explains:

quibus de causeis, [q]uom omnium bonarum feminarum simplex similisque esse laudatio soleat, quod naturalia bona propria custodia servata varietates verborum non desiderent, satisque sit eadem omnes bona fama digna fecisse, et quia adquirere novas laudes mulieri sit arduom, quom minoribus varietatibus vita iactetur, necessario communia esse colenda, ne quod amissum ex iustis praecepteis cetera turpet.

For these reasons, since the praise of all good women is normally simple and similar—because their natural goodness, preserved by its own guardianship, does not require a proliferation of words—and since it is enough that they all have done the same worthy deeds with a good reputation, and

---

[66] Dated by Mommsen to the reign of Augustus on the basis of orthography and semantics. *CIL* vi. 10230. See also Saller (2001) 104.

[67] *modestia, probitate, pudicitia, opsequio, lanificio, diligentia, fide*: *CIL* vi. 10230.

because it is difficult to find new kinds of praise for a woman, since their lives are disturbed by little variation, we praise their common virtues by necessity, lest, if something from among the proper precepts is left out, it should taint the rest.

The series of explanatory clauses is somewhat bewildering, as the son piles up excuses for why he must say the same things already said by everyone else. There is tension here concerning the mechanisms of praising female virtue, as the author moves from the fact that women's natural goodness does not require words to express it, to the idea that it must be expressed lest someone think that it does not exist. The self-consciousness about the feminine domestic ideal is striking: the author is insistent not only that all good women are good in the same way, but also that this is due to the fact that their lives, implicitly in comparison to the men around them, are unchanging. History, it seems, has no impact on women, so that, never given the opportunity to develop other attributes in reaction to changing circumstances, they content themselves with those virtues which are recognized as incontestably their own. Yet even as the son articulates the separateness of women's lives, the idea that they exist in a place which has its own rhythm, values, and boundaries, he insists that it can and must be described in this public forum. Murdia's epitaph is thus a singularly Augustan document, as it takes female domesticity simultaneously as natural, preconceived, universal, and transhistorical, and also as something which requires continuous discursive policing.

This book, then, is about the motivations for, and mechanisms of, that policing—about the ways in which the Augustan period both created, and was created by, the image of the good woman within the good home. Although Murdia's epitaph is in no sense overtly political, it nevertheless preserves a fragment of value-laden discourse which cannot be separated from the political moment which brought it into being. This is what I mean when I call it an 'Augustan' text. Recent scholarship has emphasized the instability, not just of that term, but also words like 'politics', 'literature', 'resistance', and 'propaganda' with which it has traditionally been associated. We have begun to see the ways in which texts generally, and particularly those produced under the early Empire, function as both records of and contributions to the social world around them, even when their authors do not intend them to be so: 'it can be precisely those things that present themselves, or are presented as, apolitical that are the most actively political in allowing power to be accumulated and exercised in ways that extend beyond the notice of those involved.'[68] For this reason, we no longer seek 'Augustanism' solely in the artefacts or documents which can be directly linked to the person of the princeps; 'the age of Augustus' was not just an episode in history, but also a concept, collectively imagined, described and propagated. This is not to say that every text had access to the same kind of authorizing power: Murdia's epitaph clearly speaks from a different position in relation to the institutions of rule than, for instance, Horace's *Odes*, or Virgil's *Aeneid*, or Augustus' own *Res Gestae*. Yet at the same time all are involved, on one level or another, in the same great cultural experiment, as they attempt to synthesize established social practices with ideals and ideologies drawn from an imagined Roman past, and reworked for an imagined Roman future.[69] Instead of seeing the Empire as solely a political system imposed by the force of arms, therefore, we must also see it as a set of ideas which gradually and inexorably gained the force of truth.

That some of those ideas should have to do with women and the home should not, perhaps, surprise us. After all, as Lynn Hunt has observed in the context of the French Revolution, 'politics do depend on imagination and hence to some extent on fantasy, and family experience is the source of much of that fantasy.'[70] This was as true for Roman boys as for French ones: we may remember the great republican matrons like Cornelia, mother of the Gracchi, who, in Cicero's formulation, raised her sons 'not so much at her breast as in her conversation'.[71] But my point here is that cultural

---

[68] D. F. Kennedy (1992) 34.

[69] Karl Galinsky (1996: 3–9) calls this 'the Augustan evolution'.

[70] Hunt (1992), p. xv.

[71] *filios non tam in gremio educatos quam in sermone matris* (Cic. *Brut.* 211). On the importance of mothers in training children for political careers, cf. Tacitus, *Dial.* 28.

fantasies—like any other work of imagination, collective or other-wise—are never fully under anyone's control, and often have revolutionary effects even when they appear on the surface to serve the status quo. The publication of female domesticity in the Augustan period may have had, in the first instance, deeply ideological and reactionary elements, but its effect was to transform what femininity 'meant' to Roman politics. Many recent discussions which address the performance of gender in the Roman public sphere have focused on effeminacy, and the distrust which attached to men who did not manifest their masculinity in culturally approved ways.[72] This is an important critical insight, but to a certain extent has caused us to miss the moments when femininity (rather than effeminacy, which is a different thing) emerges as a powerful force in political discourse. When Ovid writes in *Ars Amatoria* 3, *ipsa quoque et cultu est et nomine femina Virtus* ('(Manly) virtue too is herself by dress and name a woman': 3. 23), he is both speaking the literal truth—'virtue' was conventionally personified as a woman and her name is grammatically feminine—and identifying a cultural paradox, embodied in the juxtaposition of *femina* and *vir-tus*. A certain kind of femininity, far from being the despised opposite of the chest-thumping militarism of Roman politics, actually lay at the heart of what it meant to be a citizen in the early Roman Empire.

TEXTS AND CONTEXTS: ON METHODOLOGY

In *The Practice of Everyday Life*, Michel de Certeau observes that every theory since Kant has attempted to grapple, largely unsuccessfully, with the question of how to articulate the relationship between the world of language and that of experiential reality.

---

[72] e.g. Edwards (1993) 63–97; Skinner (1993); Gleason (1995); Corbeill (1996) 128–73 and (2002); Richlin (1997); Connolly (1998); Gunderson (1998) and (2000).

A particular problem arises when, instead of being a discourse on other discourses, as is usually the case, theory has to advance over an area where there are no longer any discourses. There is a sudden unevenness of terrain: the ground on which verbal language rests begins to fail. The theorizing operation finds itself at the limits of the terrain where it normally functions, like an automobile at the edge of a cliff. Beyond and below lies the ocean.[73]

It is not, I think, accidental that de Certeau chooses the metaphor of landscape here to describe the difficult-to-define relationship between the material world and the words used to describe it. As is frequently noted, 'space' is a concept both useful and slippery because it has both material and discursive aspects; it is simultaneously experienced as a part of everyday existence and understood symbolically through a network of representations.[74] The Roman Forum, for instance, might be at once an actual place to which men of a certain class went every day to conduct business and an emotive image of republican civic life. Transformations in the landscape, therefore, might be effected on different levels, all of which may be identified operating in Rome under Augustus: actual physical changes in the urban environment, such as the building of the Forum Augustum;[75] new representations of space within space, such as the map of the world which adorned Agrippa's portico;[76] a fresh interest in textual descriptions of space and its meaning, such as those found in the first books of Livy's *Ab Urbe Condita*.[77] Discussions of space generally, therefore, and particularly of space in the age of Augustus, have become a particularly productive meeting point of archaeologists and literary critics, both of whom seek to understand

[73] de Certeau (1984) 61.
[74] For a useful history of the growth and scope of 'landscape history' in classical studies, see Shipley (1996). The essays in Pearson and Richards (1994) suggest a number of productive ways in which the landscape of the classical world may be read, especially in contrast with other cultures and moments of time.
[75] On which, see Zanker (1968); Ganzert and Kockel (1988); Kellum (1996).
[76] Nicolet (1991) 95–122.
[77] Jaeger (1997) 13–14; Edwards (1996) 31–43, 82–88; Laurence (1997). For Propertius' response to the Augustan building programme, see Fantham (1997a).

what ancient people 'made', materially and discursively, of the world around them.[78]

Investigations of space have also been seen as a way of moving beyond the, very real, bias of the historical record toward economic and sexual privilege.[79] The material environment was something which every inhabitant of Rome had in common: we are thus free to imagine 'readers' of the city from many different ranks of society and walks of life. Indeed, the use and abuse of Rome's public spaces provide our best access to what might be called public opinion before the advent of the modern media, in such public performances as the burning of Caesar's body in the Forum, or the street rioting which afflicted Rome during crises in the grain supply. Houses were less liable to be claimed by the public, although the late Republic did see a number of remarkable house-sieges and house-destructions in which the populace made itself felt within the space of individual homes. But clearly houses in Rome, while not private in the sense that only personal or intimate business was conducted there, were private property, the distinction between this and public property being one of the fundamental principles of Roman law. There was thus a wide variety of living spaces and living styles in Roman Italy, and it has been quite correctly pointed out that an individual's understanding of his or her 'personal space' probably varied widely with class.[80] In Roman Pompeii, for instance, those living in one of the non-elite dwellings which did not have access to its own cooking facilities would have had to find food elsewhere, either at one of the numerous cookshops or in the house of a wealthy patron. The inability to consume a cooked meal 'in private' must have given a

[78] Recent decades have seen a new interest in blurring the traditional boundary between archaeology and philology, between 'the dirt and the word'. See Vermeule (1996); Moreland (2001). For a concrete example of how archaeologists and philologists may collaborate on a single interpretive project, see Alcock *et al.* (2001).

[79] e.g. Culham (1987). For the history of 'spatialized' feminism, see McDowell (1996); also, for a general introduction to feminist geography, see the Women and Geography Study Group (1997).

[80] Wallace-Hadrill (1994*a*); Laurence (1994) 78–81; Brothers (1996) 48–51; Ellis (2000) 166–87.

particular cast to how a person lower on the social scale conceptualized the meaning of eating, space, and society. Similarly, we know
that there were a certain number of women who were engaged in
trade, or other kinds of work, which no doubt gave them a different
perspective on the relationship between their own femininity and the
domestic ideal espoused in early imperial ideology.[81]

This book is not about that different perspective. This is not
because I think it unimportant, or because I think that we have
dealt successfully with all of the questions which an investigation of
such different perspectives might answer. Far from it: we are still a
long way from a complete understanding of the material and historical reality of women's lives in antiquity, especially women outside
the social elite. But we are also, I would argue, still a long way from a
complete understanding of the ideals, images, and ideologies which
both shaped and were shaped by that reality. To the extent that the
representations of women found in classical texts may be understood
as fragments of larger social narratives—the discursive framework
which gave meaning to everyday thought and action—they were as
material a part of lived reality for ancient women as the space of the
house itself. Moreover, I would argue that one significant aspect of
the feminine domestic ideal as it is expressed in Roman texts is the
extent to which it does *not* vary by class. Of course, our textual
record, even including funerary inscriptions, does not represent
every rank of society equally, but it is nevertheless striking how
consistently the same virtues recur, in texts which range from funerary epitaphs for freedwomen to descriptions of women in the imperial house. The obsessive return to woolworking makes an
interesting case in point, since it was clearly a skill more symbolic
than necessary in certain cases. The uniformity of the praise of
female virtue, therefore, should not cause us to believe that all
women were in fact the same, or believed themselves to be the
same; rather, we should measure the uniformity which is found
on the level of representation against the variety which we know

[81] See Kampen (1981) 29–32, 130–6; Dixon (2001*a*) 113–32.

historically must have been there. The point is not that texts give us only one voice whereas material and historical records give us many, but rather that part of the ideological message of those texts is to portray women's lives as 'simple and similar' when in actual fact they were not.[82] We must understand that the domestic ideal was a construct which did not 'truthfully' represent any woman's life, even at the same time as it purported to represent them all.[83] The question which we need to ask, then, is: what interests were served by representing female domestic virtue as independent of social relations, as being beyond the reach of the kinds of hierarchical divisions which had long afflicted Roman public life? How and why did domestic femininity become a matter seemingly independent of, but entirely permeated with, the politics of the early imperial state? These are the issues which I have tried to address in the pages which follow.

This book, then, is about a set of ideas which are imbued with history but have not been understood as 'historical' themselves, and which are grounded in the material environment but are not only expressed materially. Thus, while in the chapters which follow I will make reference to both events and artefacts, my primary focus is the textual representation of those events and artefacts, and the language used to describe them. It is, however, because of the desire to maintain as clearly and closely as possible the connection with daily life that I have not chosen to focus my discussion on the 'high' literary texts of the early Empire, but rather have turned my attention to works which have generally not seen the kind of analysis to which I subject them here. This is not, I hasten to add, because I think works like the *Aeneid* incidental, either to the expression of early imperial politics or to our study of them; indeed, it is because

---

[82] A point made by Dixon (2001*a*) 131–2.

[83] Here again we may see points of comparison with the history of the middle-class domestic ideal in the 19th cent., which, it has been argued, came into being as a challenge to the traditional aristocratic hierarchy and its definitions of virtue. The home became at once the site of emotional work and nurturance—thus freeing the market-place for self-interest and capitalist competition—and the thing which defined superiority, in moral rather than economic terms. On 'The Rise of the Domestic Woman' in the 19th cent. through such media as conduct books, see Armstrong (1987) 59–95.

they are so explicitly and completely taken up with 'Augustanism' that I have looked elsewhere for my primary texts. One of the points which I wish to make here is that gender and the domestic ideal have long lurked just below the surface of our understanding of early imperial Rome, occasioning—as in the case of the simile in *Aeneid* 8 with which I began—little scholarly comment, but none the less profoundly shaping both what we know and how we know it. This Trojan horse effect is not accidental. Early imperial culture worked extremely hard to make domesticity invisible, to make it unquestioned, natural, and transhistorical. Thus, although we may see it manifested in texts like *Aeneid* 8, which explicitly address imperial ideology, its more insidious and powerful forms are those which purport not to be ideological, those which aim simply to report or reflect the 'truth' about the world. For this reason, I consider a number of texts below—Vitruvius' *de Architectura*, Seneca the Elder's *Controversiae* and *Suasoriae*, Valerius Maximus' *Facta et Dicta Memorabilia*, Columella's *de Re Rustica*—whose primary role is as vehicles of learning rather than as objects of aesthetic beauty. It is in such vehicles, I maintain, that we may see most clearly the ways in which the domestic ideal is communicated as one of the assumptions which make knowledge possible. The Romans considered themselves a practical people, preferring, as Quintilian says, to follow concrete examples rather than abstract precepts (*Inst.* 12. 2. 29–30); it follows, therefore, that we should look for underlying networks of images, ideals, and truths as well as traditional political theory in seeking the principles which made Roman politics work.

For the early Roman Empire, I argue, one of those principles was female domesticity. The Roman household has been the subject of a good deal of scholarly interest in recent decades, spearheaded by the work of social historians who have worked hard to distinguish between ancient and modern constructions of 'family' and 'home'.[84] Thus, for

---

[84] See, for instance, B. Rawson (1986*a*); Bradley (1991) 3–11; Dixon (1992) 1–35; Saller (1997); Gardner (1998) 1–5. Dixon (1991) emphasizes the similarities in ancient and modern 'sentimental ideals', despite the actual historical differences between the two conceptions of family.

instance, Richard Saller has noted that '*domus* was used with regard to household and kinship to mean the physical house, the household including family and slaves, the broad kinship group including agnates and cognates, ancestors and descendents, and the patrimony.'[85] With such a wide range of meanings, ambiguity (both accidental and deliberate) was always a possibility, leading to the kind of jokes which Ovid makes in the *Fasti* and *Tristia* about the relationship between imperial house and imperial household.[86] There has been a debate in recent years over when exactly the term *domus augusta* came into being, and what it signifies when it does;[87] my own feeling is that, although we do not find it used until the very end of Augustus' rule, we should not put too much weight on that fact. The overlap between power, place, and family relationships which it articulates had been part of Augustan ideology since the beginning, as may be seen in the construction of the Palatine domestic-and-civic complex in the early 20s BCE. It may very well be true that the imperial family as a stable institution of the Roman state did not fully coalesce until the accession of Tiberius,[88] but this does not mean that the ideas which enabled that to occur were not already in circulation long before. Indeed, the emergence of the *domus Caesarum* as a force under the early Empire may be seen as the end result of the cultural causes outlined in the following chapters.

Although this book is deeply indebted to social history, therefore, it differs significantly from previous studies of the Roman household. Obviously, it shares with them an interest in 'the private life' of Rome, as well as a desire to foreground the stories, particularly of women, which do not often get told in traditional political histories. Ultimately, however, this is a study of representation rather than

---

[85] Saller (1984) 342.

[86] Millar (1993); Fantham (1986) 264–5.

[87] Fullerton (1985) 480–2; Corbier (1995) 190–2; Flory (1996) 292–303; Wardle (2000) 479–83; Dettenhofer (2000) 180–3.

[88] Which is the argument of Flory (1996). Severy (2003) places its beginnings in 13–12 BCE, but even she notes that earlier 'changes in the conceptual relationship between family and community, and the degree to which private matters had become part of public affairs, created a potent atmosphere for the promulgation of [Augustus'] family in the years that followed' (p. 61).

reality—although, in truth, I hope that the following pages will do something to challenge the conventional dichotomy between those two terms. This is one reason why I have chosen 'domesticity' to describe one of the subjects which the book investigates, and not just because it is an English word which employs the relevant Latin root. Miriam Peskowitz defines domesticity as 'the relations of women, labor, and home',[89] or, in other words and more generally, one type of confluence of identity, action, and place. Such confluences are, I think, extremely important in writing the history of the ancient world, which comes to us fragmentary and incomplete, and which we make more fragmentary through disciplinary boundaries, territorial notions of expertise, and the need to hold tight to what we are sure we know. Recent decades have seen a great deal of important work, especially by scholars interested in the history of women and those outside the elite upper class.[90] Part of the power of such studies is the extent to which they challenge the constitution of ancient history as we have been taught it, and demand that we broaden our definition of what, and who, we consider 'historical'. But in such a project we are working, not just against the authors of more traditional histories who went before us, but often (in a somewhat different way) against our sources themselves. It is very difficult to write the 'real' history of women, slaves, working men, foreigners, and other marginalized groups, both because they often do not appear in ancient texts, and because, when they do appear, they are so clearly figments of an elite male author's imagination. My hope here, however, is to probe Rome's cultural fantasies about women and the home a little deeper, and to ask if, rather than being an inevitable and eternal part of western culture, they too have a history. By describing that history, I think, we may both acknowledge, and contain, the power of traditional ideals of femininity.

Finally, a word or two about periodization. Some years ago now the question was asked 'Did women have a Renaissance?', which

---

[89] Peskowitz (1997) 95.

[90] e.g. Kampen (1981); Joshel (1992*a*); the essays in Joshel and Murnaghan (1998*b*), esp. Butler (1998); Dixon (2001*a*), esp. 3–15, 113–32, and (2001*b*).

articulated the difficulty of understanding women's history through models based on 'male' politics and culture.[91] The question was subsequently reinterpreted for the ancient world by Phyllis Culham, as 'Did Roman women have an Empire?'.[92] Culham's answer to the latter is a qualified yes, at least in part because of some of the cultural formations I discuss below. It is certainly true that periodization has its uses, especially for projects such as this one, which attempt to interpret ancient authors' own methods of categorization: modern historians who would make the age of Augustus a turning point in Roman history are, after all, only following in the footsteps of their ancient predecessors. At the same time, however, even Augustus acknowledged that he needed Cicero, to give oratorical legitimacy to the princeps' early military triumphs.[93] This may be a rather chilling representation of the relationship between the greatest voice of the Republic and the man who founded the Empire, but the idea—that the two political systems were and are inextricable from one another—is true in more than merely chronological terms. There is a fair amount of Cicero in the pages which follow, particularly in Chapters 1, 4, and 5, which has as much to do with the imagined connection between the two eras he and the first princeps embody as the particular historical relationship between the men themselves. The 'age of Augustus', as I noted earlier, came to be not just an episode in history but a potent ideological symbol, as subsequent eras attempted to understand the imperial present by looking back to the moment of imperial birth.[94] Thus, texts such as those I consider in Chapter 5, which were produced under 'the new Augustus' Nero, should be seen as participating in the continuing refinement of what imperial rule meant to Roman authors writing about the family. Periodization, then, is certainly an important part of this

---

[91] Kelly (1984).   [92] Culham (1997).

[93] Plutarch cites Augustus' memoirs for this sentiment: *Comparison of Demosthenes and Cicero* 3. 1.

[94] On the representation of the Augustan period in both contemporary and later histories, see Gabba (1984). For the ways in which the idea and image of Augustus influenced later emperors, see Gross (1981).

project, but only insofar as we are free to interrogate it as a textual, historical, and ideological strategy.

The first chapter of the book, 'Reading and Writing Gender on the Augustan Palatine', considers Augustus' 'domestic' complex which was one of the first of his major building projects to be completed and which incorporated both his house and a number of more clearly civic structures. I argue that both the complex itself and textual representations of the princeps' relationship to it use femininity and female roles to make 'domesticity' an imperial virtue, inseparable from the civic virtues on which Augustus is generally supposed to have built his *auctoritas*. The intimate association of the first emperor with the women of his household and their performance of traditional domestic roles assisted in constructing a picture of him as a man whose allegiance to home and family kept him from forgetting his role as a 'private' figure, even as his position trumped all other roles in Roman public life. In this sense, the imperial house on the Palatine represented not an actual private space but a performance of privacy, by the princeps, for the benefit of the Roman people.

While the first chapter considers imperial privacy directly, then, the second turns to the more subtle ways in which domesticity was represented in a contemporary text. The past decade has seen a sustained attack on the idea that Romans in the late Republic and early Empire had a concept of private or gendered space, an attack which has principally used the *de Architectura* of Vitruvius to read the architecture of Roman houses. The second chapter, therefore, 'Other Men's Wives: Domesticity and Display in Vitruvius' *de Architectura*', addresses itself to Vitruvius' text, arguing that the absence of privacy and gender from his descriptions of the Roman house cannot be separated from the ethnographic tropes which pervade his book on domestic architecture; it is clear that the Augustan architect understood the patterns of Roman building for, and behaviour within, the home as inextricably linked to Roman national character. This, in turn, must be seen in the context of Roman descriptions of Greek domestic architecture and behaviour which are set up as foils to their more sophisticated and culturally developed conquerors. Vitruvius, I argue, must not be understood as providing a faithful blueprint for the architecture of social relations within the Roman home, but rather as reflecting the idea prevalent in Augustan culture that the structure of domestic life could be used to read imperial culture.

The third chapter, entitled 'Women, History, and the Law', concerns the ways in which law and the history of law became important in Augustan ideology as a means of situating women within the public/private dichotomy. Particular kinds of gendered legal discourse and stories about laws, origins in Rome's distant past were central to the construction of a new Roman state, a point which is perhaps most compellingly illustrated in the Augustan programme of social legislation. This, for the first time in Roman history, made adultery a criminal offence and offered rewards to those who married and produced children. The second half of this chapter concerns the historian Livy's reconstruction of the debate over the repeal of the *lex Oppia* in which the historian seizes the opportunity to present opposing views of the 'place' of law within Roman society. Thus this chapter reads, on the one hand, a direct intervention by the state in the construction of domestic life and, on the other, one representational response to the contemporary cultural debate about female behaviour and public discourse.

Building on the questions of history and historical representation raised in Chapter 3, the fourth chapter, entitled 'A Domestic Disturbance: Talking about the Triumvirs in the Early Empire', considers the representation in imperial prose of domestic life during the civil wars which immediately preceded the age of Augustus. Using both traditional historical sources, such as Appian and Cassius Dio, and the rhetorical handbooks of Valerius Maximus and Seneca the Elder, I argue that stories of domestic virtue and vice during the civil wars surface in our sources less as 'real' history than as a means to characterize the late Republic as a time when private life was tragically invaded by politics. In this way, the social conflict in the Roman state which immediately preceded the transition to Empire is seen as fundamentally concerned with the relationship between public and private life, a crisis in domesticity which supposedly necessitated the political concern with domestic values under the early Empire.

'Natural Urges: Marriage, Philosophy, and the Work of the House', the final chapter, addresses what might be called popular philosophy in the early Empire. Here I turn away from the more 'public' forms of historical commemoration discussed in Chapters 3 and 4 to texts which offer a more 'private' view of the home and its relationship to individual virtue. Michel Foucault famously drew attention to the importance of philosophers such as Musonius Rufus in writing the history of ancient domestic life, but has been criticized for making too many generalizations about 'Roman society' built on the foundation of elite texts springing from the Greek intellectual tradition. In this chapter, I argue that philosophical and pseudo-philosophical works do testify to the concern of early imperial culture with the 'science' of domesticity, yet an examination of another, more self-consciously Roman, text offers a significantly different perspective on the question. This chapter thus contrasts a rereading of the work of Musonius Rufus with books 11 and 12 of Columella's *de Re Rustica*—a work which uses Cicero's Latin translation of Xenophon's *Oeconomicus* to construct its own vision of the ideal household. I argue that a reading of Columella offers a different, more complex, 'philosophical' version of early imperial ideas about the role of women and the home in Roman social life, and makes clear the fundamentally political nature of the move toward 'privatization' in the Roman family.

Finally, this study closes with an epilogue entitled 'Burning Down the House: Nero and the End of Julio-Claudian Rule'. Here I argue that Nero, the last member of Augustus' family to rule Rome, is represented as a negative mirror image of his ancestor: whereas the first Julio-Claudian made Rome into the image of a good home, the last constructs it as a bad one, and thus brings a fitting end both to his own dynasty and the kind of 'domestic politics' which characterized the early Empire. This picture of Nero serves not only to cast in a particular light the legacy of the Julio-Claudian emperors, but to mark explicitly a shift in the goals and nature of imperial rule. At the same time, however, Nero's transgressions, and the terms in which they are remembered, serve to underscore the gendered politics of Augustan private life.

Some years ago now, Josine Blok argued that future studies of women in antiquity must look to the ways in which ancient gender roles do not present distinct historical problems, but are both the cause and the result of different, sometimes seemingly unrelated, cultural forces.[95] Ideas about what constituted 'correctly' gendered practice were a part of the fabric of daily life in the ancient world, and, as such, continuously affected, and were affected by, the functioning of other social formations. In the chapters which follow, I do not discuss every early imperial text which speaks about domestic life, nor every text which relates to Augustanism and its politics. Rather, I have tried to isolate certain textual moments which lay the discourse of domesticity open to view, and illustrate the connection between it and the political and social changes which transformed the Roman state under the Julio-Claudian emperors. In this way, I hope to show that, far from existing in some isolated world of transcendent and transparent domestic values, women and women's place were continually the site of struggle and negotiation as a part of early imperial culture.

---

[95] Blok (1987).

1

Reading and Writing Gender on the Augustan Palatine

IF there is anything that the last few decades of scholarship on Augustan Rome have taught us, it is that the first princeps had a high regard for symbolic gestures. By this I do not just mean such acts as, for instance, his restoration of the Roman state to 'normal' governance in 27 BCE, while at the same time he retained extraordinary and hitherto unheard-of governmental powers. Nor am I referring only to his regime's well-known interest in, and use of, artistic images in the furtherance of its ideological programme, as outlined by Paul Zanker.[1] Rather, I would like to put the point more generally, and say that we may see as one of the signal qualities of Augustan culture the understanding that the symbolic in its most basic form—that which is used in place of something else—is a powerful tool, in that it may at once evoke that which it stands for and also subtly bring to bear any number of other, technically unrelated, images and ideas. In this chapter, I argue that domesticity is one of those Augustan symbols, an idea which may articulate some real historical truth about the person of the first princeps and how he lived, but also serves to mask a deeper and much less 'personal' politics. Here I look at the gendering of Augustan space, particularly that of the imperial house on the Palatine hill, through a network of interrelated texts and structures: from the porticoes of Livia and Octavia, to Cicero's *de Domo Sua*, to Augustus' own autobiography,

---

[1] Zanker (1988).

we can see some of the ways in which women were used in conversations about, and constructions of, the urban environment as a means of mediating between civic and domestic ideals. Thus they played an indispensable symbolic role in the emergence into public discourse of an 'imperial' private life.

In 3 CE, we are told, Augustus' Palatine home was damaged by fire, thus proving, incidentally, that not even the most important citizens were spared the hazards of living in ancient Rome. Offers of money to cover the costs of repairs poured in, but Augustus would accept only nominal sums: a gold coin from communities, a silver one from individuals (Cass. Dio 55. 12. 4). When the house was restored, however, he seized the opportunity to make some changes—not, apparently, so much in the structure itself, but in its status (Cass. Dio 55. 12. 5):

ὁ δὲ Αὔγουστος τὴν οἰκίαν οἰκοδομήσας ἐδημόσιωσε πᾶσαν, εἴτε δὴ διὰ τὴν συντέλειαν τὴν παρὰ τοῦ δήμου οἱ γενομένην, εἴτε καὶ ὅτι ἀρχιέρεως ἦν, ἵν᾽ ἐν τοῖς ἰδίοις ἅμα καὶ ἐν τοῖς κοινοῖς οἰκοίη.

Augustus, having had the house built, gave the entire thing to the people, either because a joint contribution had been made by the populace, or because, being the high priest, he would make his home in spaces at the same time private and public.

Cassius Dio appears here to have conflated events somewhat. Augustus at this point had been Pontifex Maximus for more than fifteen years, so the second explanation offered above seems a bit belated; perhaps the historian is thinking of the princeps' dedication of a shrine to Vesta in the house upon his assumption of the high priesthood in 12 BCE.[2] On the other hand, as Dio has just noted, most of the money which went towards the project of rebuilding was drawn from Augustus' own pocket, the contribution of the populace being held to a minimum. Whichever of Dio's explanations is

---

[2] Of course, the pontificate carried with it an official residence: the Regia, attached to the House of the Vestals below in the Forum. The princeps apparently had no intention of leaving his Palatine compound to move into the centre of Republican civic life. On the shrine to Vesta, see Ovid, *Fasti* 4. 949–54.

preferred, however, the significant fact is represented in τὴν οἰκίαν . . . ἐδημόσιωσε πᾶσαν. Since Augustus seems to have intended to go on living there, it is clear that what is meant is different from the donation, for instance, of Caesar's gardens to the people, an act which was done posthumously as part of the general settlement of the dictator's property in his will (Suetonius, *Div. Iul.* 83).[3] Whereas the gardens were communal property in the sense that they were available for use by the general populace, the house cannot have been entirely open to all comers; rather, the declaration was a symbolic act, meant to create, as Dio says, a dwelling space both private and public.

In fact, Augustus seems to have been working up to this point for some time, since the beginning of the transformation of the Palatine immediately following the battle of Actium. We are told by Dio, Suetonius, and Velleius Paterculus that the land eventually given over to the temple of Apollo and its accompanying porticoes had originally been purchased by the princeps to increase the size of his personal dwelling; the site was hit by lightning, which was taken by its owner as a sign that it should be used instead to create a sacred site.[4] There remained, however, a clear connection between the house and the rest of the Palatine complex, the grand temple of Apollo Palatinus, the Greek and Latin libraries containing the accumulated knowledge of the Empire, the Porticus Apollonis with its fifty statues of the daughters of Danaus. In fact, there seems to have been a ramp connecting the personal house of the princeps with the temple of Apollo; at the very least, there was clearly an understanding that the complex as a whole reflected the power and majesty of the imperial house even before its more public and more private spaces were formally integrated.[5] Ovid rather wickedly asks in *Tristia* 3. 1 to

---

[3] On the ways in which the gardens were used as public space even before Caesar's death, see D'Arms (1998); on the posthumous donation, Boatwright (1998) 74–5.

[4] Vell. Pat. 2. 81. 3; Dio 49. 15. 5–6; Suet. *Div. Aug.* 29. 3.

[5] Zanker (1983); Favro (1996) 100–1; Strothmann (2000) 62–4; Severy (2003) 47. For an overview of imperial ownership of the Palatine, see Millar (1977) 18–24; for some later developments of the space and its usage, Thompson (1981) and Severy (2000) 322–5.

be forgiven, not by the emperor, but by his house on the Palatine hill—a neat example of the exiled poet's obsession with the inter-relationship of power and place. Later Cassius Dio notes that, because Augustus had established his 'headquarters' on the Palatine hill, wherever the emperor subsequently dwelt, even temporarily, was known as the Palatium.[6] The word was thus well on its way to becoming our English 'palace', even before the Domus Tiberiana, Caligula's rebuilding, and Nero's contribution of the Domus Transitoria. The Palatine complex thus serves to underscore certain concrete issues about the relationship between public and private space in the Augustan age, and also, in a symbolic sense, to address the question of what it means for a single individual to take to himself alone the power which used to belong to an entire community.

Augustus' Palatine complex has been the subject of a substantial amount of critical investigation, especially by those who are interested in exploring how the princeps used space to articulate his social and political role; constructed in the heat of the civil war with Antony and dedicated in 28 to commemorate the battle of Actium,[7] it constitutes one of the first major architectural statements which he made as sole ruler of Rome. On one level, the ideological investments of the various constructions are quite clear: one door of the temple of Apollo Palatinus, for instance, featured a relief of the Gauls being driven back from Delphi, a reference, no doubt, to the god's role in repelling the more recent 'barbarian invaders' of Rome. The temple, moreover, was decorated with terracotta plaques depicting Heracles (ancestor of Antony) and Apollo (patron of Augustus) struggling heroically over the Delphic tripod; Cleopatra/Isis is

---

[6] 53. 16. 5–6.

[7] Gurval (1995: 87–136) attacks the widely accepted idea that the temple complex was meant to evoke Actium specifically, arguing that Augustus did not wish to associate himself too closely with the victory over Antony due to the mixed emotions aroused in the Roman populace by civil war. I am not persuaded by Gurval's argument (perhaps because I am more inclined to believe in the existence of 'Augustan ideology' than he) but even if we disassociate the complex from Actium, its blending of public and private space and use of gendered imagery remain important political statements.

portrayed being menaced by Sphinxes in the decorations which frame the picture.[8] Other plaques depict anonymous female figures, some decorating an aniconic depiction of Apollo, and others again show Perseus with Athena and the Gorgon's head.

Perhaps most famously, the Danaid portico has also been interpreted as an allegory of Actium. The daughters of Danaus were notorious for having married their cousins; on their wedding night, at the order of their father, forty-nine of the fifty new brides then assassinated their husbands. For this crime they were generally thought to have suffered punishment in Hades.[9] Although there are a number of different versions of the myth which circulated in antiquity—perhaps the most famous is represented in Aeschylus' *Suppliants*—all seem to agree that the Danaids had been caught in a territorial power struggle between Danaus, later king of Argos, and his brother Aegyptus in Egypt. In an attempt to isolate his brother and maintain his own superior position, Aegyptus insisted on the marriage between the two sets of cousins, perhaps fearing that Danaus might be able to draw on the help of future sons-in-law or grandsons to support his claims to the throne.[10] The presence of the fifty Danaid statues, alongside a fifty-first of their father with an upraised sword, as part of the Augustan Palatine complex has long puzzled scholars, for they represent a disturbing yet surprisingly prominent element in the decorative scheme; since they are at once murderesses and dutiful daughters, it is difficult to know whether we should imagine them as the victims or the villains of the story.[11]

---

[8] Kellum (1993) 76–8.

[9] See Keuls (1974: esp. 43–60) for a discussion of the different versions of the myth, focusing especially on the different fates experienced by the women.

[10] This is the story recounted by D Servius on Virgil, *Aeneid* 10. 497, apropos of the sword-belt of Pallas. Although Aeschylus is notoriously vague about the circumstances leading up to the flight of the Danaids from Egypt, the king of Argos does note at line 338 of the play that intermarriage is one sure way of maintaining a family's power.

[11] In this context it is worth noting that the Danaids also put in a brief but memorable appearance in Virgil's *Aeneid*, at 10. 495–9: they are the perpetrators of the scene represented on Pallas' sword-belt, which is taken from his body by Turnus and ultimately leads to the latter's destruction by Aeneas in the poem's final moments. It has been noted that Virgil describes the belt as showing the dead bodies of the bridegrooms and not the murderous brides, where the portico seems to have shown the brides and not the grooms

Many critics, however, have argued that we should see in the Danaid portico a reference to Augustus' triumph at Actium, as another instance of a conflict between civilization and barbarism which is ultimately resolved by the power of the gods. Thus, in one interpretation, we should see the Danaids as heroines, and their subsequent rejection of the 'foreign' marriage at the behest of their father as a mirror of Rome's rejection of Antony under the command of—*pater patriae*—Augustus.[12]

Such an interpretation of the Danaid portico, however, brings to the fore one of the central questions of the Palatine complex as a whole, namely what it means for Augustus' social and political project that gender is such an important part of the ideological story which it tells. Cleopatra, the nameless figures on the terracotta reliefs, and the Danaids all work together to 'populate' the complex with powerfully charged images of women, both good and bad; it is worth noting that the image of the Gauls attacking Delphi on the door of the temple was matched by a relief showing the punishment of Niobe, whose children were struck down by Apollo and Diana because she had insulted their mother. As in the Danaid portico, the implied comparison between a territorial or political struggle (the Gauls at Delphi; Antony at Actium) and a domestic or dynastic one (the families of Niobe and Leto; the Danaids, their father, and their cousins) serves to complicate a straightforward reading of the monument as a statement about a 'public' figure. In this sense, we cannot ignore the fact that the Palatine complex was not—like the Forum Augustum, for instance—simply a public space; it also functioned as the emperor's home, the space of his house, family, and private life. As we will see, Augustus' representation of himself as embodying a

---

(*pace* the scholium on Persius 2. 56 which indicates that the men were there too). Here the Danaids are clearly the villians—their crime is described as *nefas*—but the fact that only their dead victims are represented in Virgil's description has been seen as a response to the importance accorded the women in the Palatine portico. See Spence (1991); O'Higgins (1995); Harrison (1998).

[12] Simon (1986) 19–24; Lefèvre (1989) 12–19; Spence (1991). Others, however, have seen the Danaids and their father as representing Antony and his 'barbarian' allies: Kellum (1993) 80–1; Harrison (1998) 233–42.

certain kind of domesticity was not only an important aspect of his self-description as a public figure, but was also inseparable from the representations which he encouraged of the female members of his family. Thus, although the Palatine complex was by no means the only Augustan monument which used gender to make its ideological point, its explicit role as both house and civic space means that it highlights the complications of 'locating' femininity between the two. The extent, therefore, to which the Palatine complex both is and is not domestic, and is and is not feminized, constitutes an important example of the ways in which gender might be used to read privacy, and vice versa, in the Augustan age.

GENDERING THE AUGUSTAN LANDSCAPE: PRIVACY, PORTICOES, AND POLITICS

At *Tristia* 2. 301–2, the poet Ovid offers the observation, *omnia perversas possunt corrumpere mentes; / stant tamen ipsa suis omnia tuta locis* ('everything has the power to corrupt perverted minds; and yet everything is safe in its own place'). Not surprisingly, he is talking about women; the *perversae mentes* in question belong to the female readers of the poet's earlier *Ars Amatoria*. Ovid claims that he has been exiled from Rome due to these women's transgressions against the moral and social codes of Augustus' regime—transgressions for which, the poet insists, he should not be held accountable. Like a priest who has tried in vain to prevent a woman from rushing into his temple's inner sanctum (*Tristia* 2. 305–6), Ovid could not keep her from his text, nor could he control what use she made of it. The fault is not in the *Ars Amatoria*, but in the inherently indecent quality of the female mind; as long as the text's meaning is 'located' correctly, it is perfectly safe. Yet lines 301–2 also fall close to the end of a long catalogue in *Tristia* 2 of places in Rome where women may go to find or make mischief. The theatres, the Circus, even the temples of the Olympian gods, Ovid insists, have been the sites of lewd female behaviour. In this context, the meaning of *stant . . . suis omnia tuta locis* appears rather less metaphorical, and the 'places' in question are literally the public spaces of urban Rome. Given Augustus' well-known pride in his transformation of the capital city, and his personal connection to many of the specific places named, the rhetorical motivation of the list is quite clear. The *Ars Amatoria*, it is implied, is as innocent of influencing female behaviour as Augustus' temple of Mars Ultor (line 295), and, if the poet is to be held responsible for all the activities which are enabled by his poem, the *princeps* must answer for his buildings. If Ovid is guilty, then so is Augustus—but, in fact, both are innocent, because it isn't their fault if women choose to go where they should not. They would be safe if they stayed in their own places.[13]

Much recent scholarly discussion of *Tristia* 2 has focused on the role which it assigns to Augustus as a reader, a rather incompetent one who must be taught not only how to read Ovid's poetry but poetry in general.[14] Yet the connection which the poem draws between Augustus' role in constructing Roman spaces and Ovid's role in constructing his poetry suggests another alternative. It offers the idea that Augustus is also an author, of a text which may be found and read in the streets of Rome and whose meaning may or may not be fully within its creator's control. The analogy between the city of Rome and the *Ars Amatoria* is assisted by a pun on the word *locis*, which could mean either literal places or passages in a written work. If Ovid's medium is poetry, Augustus' is the space of the capital city, and each is equally implicated in the construction of social mores. In Augustus' city, each thing has 'its own place', the proper occupation of which guarantees moral and social stability, which translates in

---

[13] There is a rather neat slide in Ovid's language here. Like the English word 'safe', the Latin *tuta* may look either inward or outward: i.e. to be safe for something or safe from something. If *suis omnia tuta locis* is to be understood as referring to the text of the *Ars Amatoria*, then *tuta* is reflexive: the book is safe—harmless—for reading. But with the emphasis of the surrounding lines on women's movement through the literal places of the city, *tuta* seems to point back at the women: they are not safe from corruption in public places.

[14] e.g. Nugent (1990); Barchiesi (1993); G. D. Williams (1994*a*) 154 ff; Sharrock (1994).

turn to the 'safety' that Ovid invokes in these lines.[15] Like the poet's safety, threatened by the misreading of the *Ars Amatoria*, social safety is threatened by the misreading of space: thus, *Tristia* 2 emphasizes the ways in which women will see in certain temples not divine majesty, but the sordid pasts of the gods whom they were built to honour: 'when she stands in the temple of Jupiter, in the temple of Jupiter it will occur to her how many that god has made into mothers... looking on Pallas, she will ask why the virgin brought up Erichthonius, born from vice.'[16] Ovid sympathizes with the *princeps* as one author to another: isn't it difficult when people don't understand your work?

Ovid, of course, is being deliberately disingenuous. Nevertheless, it is clear that *Tristia* 2 is playing here on a particularly powerful form of social discourse in early imperial Rome. By this time, Augustus was widely known as a builder. When Ovid penned these lines, just about all of the projects which we associate with the 'Augustan' transformation of Rome were either complete or well under way: the Ara Pacis and the Horologium, the porticoes of Livia and Octavia, the Forum Augustum, the temple of Apollo on the Palatine, the great Mausoleum looming beside one of the major roads into and out of Rome. Recent scholarship has made much of these different but coordinated structural statements, each one calculated to make a particular dynastic or ideological point and together forming a continuous architectural narrative about Augustus, his family, and their rule. Thus, for instance, the celebration of past heroes of the Julian *gens* in the northern hemicycle of the Forum Augustum finds its counterpart in the parade of present family members in the great friezes of the Ara Pacis and, in a slightly odd

[15] There is a pointed contrast between 'safe places' for women as they are constructed by Augustus and the 'safe place' of exile for which the *Tristia* continuously begs (in *Trist.* 2 alone at 185–8 and 577–8); while Tomis's perpetual warfare and winter, as Ovid would have it, are a genuine threat to the poet's life, the 'danger' posed by love affairs to women is purely a social construction.

[16] *cum steterit Iovis aede, Iovis succurret in aede / quam multas matres fecerit ille deus... Pallade conspecta, natum de crimine virgo / sustulerit quare, quaeret, Erichthonium* (289–90; 293–4).

way, the space provided for future generations in the Mausoleum. The triumph of a virtuous *Romanitas* over the luxurious and barbaric East is expressed as much by the Horologium's Egyptian obelisk as by the decorative scheme of the temple of Apollo Palatinus and the Greek trophy art displayed in the portico of Livia. Strabo, writing under Tiberius, seems to have got the message: he credits 'Pompey, Julius Caesar, Augustus, his children and friends, his wife and sister' with the transformation of the city, and notes in his conclusion to the chapter, 'If, in turn, as you go to the ancient Forum, you should see the others set parallel to it one after the other, and the basilicas and the temples, and you should also see the Capitoline and the art works there and on the Palatine and in the portico of Livia, you would easily forget about anything existing anywhere else. This, then, is Rome.'[17]

The prominent role of Livia and Octavia as patrons of buildings in Strabo's description, the emphasis on the imperial family in the monuments noted above, and the more general equation of female fertility with the triumph of Roman imperialism in Augustan ideology[18] bring us back to Ovid's tongue-in-cheek representation of Rome's gendered landscape. The apparently transgressive point which *Tristia* 2 makes is that the changes which the princeps and his family have made in the city speak to, for, and about women— that is, for Ovid, women's sexuality. But this is, in some senses, no more nor less than the message of the Augustan building programme itself, which seeks to harness women's identities, influence, and bodies to support an ideological line. The friezes of the Ara Pacis, for instance, unusually represent the women and children of the imperial family alongside the men, a gesture which would connect

---

[17] πάλιν δ' εἴ τις εἰς τὴν ἀγορὰν παρελθὼν τὴν ἀρχαίαν ἄλλην ἐξ ἄλλης ἴδοι παραβεβλημένην ταύτῃ καὶ βασιλικὰς στοὰς καὶ ναούς, ἴδοι δὲ καὶ τὸ Καπιτώλιον καὶ τὰ ἐνταῦθα ἔργα καὶ τὰ ἐν τῷ Παλατίῳ καὶ τῷ τῆς Λιβίας περιπάτῳ, ῥᾳδίως ἐκλάθοιτ' ἂν τῶν ἔξωθεν. τοιαύτη μὲν ἡ Ῥώμη. (Strabo, *Geography* 5. 3. 8).

[18] A theme which is emphasized visually by the parallel figures of Roma (in military garb) and Tellus (with babies) on the eastern façade of the Ara Pacis. It is also repeatedly put forward as a principle in Horace's poetry: see esp. *Carmen Saeculare* 13–24, 29–32; *Odes* 3. 6. 33–41.

their (real) reproductive bodies with the (symbolically) reproductive body of Tellus-Italia on the east façade.[19] This in turn has been connected with the ideological statement made by the social legislation of 18–17 BCE.[20] Similarly, Livia as imperial spouse might dedicate a shrine to Concordia and rely on a neat ambiguity between 'concord' as a virtue of matrimony and as an attribute of good government.[21] The rehabilitation of Venus, from rather risqué goddess of love to matronly progenetrix of the Julian line, is one of the cornerstones of early imperial propaganda, expressed most noticeably in the temple to Venus Genetrix anchoring the Forum Iulium.[22] Near by, more subtly, there is a clear gendered contrast within the Forum Augustum, where heroic statues of great male historical figures (the Summi Viri), all carefully differentiated in appearance and title, are contrasted with female caryatid figures on the upper-level frieze, anonymous and meant to recall the subjugation of foreign peoples by (masculine) military might.[23] Indeed, it has been argued that the Forum itself is intentionally modelled on the male reproductive organ, inserting itself into the 'female' Forum Iulium to express the dominance of Augustus over his adoptive father.[24]

Yet Ovid's version of the gendered environment of Augustan Rome makes a salutary counterpoint to such heavy-handed propaganda. For Ovid, women inhabit the landscape as readers and creators of meaning as well as objects of representation; it is by their *perversae mentes* that the Augustan message of moral rebirth is

[19] For an exhaustive discussion of the connections between the 'Tellus' figure, the babies, and the fertility imagery of the monument, see Spaeth (1996) 125–51. The exact identification of the figure is uncertain.

[20] Kleiner (1978); see also Kampen (1991) 226.

[21] Kellum (1990); Flory (1984); Purcell (1986), esp. 88–94.

[22] This temple was completed by Augustus.

[23] Kellum (1997) 167–8; on the Summi Viri, see Luce (1990) and Severy (2003) 169–71.

[24] Kellum (1996). Severy (2003) 169–80 offers a compelling reading which argues that the Forum Augustum intentionally evoked both traditional public spaces like the Senate House and the private world of the atrium house.

resisted, reconsidered, and (ultimately) rejected.[25] Far from being passive objects, or even passive recipients, of ideological statements, women for Ovid are a disruptive presence in the landscape, as they refuse to see what they are supposed to see, to imagine what they are supposed to imagine, and to do what they are supposed to do. Gender, in this sense, appears less an organic part of Augustan material culture and more an unstable force needing to be contained and controlled—a category of analysis, as Barbara Kellum has noted, which holds 'the potential... for questioning the fixity of binary absolutes, whether it is the supposed opposition between male and female, between official and private, between "high" and "low" art, or between the ribald and the serious'.[26] Kellum's point is well taken, and holds true, as she notes, not simply for the scholar seeking to destabilize modern categories in relation to the ancient world, but as an aspect of ancient experience itself; that is, the argument is not simply that gender can help to deconstruct modern prejudices and binary assumptions which we carry with us to the ancient world, but that the ancient world had its own categories and assumptions within which gender might be a (sometimes deliberately) destabilizing force. There is perhaps a reason why the only time Pliny the Elder makes specific reference to a gendered space in Rome, it is in the context both of a famous Augustan building and of a kind of spatial cross-dressing: noting that the cult images of the temples of Jupiter Stator and Juno Regina were accidentally switched in the course of installation, he remarks 'in the one of these [buildings], which is the temple of Jupiter, the painted decoration and all the other ornament is made up of feminine themes; for it had been made for Juno... and also in the temple of Juno the decor is that which ought to be in the temple of Jupiter.'[27] These were, in fact, the two temples which

[25] Thus, in addition to what is noted above, *Trist.* 2. 309–12 asks us to consider how innocent, or not, it may be for respectable matrons to view *nudas... et veneris stantis ad genus omne* ('women naked and ready for every kind of lust'), leaving it to the reader to decide whether the bodies in question are real or sculpted.

[26] Kellum (1997) 181.

[27] *in Iovis aede ex iis pictura cultusque reliquus omnis femineis argumentis constat; erat enim facta Iunoni... ergo et in Iunonis aede cultus est qui Iovis esse debuit* (*NH* 36. 43).

stood within the portico of Octavia, and were probably among those restored by the princeps in his quest to create divine spaces in Rome worthy of the gods they honoured.

Indeed, that Octavia and Livia, the two most notable female builders in the imperial house, were most famous as patrons of porticoes is itself not an unambiguous fact. The Porticus Liviae and Porticus Octaviae were considered two of the more significant Augustan buildings, and they each contained, to judge from Pliny's descriptions in the *Natural History*, impressive collections of (mostly imported) art.[28] The display of such art had been for some time one of the primary roles of Rome's porticoes, although the imperial versions probably found their most influential model in that of Pompey in the Campus Martius.[29] On one level, the connection of the imperial women with such structures is not surprising, since, as spaces not specifically devoted to civic life, they may have been considered more appropriate for a woman's patronage. On the other hand, there is some evidence that the portico was considered morally suspect as a space, due in part to its association with the luxurious and notionally corrupting art work which had poured into Rome as a result of imperial expansion.[30] Velleius Paterculus remarks on the appearance of porticoes after the end of the second Punic war (2. 1. 1):

vetus disciplina deserta nova inducta; in somnum a vigiliis, ab armis ad voluptates, a negotiis in otium conversa civitas. tum Scipio Nasica in Capitolio porticus, tum, quas praediximus, Metellus, tum in circo Cn. Octavius multo amoenissimam moliti sunt, publicamque magnificentiam secuta privata luxuria est.

---

[28] On Octavia and Livia's building projects, especially the porticoes, see Kleiner (1996) 30–4.

[29] Coarelli (1972).

[30] See Lintott (1972); Pollit (1978); Néraudau (1985: 28–9) emphasizes the importance of the porticoes as sites for looking at art and at women. In fact, it may be Ovid's particular interest in the overlap between the parallel passions for art and for sex—as well as his understanding of the gaze as gendered—which leads him to put so much emphasis on the porticoes as spaces for amatory adventures: on the theme in his work generally, see Sharrock (1991) and Myerowitz (1992). On (male) scopophilia within other types of Roman space, see Fredrick (1995).

The old rule of order was abandoned and a new one brought in; the state turned to sleep from watchfulness, to pleasure from military discipline, to idleness from business. Then Scipio Nasica built his portico on the Capitol, then Metellus built the one already described, then Cn. Octavius constructed in the Circus the most lovely of them all, and private indulgence followed on from public extravagance.

Moreover, the extent to which the structure was devoted to leisure rather than business seems to have meant that it was a space, both real and imagined, in which irregular sexual relationships might be conceived. Catullus in poem 55 encounters loose women who attempt to seduce him in the portico of Pompey; Propertius may have gone to the one on the Palatine hill to meet Cynthia;[31] Ovid's *Ars Amatoria* (1. 67–74) puts Rome's porticoes, including those of Livia, Octavia, and the Danaids on the Palatine hill, first in its list of good places to pick up women.[32] Subsequently, he asks rhetorically in *Tristia* 2's moral tour of Rome, 'since certain women spend time there in order to meet a lover, why does a single portico stand open?'.[33]

In this sense, the choice of the portico form for Livia and Octavia's building projects seems a little dangerous—as, indeed, does the choice of a portico decorated with fifty sculpted domestic murderesses to round out the Palatine complex. Yet it is clear that Livia's portico, at any rate, was specifically designed to make a statement about morality, both domestic and civic.[34] We are told by Ovid and Cassius Dio that the Porticus Liviae came into being when the wealthy equestrian Vedius Pollio died and left his house to Augustus with the instructions that it should be used 'to build a very beautiful structure for the people'. In response, Augustus razed the house and

[31] This depends on whether or not we consider Propertius 2. 31 and 32 to be parts of the same poem; at the very least, however, they should be taken closely together.

[32] On the significance of this within the *Ars Amatoria*'s representation of the Augustan landscape, see Néraudau (1985); Davis (1995).

[33] *cum quaedam spatientur in hoc, ut amator eodem / conveniat, quare porticus ulla patet?* (285–6).

[34] For an excellent discussion of the ideological investments of the structure, see Flory (1984); also Grimal (1943) 155 and 188–91; Kleiner (1996) 32; Severy (2003) 132–8.

put the portico in its place, thwarting Pollio's wish for a monument by inscribing it with the name of Livia rather than that of the site's former occupant (Dio 54. 23. 5–6). Ovid also describes the incident in the *Fasti* (6. 639–48):

disce tamen, veniens aetas, ubi Livia nunc est
    porticus, immensae tecta fuere domus;
urbis opus domus una fuit, spatiumque tenebat,
    quo brevius muris oppida multa tenent.
haec aequata solo est, nullo sub crimine regni,
    sed quia luxuria visa nocere sua.
sustinuit tantas operum subvertere moles
    totque suas heres perdere Caesar opes.
sic agitur censura et sic exempla parantur,
    cum vindex, alios quod monet, ipse facit.

Learn, nevertheless, you ages to come, that the site where
        the portico of
Livia now stands was once covered by an enormous house.
This single house was like the structure of a city, and occupied a
    space
    greater than that held by the walls of many towns.
This was made level with the ground, not because of some
        treasonous crime,
    but because it seemed to be harmful in its luxury.
Caesar bore the destruction of so great a construction
    and lost so much wealth to which he was heir.
In this way an accounting should be made and an example produced,
    as the avenger himself does what he admonishes others to do.

The moral message of the structure is made abundantly clear in Ovid's formulation: Vedius' house was scandalously large and luxurious, so that the gesture of dedicating a public monument in its place was a noteworthy gesture of both generosity to the public and personal self-denial. Where the house was a symbol of private excess, the portico is an expression of civic-minded philanthropy. The point is driven home by the choice to inscribe Livia's name on the monument rather than Vedius' or, indeed, Augustus' own. As Dio notes, even though Vedius' will requested a structure explicitly for use by the public, his secret goal was a memorial to himself; by having Livia named as the patron for the portico, Augustus not only denies Vedius the opportunity for (posthumous) self-aggrandizement, but performatively gives up his own in favour of his wife. This is perhaps why Ovid's description of the structure in the *Ars Amatoria* focuses explicitly on its name: *nec tibi vitetur quae, priscis sparsa tabellis, / porticus auctoris Livia nomen habet* ('nor should you shun the colonnade "Livia", which, strewn with ancient paintings, has the name of its founder': *AA* 1. 71–2). The point, as in Dio, is that it is *not* the Porticus Augusti.[35]

Livia's name, then, works along with the portico structure: on the one hand, to refuse the sort of luxurious private extravagance represented by Vedius' house, and, on the other, to celebrate a different kind of 'domestic' model, one which benefits the public rather than an individual man. In the sense that Livia here stands for Augustus, of course, the self-effacing gesture is a hollow one, but the gesture none the less remains, along with an important sense of the princeps as a part of a loving and loyal marriage.[36] This sense would be reinforced if, along with the majority of scholars, we take the small square structure represented on the marble plan at the centre of the portico as Livia's shrine to Concordia.[37] Ovid certainly associates the

[35] On the fact that 'naming a building for someone else, particularly a family member, was unprecedented' before the portico of Octavia and the theatre of Marcellus, see Severy (2003) 91 and (on the ideological investments of the complex generally) 90–4.

[36] For a discussion of Livia's ambiguous position between public and private, and the effect which it had on ideals of femininity for imperial women, see Purcell (1986); Severy (2003) 232–43. On the historiography of imperial women and their public roles, see Fischler (1994). One piece of evidence which shows the further movement of imperial women's 'domestic' roles into the public sphere is the *senatus consultum de Cn. Pisone Patre*, a recently discovered senatorial decree of 20 CE. This document, which survives in several inscriptions, uses the idea of the imperial house and the language of familial relations to frame the condemnation of Cn. Piso for conspiracy and treason. The women of the imperial house play a particularly prominent role in the decree: Severy (2000).

[37] The Severan marble plan is a giant marble map of Rome, created *c.*200 CE, which shows buildings and other architectural features in outline form. Unfortunately, today only fragments remain. On the relationship between the Aedes Concordiae, dedicated by Livia within the Portico, and the Templum Concordiae, restored by Tiberius in the Forum Romanum, see Barrett (2002) 201–2 and 315–16.

portico and the shrine, and notes of the latter *quam caro praestitit ipsa viro* ('which she herself offered to her dear husband': *Fasti* 6. 638). As I noted earlier, Concordia encompasses a happy ambiguity as either a conjugal or civic virtue; but in this instance, even if we read it with Ovid as strictly 'domestic' in import, it still manages to communicate a 'political' message, about Augustus, Livia, and the ways in which their bond might stand against the kind of private immorality represented in Vedius' house. It is worth noting, moreover, that Octavia's portico also replaced a monument which had been, in its day, associated with luxury and the glorification of an individual: the Porticus Metelli was built by Caecilius Metellus Macedonicus after his victory over the Macedonians in 148 BCE, and contained, along with a famous statue group made by Lysippus for Alexander the Great, the first marble temple in Rome. For this, although he is otherwise rather complimentary to Metellus' character, Velleius Paterculus calls him *vel magnificentiae vel luxuriae princeps* ('the leader in magnificence or perhaps intemperance': 1. 11. 5) and lists his portico as one of those whose construction marked the transition to luxurious decline in Rome (2. 1. 1.: see pp. 59–60 above). The gesture made by replacing this colonnade with one dedicated by Augustus' sister is similar to that made by replacing the house of Vedius Pollio with the Porticus Liviae, in the sense that a structure which originated as luxurious self-advertisement gives way to one genuinely and freely offered to the people of Rome.

Livia and Octavia thus fulfil here a role which could not have been played by, for instance, Agrippa, although he too was a patron of porticoes; because they are women, their relationship with political power always appears tangential and their building projects, therefore, untainted by hope for personal gain. The fact that they can be nothing more than private citizens means that they may act unambiguously for the public good. Such an irony is an example of the ways in which gender as a destabilizing force might work for Augustan ideology as well as—in Ovid's tongue-in-cheek version in *Tristia* 2—against it. By using women in his construction of a new Roman landscape, the princeps may have given Ovid the opportunity to portray the city as a buffet of likely ladies, but he also could construct a kind of politicized privacy, a way for an individual to have power and influence outside of the traditional structures of republican civic life. Indeed, on a brutal level, this is the story told by the Danaid portico, with its fifty murderous brides and their father with his drawn sword (*Belides et stricto stat ferus ense pater*: Ovid *AA* 1. 74, and cf. *Tristia* 3. 1. 62), which Ovid explicitly connects with the porticoes of Octavia and Livia as a 'gendered' Augustan monument.[38] Danaus' drawn sword has not generally struck commentators as odd, although it probably should have: after all, *he* didn't kill anyone on his daughters' wedding night.[39] His drawn sword seems, in this context, a bit impotent, especially since his daughters were forced to their crime because he had been unable to prevent the marriage. The story of the Danaids thus does not simply carry the message that women's 'private' actions may have political effects, but that they may be politically effective where men's are not. As an extension of the imperial house on the Palatine hill, therefore, the Danaid portico, like the porticoes of Livia and Octavia, illustrates the extent to which a certain kind of gendered domestic virtue may be a force to be reckoned with on the public stage.

AUGUSTUS, CICERO, AND THE HOUSE ON THE HILL

The Danaid portico on the Palatine thus appears not simply as an allegory of the battle of Actium but as a celebration of the politicization of a family bond, as the daughters' obedience to their father becomes the (rather bloody) solution to the dynastic and territorial

---

[38] Gendered, of course, in his terms, as a site of love affairs. Ellen O'Gorman (1997) has discussed the appearance of the Danaid portico in *Ars Amatoria* 1 and *Tristia* 3. 1 as a site of contestation between Ovid and Augustus in the role of *magister*.

[39] No trace of this statue has been found, although some figures which might be those of the Danaids were excavated in the area of the temple of Apollo on the Palatine: Tomei (1990) and (1997) 56–7.

quarrel between Danaus and Aegyptus. In the sense, then, that the theme of its decorative scheme blends public and private life, the portico is a fitting symbol for the Palatine complex as a whole, which functioned as both the residence of the imperial family and a focus of civic life. Of course, it has been noted that under the Roman Republic the house was never what we might term 'private' space, so that Augustus' creation of a simultaneously public and domestic complex on the Palatine follows on neatly from the role which the house had come to play in Roman society during the last centuries BCE.[40] The sense of continuity from late republican precedents must have been strengthened by the fact that the hill had long been a favoured site for elite houses, although the vast majority of the republican structures were lost in the later building and rebuilding under the Empire. Famous names from the last two centuries BCE, however, crop up repeatedly in the textual record connected with residences on the hill above the Forum: the orator Q. Hortensius Hortalus, whose house was later owned by Augustus; the general Q. Lutatius Catulus, in whose atrium the princes Gaius and Lucius were tutored by Verrius Flaccus when it too had become part of the palace;[41] C. Sempronius Gracchus and P. Cornelius Sulla; P. Clodius Pulcher and T. Annius Milo.[42] Indeed, one of the most paradigmatic stories about the complex relationship between individual, house, and community in republican Rome took place on the Palatine: when M. Livius Drusus was building his house on the hill in the early first century BCE, the architect offered to build it so that 'it might not be overlooked and be safe from all witnesses'. In a display of openness praised by later generations, the tribune responded, *si quid in te artis est, ita compone domum meam, ut, quidquid agam, ab omnibus perspici possit* ('if you have any kind of skill, you will build my house so that, no matter what I am doing, everyone can see it').[43]

---

[40] Royo (1999) 9–45.   [41] Suetonius, *Gramm.* 17.

[42] For a thorough list of occupants from the 2nd cent. to 36 BCE, see Royo (1999) 70–5.

[43] Velleius Paterculus 2. 14. 3; cf. Plutarch, *Mor.* 800 F.

The story of Drusus underscores the role of the house as a performance of self for the benefit of other members of the community—as, in other words, a kind of public space. For the Roman man active in politics, the visibility of his virtue in the private sphere was an indispensable part of his public persona; it was not so much being good as being seen to be good which mattered in the conduct of civic life.[44] It is not surprising, therefore, that the Palatine generally, and the site of Drusus' house particularly, would become the location of perhaps the most significant material and textual battle over public and private space which the Roman Republic ever witnessed. In 62 BCE, the orator Cicero purchased the house which then stood on the site of Drusus'. It had belonged, so Cicero tells us, to Crassus' father and was apparently rather beyond its new owner's means: having bought the house, the orator jokes in a letter to P. Sestius that he is now in search of a conspiracy to join in order to pay it off (*ad Fam.* 5. 6. 2). In fact, the house was read as an index of the extent to which Cicero had overstepped himself both socially and politically: he reports an exchange in the senate in which Clodius refers to him as *hic rex*[45] and charges, *domum ... emisti* ('you bought a house'), to which Cicero retorts, *putes ... dicere 'iudices emisti'* ('you would think you were saying I'd bought the jury': *ad Att.* 1. 16. 10). In private, however, Cicero defends the purchase to Atticus, saying *homines intellegere coeperunt licere amicorum facultatibus in emendo ad dignitatem aliquam pervenire* ('People are beginning to understand that it is permissible to arrive at a certain status through buying things with the help of friends': *ad Att.* 1. 13. 6). Unfortunately, the vicissitudes of Cicero's career came to be reflected in the material history of his dwelling on the Palatine: when he was exiled from Rome in 58, it

[44] This point has been driven home in recent years especially by scholars interested in the elite Roman male's self-presentation in rhetorical contexts: most famously, Gleason (1995), esp. ch. 3 ('Deportment as Language'), but see also Gunderson (1998); Walters (1998); Corbeill (2002).

[45] *quousque ... hunc regem feremus?* ('how long ... shall we tolerate this king?'). A similar criticism was apparently made of the orator's villa in Tusculum, which was not only substantial but had the additional cachet of having once been owned by the Catuli, an old senatorial family (*ad Att.* 4. 5. 2).

was destroyed under the auspices of the first Triumvirate; the site was acquired by Cicero's long-time enemy Clodius and built over with a portico and shrine to Libertas; after Cicero returned to Rome in 57, he sued to have the land returned to him and the house rebuilt.

The speech which Cicero wrote for the hearing of this case before the Pontifical College, *de Domo Sua*,[46] offers a remarkable example of the ways in which a house might be used in the late Republic as a potent material and discursive symbol of a man's position in public life.[47] Looking forward, however, it is also worth noting the extent to which the speech writes and rewrites the terms within which structures other than the house might be read. Most strikingly, given the importance later ascribed to Augustus' Danaid portico on the Palatine hill, one of the major questions on which speech turns is whether a Palatine portico—in this case, the Porticus Catuli—should be considered public or private space, and one of the major rhetorical structures through which that question is answered is the contrast between different 'types' of women. This is not, I hasten to add, to argue that there was a particular material relationship between the houses of Cicero and Augustus, which is a question notoriously fraught with difficulty.[48] Even if we assume, on the basis of good but circumstantial evidence, that the so-called Houses of Livia and Augustus on the Palatine were in fact part of the first 'imperial' residence, we are still left with the question of locating Cicero's dwelling, of which no material trace remains.[49] We are forced, therefore, to fall back on textual evidence, principally the speeches and letters of Cicero, which offer a frustratingly ambiguous picture of how the hill was structured in the middle of the first century BCE. But this ambiguity, I would argue, is primarily testimony to the

[46] The case went to the pontiffs because Clodius claimed to have dedicated the site to Libertas; Cicero needed to have the dedication declared void before he could reclaim and rebuild his house.

[47] See Berg (1997) and Hales (2000) for the 'republican' nature of Cicero's battle for his house.

[48] Recent attempts to match the material and textual record on Cicero's house are Cerutti (1997) and Papi (1998). Cf. Berg (1997) 127–32.

[49] On the Houses of Augustus and Livia see Carettoni (1983); Barton (1996a) 91–3.

extent to which the landscape was continuously rhetorically manipulated for particular social and political ends. For instance, much has
been made of the fact that Cicero notes in the *de Domo Sua* that his
house stood 'within the sight of almost the entire city' (*in conspectu
prope totius urbis*: 100), a statement which has been taken to mean that
it stood on the side of the Palatine which overlooks the Forum Romanum. This may well be true, but it seems equally likely that Cicero is
attempting to evoke the story of Drusus (and its message of staunch
republican virtue) told above, of a house with nothing to hide. The
extent to which Cicero's house, or Drusus' for that matter, was 'really'
able to be seen by everyone in Rome is caught up in the rhetorical value
of representing it to be so. Indeed, the act of stating its 'viewability' to
the populace might on some level substitute for the material reality of a
prominent position on the hill, since it would serve to call attention to
it over other, equally or more visible, structures in the same place.

This is not to say that we should abandon hope of using textual
evidence to reconstruct a picture of the Palatine hill before the great
imperial structures whose remains now dominate the site. Rather it is
to point out that Rome generally, and in particular the ideologically
charged Palatine, existed in a complicated nexus of material and
discursive constructions; the experience of the landscape, both of
those who lived there and those who did not, was informed not only
by the buildings which were actually there but by the rumours, dec-
larations, stories, innuendoes and other verbal representations which
sought to give particular meanings to the built environment. I would
argue that it is on this level, regardless of what material relationship
there was between the structures, that we may see a real continuity
between Cicero's dwelling on the Palatine and Augustus', between
(ironically) the house as the last gasp of republican pride and the
house as 'palatial' symbol of the emperor's power. Both Cicero and
Augustus recognized that textual manipulation was an important
component in affecting, and effecting, changes in the city's physical
landscape.[50] More than that, however, both orator and emperor seem

---

[50] On Cicero, see Vasaly (1993); on Augustus, Hardie (1992), and Leach (1997); on
both, Edwards (1996) 1–26.

to have understood that the house, both its actual structure and rhetorical representations of it, might be used systematically to construct and reconstruct the imagined relationship between an individual and the city as a whole, between the private man and his public role. Because of Cicero's importance as a figure in the late Republic, and the highly politically charged nature of the battle for his home on the Palatine, it must have been hard to ignore his presence and example when considering the meaning of a house on the hill.[51]

As I noted earlier, it is clear that, in one sense, the conflict over Cicero's house on the Palatine was a natural offshoot of the 'public' role which the elite house had long played in republican life. In the *de Domo Sua*, Cicero himself underscores the continuity, noting that the destruction of his dwelling was in the tradition of punishments inflicted on men who attempted to set themselves up as tyrants in Rome, from Spurius Maelius to Marcus Manlius, whose desire for personal power was rewarded by the obliteration of their personal property.[52] The sites of these houses were sometimes left empty, sometimes rededicated to public use: the house of Spurius Cassius was replaced with a temple to Tellus,[53] that of Manlius with a temple of Moneta;[54] the area called the Vacci Prata, once the place of Marcus Vaccus' house, may have been a public garden.[55] Closest to home (literally) for Cicero was Fulvius Flaccus' house on the Palatine, destroyed after his condemnation for conspiracy with

[51] Indeed, the very fact that there is no extant reference to the material relationship between the orator's house and the emperor's is itself a kind of evidence. If Suetonius (*Gramm.* 17) is to be believed and the imperial house eventually extended to include the former house of Catulus, it must have come close to encroaching on Cicero's, whose residence, as we will see below, was closely connected with Catulus' portico which was, in turn, close to his house.

[52] As Valerius Maximus says in a similar catalogue, *quantum ergo odii adversus hostes libertatis insitum animis antiqui haberent parietum ac tectorum in quibus versati fuerant ruinis testabantur* ('thus the ancients showed how much hatred they had in their hearts for the enemies of freedom by the ruins of walls and roofs within which [such enemies] used to live': 6. 3. 1c).

[53] Cicero, *de Dom.* 101; Val. Max. 6. 3. 1b.

[54] According to Val. Max. 6. 3. 1a and Livy 6. 20. 13; Cicero's version has the house replaced by two sacred groves (*de Dom.* 101).

[55] *de Dom* 101; Livy 8. 19. 4.

Gaius Gracchus and subseqently replaced by a portico built by Quintus Lutatius Catulus from the spoils of his victory over the Cimbri. It was this portico which Clodius rededicated as a shrine to Libertas and extended over part of Cicero's property after the orator's exile, a gesture whose symbolic force is delineated in the *de Domo Sua* (100–2):

in conspectu prope totius urbis domus est mea, pontifices: in qua si manet illud non monumentum urbis, sed sepulcrum, inimico nomine inscriptum, demigrandum mihi potius aliquo est quam habitandum in ea urbe, in qua tropaea et de me et de republica videam constituta. . . . ista autem fax ac furia patriae, cum urbem Pisone et Gabinio ducibus cepisset, occupasset, teneret, uno eodemque tempore et clarissimi viri mortui monumenta delebat et meam domum cum Flacci domo coniungebat, ut, qua poena senatus adfecerat eversorem civitatis, eadem iste oppresso senatu adficeret eum, quem patres conscripti custodem patriae iudicassent.

My house is visible from almost every part of the city, pontiffs: if it is to remain here not as a monument to the city, but as its tomb, inscribed with an enemy name, I must emigrate to some other place rather than live in a city where I must look upon a trophy set up both over me and over the Republic. . . . But that flaming scourge and avenging demon of his country, when, with Piso and Gabinius as his generals, he had captured, occupied, and held the city, at once both obliterated the monument of a very great man now dead and joined my house with that of Flaccus, so that, by the same penalty with which the senate had punished one who had overthrown the country, that one—when he had crushed the senate—punished one whom the conscript fathers had judged the saviour of the nation.

Clodius had managed both to destroy Catulus' memorial and to create a link both mental and material between Flaccus' fate and Cicero's. But the particular irony, as Cicero would have it, is that where Flaccus lost his house because he was a traitor, he himself lost his because of his patriotism, and where the construction of Catulus' portico was undertaken to commemorate a glorious Roman victory, Clodius' celebrates an enduring Roman shame. Clodius is thus doubly a traitor: not only has he notionally invaded the city, over-thrown its institutions, and destroyed its material fabric, but, by taking upon himself the responsibility for rebuilding the site on the Palatine, he has attempted to usurp the material manifestations of public power.

Despite its dedication to the goddess Libertas, therefore, Clodius' portico is no more nor less than a manifestation of its dedicator's arrogance and private appetites. Cicero argues that, under the *lex Papiria*, Clodius could not have dedicated his portico without the mandate of the people, a mandate which he did not bother to seek since he knew he would not receive it (127–8); he contrasts the behaviour of Clodius with that of C. Cassius, who in a spirit of genuine public-mindedness dedicated a statue to Concord in the Senate House—*ille in curia quae poterat sine cuiusquam incommodo dedicari: tu in civis optime de re publica meriti cruore ac paene ossibus simulacrum... collocasti* ('he (sc. Cassius) [set his statue] in the Senate House, which was able to be dedicated without any distress to anyone: you placed an image in the blood or even on the very bones of a citizen who had done his utmost for the Republic': 131). Most particularly, Cicero continuously insists that Clodius' religious pretensions are a sham, an excuse concocted because he was 'aflame with lust for the site, with lust for the dwelling' (*cum loci illius, cum aedium cupiditate flagraret*: 107).[56] What he really wanted was not a public religious space but a bigger house: 'But see the man's unbearable audacity along with his precipitate and unbridled greed. Was such a man ever thinking about a memorial or sacred site? He wanted to live in luxury and splendour and to join together two great and worthy houses'.[57] The proof, as Cicero would have it, is that Clodius has actually devoted very little of the Palatine property to the extension of Catulus' portico, since he hoped to keep most of it for his own private use (116):

---

[56] Cicero, in fact, likes the image so much he uses it again later in the same paragraph: *meam domum, cuius cupiditate inflammatus erat.*

[57] *at videte hominis intolerabilem audaciam cum proiecta quadam et effrenata cupiditate. monumentum iste umquam aut religionem ullam excogitavit? habitare laxe et magnifice voluit duasque et magnas et nobiles domos coniungere* (115).

domus illa mea prope tota vacua est: vix pars aedium mearum decima ad
Catuli porticum accessit. causa fuit ambulatio. . . . in Palatio, pulcherrimo
prospectu, porticum cum conclavibus pavimentatam trecentum pedum
concupierat, amplissimum peristylum, cetera eius modi, facile ut omnium
domos et laxitate et dignitate superaret.

My house is almost completely unconsecrated: scarcely a tenth part of it has
been added to the portico of Catulus. The reason was a pleasure-
walk. . . . He desired to have, on the Palatine with its breathtaking view, a
paved portico of three hundred feet, with private side rooms, an extremely
large peristyle, and everything else styled in such a way that it might easily
outdo every other house in spaciousness and display of status.

Clodius may have built a portico, but it is not, like Catulus',
dedicated to the greater glory of the city; it is instead an *ambulatio*,
a private walkway, meant to display Clodius' personal importance
and satisfy his private desires. As Cicero cries in conclusion to this
section of the speech, *hanc vos, pontifices, tam variam, tam novam in
omni genere voluntatem, impudentiam, audaciam, cupiditatem com-
probabitis?* ('Will you, pontiffs, give your approval to such a multi-
farious hunger—unprecedented in any form—to such impudence,
audacity, and greed?': 116).

The invocation here of such 'consuming passions' (*voluntas, impu-
dentia, audacia, cupiditas*) is traditional in the criticism of luxury by
Roman moralists, a criticism which is in turn often associated with
femininity. It is not surprising, therefore, that one of the most potent
symbols of Clodius' brazenness in the *de Domo Sua* appears as a
woman, and offers Cicero the opportunity to use traditional ideals of
femininity to drive home the particular spatial and social message of
his speech. In the same way that Cicero dispenses with Clodius'
extension of the portico by representing it as an *ambulatio*, a private
pleasure-walk rather than a public monument, his representation of
the shrine to Liberty is as a (deeply ironic) celebration of Clodius'
personal licentiousness rather than the freedom of the Roman
Republic: *signum magis istorum quam publicae libertatis* ('a symbol
of the liberty of those of his ilk more than of the state': 112). The
rhetorical mechanism for this effect is a description of the history of

'Liberty's' statue, which, it transpires, was originally a funerary monument to a Tanagrean prostitute, or so Cicero would have it (111). The statue was carried off as spoil from Greece, along with numerous other works of art, by Clodius' brother Appius Claudius. This booty he first deposited not in a public place, but in his own house, no doubt 'for the glory of the Roman people' (*honoris populi romani causa*), Cicero notes sarcastically; subsequently, when he became concerned that he might have to return what he had stolen, he turned the statue over to Clodius for his shrine in the portico. The point is that although Appius Claudius was supposedly collecting the booty for public display when he was curule aedile, he actually wanted it all for his own personal use; Cicero says that he managed to avoid the aedileship and put the money thereby saved into 'two places, some in his coffers, some in his pleasure gardens' (*aedilitatem duobus in locis, partim in arca, partim in hortis suis, collocavit: de Dom.* 112). Like his brother, therefore, his goal was to rob the state for his private pleasure.[58]

Clodius' 'Liberty', therefore, is nothing more than a foreign prostitute—*Tanagraea quaedam meretrix* (111)—who has driven out from the Palatine site not only Cicero, but the domestic gods to whom the place rightly belongs: *ista tua pulchra Libertas deos penates et familiares meos lares expulit, ut se ipsa tamquam in captivis sedibus collocaret?* ('Did that pretty Liberty of yours drive out the penates and my familial lares, in order that she should settle herself as if in a captured dwelling?': 109). As a woman and a foreigner, Libertas' statue represents the forces of Clodius' personal debauchery arrayed against the lares and penates which adorn a Roman citizen's house. Moreover, the statue's role as an imported eastern luxury marks her as a monument to the selfish and immoral consumption of the Empire's wealth by men such as Clodius, his brother, and their friends.[59] This point is also made elsewhere in the speech, when Cicero laments the treatment of his family (*de Dom.* 59–60):

[58] See Nisbet (1939: 163–4) for a fuller explication.
[59] See Pollitt (1978) for an analysis of Roman attitudes to 'foreign' art. It was a traditional notion that Roman culture had been corrupted by the art which had begun to

quid enim vos uxor mea misera violarat, quam vexavistis, raptavistis, omni crudelitate lacerastis? quid mea filia, cuius fletus adsiduus sordesque lugubres vobis erant iucundae, ceterorum omnium mentis oculosque flectebant? . . . sed quid ego vestram crudelitatem exprobro, quam in ipsum me ac meos adhibuistis: qui parietibus, qui tectis, qui columnis ac postibus meis hostificum quoddam et nefarium, omni imbutum odio bellum intulistis? . . . non existimo Campanum illum consulem cum saltatore collega, cum alteri totam Achaiam, Thessaliam, Boeotiam, Graeciam, Macedoniam omnemque barbariam, bona civium Romanorum condonasses, alteri Syriam, Babylonem, Persas, integerrimas pacatissimasque gentes, ad diripiendum tradidisses, illos tam cupidos liminum meorum et columnarum et valvarum fuisse.

But what harm did my unhappy wife do you, she whom you tormented, ravished, tortured with every form of cruelty? What did my daughter do, whose continuous weeping and mourning garments were so pleasant to you, although they moved the spirits and eyes of everyone else? . . . But why should I bring up the cruelty which you showed to me myself and my family, when you are the men who brought genuinely inimical and unholy war—war infected with every kind of bile—against my walls, my roof, my columns, and door-posts? . . . I don't think that the Campanian consul and his dancer colleague were so desirous of my thresholds, columns, and doors, when you had given to one of them as a gift all of Achaea, Thessalia, Boeotia, Greece, Macedonia, and all foreign territory, the property of Roman citizens, and handed over to the other Syria, Babylon, and Persia—stalwart and peaceful peoples—for his plundering.

The 'Campanian consul and his dancer colleague' here are L. Calpurnius Piso and A. Gabinius, the two consuls of 58, who were awarded control of the provinces named on the same day and through the same machinations that Clodius used to engineer the banishment of Cicero.[60] The pillaging of Cicero's house and the torment of his family by Clodius in Rome are thus made parallel to the torment experienced by the peoples governed by Clodius' henchmen in the rest of the Empire. This comparison is assisted by the fact

pour into Rome following the conquest of Carthage: see e.g. Sallust, *Bell. Cat.* 11. 5 and Livy 25. 40. 2–3.

[60] Nisbet (1939), pp. xiv–xv.

that almost all of the provinces listed above have grammatically feminine names, and were traditionally personified as female—as, for instance, on the reliefs of the Sebasteion at Aphrodisias.[61] Cicero's staunchly Roman wife and daughter were made by Clodius to suffer the same fate as captive 'barbarian' peoples at the edges of the Empire.

The connection between this passage and the description of Liberty's statue is thus made through the references to the plundering of eastern provinces, as well as the contrast between the good women of Cicero's family—intimately associated here with the physical structure of the house—and the *meretrix* Libertas who occupies Clodius' new portico.[62] The point which Cicero is making in chs. 59–60 is reiterated when he returns to the theme in 111, namely that Clodius and his friends have not only consumed the wealth of the Roman Empire (*bona civium Romanorum*) to indulge their personal desires, but they have then turned their attention to 'making war' on Cicero's home and family. The particular emphasis on *hostificum quoddam... bellum* underscores the point that they have attacked his house as though they, or it, were a foreign nation; he later makes the parallel explicit by noting the Roman practice of razing the cities of defeated peoples and comparing it with the treatment given his house (61). The representation of the house as city is further assisted through the image of Cicero's 'tormented, ravished, and tortured' wife and his weeping daughter, who recall the stock images of female suffering following defeat in war. Cicero's house was not simply a place where he and his family lived, but here is assimilated to a city-state whose tragic fall may be described in the same terms used elsewhere to characterize the destruction of Troy or Alba Longa.[63] In the same way, then, that Libertas, as both prostitute and looted foreign art, represents the ways that Clodius' 'public' portico is in fact devoted to 'private' immorality, the sufferings of the good

---

[61] Smith (1988) 50–77.   [62] Treggiari (1999), 53–6; cf. Treggiari (1998).
[63] Paul (1982); Rossi (2002).

women in Cicero's house serve to characterize it as 'national' rather than simply domestic space.

There is, in this sense, a neat rhetorical shift in the *de Domo Sua*'s reading of power, space, and morality on the Palatine, a shift which is effected, in part, through the contrasting images of women noted above. Clodius would represent Cicero as a new Flaccus, who lost his private property as punishment for his private ambition, and himself as a new Catulus, dedicating a portico as a public and pious gesture to the greater glory of Rome. But the *de Domo Sua* reverses the roles and their meanings, so that Cicero's destroyed house becomes a public monument and Clodius' portico a symbol of his personal greed. Thus, Cicero repeatedly insists on representing the new Palatine portico which has replaced his house as a monument not simply to his individual grief but as a symbol of public disaster;[64] he calls Clodius 'not an enemy of mine, but a communal foe' (*non ab inimico meo, sed ab hoste communi*: 101); he insists that all who had 'polluted' (*contaminaverunt*) themselves by taking part in the dissolution of the house and its contents have been subject to both public and private prosecution (*nullius neque privati neque publici iudicii poenam effugere potuerunt*: 108). He concludes the speech by insisting that it is not the destruction of his material property which concerns him—'I have always thought that it is not so much the easy acquisition or quantity of goods which should be sought, but rather moderation in their use and calm in their loss'[65]—but the symbolic affront to himself and the state: *domo ... carere sine maxima ignominia rei publicae, meo dedecore ac dolore non possum* ('I cannot

___

[64] *sin mea domus non modo mihi non redditur, sed etiam monumentum praebet inimico doloris mei, sceleris sui, publicae calamitatis. . . .* ('if my house is not only not returned to me, but even provides my enemy a monument of my grief, his own wickedness, the state's disaster . . .': 100); *hanc vero in Palatio atque in pulcherrimo urbis loco porticum esse patiemini, furoris tribunicii, sceleris consularis, crudelitatis coniuratorum, calamitatis rei publicae, doloris mei defixum indicium?* ('will you indeed allow this portico to stand on the Palatine and in the city's most lovely spot, as a permanent sign of a tribune's madness, a consul's wickedness, the cruelty of conspirators, the disaster of the Republic, and my own grief?': 103).

[65] *quorum [sc. bonorum] ego non tam facultatem umquam et copiam expetendam putavi, quam et in utendo rationem et in carendo patientiam* (146).

lose my house... without the greatest disgrace upon the state, without my own shame and grief': 146). If the house is to be restored, moreover, it should be done not because Cicero wishes it, but only 'if my return is gratifying and pleasing to the immortal gods, the senate, the Roman people, the rest of Italy, the provinces, the foreign nations, and to you yourselves' (*si dis immortalibus, si senatui, si populo Romano, si cunctae Italiae, si provinciis, si exteris nationibus, si vobismet ipsis... gratum et iucundum meum reditum*: 147). Insofar as Cicero's house is synonymous with his *dignitas*, and his *dignitas* with the power and prestige of the Roman Republic, the entire world ought to join together to see the orator restored to his home.

In other words, although Cicero's house may have looked like a private structure, it was in fact a state monument; Clodius' portico may look like a public building, but it is in fact dedicated to the use and abuse of its owner alone. The *de Domo Sua*, then, certainly draws on the tradition which understands an elite house as, on some level, 'public' space. Yet it is also important to take note of the innovation which is expressed in the speech's representation of Cicero's dwelling not simply as an expression of his own individual position, but as directly reflecting the authority and status of the Roman people. Whereas his earlier reading of the Palatine house was as a support of his personal *dignitas*, in the *de Domo Sua* he repeatedly invokes the *dignitas* of the Res Publica, or of the Roman people: e.g. *hanc vero, pontifices, labem turpitudinis et inconstantiae poterit populi Romani dignitas sustinere... ut domus M. Tullii Ciceronis cum domo M. Fulvii Flacci ad memoriam poenae publice constitutae coniuncta esse videatur?* ('Shall the dignity of the Roman people, priests, really be able to withstand the stain of disgrace and disloyalty... that the house of M. Tullius Cicero should seem to be joined with that of M. Fulvius Flaccus with regards to the memory of a publicly assessed punishment?': 102).[66] The point is that Cicero would have his house understood as public space not simply because the public may be admitted there, or because it represents his role as a public figure, but

---

[66] Cf. *de Dom.* 1, 89.

because it may be construed as representing the state itself. Thus, its original destruction at the hands of Catiline's men, serves as metonymy for what they wished to do to the country generally,[67] and its subsequent restoration was done at public expense. As the orator would proclaim later, after the house had been rebuilt by order of the senate, 'there are many houses in this city, senators, practically all of them, I expect, held by unassailable right—by private right, by hereditary right, by right of authority, by right of seizure, by mortgage—[but] I would deny that there is any other house which is maintained equally by private and unassailable title, and also by every significant public, human, and divine law... The full senate decreed that whoever attacked my house would be judged to have attacked the state.'[68]

While it is important never to underestimate Cicero's impulse toward self-aggrandizement (in the same speech he reports that someone recently asked him to which country he belonged and he answered, 'to one which could not exist without me'), the orator's testimony in *de Domo Sua* and *de Haruspicum Responsis* illustrates, I would argue, a kind of middle stage between the houses of great public figures in the Republic proper and the imperial house which was about to come into being on the Palatine hill. If Cicero's representation of the senate's actions in the quotation above is to be believed, it would seem that Rome's governing body had followed

---

[67] *domus ardebat in Palatio non fortuito, sed oblato incendio: consules epulabantur et in coniuratorum gratulatione versabantur, cum alter se Catilinae delicias, alter Cethegi consobrinum fuisse diceret. hanc ego vim, pontifices, hoc scelus, hunc furorem meo corpore opposito ab omnium bonorum cervicibus depuli...* ('My house on the Palatine was burning, not by accident but because of arson: the consuls were dining out and basking in the congratulations of the conspirators, as one of them remarked that he had been Catiline's darling, and the other that he was Cethegus' cousin. This was the violence, the evil, the madness which I warded off from the necks of all good men by interposing my own body...': 63).

[68] *multae sunt domus in hac urbe, patres conscripti, atque haud scio an paene cunctae iure optimo, sed tamen iure privato, iure hereditario, iure auctoritatis, iure mancipi, iure nexi: nego esse ullam domum aliam aeque privato iure atque optima lege, publico vero omni praecipuo et humano et divino iure munitam... decrevit idem senatus frequentissimus, qui meam domum violasset, contra rem publicam esse facturum* (*de Haruspicum Responsis* 14–15).

in actuality the lead which the orator had laid out rhetorically in the *de Domo Sua*: they made his house legally synonymous with the Roman state, a dramatic statement about its role as 'public' space. Augustus himself would never insist on the same honour for his own Palatine dwelling, but it is worth noting that Cassius Dio connects Augustus' receipt of tribunician inviolability with the offer of a house (Dio 49. 15. 5–6):

ἀλλὰ ταῦτα μὲν ἄλλως ἐθρυλεῖτο, τότε δὲ οἰκίαν τε αὐτῷ ἐκ τοῦ δημοσίου δοθῆναι ἔγνωσαν· τὸν γὰρ τόπον ὃν ἐν τῷ Παλατίῳ, ὥστ' οἰκοδομῆσαί τινα, ἐώνητο, ἐδημοσίωσε καὶ τῷ Ἀπόλλωνι ἱέρωσεν, ἐπειδὴ κεραυνὸς ἐς αὐτὸν ἐγκατέσκηψε. τήν τε οὖν οἰκίαν αὐτῷ ἐψηφίσαντο, καὶ τὸ μήτε ἔργῳ μήτε λόγῳ τι ὑβρίζεσθαι· εἰ δὲ μή, τοῖς αὐτοῖς τὸν τοιοῦτό τι δράσαντα ἐνέχεσθαι οἷσπερ ἐπὶ τῷ δημάρχῳ ἐτέτακτο.

But even while there was all this useless babble, they voted to give him a house out of state property; for the site on the Palatine which he had purchased in order to build a house, he had made public and dedicated to Apollo, since it had been struck by lightning. They therefore voted him the house, and also that he should not be shown violence by either deed or word; anyone who did this would be punished in the same way as if he had offended against a tribune.

Cicero may have received protection for his house, but Augustus enjoyed it for his person, a distinction which reflects the different moments the awards were made as much as the individuals who were so rewarded. The extent to which the princeps was able to gather to himself the powers of both tribunate and consulship was an index of how little of the old republican system of checks and balances was left in place by 28 BCE. On the other hand, the fact that the offer of a publicly funded house and the personal protection afforded a tribune went hand-in-hand indicates the ways in which both represented a blending of public and private, of individual and state. The gesture would later be fully realized in Augustus' dedication of his dwelling on the Palatine to the people of Rome. Like Cicero's, then, Augustus' house would became more than simply the site of public business, more than simply the representation of a man's role in public life, but a symbol of Rome itself.

PUBLICIZING PRIVATE LIFE: GENDER AND THE IMPERIAL HOUSE

The variety of types of women in Cicero's *de Domo Sua* is, I would argue, an index of the ways in which gender might be used—indeed *was* used—to represent the complexities of public and private space on the Palatine hill. We can see here that the issue is not as simple as finding good wives and daughters used to embody the pure privacy of Cicero's house, or the prostitute Libertas used to articulate Clodius' portico as public space. In fact, as I have argued above, the situation is exactly the reverse: the Tanagrean statue illustrates the ways in which Clodius and his henchmen have taken public property and used it to satisfy their own private desires; the sufferings of Cicero's female family members help to make his house rhetorically into a conquered city, one step on the road to representing it as synonymous with Rome itself. In the same way that Livia's portico uses female domestic virtue to purify the site of Vedius Pollio's luxurious house in the name of public morality, the restoration of Cicero's house on the Palatine and of its tragically dispossessed womenfolk are triumphs not so much of the house's owner as of the republican state. The complications of reading gender in the Danaid portico, of understanding why and how the Augustan structure employs a story about female domesticity to make an ideological point, must be seen within the context of this wider concept of using women to represent a purer, 'publicized', domestic practice. Indeed, turning to a more direct consideration of the imperial house itself (that is, the residential structure which formed part of the Palatine complex), it is clear that its function was as far more than a mere place for the first family to live, and that its female members were far from incidental in constructing a vision of what it meant for the first citizen in Rome to live anywhere at all.

As has been noted, the Palatine hill had long been the site of elite residences, including, apparently, some strikingly sumptuous ones:

Cicero spent three and a half million sesterces on his (*ad Fam* 5. 6. 2). In the *de Domo Sua*, the orator declared that Clodius was unable even to secure for his friends the support of 'your own Palatine' (*Palatinam tuam*: 19), indicating the extent to which the space was understood as synonymous with politically important, if morally suspect, homes. Augustus, however, seems to have insisted on a sumptuous display of wealth in the public spaces of his Palatine complex while reserving for the imperial residence a rather modest and self-effacing house which once belonged to the orator Hortensius. Suetonius famously describes it (*Div. Aug.* 72):

in ceteris partibus vitae continentissimum fuisse constat ac sine suspicione ullius vitii. habitavit primo iuxta Romanum forum supra scalas anularias, in domo quae Calvi oratoris fuerat; postea in Palatio, sed nihilo minus aedibus modicis Hortensianis, et neque laxitate neque cultu conspicuis, ut in quibus porticus breves essent Albanarum columnarum et sine marmore ullo aut insigni pavimento conclavia.

In all other aspects of his life it is agreed that he was most self-controlled and without suspicion of any vice. He lived first next to the Roman Forum, above the ring-makers' stairway, in the house which had belonged to the orator Calvus; afterwards, he lived on the Palatine, but still in the modest house of Hortensius, which was noteworthy neither for its size nor decoration, as it had short porticoes of Alban columns and little rooms without any marble or decorated pavement.

Whether or not this second house should be considered the same as that of which parts still remain on the Palatine hill is not certain; the lavish paintings which it contains seem hard to reconcile with Suetonius' description of the humbleness of Hortensius' house.[69] But it is clear that, whatever the truth of the matter, Suetonius

---

[69] It is perhaps worth noting that when Suetonius later mentions that some of Augustus' furnishings still survive in his own day, he does not indicate that he has seen the actual house in which the princeps lived. The only contemporary description of the inside of an Augustan imperial residence is the epigram of Antipater of Thessalonica, preserved in the *Palatine Anthology* (9. 59), in which the poet apparently describes an eleborate ceiling painting in the house of Augustus' adopted son Gaius. For commentary, see Gow and Page (1968) ii. 57. It is, of course, hard to know what relationship the text bore to material reality.

represents a tradition which saw a distinct contrast between the lavish marbles, mosaics, and colonnades which marked the public part of the complex and the simplicity of the space where the princeps actually lived.[70]

From our perspective, of course, the distinction between the public and private spaces on the Palatine appears artificial, since we can see how the temple, the libraries, the porticoes, and so on functioned to extend and enhance the domestic space to which they were connected.[71] This is particularly visible with hindsight, since as early as Tiberius and Caligula the imperial residence had taken on 'palatial' proportions. But the very artificiality of the distinction between public and private spaces in the Palatine complex underscores its significance. Augustus, in contrast with his successors, maintained humility and self-control in the spaces which reflected his identity as a private citizen. Suetonius notes that even in his day, material evidence of the first emperor's domestic modesty was still available for viewing: *instrumenti eius et supellectilis parsimonia apparet etiam nunc residuis lectis atque mensis, quorum pleraque vix privatae elegantiae sint* ('the frugality of his household equipment and furniture is still visible even now from the surviving couches and tables, which are scarcely of a quality for private life': *Div. Aug.* 73). The historian's testimony that more than a century later the furniture still existed, and was still closely associated with Augustus, indicates its role not simply as a characterization of its original owner but as an ideological statement about his position in public life. When Suetonius notes that the furniture which he saw

[70] Plutarch preserves a story which indicates that there was a similar contrast between Pompey's theatre complex and the house which he built near it: the person who moved into it after his death was amazed by its small size and enquired 'where did Pompey the Great dine?' (*Pomp.* 40. 5). It is possible, however, that the story is a later interpolation which retrojects the model of Augustus into the image of Pompey. Nevertheless, it is clear that Pompey's earlier complex was in many ways the precursor to a number of Augustan building projects: see Gros (1987).

[71] Thus, I. M. Barton (1996a) 94: 'What Augustus was doing, in effect, was to adapt his house to the needs of a situation in which the whole Roman poeple—Senators and all—had become the clientes of one man, the princeps'. See also Strothmann (2000) 81–9.

'was scarcely of a quality for private life' he sketches the outline of the paradox: in truth it was not private, but a performance of privacy for public consumption. Indeed, even the late gesture of making the house into public property must have only served to highlight the fact that, until that moment, the emperor—even as Pontifex Maximus, with the time-honoured right to live in the Domus Publica[72]—had dwelt in his own house, in (comparative) poverty.

The extent to which Augustus sought systematically to characterize himself and his household through a performance of traditional Roman domesticity is repeatedly emphasized in Suetonius' description of the princeps as a private individual, a description to which the *Divus Augustus* devotes almost as much space as the narrative of his public deeds.[73] Indeed, Suetonius articulates the two sides of the emperor in explicitly spatial terms, noting *referam nunc interiorem ac familiarem eius vitam* when he turns to his life at home. The following chapters then offer a rather surprising level of detail about the imperial house: the fact that Augustus slept in the same bedroom during winter and summer, for more than forty years, that his bed was a simple and unadorned affair; that he liked to decorate with antiques and objects of curiosity rather than statues and paintings (*Div. Aug.* 72–3). The unaffected Roman virtue displayed by the house reflects the virtuous private life of the princeps. The extent to which the house and its owner are imagined to be intertwined with one another is perhaps most strongly expressed when Suetonius notes Augustus' habit of wearing only 'domestic' clothing except

---

[72] Note that Julius Caesar, when Pontifex Maximus, lived there: Royo (1999) 21.

[73] Suetonius is explicit in making the transition from one to the other: *quoniam qualis in imperiis ac magistratibus regendaque per terrarum orbem pace belloque republica fuerit, exposui, referam nunc interiorem ac familiarem eius vitam quibusque moribus atque fortuna domi et inter suos egerit a iuventa usque ad supremum vitae diem* ('since I have explained what kind of man he was in military commands, public offices, and in ruling the Republic throughout the world in both peace and war, I will now discuss his private and family life, and with what morals and luck at home and amongst his kin he conducted himself, from childhood until the last day of his life': *Div. Aug.* 61). Of course, he is equally interested in the private lives of his other subjects, but that too may in part be Augustus' legacy.

on special occasions: *veste non temere alia quam domestica usus est, ab sorore et uxore et filia neptibusque confecta . . . et forensia autem et calceos numquam non intra cubiculum habuit ad subitos repentinosque casus parata* ('unless he had a good reason, he never wore anything other than his indoor clothes, which had been made by his sister or wife or daughter and granddaughters . . . but he also always had outdoor clothes and shoes in his bedroom, ready in case of sudden and unexpected events': *Div. Aug.* 73). The ideological point of this information is clear, that by choice the princeps was a simple, house-centred man; only when forced to it did he don the mantle of his public persona.

Of course, the 'fact' that Augustus almost always wore clothing made by the women of his family speaks not only of his domestic behaviour but also of theirs. The point is fleshed out further elsewhere in Suetonius' account (*Div. Aug.* 64):

filiam et neptes ita instituit, ut etiam lanificio assuefaceret vetaretque loqui aut agere quicquam nisi propalam et quod in diurnos commentarios referretur; extraneorum quidem coetu adeo prohibuit, ut L. Vinicio, claro decoroque iuveni, scripserit quondam parum modeste fecisse eum, quod filiam suam Baias salutatum venisset.

He taught his daughter and granddaughters that they should be accustomed even to work with wool, and he forbade them to say or to do anything that could not be reported with complete honesty in the daily diaries; in fact he was so strict about preventing their meeting with young men from outside the family that he once wrote to Lucius Vinicius, an honourable and decent young man, that he had displayed too little respect for propriety, because he had come to Baiae to pay a call on his daughter.

The spatial terms here are clear, not simply in the domestic dispatches which report the activities of the household to a wider readership, but in the disgraceful visit of Lucius Vinicius, whose crime was to be an *extraneus* (literally, 'an outsider') despite his otherwise unimpeachable character. Again, we see the emperor as displaying an obsession not simply with good domestic behaviour, but with the appearance of good domestic behaviour; what is judged correct within the house is determined by what may be told without scandal to those outside it. But equally important is the point that, like the descriptions of the house itself, the actions of the imperial women as part of the household are here made part of the characterization of Augustus: their correct performance of traditional domestic values reads as part of the princeps' own commitment to a virtuous Roman home.[74] In the same sense that the presence of the *meretrix* Libertas in Clodius' portico serves to represent it as a morally suspect space, the presence of good women in the imperial house is the basis for understanding it as solidly, one might even say stolidly, pure of taint.

Indeed, the appearance in the passage above not only of the *diurni commentarii,* apparently an Augustan invention, but also of the letter reprimanding Vinicius, points to one of the phenomena which characterized the Augustan period both in its own time and for later historians, namely the sheer volume of textual material produced by and about the imperial house. We cannot know how far and to whom the 'daily diaries' cited above circulated, although the implication that they were for public consumption is clear, but the collections of letters between the emperor and members of his family are well attested. Pliny the Elder, Aulus Gellius, Quintilian, and Suetonius all make reference to letters by the princeps; the latter two even claim to have read some written in his own hand.[75] Suetonius preserves numerous, rather tantalizing, quotations of communications from Augustus to Tiberius, to Gaius, to Germanicus, as well as to Julia and Agrippina. Some of the frankest and most extensive fragments are from his letters to Livia, in which he offers unflattering opinions about Claudius (*Div. Claud.* 4. 1–6); similar ones also appear to have existed concerning Tiberius, although these do not seem to have circulated so widely.[76] But what might be

[74] On the irony of 'publicizing' such 'private' information, see Kleiner (1996) 30.

[75] Quint. *Inst.* 1. 7. 22; Suet. *Div. Aug.* 71. 2. For testimonia and fragments, see Malcovati (1928) 6–31.

[76] Suetonius tells the story that, after Augustus' death and during a quarrel with her son, Livia produced from a hiding place 'small volumes' (*codicillos*) by her deceased husband which spoke about Tiberius' 'unpleasantness and intolerance' (*acerbitate et intolerantia*): Suet. *Tib.* 51. 1.

construed even loosely as 'political' in the letters shares space with the much more banal: he appears, for instance, to have written a great deal about what he was eating.[77] Pliny the Elder cites a letter in which the princeps claims to have been cured of ill health by bitter vetch.[78] The single extant letter to Julia is a simple note to accompany a gift of money (*Div. Aug.* 71), although Macrobius refers to a letter reproving her for her choice of companions (*Sat.* 2. 5. 6). The princeps also wrote to Tiberius about how much he won at dice (*Div. Aug.* 71); to Gaius about his (own) birthday (Aulus Gellius 15. 7. 3); to Agrippina about simplicity in rhetorical style (*Div. Aug.* 86).[79] Indeed, I would argue that the much-discussed colloquialisms in his writing style (who could forget 'quicker than boiling asparagus'?) must be understood as a rather sophisticated form of self-characterization.[80] Not unlike the 'untrained' speakers who appeared before juries in classical Athens, Augustus knew the ideological value of sounding like an ordinary man.

The fact that so many of the epistolary fragments are preserved in Suetonius is not a surprise, since he is well known for his love of (often prurient) personal detail. Augustus, however, seems to have offered the biographer an unprecedented volume of material from which to construct the picture which emerges from the *Divus Augustus*, of a man whose simple, unaffected, private persona contrasts sharply with the grandeur of his role in public life. It has recently been observed that we do not give sufficient credit to Augustus as an Augustan author—as, that is, one of the many writers

---

[77] e.g. *Verba ipsius ex epistulis sunt:* '*Nos in essedo panem et palmulas gustavimus*' ('These are his own words from a letter: "I ate bread and some small dates in my travelling-carriage" ': *Div. Aug.* 76).

[78] *NH* 18. 139.

[79] The subjects of the letters are in themselves curious. Note that the two letters to his male relatives concern trivial matters, but he writes to his granddaughter about rhetoric, a traditionally masculine and 'public' preserve. This reflects both the importance which Augustus himself was willing to accord to his female relatives and the very real historical role which Agrippina and her offspring would play in the continuation of the Julio-Claudian dynasty (on which, see my Epilogue, pp. 285–304).

[80] Suet. *Div. Aug.* 87; Aulus Gellius 10. 24. 1; cf. Quint. *Inst.* 1. 6. 19. For Augustus' concern with his own eloquence, see Millar (1977) 203–4, and on his 'private' letters, Millar (1977) 215.

whose texts served to produce an idea of who the princeps was and what his rule might mean.[81] Certainly, much attention has been paid to works like the *Res Gestae*, public statements about a public identity, but less notice has been given to the first emperor's publication of his private persona, through texts like the letters and his autobiography. My point is not that there is no reality to the image of Augustus which emerges from such 'personal' documents, but rather that we must take into account the deliberation (equal, I would argue, to the deliberation of the *Res Gestae*) with which that image was constructed.[82] We may note, for instance, the fact found in Suetonius that he always relied on a written text to assist him in speaking: *sermones quoque cum singulis atque etiam cum Livia sua graviores non nisi scriptos et e libello habebat, ne plus minusve loqueretur ex tempore* ('even his discussions with individuals, and also the more serious ones with his wife Livia, he did not conduct without having written them down, and [reading them] from a small book, lest he should say too much or too little when speaking off the cuff': *Div. Aug.* 84). Like his concern for what was recorded in the 'daily diaries' above, the point is that nothing, not even conversations between husband and wife, was to be left up to chance. Indeed, one of the most programmatic statements about the princeps' relationship to authority comes to be represented in the literary-historical tradition as a conversation between Augustus and Livia, namely when she urged him to exercise clemency towards L. Cinna and his co-conspirators after their plot to depose him.[83] Whether or not the conversation ever took place is beside the point; its significance lies in the way that it represents as natural the politicized and public nature of the domestic relationship.

Like descriptions of the imperial house, therefore, representations of the imperial house*hold* seem to have played an important role in the characterization of the first emperor. This characterization is

[81] Ando (2000) 138–52.

[82] For the different ideological investments of the autobiography and the *Res Gestae*, see Yavetz (1984) 1–3.

[83] As found in Seneca, *de Clementia* 1. 9 and Cass. Dio 55. 14–22.

particularly assisted by the, at first surprising, prominence of the women of Augustus' family in the 'official' textual record. I have already cited the letters to Livia, Agrippina, and Julia, and their role as heroines (or not) in the household diaries; it is worth noting that Augustus' first public act was to deliver his grandmother's funeral *laudatio* at the tender age of twelve.[84] It appears to have been the first episode in a lifetime of self-representation through the praise of female relatives. Of course, the women of the imperial household were not always cooperative with the princeps' desire to demonstrate domestic virtue. Augustus' relationship with his daughter Julia was famously fraught, and her behaviour hardly that of a model Roman woman.[85] But even this seems to have been incorporated into the historical tradition as a monument to Augustus' tragic and stalwart performance as a father rather than a failure on the part of imperial domesticity. Julia's supposed adultery became in later historians an established part of the rhetorical trope which emphasized the tribulations of Augustus, often used to make the point that even those who have risen high cannot escape the vicissitudes of fortune.[86] Macrobius preserves a humorous aphorism of Augustus' which makes clear the extent to which his domestic trials had been incorporated into his public persona: *itaque inter amicos dixit duas habere se filias delicatas, quas necesse haberet ferre, rem publicam et Iuliam* ('in fact, among friends, he said that he had two darling daughters who gave him trouble, the Republic and Julia': Macrobius, *Sat.* 2. 5. 4). Seneca the Younger articulates the situation in terms of a conflict between the duties of the emperor, who was required to publicize and punish his daughter's misdeeds, and the emotions of a father, who would have liked to conceal them. The point is that he did publish them, at the same time continuing to maintain a stance of being personally distraught by Julia's betrayal—the tragic irony of his own daughter being convicted under his own moral legislation used

[84] Suet. *Div. Aug.* 8; Quint. *Inst.* 12. 6. 1; Nicolaus of Damascus, *Life of Augustus* 3.
[85] She was banished in 2 BCE for adultery.
[86] e.g. Seneca, *de Clem* 1. 10. 3, *de Brev. Vit.* 4. 5, *de Ben.* 6. 32. 1; Pliny, *NH* 7. 149; Tacitus, *Ann.* 3. 24; Suet. *Div. Aug.* 65. 1.

as an opportunity to prove both the continuity and contrast between his public and private personae.

Among the self-representational documents which the princeps produced, however, his thirteen-volume autobiography must necessarily stand out, and the power and importance of female domesticity in Augustus' life appears as one of its major themes. The text itself is no longer extant, but it is universally agreed that Nicolaus of Damascus' *Life of Augustus* must have been closely based on it, especially sections 1–18 and 28–31 (the narrative of Caesar's assassination which occupies the middle section seems to have been drawn from a different work).[87] In these sections, after Augustus himself, his mother Atia is one of the most prominent characters in the work—almost as prominent as Julius Caesar, who lurks paternally through most of the narrative. Of course, the fragments of Nicolaus' *Life* begin when Augustus is less than 10, and break off when he is less than 20; since, moreover, his biological father was dead, his mother is necessarily prominent as the adult mainly responsible for the young man's upbringing. On the other hand, she is represented as taking a singularly active role in directing his activities, e.g. after he assumes the *toga virilis* at 14 (Nic. Dam. 10):

καίπερ δὲ κατὰ νόμον εἰς ἄνδρας ἐγγεγραμμένον διεκώλυεν ἡ μήτηρ ἔξω τῆς αὐλείου θύρας χωρεῖν, πλὴν ὅπη καὶ πρότερον, ὅτε παῖς ἦν, ἐφοίτα, δίαιτάν τε τὴν αὐτὴν ἔχειν ἐπηνάγκαζε κοιτάζεσθαί τε ἔνθα καὶ πρότερον ἐν τῷ αὐτῷ δωματίῳ. νόμῳ τε μόνον ἀνὴρ ἦν, τά δ' ἄλλα παιδικῶς ἐπεστατεῖτο.

Although under the law he had been enrolled among the men, his mother prevented him from going out of the house, except to frequent the places where he had gone before, when he was a boy, and she required him to keep to the same manner of living and to go to bed in the same bedroom as before. By law alone he was a man; in all other respects he remained as a child.

The point is clearly to emphasize the protection which the boy enjoyed, especially since this passage is followed in Nicolaus'

[87] Dobesch (1978); Bellemore (1984), p. xxii. On the autobiography more generally, see Blumenthal (1913) and (1914).

narrative by the fact that he could only attend religious ceremonies at night due to the unwonted attention from women which he attracted during the day (Nic. Dam. 12). The underlying message, therefore, is in the contrast between the loose women of the streets and the cosy safety provided by his mother's house. In a similar vein, when he returns to Rome in 45 BCE after seeing Caesar in Spain, it is noted that he lived near his mother and Philippus (his stepfather), spending most of his time with them (Nic. Dam. 34); this is again immediately followed by a passage in praise of his sexual self-control (Nic. Dam. 36). The safety of his mother's home is also the theme of her letters after Caesar's assassination, when she repeatedly urges him to return to her—explicitly, in ch. 52, to her household (ἐγέγραπτο . . . ἑαυτὸν ἐκείνῃ τε ἀποδοῦναι καὶ τῷ σύμπαντι οἴκῳ).

Atia's role in the autobiography seems at first to represent her son in a curiously unheroic light: rather than a warrior and politician to be reckoned with, the first emperor comes across in the *Life of Augustus* as a boy still in need of his mother's protection. On the other hand, Nicolaus of Damascus' narrative also depicts her as an intelligent witness to, and active player in, contemporary Roman politics: following the assassination, Augustus relies on his mother's letters to provide details about the political situation in the capital city, and we are told that it was she who was charged with arranging Caesar's funeral.[88] The description, moreover, of her conflicting emotions about Augustus' assumption of Caesar's name (Nic. Dam. 54) not only represents her as having a clear sense of the political risks of such a move, but echoes the argument between her husband and son described in the chapter before. She is not, in short, simply an over-protective mother, but a lively and intelligent ally to her son. Atia has not received a great deal of attention from critics, perhaps because, after the autobiography, she seems to have faded out of the tradition in favour of other imperial women. Still, an enigmatic epigram by Domitius Marsus is preserved in which she is

---

[88] Ch. 48. She was forestalled by the mob who seized the body and carried it to be burned in the Forum.

made to suggest that her son might be a god, a political as much as religious statement;[89] Tacitus later cites her as a strong influence on the young Augustus, on a par with Cornelia, mother of the Gracchi, and Caesar's mother Aurelia (*Dialogus* 28. 6). Indeed, on some level Augustus' relationship to his female relatives appears to be modelled on that of Caesar, who used the *laudatio* at his aunt's funeral to celebrate the family's connections to the stock of the kings and of the gods themselves.[90] But Atia's function in the autobiography seems to have been more complex than as a means of gesturing to a glorious family history; rather (like Livia, Julia, Octavia, and Agrippina in the later texts about the imperial household), her role is to advertise a particular relationship between Augustus and the world of the *domus*.

The publication of Augustus' autobiography was a dramatic gesture of self-representation, on par, on one level, with Caesar's *Civil War*. But whereas Caesar appears in that text, and in the *Gallic War*, as a grown man and a great general, Augustus appears in his autobiography as little more than a child, still within his mother's care. To a certain extent, of course, this appearance is due to accidents of survival, since the fragments of Nicolaus of Damascus' *Life of Augustus* break off before Atia's death in 43 BCE and the civil war with Antony. Yet even if the narrative at that point became much less 'domestic', the impression left by the text would still be that the reader had watched a boy grow into a man—a narrative calculated, I would argue, to present the illusion of a certain personal intimacy with the world's most powerful man.[91] The publication of the

---

[89] *ante omnes alias felix tamen hoc ego dicor, / sive hominem peperi femina sive deum* ('Nevertheless, I am called fortunate before all other women because of him (sc. my son), whether I, a mortal woman, bore a human being or a god'), see Courtney (1993) 304; Fogazza (1981) 44. 3. See Flory (1995) 127–34 for a discussion of the epigram in the context of early imperial politics.

[90] *est ergo in genere et sanctitas regum, qui plurimum inter homines pollent, et caerimonia deorum, quorum ipsi in potestate sunt reges* (' "there is therefore in my family both the virtue of kings, who hold supreme power among men, and the holiness of the gods, who have even kings in their power" ': Suet. *Div. Iul.* 6).

[91] It has been suggested that the autobiography's focus on Augustus' early life is in order to underscore his moral rectitude when a young man and subject to temptation,

autobiography, moreover, sits in contrast with what Augustus did *not* choose to publish, that is, among other things, the proceedings of the senate while he was in power (Suet. *Div. Aug.* 31). The reading public, it seems, was to be offered the details of the princeps' digestive system and relationship with his mother, but not what business was conducted by the (still nominally) elected government. The publication of the senatorial proceedings had been instituted only a few decades earlier, by Julius Caesar as one of his populist gestures upon becoming consul in 59 BCE. Indeed, Caesar's openness in his memoirs about his political and military career was praised by Cicero (*Brutus* 262), and Suetonius seems to have had access also to a collection of Caesar's speeches against Cato, a poem entitled 'The Journey' (*Iter*), and a number of personal letters (Suet. *Div. Iul.* 56). But here again we find Augustus exercising control over the textual traces of his adoptive father which were to be left to later generations: the writings from the dictator's boyhood and adolescence were suppressed, by direct and personal order of the princeps.[92] The rehearsal of Augustus' own boyhood in the imperial autobiography was apparently designed to be unique.[93]

The show of a certain kind of domesticity, therefore, seems to have been an important aspect of Augustus' self-definition, as a man whose life as a private citizen was at the same time virtuously distinct from the pomp and circumstance of his role as princeps and continuously implicated in it. This is the message of the complex which was constructed on the Palatine in the early 20s BCE, a complex which was both house and forum, both private and public space—

and before he emerged into the public eye (Lewis (1993) 673–4). This is a fine reading, and—put a slightly different way—supports my overall point here: by focusing the reader's attention on the personal morality of the young hero, the text distracts from his later, more problematic, public deeds. Cf. Bellemore (1984), pp. xxiii–xxv.

[92] *quos omnis libellos vetuit Augustus publicari in epistula, quam brevem admodum ac simplicem ad Pompeium Macrum, cui ordinandas bibliothecas delegaverat, misit.* (Suet. *Div. Iul.* 56. 7).

[93] Lewis (1993: 686–9) makes the observation that, structurally, Augustus' autobiographical writings are closer to Sulla's than Caesar's, insofar as they echo the former's interest in ancestry and family while the latter focus solely on the author's public career. The overall tone of the work, however, is uniquely Augustan.

categorical distinctions which were on some levels deliberately confused and on others kept rigidly distinct. It is also the message of Augustus' autobiography which, not coincidentally, appeared only a few years later: Suetonius tells us that it only went down to the conclusion of the Cantabrian war, and scholarly consensus places its publication in 22 BCE. Both the material constructions on the Palatine and the textual remains left by the imperial house, moreover, give particular primacy to the role which women might play in deconstructing the dichotomy between the domestic and civic spheres. From the Danaid portico, whose sculptural programme represents marriage, conjugal murder, and filial obedience as 'political' acts, to the more general and widespread use of gender in almost every major Augustan structure, to the textual display of domestic virtue by Augustus in company with the female members of the imperial house—all manage to draw on a sense of women as the best representatives of what we might call 'politicized domesticity': the idea that certain relationships may transcend the divide between public and private life. This is an idea which was, in the first instance, very much grounded in material space, and never really lost the sense that what was at issue was the very real experiential difference between the house and the forum. It is for this reason that the Palatine—the house on the hill, Augustus' new centre of civic life away from the republican-inflected Forum Romanum—became such an important 'location' of both material and textual representations of imperial domesticity. But it also, as we will see in the next chapter, had significant impact on much more abstract representations of space, gender, and society in Augustan Rome.

2

Other Men's Wives: Domesticity and Display in Vitruvius' *de Architectura*

THE *de Architectura* of the Augustan architect Vitruvius has been, over the centuries, remarkably influential. Although it is difficult to assess what impact it may have had in its own time, its rediscovery in the Renaissance paved the way for a whole set of new, more 'classical' architectural forms, and it remains a standard handbook for their study. At the same time, however, it seems that some early readers of the text found it as frustrating as enlightening: the fifteenth-century architect Leon Battista Alberti complains that the Latin is obscure, the text corrupt, and the information so garbled that the author 'might just as well not have written at all, rather than write some-thing that we cannot understand'.[1] Indeed, as Linda Pellecchia has shown, in the absence of physical evidence with which to compare Vitruvius' text, Renaissance architects interpreted his description of the atrium house in a wide variety of ways, which bear little or no resemblance to the real Roman houses which were subsequently excavated in the bay of Naples.[2] Pellecchia's study thus illustrates an important point, which is that the *de Architectura* was and is only a text, a vehicle of representation whose meaning is not as transpar-ent as it may seem on the surface. Indeed, recent archaeological work has shown that, particularly in the case of the house, Vitruvius' schemata are far from straightforward descriptions of historical

---

[1] L. B. Alberti, *De re aedificatoria* 6. 1. Translation from Rykwert *et al.* (1988) 154.
[2] Pellecchia (1992).

truth, since it is clear that both house structures and house usage in the ancient world were actually far more diverse and complex than he would lead us to think.

Vitruvius' work is not just the only architectural handbook to have survived from classical antiquity; it also has the distinction of having been written at a moment when architecture and building were being given new significance under imperial rule. Augustus, as discussed in the last chapter, was showing himself to be a builder, and one whose constructions were to bear a substantial amount of ideological weight. Recent scholarship has therefore emphasized that the *de Architectura* must be read in its own historical context, as a work which attempts to make a special place for itself not only in the history of architectural theory but also in the construction of Augustus' new Roman state. Thus, for instance, Indra Kagis McEwen's recent book argues that the *de Architectura* is imbued throughout with a sense of its own embodiment: she argues that the 'body of knowledge' (*corpus disciplinae*) represented by the text also serves as a figure for the power represented in the person of Augustus, and the political 'body' of the empire as a whole.[3] Yet, given on the one hand its investment in imperial building and ideology, and on the other its apparent interest in bodies and space, it is doubly surprising how little attention the text gives to questions of gender—even where (as in the case of domestic space) other historical and material evidence indicates that the Romans 'made a place' for women. Although there has been a fair amount of recent scholarship criticizing the centrality of gender to Vitruvius' description of the Greek house, and urging us to see his representation of Greek gender roles as a construct,[4] there has been little corresponding discussion of the absence of Roman women from the text. Especially since the Augustan period was one in which gender and domestic roles were undergoing a substantial reformulation, the question which we ought to be asking of Vitruvius' text is not just why is so much prominence given to 'other' women in the description

---

[3] McEwen (2003).   [4] On which, see below, pp. 132–8.

of 'other' types of house, but also why so little is given to the women who inhabited the houses which Vitruvius himself called home.

One way of approaching this question, I think, is to look at the places where gender does appear in Vitruvius' text, and to ask not just what relationship it bears there to 'real' social mores, but what purpose it serves in the overall logic of the text. As an opening example, we might consider what is perhaps the best known instance of gendered architectural language in the *de Architectura*, which occurs (not coincidentally) immediately following his first usage of *corpus* to describe the 'body' of architectural knowledge in the preface to book 4. In the opening chapter of the book, then, he goes on to describe the origins of the architectural orders, which (for Vitruvius) are combinations of particular proportions and forms associated with particular cultures and moments in time. Vitruvius also, however, insists that the three different orders, Doric, Ionic, and Corinthian, must be understood as representing gendered bodies: the Doric was given the shape, strength, and beauty of the male body (*virilis corporis proportionem et firmitatem et venustatem*: 4. 1. 6), while the Ionic was modelled on the grace of the female (*ad mulieb-rem . . . gracilitatem*), given curling 'hair' as its capital to imitate a woman's style, and 'dressed' in columns fluted like the folds of a matron's robe (*uti stolarum rugas matronali more*: 4. 1. 7). Out of these two orders, the male and the female, was 'born' (*est procreatum*: 4. 1. 3) the third or Corinthian, which was created when a basket was placed on the grave of a young virgin; an acanthus plant grew up around it and inspired the architect Callimachus to invent the new order (4. 1. 8–11). Thus, although the Corinthian order reflects the Ionic in having the grace of a young girl (*virginalis habet gracilitatis imitationem*), it also allows more beautiful effects (*venustiores*, echoing *venustatem* in the description of the Doric: 4. 1. 8); its traditional capital, however, takes its shape from the original basket and plant combination placed on the Corinthian maiden's grave, rather than from any part of the human form.

It is difficult to know exactly what we are to make of this peculiar family narrative, with its Doric father, Ionic mother, and dead

Corinthian daughter—especially since there appears to be little real historical fact in anything that Vitruvius says here.[5] For my purposes, however, I would simply like to emphasize the ways in which Vitruvius' narrative of the orders causes gender, and in particular domestic femininity, to disappear: while the Doric assumes the form of a heroic man, the Ionic takes on that of a matronly woman, but their offspring is represented as a peculiar combination of the sterile body of a virgin and the vegetable commemoration of her death. It is worth noting, moreover, that by the time of Vitruvius' writing the Corinthian order was the one most beloved in Roman architecture, so that the story of the orders contains a strong sense of progress from the (Greek) past to the (Roman) present.[6] In other words, I would argue that we can see in Vitruvius' narrative here a small example of what we will see more strongly expressed in other parts of the text: an effort to use domestic femininity as a way to talk about politics and history, but also as something which cannot be fully integrated into the Augustan architect's model of public life. Only 'other' people, for Vitruvius, have gender; among the Romans, all places—including the domestic spaces traditionally associated with women—are simply pieces of a larger imperial space, meant to display masculine virtues and values. That his version of public life does not include certain kinds of domestic femininity marks him, I think, as an early Augustan author, or at least one who does not reproduce parrot-fashion the ideological messages that the new regime was seeking to promote. At the same time, however, Vitruvius does see the display of domestic femininity as a meaningful political statement. In this sense, the *de Architectura* reveals how the advent of Augustus changed the representational relations of gender, power, and private life.

[5] On the passage, see Rykwert (1996) 317–49; cf. McEwen (2003) 212–24.
[6] Wilson Jones (2000) 135: 'Corinthian is the Roman order'.

GENDER AND PERFORMANCE IN THE ROMAN HOUSE

Let me begin with one small example of how the early Empire used 'good womanhood' to construct domestic space. The House of Marcus Lucretius Fronto in Pompeii is neither the largest nor the most richly decorated in the ancient city.[7] Nevertheless, it preserves some of the best examples of third- and fourth-style wall painting to have survived, as well as an architectural plan (Fig. 1) which conforms closely to our expectations of an elite Roman house: narrow *fauces*(a) lead from the street into a Tuscan-style *atrium* (b), off which opens a *tablinum* (h), where the master of the house traditionally met with clients, which in turn opens onto a colonnaded garden beyond. Off the atrium and garden are rooms identified as *triclinia* (dining rooms: f, t, s) and *cubicula* (bedrooms: c, g, i), as well as some service areas (p, q, r) tucked neatly out of sight. Recent years have given birth to a

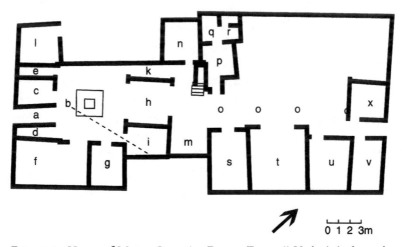

FIGURE 1. House of Marcus Lucretius Fronto (Pompeii V. 4. a) (redrawn by Bryan Burns, after Peters (1993) 137)
--------line of sight from atrium to image of Pero and Mycon

[7] On the house, see Peters (1993).

number of 'social' readings of the Roman house, which emphasize the ways in which elite domestic structures such as this one use architecture to create a hierarchy of access, as lower-ranking visitors who might come into the atrium to conduct business with the master of the house would not necessarily be allowed to progress further to the more intimate social spaces around the peristyle beyond. While the atrium functions as a more 'public' space, then, the garden area is more 'private', not in the sense that it is restricted to members of the household alone, but in that access is limited to more privileged visitors and controlled by the owner of the house.[8] Unlike that of other societies to which they might be compared, however, Roman concepts of public and private space did not map cleanly onto the division between the sexes. Private space, in other words, was not especially associated with women, nor were the female members of the household restricted to it for their activities; rather, in the words of the biographer Cornelius Nepos, 'the mother of the family holds a central place in the house and mixes with the crowd'.[9]

In the House of Lucretius Fronto this point is illustrated by a small room which opens off the atrium, whose entrance, like that of the *tablinum* with which it shares a wall, faces the *fauces*, so that its interior would have been visible immediately upon entering the house from the street.[10] Particularly noticeable is the mythological panel which adorns the centre of the south wall, which is the only

---

[8] Among others, Coarelli (1989); Thébert (1987); Clarke (1991); Wallace-Hadrill (1994*b*); Nevett (1997); George (1997); Grahame (1998); Fredrick (2002*a*) 253–9. For a more conceptual/textual approach, see Riggsby (1997); Ellis (2000) 166–79.

[9] *materfamilias primum locum tenet aedium atque in celebritate versatur* (*Lives of the Foreign Generals*, pref. 6).

[10] I should note here that the room did clearly have a door (there are substantial postholes cut into the threshold), so that a visitor would only be able to see into it from the atrium if the door were left open. It seems likely, however, that the doors would be closed to make the space more private at some times and left open for it to be more public at others—thus conforming to the 'temporal' model of domestic activities for which archaeologists have argued (Laurence (1994) 122–32; Berry (1997) 194). Indeed, Riggsby (1997) argues on the basis of textual evidence that *cubicula* of this kind had a very particular and prominent 'public' role to play in Roman society, and, given the room's location, I think we can do away with the idea that it was a truly 'private' space, such as a child's bedroom (as proposed in Clarke (1991) 159). Clarke (2003: 254–9) discusses the different meanings which the room's decorative programme would have had for different viewers.

one of the room's paintings able to be seen by a visitor standing on the far side of the atrium. It depicts the story of Pero, a young woman whose father, Mycon, was unjustly imprisoned and condemned to starve to death; the daughter, however, saved his life by visiting him in his cell and feeding him the milk from her breast.[11] Although now badly decayed, we can determine from other examples preserved in Pompeii that the picture in the House of Lucretius Fronto shows the woman seated before a barred window, offering her breast to the old man lying across her lap (Fig. 2). It is a remarkable image, and not just because wall paintings of women behaving virtuously are rare, but because it is extremely explicit in its moral message: not only are both figures carefully labelled to identify who they are, but the picture also comes equipped with a short ecphrastic poem which explains the significance of the painting. The three elegiac couplets praise the heroism of Pero, who gives to her father the nourishment made for her own children, and concludes by invoking two great feminine virtues illustrated here: *tristis inest cum pietate pudor* ('there is sad modesty in her along with piety'). The reference to *pudor* seems to be meant to empty the scene of erotic connotations[12]—despite how it looks, this is not incest—a task which is assisted by the invocation of the more appropriate family sentiment *pietas*. Indeed, the story of Pero was closely associated with that virtue, appearing in both Roman and Greek versions as exempla of 'piety' in Valerius Maximus (4. 4. 7). According to the elder Pliny, moreover, the site of the Roman version (which has the woman's mother in prison rather than her father) would later become that of the temple of Pietas (*NH* 7. 36).

The fact that the painting of Pero and Mycon is given such prominence in the House of Lucretius Fronto makes a statement about the centrality of women, both to the Roman family and to the

---

[11] For a full list and description of ancient examples of the scene (including two decorative terracotta groups from Pompeii), see Deonna (1954).

[12] On female *pudor* and its relationship to sexual respectability, see Kaster (1997) 9–10.

Roman house.[13] The story places Pero simultaneously in the position of mother and daughter, emphasizing the role which women have as guarantors of the continuing cycle of generations—reproducing

FIGURE 2. Wall painting of Pero and Mycon (photograph by author; used by authorization of the Italian Ministry for Cultural Heritage and Environment)

[13] It is worth noting that my comments here on the ways in which the image of Pero and Mycon should be seen as a public invocation of domestic virtue also hold true for the two other extant examples of the painting found in Pompeii: although both were removed from their findspots by 19th-cent. excavators, one was originally located on the wall of a *triclinium* opening from a shop at 9. 2. 5; the other was part of the decorative scheme of an *oecus* on axis with the atrium of the 'Casa di Bacco' at 7. 4. 10. For descriptions of

the next while still supporting the last.[14] In this sense, the picture of Pero and Mycon serves to advertise the importance of a strong and virtuous family life to the owner of the House of Lucretius Fronto, a statement about domestic values in the domestic space which the visitor has just entered. At Rome, however, *pietas* had also long been a civic virtue as well, a point which is made by the ancient sources on the story of Pero and Mycon: Pliny the Elder tells us that the temple of Pietas, built on the site of the prison where the story takes place, was vowed by M. Acilius Glabrio in 191 BCE, in gratitude for his victory over Antiochus at the battle of Thermopylae.[15] *Pietas* is embodied as much in the military victory on behalf of the state as in the appropriate gratitude to the gods symbolized by the building of the temple, and in the family loyalty which had been so strikingly displayed on the spot where it was built. The different aspects of *pietas* (*erga deos, erga parentes, erga civitatem*) were all clearly intermingled even before Augustus adopted it as one of his own public and private virtues, but it seems likely that his influence collapsed the distinctions even further.[16] The image of Pero and Mycon, then, is appropriate to its context in the House of Lucretius Fronto as an invocation of both civic and family virtue, generated within domestic space but directed to the attention of a wider audience. It illustrates, moreover, the extent to which femininity could be a part of the performance which was continuously enacted on the stage of the Roman house, and which played such an important role in constituting Roman private space as part of the theatre of public life.[17]

the architecture and original decorative schemes of these two spaces, see Carratelli *et al.* (1990–9) vol. viii, pp. 1052–67 (for the shop at 9.2.5) and vol. vi, pp. 978–80 (for the 'Casa di Bacco' at 7.4.10). The findspots of two other examples cited at *LIMC* 328 are unknown.

[14] Deonna (1956).

[15] Although the temple was not actually dedicated until 181, by his son: Deonna (1954) 365.

[16] On *pietas* within the family and its relationship to *pietas* in civic life, see Saller (1994) 102–32.

[17] Constructions of gender in Roman wall painting and their relationship to domestic architecture are the topics of a number of recent studies. See Fredrick (1995); Bergmann (1996); Koloski-Ostrow (1997).

The role of the Roman house as a public presentation of its owner has been the subject of a great deal of recent scholarship, which has emphasized the extent to which a politically active man's house was intimately associated with his *dignitas* throughout the late Republic and early Empire.[18] This was true both actually, in the sense that it was here that a patron would receive his clients and other associates, and metaphorically, as the house might symbolize an individual's relationship with the city as a whole. Thus, Cicero notes in the *de Officiis*, 'Status may be enhanced by a house ... care must be taken in regard to the house of an illustrious man, where many guests will need to be received and a crowd of people of different stations will be admitted, that there should be enough space; but on the other hand, a large house may be embarrassing to its owner, if there is no one in it'.[19] In a similar vein, the *de Architectura* of Vitruvius, who lived through the end of the Republic and the early years of Augustus' reign, also describes the need for the house to act as a kind of mirror of the societal role of its owner. He notes in his book on domestic architecture (6. 5. 1–2):

cum ad regiones caeli ita ea fuerint diposita, tunc etiam animadvertendum est, quibus rationibus privatis aedificiis propria loca patribus familiarum et quemadmodum communia cum extraneis aedificari debeant. namque ex his quae propria sunt, in ea non est potestas omnibus intro eundi nisi invitatis, quemadmodum sunt cubicula, triclinia, balnea ceteraque, quae easdem habent usus rationes. communia autem sunt, quibus etiam invocati suo iure de populo possunt venire, id est vestibula, cava aedium, peristylia, quaeque eundem habere possunt usum. igitur iis, qui communi sunt fortuna, non necessaria magnifica vestibula nec tabulina neque atria, quod in aliis officia praestant ambiundo neque ab aliis ambiuntur. ... item feneratoribus et publicanis commodiora et speciosiora et ab insidiis tuta, forensibus autem et disertis elegantiora et spatiosiora ad conventos excipiundos, nobilibus vero, qui honores magistratusque gerundo praestare debent officia

---

[18] Wiseman (1987); Dwyer (1991); Bergmann (1994). On senatorial houses, specifically under the Empire, see Eck (1997), esp. 184–5.

[19] *ornanda enim est dignitas domo... sic in domo clari hominis, in quam et hospites multi recipiendi et admittenda hominum cuiusque modi multitudo, adhibenda cura est laxitatis; aliter ampla domus dedecori saepe domino fit, si est in ea solitudo* (*de Off.* 1. 139).

civibus, faciunda sunt vestibula regalia alta, atria et peristylia amplissima, silvae ambulationesque laxiores ad decorem maiestatis perfectae.

When [the different rooms] have been laid out in relation to the quarters of the sky, then it must be considered by what rationale, in private houses, places reserved for the owners of the house and those commonly shared with outsiders should be built. For the 'reserved' places are those into which not everyone can come without an invitation, such as bedrooms, dining rooms, baths and other places which have related functions. The 'common' rooms, however, are those into which ordinary people can come by right, even if uninvited; these are the vestibule, the inner courtyard, the peristyles, and other places which are able to be devoted to the same kind of use. For this reason, a person who is 'common' in his place in life does not need to have magnificent vestibules, or meeting rooms, or central courtyards, because he performs his duties by visiting others rather than being visited himself. . . . In the same way, houses for moneylenders and tax-collectors must be spacious and attractive and safe from ambush; for lawyers and rhetoricians they must be stylish and sufficiently large to hold meetings; but for gentlemen who must perform their duties to the citizenry by holding offices and magistracies, great grand halls must be made, courtyards and very large peristyles, woodlands and wide open walks, all finished off as an ornament to their noble status.

Andrew Wallace-Hadrill most famously used passages like this one to argue that what we might call Victorian notions of public and private life do not, for the Romans, map cleanly onto public and private architecture.[20] He points out, quite correctly, that whereas the modern world harbours an ideal of a domestic space impermeable to the cares, concerns, and inhabitants of the 'outside' world, the Romans conducted a great deal of commercial and civic business within the walls of their homes. Thus the house must function, in Vitruvius' description, as a public space, not serving the particular private needs of an individual family, but expressing the role and status of the owner in the community. For this reason, it necessarily took on the shape of a public space, to the extent that, Vitruvius goes on to note, certain houses might not be dissimilar in form and

---

[20] Wallace-Hadrill (1994*b*) 8–14; 44–7.

decoration to the buildings of public life (6. 5. 2). The Roman house, even particular spaces within the house, did not preserve 'privacy' in the same sense that it does in the modern world—rather than a space apart from the sphere of public life, the domestic structure was an extension or elaboration of the work which its owner did as a member of the larger community.

Modern scholarship has dwelt a great deal on this point, as a corrective to post-industrial notions simplistically applied to the ancient world. Readings of Vitruvius over the past decade have turned to considering his work less as a simple collection of dry architectural facts and more as a 'scientific' explanation of the relationship between the social world and the built environment. In this sense, he is one of the most Augustan of authors, even though his work was probably begun before the princeps' return to Rome after Actium.[21] Yet I think we may go even further than we have done in recovering Vitruvius as an author whose text, while certainly concerned to communicate particular architectural truths, is also attempting to construct and communicate a vision of the contemporary imperial landscape. This attempt may not be so obvious in the *de Architectura* as it is in Ovid's *Ars Amatoria*, or even in Livy's *Ab Urbe Condita*, but, in part because of this, it has the effect of being more persuasive. As I noted in the Introduction, to my mind it is within texts which draw on the language of fact that we can see the most insidious manifestations of Augustan ideology. I would thus argue that, especially given what we have seen of the importance accorded to 'the domestic' in the first decade of the princeps' rule

---

[21] We actually do not know when the book was published. Vitruvius' silence on specific Augustan constructions is usually cited as evidence that it pre-dates the heyday of Augustus' building activities in the city of Rome, although this may be evidence of tact rather than ignorance. Indeed, the foundations of Augustus' building programmes had been well laid by his adoptive father, so that it does not seem unrealistic to suppose that Vitruvius had a sense that architecture was, and would continue to be, an important theoretical and practical skill under the new regime. Moreover, the preface to the book refers to Octavian as Augustus, indicating that it, at any rate, must have been written after 27 BCE. Elizabeth Rawson sets the actual date of publication in the 20s: E. Rawson (1985), p. vii. See also Schrijvers (1989).

(that decade which saw the construction of the Palatine complex discussed in the last chapter), it is worth examining what Vitruvius has to say about the meaning of domestic space and what relationship it has to gender, imperial power, and private life.

Indeed, although Vitruvius may not have a sense of the elite house as 'private' space, it is nevertheless clear that he understands there to be a separate and significant category which *he* calls 'private architecture'.[22] Indeed, the dichotomy between public and private building is one of the most fundamental structuring devices in the *de Architectura*, as the text moves from methodology and building technologies in books 1–3, to the decoration and construction of public buildings in books 4–5, to the decoration and construction of private buildings in books 6–7, and back to methodology and technology in books 8–10.[23] In 1. 3. 1, Vitruvius remarks that *aedificatio* ('building'), the first and most important part of architecture, 'has been divided into two parts, of which the first is the placement of city walls and communal works in public places, and the second is the planning of private structures'.[24] The shift of topic between civic structures in book 5 and domestic construction in book 6 is made explicit, as the author writes at the end of 5, 'In this book, I have written those things which it occurred to me were necessary for the usefulness of public places in cities, in what way they should be laid out and built; in the subsequent book, however, I will consider the conveniences and proportions of private build-

---

[22] This is an important instance of the difference between *privatus* in Latin and the English word 'private': whereas the latter, especially in regard to architecture, is closely associated in the modern West with the nuclear family, Vitruvius reflects traditional Roman thinking which uses *privatus* to denote anything not owned and controlled by the state. See Riggsby (1997: 48–50) for a discussion. In this sense it is curious, and telling, that it is private rather than public architecture which is so closely associated with the development of human culture in Vitruvius' text.

[23] For a discussion of this and other unifying structural devices in *de Arch.*, see Callebat (1989).

[24] *aedificatio autem divisa est bipertito, e quibus una est moenium et communium operum in publicis locis conlocatio, altera est privatorum aedificiorum explicatio.*

ings': 5. 12. 7.[25] A similar note occurs at the beginning of book 6. The book on house construction, moreover, opens with a remarkable chapter concerning the influence of climate on building which draws on the tradition of ancient ethnographic literature such as the Hippocratic *Airs, Waters, Places* (*c.*400 BCE) and links styles of house-building with levels of cultural development. Book 6 is the only book in the *de Architectura* which offers such a cosmological overview, indicating that it is linked in the author's mind with the explicit change of subject from public to private construction. The *de Architectura* thus sees domestic architecture as both primary and primal, both a particular category of construction and a fundamental expression of the human relationship with the built environment.

   Given both the importance accorded to private building in the text generally, and its role as a microcosm of human society in particular, it is surprising how little attention the *de Architectura* gives to questions of gender. Despite his detailed descriptions of the different rights and requirements of different classes at Rome, Roman women are almost entirely absent from Vitruvius' text. Even when he speaks of those spaces reserved for the owners of the upper-class house, his vocabulary indicates that he does not mean 'the family' in either a modern or a Roman sense; rather, he speaks of *propria loca* patribus familiarum—that is, 'places belonging to *male heads of household*'. Yet, as we have seen, there was a close connection in traditional Roman culture between women and the house, between virtuous femininity and the place it was most often displayed. This may be seen not just in the female *domestica bona* ('domestic virtues') which were traditionally praised in epitaphs, but also more concretely in the formation and decoration of the space of the house

---

[25] *quae necessaria ad utilitatem in civitatibus publicorum locorum succurrere mihi potuerunt, quemadmodum constituantur et perficiantur, in hoc volumine scripsi; privatorum autem aedificiorum utilitates et eorum symmetrias insequenti volumine ratiocinabor.* Cf. 6. pref. 7: *igitur, quoniam in quinto de opportunitate communium operum perscripsi, in hoc volumine privatorum aedificiorum ratiocinationes et commensus symmetriarum explicabo* ('therefore, since in the fifth book I fully considered the convenient disposition of public buildings, in this book I will explain the reasoning and even proportions of private buildings').

itself. We have historical evidence indicating that, along with the ancestor masks celebrating the male head of household, looms and a representative marriage bed were also kept in the atrium.[26] Since this was the place where most of the 'public' business of the elite house took place, where the *paterfamilias* would meet with clients and generally conduct his affairs, the presence of such artefacts of virtuous womanhood here indicates the importance which femininity had in the social role of the home.[27] There is a story that the great republican matron Fulvia, during the riots which followed the murder of her first husband P. Clodius Pulcher, contributed to the public chaos when she whipped up the emotions of the crowd by displaying her husband's mutilated body in the atrium of their house.[28] The place of the display was surely calculated to maximize Fulvia's authority as grieving widow as well as to demonstrate the loss to the people of their *popularis* champion; woman and crowd found in Clodius' atrium both a meeting place and a common cause. The story thus underscores the role of the central courtyard of the house as a place where virtuous femininity encountered civic life, as part of the public display of the Roman home.[29]

In fact, critics have argued that it is because of the 'public' nature of gender in the elite Roman house that it does not make an impact

[26] Treggiari (1994: 316–19) collects and discusses the evidence, which includes Catullus 64. 47–8 (where the marriage bed is described as being prepared 'in the middle of the palace'); Horace, *Epistles* 1. 1. 87; and Aulus Gellius 16. 9 (on the '*lectus adversus*', so called because it stood opposite the front door). Whether the bed in question was real or a small symbolic image is an open question.

[27] Asconius, *Mil.* 38, notes that when a mob broke into the house of M. Aemilius Lepidus, they destroyed the portraits, the bed, and the woven cloth being produced in the atrium.

[28] *infimaeque plebis et servorum maxima multitudo magno luctu corpus in atrio domus positum circumstetit. augebat autem facti invidiam uxor Clodi Fulvia quae cum effusa lamentatione vulnera eius ostendebat* ('Mourning greatly, a huge crowd of humble people and slaves surrounded the body, placed in the atrium of the house. But Fulvia, the wife of Clodius, increased the horror at the deed when, with copious tears, she displayed his wounds': Asconius, *Mil.* 32).

[29] Vitruvius' vision of the atrium as simply a place of gentlemanly business has been challenged by recent studies of artefact assemblages, which show that the atrium had numerous functions, including being used for storage and varying kinds of handwork: Berry (1997); Allison (1997). Cf. George (1997), esp. 303–6.

on Vitruvius' description in the *de Architectura*. The desire for good women to display their goodness meant that they were not kept away from the house's public areas, but rather were subsumed into the interior decor as additional testimony to the power of the *paterfamilias*.[30] Unlike classical Athens where the mark of a good woman was 'not to be spoken of, for praise or blame', the virtue of a Roman wife was trumpeted as one more of the status symbols with which the elite house was filled.[31] We should not, then, expect to find gendered places in Vitruvius: the critical distinctions in ranking space for the Roman architect are not between the sexes, but between the different audiences who will be entering and viewing the interior of the house.[32] On one level, this analysis is clearly correct. It is true that Vitruvius reflects a fairly traditional—based on what is said elsewhere—republican view of how status ought to be reflected in household architecture and decoration. His authorial eye, like that of Cicero and others, is focused on what a house says about its owner. Thus, in concluding his chapter on domestic architecture, he notes: *ergo si his rationibus ad singulorum generum personas . . . ita disposita erunt aedificia, non erit quod reprehendatur* ('therefore, if structures are laid out by these rules in accordance with the role of each individual type [of person], there will be nothing to criticize': 6. 5. 3). *Persona* ('role') is the language of performance, in the theatre or public sphere,[33] underscoring the idea that what is at stake is the correct presentation of identity for a viewing audience. It is curious, however, given how important the virtuous *materfamilias* could be as

---

[30] Wallace-Hadrill (1996).

[31] The phrase is from Pericles' funeral oration in Thucydides: 2. 45. 2. Compare this, again, to the funeral epitaph of Murdia from the Augustan period, in which her son expresses his dismay at the endless but necessary repetition of female virtues (see Introd. pp. 31–2). It goes without saying that neither one of these statements directly describes the reality of women's lives in its historical period; nevertheless, such ideal or ideological constructs were a significant aspect of the cultural environment in which ancient women existed.

[32] Wallace-Hadrill (1994*b*) 8–9; 185–6.

[33] The word could also be used of an ancestor mask, used in funerals and displayed in the atrium of an elite house, which again underscores the importance of the 'show' of family honour to a wider audience.

part of the household's supporting cast, that she receives no mention in Vitruvius—no discussion, for instance, of how large an atrium ought to be to house the conjugal bed, or whether it would contain enough light to weave effectively.[34] Women, moreover, play an important part in Vitruvius' description of the Greek house, underscoring their peculiar absence from the Roman, as though only Greeks lived with wives, or mothers, or daughters. The one place we might expect to find Roman women, the house, has been emptied of gender by Vitruvius, leaving it as a strikingly hypermasculine space, built to speak to and about men alone.

The argument might well be made that Vitruvius here is simply reflecting the patriarchal bias of his culture, which prioritized the pursuits of the male public sphere to such a degree that it caused everything else to disappear. On the other hand, women are not entirely absent from the *de Architectura*. Indeed, one of their most noticeable appearances occurs very early in the book, in the chapter on architectural knowledge which follows the preface and dedication to Augustus. Here, Vitruvius discusses a subject clearly close to his heart, since it is the proliferation of untrained and ignorant builders which was the motivating factor for writing the book. The author explains that one of the marks of a good architect is that he understands not just how to do something, but why he does it. For instance, if someone uses caryatids (*statuas marmoreas muliebres stolatas*, or 'marble statues of robed women') instead of columns to support a roof, he ought to be able to explain why. Vitruvius goes on to prove the didactic worth of his book, as well as his own expertise, by providing just such an explanation (1. 1. 5):

Caria, civitas Peloponnensis, cum Persis hostibus contra Graeciam consensit. postea Graeci per victoriam gloriose bello liberati communi consilio Cariatibus bellum indixerunt. itaque oppido capto, viris interfectis, civitate declarata matronas eorum in servitutem abduxerunt, nec sunt passi stolas neque ornatus matronales deponere, uti non una triumpho ducerentur, sed aeterno servitutis exemplo gravi contumelia pressae poenas pendere vider-

---

[34] In fact, he worries about light and textile production elsewhere: see 6. 4. 2.

entur pro civitate. ideo qui tunc architecti fuerunt aedificiis publicis desig-
naverunt earum imagines oneri ferundo conlocatas, ut etiam posteris nota
poena peccati Cariatium memoriae traderetur.

Caria [i.e. Caryae], a city in the Peloponnese, conspired with the Persians in
their war against Greece. Afterwards, the Greeks, gloriously freed of war by
victory, declared war on the Carians by common consent. After the city was
captured, then, the men killed, and the state surrendered, the Greeks
handed over the Carian matrons into slavery, and they did not allow
them to take off their *stolae* and matronly decorations, in order that they
should not only be led in triumph, but, as an eternal example of slavery,
oppressed by heavy shame, they would seem to pay the penalty for their
city. Therefore, those who were architects then designed for public buildings statues of them, set up to carry burdens, in order that the punishment
of the Carians' error—having been made known to posterity—might be
handed down as part of history.

Vitruvius' aetiology of the caryatids has puzzled scholars on a number of levels. First and foremost is the fact that the story cannot be
historically accurate, since Caryae in Greece continued to thrive as a
community well into the fourth century BCE, long after Vitruvius in
his story has it destroyed by its fellow Greeks.[35] The most famous
Greek caryatids which survive, moreover, are those decorating the
Erechtheion on the Athenian Acropolis, which may or may not
express the kind of subjugation described by Vitruvius.[36] Perhaps
more directly to the point is the fact that language used to describe
the episode in the *de Architectura* is strikingly anachronistic: the
Greeks did not hold triumphs, nor did Greek women wear *stolae*,
the traditional garb of respectable Roman matrons. Yet the author
describes the women of Caria as dressed like *matronae* not once but
twice (*muliebres stolatas; nec sunt passi stolas . . . deponere*), compound-
ing and drawing attention to the mistake. In other words, Vitruvius
seems to have stumbled here: instead of showing that he has the

---

[35] It has been suggested that Vitruvius here is thinking of Caria, a Persian satrapy,
rather than Caryae in Laconia. The former, however, was located in Asia Minor rather
than Greece proper, which is an important part of the story as Vitruvius tells it. See
Plommer (1979); King (1998).
[36] See Ridgway (1999: 145–50) for a discussion.

correct explanation at his fingertips, he has put forward an obviously erroneous story; instead of supporting his argument that a good architect knows his history, he has revealed that he himself does not know the correct explanation for the caryatids.

The peculiarly Roman flavour of Vitruvius' description of sixth-century Greece has not escaped scholars, some of whom have tried to rescue the author from the charge of ineptitude by connecting the caryatid description with the text's own cultural moment. B. Wesenburg, for instance, argues that the story quoted above has little to do with the Persian wars and everything to do with Augustan ideology: the point was to emphasize the connection between the caryatids and military triumph, so that the female support figures which decorated the Forum Augustum would be read as a reference to the spoils of imperial conquest which had made the structure possible.[37] This is an important argument, although I am somewhat wary of drawing too close a connection between the *de Architectura* and the Forum Augustum, since it is unclear whether the latter was even begun, let alone completed, when the former was published. Moreover, it seems to me that too little has been made of the *stola* and its significance in Vitruvius' description. Augustus would later take active steps to restrict the *stola* to virtuous *matronae* alone, so that women who were convicted under the *lex Iulia de adulteriis* were prohibited from wearing it; the move was clearly connected with the regime's general concern with the public display of civic identity through costume.[38] This may also be seen in the terms of the *lex Julia theatralis*, which not only created a detailed map of Roman society by designating where certain groups (women, freedmen, *equites*, soldiers) might sit in the theatre, but also controlled what they might wear there.[39] The official portraits of the women of the imperial house frequently show them dressed in the *stola*, as on the

[37] Wesenberg (1984).

[38] He also took steps to revive the popularity of the toga for men (Suet. *Div. Aug.* 40. 5). See Sebasta (1998).

[39] Men in cloaks (which hid their togas) were prohibited from sitting in the theatre where they would be seen: E. Rawson (1987). See also Kolendo (1981); Edmondson (1996).

Ara Pacis where their display of traditional female dress coordinates with the male figures' display of the toga, and the children's display of the toga praetexta. The *stola* was thus not simply a woman's garment, but a *good* woman's garment, associated not just with female members of the upper classes, but with female members who correctly performed their duties as wives, mothers, daughters, and sisters. The story of the caryatids in Vitruvius, therefore, turns on the idea that power, military power, may be manifested in the public display, not just of women, but of women clothed to emphasize their role as representatives of virtuous domestic life.

Indeed, the strange fact that Vitruvius' aetiology of the caryatids 'clothes' Greek women in Roman dress is especially noticeable because he immediately follows it with another story which makes a similar point. He recounts the tale of the Spartans who, after defeating the Persians, set up a colonnade in which they used as columns images of captives outfitted in their native dress (*captivorum simulacra barbarico vestis ornatu*: 1. 1. 6). This they did in order that their enemies might fear them more, and that their fellow citizens might be inspired by their example to support the cause of freedom (*cives id exemplum virtutis aspicientes . . . ad defendam libertatem essent parati*: 1. 1. 6). As in the caryatid story, the tale of the Spartans and the Persians underscores the idea that the display of 'other' bodies—women or barbarians—as architectural elements is meant to remind the viewer of the power which both caused their subjugation and created the monument of which they are a part; both femininity and foreignness here identify the subject status of the figures used in place of columns. This is true in spite of the differences in the appearance of the two groups: while the women of Caria are improbably dressed as though they were good Roman wives and mothers, the clothing of the Persians emphasizes their ethnicity. The idea would seem to be that, while barbarism has a costume which is specific to time and place, the visual language of virtuous femininity is necessarily Roman. It is also, however, worth noting the different visual messages which Vitruvius sees in the different types of monument. Whereas the use of caryatids in building is meant to drive home the shame of the Carians, the Persian portico is imagined to inspire the local citizenry with greater will to fight: in Vitruvius' own formulation, the caryatids are 'a reminder of slavery' (*servitutis exemplo*: 1. 1. 5), while the Persians are 'a reminder of bravery' (*exemplum virtutis*: 1. 1. 6). The caryatids constitute a threat, of what happens to those who follow the losing side, while the representation of the Persians is imagined more simply as a sign of triumph. On the one hand, then, the pairing of the stories in Vitruvius' text drives home the point that gender—even gender displayed through Roman signs like those given to the women of Caria—is something which describes 'other' people, a way of constructing column-supports which are emphatically 'not us'; on the other, the caryatids also embody the message that 'our' women may end up paying the price for 'our' losses in politics and war.

Vitruvius may get the caryatids wrong for their time, then, but he gets them right for his own: insofar as the exhibition of women appears as a sign of political authority, the passage displays a Roman and Augustan sensibility which would surely not have been lost on the reader. The primacy which women are given here as public symbols (the women of Caria bear the representative weight of the punishment for their city's betrayal) puts forward the question of gender, and when and where it is found, at the very outset of the *de Architectura*. The fact that the caryatids appear in Vitruvius' formulation in the guise of good Roman matrons, as representatives of good Roman families, points us toward women and issues of public and private display. Yet the caryatids also carry weight as part of the *de Architectura*'s scientific project, since their history constitutes the first 'fact' produced to illustrate the knowledge which the architect needs and to prove the qualifications of the author to provide it. In this sense, it seems appropriate to ask how our understanding of the rest of the text may be influenced by our reading of this story. If, for instance, the caryatid story is only 'true' in its own Augustan context, what does that mean for the rest of the expertise put forth in the book? Because of its methodology and subject matter, the *de Architectura* is particularly attuned

to the construction of architectural ideologies, in which, as we have
seen, Augustan women played a significant symbolic and material
role as representatives of what we might call the politics of private
space. Before turning back to the question of how Vitruvius understands the 'place' of women, then, I would like to discuss briefly what
Augustus means to the *de Architectura*, and how that meaning may
be seen as inextricably linked to what the text will go on to say (and
not say) about gender and the Roman home. For while Vitruvius,
like Augustus himself, sees the construction of private spaces as an
important part of the imperial project, it is also clear that within the
text of the *de Architectura* domestic femininity comes to identify a
different, and rather less positive, kind of private life.

VITRUVIUS AND THE IMPERIAL MUSE

Cicero, as has been noted, does not seem to think of architecture as a
proper pursuit for a gentleman. Certainly it is true that we have
evidence of noblemen, such as the orator's brother Quintus,[40] who
dabbled in architecture as part of their role as wealthy property
owners and public benefactors, and it is certainly clear that the
financing of building projects had long been one of the ways in
which the politically ambitious ingratiated themselves with the
Roman plebs.[41] But Cicero makes his opinion of the actual profes-
sion as a whole clear in the *de Officiis*, where he places it somewhere
between acting and agriculture and on a par with medicine and
teaching—professions which, as he says condescendingly, 'are respectable for those whose social standing they become' (*sunt iis,
quorum ordini conveniunt, honestae*: 1. 151). For Vitruvius, on the

---

[40] *ad Quint. Frat.* 3. 1. 2.
[41] Thus, for example, Pompey's huge theatre, portico, and temple complex in the
Campus Martius was constructed in 55 BCE to regain popularity after his election to the
consulship (with Crassus) which had been tainted by street riots and heavy-handed
political manœuvring. On the historical circumstances, see Seager (2002) 130–4; on
the ideological import and influence of the complex more generally, Gros (1987).

other hand, the architect must be a man of letters as well as a draughtsman; a student of philosophy, history, music, and law, as well as familiar with mathematics and astronomy.[42] It is not strictly a nobleman's course of study (the traditional focus on public speaking is quite noticeably absent) but neither is it any longer simply that of the slaves and freedmen who seem to have occupied the role of professional architect most frequently in the first century BCE.[43] And although some of the subjects named have concrete applications to the science of building, others are less direct. Philosophy, for instance, is recommended for its beneficial effect on character: 'but philosophy provides the architect with a noble spirit, and sees to it that he is not arrogant, but rather affable, fair, and trustworthy.'[44] Indeed, Vitruvius notes that, far from being a matter of acquiring a few easy skills, the title of architect belongs only to a select few: only those 'who from childhood, by climbing the steps of these studies, nourished in the knowledge of the many arts and sciences, have made their way to the highest temple of architecture'.[45] This is architecture not merely as an occupation, but as a way of life.

Needless to say, Vitruvius has a particular investment in elevating his subject, and his lofty rhetoric may disguise a certain anxiety about his own standing and status as an authority. Yet it is certainly true that, as Vitruvius himself informs us, Varro's *de Novem Disciplinis* included a book on architecture (*de Arch.* 7. pref. 14), so that the

[42] *et ut litteratus sit, peritus graphidos, eruditus geometria, historias complures noverit, philosophos diligenter audierit, musicam scierit, medicinae non sit ignarus, responsa iurisconsultorum noverit, astrologiam caelique rationes cognitas habeat* ('And as he should be a literate man, skilled in drawing [and] learned in geometry, he should know a fair amount of history, listen carefully to philosophers, understand music, not be ignorant of medicine, be acquainted with the principles discussed by experts in law, [and] know about astronomy and the rules of heavenly design': 1. 1. 3).

[43] Particularly remarkable is the fact that the education which Vitruvius prescribes for the ideal practitioner of his art is neither that of the other architects of whom we have historical evidence, nor apparently that of the author himself: J. C. Anderson (1997) 3–10.

[44] *philosophia vero perficit architectum animo magno et uti non sit adrogans, sed potius facilis, aequus et fidelis* (1. 1. 7).

[45] *qui ab aetate puerili his gradibus disciplinarum scandendo scientia plerarumque litterarum et artium nutriti pervenerint ad summum templum architecturae* (1. 1. 11).

de Architectura was not the first volume to insist that architecture should be given a place alongside literature, history, and philosophy as one of the fundamental building blocks of a formal education.[46] Vitruvius' rationale for making his subject an aspect of true learning is delineated in *de Architectura* book 1, as he describes the project on which he has embarked: 'Indeed, concerning the power of this art and those theoretical principles which lie within it, I may offer, I hope, to lay them out confidently in these volumes with the greatest authority, not only for those who are engaged in building, but for all intelligent people.'[47] What Vitruvius proposes to describe in his book is *de artis... potestate quaeque insunt in ea ratiocinationes*; that is, not so much the practical knowledge needed to construct specific buildings as the fundamental principles on which architecture rests. This is why he imagines that his book will be useful to everyone, and not simply those who are interested in building: he is offering a theoretical system, an explanation of how the built environment comes to be what it is and mean what it does. As he says in a remarkable, albeit rather obscure,[48] passage in book 1 (1. 1. 3):

cum in omnibus enim rebus, tum maxime etiam in architectura haec duo insunt, quod significatur et quod significat. Significatur proposita res, de qua dicitur; hanc autem significat demonstratio rationibus doctrinarum explicata.

For as in all matters, so especially in architecture, there are two sides: that which is signified and that which signifies. The matter under consideration is the signified; but what signifies is the concrete manifestation, carried out according to the principles of science.

The *de Architectura*, therefore, understands that there are two matters of primary importance, *quod significat* and *quod significatur*, the

[46] On the relationship between Varro's work and Vitruvius, see Geertman (1994) 11–16.

[47] *de artis vero potestate quaeque insunt in ea ratiocinationes polliceor, uti spero, his voluminibus non modo aedificantibus sed etiam omnibus sapientibus cum maxima auctoritate me sine dubio praestaturum* (1. 1. 18).

[48] On the different interpretations which have been offered for the passage, see Gros (1997) 67–8.

building itself and the ideas behind it. Architecture is understood to be important for 'all wise people' both for practical purposes and as a means of understanding the science of space.[49]

It is in this context that Vitruvius' role as an Augustan author must be understood. The princeps' role as a builder has been the subject of much critical study, and it has been concluded that his famous boast—that he 'left a city of marble where he had found a city of brick'[50]—is not without a strong basis in material fact. From the ostentatious restoration of a reported eighty-two temples[51] to the transformation of the Palatine, it is clear that Augustus had a finely tuned sense of the kind of statements which could be made by the built environment. Indeed, the connection between architecture and the emperor's power is made explicitly in the opening preface of Vitruvius' handbook, where the author praises the princeps and describes how the work was inspired by his example (1. pref. 2):

cum vero adtenderem te non solum de vita communi omnium curam publicaeque rei constitutionem habere sed etiam de opportunitate *publicorum aedificiorum*, ut civitas per te non solum provinciis esset aucta, verum etiam ut maiestas imperii *publicorum aedificiorum* egregias haberet auctoritates, non putavi praetermittendum, quin primo quoque tempore de his rebus ea tibi ederem ...

But when I observed that you not only took care of the common life of all people and the organization of the state but also of the suitability of *public buildings*—so that not only might our civilization be augmented by you with new territories but also that the majesty of Empire might have the additional authority of *public buildings*—I did not think that the chance should be allowed to pass by of putting before you my thoughts on these matters at the earliest opportunity...

---

[49] On the relationship between practical and theoretical knowledge in Vitruvius, see Frézouls (1989) and Geertman (1994). A specific example of what Vitruvius means here occurs at book 2. 1. 5, where the author notes about the hut of Romulus, along with other rustic shrines in the city, *commonefacere potest et* significare *mores vetustates* ('it is able to impress [us with] and *signify* ancient customs').

[50] *excoluit adeo, ut iure sit gloriatus marmoream se relinquere, quam latericiam accepisset* (Suet. *Div. Aug.* 28. 3).

[51] As reported in the *Res Gestae* (20).

Vitruvius does not presume to tell Augustus what or how to build.
Indeed, the first preface of the *de Architectura* makes much of the fact
that the princeps has already built, creating a link between power and
space which the author-architect proposes to elaborate and exploit.
What Vitruvius sets out to do, then, is not to describe the imperial
building projects, but rather to interpret them; they form the basis of
his work not because they are technically sophisticated, but because
they embody the constructed environment's ability to signify larger
principles.[52] The point is not simply that the princeps has built
more, better, and bigger, and thus provided a greater opportunity
for the exploration of architectural techniques, but rather that he has
revealed the ways in which architecture can mean something more
than the construction of buildings. The *de Architectura*'s insistence
on the importance of architectural theory—the ideas which lie
beyond the constructed space itself—is thus connected with the
transformations wrought on the capital city under the auspices of
Augustus.

Pierre Gros has pointed out the extent to which the quotation
above trades on the language of contemporary ideology, as the
princeps' lavish building programmes, like his position as head of
the state, are legitimized by reference to *auctoritas*.[53] In this sense,
the double reference to *publicorum aedificiorum* is to the point:
Augustus has built extravagantly, not for himself, but on behalf of
the state. It is curious, however, that the opening preface of the
de Architectura goes on to make what seems at first to be the same
point as that in the quotation above, but this time making reference
to both public *and* private architecture. In the final paragraphs of the
preface, the author notes that he owes his career in military engin-
eering to the joint sponsorship of Augustus and his sister Octavia. He
goes on (1. pref. 3):

[52] It has been recognized that the preface to *de Arch.* performs a neat balancing act
between presuming to teach Augustus and using him as an example to teach others: he
appears both as the text's ideal audience and as the reader who does not need to learn the
information it contains. For discussion, see Gros (1994) and Novara (1994).
[53] Gros (1989).

cum ergo eo beneficio essem obligatus, ut ad exitum vitae non haberem inopiae timorem, haec tibi scribere coepi, quod animadverti multa te aedificavisse et nunc adificare, reliquo quoque tempore *et publicorum et privatorum aedificiorum*, pro amplitudine rerum gestarum ut posteris memoriae traderentur, curam habiturum. conscripsi praescriptiones terminatas, ut eas adtendens et ante facta et futura qualia sint opera per te posses nota habere.

Since, therefore, I owe it to that favour that I will never as long as I live be in fear of poverty, I began to write these things for you, because I noticed that you had already built, and were still building, many things, and that you also are concerned about *both public and private buildings* for the future, that memorials should be left to your descendants which are on a scale equal to your achievements. I have composed specific precepts, so that, considering them, you should be able to know for yourself what kind of works you have already accomplished and will accomplish in the future.

As before, Vitruvius represents his text as an explication of Augustus' architectural achievement, but here the type of building is specifically designated both public and private. On one level, it is tempting to see this intrusion of the domestic as connected with the turn of the second half of the preface to the 'personal' relationship between Vitruvius and Augustus—a relationship mediated, not coincidentally, by the princeps' sister. Whereas the earlier passage emphasized the contribution which Augustus has made to the *civitas*, a contribution mirrored in the *publica aedificia* which he has caused to be built, here the theme is Augustus as both public and private benefactor, and builder of both public and private structures. The fact that *posteris memoriae traderentur* ('memorials to be handed down to your descendants') are constituted by buildings in both spheres emphasizes Augustus' dual achievements as greatest personal and political authority in the Roman state. Equally important, however, is the fact that *publica et privata aedificia* are the two halves of *aedificatio* as the author will define it. The dichotomy which goes on to be important in structuring the text of the *de Architectura* is instantiated here in the preface, both sides of the equation placed squarely within the purview of the first emperor. Indeed, there would seem to be an ambiguity or overlap in the final sentences between the material structures produced under the auspices of Augustus and the textual 'monument' to which this passage serves as preface. The *ante facta et futura . . . opera per te* to which Vitruvius refers in the final clause might both be the imperial building projects already mentioned, and the *praescriptiones terminatas*, inspired by the princeps, which the treatise is imagined to contain. In the same way that Augustus was responsible both directly and indirectly for the transformation of the Roman landscape, he is implicated in the process of 'building' the two halves of the text of the *de Architectura*.

As was explored in the last chapter, Augustus' role straddling the boundary between public and private builder was particularly highlighted by the construction of his house, temple, and portico complex on the Palatine. I have already noted that we cannot be certain exactly when Vitruvius published his text, but since the Palatine project was among the very first undertaken after the princeps' return from Actium, it is certain to have been well under way, even if not complete, by the time of the *de Architectura*'s appearance. Vitruvius' desire to underscore the double architectural role of the princeps might well have been inspired by the particular projects which he saw being undertaken in the aftermath of the civil war. On the other hand, however, it is also clear that building 'privately', to the extent that it might signify a kind of spatial hoarding, was anathema to the new regime's preferred forms of self-representation. We may note, for instance, texts such as Horace's *Ode* 2. 15, whose profound connections with Augustan ideology have long been recognized[54] and which drums the terms public and private particularly hard. The ode opens with a vision of traditional rural life threatened by the construction of, literally, 'royal piles' (*regiae moles*: 1–2), going on to lament the banishment of the elm tree in favour of sterile planes, and the displacement of the fertile olive grove by fragrant but useless flower gardens (4–8). The third stanza brings this section of the

---

[54] e.g. West (1998): 'It has no addressee but everyone would have known that it was about Augustus' (p. 109).

poem to a close intoning *non ita Romuli / praescriptum et intonsi Catonis / auspiciis veterumque norma* ('this was not taught by the auspices of Romulus and unshorn Cato, nor by the rule of the ancients': 10–13). The lament over modern morals, the imagined demise of hardy country life, and the expressed desire to return to a time of more rigorous and productive virtue, are all almost stereotypically Augustan and are linked with domestic architecture through the spreading villa invoked in the first lines. The final two stanzas of the poem, moreover, articulate the point explicitly through the difference between virtuous public, and greedy private, building (lines 13–20):

> *privatus* illis census erat brevis,
> *commune* magnum: nulla decempedis
>   metata *privatis* opacam
>   porticus excipiebat Arcton,
>
> nec fortuitum spernere caespitem
> leges sinebant, oppida *publico*
>   sumptu iubentes et deorum
>   templa novo decorare saxo.

> Among them, a *private* fortune was small,
> the *common* property large: no colonnade, measured out
>   in ten-foot lengths, seized the shady northern bear
>   for *private individuals*,
>
> nor did the laws allow them to scorn
> the chance turf, ordering them
>   to decorate towns at *public* expense
>   and the temples of the gods with fresh stone.

Ode 2. 15 has not stirred much critical interest, at least partially because it appears so unimaginatively to rehearse Augustan ideology in exactly the same terms as are found elsewhere.[55] The final stanza's reference to temple renovation, for instance, has been seen as referring to Augustus, who boasts in the *Res Gestae* that he restored

---

[55] Romano (1994).

eighty-two temples in Rome, adding that he did so only under the authority of the senate (*RG* 20). Indeed, the *Res Gestae* is very careful in its representation of the emperor's building to characterize it as public service rather than self-aggrandizement: Augustus repeatedly highlights buildings which he did not inscribe with his own name, instead leaving them dedicated to others.[56] In Horace's *Ode* 2. 15, the point is driven home by the word *excipiebat* in line 16, which both delineates a neat hunting metaphor (with Arcton as 'bear') and indicates the grasping greediness of a man who wishes to own the constellations for himself. Indeed, although Nisbet and Hubbard obelize the first word in line 13 on the grounds that *census* needs no modification to indicate a personal fortune,[57] we may see the significance of *privatus* in its contrast with line 14's *commune*—not just in the comparison between private and public wealth, but in the spatial metaphors embedded in the words. Where *privatus* looks back to *privo* (and thus signifies literally 'to be deprived'), indicating the strict limits on individual wealth in ancient days, *commune* is made up of *con-* and *munis, -e* ('ready to be of service') which is cognate with words like *munus, -eris*, n. ('a service or duty'). Indeed, Varro at *de Lingua Latina* 5. 141 and 179 would—albeit erroneously—derive *munus* from *munio, -ire* ('to build a defensive wall'), so that the shared obligations in *commune* would be specifically architectural in nature. Even if Horace here is not following Varro's line of reasoning, there is still a sense of openness in *commune*, while *privatus* indicates the attenuated space of private property in old Rome. Unlike Vitruvius, Horace refuses to allow that any building for private purposes might be acceptable.

Horace's *Ode* 2. 15, therefore, indicates the extent to which private building in the modern day might be understood as luxurious self-aggrandizement, in contrast with the communal architectural

[56] e.g. the Capitolium and theatre of Pompey, *sine ulla inscriptione nominis mei* ('without any inscription of my name': *RG* 20); the Porticus Octavia, *porticum ad circum Flaminium, quam sum appellari passus ex nomine eius qui priorem eodem in solo fecerat Octaviam* ('the portico near the Circus Flaminius, which I allowed to be called "Octavia", from the name of him who had made the earlier one on the same site': *RG* 19).
[57] Nisbet and Hubbard (1978) 248.

gestures which marked the heroic Roman past. The point is to celebrate building which reflects the glory of the city generally, rather than that which consumes space for the benefit of a single individual. In Vitruvius' *de Architectura*, however, private building is from the outset associated with a public goal: even though Augustus' architectural projects do reflect his personal achievements, those achievements and their material monuments are praised as a legacy to the future rather than a representation of self for the present. In this sense, despite the rather republican description of the house which will later be found in book 6, Vitruvius' preface gives an Augustan frame to the project as a whole, and particularly to the two halves of *aedificatio*, public and private. The princeps' identity, as the primary personal and political authority in Rome, is expressed materially in his dual roles as public and private builder, an overlap which Vitruvius then reflects in the constitution of his text. When Vitruvius turns to private building in book 6 of his treatise, therefore, we should not be surprised to discover that social and political authority are encoded in the material structures described by the author: not only is he heir to the republican vision of the house as a kind of public space, but he has also already suggested that, in the case of Augustus, private building may serve the state as well as the individual. This is not to say that the house later described in the *de Architectura* is imagined to bear a structural resemblance to the residence of the imperial family. Rather, it is to try to point us toward 'what is signified' in the descriptions of the private dwellings found in book 6. Here again, however, we will see that the display of domestic femininity in the *de Architectura* is used as a complex cultural and textual signal, rather than as a straightforward symbol of virtuous private life.

PRIVACY, GENDER, AND CULTURE IN VITRUVIUS 6

Like several other books of the *de Architectura*, book 6 opens with a short, paradigmatic narrative which serves to introduce the author's prefatory comments—an exemplum which Vitruvius will go on to embroider and elaborate before he engages with the architectural substance of the book. In book 6, the opening narrative concerns the Socratic philosopher Aristippus of Cyrene (6. pr. 1).

Aristippus philosophus Socraticus, naufragio cum eiectus ad Rhodiensium litus animadvertisset geometrica schemata descripta, exclamavisse ad comites ita dicitur: 'bene speremus! hominum enim vestigia video.' statim- que in oppidum Rhodum contendit et recta gymnasium devenit, ibique de philosophia disputans muneribus est donatus, ut non tantum se ornaret, sed etiam eis, qui una fuerunt, et vestitum et cetera, quae opus essent ad victum praestaret.

Aristippus the Socratic philosopher, when he was washed ashore at Rhodes following a shipwreck, noticed geometrical diagrams inscribed [on the earth], and, it is said, exclaimed to his companions: 'Let us take hope! For I see traces of human beings.' Immediately, he made for the city of Rhodes and went straight to the gymnasium; there, as he discoursed about philoso- phy, he was given rewards, so that he was not only able to take care of himself, but also able to provide clothing and other necessities of life to those who were together with him.

The moral, as Vitruvius goes on to explain, is that the only truly portable property is knowledge: *doctum ex omnibus solum neque in alienis locis peregrinum neque amissis familiaribus et necessariis inopem amicorum, sed in omni civitate esse civem difficilesque fortunae sine timore posse despicere casus* ('the learned man alone of everyone is not a stranger in foreign lands, nor, if he has lost his family and property, is he bereft of friends; rather, he is a citizen of every state and is able without fear to scorn the hard turns of fortune': 6. pr. 2). This subsequently leads into a short sketch of the author's own education and career, the observation that he did not pursue architecture for the sake of financial reward, and a programmatic lament that unqua- lified architects are allowed to go on practising—a situation which he hopes the present volume will do something to remedy. In short, the opening story of Aristippus seems to have little to do with what follows in the preface to book 6, except insofar as it serves to emphasize and elevate the position of the learned man, nor does it appear to have anything to say about domestic architecture, the subject of the book as it was announced in the concluding sentence of book 5 (*privatorum autem aedificiorum utilitates et eorum symmetrias inseqenti volumine ratiocinabor.* 5. 12. 7).

This apparently tenuous connection between the opening exemplum and what follows in the body of the book is not entirely unprecedented in the *de Architectura*; we might compare, for instance, book 2, on building materials, which begins with the famous story of Alexander the Great and his architect Dinocrates, who offered to carve Mt. Athos into the figure of man holding a great city in the palm of his hand. In book 6, however, the focus of the story of Aristippus on how different cultures compare and communicate with one another is actually picked up in the chapter which follows the preface. In 6. 1, by way of introduction to his discussion of the technical details of domestic architecture, Vitruvius offers a description of the ways in which climate may be understood to influence building. One expects here, I think, a simple argument that hotter regions require houses with more shade, but instead, the author provides a lengthy analysis of the effect of environment, not immediately on architecture, but upon human character. Drawing heavily on the language of ethnographic and medical literature like the Hippocratic *Airs, Waters, Places*, Vitruvius argues that the people of the south are intelligent but cowardly, due to the dry heat of their countries, while northerners are made fierce and rash by the dampness and chill. Only Italy, perhaps not surprisingly, is perfectly situated to balance cold and hot, wet and dry, so that her peoples are *temperatissimae... et corporum membris animorumque vigoribus pro fortitudine* ('most balanced... both in the limbs of their bodies and in the courageous strength of their spirits'). Unlike the peoples around them, the Italians enjoy a perfect climate, which in turn produces a population whose balanced temperament and physical ability means that it is able to act as a kind of golden mean for the entire world: *itaque consiliis refringit barbarorum virtutes, forti manu meridianorum cogitationes. ita divina mens civitatem populi Romani*

*egregiam temperatamque regionem conlocavit, uti orbis terrarum
imperio potiretur* ('Therefore [Rome] curbs the physical strength of
barbarians with its wisdom, and the thoughts of the southerners with
its powerful hand. Thus the divine mind placed the civilization of
the Roman people in an excellent and moderate place, so that it
might rule the globe of the world with its power': 6. 1. 11). Italy is, as
Vitruvius' contemporary Strabo would put it in a similar passage,
'naturally fit for rule'.[58]

What has all this to do with architecture? Well, Vitruvius says, in
as much as different environments have been assigned to different
peoples, so that they are different in temperament and physical
type, dwelling places must be constructed to suit the particular
characters of the nations and races for whom they are built. Nature
makes people who they are, and architecture responds accordingly
(6. 1. 12).

quodsi ita est, uti dissimiles regiones ab inclinationibus caeli variis generibus
sint comparatae, ut etiam naturae gentium disparibus animis et corporum
figuris qualitatibusque nascerentur, non dubitemus aedificiorum quoque
rationes ad nationum gentiumque proprietates apte distribuere, cum habea-
mus ab ipsa rerum natura sollertem et expeditam monstrationem.

But if this is indeed the case, that regions dissimilar in environment are
provided to the different nations with the result that the natures of the
peoples arise with varying spirits and shapes and conditions of body, we
must not hesitate to arrange the layouts of our buildings also, suiting them
to the characteristics of nations and peoples, since we have from nature
herself a clever and skilled demonstration.

People in different countries need their own particular kinds of
dwellings, not directly because of external conditions imposed by
the climate but because of internal diversity created by the inhabitants. Yet although human beings may differ from one another
physically, spiritually, and intellectually, the scientific principles
upon which architecture is based speak both for and to them; the

---

[58] πρὸς ἡγεμονίαν εὐφυῶς ἔχει (Strabo 6. 4. 1).

architect, like the philosopher Aristippus, is the master of a universal language which can be moulded to suit the different needs of different national characters. Following as it does, moreover, upon the passage which praises the universality of Roman imperialism—the ability of Italy to balance and control the unbridled natures of the rest of the world—there is also an implicit connection drawn here between the power of Rome and the power of architectural discourse. The language of building, the language taught by the *de Architectura*, is able to encompass different peoples and cultural practices in the same way that the Roman Empire has embraced, incorporated, and supposedly improved them. As in the dedication to Augustus which precedes book 1, then, the introduction to book 6 underscores the continuity between the authority of the text and that of the Roman state.

With such an introduction, it seems legitimate to expect that book 6 will concern itself with cultural difference: the stage is set by the first chapter's argument linking architecture with ethnicity, styles of house-building being integrally connected to the national nature of those for whom they are built. It is noticeable that Vitruvius has waited until book 6 to make such an apparently sweeping statement about the nature of building, which would seem to underscore the extent to which the point is particular to the type of building (private) to be described in this book. For contrast we may again compare a passage in book 2, where the author notes that buildings are constructed similarly in such far-flung places as Gaul, Spain, Greece, and Pontus; the same kind of structure, in fact, can be found in the hut of Romulus on the Palatine (2. 1. 4–6). His conclusion in book 2, however, does not emphasize cultural difference, but rather chronological change: the similarities of building across the world are held to prove a single origin for the practice of architecture, now lost in the mists of time. The shift in perspective on this question for book 6, where Vitruvius emphasizes the adaptability of architectural principles rather than their common origin, makes it clear that only houses are imagined to be so closely linked with ethnic character. The point, moreover, is reinforced by an overview of book 6. Although much of it is taken up with architectural differences within the Roman landscape, so that there are separate chapters for town and farm buildings, the book does include a special chapter on 'how buildings are arranged according to the customs of the Greeks' (*quemadmodum Graecorum consuetudinibus aedificia distribuantur*). The use of the word *consuetudo* is not accidental here: it neatly signifies both different modes of architectural design and the different social customs which give rise to them. As the author's introductory comments have led us to expect, we here discover that national identity is manifested in domestic building: the Greeks construct their houses differently from the Romans, a difference which may be traced back to a fundamentally different way of living in the world.

Vitruvius' chapter on Greek domestic architecture has been the subject of a great deal of controversy, principally because his description bears little or no resemblance to the remains of Greek houses found in the material record. Various explanations have been adduced for this phenomenon (our evidence is, admittedly, scanty even for the classical period, and perhaps Vitruvius is describing what he knew of the Hellenistic house?) but an overview of the book as a whole introduces another element, namely that of cultural difference. In the same sense that the first chapter of book 6 explicitly compares the climates of other regions of the world to the 'norm' which is Roman Italy, the chapter on Greek domestic architecture must be read in relation to Vitruvius' description of the Roman house. This is not to say that there was no material basis for the *de Architectura*'s descriptions in book 6. Rather, it is to focus attention on the representation of those material facts in the light of their rhetorical setting, in a book which opens with the argument that nation and culture manifest themselves in domestic architecture. This point is reinforced in the opening sentence of the chapter on the Greek house, which begins, *atriis Graeci quia non utuntur, neque aedificant* ('since the Greeks do not use atria, they do not build them': 6. 7. 1). As in Vitruvius' insistence on the atrium as one of the primary spaces of social interaction in the Roman house, where visitors are received and 'public' business is transacted, the point is as much about the use of space as its material structure.

Indeed, the beginning of the chapter on the Greek house seems almost to work as a response to the first sentence on the social structure of the Roman house, which explains that the critical distinction within the Roman structure is that between rooms dedicated to the use of strangers and those occupied by the homeowner alone: *cum ad regiones caeli ita ea fuerint disposita, tunc etiam animadvertendum est, quibus rationibus privatis aedificiis propria loca patribus familiarum et quemadmodum communia cum extraneis aedificari debeant* ('when [the rooms] have been laid out in relation to the areas of the sky, then it must be considered by what rationale, in private houses, places reserved for the owners of the house and those commonly shared with outsiders should be built': 6. 5. 1). As has been noted, the chapter will go on to focus attention on the ways in which the elite house functions both to accommodate and to reflect the position of its owner in relation to an audience of fellow citizens, as bankers need to display their wealth, rhetoricians need space for teaching, magistrates need a place to pass judgement, and so on. Yet, as Vitruvius will note, one of the peculiarities of Greek social practice, in implicit contrast to Roman, is that visitors to the Greek house are not received into the courtyard, or really into the house at all, but into specially designated 'guest quarters' (*hospitalia*) with their own entrances, dining rooms, and bedrooms.[59] In fact, historically, the Greek house was even less open to visitors than it is in Vitruvius' time (6. 7. 4):

nam cum fuerunt Graeci delicatiores et fortuna opulentiores, hospitibus advenientibus instruebant triclinia, cubicula, cum penu cellas, primoque die ad cenam invitabant, postero mittebant pullos, ova, holera, poma reliquasque res agrestes.... ita patres familiarum in hospitio non videbantur esse peregre, habentes secretam in his hospitalibus liberalitatem.

For when the Greeks were more self-indulgent and wealthier in their circumstances, they provided dining rooms, bedrooms, and storerooms

---

[59] The fact that the guest houses are notionally separate from the main house is indicated in the description of them as *domunculae*: they exist as independent 'little houses' (6. 7. 4).

with provisions to visiting guests, and on the first day they invited them to dinner, but on the next sent chickens, eggs, vegetables, apples, and all sorts of other agricultural produce. . . . In this way, householders who were visiting did not seem to be travelling abroad, as they enjoyed separate hospitality within the guest accommodations.

Vitruvius' vision of Greek hospitality and its spaces is, as far as we can tell, unique, and, especially in contrast with stated Roman practice, rather peculiar. Visitors to the Greek home are not only restricted in their movements within the house but kept entirely separate, given their own *domunculae* in which to set up facsimiles of their own private spaces. Whereas the Romans bring the community inside their dwellings, the Greeks keep even invited guests outside the walls.

This contrast serves, I think, to highlight the point which Vitruvius is seeking to make about Greek and Roman domestic architecture, and, correspondingly, about Greek and Roman culture: that what we might term privacy—the creation of distinct and separate spaces into which those outside the household might not pass—was far more developed as a feature of Greek houses than Roman. Indeed, even in addition to the highly structured (literally) relationship between those inside and outside the family, Greek domestic life appears in Vitruvius as built around distinctions internal to the household itself. Most noticeably, the *de Architectura* is one of a handful of texts from antiquity which testify to a structure which has been the subject of more controversy than any other aspect of ancient house-design: the Greek *gynaeconitis* or 'women's quarters', a room or rooms specifically devoted to female activities such as cooking, weaving, and childcare, where the women of the household might be kept out of sight of the more public spaces of the house. According to Vitruvius, while the Roman house is constructed around a central atrium, Greek domestic architecture features two sections: one larger and more open for the men and their guests (the *andronitis*: 6. 7. 3–4) and one smaller and more private for the women and the household servants (the *gynaeconitis*: 6. 7. 2).[60] The architect-author

---

[60] For a more detailed discussion of the differences between the two kinds of house, see Ruggiu (1995) 289–310.

carefully links the names of the two wings to those who populate them, noting that the *gynaeconitis* is where the ladies sit with the spinning-women, and that it also includes bedrooms, dining rooms, and servants' quarters. The *andronitis*, similarly, contains peristyles, libraries, art galleries, and *triclinia*, and takes its name from the banqueting halls from which women are excluded—a fact which Vitruvius seems to think bears repeating, since he explains it twice in two sequential paragraphs: *in his oecis fiunt virilia convivia; non enim fuerat institutum matris familiarum eorum moribus accumbere* ('in these spaces men's banquets are held; for it was not according to their customs for the ladies of the household to lie down at table': 6. 7. 4) and *Graeci enim andronas appellant oecus, ubi convivia virilia solent esse, quod eo mulieres non accedunt* ('for the Greeks call this space the andron(itis), where the men's banquets are accustomed to be held, because women do not go there': 6. 7. 5). Like the guest *domunculae*, therefore, both the men's and women's quarters are almost completely self-contained, and separated from one another both spatially and by the kinds of activities performed there.[61]

For many years, the testimony of Vitruvius and similar texts was accepted without question, and the idea that the Greek home contained a separate living space for women was firmly entrenched in discussions both of ancient domestic architecture and of the social structures of classical Greece and Rome.[62] More recently, however, scholars have begun to emphasize the disjunction between surviving written and material evidence (despite the best efforts of archaeologists, no physical evidence of the *gynaeconitis* has been found) to insist that the situation was not as straightforward as our texts make it appear.[63] Carla Antonaccio makes the particularly cogent argument that we must be wary of understanding either architecture or literature transparently to represent historical reality, and that social practice always has the capacity both to embrace and resist cultural norms.[64]

---

[61] One excellent representation of the Roman view of the Greek house generally, and the *gynaeconitis* in particular, may be found in Plautus' *Mostellaria*, in which a number of jokes are made about the segregation of women: see Milnor (2002) 17–19.

[62] e.g. Walker (1983).   [63] e.g. Jameson (1990); Nevett (1994).

[64] Antonaccio (2000); cf. Goldberg (1999).

This is not the place, nor am I qualified, to pronounce on the reality or otherwise of the *gynaeconitis* as a feature of ancient Greek architecture. What I would like to point out, however, is the extent to which Vitruvius' description of gender relations in the Greek house conforms to his understanding of Greek culture as it is expressed in domestic architecture generally. That understanding, moreover, cannot be separated from the author's goal of finding in Greek domestic structures a counterpoint to the Roman, not simply structurally but in the ways that they express different cultural values. In this sense, I think it is profitable to consider the *de Architectura*'s representation of 'women's quarters' in the Greek house as structured by the requirements of the text as much as by historical reality. My point is not to deny the *gynaeconitis* any basis in material fact, but rather to underscore the rhetorical ends which the production of such a fact might serve in Vitruvius' text.

By way of illuminating the issues at stake here, let me begin with a passage which is often taken as evidence of gender segregation in the Greek household—a passing reference that manifests the difference between Greeks and Romans which is found more explicitly articulated in authors such as Vitruvius.[65] In Cicero's second Verrine oration, the orator recounts a scandalous event which took place when the defendant was serving as assistant governor of Cilicia (*2 Verr.* 1. 63). Along with his henchman Rubrius, Verres made his way to a town called Lampsacus on the shore of the Hellespont. Upon their arrival, Rubrius quickly discovered that one of the town's most respected citizens, a certain Philodamus, was known to have an extremely beautiful daughter, whereupon Verres and his crew decided to invite themselves over to the old man's house for dinner. Philodamus, concerned for his family's welfare but anxious not to offend the Roman dignitaries, prepared a lavish banquet but made arrangements for the entire household, excepting himself, to be otherwise engaged when the guests arrived. The party commenced, but trouble quickly ensued, as Cicero reports (*2 Verr.* 1.66):

---

[65] e.g. Wallace-Hadrill (1996: 109–10), who discusses the passage but does not quote it in full, so that the nuance which I point out below is lost.

Posteaquam satis calere res Rubrio visa est, 'Quaeso,' inquit, 'Philodame, cur ad nos filiam tuam non intro vocari iubes?' homo, qui et summa gravitate et iam id aetatis et parens esset, obstupuit hominis improbi dicto. instare Rubrius; tum ille, *ut aliquid responderet*, negavit moris esse Graecorum ut in convivio virorum accumberent mulieres.

When it seemed to Rubrius that things had warmed up sufficiently, he said, 'I wonder, Philodamus, why you don't ask for your daughter to be called in to see us?' The gentleman, not only a father, but high-minded and already elderly, was dumbfounded by the suggestion of this shameless man. Rubrius persisted; Philodamus then responded, *in order that he should say something*, that it was not the custom among the Greeks for women to join the men at dinner.

On the surface, this passage does seem to record actual firsthand testimony of the practice of gender segregation within the Greek house, articulated in the same terms as Vitruvius' *de Architectura*: the Greek dining room is off-limits to women. To my mind, however, such an interpretation misses the point, both of the story as a whole and of the phrase *ut aliquid responderet* italicized in the passage above. The idea which lies behind the story as Cicero tells it is that Verres is, and is known by his host to be, a lecher; no one is safe with him, not women or boys. Hence Philodamus carefully dispatches his entire family, including his son, to other locations for the duration of the infamous party. The old man's daughter is not at dinner because Verres can't be trusted, not because the house is segregated by gender. Far from expressing a truth about Greek culture, the 'fact' that men and women dine separately in Lampsacus is produced on the spur of the moment as an excuse: 'in order that he should say something'. Not wanting to insult his temperamental guests, Philodamus takes refuge in cultural difference, producing a story—visible in Cicero's speech *as* a story—which he thinks will protect his daughter from the leering foreigners. The subsequent production of it in the second Verrine then serves to mark Cicero's greater understanding of what happened in Lampsacus, an understanding which he expects his audience to share: he expects that they will recognize both the desperation which led the father to produce the tale and the cultural mythology which made it believable. The significance, therefore, of this moment in the second Verrine lies not in the historical reality of Philodamus' statement, but in the way it represents self-representation; it gives us a window, not necessarily onto actual Greek customs, but onto the kinds of Greek customs which it seemed likely that Romans such as Verres and Rubrius would believe.

In fact, the *de Architectura* is not alone in seeing the presence of 'women's quarters' in the Greek house not just as a curious fact but as evidence of a fundamental difference between Greek and Roman society. As early as Plautus we find jokes which turn on the structural and social oddity of a house built around a *gynaecium* (a synonym for *gynaeconitis*).[66] Cicero in the second Philippic makes reference to the *gynaecium* of Antony's wife Fulvia, where Deiotarus, king of Galatia, was forced by Antony to pay ten million sesterces for the return of his kingdom: the transaction 'was done in the *gynaecium*, in which many things have been, and are being, sold' (*facta in gynaecio est, quo in loco plurimae res venierunt et veneunt*: 95). This is the only use of the word in all of Cicero, and its appearance in the carefully crafted rhetoric of the second Philippic is testimony to its weighted meaning. Here Cicero's use of the word must fit into the picture which Cicero is trying to construct of Antony as a false Roman; in this sense, Fulvia's imagined *gynaecium* is an early shot in the war of propaganda waged later between Antony and Octavian, in which Antony would be cast as a debauched eastern monarch, his Roman blood corrupted by the embraces of the Graeco-Egyptian Cleopatra.[67] Indeed, the ability of the *gynaecium* (or *gynaeconitis*) to embody single-handedly the difference between Rome and the foreign other is manifested in the preface to Cornelius Nepos' *Lives of the Foreign Generals*, where the author attempts to illustrate the distinction between Greek and Roman culture. He enumerates a number of things either permitted or celebrated in Greece which the Romans would judge 'far from good conduct' (*ab honestate remota*:

[66] For a fuller exploration of spatial language in Plautus, see Milnor (2002).

[67] More specifically, however, it is clear that Cicero is using the *gynaecium* ironically: while Greek women sit meekly secluded, away from public life and influence, Fulvia makes her quarters into a market where kingdoms are for sale. The *gynaecium* evokes the idea of the over-protected and restricted lives of Greek women, ironically juxtaposed with the reference to 'things for sale' which hints at prostitution.

pref. 6), including male–male love affairs, Cimon's marriage to his sister, and the high social standing of actors and athletes. On the other hand, there are things which are perfectly correct at Rome, yet shameful in Greece (pref. 6–7):

quem enim Romanorum pudet uxorem ducere in convivium? aut cuius non mater familias primum locum tenet aedium atque in celebritate versatur? quod multo fit aliter in Graecia. nam neque in convivium adhibetur nisi propinquorum, neque sedet nisi in interiore parte aedium, quae gynaeconitis appellatur, quo nemo accedit nisi propinqua cognatione coniunctus.

For what Roman would be ashamed to bring his wife to a dinner party? And in what family does the mother of the household not occupy a central place in the home and move about through the crowd? But the situation is very different in Greece. For she is not invited to dinner, unless it is with close relatives, nor does she sit anywhere other than the innermost part of the house, which is called the *gynaeconitis*, into which no man goes except a near relation.

Contrasting the *primum locum . . . aedium* which the Roman woman holds with the confinement of Greek women to the *gynaeconitis*, Nepos here provides both a social and an architectural critique of the different domestic practices of Greeks and Romans. Unlike the wide-ranging list of 'normal' Greek activities which would meet with disapproval at Rome, female seclusion is the only practice adduced to illustrate something which the Romans do as a matter of course which the Greeks would find shocking. Nepos thus represents the women's quarters in the Greek house as paradigmatic of the difference between Greek and Roman cultures, an example sufficiently compelling that it stands on its own.[68]

   In short, it seems as though the *gynaeconitis* appears in Latin literature not simply as a material structure but as a cultural symbol: in texts from Plautus to Cicero to Cornelius Nepos, references to it

---

[68] Nepos' remarks on Greek domestic practice in his preface, in fact, are contradicted by the behaviour of the few women who do appear in the following biographies, like the politically dangerous Olympias (*Eumenes* 6).

appear as much to articulate the ways in which Greek culture is distinct from Roman as to describe the real structure of the Greek house. As in the story from the second Verrine quoted above, the *gynaeconitis* appears in these contexts as much as a rhetorical strategy as a material fact. When it surfaces in Vitruvius, therefore, it again serves to situate the passage in which it appears as part of a discourse of difference, one piece of the overall thrust of the book toward expressing the ways in which culture is manifested in domestic architecture. Yet it is also important to note the difference between what Vitruvius has to say on this subject and, particularly, the passage from Cornelius Nepos quoted above. Whereas Nepos is explicit, not just about the lives of Greek women in the house, but also about those of Roman *matres familiae*, Vitruvius describes only the Greek; when it comes to the Roman house, he is entirely silent on the subject of gender. Again, I would by no means deny that this may have had something to do with the different material practices of the cultures in question. It seems likely that there was some kind of structural differentiation between the sexes which could be found, on whatever level, in the Greek house, and which was not present in the Roman. Yet at the same time we cannot ignore the extent to which both the idea of the house and the representation of women have already been loaded in the *de Architectura* with meaning—meaning which speaks not just to cultural difference, but to imperial power. Vitruvius has made it clear in the introduction to book 6 that what is communicated in the following chapters is not simply a set of unbiased ethnographic facts, but descriptions of cultures in relation to one another: since Italians inhabit the perfectly balanced centre of the world, they are naturally superior, and the architecture which is most closely associated with their state of nature, that of their houses, also reflects that superiority. In contrast, the high level of seclusion and need for privacy in the Greek house, including the separation of the sexes, expresses the particular nature of Greek culture. The absence of gendered spaces in the Roman house, correspondingly, illustrates the perfectly blended and balanced state of Italian domestic life.

The description of the Greek 'women's quarters' found in the *de Architectura*, then, functions within the text as a sign of the difference between Rome and Greece, a difference which legitimizes the imperial rule of the one society over the other. Similarly, of course, the fact of the *gynaeconitis*, apparently already recognized among the Romans as a strange feature of Greek domestic architecture, is marshalled by Vitruvius to 'prove' his original point in book 6: different cultures do in fact structure their houses differently, yet the architectural principles on which they are built remain the same. Given the importance which the text accords to the description of gendered space in the Greek house, however, it is worth remembering the earlier instance in the *de Architectura* in which women appeared as, literally, a monument to the triumph of one society over another. The story of the caryatids, displayed to commemorate their city's defeat, established at the very beginning of Vitruvius' text the terms in which women may be understood as features of architecture, as a means of representing—through the power of representation—the subjugation of the viewed to the viewer. The objectification in the *de Architectura* of the Greek house's gendered spaces serves a similar purpose, and communicates a similar message: the 'eye' of Vitruvius' text penetrates everywhere, into the most secret and secluded parts of Greek private space, revealing, describing, and displaying the places and people that as a culture they most wished to hide. The Roman house, in contrast, has no privacy to be violated, no secrets to be revealed; what Vitruvius shows to the reader is the public face of domestic life in Rome, whose openness makes it an easy and unproblematic subject for textual representation. The fact that the Roman house is already a public space means that its 'publication' in the *de Architectura* only serves to reinforce and underscore its own values; the fact of Greek privacy, on the other hand, means that its display in the text is an invasion and marks its subjugation to the reader's knowing eye.

Vitruvius' *de Architectura*, therefore, may very well reflect real, material differences between the construction of domestic life in Greece and Rome, but it also uses those differences to further its own rhetorical ends. The text continuously insists on the role which the house may play as a public symbol: as a representation of Augustus' achievements in the work's preface; as a sign of cultural difference and Italian superiority in the opening chapters of book 6; as a place where power may be displayed through the triumph of architectural knowledge over the desire for privacy in the description of the Greek house. All of these are clearly born from Vitruvius' very Roman understanding of the house as a space of display, where the focus is entirely on the audience and the importance of displaying the identity of the *paterfamilias*. In this process, the women of the Roman household disappear, not because they were not present but because they have been subsumed, as they historically were, into the project of demonstrating the values of the head of the house. When women do appear in the *de Architectura*, they do so in the guise of 'others', on parade to illustrate the mastery of both architectural discourse and Roman imperialism. The most significant exception to this is, importantly, the woman without whom the text would not have happened: Octavia, whose cameo appearance in the work's preface marks and mediates the personal relationship between her brother and the author. But her presence serves simply to prove the rule, that Roman women in the age of Augustus serve an indispensable role as representatives in public of private life, in contrast with the supposedly shameful display of foreign women later in the text. Octavia thus, as both member of the emperor's household and a virtuous Roman woman, offers us a glimpse of the proudly public function of femininity as part of the imperial Roman home.

3

Women, History, and the Law

THERE is perhaps no historical event more closely associated with Augustan family values than the social legislation of 18–17 BCE. The *lex Iulia de maritandis ordinibus* and the *lex Iulia de adulteriis* together formed one of the cornerstones of Augustus' 'moral revolution'—that is, the idea that the Principate represented a return to, and renewal of, the ancient domestic virtues on which the Roman state had been built.[1] The former law set up a system of rewards and penalties for marriage within and between classes, so that, for instance, members of the senatorial class were forbidden to marry freedpeople or actors, while all freeborn people were forbidden to marry anyone who had the status of a prostitute. This law also established social, political, and economic rewards for men and women who produced a certain number of children. The *lex Iulia de adulteriis* formally outlawed adultery for the first time in Roman

---

[1] The traditional view that there was a population crisis following the social turmoil of the civil wars, a practical problem to which the social legislation was a practical solution, has certain points to recommend it but does not work as a complete explanation. The adultery law, after all, has very little to do overtly with reproduction, and the inducements to having children under the *lex Iulia de maritandis ordinibus* are matched by numerous restrictions on intermarriage between classes. Moreover, the most serious penalties invoked against persons who failed to produce the requisite number of children involved the inability to leave or collect inheritances, a point which would seem to indicate that the laws were directed primarily at those who had some access to property. It seems likely that, as scholars have argued, it was the shortage of particular classes of Romans (i.e. the elite upper classes) that concerned Augustus. See Brunt (1971: 558–66) for a discussion of the late republican 'manpower shortage'. McGinn (1998*b*: 78) makes the cogent point that 'the distinction between morality and demographics is a false one to draw for the Romans', since 'demographic ends might be pursued within a framework determined by considerations of rank and gender'.

history, and not only established penalties for those caught in the act, but also set up rules for how those who discovered them should proceed. Thus, the two laws each made real legislative incursions into the sphere of family life, and the *lex Iulia de maritandis ordinibus*, at any rate, seems to have met with a significant level of resistance. Nevertheless, despite the unpopularity, and possible ineffectiveness, of the laws, the princeps clearly remained committed to them—testimony to their importance as a part of his vision of the newly constituted imperial state. The performance of the Saecular Games less than a year after the passage of the legislation would seem deliberately to underscore their mutual connection to the new imperial age of fertility and abundance, celebrated in the festival on the one hand and guaranteed by obedience to the laws on the other. The laws certainly appear prominently in Horace's *Carmen Saeculare*, written for and performed at the opening of the games, in which the goddess Ilithyia is asked to support the *patrum . . . decreta super iugandis feminis prolisque novae feraci lege marita* ('decrees of the senate concerning marriage with women and the nuptial law productive of new life': *Carmen Saeculare* 17–20). Augustus himself makes reference to the laws in the *Res Gestae* as one of his proudest achievements, and an examination of the later historical tradition, from Tacitus and Suetonius to Cassius Dio and the late antique jurists, makes it clear that the social legislation became one of the most famous and illustrative symbols of the first emperor's rule.

Other scholars have amply and admirably analysed the Augustan legislation as a social event, a cultural event, a demographic event, and an historical event, asking productively what the laws intended, what they actually effected, and how and whose particular interests were served.[2] What I would like to do here, however, is to

[2] There is a great deal of bibliography on the social legislation, including Mommsen (1899) 682–702; Field (1945); Csillag (1976); Frank (1976); Raditsa (1980); Galinsky (1981); Wallace-Hadrill (1981); de Bouvrie (1984); Bellen (1987); Cohen (1991); Edwards (1993) 34–62; McGinn (2002); and Severy (2003) 52–6 and 232–51. In recent decades, scholars have moved away from traditional legalistic and demographic explanations of the laws toward those which focus more on Augustan ideology and self-representation.

consider them as a historiographical event—as an imperial act which changed the way that authors read and represented law and the history of law in the early Roman Empire. This is not to say that I will only, or even primarily, be looking at texts which specifically mention the *leges Iuliae* of 18–17 BCE; indeed, one of the surprising facts about the social legislation is how little overt attention it receives in the contemporary literary record. The exception is Horace, whose role as 'poet laureate' of the Augustan regime is sometimes seen as proven by the extent to which his poetry delivers the same message as the social legislation, as both insist on Rome's moral rebirth under the new political order; even beyond the publicly commissioned and performed *Carmen Saeculare*, there are clear moments in the *Odes* which call for, and later praise the results of, legislation to curb immorality.[3] But when I speak of the Augustan social legislation as a historiographical event, I am not so much refering to the ways in which the laws themselves become the objects of representation in literature, but rather how they function on a par with other works of the same period as representational vehicles;[4] like other 'Augustan' texts, they too encompass certain readings of early imperial society and what it meant to live in the age of the first emperor. What I aim to do in this chapter, therefore, is to look closely both at what the laws might be construed as saying about the role of domesticity in Roman culture and at a particular moment in the work of a contemporary author—Livy's debate over the repeal of the *lex Oppia*—which also addresses this question. Although this episode in Livy's history notionally takes place in 195 BCE, I will argue that the debate which he composed for the occasion articulates

---

[3] I think especially of *Odes* 3. 6 and 24 (esp. 25–32), published before the passage of the laws, and *Odes* 4. 5 and 15, published after.

[4] In this I have been influenced by such legal theorists as J. B. White, who calls the law 'a constitutive rhetoric'—a language which, like any other language, is the site of continuous interpretive struggle, appropriation, and change: White (1985) 28–48. Feminist legal historians have been also influential in the development of 'social constructionist' approaches to law: see, for instance, Smart (1995) and the essays in Smart (1992). For a discussion of the development of legal theory over the past two decades, particularly in the light of feminist theory, see Chunn and Lacombe (2000).

certain ideas and anxieties about the gendered relationship between public and private life which both reflect, and are reflected in, the moral legislation so closely associated with the age of Augustus.

HISTORY, GENDER, AND THE AUGUSTAN LAW

In book 3 of Tacitus' *Annals*, in the lull between the death of Germanicus and that of Drusus, the historian presents one of his most famous digressions, on the development and decline of Roman law.[5] The immediate impetus for the passage is an attempt to change the stipulations of the *lex Papia Poppaea*, which had been passed late in Augustus' reign as a revision of the *lex Iulia de maritandis ordinibus*. Tacitus notes that, even under the harsher revised version of the law, the problem of celibacy and childlessness did not abate. Indeed, the laws did more harm to Roman society than good (*Ann.* 3. 25):

nec ideo coniugia et educationes liberum frequentabantur praevalida orbitate: ceterum multitudo periclitantium gliscebat, cum omnis domus delatorum interpretationibus subverteretur, utque antehac flagitiis ita tunc legibus laborabatur. ea res admonet ut de principiis iuris et quibus modis ad hanc multitudinem infinitam ac varietatem legum perventum sit altius disseram.

People did not rush to marriage or the rearing of children because of the law—solitary living was still prevalent—but there arose a great crowd of people at risk [of prosecution], since every home was being undermined by the examinations of informers. Thus, as much as up to that point it had laboured under the weight of its sins, now the house was burdened by the laws. This circumstance prompts me to discourse further on the principles of justice, and how we have come to our current vast and various quantity of legislation.

The Augustan social legislation appears in Tacitus not just as ineffective, but as a prime example of the over-legislation which has

---

[5] On the excursus, see Hahn (1933) 5–21; Woodman and Martin (1996) 236–8.

afflicted Rome; as he notes darkly, *corruptissima re publica plurimae leges* ('laws were most numerous when the state was most corrupt': *Ann.* 3. 27). The history which he then goes on to trace begins with a traditional golden-age vision of a world which neither had nor needed laws to persuade people to pursue moral lives, but quickly proceeds to the Twelve Tables (the final instance of good law at Rome, in Tacitus' formulation) and the proliferation of legislation under the Republic. Sulla attempted to fix the problem, and Pompey added to it, but finally Augustus appears to deliver the *coup de grâce*: *sexto demum consulatu Caesar Augustus, potentiae securus, quae triumviratu iusserat abolevit deditque iura quis pace et principe uteremur* ('Finally, in his sixth consulate, Caesar Augustus, secure in his power, rescinded what he had ordered in the Triumvirate, and gave us a justice system that we might use in peace and under a prince': 3. 28).[6] Although Tacitus seems to refer here to a more general code of law, the only specific measure to which he refers is the marriage legislation with which he began: *acriora ex eo vincla, inditi custodes et lege Papia Poppaea praemiis inducti ut, si a privilegiis parentum cessaretur, velut parens omnium populus vacantia teneret* ('From this the chains became more bitter, watchdogs were established and encouraged by rewards under the *lex Papia Poppaea*, so that, if a person should abandon the privileges of parenthood, the populace—as though it were the parent of everyone—should step in to occupy the empty places': 3. 28). The terror spreads far and wide throughout the Empire, threatening to overwhelm the populace, but, in the end, Tiberius steps in to remedy the problem. The historian then returns to his more standard historical narrative.

The fact that Tacitus' history of law begins and ends with the Augustan social legislation is not entirely surprising. As I have noted, the laws became very famous very quickly, soon becoming, as may be

---

[6] Woodman and Martin (1996: 258–9) note that there are two possible interpretations of the sentence, depending on whether we take *uteremur* as governing *quis* (for *quibus*) or *pace et principe*. I have taken the former reading; if the latter is preferred, the line would read 'gave us a justice system by means of which we might experience peace and a prince'.

seen here in the *Annals*, almost synonymous with Augustus' rule and
the birth of the imperial system. It may be noted that Tacitus does
not question the idea that there was a particular problem (celibacy
and childlessness) which the laws set out to fix. Rather, he objects
more generally to the use of legislation against social ills; in a neat
Tacitean reversal, the proliferation of law is actually evidence of, and
a contribution to, what is wrong with Roman society. Augustus'
measures, in their attempt to regulate family morality, serve to
undermine the foundations (*omnis domus... subverteretur*) of
the very structure they sought to protect. The legal digression in
Annals 3, moreover, follows on the heels of two episodes which
concern the *lex Julia de adulteriis*, the law outlawing adultery
which was passed along with the marriage statute as part of Augustus'
legislative package in 18–17 BCE. In *Annals* 3. 22–3, Tacitus tells the
story of Aemelia Lepida, tried and convicted for numerous crimes
including adultery, and, Tacitus notes, a great loss to her family
(3. 24). Section 24 goes on to give the history of Decimus Junius
Silanus, banished by Augustus for adultery with the younger Julia
(Augustus' granddaughter) and now restored to his kin (*D. Silanus
Iuniae familiae redditus*) through the influence of his brother and the
generosity of Tiberius. The point would seem to be that, like the
marriage statutes about to be described, the adultery legislation
historically served to destroy great Roman families rather than
preserve them. Tacitus' description makes it clear that he sees Augustus' actions against adultery to be a violation of custom, social
structures, and even history itself: *nam culpam inter viros ac feminas
vulgatam gravi nomine laesarum religionum ac violatae maiestatis
appellando clementiam maiorum suasque ipse leges egrediebatur* ('for
by calling a fault common between men and women by the heavy
name of sacrilege and treason, he overstepped the indulgence of our
ancestors and his own legislation': 3. 24).

Tacitus' sense, however, that the Augustan social legislation was a
milestone in both Roman history and the history of Roman law
actually reflects a theme which was a part of the laws from the very
beginning. Augustus himself, when describing the measures in the

Res Gestae, articulates them explicitly as an intervention in history, as an attempt to bring the past into the present: *legibus novis me auctore latis multa exempla maiorum exolescentia iam ex nostro saeculo reduxi et ipse multarum rerum exempla imitanda posteris tradidi* ('by new laws proposed by me, I restored many of the good ideals of our ancestors which were dying out in our time, and I myself have passed on to posterity examples of many things worthy of imitation': 8. 5). There is a certain rhetorical tension between the new laws and the old values they were supposed to instantiate, but it is defused by the turn to the imagined future they are supposed to serve: the laws may be new now, but they will be old in ages to come. The exempla that they propagate, moreover, are timeless.[7] The notion outlined in the *Res Gestae*, of the social legislation as part of an historical process, is also expressed in the close connection between the *leges Iuliae* and the Saecular Games. Just as the games celebrated the ebb and flow of Roman time (they were held under the Republic every hundred years, or thereabouts, to mark the advent of a new era), the laws too are imagined to regenerate and restore rather than create something really 'new'. Horace's *Carmen Saeculare* makes the connection explicit (lines 17–24):

> diva, producas subolem patrumque
> prosperes decreta super iugandis
> feminis prolisque novae feraci
>   lege marita,
>
> certus undenos deciens per annos
> orbis ut cantus referatque ludos
> ter die claro totiensque grata
>   nocte frequentes.
>
> Goddess, bring forth our young and
> prosper the decrees of the fathers concerning marriage
> with women and the nuptial law productive
>   of new life,

---

[7] See Bellen (1987) for a discussion of the ways in which the laws both invoke, and subtly change, historical precedents.

so that the certain cycle through ten times eleven years
will bring back songs and games
crowded in for three clear days and as many times
   in welcome night.

Both legislation and festival are imagined to look backward to the past they honour and forward to the future they guarantee.

But it is not simply texts 'about' the social legislation which are sensitive to the ways that it might be represented as having a place in the recurrent cycle of Roman history. Another Augustan text which seems to have been influenced by the princeps' interest in law and morality is the passage on the social legislation of Romulus found in the early imperial historian Dionysius of Halicarnassus' *Roman Antiquities*. Dionysius' depiction of Rome's founder is distinctive in a number of ways, not least of which is the fact that he departs from the Roman tradition represented in Cicero (*de Re Publica* 2. 1. 1–3), which argues that the city's constitution was developed over many centuries and cannot be traced to a single author. Romulus appears in the *Roman Antiquities* in the guise of a Greek *nomothetēs*, the single originary lawgiver who traditionally looms large in the mythology of classical Greek city-states—a representation which seems designed to help prove Dionysius' stated opinion that the Romans were fundamentally Greek, but which must also have resonated with Augustus' vision of himself as the new Romulus, the refounder of the city's corrupted institutions.[8] Most significant for our purposes is the fact that Dionysius begins from Romulus' laws concerning marriage and the family, noting that, since the tranquillity of individual households is an important component of the overall peace of the state, every prudent lawgiver in history has attempted on some level to regulate the private lives of its citizens. The historian then launches into a brief history of what states have done 'concerning marriage and interactions with women' (περὶ γάμων καὶ τῆς πρὸς γυναῖκας ὁμιλίας: *Ant. Rom.* 2. 24. 4). He disparages the steps which have been taken among 'barbarians and Greeks', who have tried

---

[8] Pohlenz (1924); Gabba (1991) 155–8; cf. Gabba (1960) 198.

everything from complete laxity with regard to sexual intercourse to
draconian oversight of women's behaviour. He finally turns to the
solution put forward by Romulus, who made man and wife equal
economic and religious partners in the marriage (2. 25. 2). This law,
according to Dionysius, is the only one which has been seen to work,
creating not just good, reliable marriages, but a stable and effective
state. The resonance between Dionysius' depiction of Romulus and
Augustan ideology has long been recognized, particularly the ways in
which the historian links the endurance of the Roman state to
morality, and morality to the stable home.[9] But equally important
for our purposes is the fact that the inclusion of Romulus as 'social
lawgiver' in Dionysius' text provides a history to Augustus' actions in
the same sphere, so that the *leges Iuliae* appear not as innovations, but
as a restoration and renewal of the kinds of laws passed under the
original Roman king.

The Augustan social legislation, then, was understood even before
Tacitus' *Annals* as historical, as an intervention in the passage of time,
as a way to bring both past and future to bear upon the present. But
another aspect of the laws which is highlighted by their appearance
in Tacitus, Horace, and Dionysius is their dependence upon, and
attempted reinforcement of, ideologies of femininity. In the *Roman
Antiquities*, Dionysius is explicit about the fact that he sees marriage
as being primarily about controlling the unstable erotic force represented by women: he notes that it has historically been understood
necessary for a state to address this issue 'in order to relieve [men] of
the many other evils which have descended upon individual households and entire states because of women'.[10] Horace puts a more
positive spin on the question in the *Carmen Saeculare* by representing stable marriage and legitimate reproduction as the guarantors of
Rome's future. The connection with femininity is made clear not just

---

[9] Indeed, the strong connections between the Romulus section in Dionysius' history
and contemporary Roman politics have led to a long-running debate over whether this
passage may not actually be considered a political pamphlet which originally circulated
separately from the rest of the work: see Balsdon (1971).

[10] καὶ πολλῶν ἄλλων ἀπαλλάξοντες κακῶν, ἃ καταλαμβάνει τούς τε ἰδίους οἴκους
καὶ τὰς πόλεις ὅλας διὰ γυναῖκας (2. 24. 4).

by the invocation of Ilithyia, goddess of childbirth, but in the way that the law itself is feminized in lines 19–20, where it (rather than the women) is represented as 'productive of new life' (*prolisque novae feraci / lege marita*). It is also worth noting that, at the opening of the Saecular Games where the song was first performed, the 110 years of the *saeculum* were represented by 110 Roman matrons.[11]

The ways in which Tacitus understands the social legislation to be gendered are perhaps less obvious. It has been noted, however, that *Annals* 3—more than any other book in either the *Annals* or the *Histories*—is persistently concerned with women, and particularly with the relationship between women and public life.[12] The book opens with the return of Agrippina from the east with the ashes of Germanicus. As she marches to Rome with her vast crowd of mourners, Tiberius is disturbed by the honorific terms in which she is praised: *decus patriae, solum Augusti sanguinem, unicum antiquitatis specimen* ('the pride of her fatherland, the only remaining blood-relation of Augustus, the last example [of the quality] of ancient times': *Ann.* 3. 7). The book also encompasses the end of the Pisonian conspiracy, in which Plancina escapes the fate of her husband because she is able to appeal to her gender and the influence of Livia (3. 17). The machinations of Agrippina and Plancina subsequently spur a debate in the senate over whether women should be allowed to accompany their husbands to provincial commands (3. 33–4), a debate which clearly echoes a famous episode in Livy over 'women's rights'.[13] *Annals* 3 finally closes with the epitaph for Junia, who, the historian notes, served as the link between a number of great republican families: she was Cato's niece, Cassius' wife, and Brutus' sister (3. 76). The presence of the social legislation in *Annals* 3, therefore, should be seen as part of the thematic interest of the book in how and why women became part of public life under the Roman Empire.

---

[11] As is recorded in the monumental inscription which commemorated the games: *CIL* vi. 32323 (*ILS* 5050).

[12] Woodman and Martin (1996) 11–17.   [13] On which, see below, pp. 154–79.

The importance of ideologies of gender to understanding the Augustan social legislation should not be underestimated. Scholars since Ronald Syme have recognized that one major aim of the princeps' moral programme was, as he says, 'to keep women in their place'.[14] Thomas McGinn has recently added an important dimension to this description by noting the ways in which the laws both depend on and enforce the existence of certain categories of women: those worthy of marriage and those not; those sexually available and those off-limits. This is particularly evident in the case of the *lex Iulia de adulteriis*, which standardizes categories such as *materfamilias* and prostitute, a move which was critical to the law's functioning since it was the status of the woman rather than the man which defined a sexual act as adulterous.[15] On one level, such official state attention to what might be called 'private morality' was no innovation in Roman culture. Scholars have argued that the office of censor, which was responsible under the Republic for demoting from his census rank any man whose moral character was suspect, was the precursor to the later moral legislation.[16] Cicero echoes a traditional sentiment when he opens book 5 of his *de Re Publica* with a quotation from Ennius: *moribus antiquis res stat Romana virisque* ('the Roman state rests on its ancient customs and on its men'). Yet it has also been pointed out that, by focusing on men (*viris*), Ennius' statement represents the discursive picture at Rome before the advent of Augustus;[17] that is, for the republican poet, it is male behaviour which is at issue, not female. Before the institution of the *leges Iuliae*, the oversight of a woman's moral health was the responsibility of the male head of her household, either her father or her husband, depending on the circumstances. For the first time under the adultery legislation, women were answerable to the state for their actions in the bedroom. This was a dramatic change in the

[14] Syme (1939) 414.
[15] That is, a sexual act by a legitimately married woman with any man is defined as adultery; a married man, on the other hand, might have sex with a prostitute, concubine, or slave and not be liable under the law. McGinn (1998*b*) 144–5.
[16] de Bouvrie (1984).   [17] Edwards (1993) 20.

way in which Roman law conceptualized both the role of state in enforcing morality and what might be termed the 'subject' of legislation. The explanation of the moral role of the censor as well as such matters as the passage of sumptuary legislation had always been that the state had an investment in seeing to it that its citizens were morally fit to take part both in the military and in the governance of the Republic.[18] Women had not before been a part of this picture, since they had no official role in Roman civic matters: the state was not concerned with them because they were not concerned with the state. Even as the social legislation appeals to traditional ideas about the sanctity of marriage and the home, therefore, it accords to women a kind of legal subjectivity which they had not before enjoyed.[19]

This becomes particularly clear when we examine some of the ways in which the laws functioned in actual practice. For instance, scholars have noted the specific and rather peculiar restrictions which the *lex Iulia de adulteriis* places on what might, and must, be done about an adulterous woman. First, the law explicitly forbids an unfaithful woman's husband from killing her, even if he were to catch her in the act; he might kill her lover if the man fell into certain specific social categories, but then only if the pair were discovered in the act of sexual intercourse, in the husband's house, and the husband was willing to dispatch the lover with his own hand. A woman's father, however, might kill his daughter's lover only if he also killed the daughter, and again only if the pair were discovered *in flagrante*, in the father's house, and the father committed the double killing with his own hand. In short, the restrictions were such that there seems to be little likelihood of this 'right to kill' ever being invoked; instead, 'the legislator's principal interest was in provoking a trial'.[20] In addition, the restrictions on what private actions a man might take are matched in the law by particular inducements to making

[18] On the censorship, see Astin (1988); Baltrusch (1989), esp. 5–30.

[19] Ruggini (1989) traces the development of female legal subjectivity over the course of Roman history. She too sees the Augustan legislation as a significant milestone in this process. Cf. McGinn (2002) and Severy (2003) 52–6.

[20] McGinn (1998*b*) 205.

public the actions of an adulterous wife even if the husband was personally inclined to forgive her: a man who failed to divorce his wife within
sixty days of discovering her infidelity was liable under the law to a charge
of *lenocinium* (pimping). Once the adultery was exposed, anyone might
bring a criminal accusation; although the law gave special privileges to a
husband or father who wished to prosecute the woman, it also allowed
for members of the general population to bring charges, which presumably they would do in the hope of receiving part of the property
confiscated if she was convicted. The point would seem to be that the
law sought concretely and specifically to expose an unfaithful woman to
public scrutiny, rather than allowing, as had been traditional under the
Republic, the situation to be handled within the sphere of the family.
Like the *lex Iulia de maritandis ordinibus*, which made marriage and
reproduction into a matter of state interest and control, the adultery
legislation understands the regulation of domestic life as too important
to be left in the hands of individual citizens.

Indeed, our sources do testify to the emergence of adultery trials
under the Empire as one avenue by which women crossed over the
traditional boundary separating them from civic life—though not,
perhaps, always in the way they, or we, might have wished. As in
Annals 3. 22–3 with the trial of Aemilia Lepida, we hear of a number
of women appearing before the senate on charges of marital
infidelity, either by itself or in combination with other accusations.
It has been noted that such charges oftentimes seem to have little to
do with the actual commission of an adulterous act, becoming
instead one way of disgracing a woman, her family, and friends by
attacking her sexual morality. The frequency with which adultery
appears among the accusations along with *maiestas* ('treason'),
a genuinely political charge, is an indication of the potential cross-
over between public and private crime, and it is perhaps worth
noting that no woman who appears in our sources accused under
the *lex Iulia de adulteriis* is acquitted.[21] But if the Augustan social
legislation produced a new form of symbolic attack against women,

---

[21] Marshall (1990*b*).

it also produced a new form of symbolic honour. Under the *lex Iulia de maritandis ordinibus*, women might receive certain rights and social privileges, such as freedom from male guardianship and exemption from the inheritance restrictions in the *lex Voconia*, if they produced the requisite number of legitimate children; this was called the *ius liberorum*, and it tends to appear in our sources more as a recognition of civic responsibility than a reflection of actual reproduction. We first hear of it awarded in 9 BCE to Livia, who had only two children rather than the correct three, and neither one of them was fathered by her current husband.[22] The Vestal Virgins were awarded the right,[23] as were women during the reign of Claudius who gave money to build ships during a crisis in the grain supply.[24] It was not only women, of course, who were subject to the terms of the law and who might enjoy release from them, but, perhaps because of the limited availability of a language to describe female civic honour, the *ius liberorum* seems rather quickly to have become simply a way of designating a contribution made by a woman to Roman society.

Such examples serve, I think, to illustrate the contradictions inherent in the social legislation, as it sacrifices certain norms for the sake of supporting others, and in doing so is caught in the conflict between wanting both to retain the status quo and to change society for the better.[25] Augustus' laws concerning adultery and the family must be understood to encompass a certain paradox, one born out of the attempt to construct private morality through the imposition of legislation. The 'traditional' family values which the law touts were never meant to be instantiated through legislation: to do so is to violate the very domestic integrity which the law seeks to

[22] Cass. Dio 55. 2. 5–6.   [23] Cass. Dio 56. 10. 2.

[24] Suet. *Div. Claud.* 19.

[25] There is an interesting parallel which may be drawn between the Augustan social legislation and the law passed in Athens in the middle of the 5th cent. BCE which made citizenship dependent upon descent from an Athenian mother as well as father. Osborne (1997) argues that, although the law certainly reflects a 'possessive and exclusive attitude toward Athenian citizenship' (p. 3), and was hardly progressive in its outlook or aims, it nevertheless resulted in a shift in the importance of representing Athenian women as mothers in funerary art. This, then, resulted in an unprecedented number of women being seen in public contexts and a new emphasis on the domestic as a site for masculinity.

protect. But by taking the responsibility for creating and maintaining the household out of the hands of individual men and instead making it part of the business of the state, the law makes a statement about the relationship between domestic and civic life, and how certain actions might be construed as transcending the boundary between them. But, looking back to Augustus' own description of the laws in the *Res Gestae*, we should remember the ways in which he balances his *novae leges* against the *exempla maiorum*, so that the innovation of the legislation is deflected by the sense of the Principate as a turning point in history; though the laws themselves may be new, what they represent are values which are enshrined in the Roman past and which look forward to the Roman future. If the laws overstep the boundary between public and private life, they do so only on the understanding that history requires it. The social legislation is thus 'Augustan' to the core, as it draws on a sense of both place and time to support its message: it both maps the concerns of the civic onto the domestic and defends that map by reference to the grand sweep of Roman history. Some of the practical historical consequences of this I have noted above, but it is also clear that the questions about gender, time, and the public/private dichotomy which the laws raise also had an effect on representations, not just of the social legislation itself, but more generally of legal history. In order to explore this further, I would like to look closely at a famous episode in Livy's *Ab Urbe Condita*, in which the historian offers two different and opposing views of the relationship between legislation and female behaviour. In the context of what we have seen of the contemporary *leges Iuliae*, the 'historical' event takes on new meaning, as the *AUC* attempts to understand and describe the complex interaction between women, history, and the law.

LIVY AND THE REPEAL OF THE *LEX OPPIA*

Livy is often considered one of the most important 'Augustan' writers, the only Latin historian to have survived from the period and one who seems to have had close ties to the imperial house. The princeps knew of Livy's work and was, to a certain extent, involved in it: Livy cites Augustus' help in resolving the question of A. Cornelius Cossus' consulship in an often quoted passage in book 4 (20. 5–11).[26] We also hear that he served as tutor to the future emperor Claudius, although the history which he encouraged his pupil to write seems to have got off to a rocky start.[27] Certainly Livy's careful negotiation of such politically tricky issues as Aeneas' son's real name[28] as well as his professed horror of civil war[29] reveals a sensitivity to the ideological issues of the day. Less tangibly, Livy's life's work—to write a history of Rome beginning with the ancient past in order to provide positive exempla for modern Romans—goes hand in hand with the systematic antiquarianism of the Augustan regime: both Livy and Augustus, each in his own way, imagined himself bringing the good old days back to Rome.[30] '[It is] more interesting', Christina Kraus remarks in the introduction to her edition of book 6, '... to consider the *AUC* as the gradual, often experimental construction of a written Rome ... As such, of course, the historian's project parallels/rivals Augustus' own building of a new Rome via (re)construction of its past'.[31]

The extent to which the *Ab Urbe Condita* gestures to the superior morality of earlier generations connects Livy's work closely with the Augustan social legislation, which, as the *Res Gestae* makes clear, both depends on and reinforces the idea that imperial Rome must look backwards into the past in order to move forwards into the future. In addition, although those books of Livy's history which detailed the events of the historian's own lifetime have not survived, scholars have long seen traces of the social legislation in the *AUC*'s preface, which

[26] The passage is discussed in Syme (1959) 43–7; Walsh (1961a) 30; Luce (1965); Mensching (1967); Ogilvie (1970) 563–4; Miles (1995) 42–7.

[27] He attempted a history of the civil wars starting with the death of Julius Caesar but was forced to abandon it after two books under pressure from his family: Suet. *Div. Claud.* 41. 2.

[28] Ascanius or Iulus? Livy 1. 3. 2. See Syme (1959) 47–8; Miles (1995) 38–40; cf. Weinstock (1971) 5–17.

[29] For instance, at 9. 19. 16.   [30] Wallace-Hadrill (1982a); Miles (1995) 38–54.

[31] Kraus (1994a) 8.

famously remarks that the Roman state has morally descended to a level where 'we are not able to bear either our sins or their cure' (*nec vitia nostra nec remedia pati possumus*: pref. 9).[32] It is unclear whether this is actually a reference to an earlier, and failed, legislative attempt on the part of the new imperial regime to curb social ills, which is a question tied up in the rather fraught issue of whether or not such an earlier attempt actually occurred.[33] It is less problematic to say simply that Livy's view of a declining Roman state in search of a remedy for its moral degeneration is well in keeping with the Augustan explanation of what made the social legislation necessary. And indeed, the historian also reveals a real sensitivity to what law has done to, and for, the Roman state. This is clear in the attention which he gives to the institution of particular laws, but also more generally in the way he represents 'law' as an abstract concept. Thus, for instance, in book 1 one of Romulus' first acts after the creation of religious ceremonies is the passage of a legal code; Livy notes that the random group of his and Remus' followers who comprised the city's first inhabitants 'could not in any way have been brought together into a single citizen body except by means of laws' (*AUC* 1. 8. 1). The fact that the historian does not concern himself to say what the Romulan laws actually covered (theft? murder? property exchange?) underscores the point that it was the *fact* of law rather than any particular legal stipulation which was supposed to bind the fledgling community together. The institution of the legal code, therefore, was not as significant for the individual acts which it supported or prevented, but rather as a means of defining what Rome meant.[34]

[32] This idea originated with H. Dessau (1903); cf. G. Williams (1962) 33–4.

[33] Those who believe there was an attempt at a law before 18–17 BCE base their arguments on Propertius 2. 7. 1–3. I personally am inclined to think that, had Augustus wanted to pass a law at that point, he would have had no trouble doing so, but it is difficult to be certain in the absence of other evidence. For the argument against an earlier law, see Badian (1985).

[34] The idea is, of course, not original to Livy and had by his time made its way from Greek philosophy into Roman political theory. See, for instance, Cicero, *de Leg.* 2. 12: '*Lege autem carens civitas estne ob id ipsum habenda nullo loco?*' '*Dici aliter non potest.*' (' "Then, if it lacks law, shouldn't a state for that reason be considered nothing?" "It isn't possible to say anything else." ').

There has been something of a renaissance in Livian studies over the past couple of decades, much of which has underscored the subtlety in the historian's method, language, and narrative style.[35] In particular, there has been a great deal of interest in Livy's sense of history, and the ways in which he sees it not just as a passive object of representation in his text, but as a force which simultaneously shapes and is shaped by the work of the narrative.[36] For instance, the sack of Rome by the Gauls, which concludes the first pentad, marks a triple turning point: in the story of the physical city, in the text which is 'refounded' in a new preface at the beginning of book 6, and in the historian's ability to write history; Livy notes that the sack destroyed all the documents which he might have been able to use to write his narrative, so that what comes after the Gauls in the *AUC* will be qualitatively different from what went before.[37] Moreover, characters in Livy's history often have a sense of themselves, rightly or wrongly, as historical actors, whose lives will have an impact not just on their own time but on what is to come: perhaps most notably Lucretia, whose death marks the end of book 1 and the fall of the monarchy, kills herself proclaiming that she does not wish to be an unchaste *exemplum* for women to come (*nec ulla deinde impudica Lucretiae exemplo vivet*: 1. 58. 10). Her example, in fact, does live on after her, as the death of Virginia, which brings down the Decemvirate, is explicitly compared to that of Lucretia (*sequitur aliud in urbe nefas, ab libidine ortum, haud minus foedo eventu quam quod per stuprum caedemque Lucretiae urbe regnoque Tarquinios expulerat, ut non finis solum idem decemviris qui regibus sed causa etiam eadem imperii amittendi esset*: 3. 44. 1).[38] The stories of Lucretia and Virginia thus also mark the extent to which Livy's history is able, eager even, to admit women to its project as both historical and textual

---

[35] e.g. Walsh (1961*b*); Luce (1977); Miles (1995); Jaeger (1997); Forsythe (1999).

[36] See, especially, Konstan (1986); Feldherr (1998), esp. 12–50; Chaplin (2000).

[37] Kraus (1994*b*); Feldherr (1997).

[38] 'There followed another crime, in Rome, which arose from lust, not any less than the foul episode which expelled the Tarquins from the city and its rule because of the rape and slaughter of Lucretia; thus, not only did the same end come to the Decemvirs as to the kings, but there was also the same cause for losing their power.'

markers; their stories structure not just Roman politics and their history, but the *AUC* which records them.[39]

The function of women in Livy's history is the subject of a different book, one which ought, but is still waiting, to be written. For the present, however, I would like to look closely at one particular incident in the *AUC*, which, although less famous than that of Lucretia, was also widely understood as an important moment for the history of Roman women and public life. Moreover, although it contains no direct reference to Livy's own chronological moment, what it says resonates profoundly with the social, spatial, and historical messages embedded in the Augustan social legislation.[40] Book 34 of Livy's *Ab Urbe Condita* opens with a scene set in 195 BCE describing a debate in the Roman Assembly over the repeal of the *lex Oppia*, a sumptuary law passed at the height of the second Punic war which regulated female consumption of certain luxury items.[41] The episode has something of the air of an interruption; Livy's book 33 and the rest of book 34 are taken up with the political and military situation abroad, and, indeed, the Oppian debate, which comprises nearly a fifth of its own book, is one of the few domestic incidents described between the end of the second Punic war and the beginning of the conflict with Antiochus. It is not, however, the *lex Oppia* itself which appears to have attracted Livy's attention, since he fails to mention it at the time of its ratification in 215, nor does he note its existence at any point in the intervening period between then and its repeal. Indeed, the historian himself remarks in his introduction to

[39] Hemker (1985); Arieti (1997); Claassen (1998).

[40] Purcell (1986: 83–4) notes 'the style of thought here (sc. in the debate) is deeply Augustan'.

[41] The terms of the law are quite clear in Livy: women were prohibited from wearing particoloured clothing, from riding in carriages within a mile of Rome, except on festival occasions, and from possessing more than half an ounce of gold. Whether this last was meant to regulate women's property as a whole or merely what could be worn at one time is a matter of some debate. Among others, Pomeroy (1975: 178) believes that the law confiscated women's property in excess of the prescribed half-ounce. Culham (1982) disagrees on the basis of other passages in Livy and suggests that the law only covered what could be worn about a woman's body.

the episode in book 34 that what he is about to relate is, in reality, a trivial incident, only transformed into a matter of historical interest by the emotions which it aroused: *res parva dictu, sed quae studiis in magnum certamen excesserit* ('a matter insignificant in the telling, but one which grew into a great struggle because of [people's] passions'). It seems likely that the historian's interest in the debate was at least partially aroused by the notoriety of one of the speakers: Cato the Elder held the consulship in 195 and delivers the speech opposing the repeal. Yet his opponent, L. Valerius, a tribune of the plebs, is virtually unknown, and it is his position which carries the day—a circumstance which makes it all the more striking that Livy attaches such importance to the scene. While it is possible, therefore, that the *lex Oppia* is included in Livy's history simply in order to allow Cato to display some of his famous 'severity', we cannot forget that it *is* a debate, which gives Valerius' opinions as much weight as Cato's.

One of the most remarkable aspects of the repeal, and certainly the one which has aroused the most interest in modern scholarship, is the role played in it by the Roman women. Livy begins his narrative of the debate in the Assembly by describing how, incensed by the idea that the law might remain in effect, the female population filled the streets of Rome, accosting male passers-by to urge that they support the repeal (34. 1. 5). Day by day, the throng grew larger, its numbers swelled by women pouring into the city from outlying towns (1. 6). Following the debate, moreover, the women continued to pressure the tribunes who threatened a veto of the repeal, besieging their homes and refusing to leave until the proposed veto was abandoned (8. 1–2). The story of the repeal of the *lex Oppia*, therefore, is the story of one of the first and few collective demonstrations by women in the history of the Roman state, and, as such, has become a minor locus of methodological struggle, between those who would argue for the relative freedom and independence of Roman women and those who see them as passive and oppressed by the patriarchal Roman state. While the former celebrate the unity of the women who came out against the law and their ability to influence the political scene by collective action,[42] others point to the misogynist tone of both Cato's and Valerius' speeches and argue that the issue in the repeal of the *lex Oppia* is not exactly women's liberation.[43]

It is worth noting, however, that comparatively little of Livy's narrative is actually concerned with the activities of the women per se. Although they appear in his introductory remarks which set the scene for the debate, and in his final summary which details the ultimate death of the law, at base it is the paired speeches of Cato and Valerius on which the historian's attention is focused. Livy does not give us any insight into how (or, really, why) the women orchestrated the protests; he does not describe their reaction to the debate or to the ultimate success of their agitation; he does not name for them a leader, or leaders, as representative personalities to be measured against the vividly drawn antagonists in the Assembly debate. As in much of Roman history, the women are a shadowy presence on the historical stage, who appear and disappear without explanation and whose actions are mysterious even to men of the time. The nameless and faceless women who appear in Livy's narrative thus exist most potently not as individual actors in the unfolding drama, but as an inscrutable and irresistible force to which the men are compelled to react. The story, then, is not so much about the real, historical actions of the women, but about how those actions come to be understood in the arena of the Assembly. While Cato, on the one hand, argues that the women's presence in the streets illustrates exactly the kind of disorderly female conduct which the *lex Oppia* was meant to restrict, Valerius responds by insisting that the women are merely behaving exactly as members of the Roman body politic are wont to do when they feel that they have been wronged. Livy

[42] Thus, as early as 1920, H. W. Flannery compared the protests against the *lex Oppia* with the women's suffrage movement in his own time, and the *lex Oppia* protests make a prominent appearance in Daube's *Civil Disobedience in Antiquity* (1972), where the author enquires 'why is [Valerius] not on Women's Liberation buttons?' (p. 27). Cf. Herrmann (1964) 52–67.

[43] The 'pessimists' include Hemelrijk (1987); Ruggini (1989) 608–9; and Wyke (1994) 138–9.

offers us the 'facts' of the story—there was a law, a proposal to repeal, and a protest—and then two dramatically different interpretations of what significance might be attached to them. Thus, on a certain level, Cato and Valerius function as readers of the events described in Livy's spare introduction, readers who provide different models for understanding not only the law but also, and especially, the presence of the Roman women in the streets of the capital city. Though each man is overtly arguing either for or against the proposed repeal, therefore, what emerges from these two carefully crafted rhetorical set-pieces are two different understandings of the 'space' of Roman politics; as the women's occupation of public space becomes a metaphor for their participation in public life, the two speakers seize the opportunity to map, discursively, the outlines of the Roman state.

Even a broad overview reveals that Livy's narrative of the repeal of the Oppian law is not as simple as it seems. For instance, scholars frequently note that it is Valerius' speech which effects the repeal of the law.[44] In some sense, this may be true: Valerius may certainly have influenced the votes of some of those listening in the audience. Yet Livy's focus after the conclusion of the debate is not the vote on the proposal to repeal, but on the threatened veto by certain tribunes, which must be withdrawn before any vote takes place. It is only with the continued agitation of the Roman women, who besiege the homes of the recalcitrant officials, that they are persuaded to withdraw their objections: *maior frequentia mulierum postero die sese in publicum effudit unoque agmine omnes Brutorum ianuas obsederunt, qui collegarum rogationi intercedebant, nec ante abstiterunt quam remissa intercessio ab tribunis est* ('a greater crowd of women poured into public the next day and in a single army besieged the doors of the Bruti, who were vetoing the proposal of their fellow tribunes, nor would the women retreat until the veto was withdrawn by the tribunes': 8. 2). The proposal then passes easily. In reality, then, the repeal of the law does not happen because of the speeches in the

---

[44] Many scholars make the mistake of believing this: see Pomeroy (1975) 180.

Assembly: the tribunes are not persuaded by the eloquence of either Cato or Valerius, but by the threat posed by the mob of women in the streets.[45]

This is particularly remarkable given the attitudes and arguments presented in the two speeches of the debate. Cato expresses concern that women, loosed from the bonds of laws such as the *lex Oppia*, will quickly become more than the men can handle: he warns the Assembly that 'as soon as they become our equals, they will straight away be our superiors' (*extemplo simul pares esse coeperint, superiores erunt*: 3. 3). Valerius, on the other hand, scorns such paranoia, and reassures the crowd that women must accept whatever men decide is best for them; under such circumstances, he argues, it behoves the more powerful sex to be generous to the weaker, and to allow them the petty pleasures prohibited under the Oppian law. In other words, Cato argues that women are dangerous, and therefore the law should not be repealed; Valerius counters with the position that women are not dangerous, and therefore the law should be repealed. The 'frame' of Livy's narrative, however, seems to convey the message that women are dangerous, and therefore the law was repealed, thus showing the error of both speakers' arguments. Perhaps more importantly, the speeches themselves are revealed as historical distractions from the real action, since what Cato and Valerius said had almost no real effect. Thus, rather than presenting a right argument and a wrong one, I would argue, Livy explores the difficulties involved in asking the question in the first place.

Livy sets the scene for the paired speeches of Cato and Valerius by describing the gathering of the Roman people in the public places of the city. Such concern with the urban landscape is typical of Livy, but here it is particularly noteworthy, since space, and who has the right to occupy it, will become one of the major themes of the speeches which follow.

ad suadendum disuadendumque multi nobiles prodibant; Capitolium turba hominum faventium adversantiumque legi complebatur. matronae

---

[45] See Chaplin (2000) 99–100.

nulla nec auctoritate nec verecundia nec imperio virorum contineri limine poterant, omnes vias urbis aditusque in forum obsidebant, viros descendentes ad forum orantes. . . . augebatur haec frequentia mulierum in dies; nam etiam ex oppidis conciliabulisque conveniebant.   (*AUC* 34. 1. 5–6)

Many well-born citizens came forward to argue for and against the measure; the Capitoline was full of a crowd of men, some in favour and some opposed. The women could not be kept in their houses by the authority, respect, or orders of their husbands, and they invaded all the streets of the city and the entrances to the Forum, addressing men descending into the Forum. . . . This mob of women grew day by day; for they even came in from provincial towns and outlying areas.

The *turba hominum* is set against the *frequentia mulierum*, as the one occupies the Capitoline and the other surrounds the Forum and fills the streets. In a pairing of internal and external that will be seen again in Cato's speech, Livy imagines the crowd of women originating from two places: exploding out of the innermost domestic spaces of Rome proper, and pouring into the city from outlying areas. The verb which Livy uses to describe the women (*obsidebant*) will also be echoed in Cato's speech, as he compares the women to an invading army—it is a word commonly used for besieging a city. It is difficult to be certain where Livy imagines the following debate taking place: although city space becomes an important part of the rhetoric of the debate, Livy never makes the specific location of the gathering explicit. His mention of the Capitoline as full of both supporters and opponents of the measure (1. 4) may indicate that he imagines the speeches delivered there.[46] Yet the place which looms large both in Livy's description and in Cato's speech is not the Capitoline but the Forum, the emotive centre of Rome, the heart of Roman politics. This focus reinforces the sense of siege which *obsidebant* sets up, since the women have not entered the Forum in Livy's formulation; rather, they fill the streets around it, leaving it as the beleaguered centre of the otherwise occupied city.

---

[46] The steps of the temple of Jupiter Optimus Maximus were often the place of gatherings to discuss questions to be put before the Assembly: Taylor (1966) 19–21.

The Speech of Cato: Place . . .

Livy has set the scene for the debate, and now Cato rises to speak. Much of the scholarship on the Oppian law debate has focused on the speech of Cato, generally because critics are interested in determining the historical accuracy of the scene. If the speech is genuine in any form, it is the earliest oration by Cato on record,[47] and it certainly displays the concerns about foreign luxury and the decline of morality for which Cato was known. Most critics agree, however, that the speech was composed by Livy, only loosely based on the tradition that Cato gave a speech on the occasion.[48] In support of this contention, it is notable that on various other occasions, Livy is careful to explain that the texts of certain Catonian speeches do survive in his time: see, for instance, *AUC* 39. 54. 11 for Livy's comment on Cato's *de Pecunia Regis Antiochi*; 39. 42. 6–7 for the *acerbae orationes* from Cato's censorship; and 45. 25. 2–4 for the oration in favour of the Rhodians.[49] In fact, in this last case, Livy explains that he will not include the text of the speech since he does not wish to reproduce a mere *simulacrum* of the great Cato, especially since his readers can find Cato's original in book 5 of the *Origines*. While it is certainly possible that a few words or phrases were drawn from fragments of the original Oppian Law speech, the fact that there is only one sure archaism,[50] and at least one anachronism,[51] supports the conclusion that the speech is at most minimally Catonian.

---

[47] Malcovati (1955) 12–14.

[48] Briscoe (1981) 39–43; Perl (2002). For the opposing minority view, see Pais (1910) 123 ff. It has been suggested that Ennius included a version of the speech in his *Annals*, on the basis of a very inconclusive fragment from book 11 (Nonnus 195. 10). The idea that the setting is the repeal of the *lex Oppia* is dismissed by Skutsch (1985) 525.

[49] Briscoe (1981) 42.

[50] *faxitis* at 4. 21. Briscoe (1981: 54) points out that the word is used here in a context in which it is found several times elsewhere in Livy's work, and so does not indicate a genuine Catonian element here.

[51] This is Cato's comment at 4. 3 about the negative influence of treasures seized in Asia: the Romans would not march so far east until the war with Antiochus in 190, five years after the speech is set. See Luce (1977) 252–3 and Scullard (1951) 257.

In Livy, it is clear from the first sentence of Cato's speech that places, and the presence of women in them, are important to the rhetoric of the debate:

si in sua quisque nostrum matre familiae, Quirites, ius et maiestatem viri retinere instituisset, minus cum universis feminis negotii haberemus: nunc domi victa libertas nostra impotentia muliebri hic quoque in foro obteritur et calcatur, at quia singulas sustinere non potuimus universas horremus. (*AUC* 34. 2. 1–2)

If each of us, Assemblymen, undertook to uphold the law and the authority of a man in regard to his own wife, we would have less trouble with women as a whole; now, with our freedom having been conquered in the home by feminine weakness, here in the Forum too it is ground down and trampled, and because we cannot hold them back individually, we are afraid of them collectively.

The consul here articulates the dichotomy to which he will continually return over the course of the speech, namely that between home and forum, the place of women and that of men. *Impotentia muliebris* has triumphed within its own domestic space and has now made its way into public, 'grinding down' and 'trampling' male liberty as though it were an equestrian soldier. Our ancestors, Cato notes, did not allow a woman to conduct even private business without a male overseer—but 'we, the gods help us, now even allow them to take a hand in the state and also to enter into the Forum and to join in our meetings and assemblies'. Later on, he will insist that it is inappropriate not only for women to appear physically in public, but even to allow their thoughts to stray to the measures passed or repealed in the Forum: the only law about which they should concern themselves, he avers, is the 'law' of modesty. Female domesticity is thus simultaneously a concrete location, a kind of behaviour, and a state of mind.

Cato, therefore, sees the situation at hand as a struggle both of gender and of place: the women are a threat not simply in themselves, but as a hostile force which is attempting to take the space of the Roman Republic for itself. Thus, throughout the speech, Cato will continually represent the women and their actions using military metaphors: he speaks of the *agmen mulierum* through which he must make his way in order to enter the Forum, 'an army of women' which is guilty of 'invading the streets' (*obsidendi vias*); he imagines the women demanding to be carried through the city, *velut triumphantes de lege victa et abrogata et captis ereptis suffragiis vestris* ('as though triumphing over the defeated and repealed law and the captured votes snatched from you': 3. 9). By moving out of their houses and into the streets, the women represent a threat to the *res publica* parallel to that of a foreign enemy, a hostile invasion from a place that is not 'us' but 'them'. This, then, is the discursive 'map' of politics and political space which Cato employs in his discussion, a map in which the civic is constituted in opposition to the domestic, the private spaces of women in opposition to the public spaces of men. It is this boundary line which the women have crossed, threatening not only individual men and this individual law, but the state itself and the Law on which it is founded.

Indeed, Cato goes on to warn darkly that the repeal of the *lex Oppia* is dangerous not simply in and of itself, but would compromise the integrity of the entire Roman legal system: since the women's private interests will have been seen to be stronger than the public good, other individual concerns will quickly triumph over other individually onerous laws.

si quod cuique privatim officiet ius, id destruet ac demolietur, quid attinebit universos rogare leges quas mox abrogare in quos latae sunt possint? (34. 3. 5)

If any law which stood in the way of someone's private needs was to be destroyed and cast down, what good would it do for the whole group to pass laws which were quickly able to be repealed by those against whom they were passed?

The contrast here between *privatim* and *universos* is echoed throughout the speech, most notably in the juxtaposition in his opening statement of *singulas* and *universas* (2. 1) and again in 2. 8, when he speaks of his respect for individual women (*singularum*) rather than for the sex as a whole (*universarum*). Of course, here in 3. 5, the collective to which

Cato is appealing is that of the male population which makes the laws, the triumph of whose private interests would be a public disaster: by even considering the repeal of the *lex Oppia*, the Assembly is breaking ranks and endangering the *res publica*. This rhetorical turn of Cato's is thus the flip side of his argument about women's behaviour: while it is dangerous to allow women to act collectively, men must do so if the state is to survive. The women are thus represented as challenging, not just male authority, but the solidarity of citizenship; they represent privacy and its demands, and as such constitute a danger to the very foundations of public life.

It is perhaps this last rhetorical turn which gives Cato's words much of their power: he is not merely appealing to the men in the audience to stand publicly together, he is doing so in subtle contrast to the body of women, whose ability to unite as a sex is both impressive and threatening. Early in the speech, Cato makes a telling comment on the situation before him:

equidem fabulam et fictam rem ducebam esse virorum omne genus in aliqua insula coniuratione muliebri ab stirpe sublatum esse; ab nullo genere non summum periculum est si coetus et concilia et secretas consultationes esse sinas. (34. 2. 3–4)

For my part, I used to think that it was a myth and a fictitious story that the whole race of men on a certain island was completely destroyed by a conspiracy of the women; from no group is there not the highest danger if you allow there to be gatherings and assemblies and secret meetings.

Cato is referring, of course, to the story of the Lemnian women, a myth well established in the Graeco-Roman literary tradition: aroused by the anger of Aphrodite, the women of the Greek island killed all the male inhabitants. As Briscoe notes, the redemptive elements of the story, such as Hypsipyle's rescue of her father, are left out of Cato's narrative; it is the threat of destruction of one sex by the other which interests the orator and in which he sees a parallel with the situation at hand.[52] The myth, then, occupies the place of

---

[52] Briscoe (1981) 46.

an historical *exemplum* in Cato's speech, a warning of what can happen if such female activities are left unchecked.[53]

What is even more striking, however, is the language which Cato uses to describe the events on Lemnos. He employs the word *genus* for those whom the women murdered—'the whole race of men' (*virorum omne genus*), meaning, of course, everyone of the male gender. *Genus* can certainly be used to mean sex, although this is not its primary meaning. Yet Cato immediately uses it again and in a much different context. He adds to his comment on the story of the Lemnian women the generalized statement that there is the highest danger from any *genus* which is allowed secret meetings, meaning, of course, to make the point that any group of people can be a threat to the state if given the chance. The double use of the word *genus*, however, serves to characterize women and men not as two mutually dependent halves of the human race (or, indeed, as a weaker half entirely dependent on a stronger half, which is the way Valerius would tell it) but as competing 'kinds' of people which want to have the state for their own. In the same way that certain classes struggled for control and influence in the Roman state, so does Cato see the conflict between the genders. It is essentially political, and not unlike other public struggles fought throughout the history of the Republic between different 'kinds' of men.

The group of women, therefore, in Cato's understanding, are not a threat because they are so very different from men: rather, it is their facility at behaving exactly like men which makes them dangerous. Thus, in the story of the Lemnian women, Cato uses the word *coniuratio*, a conspiracy, and warns of *coetus*, *concilia*, and *secretae consultationes*—all words drawn from the sphere of Roman public life. In fact, throughout his oration, Cato consistently describes the activities of the women using two metaphors taken directly from the

[53] Chaplin (2000: 97) notes that this is a rare reference to Greek 'history' in Livy, and argues that this is part of the characterization of Cato as a representative of older history and knowledge. I think that it is important, however, that Cato himself represents the story of the Lemnian women as fictional, at least until it is 'proven' by present events. In this sense, it occupies a different category of past event from those cited by both Cato and Valerius from *Roman* history.

sphere from which he seeks to exclude them. First, he employs the language of a political conspiracy: in addition to the passage noted above, the protest is 'sedition' (*seditiones*, 2. 7 and *seditioni*, 3. 8), and an attempt to influence the vote (*legem abrogandam censent*, 2. 13 and *legem et suffragia rogant*, 4. 18). Most tellingly, Cato compares the situation at hand with the dramatic events of the struggle of the orders, when the plebs threatened to abandon Rome entirely should their demands not be met: *ut plebis quondam sic nunc mulierum secessione* ('as once there was a secession of commoners, now there is one of women': 2. 7).[54] This is in the same spirit as the double use of *genus* noted above: the struggle between the men and the women is akin to that between other rival groups throughout the history of the Republic. None the less, the parallel seems at first rather bizarre, since the women have not threatened anything like secession, nor have they that ability which in Livy's narrative lent power to the plebs' actions in the fifth century—namely, the fact that the lower classes made up a substantial proportion of the military strength of the early Roman Republic.[55] Cato's comparison makes more sense, however, when understood together with the reference to the story of Lemnos, in which the women decide that men are dispensable and opt for a single-sex city. If women are understood to have the capacity to perform public roles and take political action, what use is there for men? The plebeian secessions thus are a powerful rhetorical tool to raise the spectre of the establishment of an alternative Roman state,[56] one in which men have no power and no place.

Cato's language, therefore, seems to belie his point that women have no place in public life by presenting the confrontation at hand in the same terms as political conflicts between men in the Roman past. By articulating the actions of the women in these terms, Cato presents them as particularly threatening, in that they are represented

---

[54] See Desideri (1984: 63–4) for a discussion of the similarities between the plebeian and the women's movements.

[55] Whether or not this is in fact historically true is a matter of some debate: see Cornell (1995) 257–8.

[56] This is precisely what was threatened in the secession of the plebs. They took up residence on the Aventine and formed their own government: Cornell (1995) 256.

as competing as equals in the male sphere. Indeed, although Cato
appears at first to be arguing that that dichotomy should not be
transgressed for ethical or moral reasons, it soon becomes clear that
his point is much more pragmatic. Women must be made domestic;
their presence in public is threatening because it illustrates the point
that their assignment to the private sphere is arbitrary and therefore
unstable. Yet it is on this separation of worlds along the lines of
gender that the city's stability rests, and it is for this reason that the
state cannot afford to leave the control of women's behaviour in
individual male hands where it has always been. The *lex Oppia*
cannot be repealed, Cato insists, because men's ability to confine
women within the domestic sphere has been compromised—compromised, ironically, by the law itself. Cato concludes grimly with
the point that his audience is naïve if it thinks that the repeal of the
law will allow them to go about their lives as they did before its
passage.

adversus te et rem tuam et liberos tuos exorabilis es: simul lex modum
sumptibus uxoris tuae facere desierit, tu nunquam facies. nolite eodem loco
existimare, <Quirites>, futuram rem quo fuit antequam lex de hoc ferre-
tur. et hominem inprobum non accusari tutius est quam absolvi, et luxuria
non mota tolerabilior esset quam erit nunc, ipsis vinculis sicut ferae bestiae
inritata, deinde emissa.   (34. 4. 18–20)

You are sympathetic [to the proposal] in opposition to yourself, your own
business, and your children: as soon as the law ceases to place a limit on the
extravagances of your wife, you will never do it yourself. Do not think,
Quirites, that things will be in the future as they were before the law
concerning them was passed. It is safer for a bad man not to be accused than
to be acquitted, and luxury undisturbed would be more tolerable than it will
be now, enraged like savage beasts by the chains themselves, and then released.

The law, then, is self-perpetuating: for Cato, the very fact that it
exists makes its repeal impossible. The central irony of the speech
thus becomes clear. Having begun by bemoaning the invasion of the
public sphere by private interests (the women and the men who
sympathize with them), he ends by advocating ongoing legal control

of matters formerly left to individual discretion. The only way to stop the collapse of the public/private boundary is for the state to continue to transgress it.

In this sense, although Cato's first argument about the necessity of maintaining an impermeable boundary between domestic and civic life represents a deeply anti-Augustan sentiment, one aspect of his vision of the law does look forward to the later social legislation: the idea that, under certain circumstances, the state has a duty to contain and control private life, represented here (as in the Augustan social laws) by femininity and the domestic sphere. Like the Augustan social laws too, however, the *lex Oppia* and Cato's speech defending it contain a central paradox. The point of the law was to subordinate private, feminine needs to the public good, but in doing so it gave those needs a public visibility—a 'place' in the discourse of the law. The women's protest in the streets of the city thus becomes a physical manifestation of the transgression embodied in the law; Cato's use of military and political vocabulary to describe the women's actions similarly reflects what the *lex Oppia* and the protest together have done to the language of public and private. There is a significant tension between what Cato wishes to argue, that women are 'out of place' in public, and the way he is forced to argue it—by using terms taken from the sphere of civic life. In this sense, the women's behaviour is represented by Cato as turning on a question of identity: despite what he may say, Cato does in fact want the women to act as a group, of 'well-behaved matrons', undifferentiated in character but isolated within individual homes and families. They themselves, however, have seized upon a different self-description, that of 'disorderly females', which has enabled the group action so alarming to the consul. His own discourse, then, forces Cato to acknowledge the fact that the description 'women' (of whatever sort) implies—or even *ap*plies—a collective consciousness which may transcend the pale and petty isolation of private life. Within the consul's own speech, there is no resolution to this tension, but Livy's story of the *lex Oppia* is only half-done. Turning to the speech of Valerius, then, we may see how he reformulates his opponent's vision of both the

lex Oppia and the female protests it engendered, and thereby sketches
a different and even more truly Augustan picture of the relationship
between women and public life.

...and Time: The Speech of Valerius

After Cato's oratorical *tour de force*, Valerius' response is mild to the
point of being sarcastic. From the beginning, it is clear that the
tribune's speech is carefully crafted to answer the consul.[57] Valerius
begins by ridiculing the dramatic rhetorical flourishes noted above:

coetum et seditionem et interdum secessionem muliebrem appellavit quod
matronae in publico vos rogassent ut legem in se latam per bellum tempor-
ibus duris in pace et florenti ac beata re publica abrogaretis.   (*AUC* 34. 5. 5)

He called it 'an assembly' and 'sedition' and, now and then, 'a women's
secession' just because the matrons are asking you publicly to repeal, in a
time of peace and a flourishing and successful state, a law which was passed
against them in harsh times and because of war.

In the same vein, Valerius' following statement that even if Cato's
speech may have sounded harsh, the consul's spirit is mild (*cum
ingenio sit mitis*: 5. 6) has puzzled commentators; it makes more
sense, however, if understood to be a sly joke on the rhetorical pose
of personal victimization which Cato displays in his speech. As he
goes on, Valerius continues to answer Cato's speech both substan-
tively and rhetorically. He drums the word *publicus* (*in publicum*
(5. 7); *in publico* (5. 7); *bono publico* (5. 7); *in publicum* (5. 9)) and
notes that these particular actions which benefited the state were
taken by the women collectively (*consensu omnium* (5. 9); *matronae
universae* (5. 10)). He even responds to Cato's vision of the *agmen
mulierum* which invades the Forum by citing a historical instance in
which the women defended Rome against an army—an instance,

---

[57] The conflict represented here between the 'conservative' consul and the 'progressive'
tribune draws on a trope of republican history which would have been familiar to Livy's
readers.

perhaps not accidentally, in which the city was about to be invaded by one of its own.[58]

But if Cato defines the space of the Republic in relation to the domestic, Valerius too offers an opposing term against which the Roman state may be defined. Towards the end of the speech, he makes a telling comment on the women's living conditions under the law:

at hercule universis dolor et indignatio est, cum sociorum Latini nominis uxoribus vident ea concessa ornamenta quae sibi adempta sint, cum insignes eas esse auro et purpura, cum illas vehi per urbem, se pedibus sequi, tamquam in illarum civitatibus, non in sua imperium sit. (34. 7. 5–6)

But, by Hercules, they all experience grief and anger, when they see that those decorations which have been taken from them are given to the wives of our Latin allies; when they see those women decorated with gold and purple cloth; when they see them carried through the city, while they themselves follow along on foot, as though imperial power lay in those other women's cities and not in their own.

Again, the particular rhetoric here is worth noting: the ornaments have not just been forbidden by the law, but 'taken away' (*adempta*) from Roman women like the spoils of war and 'given up' (*concessa*) to the wives of the Latin allies; the matrons of Rome are represented as following along like attendants behind the chariots of these ladies from abroad. Here again, as in Cato's speech, we find the language of 'them' and 'us', but the frame of reference has changed: the Roman women have been claimed *as Romans* in opposition to the foreigners who pass through the streets of the triumphant imperial nation. Valerius has remarked earlier on the perfidy of the Latin allies, who deserted Rome in her most recent time of need; the picture

---

[58] *regibus exactis cum Coriolano Marcio duce legiones Volscorum castra ad quintum lapidem posuissent, nonne id agmen quo obruta haec urbs esset matronae averterunt?* ('After the expulsion of the Kings, when the Volscian troops under Marcius Coriolanus' command had made camp at the fifth milestone, did the matrons not turn aside that army, by which this city would have been destroyed?': *AUC* 34. 5. 9). The attempted invasion occurred in 488 BCE (see *AUC* 2. 40).

here of Latin women behaving as though their countries had won the *imperium* is calculated to sting. The tribune thus reminds his audience (an oratorical turn particularly appropriate in the aftermath of the bloody and traumatic second Punic war) exactly where the boundary of the Roman state lies, whom it includes and whom it does not. Valerius thus redescribes Cato's map of Roman space, offering an alternative dichotomy to house versus forum, namely, home versus abroad. For Cato, women cannot have a part in 'Rome', because Rome is the Assembly, the law courts, and the other places of civic life—places which are defined against the private domestic interiors which are the space of women. Valerius, however, argues for a different conception of Rome as a political entity, redrawing the line between 'us' and 'them' and claiming Roman women through a nationalist discourse which opposes the native Roman to the foreign other.

More importantly, however, Valerius' speech contrasts with Cato's in that it is intimately concerned with history, particularly historical change. The tribune begins, after the few oratorical shots noted above, by pointing out that the *lex Oppia* was a law passed for particular reasons, under particular circumstances: Hannibal was breathing down Roman necks, the allies had deserted, there was no money to build new fleets, hire new soldiers, or feed the populace. Then everyone, women and men, suffered restrictions on consumption. Now that the war has been won, however, everyone should be able to look forward to their repeal: *quae in pace lata sunt, plerumque bellum abrogat; quae in bello, pax, ut in navis administratione alia in secunda alia in adversa tempestate usui sunt* ('Things which were passed in peaceful times are often repealed in time of war; those passed during war are repealed in peace—just as, in guiding a ship, some things are useful in fair weather and others in foul': 34. 6. 6). The ship of state metaphor is hardly a rhetorical novelty, but the principle which Valerius is urging is perhaps more subtle than it at first appears. He is not only arguing that the women deserve to share equally with men in the renewed prosperity of the Roman state, but that, in fact, the *lex Oppia* has already acknowledged that right, by insisting that they share equally with men in its misfortunes: *cui non apparet inopiam et miseriam civitatis... istam legem scripsisse ...?* ('to whom is it not obvious that the poverty and distress of the state wrote that law?': 34. 6. 16).

Valerius thus not only responds to Cato's spatial model of Roman politics, he adds the element of time as well. As noted above, Cato uses the myth of the Lemnian women in the place of a historical exemplum to support his claims about the danger posed by women's activities in public (34. 2. 3–4). This is particularly remarkable in that later in the speech Cato rejects exempla from actual Roman history as beside the case: at 3. 7 he mentions the abortive ransoming of the captives of Hannibal in 216[59] and at 3. 8 the arrival of the Idaean Mother in 205[60] in order to show the ways in which the women's present behaviour is *unlike* past situations. His detailed citation of the unsuccessful attempt by Pyrrhus' envoy Cineas to bribe the citizens of Rome in 279 is particularly worth noting.[61] Cato narrates the story in order to reject it as an example that characterizes women's ability to withstand the temptations of luxury. If the same event were to occur today, he says, it would have a different outcome (4. 6–7). The story proves Cato's point only when transported from factual historical events into the realm of imagination—not what did happen, but what would have happened. Roman history, therefore, is brought forward by Cato only to be dismissed as a model for thinking about the present situation, leaving the Lemnian women, rescued from fiction to become fact, as the historical foremothers of the women of 195.[62]

---

[59] See *AUC* 22. 58–61 for Livy's account of the affair.

[60] See *AUC* 29. 10.

[61] The relevant book of *AUC* is lost, although the story appears in the summary of book 13. Cf. Plutarch, *Pyrr.* 18. 4; Valerius Maximus 4. 3. 14; Zonaras 8. 4. 9.

[62] Chaplin (2000: 97–105) deserves credit for recognizing that the debate over the *lex Oppia* turns on the question of how to read history. She argues that Cato shows a greater knowledge of historical exempla than Valerius, and is therefore meant to be understood as a 'warner figure' whose advice, while correct, is destined to be ignored by his audience—thus leading to the inevitable moral decline Livy described in the preface to the work as a whole. Especially given the different kinds of history which the two cite,

Whereas Cato 'proves' the threat posed by the Roman women by citing the mythical exemplum of Lemnos and rejecting actual historical events, Valerius carefully situates both the women's behaviour and the *lex Oppia* within Roman history. Thus, at 34. 5. 7 he asks, *quid tandem novi matronae fecerunt...?* ('What then are the matrons doing which is so novel?') and as an answer provides five historical exempla in rapid succession (5. 8–11). *Novus*, of course, was a value-laden word for the Romans, and Valerius knows the importance of defusing it. He remarks at 5. 11, *nec mihi causas aequare propositum est: nihil novi factum purgare satis est* ('I don't propose to equate the causes [for the women's behaviour in the past and in the present]: it is sufficient for me to prove by way of defence that nothing new is being done'). In fact, Valerius is not merely defusing *novus*, he is turning it back against Cato's argument. When he comes to consider the circumstances surrounding the original passage of the *lex Oppia* (6. 7–8) he will remind his audience that the law does not date to the time of the kings, or the Twelve Tables, or even to the time of their grandfathers. *quis igitur nescit novam istam legem esse...?* ('Who, therefore, doesn't know that this is a new law?' 6. 9). Thus, Valerius transfers the accusation of novelty from the women to the law and makes the point that what is historically anomalous here is not the women's behaviour, but the *lex Oppia* itself. While Cato would reject the women's actions and normalize the law as a part of his narrative of declining Roman morality, Valerius uses historical exempla to tell a story which situates the women squarely within Roman history.

There is a subtle contrast between the different exempla drawn from Roman history which Cato and Valerius employ in their speeches, as each speaker considers other historical moments in which women have gathered together in public. Cato begins by citing an incident at 34. 3. 7 which took place in 216 when Hannibal was demanding ransom for captives taken at the battle of Cannae.

however, and the different uses to which they put it, I would argue that Livy here is actually offering a much more subtle message about how, and why, present events may be situated within a narrative of the past.

Both women and men poured into the streets to beg government officials to produce the money to bring the soldiers back, but, as Cato reminds his audience, the Assembly refused to pay. In contrast, Valerius cites two instances at 34. 5. 9–10: one when the Gauls demanded money after capturing the city in 387,[63] and the other during the worst part of the second Punic war in 214,[64] when the women gathered together to give voluntarily their personal funds to assist the state treasury. Although the stated morals of these stories have to do with the legitimacy, or illegitimacy, of women's public gatherings, it is clear that their subtext is primarily about money, public and private. Since part of Cato's argument in favour of retaining the *lex Oppia* rests on the idea that money spent on private luxuries (especially female luxuries) is sapping the state's vital resources, it is not surprising that he chooses to cite a historical instance of the government's decision to consider the public good rather than individual concerns in the allocation of funds. Valerius, on the other hand, retorts with moments from history when the money has flowed in the opposite direction and women's private funds have been vital in maintaining the Roman state. Valerius continues this line of argument in discussing the nature of the *lex Oppia* and the ends which such sumptuary legislation serves. Indeed, Valerius remarks, the consumption which the *lex Oppia* governs is not really 'consumption' at all.

sed in purpura, quae teritur absumitur, iniustam quidem sed aliquam tamen causam tenacitatis video; in auro vero, in quo praeter manupretium nihil intertrimenti fit, quae malignitas est? praesidium potius in eo est et ad privatos et ad publicos usus, sicut experti estis.   (34. 7. 4)

In the case of purple cloth, which is used and worn out, I see a reason—an unjust one, but nevertheless a reason—for stubbornness; but as for gold, in which nothing is consumed except for the manufacturing, what harm is there? Rather, there is protection in it for both private and public ends, as you know well.

<hr>

[63] See *AUC* 5. 50.   [64] See *AUC* 24. 18.

Valerius is answering Cato's argument that money spent by women on luxury goods is, at best, wasted and, at worst, a threat to male power in the public sphere. But Valerius questions this understanding of women and money spent on adornment. Purple cloth, perhaps, may be understood to be truly consumed, since it can be worn out and rendered worthless through use, but gold is worth the same whether in the form of a coin or an earring. For the women's purposes it requires only the small amount of money spent to transform it from the former to the latter. In fact, money spent on gold jewellery is not only not lost, it counts as safety gained: women are something like banks and can be counted on to bring forth the stored wealth of their gold jewellery in times of crisis. Valerius' historical exempla have proved this, as he reminds his audience of what they have learned from their experience and in his speech— *sicut experti estis*. What is represented in female jewellery, then, is not private consumption but a resource both private *and* public; the Roman women's adornment is at once a symbolic and very real display of the nation's power.

On the one hand, therefore, Cato sees the Roman women as embodying that which the civic sphere must exclude, the private concerns against which the Assembly must stand if it is to survive. There is no place for women in public life because they are indistinguishable from the spaces they ought to occupy; just as the boundary between house and forum must be maintained, so must that between female and male. Valerius, on the other, places women squarely within the *res publica*, an indispensable part of Roman civic life. Yet although he takes pains to answer Cato's spatial model of politics, Valerius' speech is much more concerned with time; it is history which makes the final, arbitrating difference between considering the Roman women as friends or foes. In the narratives of Rome's past which the tribune tells (stories which, it should be noted, also appear as events in their own right in the pages of Livy's *Ab Urbe Condita*) the work of women becomes a part of the teleological story of the city, carefully traced from its most humble beginnings to the imperial glory of the historian's present day. Thus, as we saw in the case of the Augustan social legislation, place and time are intertwined with one another, but it is the latter which gives the former its true meaning. Indeed, the centrality of women to Valerius' history of Rome, especially to the extent that it reflects their centrality to Livy's, is profoundly Augustan in sensibility—much more so than the model of the *res publica* which Cato puts forward, although it is the latter who defends the act of legislating private life. For this reason, even though I would argue that Livy's story of the repeal of the *lex Oppia* must be understood on some level as a response to contemporary history, I would urge against seeing it as either pure criticism or strict support of the Augustan social legislation. Rather, we should see in this episode one historian's attempt to work through questions about the relationship between gender and the law which had been raised by the new regime's very public interest in women, the family, and the home. Ultimately, the message of the opening chapters of book 34 of *AUC* is that Roman women are a force to be reckoned with, and that, one way or another, the state and its servants must give them a place in public life, even if that means rewriting the terms in which public life itself is constituted. In this, the repeal of the *lex Oppia* echoes the contemporary *leges Iuliae*, and offers a profoundly 'Augustan' vision of the relationship between gender, law, and politics.

THE AFTERLIFE OF THE DEATH OF THE *LEX OPPIA*

Livy's vision of the repeal of the *lex Oppia* seems to have had influence. It is difficult to be certain whether later authors who cite the debate in passing, such as Valerius Maximus, the author of *de Viris Illustribus*, or Orosius,[65] are drawing on Livy's account or some other source which is lost to us. Yet the strong moral tone of these citations suggests that Livy at least had influence in making the

---

[65] Val. Max. 9. 1. 3; *de Vir. Ill.* 47; Oros. 4. 20. 14.

scene into an important exemplum for use in discussing women, legislation, and the moral health of the Roman state. The speeches composed for the same occasion which are found in Zonaras (whose story concerning the repeal of the *lex Oppia* was probably extracted from the pages of Cassius Dio) echo Livy's in many particulars, although much of the subtlety of the scene as it appears in *AUC* 34 is lost. But especially given the connection which may be seen between the arguments presented in the debate and the logic of the social legislation in the historian's own time, it is noteworthy that Livy's speeches for Cato and Valerius reappear in book 3 of Tacitus' *Annals*—almost immediately following Tacitus' digression on law discussed at the beginning of this chapter. The beginning of Livy's book 34 was the model for a debate in the senate at *Annals* 3. 33–4, which takes place in 21 CE over a proposal that wives of governors should be forbidden from joining their husbands in the provinces.[66] Caecina Severus, whose 'severity' matches that of Cato, makes the motion and delivers a speech in support of it; Valerius Messalinus, a descendant of the earlier tribune, responds in opposition and is followed by Drusus, who also speaks against the proposal. The proposal is then abandoned, not because of the persuasiveness of either speaker, but, as in the eventual repeal of the *lex Oppia*, because of the intervention of an external force—in this case, the *auctoritas* of Drusus.

The connection with Livy's book 34 here is first noticeable because both speakers refer explicitly to the *lex Oppia*; this should not simply be taken, as by some scholars, merely as proof that the *lex Oppia* was the primary exemplum in Roman history for discussing women and public power. Rather, it should also be understood as a reference to Tacitus' source for his construction of the debate.[67] It is also remarkable that the two sides of the question are presented by a

---

[66] Ginsburg (1993); L'Hoir (1994). Cf. Woodman and Martin (1996) 283 ff.

[67] While it is not beyond belief that this debate actually took place, it is unlikely that the speeches presented by Tacitus were actually delivered on the occasion: the debate has numerous Livian echoes and fits neatly into the thematic structure of *Annals* 3. See Marshall (1975); Baldwin (1972) 90; Ginsburg (1993) 88; Woodman and Martin (1996) 284–6.

Valerius and a man whose cognomen is Severus: Cato the Elder was known for his severity, and is mocked by the earlier Valerius for his *severissimis moribus* (*AUC* 34. 6. 2). Caecina's fellow senators even complain after his speech, *neque Caecinam dignum tantae rei censorum* ('nor was Caecina worthy of [the office of] the censors in such a matter': *Ann.* 3. 34. 1).[68] There are significant verbal echoes, such as the only use of the verb *constringo* in Tacitus at *Ann.* 3. 33. 4 reflecting Livy's use of it at *AUC* 34. 3. 1,[69] and the unusual word *coniunx* (*Ann.* 3. 33. 1; *AUC* 34. 7. 1).[70] The senators' objection that Caecina's proposal is irrelevant to the debate (*plures obturbabant neque relatum de negotio*: *Ann.* 3. 34. 1) may also be a subtle signal that there is more going on here than a straightforward historical narrative.[71]

More interesting, perhaps, are the ways in which Tacitus' scene in *Annals* 3 reflects Livy's in the positions taken up by the speakers. Caecina argues that women are dangerous, and likely to overwhelm the provincial government of their husbands with their greed for money and power. He imagines the governor's wife who conducts business (*negotia*) for herself and replaces her husband as the army's commander. Although the image is drawn from Plancina's recent antics in the provinces[72] (to whom Caecina obliquely refers at 33. 3), Caecina's vision of 'two commanders' departures to be attended; two official residences' (*duorum egressus coli, duo esse praetoria*: 33. 4) certainly recalls Cato's picture of an alternate women's Rome. Messalinus, on the other hand, points out that times have changed and that women are useful in the provinces now that the Empire is at peace. Like the earlier Valerius, Messalinus argues that as the state passes from war to peace, the lives of its citizens should change too,[73] thus preserving the 'historical specificity' message of the tribune's speech. Messalinus goes on to argue that since men are not free of corruption without women, and are still allowed to govern provinces, there is no logical reason why women should be kept at home. Women share everything else with their husbands (*cetera promisca*

---

[68] L'Hoir (1994) 15.   [69] Ginsburg (1993) 90.
[70] Woodman and Martin (1996) 291.   [71] Ibid. 299.
[72] *Ann.* 2. 55.   [73] Woodman and Martin (1996) 301.

cum marito: 34. 2)—why separate the couple merely because the husband must travel abroad? Again, Messalinus is echoing Livy's Valerius, imagining the couple as partners rather than competitors.

In some ways, it is not surprising that Tacitus should turn to Livy's scene of the *lex Oppia* repeal as a model. Judith Ginsburg[74] has made the cogent argument that part of the point here is to compare this debate unfavourably with the earlier one, as Tacitus attempts to show the degeneration of the senate and its tradition of moral oratory. Certainly, one of the themes of *Annals* 3 seems to be the present's relationship with the past: it contains two famous historical digressions in the author's voice, on legal history (§§26–8) and luxury (§55); Tacitus takes various opportunities for making a comparison between the fortunes of old and new senatorial families;[75] the book concludes (§76) with the funeral procession of Junia, for which the effigies of twenty great republican families were brought out. But, as I noted earlier, *Annals* 3 is also deeply concerned with women, and the relationship between women and public life. Indeed, the two themes may be seen as tied closely together, as the book repeatedly makes reference to the ways in which women survive the processes of history which men do not. Agrippina, Plancina, Livia, and Junia are all left behind, for better or worse, by the political vicissitudes which took their husbands' lives; they remain in the end as witnesses to events, both protected and prohibited from full participation in civic affairs. The final image of the book is particularly telling in this context. Despite having been snubbed by the dead woman's will, the emperor Tiberius generously allows her a *laudatio* from the rostra and a large funeral procession, which is missing only the masks of Brutus and Cassius. Although the historian notes that the latter two are conspicuous in their absence (*Ann.* 3. 76), I would argue that there is a certain play here on omission and survival: Tiberius is left out of the will, and Brutus and Cassius have disappeared from the

---

[74] Ginsburg (1993) 86–96.
[75] Such as the deaths of Lucius Volusius and Sallustius Crispus at 3. 30.

funeral procession, but Junia herself is inscribed permanently and in pride of place as part of Tacitus' narrative of Roman history.

To the extent, then, that *Annals* 3 is generally concerned with gender, history, and public life, Livy's narrative of the repeal of the *lex Oppia* is understandably an important touchstone for Tacitus, a famous moment in history *and* historiography when such issues had come to the fore. We cannot know, of course, whether the later historian additionally understood that Livy's composition for the occasion was not a historical record of the second century BCE but a product of Livy's own time—whether, that is, he too saw in the repeal of the *lex Oppia* a debate over more contemporary, intimately imperial, legislation. Yet the close connection in his narrative between the discussion of Augustus' social laws and the debate in the senate suggests that, at least in his own mind, Tacitus saw a relationship between the two. It is worth noting, in this context, the ways in which Tacitus reformulates the terms of Livy's original episode to serve his own textual purposes. For Livy, as I have remarked above, the presence of women in the streets of Rome is a crucial part of the debate over the *lex Oppia*; it becomes the springboard for a larger discussion about women in the public sphere of Roman life. Cato's apocalyptic fantasies as he presents them to the Assembly begin with the actual presence of women surrounding the Forum and end with their imagined invasion of all Roman public institutions. Physical space thus becomes metaphorical place. As women pour into Rome from outlying municipalities to pressure the Assembly in the streets of the city, it becomes abundantly clear 'where' is at stake in the conflict at hand. Although Cato's speech was composed by Livy in the early years of the Principate, then, it reveals a substantially republican way of thinking about the places which power occupies.

Tacitus' version of this scene is also about space, place, and power; but the places in question have clearly changed. Women should not be taken to the provinces, Caecina argues, because there they grow powerful and take over the roles of men. The example of Plancina is explicit; the example of Agrippina, who returns to Rome with the ashes of her husband and a huge popular following at the beginning of *Annals* book 3, must also be remembered. Where does power live? Where is it negotiated? Caecina concludes his speech, *nunc vinclis exsolutis, domos, fora, iam et exercitus regerent* ('now with their chains loosened, they rule homes, fora, and even armies': 3. 33. 4).[76] The dichotomy which Cato figured as home versus forum has gained a third term, and the simple exclusion of women from the public places of Rome is no longer an answer. The task seems now to be to keep them in Rome and away from the edges of the Empire. In response to Caecina, Messalinus points out that there is no safety in leaving your wife at home in Rome either. He remarks at the end of his speech, *sic obviam irent iis quae alibi peccarentur ut flagitiorum urbis meminissent* ('thus, while you go against sins committed elsewhere, remember the offences of this city!': 3. 34. 5). Again, we may see here a sensitive reformulation of the terms in which Livy's speakers originally framed this question: for Cato, the women were like foreign invaders of the city of Rome; for Valerius, they were staunch members of the Roman body politic and thus deserving of greater privileges than women from subject states. In each case, however, the women's position is understood in relation to the 'foreign outsider', notionally located just beyond the city wall. Tacitus' speakers, on the other hand, are forced to consider women's roles in a state which extends to the edge of the known world, so that the territory of politics has expanded beyond the boundaries which Cato and Valerius had used to frame their discussions of women's place. The Empire in its later days is everywhere a dangerous place—the temptations of power exist both at home and abroad.

Alibi / urbs is the geographical structure around which Tacitus' history is framed, as he moves back and forth between foreign wars and events in Rome; it might be argued that the question of literally where power comes from is one of the themes of the *Annals*. The debate in the senate analysed here attempts to place women within a power structure that relies on the provinces for its brute military

[76] Tacitus' narrative of the scene is rendered completely in *oratio obliqua*. For the sake of clarity, I have translated passages from the speeches as though they were direct quotations.

force and on Rome for its political legitimacy. Thus, the rewritten version of the *lex Oppia* debate found in *Annals* 3 reveals the ways in which Tacitus is operating with a conception of place and power different from Livy's: Rome has become a vast provincial empire and in it women are active political players. Tacitus has transformed Cato's description of the conflict between house and forum into one which contrasts the capital and the provinces it governs, and in doing so constructs a new means of asking the question of where women belong in the Roman state. Yet his understanding of the ways in which law and history may be used to frame a discussion of the relationship between women and politics is drawn from Livy's description of the repeal of the *lex Oppia*, which in turn reflects a particularly Augustan model of the gendered discourses of public life.

4

A Domestic Disturbance: Talking About the Triumvirs in the Early Empire

IN the last chapter, I argued that the social legislation was perhaps the single most important ideological gesture expressing the 'domestication' of politics in the Augustan period. As a gesture, however, it was also bound up with other ideological formulations put out by the new imperial regime, particularly the ways in which that regime was attempting both to affect and to effect the writing of history. We may see in Livy's narrative of the repeal of the *lex Oppia* the success of that attempt, an acceptance of 'Augustan' terms in which the relationship between women and public life should be debated as part of a historical narrative. The reappearance of Livy's debate in Tacitus' *Annals* testifies to the persistence of those terms and their continued significance for writing the story of imperial Rome. Like the last, this chapter is also about historiography, but of a more particular kind. As I, and others, have argued, the Augustan period's sense of itself as a historical moment, as an expression of the past and a legacy to the future, had an important effect on representations of Roman time: although Augustus was supposedly taking Rome back to what it had been, he was also taking it forward to what it ought to have been all along, creating a new and better version of old and established national virtues. Thus, insofar as it was invested in advertising itself both as a faithful expression of, and as an improvement on, the political system which went before it, the early Empire's representations of the late Republic were necessarily complex and highly ideologically charged.[1]

This is particularly true of what has come to be known as the age of the triumvirs, the period following the assassination of Julius Caesar which marked the beginning of Octavian's rise to the pinnacle of political power. Scholars have long struggled with how to characterize this moment in Roman history (as the death throes of the Republic or the birth pangs of the Empire) but it is clear that it was an important period of transition, both for Octavian and the Roman state.[2] In this sense, it formed an indispensable part of the narrative which early imperial historians sought to tell, of Augustus, his early career, and the political system which he brought into being. On the other hand, the triumviral period was also marked by some of the ugliest, most brutal, acts which the Republic had seen in its hundred years of civil conflict. Those acts, then, and Octavian's complicity in them, made the age of the triumvirs an episode which many would have apparently preferred to forget: Suetonius preserves a story that the soon-to-be emperor Claudius, working under Livy's tutelage, began an account of the period with the death of Caesar in 44 BCE, but was forced, after two books, to restart with the battle of Actium under pressure from his family (*Div. Claud.* 41. 2). It is understandable, therefore, that there is a real tension which may be felt in the surviving historical accounts of the triumvirs, a tension between the desire to tell Augustus' story from the beginning and the desire to forget the devastation of his early career.[3] This chapter is about one way in which that tension found some resolution, in a history which turns away from the vagaries and violence of politics and focuses instead on moralizing stories of private life. Such a resolution, however, sheds light not just on the particular needs of

---

[1] On the historiography about the birth of the Empire, see Gabba (1984) 77–9.

[2] On the period and its significance, see Millar (1973).

[3] Morgan (2000: 55–60) discusses the difficulty with which the period presented the contemporary historian, and suggests some ways in which Asinius Pollio grappled with it.

historians and their narratives but also on the kinds of self-representation which early imperial culture was inclined to support.

In purely historical terms, the facts are these. The Second Triumvirate was formed in 43 BCE as a compromise. The assassination of
Julius Caesar the preceeding year had left a power vacuum in Roman
politics which no individual had yet succeeded in filling. Two of the
major candidates for succession, therefore, Caesar's lieutenant Mark
Antony and the dictator's adopted son Octavian, concluded an
uneasy peace, and, along with the senator and general Lepidus,
formed a three-man alliance to rule over the Roman state, following
the pattern of Caesar, Pompey, and Crassus two decades before. Not
unlike the first, the Second Triumvirate was not sufficiently stable to
last for ever: Octavian would ultimately depose Lepidus and declare
war on Antony—that war which would come to its conclusion at the
battle of Actium and leave the field clear for Octavian to become
Augustus and transform Rome into his own imperial state. While the
Second Triumvirate was still in place, however, in the period between
its birth in 43 and the defeat of the tyrranicides in late 42, Octavian,
Antony, and Lepidus set about ridding themselves of some of the
more irritating of their personal and political enemies. They did this
by means of proscription, an idea which appears to have originated
with Sulla, in the civil wars between him and Marius earlier in the
first century BCE. Proscription was a simple but none the less dia-
bolical process, whereby those in power would publish a list of those
whose lives were forfeit to the state; anyone could then kill the
proscribed men without fearing punishment, and, indeed, the killer
could often expect a reward, both officially, in the form of pay for
what he had done, and unofficially, in what he could carry off from
his victim's property. Needless to say, this created chaos in Rome,
particularly among the socially and politically prominent: not only
were they the most likely to be proscribed in the first place, due to
their position, but they were also the most 'valuable' victims, both to
the killers who would loot their homes and to those in power who
could confiscate after the owner's death the less portable parts of his
property. The proscriptions of the Second Triumvirate thus struck

the Roman upper classes especially hard and, in part because of this, came to be remembered as one of the darkest moments in the late Republic, when the collapse of the social order was made manifest in the wholesale slaughter of the city's most prominent men at the command of those charged with maintaining the peace.[4]

It is not surprising, in this sense, that the triumviral proscriptions should enjoy a powerful presence in the later historical record, although most authors are inclined to absolve Octavian of his role in the terror. The princeps himself in his autobiography seems to have attempted to foster a sense of youthful miscalculation around his actions as a member of the Triumvirate,[5] a trope picked up in later texts.[6] Yet the most prominent role which the proscriptions play in early imperial texts is not so much as an episode in Roman politics but as a backdrop for stories about domestic relationships: the public history of senate and state, tyrannicides and troops, fades into the background, giving way to a portrait of the Roman home and a cast of characters drawn from the sphere of private life. Thus, for instance, at *Bellum Civile* 4. 14, the second-century historian Appian sets the scene for his narrative of the triumviral proscriptions by remarking that it was a terrible time, not simply because of the numbers of killed, but because of the form which the killing took on:

ἰδέα τε πᾶσα κακῶν ἦν, οὐχ ὡς ἐν στάσεσιν ἢ πολέμου καταλήψεσιν. οὐ γάρ, ὡς ἐν ἐκείνοις, τὸν μὲν ἀντιστασιώτην, ἢ πολέμιον ἐδεδοίκεσαν, τοῖς δ' οἰκείοις σφᾶς ἐπέτρεπον, ἀλλὰ καὶ τοῦδε τῶν σφαγέων μᾶλλον

---

[4] See Hinard (1985) 303–12.

[5] Plutarch quotes him twice as having cited simple fear of the tyrannicides as the motivating force behind the original formation of the three-man governing body (*Cicero* 45. 5; *Brutus* 27. 2). In the exchange of speeches quoted in Appian's *Bellum Civile* (the longest extant passage from Augustus' autobiography, although imperfectly (Appian admits) rendered in Greek) the princeps allows Lucius to cast the fundamental illegality of the Triumvirate in his teeth without contradiction, a fact which Lucius underscores by remarking 'not even you will deny [this accusation]' (*BC* 5. 43). But, again, the continued threat represented by Brutus and Cassius is used as explanation and excuse.

[6] Thus, for instance, Seneca the Younger contrasts the brutality represented in the proscriptions with later acts of clemency, noting *iam unum hominem occidere non poterat, cui M. Antonius proscriptionis edictum inter cenam dictarat* ('now he was not able to kill a single man, he to whom Mark Antony had recited the edict of proscription during dinner': *de Clem.* 1. 9. 3).

ἐδεδοίκεσαν, οὐδὲν μὲν αὐτοὺς ὡς ἐν πολέμῳ καὶ στάσει δεδιότας, σφίσι δὲ
αὐτίκα γιγνομένους ἐξ οἰκείων πολεμίους, ἢ δι' ὕπουλον ἔχθραν ἢ ὑπὸ τῶν
ἐπικεκηρυγμένων σφίσι γερῶν ἢ διὰ τὸν ἐν ταῖς οἰκίαις χρυσόν τε καὶ
ἄργυρον.

Every kind of evil occurred, not just as happens during a revolution or
occupation by an enemy army: for during events such as those, people fear
the opposing party or the enemy, and trust in the members of their own
households; but now they feared these more than the murderers, and since
the former were in no way afraid for themselves—as they would be during
war or revolt—they straight away were transformed from the master's
household into his enemies, either because of some festering hatred, or
for the sake of the rewards which had been proclaimed, or for the gold and
silver contained within the house.

It is this, to Appian's mind, which made the proscriptions of 43–42
BCE so shocking: not so much the fact of the condemnations (which,
after all, had been seen in Rome before) but the ways in which the
condemnations transformed homes into battlefields, masters into
subordinates, subordinates into the saviours or betrayers of those
whom they formerly served. Certainly, Appian goes on, there were
extraordinary acts of heroism on the part of some wives, children,
brothers, and slaves, as they attempted to save the heads of their
respective households from the enmity of the triumvirs. Yet the very
fact that a man's dependants were now in such positions of power, to
destroy or preserve, is a manifestation of the unprecedented social
reversals which characterized the period. In choosing to become
either a man's worst enemies or his best friends, wives, slaves, and
children became actors in the civic drama being played out in the
streets of Rome. The point made by the passage quoted above,
therefore, is that the proscriptions were a time when the turmoil
consuming the state consumed the home as well: the period marked
a crisis in Rome, not simply in political but in domestic life.[7]

   Appian will go on to illustrate this point with more than eighty
short anecdotes, detailing the particular fates of individuals and

---

[7] On this passage in Appian, see Magnino (1998) 166–7.

which members of a man's household assisted or betrayed him. Thus, the historian concludes particular subsections with statements such as, 'these, then, are representations of good and bad sons' (*BC* 4. 21) or, 'let those things just written serve as examples of bad wives' (4. 24). The stories, therefore, are clearly paradigmatic; indeed, Appian himself declares that there are many more which he could tell, but that he has deliberately chosen those 'which are especially extraordinary and amazing, and produce belief in the matters just laid out' (4. 16). It is a strongly drawn typology, with a feeling of lists and categories echoing Valerius Maximus more than Thucydides, and noticeably different in style from the more traditional narrative history which precedes it in Appian's text. Yet the historian also notes that he is actually just following in the historiographical footsteps of his predecessors: πολλὰ δέ ἐστι, καὶ πολλοὶ Ῥωμαίων ἐν πολλαῖς βίβλοις αὐτὰ συνέγραψαν ἐφ᾽ ἑαυτῶν ('these [stories] are many, and many Romans have written the same things in many books, one after the other': 4.16). Exactly who these 'many Romans' were we can only speculate,[8] though Appian's comments here are supported by Cassius Dio, who also declares that repeating all the domestic stories to have survived from the period of the triumviral proscriptions is a project much too vast to take on (47. 10. 1).

Appian's vision of the 'crisis' in Roman private life occasioned by the proscriptions has achieved a certain currency in modern historiography. Thus, one scholar notes that, with the proscriptions, 'a place [the household] which had offered an escape and a secure base of support to the Roman man of affairs became just one more potential source of treachery and betrayal'[9] while another sees the time as 'una tappa drammatica...dello sfilacciamento dell'ethos familiare' ('a dramatic stage...in the fraying of family values').[10] Perhaps most dramatically, and most influentially, Sir Ronald Syme

---

[8] There has been a great deal of interest over the years in identifying Appian's source materials for the *BC*, but it is certain that at least some of it must have come from Asinius Pollio. Gabba (1956: 213–19) suggests that all of Appian's material was drawn from Pollio's lost *History*, a controversial position: see Gowing (1992) 39–50. For some other possible authors, see Nisbet (1995).

[9] Cluett (1998) 71.   [10] Canfora (1980) 436.

writes in *The Roman Revolution*, 'The Caesarian leaders had defied public law; they now abolished the private rights of citizenship... Roman society under the terror witnessed the triumph of the dark passions of cruelty and revenge, of the ignoble vices of cupidity and treachery. The laws and constitution of Rome had been subverted. With them perished honour and security, family and friendship.'[11] In modern historical texts as well as ancient ones, then, the triumviral proscriptions are imagined as a crossroads in Roman morality as much as in Roman politics, and the extent of the rot which had consumed republican governance is measured by its penetration into the sphere of private life.

That there was something very wrong in Roman society during the age of the triumvirs is difficult to dispute, and the innumerable tales of domestic virtue and vice found in early imperial sources are certainly based on some kind of historical truth, as is made clear by the existence of such eyewitness testimony as the famous funerary inscription known as the *laudatio Turiae*. Nevertheless, the sheer number of these stories is striking, and the extent to which they proliferated in early imperial prose is shown in the comments of Appian and Cassius Dio noted above. Moreover, it is worth noting that when Dio turns to these tales, he remarks that certain ones have survived despite the fact that they are not attached to historically significant people. Indeed, he cannot even provide names for the heroes of two of the episodes he chooses to tell (47. 10. 6). But even though the stories have been detached from the individuals whose actions they represent, they have nevertheless clung to their historical moment; they have remained stories about the triumviral proscriptions, and would do so for as long as they remained part of the Roman literary tradition. They thus function as a means of characterizing, not particular people, but a moment in time, and would continue to be remembered and retold as episodes in the story of the birth of the imperial state. The fact that women, and other characters drawn from the private sphere, are such significant players in the

---

[11] Syme (1939) 190. Cf. Hinard (1985) 309.

proscription tales both accords them a very real role in one of the signal episodes of late republican history, and marks the period as somehow distinct from the standard record of public events.

In this sense, I think that it is appropriate to view the proscription tales not simply as a curious tangent to our standard histories of the late Republic, but as a historiographical phenomenon—a series of fictions, yes, but fictions which articulate in early imperial texts some kind of truth about the age of the triumvirs which more traditional historical narrative cannot.[12] As scholars such as Hayden White have pointed out, the form in which history is communicated is an important part of the story which it seeks to tell, drawing as it does upon readers' expectations of how certain plots, themes, and generic structures develop: is this story a comedy? A tragedy? A romance? How am I as reader supposed to respond, given what I already know about the type of story being told?[13] I would argue that the proscription stories represent an intrusion into traditional history, not just of subject matter but of generic type, as continuous narrative gives way to disjointed episode, the names of 'great men' fade in the presence of anonymous women and slaves, and the story of the state is subsumed by the story of the home. If this is true, it seems important to ask, not just what the proscription stories meant to an early imperial audience, but what were the political and historical factors that allowed them to flourish. It is significant that one place that the style of historical narrative and the subject matter of the proscription tales come together is in rhetorical exercises and education, since oratory, like history, was a genre whose roots were deeply

---

[12] Indeed, in this context it is worth noting a different solution to the problem of historicizing Augustus, which is that represented in Pompeius Trogus' *Historiae Philippicae*, written under the early Empire. This is the first 'world history' written in Latin, and it remained the only one for more than 400 years. Trogus' work only survives in a later epitome, but it is clear that Rome as a city played a small role in his text—except, significantly, as the cradle of Augustus, who is imagined as the current heir to the world-empire founded many millennia ago by the Assyrian king Ninus. Since he sees human history as moving naturally from empire to empire, and monarchy to monarchy, Trogus has little difficulty with the accession of Augustus and the triumph of Roman imperialism. He does not, of course, discuss the civil wars. On Trogus, see Alonso-Núñez (1987).

[13] H. White (1978), esp. 51–80 ('Interpretation in History').

embedded in the soil of Roman politics. The fact, then, that this moment in the demise of the Roman Republic is understood by later authors to be intertwined inextricably with the history of the Roman family testifies not simply to the real story of the civil wars, but to the terms established in the early Empire for understanding the relationship between history, politics, and domestic life.

DOMESTICATING CIVIL WAR: THE PROSCRIPTIONS AND HISTORY

It is unfortunate, but not entirely surprising, that we have no extant contemporary accounts of the age of the triumvirs, the last decade-and-a-half before the coming of the 'Augustan settlement' to Rome. The death of Cicero, most famous victim of the proscriptions, cuts off in 43 our best source for the politics of the late Republic, and Appian reports that, after the defeat of Sextus Pompey in 36 BCE, Octavian ordered all documents concerning the recent civil conflicts to be burned (*BC* 5. 132). Although Livy certainly wrote of the period, those books of the *Ab Urbe Condita* are preserved only in the periochoi and the few fragments quoted in later texts. Tacitus' description of the death of Cremutius Cordus (*Annals* 4. 34–5), condemned for praising Brutus and Cassius in a history of the civil wars, is well known, and testifies to the difficulties and dangers of writing about the civil wars under the early Principate. Indeed, other than such tantalizing snippets as Cornelius Nepos' *Life of Atticus*, the earliest actual history of the time to come down to us is that of Velleius Paterculus, written under Tiberius. Velleius makes an interesting case study in the politically delicate historiography of the period: he makes a concerted effort to paint Antony as the real villian of the proscriptions, maintaining that Octavian saved as many as he could from the enmity of his fellow triumvirs; his lament for Cicero, hailed as 'the voice of the people' (*vox publica*: 2. 66. 2), seems heartfelt, but would not have been out of keeping with Augustus' own later assessment of the great orator as 'a learned man . . . and a patriot'.[14] Velleius' final comment stands as a suprisingly eloquent summation of the quandary with which the period presented the early imperial historian: 'no one has even been able to weep sufficiently for the events of this whole era, let alone find a way to express it in words' (*huius totius temporis fortunam ne deflere quidem quisquam satis digne potuit, adeo nemo exprimere verbis potest*: 2. 67. 1).

Velleius, however, is not content to leave this as his last word on the age of the triumvirs and their activities in Rome. Having remarked that the horror of the times transcends the ability of language to express it, he adds that there is *something* which begs narration: not the behaviour of the killed, or indeed of the killers, but rather of those whose connection to those condemned was personal rather than political (2. 67. 2):

id tamen notandum est, fuisse in proscriptos uxorum fidem summam, libertorum mediam, servorum aliquam, filiorum nullam; adeo difficilis est hominibus utcumque conceptae spei mora.

Nevertheless, this must be mentioned: the highest loyalty was displayed towards the proscribed by their wives, a fair amount by their freedmen, a little bit by their slaves, and none whatsoever by their sons—to such an extent delay is hard for people in the realization of their expectations, however they have been conceived.

The similarity with Appian's reading of the period is clear, although Velleius focuses on the positive rather than the negative. In explicit contrast with what cannot be said about the civic sphere,[15] Velleius here offers an analysis of domestic virtue and vice. As in Appian's *Bellum Civile*, what surfaces in the historian's narrative is not politics but the deeds done within the sphere of the household.[16] The list of

---

[14] λόγιος ἀνήρ . . . καὶ φιλόπατρις (Plut. *Cic.* 49. 3). Cf. Plutarch's *Comparison of Demosthenes and Cicero*, in which he quotes Augustus' *Memoirs* as saying that, when a young man, Octavian needed Cicero as Chares, Diopeithes, and Leosthenes had needed Demosthenes (3. 1).

[15] On the proscriptions as a crisis in speech (historical, oratorical, and political) see Richlin (1999).

[16] There is a parallel for this passage to be found in book 1 of Tacitus' *Histories*, where the author remarks on the social chaos which attended the assassination of Nero and the transition to Flavian rule. As in Velleius, Tacitus turns away from the atrocities of the

dependants seems to be offered in reverse order of who stood to gain most from the death of the *paterfamilias*; there is a pointed contrast, at any rate, between *uxorum fidem summam* and *filiorum nullam*, between the family members who were stalwart in adversity and those who were not. Velleius reinforces his point that the most important battleground of the triumviral proscriptions was the private sphere rather than the public by remarking that Antony had his uncle, and Lepidus and his fellow consul Plancus a brother each, placed on the list to be killed, *velut in dotem invitamentumque sceleris* ('as a kind of endowment and enticement for wickedness': 2. 67. 3). He rounds off the chapter by repeating the apropos joke shouted by the soldiers at Lepidus and Plancus' triumph: *de germanis, non de Gallis duo triumphant consules.*[17] The 'enemy' of the proscriptions was not the usual foreign barbarian but the members of the generals' own families.

Velleius himself does not actually offer any of the particular virtuous and vicious family stories from the age of the triumvirs to which he refers in his history, but we can get a taste of them from his contemporary Valerius Maximus. In book 6. 6–8 of the *Facta et Dicta Memorabilia*, when Valerius is attempting to exemplify the quality of *Fides*, he divides it into three subsections which illustrate the general principle: the first shows men's loyalty to the state; the second, wives' loyalty to their husbands; and the third, slaves' loyalty to their masters. This triple division is itself curious. It would appear to express a kind of continuum, moving from a strictly civic virtue to a strictly domestic one, from a loyalty which is inextricable from

---

public sphere to virtues displayed in the private: *non tamen adeo virtutum sterile saeculum ut non et bona exempla prodiderit. comitatae profugos liberos matres, secutae maritos in exilia coniuges: propinqui audentes, constantes generi, contumax etiam adversus tormenta servorum fides* . . . ('The age was not so bereft of virtue that it did not provide some good examples also. Mothers accompanied their children in flight, wives followed their husbands into exile; relatives were daring, sons-in-law were reliable, slaves displayed loyalty which stood even against torture . . .': 1. 3. 1). I would argue that this echo is not coincidental, in that Tacitus is deliberately drawing on the historiographical tropes used to describe Augustus' rise to power in order to colour Nero's fall.

[17] 'Over brothers, not over the Gauls, do these two consuls triumph.' The pun does not translate, but the point is that *germanus* means 'brother' as well as an inhabitant of Germania.

Roman identity to one which is entirely outside of it.[18] But the particular content of the sections is most striking. In the first, men's loyalty to the state, the Punic wars dominate, providing the content for five of the seven stories told, including both of the 'foreign' exempla. When we turn to the wives and slaves, however, it is the triumviral proscriptions which loom large: five of the total of ten tales are of this period, including two of the three examples of women's loyalty to their husbands. Considering that Valerius had all of Roman history from which to draw his exempla, the fact that the triumviral proscriptions stand out in this part of the book is worthy of note. This is especially true since this is the only place that such stories appear: they are noticeably absent where Valerius discusses 'bravery', 'fortitude', and even 'conjugal loyalty', where they would seem to fit equally well, if not better. The proscriptions, however, only appear under the heading of *Fides*, in service of a quality which may be understood as civic, or domestic, or both. Valerius' schema itself makes this clear. Like Velleius and Appian, the *Facta et Dicta Memorabilia* understands the civil conflicts of the age of the Triumvirs as intimately connected to the history of Roman domestic life.

The irony of representing political change through descriptions of the domestic sphere is evident in the rhetoric which Valerius uses in telling the tales of Turia and Sulpicia, the loyal wives who appear in his catalogue under the heading of *Fides*. In the case of Turia, who concealed Vespillo in the rafters of her bedroom, Valerius remarks that her loyalty was such that *cum ceteri proscripti in alienis et hostilibus regionibus per summos corporis et animi cruciatus vix evaderent, ille in cubiculo et in coniugis sinu salutem retineret* ('while the rest of the proscribed scarcely escaped into alien and hostile places by means of the worst agonies of their bodies and spirits, he kept safe in the bedroom and the bosom of his wife'). The snug domesticity of the innermost recesses of the house (the *cubiculum*) and the recesses

---

[18] On the significance of the section, both to Valerius' text and to Roman culture, see Lehmann (1998) 20–2.

of Turia's embrace (her *sinus*) strongly contrast with the emphatically foreign places (*alienis et hostilibus regionibus*) to which other men were forced to flee. Indeed, there is almost a comic element to the story, as Vespillo hides like an adulterer caught in the act. The contrast is thus not just between his unheroic retreat and his wife's staunch bravery, but between the conjugal fidelity the story describes and the image of marital betrayal it employs. There is also a delicate irony in the language used of Sulpicia's choice to defy the wishes of her mother and follow her husband into exile: Valerius says *nec recusavit se ipsam proscribere ut ei fides sua in coniuge proscripto constaret* ('nor was she reluctant to proscribe herself in order that her loyalty to her proscribed husband should stand firm'). *Proscribere* and *proscripto* underscore the gendered anomaly of Sulpicia's actions; by choosing to join her husband in flight, she chooses to write herself into the world of politics. Valerius, therefore, appears to be alert to the paradox represented in his stories of wifely *fides* during the proscriptions, namely that the highest expression of family loyalty involved transcending the divide between domestic and civic life. Although Turia saves her husband by taking him out of his world and into hers, while Sulpicia chooses to give up the gendered privilege of being beyond the reach of politics, the point remains that the political conflict resulting in the proscriptions was one in which domestic virtue had resonances beyond the marital relationship—indeed, beyond the realm of the household entirely.

It is, of course, the irony in these stories that attracts the attention of the compiler and which is imagined to make them appealing to the reader. Yet it is striking that a single moment in Roman history—and, indeed, in relatively recent Roman history, during a time about which Valerius has little else to say[19]—should furnish such a preponderance of this kind of ironic story. Moreover, to the extent that it is possible to construct a coherent narrative of Valerius' soundbite version of Roman history, this vision of the late Republic

[19] Valerius' reluctance to discuss the recent civil wars, and especially Octavian's activities as a triumvir in Rome, has been noted: see Bloomer (1992) 223–9; Freyburger (1998); Weileder (1998) 175–9.

as a time of conflict in and around the domestic sphere finds its counterpart in his understanding of the Empire as a return to 'normal' family life. The first Caesars are repeatedly represented in the *Facta et Dicta Memorabilia* as the saviours and champions of the traditional Roman family.[20] The book is dedicated to Tiberius, who is represented as nurturing and disciplining the nation like a benevolent father (1. pref.), Drusus is praised for having confined his sexual activity to his wife (4. 3. 3), and the love between the two brothers is compared to that between Castor and Pollux (5. 5. 3). The divine Augustus appears less in the context of his own family than that of other people: he gives a son his rightful role as his father's heir (7. 7. 3), in a paternal spirit made clear by Valerius' comment *patris patriae animo usus*;[21] he preserves the inheritance of two others who have been disowned by their mother (7. 7. 4); he refuses to allow an imposter to claim Octavia as his mother (9. 15. 2). Perhaps most notable in this context is the story of the man who, under Sulla, was able to claim Cn. Asinius Dio as his father, displacing the old man's rightful son (9. 15. 5). Valerius comments, 'but after Caesarean justice brought the state back from Sullan violence—the rudder of Roman power having been received by a more just leader—[the fraudulent son] gave up his life into public custody.'[22] The passage from Sullan civil war to imperial peace is represented as that from a false and disturbed family structure to one more just, more stable, and more legitimate. The political change from Republic to Empire is articulated as a change for the better in the patterns and expression of life in the Roman home.

On one level, it is clear that Velleius and Valerius are here simply drawing on the tropes of the historiographical tradition in order to represent the social chaos of the late Republic. The idea that a compromised boundary between public and domestic life is one of

---

[20] Bloomer (1992) 227; Wardle (2000). On the historian's somewhat more nuanced view of Julius Caesar, see Wardle (1997).

[21] 'having employed the spirit of the father of the fatherland'.

[22] *verum postquam a Sullana violentia Caesariana aequitas rem publicam reduxit, gubernacula Romani imperii iustiore principe obtinente, in publica custodia spiritum posuit.*

the hallmarks of civil conflict goes back as far as Thucydides, who, in his narrative of the stasis at Corcyra, remarks on the unorthodox role which the women played: 'the women joined in with them daringly, throwing down tiling from the roofs and sustaining the disturbance in a manner contrary to [their] nature' (αἵ τε γυναῖκες αὐτοῖς τολμηρῶς ξυνεπελάβοντο βάλλουσαι ἀπὸ τῶν οἰκιῶν τῷ κεράμῳ καὶ παρὰ φύσιν ὑπομένουσαι τὸν θόρυβον: Thuc. 3. 74). As has been remarked, the participation of the women here would seem to be part of the profound disturbance of social mores which the historian sees as accompanying civil war;[23] in the same passage, he also notes that both sides in the conflict attempted to recruit slaves from the fields by promising them their freedom (3. 73). What distinguishes Thucydides from the early imperial versions of the history of the late Republic, however, is the extent to which their stories of domestic turmoil come to substitute for the 'real' events of the time. While Thucydides seeks to colour the political and social history of Corcyra with the shocking behaviour of her citizens, Velleius, Valerius, and Appian turn away from the story of the public sphere in order to focus on the private; their tales of the proscriptions, unlike the revolution at Corcyra, are divorced from politics and rendered as narratives of domestic triumphs and tragedies. Moreover, it is worth noting that, whereas Thucydides sees the women's actions at Corcyra explicitly as contrary to what he considers their 'naturally' domestic nature, the stories of the triumviral proscriptions express dependants' actions as arising out of their roles in the household. Thus, we find wives who have adulterous affairs and then turn their husbands over to the triumvirs, the betrayal in the bedroom presaging the betrayal to the court. Similarly, virtuous behaviour is represented as conforming to domestic values in spite of the explosion of politics into the home: Seneca the Younger remarks of a heroic slave, *quanti viri est... in publica crudelitate mitem inveniri, in publica perfidia fidelem!* ('How great a man is this... to be found kind in the face of public cruelty, faithful in the face of public betrayal!': *de Ben.* 3. 25).

---

[23] See Wiedemann (1983) 169.

Tales of domestic behaviour during the triumviral proscriptions thus form a kind of alternative history, expressing a sense of social turmoil without referring to a specific politics—a series of stories about the household which might be told even in the face of unspeakable public horror.

John Henderson has pointed out that the proscriptions must be understood as a historiographical phenomenon as much as anything else, insofar as writing and history on a number of different levels become the central issues of the story.[24] In the first instance, the fact that proscription itself was already a historical phenomenon, primarily associated with Sulla, meant that the subsequent execution lists were read and written about explicitly as a citation—even, if Appian's version of the proscription edict is anything like the original, by the triumvirs themselves. Cassius Dio drums this point particularly hard, noting that Sulla's activities were always on the minds of both triumviral perpetrators and victims, as a model to be outdone on the one hand and an image to be feared on the other. Ancient historians dwell on echoes of the earlier in the later horror, not simply to prove that history repeats itself, but to emphasize the role which history played in producing meaning for the actors within the drama. Thus, when Quintus Lucretius Vespillo is attempting to escape his proscription by the triumvirs, he encounters a troop of guards at the same gate where his father was executed during Sulla's purge; he is so overcome by the coincidence that he faints and almost gives himself away. His reading of his family's history, and of himself as a historical actor, is nearly the death of him. The literal mark, moreover, which proscription made on the historical record was also underscored by the fact that it was itself documentary, a written text whose form, if not its deadly power, might be echoed in the textual product of the later historian: 'Full transcription of the narrative of proscription entangles the writing *of*, with the writing *in*, the account.'[25] The lists of the dead and escaped which appear in Appian and Cassius Dio thus explicitly and ironically reflect the earlier lists

---

[24] Henderson (1998).   [25] Ibid. 30.

which condemned them. The sense of competing authorship between historian and dictator in this context is neatly summed up in
the historian Pollio's joke from the triumviral period: *non est enim
facile in eum scribere qui potest proscribere* ('it isn't easy to write against
someone who can write you up').[26]

Such questions are especially evident in descriptions of the death
of Cicero, which quickly became grist to the mill of historians,
particularly those interested in oratory. Thus, Velleius Paterculus
proclaims that Antony's sentence of death merely ensured that the
fame of Cicero's speeches would last as long as the race of man (2. 66.
5); a fragment of Cornelius Nepos' *de Historicis Latinis* wonders
'whether the Republic or history should mourn his death more.'[27]
Seneca the Elder, declaring Cicero 'the only thing which the Roman
people had to equal its imperial power',[28] expresses the opinion that
the end of his age marked the end of great oratory at Rome: *omnia
ingenia quae lucem studiis nostris attulerunt tunc nata sunt. in deterius
deinde cotidie data res est* ('all genius which was to bring light to our
pursuit was born then. Ever since, the subject has been declining
every day': *Controv.* 1. pref. 7). Indeed, Cicero's death forms the basis
of not one but two of the seven *Suasoriae* preserved in Seneca's
collection, and are the only examples therein drawn from Roman
rather than Greek or Hellenistic history. Again, there is much play on
competitive forms of authorship, especially within the section
devoted to whether Cicero should agree to burn his writings in
exchange for his life, a subject which Seneca seems to think a bit
too emotionally charged on behalf of the writings.[29] Here we find
Argentarius urging, *sine durare post te ingenium tuum, perpetuam
Antonii proscriptionem* ('Allow your genius to endure after your
death as a perpetual proscription of Antony': 7. 8) and, though
Seneca condemns it on stylistic grounds, Pompeius Silo's epigram:

---

[26] Macrobius, *Sat.* 2. 4. 21.

[27] *interitu eius utrum res publica an historia magis doleat* (*de Hist. Lat.* fr. 58).

[28] *quod solum populus Romanus par imperio suo habuit* (*Controv.* 1. pref. 11).

[29] *omnes pro libris Ciceronis solliciti fuerunt, nemo pro ipso* ('Everyone was worried
about Cicero's books but no one about the man himself': *Suas.* 7. 10).

pro facinus indignum! peribit ergo quod Cicero scripsit, manebit quod Antonius proscripsit? ('Oh unworthy crime! So will what Cicero wrote perish, and what Antony wrote survive?': 7. 11). Arellius Fuscus Senior is also reported to have proclaimed, *quoad humanum genus incolume manserit, quamdiu suus litteris honor, suum eloquentiae pretium erit... admirablile posteris vigebit ingenium <tuum>, et uno proscriptus saeculo proscribes Antonium omnibus* ('As long as the human race remains intact, as long as there is due honour to literature, as long as there is the appropriate reward for eloquence... your genius will thrive as a source of wonder to our descendants, and, proscribed for a single generation, you [Cicero] will proscribe Antony for ever': 7. 8).[30]

As this final statement makes most clear, what is imagined by Seneca's speakers to be at issue here is not simply competing claims of authorship, but competing claims on the historical record: whose writing ultimately wins is measured by what story is preserved. This question is thrown into particular relief when we consider the stories of domestic heroism preserved in Valerius Maximus and others, since those who star in them do not otherwise tend to make a mark on history. Valerius, in fact, seems to allude to the issue in several of the stories he tells of the triumviral proscriptions. In his story of Urbinius Panapio, for instance, a slave impersonates his master and is killed in his place by the soldiers sent to execute him (6. 8. 6). Valerius remarks that it isn't actually much of a tale:

brevis huius facti narratio, sed non parva materia laudationis: nam si quis ante oculos ponere velit subitum militum accursum, convulsa ianuae claustra, minacem vocem, truces vultus, fulgentia arma, rem vera aestimatione prosequetur, nec quam cito dicitur aliquem pro alio mori voluisse, tam id ex facili etiam fieri potuisse arbitrabitur. Panapio autem quantum servo deberet amplum ei faciendo monumentum ac testimonium pietatis grato titulo reddendo confessus est.

---

[30] Cf. Martial, *Epigr.* 5. 69. 7–8: *quid prosunt sacrae pretiosa silentia linguae? / incipient omnes pro Cicerone loqui* ('What good does it do, the expensive silence of the holy tongue? Everyone will begin to speak in place of Cicero').

The telling of this deed is short, but it supplies no small amount of material for praise: for if someone should wish to conjure up before his eyes the sudden attack of the soldiers, the shattered bolts of the doors, the threatening yell, the savage faces, the glittering arms, he might proceed through the matter with a fair judgement, nor will it be thought that, as quickly as it can be said that someone has chosen to die for another, so easily is it also able to be done. Panapio, in fact, showed how much he owed to the slave by setting up a grand monument to him and creating a document of his loyalty with a grateful inscription.

The phrase *materia laudationis* does not seem to have been accidentally chosen, since the following description is emphatically visual (*ante oculos*), having something of the air of an ecphrasis in its shattered bolts, savage faces, and glittering arms; it seems just possible that Valerius is actually describing what appeared on Panapio's *amplum . . . monumentum*. At the very least, the picture which Valerius creates sets up the reader for the information that material evidence of the tale exists, courtesy of the surviving master. The *testimonium* which first commemorated the story then finds its echo in Valerius' retelling, each an enduring written and visual record of the heroic slave.

The tale which follows in the *Facta et Dicta Memorabilia* also seems to allude to the ways in which the proscriptions were a time of struggle not only within the social hierarchy but within the hierarchy of writing and record-keeping. This is the final example which Valerius offers under the heading of *Fides*, and he does so noting that he would have been satisfied with the list, 'except that admiration for the deed forced me to add one more': *contentus essem huius exemplis generis, nisi unum me [a]dicere admiratio facti cogeret* (6. 8. 7). He goes on to tell at some length the story of Antius Restio, proscribed by the triumvirs, whose slave hid his master and deceived the soldiers who came looking for him. In outline, this tale is no different from the others which have survived from the proscriptions, but what makes the story most remarkable to Valerius' mind is the fact that this was a slave who had been subjected to the harshest punishments, *ab eo vinculorum poena coercitus, inexpiabilique litter-*

arum nota per summam oris contumeliam inustus ('punished by [Restio] with chains, and burned with an inexpiable trace of letters to mark his extreme humiliation on his face').[31] Nevertheless, he assisted his master in his time of need (6. 8. 7):

iis enim quorum felicior in domo status fuerat lucro intentis, ipse, nihil aliud quam umbra et imago suppliciorum suorum, maximum esse emolumentum eius a quo tam graviter punitus erat salutem iudicavit.

For, while those whose position in the household had been more fortunate were intent on monetary profit, he himself—who was nothing other than a shadow and representation of his punishments—judged that the greatest gain was to be found in the safety of the man by whom he had been so terribly punished.

The phrase *nihil aliud quam umbra et imago suppliciorum suorum* is particularly striking, and underscores the fact that the slave had been branded, rendering him literally readable as a servant who did not respect the hierarchy of the household. Indeed, when the executioners finally turn up, the slave manages to convince them that he has killed the master himself, in revenge for the punishment whose traces he bears on his face. The irony of the story, therefore, lies not only in the way that the slave repays poor treatment with good, but also in the mis-writing and subsequent mis-reading of the brand on his forehead: although he has been labelled by his master, and is understood by the soldiers, as a bad slave, he actually acts like a good one. His heroic behaviour and its record in Valerius' text have thus redeemed him from the earlier *inexpiabili . . . litterarum nota* which marked his body.

---

[31] The use of the word *inexpiabilis* to describe the mark of the brand is curious, since it does not elsewhere mean, as we would like it here, 'indelible'. In Cicero (*Tusc.* 1. 27 and *Rep.* 3. 19) we find it used of punishments for religious offences which cannot be resolved in any other way. I suspect, although I am not willing to argue it here, that the word refers to Restio's behaviour in branding the slave, rather than to the offence which the slave committed to earn the brand, since the focus of the story is on the cruelty of the master rather than the misbehaviour of the servant. The story which the slave subsequently offers the soldiers, moreover, is that *ibi illum datis sibi crudelitatis piaculis uri* ('[his master] was burned there in atonement for the cruelty done to himself')—the word *piaculis* picking up the *inexpiabilis* from before.

The story of this slave, in fact, reappears numerous times in the literary and historical record as one of the most paradigmatic examples of slave-heroism during the triumviral proscriptions. Martial refers to him in a somewhat enigmatic epigram: *proscriptum famulus servavit fronte notata. / non fuit haec domini vita, sed invidia* ('A slave with a branded forehead saved a proscribed man. This did not give life to his master, but resentment.': 3. 21). The second line is too compressed for clarity (Bridge and Lake's 1908 commentary glosses it as 'what he really gave his master, however, was not life but the hatred of men for one who could so treat a faithful slave', p. 57) though the sound play between *vita* and *invidia* appears to be the joke. More interesting for our purposes, though, are the first and last words in line 1, which play on the contrast between the proscription edict and the brand on the slave's forehead.[32] The emphasis here is on the mutual victimization of master and slave by writing, with the added ironic circumstance that the master was the original 'author' of the slave's suffering. Thus, in Appian, the slave says to the soldiers, Ῥεστίωνα...ἔκτεινα, τὸν ἐμαυτοῦ δεσπότην, τάδε μοι τὰ στίγματα ἐγχαράξαντα ('I have killed Restio, my master, the man who inscribed these marks on me': *BC* 4. 43). We may certainly see in this story a kind of psychological palliative to the slave-owning Romans,[33] in that it insists that even one who has been treated poorly will remain loyal to his master in a crisis. But the fact that Restio goes from the one who writes (the brand on the slave) to the one who is written about (by the triumvirs in the proscription edict) is also part of the exchange of roles between domestic dependant and *paterfamilias* which characterizes the historiography of the period. And although Restio's name is the only one preserved in the story, it is, as Martial's epigram makes clear, the slave who is its hero. The

---

[32] In his retelling of the story, Macrobius makes the same joke, writing, *Antium enim Restionem* proscriptum...*servus compeditus* inscripta *fronte*...*fugientem persecutus est*...('when Antius Restio was *proscribed*...a shackled slave with an *inscribed* forehead...pursued him as he ran...': *Sat.* 1. 11. 19). The story also appears in Cassius Dio (47. 10. 4).

[33] Which is the argument of Parker (1998).

master might just as well have died for all the historical credit his
continued life produced.

The triumviral proscriptions were not, of course, the only moment in Roman history which supplied tales of heroic slaves, but
they do produce a surprising volume of examples—examples which
then go on to have a remarkable purchase on the literary and
historical record. The story of Antius Restio's slave, for instance, is
still in circulation at the time of Macrobius, writing in the early fifth
century, and is still explicitly identified with the triumviral proscriptions (*Sat.* 1. 11. 19). In this sense, the question which seems to
haunt the stories discussed above, namely who writes and who is
written into history, is clearly answered by the later textual record:
'insignificant' people emerge as heroes while elite men fade into
insignificance. The fact that it is women and slaves who figure
most prominently in the proscription stories does not seem accidental. These were the two principal categories against whom elite male
identity was measured in Graeco-Roman culture: on a fundamental
level, a free man was defined by his ability to rule over the subordinate members of his household.[34] Women and slaves are thus, in a
sense, the traditional 'set dressing' of standard history, whose presence served to bolster the elite male's ability to represent himself as
such. Their emergence, then, in the proscription tales serves not only
to underscore the irony of the master's disempowerment, but to
mark a shift in the focus of stories about the past, from the traditionally foregrounded public sphere to the domestic which had
always lain quietly behind.

Indeed, Sir Ronald Syme rather famously theorized that the stories
'went a long way towards compensating the lack of prose fiction
among the Romans'.[35] Such a description underscores the extent to
which the proscription narratives do not fit neatly into traditional
modes of writing about the Roman past; while they purport to be

[34] See Joshel and Murnaghan (1998*a*). Fitzgerald (2000: esp. 69–86) discusses the
ways in which the Romans continually used the image and idea of the slave to 'think
through' other kinds of social relations.
[35] Syme (1939) 190 n. 6.

historical records of actual events, their moralizing tone, stylized narratives, and stereotyped characters all seem to be drawn from a different, more fictional, genre. In part, of course, this is because of where we find them: Valerius Maximus' compendium, for instance, is a work which continuously and deliberately walks the line between the real and the imaginary, in an effort to create a moral, rather than narrative, history of the world.[36] Yet even 'real' historians—Velleius Paterculus, Appian, Cassius Dio, and the 'many others' who have not survived—see the proscription tales as expressing a kind of truth about triumviral history, a truth which has less to do with the facts they communicate and more with the way they express the general spirit of the age.[37] There was clearly something difficult about writing about the triumvirs, a difficulty which comes to be expressed in how the boundaries of 'the historical' are defined. It is not, however, only in stories about the proscriptions that we may see this process in operation; we may also see it delineated in texts much closer to the chronological site of the action, texts which are not, strictly speaking, 'histories' of the period but which also attempt, in their own terms, to define what can and should be remembered of the triumviral age. In the next section, I will consider two of these texts.

EFFICACIOUS VIRTUE: PRIVACY AND TRIUMVIRAL POLITICS

Cornelius Nepos' biography of Titus Pomponius Atticus is one of the few pieces of Latin prose to have survived from the Second Triumvirate, and it has been described as 'one of the best introduc-

---

[36] For a comparison of Valerius' exempla history with the continuous narrative style of Velleius Paterculus, see Jacquemin (1998). Cf. Maslakov (1984).

[37] As C. J. Carter (1975: 39–40) notes, 'But if Valerius has little value to the historian of events, he has something to contribute to the historian of ideas, providing evidence of a first-century attitude to the past, the manner and quality of that understanding and the uses to which it was put.' Cf. Weileder (1998) 28–38; Coudry (1998).

tions to the period'.[38] Mostly written before Atticus' death in March 32 BCE, the text was produced as one of Nepos' *Vitae* of Roman historians, of which only the unfortunately abbreviated *Cato* also survives.[39] The *Atticus* is unique on a number of different levels: the only biography of an *eques* in all of Roman literature; the only fully-fledged description of a career which spanned all of the great civil conflicts of the first century BCE; the only depiction of Atticus from a point of view other than Cicero's. It is clear, moreover, even discounting the worshipful perspective of his friend and biographer, that Atticus was a singularly important figure in the politics of the late Republic, having befriended just about every important personage from Sulla to Octavian. His daughter was married to Octavian's right-hand man Agrippa, a match rather surprisingly arranged by Antony during the Triumvirate; his granddaughter was engaged at a very young age to the future emperor Tiberius. Such familial alliances under the Republic were powerful signs of social standing and political influence, and Nepos adds in his postscript (written shortly after his subject's death) that *both* Antony and Octavian were careful to keep Atticus abreast of their activities during their war with one another: *numquam ad suorum quemquam litteras misit quin Attico scriberet quid ageret, in primis quid legeret quibusque in locis et quam diu esset moraturus... neque vero a M. Antonio minus absens litteris colebatur* ('[Octavian] never sent a letter to one of his friends without writing to Atticus about what he was doing, in particular what he was reading, to what places he was going and how long he was going to stay there... nor was he any less cultivated by Mark Antony through letters, even though they were far apart': Nep. *Att.* 20. 1). Even Nepos seems a little surprised by Atticus' ability to maintain such intimacy with both sides: 'The significance of this will be more easily seen by one who is able to judge how much wisdom it requires to

---

[38] Millar (1988) 40.
[39] On the connection between Nepos' *Lives of the Foreign Generals* (as well as, to a lesser extent, the rest of his work) and contemporary politics, see Dionisotti (1988).

maintain the intimacy and goodwill of these men ... when they each desired to be the leader not only of Rome but of the entire world'.[40]

Atticus' enduring influence with public figures is particularly striking since it appears that he never held public office, a point which Nepos goes out of his way to stress: *neque ... se civilibus fluctibus committeret, quod non magis eos in sua potestate existimabat esse qui se his dedissent, quam qui maritimis iactarentur* ('he would not entrust himself to the ups and downs of politics, because he judged that those who gave themselves up to them were not any more in control of their own lives than those who were tossed about on the sea': 6. 1). This statement is followed by an almost comical *cursus honorum* in the negative, in which Nepos details all of the things which Atticus did not do in public life (6. 3–4).

honores non petiit. ... ad hastam publicam numquam accessit. nullius rei neque praes neque manceps factus est. neminem neque suo nomine neque subscribens accusavit, in ius de sua re numquam iit, iudicium nullum habuit. multorum consulum praetorumque praefecturas delatas sic accepit, ut neminem in provinciam sit secutus.

He did not seek offices. ... He never went to a public auction of property. He did not act as a guarantor or agent in any matter. He did not prosecute anyone, either under his own name or as a joint prosecutor, he never went to court over his own property, he never conducted a trial. He did accept the post of prefect, offered to him by numerous consuls and praetors, but only under the condition that he did not have to follow anyone to his province.[41]

Indeed, the overriding theme of the biography is Atticus' role as a private citizen, a friend to all and an enemy to none. This trend was established early on in Atticus' career, when he retreated to Greece rather than join either Sulla's or Cinna's camp; when Sulla—*captus*

---

[40] *Hoc quale sit, facilius existimabit is qui iudicare poterit quantae sit sapientiae eorum retinere usum benevolentiamque ... cum se uterque principem non solum urbis Romae sed orbis terrarum esse cuperet* (20. 5).

[41] i.e. the appointment in Atticus' case was purely honorary, since the only place such a prefect could exercise authority was in the province to which he had been assigned (Horsfall (1989) 71).

adulescentis et humanitate et doctrina[42]—subsequently arrived in Athens, Atticus entertained him with conversation and poetry but politely declined his offer to accompany him on his return to Italy. Later, back in Rome, Atticus remained similarly neutral during Caesar's conflict with Pompey, during the chaotic aftermath of Caesar's assassination, during the triumviral period, and, as we have seen, during the final conflict between Antony and Octavian. A paradigmatic episode occurred during the brief moment in 44 BCE when the tyrannicides had the upper hand and a friend of Brutus came to Atticus for a contribution to their cause. Atticus, however, declined: *at ille, qui officia amicis praestanda sine factione existimaret semperque a talibus se consiliis removisset, respondit: si quid Brutus de suis facultatibus uti voluisset, usurum quantum eae paterentur, sed neque cum quoquam de ea re collocuturum neque coiturum* ('But he, in as much as he judged that obligations to friends ought to be carried out without joining a faction, and had always kept himself aloof from such plans, replied that if Brutus should wish to make use of any of his possessions, he might employ them to their limit, but that he himself would not meet or conspire with anyone about this matter': 8. 4).

The phrase *officia amicis . . . sine factione* neatly sums up the character which Nepos attributes to Atticus: again and again throughout the biography we are shown the hero performing acts of 'friendship' which might have been construed as political were he not so resolutely a private individual. Whether this was merely the product of a modest personality or a more calculated stance is an open question, even within Nepos' admiring biography. We are told that Atticus was particularly kind to Antony's wife Fulvia during Antony's enforced absence from Rome, since 'he judged it the greatest advantage to be recognized as thoughtful and grateful and at the same time for it to be apparent that he was accustomed to be a friend, not just to the fortunate, but to all humankind' (*maximum existimans quaestum*

---

[42] 'captivated by the urbanity and learning of the youth' (4. 1).

memorem gratumque cognosci simulque aperire se non fortunae, sed hominibus solere esse amicum: 9. 5). Nepos quickly follows up this statement with a protestation that his hero was not thinking of the future—after all, at the time, no one thought Antony would be restored to power (9. 6)—but the sense of rather chilling calculation remains in *maximum existimans quaestum . . . hominibus solere esse amicum*. And, indeed, during the proscriptions, when his wealth and close relationship with Cicero made him a target, his earlier services to Antony's family saved him from harm (10. 4); this enabled him, in turn, to save others (12. 3). Again, however, Nepos stresses that his hero's activities on behalf of the proscribed were purely personal both in motivation and execution: *nulla in re usus sit ea, nisi in deprecandis amicorum aut periculis aut incommodis. quod quidem sub ipsa proscriptione perillustre fuit* ('he never used his influence except to intercede against the dangers or inconveniences of his friends. This was especially evident during the time of the proscriptions': 12. 2–3).

The fact that Atticus is, on the one hand, saved by his association with Fulvia, and, on the other, able himself to use his identity as a non-political individual to preserve the lives of others, fits well with what we have seen of the historiography of the triumviral proscriptions in other texts, where the strength of private loyalties and familial associations become the most important part of the story. In fact, Nepos' continued insistence on Atticus' refusal of public life in favour of domestic tranquillity—a refusal belied by his obvious influence over the statesmen and generals around him—almost seems like the historiography of the proscriptions writ large, as, like the slaves and wives in Valerius Maximus, Atticus' separation from civic life gives him a kind of power over those within it. The connection which the biography makes between Atticus and Fulvia, and later between Atticus and Brutus' mother Servilia (11. 4), is telling in this context. Both women were among the great republican matrons whose relationships with important men gave them real standing and influence over events in the public sphere, especially during times when the situation in the capital was too volatile to hold their husbands or sons.[43] Thus, for instance, Servilia appears in several letters of Cicero working both with and on behalf of her son after the dramatic events of 44 BCE: writing to Brutus of a meeting in July of 43 to discuss whether the tyrannicides should bring their armies to Italy, Cicero called her 'a very wise and industrious woman, whose attention is always turned to you'.[44] Fulvia, similarly, was a powerful figure, in ways that made her distinctly unpopular in the later historical record; indeed, during the very time[45] that Nepos has Atticus comfort her as she was 'harassed by lawsuits and troubled by great worries' (*litibus distineretur magnisque terroribus vexaretur.* 9. 4), Appian offers a vivid account of her attempts to pressure the votes of senators on behalf of her husband (*BC* 3. 51). There is, in other words, a certain irony embedded in Nepos' account of Atticus' non-politicized sphere of influence, especially after 44, since, by turning to the womenfolk of the various political players, he appears to have turned to where much of the real power lay.

The parallel which may be drawn between Atticus and certain triumviral women is not, I think, accidental. By this I do not mean that Nepos wishes to 'feminize' Atticus, although on some level this is exactly what he does. But I would say instead that the biography makes an overall point about triumviral politics, and the way in which they would be remembered, by foregrounding not just women but a man who refused the roles which had long defined elite Roman males. Atticus' rejection of the sphere where Roman men traditionally proved their masculinity should have made him rather suspect, especially placed in Nepos' book alongside heroes such as Cato, who 'was an intelligent farmer, an experienced

---

[43] For a number of different reasons—some political, some economic, some (I would argue) historiographical—certain elite women appear prominently in the historical record of the late Republic. Although it is clear that, in real historical terms, women did achieve a certain poistion of prominence in this period, it is also important to recognize the 'great republican matron' as a historiographical trope. See Dixon (1983) on the history; Hillard (1989) and (1992) on the historiography.

[44] *prudentissima et diligentissima femina . . . cuius omnes curae ad te referuntur* (*ad Brut.* 24. 1).

[45] i.e. in the winter of 44–43 BCE.

advocate in law, a great general, a persuasive orator, and a great lover of literature'.[46] Atticus, on the other hand, pursued what Nepos calls at one point *quies tantopere Caesari...grata* ('a quietude...most pleasing to Caesar': Nep. *Att.* 7. 3), yet was not absent from the business of politics due to laziness but rather because of a reasoned choice.[47] The public sphere is a stormy sea (10. 6); Atticus judged it better to remain within the world of private, individual relationships and not take a chance by joining one side or the other. But his choice not to choose is understood not as cowardice or indecision, but as expressing an allegiance to a higher set of values. Like those of the women discussed above, his loyalties are constructed in Nepos' biography as originating from personal virtues untainted by the touch of politics: friendship, kindness, love, mercy. And like those women also, Atticus not only survived (as so many others did not) but managed to throw his net of protection around others whose political choices had brought them to the brink of personal destruction.

The 'domestic politics' of the period, then, meant both that someone whose natural place was in public life could make a statement by refusing to participate, but also that someone whose natural place was in the home could make a statement by acting in public life. The extent to which this was true is visible in the stories of domestic heroism during the proscriptions which I have discussed above, but also, and more dramatically, in a text known as the *laudatio Turiae*, recognized as perhaps the closest parallel to Nepos' life of Atticus to have survived.[48] The *laudatio* is a lengthy, although now fragmentary, funerary inscription set up sometime during the last two decades BCE by a husband to commemorate his wife; the names of both *laudator* and *laudata* are unfortunately lost, and the early attempt to associate the pair with Q. Lucretius Vespillo and his wife Turia, known to us from a story of the proscriptions in

---

[46] *et agricola sollers et peritus iuris consultus et magnus imperator et probabilis orator et cupidissimus litterarum fuit* (*Cato* 3. 1).

[47] *iudicari poterat non inertia, sed iudicio fugisse rei publicae procurationem* (*Att.* 15. 3).

[48] Millar (1988) 42.

Valerius Maximus and Appian, has been largely discredited.[49]
Nevertheless, it is clear that the life commemorated spans the
triumviral period, and, indeed, it is the triumviral period which
looms largest in the inscription. There is a surprising amount of
information provided in the text about the political situation in
Rome between Caesar's invasion of Italy and the end of the Second
Triumvirate—surprising because women's epitaphs generally do not
embed themselves strongly in their particular historical moment.
The kinds of domestic values usually praised in women are transhistorical, or are at least imagined to be so:[50] in the famous funeral
epitaph of Murdia, as I noted in the Introduction, the dead woman's
son is rather apologetic for having to repeat the same catalogue of
virtues found in this context everywhere else.

The *laudatio Turiae* does not lack similar praise of domestic
virtues, including the omnipresent woolworking. Yet the *laudator*
goes on to insist that there is a great deal more to be said about his
wife than such a catalogue encompasses (1. 30–6).

domestica bona pudici[t]iae, opsequi, comitatis, facilitatis, lanificii stud[i,
religionis] sine superstitione, o[r]natus non conspiciendi, cultus modici cur
[memorem? Cur dicam de tuorum cari]tate, famlliae pietate, [c]um ... cetera innumerabilia habueris commun[ia cum omnibus] matronis dignam
f[a]mam colentibus? Propria sunt tua quae vindico, ac [perpaucae in
tempora] similia inciderunt, ut talia paterentur et praestarent, quae rara
ut essent [mulierum] fortuna cavit.[51]

    [49] See Horsfall (1983) 91–2.
    [50] Forbis (1990), in fact, argues that the Empire saw a significant shift in the kinds of
female values praised in 'public' inscriptions, as there developed a vocabulary for
describing women as benefactors and patrons.
    [51] It is a great pity that we are missing the word between *essent* and *fortuna*, as well as
those between *ac* and *similia* in the earlier line. Editors have been torn between making
these statements about the lot of human beings in general and restricting them to women;
thus, Mommsen in *CIL* suggested *ac [quorum pauci in] similia inciderunt ... quae rara ut
essent [hominum] fortuna cavit*, while Wistrand (1976: 20, 39) offers what I have here. My
feeling is that, given the sentences preceding are explicitly concerned with the virtues
which the *laudata* displayed as a woman and a wife, it makes better sense for the closing
statements to continue to speak in gendered terms. It may also be noted that the *laudatio
Murdiae* contains a similar statement emphasizing the scarcity of opportunities for

Why should I mention your domestic virtues of modesty, obedience, kindness, affability, enthusiasm for spinning, piety without superstition, adornment without ostentation, and moderate refinement? Why should I speak about your affection for your relatives and your devotion to your family... when you had all the rest of the innumerable virtues in common with all married women who seek to preserve a worthy reputation? The virtues which I celebrate are your very own, and very few women have fallen into similar times, such that they might suffer through and triumph over circumstances like these, which the fortune of women is careful to make unusual.

The traditional *domestica bona* are held up in implicit contrast with the other, more particular, virtues which the inscription goes on to celebrate, virtues which are imagined to have been the product of the times through which the pair was forced to live. Thus, for instance, when the husband was first forced into exile, probably during the civil war between Caesar and Pompey in 49–48,[52] the wife provided for his needs by sending him her jewellery;[53] she also personally interceded with those in power to effect his return (2. 6a–8a). She then, rather remarkably, appears to have defended the couple's property from a crowd of thugs organized by Milo, whose house had been bought by the husband after Milo's exile from Rome in 52. Such house-sieges were not uncommon in the late Republic, particularly during the messy riots of the late 50s, but this is the only instance in which we find a woman actually holding off the attackers: it makes a particularly concrete example of the extent to which civil conflict not only compromised the boundary between the home and the world of politics, but also made it necessary for domestic actors to take part in events connected with public life.

women to display exemplary virtue. Flach's (1991: 86–7) supplement of *propitia* to describe *fortuna* seems to me to have little to recommend it: where the noun appears elsewhere in the speech (2. 27), it is unmodified by an adjective, and given that the point here seems to be to emphasize the wife's resolution in the face of adversity, it would ring strangely ironic to describe fortune as 'well-disposed'.

[52] Durry (1950) 60.

[53] *ornamentis [vitam meam instruxisti,] cum omne aurum margaritaque corpori [tuo detracta trad]idisti mihi* (2. 2a–4a).

There is a section missing between the wife's defence of the couple's property and what follows, but we can construe that the *laudator*, or the *laudata* on his behalf, was able to negotiate a recall to Rome. Unfortunately, following Caesar's assassination, either his wealth or political associations appear to have caused him to run foul of the triumvirs and he found himself among the proscribed. Although the *laudator* does not mention proscription per se, the implication is clear: *Quid nunc interiora [no]stra et recondita consilia s[e]rmonesque arcanos eruam? ut repentinis nu[n]tiis ad praesentia et inminentia pericula evocatus tuis consiliis cons[er]vatus sim? ut neque audac[i]us experiri casus temere passa sis et mod[es]tiora cogitanti fidu receptacula pararis?*... ('Why now would I drag into the open our secret and hidden plans and our covert talks? When, roused up by sudden revelations of immediate and threatening danger, I was preserved by your advice? When you did not allow me rashly to attempt a bolder design and, when I had resigned myself to a more circumspect approach, prepared a safe hiding place?...': 2. 4–7). Here we indeed seem to have a real instance of the kind of connubial heroism described in such detail by later authors, although the *laudata* not only spirits her husband away to safety, but actually attempts to intercede with Lepidus on his behalf. The scene is vividly depicted (2. 12–21):

Reddito me iam] cive patriae beneficio et i[ud]icio apsentis Caesaris Augusti, [quom abs te ----] de restitutione mea M. L[epi]dus conlega praesens interp[ellaretur et ad eius] pedes prostrata humi n[on] modo non adlevata, sed tra[ducta et indignum in] modum rapsata, livori[bus c]orporis repleta, firmissimo [animo eum admone]res edicti Caesaris cum g[r]atulatione restitutionis me[ae atque vocibus eti]am contumeliosis et cr[ud]elibus exceptis volneribus pa[llam conquereris,] ut auctor meorum peric[ul]orum notesceret.... Quid hac virtute efficaciu[s], praebere Caesari clementia[e locum et cum cu]stodia spiritus mei not[a]re inportunam cudelitatem [Lepidi firma tua] patientia? Quoi no[cuit mox ea res].

After I had been restored as a citizen of my country through the kindness and good judgement of Caesar Augustus while he was still absent, you confronted his associate M. Lepidus, who was present in Rome, about my

return. As you lay prostrate on the ground at his feet, not only were you not
helped up, but you were dragged away and pushed out in an undignified
way; but even though your body was covered in bruises, you reminded him
with the most stalwart spirit about Caesar's edict and congratulations on
my restoration, and although you experienced insulting words and cruel
wounds, you spoke openly about your sufferings so that the one responsible
for my tribulations should be known.... What could have been more
efficacious than this [display of] virtue, as you provided Caesar the opportunity to show his kindness and, at the same time that you took care of my
continued existence, you illustrated by your unceasing forbearance the
perverse cruelty of Lepidus? This matter was soon to do him harm.

We know that the inscription was put up well after the accession of
Augustus, and it is therefore not surprising that the *laudator* here
conforms neatly to the imperial line on the proscriptions, so that
Lepidus appears as the real villain, acting on his own against his
colleague's wishes. The idea that Lepidus' behaviour in this situation
was one factor in his fall seems likely to be a rhetorical embellishment, but the wife's role in 'publishing' his treatment of her underscores the paradoxical effect which her loyalty to her husband has had
on events in the public sphere—more effective because of her virtue
(*virtute efficacius*), indeed.

   The *laudatio Turiae* thus provides a parallel not only for the stories
of domestic heroism which characterize the triumviral period in later
histories, but also for the kind of 'efficacious virtue' which Nepos
attributes to Atticus: both Atticus and the *laudata* are outside the
sphere in which the political battles of the late Republic were fought,
the former by choice and the latter by necessity. But private virtue—
Atticus' role as a good friend and the *laudata's* role as a good wife—is
under these historical circumstances translated into political gain.
Indeed, it transpires that only the most 'private' of citizens is able to
act publicly. Atticus did not survive to see the Principate, so we
cannot know what Nepos might have said about his behaviour under
different historical circumstances; it is interesting in this context,
however, that the *laudatio* takes a turn to the domestic at the
moment of Augustus' triumph. At 2. 25, the *laudator* notes *pacato*

orbe terrarum, res[titut]a re publica, quieta deinde n[obis et felicia]
tempora contigerunt ('When the world had been made peaceful, and
the Republic restored, we passed into quiet and happy times'), after
which the speaker dwells principally on the distress occasioned by
the couple's inability to have children. The introductory language
strongly echoes official descriptions of the transition to imperial rule
(the *pax Romana*, the restored Republic, and the happy prosperity of
the Augustan age are all ideological staples of the time) which is one
way in which the speech is clearly a product of its own historical
moment.[54] But perhaps more subtly, the fact that the wife is represented as now free to concern herself with motherhood, having put
her activities during the triumviral period behind her, also neatly
accords with the official Augustan version of what the new state
brought to the Roman home. Women like the *laudata*, who were
forced out of their homes by the turmoil of civil war, are now
returned to them; families in danger of collapse under the pressure
of politics are reconstituted as domestic units once again. This is not
to say that such a narrative does not, on some level, reflect a kind of
historical truth. The point is that both the threat to the home during
the Triumvirate and its resolution by the Principate are ideologically
overdetermined symbols, so that to tell, and retell, such a historical
truth is part of reinforcing a particular vision of present reality.

QUARE EST SECUTA VIRUM? RHETORICAL
'HISTORY' AND CIVIL WAR

It is perhaps the dramatic quality of the husband's voice which has,
until very recently, allowed the *laudatio Turiae* to go largely uncriti-
cized as a transparent document of social life during the mid-first
century BCE. By this I do not mean that it has escaped the notice
of historians, who have long mined the text for information on

---

[54] For parallels with contemporary history and literature, see Cutolo (1983/4). Cf.
Saller (2001) 103–4.

everything from Roman inheritance law to the popularity of Stoic philosophy. But it is only in the past decade that scholars have begun to take seriously its generic context, namely the fact that, before it was an inscription, it was a speech. This is made clear not only by the style and tone of the document but also by the author's repeated reference to it as an *oratio* (e.g. *ultimum huius orationis*: 2. 67). Although it has survived to us as a written document, therefore, it actually emerges from the oratorical tradition which lay close to the heart of Roman republican political culture. Scholars have long recognized the role which such funerary speeches played as 'historical' documents, first performed in public contexts and then preserved in family archives or as part of monuments.[55] Cicero and Livy, however, both complain that such texts play a significant role in the falsification of history because of the rhetorical embellishment to which they were prone, testifying to both the value and danger in taking *laudationes* as elements of 'real' history. As Cicero notes, it is not just individual family histories which are at stake, but the larger picture of the Roman past: *his laudationibus historia rerum nostrarum est facta mendosior* ('because of these speeches of praise, our common history has been rendered somewhat false': *Brut.* 62). It is clear, moreover, that such speeches could be real and important vehicles of not just personal but political propaganda, even when delivered on behalf of women: I have already mentioned Julius Caesar's oration on his aunt Julia, in which he made the connection between his family and Venus; we do not know the content of Cicero's *laudatio* for Cato's sister Porcia, but the fact that Atticus distributed copies to Brutus and Domitius Ahenobarbus makes it appear to be more significant than a simple speech.[56]

Of course, the *laudatio Turiae*, and its hero and heroine, did not participate in contemporary politics to the same extent as these last examples. My point is, however, that we ought to see the text as both creating and being created by the same kinds of cultural *mythoi*

---

[55] Crawford (1941/2). On the close relationship between rhetoric and history, especially in the works of Cicero, see Cape (1997).
[56] Cic., *ad Att.* 13. 37. 3, 48. 2. Cf. Horsfall (1983) 89–90.

which gave shape and meaning to the proscription tales found in authors such as Valerius Maximus. Those cultural *mythoi*, I would maintain, encompass a certain kind of imperial politics, which may not be as transparent as Julius Caesar's claim to descent from Venus, but are still just as real. Like those tales, the *laudatio*, as well as Nepos' biography of Atticus, function as a kind of para-history, refracting the story of events in the public sphere through the experiences of private individuals, and creating a narrative which focuses on the domestic rather than the civic, the moral rather than the political. Yet this is as much a representational as a real effect, a phenomenon whose traces may be seen as much in the way such stories are told as in what they tell. Despite apparent attempts on the part of the imperial house to censor, or at least control, the history of the period, stories about Rome's experiences under the triumvirs continued to circulate, but the disruption in both history and historiography is evident. Women, and slaves, and private men like Atticus, emerge in the story of the triumviral period as heroes both because the actual social boundaries between public and private life had been compromised, and because traditional modes of historical writing were forced to give place to a different idea of who and what made history.

An additional and, I would argue, significant example of both effects may be found in the story of Hortensia, scion of a famous republican oratorical family. The fullest version of the tale is found in Appian, who uses it along with the story of Lepidus' triumph to provide a kind of 'breathing space' in the middle of his catalogue of proscription tales.[57] In 42 BCE, short of the money they needed to fund the war effort against Brutus and Cassius, the triumvirs imposed a tax on 1,400 of the wealthiest women in Rome. This act incensed the *matronae*, who appealed to the wives and mothers of Octavian and Antony. Dismissed by Antony's wife Fulvia, they made their way into the Forum, where the triumvirs were conducting business. Hortensia, who had been selected as the spokesperson for the women, then addressed the tribunal, delivering a speech which,

[57] Gowing (1992) 259–60.

at least in the version preserved in Appian, drums the issue of separate public and private spheres hard. Fundamentally, she argues, the tax imposed by the triumvirs is wrong, not just because it would rob women of their financial independence, but because by robbing them it transgresses the traditional boundary between the world of men and that of women:

ὑμεῖς δ' ἡμᾶς ἀφείλεσθε μὲν ἤδη γονέας τε καὶ παῖδας καὶ ἄνδρας καὶ ἀδελφοὺς ἐπικαλοῦντες, ὅτι πρὸς αὐτῶν ἠδικήσθε· εἰ δὲ καὶ τὰ χρήματα προσαφέλοισθε, περιστήσετε ἐς ἀπρέπειαν ἀναξίαν γένους καὶ τρόπων καὶ φύσεως γυναικείας. εἰ μὲν δή τι καὶ πρὸς ἡμῶν, οἷον ὑπὸ τῶν ἀνδρῶν, ἠδικῆσθαί φατε, προγράψατε καὶ ἡμᾶς ὡς ἐκείνους. εἰ δὲ οὐδένα ὑμῶν αἱ γυναῖκες οὔτε πολέμιον ἐψηφισάμεθα οὔτε καθείλομεν οἰκίαν ἢ στρατὸν διεφθείραμεν ἢ ἐπηγάγομεν ἕτερον ἢ ἀρχῆς ἢ τιμῆς τυχεῖν ἐκωλύσαμεν, τί κοινωνοῦμεν τῶν κολάσεων αἱ τῶν ἀδικημάτων οὐ μετασχοῦσαι;   (App. *BC* 4. 32)

You have already taken from us our fathers, our sons, our husbands, and our brothers, whom you claim have committed crimes against you; if you remove our property as well, you will degrade us to a position unworthy of our station, our customs, and our womanly nature. If you say that you have been wronged in some way by us, just as by our husbands, proscribe us as you did them. But if, being women, we have not voted to make any of you an outlaw, have not demolished your houses, have not destroyed your armies nor led one against you, have not prevented you from gaining offices or honours—why then are we to share the punishments, we who did not take part in the crimes?

Hortensia is not here asking for the vote. Indeed, she is arguing the exact opposite point, that the separate spheres of men and women should protect the wealthy matrons of Rome from punitive taxes such as the triumvirs have imposed. Like Valerius in his speech on the repeal of the *lex Oppia*, moreover, Hortensia here represents economic independence as one of the fundamental rights of the female sex at Rome: she goes on to note that, certainly, women in the past have offered their jewellery to save the state, but then they did it voluntarily and not under the threat of violence. More to the point, she adds, while the women would be happy to contribute to a war against a foreign power, they have no intention of supporting the current civil conflict, as they have not supported any of those in the recent or more distant past.[58] She concludes, bitingly, that even Sulla the tyrant did not tax Roman women, while, on the other hand, '*you say that you are restoring the Republic*' (ὑμεῖς δέ φατε καὶ καθίστασθαι τὴν πολιτείαν: *BC* 4. 33). This last seems especially pointed in light of later ideology: Augustus' restoration would indeed advertise itself as a return to the traditional divide between public and private life, even though (as I have argued) that advertisement itself encompassed the paradox of using domestic life for political ends. But while Hortensia's statement at first seems like a particularly nasty dig at Octavian-as-triumvir, the assumption which lies behind it is completely in keeping with Augustan ideology. For Hortensia, as in later days under the Principate, one of the signs of good government is the ability of domestic life to be beyond the reach of politics.

Hortensia's speech in Appian thus serves to underscore the historian's point about what made the triumviral period in Rome so terrible, namely the disintegration of the boundary between public and private life. Hortensia's paradoxical position—that she stands up in a public assembly to defend her own exclusion from public life—has been made necessary by the prior transgression represented by the proposed tax. The triumvirs were not content with taking the lives and fortunes of those whose gender made them fair game, and so have proceeded to cross over the line which ought to separate men from women, civic from domestic, that which is vulnerable to the turmoil of civil war from that which must remain untouched. In response, she and her crowd of women have been forced to invade the Forum. Hortensia's emergence into the public sphere, however, is not limited to the fact that she stood forth and addressed the tribunal in 42 BCE. In fact, her transgression continues to be enacted repeatedly in the historical record, not just in the ways that she is embraced by Roman history, but as she becomes a heroine of Roman oratory. We are told by Quintilian that her speech before the triumvirs was

[58] They gave money neither to Caesar nor Pompey, Marius nor Cinna (*BC* 4. 33).

preserved, read, and admired by later generations, and not just, he adds, because it has the novelty of being by a woman (*Inst.* 1. 1. 6). Valerius Maximus is similarly admiring: although he condemns two other examples of 'women who pleaded before magistrates on behalf of themselves or others' as acting outside of their proper place (8. 3. 1–2), he has nothing but praise for Hortensia:

Hortensia vero, Q. Hortensii filia, cum ordo matronarum gravi tributo a triumviris esset oneratus <nec> quisquam virorum patrocinium iis accommodare auderet, causam feminarum apud triumviros et constanter et feliciter egit: repraesentata enim patris facundia impetravit ut maior pars imperatae pecuniae iis remitteretur. revixit tum muliebri stirpe Q. Hortensius verbisque filiae aspiravit; cuius si virilis sexus posteri vi<a>m sequi voluissent, Hortensianae eloquentiae tanta hereditas una feminae actione abscissa non esset.   (8. 4. 3)

But when the class of matrons was burdened by the triumvirs with a heavy tax and no man dared to provide them protection, Hortensia, the daughter of Quintus Hortensius, pleaded the case of the women before the triumvirs with both determination and success: for the eloquence of her father, rediscovered, saw to it that most of the money which had been sought was returned to them. Then Quintus Hortensius lived again in his female offspring and found breath in his daughter's words; if his male descendants had afterwards been willing to follow her path, the great legacy of Hortensian eloquence would not have been cut off at a single act by a woman.

In other words, Hortensia made an impression, not just on the history of Rome, but on the history of oratory.[59] While it is certainly

[59] In fact, we know absolutely nothing about Hortensia other than the fact that she made this speech. It seems likely, as Hemelrijk (1999) hypothesizes, that her oratorical male relatives had assisted her speech-making ability—both through formal means, by sending her to a grammarian to study, and informal, by allowing her to participate in family discussions. There appear to have been some families in which the education of girls was something of a tradition: viz. that of C. Laelius (consul, 140 BCE), whose daughter Laelia is cited by Quintilian (*Inst.* 1. 1. 6) along with Hortensia as an example of female eloquence, and whose daughters and granddaughters were equally well educated: Hemelrijk (1999) 25, 91, and 235 n. 51. Even Hemelrijk, however, acknowledges that Hortensia is an anomaly, as a woman who is praised for her proficiency in oratory rather than attacked for encroaching on male territory: see Hemelrijk (1999: 89–92) for the traditional Roman view of why women should not and could not study rhetoric. Cf. Marshall (1989).

true that her act is partially justified by her ability to embody her male ancestors,[60] it is also made legitimate by its historical moment, when men were silenced and women were forced to come forward into the public sphere. Joy Connolly has argued that Roman oratorical theory was continuously engaged in a struggle with the 'feminine' side of eloquence, which relied on misrepresentation and deception to persuade.[61] If this is true, Hortensia's speech should have been remembered with the same distaste as those of Maesia of Sentinum (called *androgyne* for her embodiment of male and female qualities) and Gaia Afrania (a 'monster' whose name became synonymous with immorality).[62] Hortensia, however, manages to come forward into the civic sphere without damaging the perceived performance of her role as a good woman. This is not just because of who she was, but because of the particular historical circumstances in which she found herself. As Valerius Maximus says elsewhere, of a different civil conflict, 'what do women have to do with a public meeting? Nothing, if our ancestral customs were preserved: but where domestic quiet is stirred up by the turbulence of sedition . . . what violence compels is stronger than what modesty urges and instructs.'[63] Hortensia's literal historical position in the Forum, the most important space of republican civic life, is thus matched by the 'place' which is made for her in oratory, its most significant mode of civic discourse. Both transgressions, however, are justified by the social chaos afflicting Rome during the age of the triumvirs.

Hortensia, then, makes an important example, not just of what kinds of stories were remembered from the triumviral period, but of the contexts in which such stories might be propagated under the

---

[60] Noted by Hallett (1989) 66.   [61] Connolly (1998).

[62] These are the other two examples of female orators cited by Valerius Maximus (8. 3. 1–2). See Marshall (1990*a*) for a discussion of their historical circumstances.

[63] *quid feminae cum contione? si patrius mos servetur, nihil: sed ubi domestica quies seditionum agitata fluctibus est . . . plusque valet quod violentia cogit quam quod suadet et praecipit verecundia* (Val. Max. 9. 7. 1–2). This is his comment on the story of Sempronia, sister of Gaius and Tiberius Gracchus, who was forced into public to identify a man who was claiming to be the illegitimate son of the assassinated Tiberius. Valerius admires her fortitude in refusing to bow to pressure to admit the interloper into her family.

early Empire. There has been a great deal of critical debate over what link should be seen between Valerius Maximus' compendium and other 'historical' texts of the same period, especially those which deal with oratory such as Seneca the Elder's *Controversiae* and *Suasoriae*. Scholars are divided on whether the *Facta et Dicta Memorabilia* was meant for general consumption or was specifically directed at those who practised the kind of mock speech-making depicted in Seneca's texts.[64] Yet even if we do not postulate a direct connection, it is nevertheless clear that both authors reflect a similar interest in, and anxiety about, Roman social values and how they should be communicated. The historical importance of oratory to republican civic life means that the arguments which Seneca's speakers put forward in their declamations have the same ability to reflect contemporary public values as the stories from the heroic Roman past preserved in Valerius' exempla. Put more generally, we might say that, as is illustrated in the story of Hortensia, oratorical occasions were sites of Roman history, not just insofar as speeches themselves often turned on the question of how to read both the immediate and distant past, but also in that oratory itself has the power to mark something as public and historical: had Hortensia not given a speech, the incident in which she appears would not have been so noteworthy, memorable, or transgressive. Her use of one of the most important tools of republican civic life to defend her own exclusion from it is both testimony of, and a contribution to, the erosion of the public/private dichotomy in the age of the triumvirs, and—equally as important— the ways in which it was remembered.

---

[64] Bloomer (1992: 255) sees declaimers and their students as the primary audience; Skidmore (1996: 103–12) understands the text to be designed for private study and individual moral guidance. Coudry (1998) situates Valerius' work within the historical tradition and sees it as an attempt to preserve and propagate certain kinds of social values—the position closest to my own. Cf. Lehmann (1998) and Loutsch (1998). It is worth noting that the *Liber Memorialis* of Lucius Ampelius, a later (3rd–4th cent. CE) but similar handbook of historical and scientific facts, is clearly aimed at general education: it is addressed to a certain Macrinus and opens, *volenti tibi omnia nosse scripsi hunc librum memorialem* ('I have written this book of notes for you because you want to know everything').

I would argue, then, that we should take a concern with history and the ways in which it might both represent and construct social values as one point of contact between the work of Valerius Maximus and the declamatory culture represented in Seneca the Elder. Given this, it is telling that the image of the last years of the Republic as a crisis in personal as well as political life is repeated and elaborated in the mock rhetorical battles recorded in the *Suasoriae* and *Controversiae*. Of course, it is certainly true that declamation under the Empire was by its very nature already deeply enmeshed in questions about the 'correct' relationship between the domestic and the civic.[65] Oratory was a subject always close to the Roman heart, but its added role as entertainment as well as education among the early imperial elite gave it an unprecedented presence in private as well as public life. Originally, practice declamations were used simply in the training of young men; under the early Empire, however, we find it increasingly as a leisure-time activity, of such personages as Maecenas, Agrippa, and Augustus himself. Declamatory skill thus became an end in and of itself, so much so that the most accomplished rhetoricians rarely if ever actually appeared in court, preferring the more controlled environment of their own houses.[66] Seneca the Elder tells the story of Albucius who, bested in court, confined his activities to private performance, remarking, 'what reason do I have to speak in the Forum, when more people hear me speaking at home than hear anyone there?' (*Controv.* 7. pref. 8).[67]

This relocation from public to private space is matched, moreover, by a peculiar obsession in subject matter with the mechanics of

---

[65] Bloomer (1997) 277–14. Erik Gunderson's recent book (2003) explores this question as one of authority, through a Freudian analysis of the paternal relationship(s) represented in the declamations. In general, he is much more interested in the ways that the texts represent a general Roman *mentalité* than in how they represent a particular kind of history. See, however, Gunderson (2003: 135–49), on paternal authority and civil war.

[66] See G. A. Kennedy (1994) 170.

[67] '*Quid habeo quare in foro dicam, cum plures me domi audiant quam quemquam in foro?*'

private life.[68] The cast of characters which populates the declamations seems closer to the world of Greek New Comedy than that of early imperial Rome: sons who squander their fathers' money, stepmothers who plot against their stepchildren, daughters who are raped and then must decide the fate of their rapists. Although some of the topics consider what might be called 'political action' (tyrannicide is a popular theme), the vast majority are focused on domestic issues: inheritance, filial piety, conjugal loyalty, murder within the home. Even those declamations which are given a civic backdrop are often given a familial twist: thus, not simply, what should the reward be for a tyrannicide?, but what should be the reward for a tyrannicide who is also guilty of beating his father? (*Controv.* 9. 4). Even the canon of laws to be applied to the individual cases—a canon which by rights should represent the point of contact between the declamations and the functioning of the courts in real life—bears only a passing resemblance to any set of laws which has survived from antiquity, Roman or Greek. The early imperial collections of rhetorical set topics may thus be characterized as persistently apolitical, not simply in the sense that they choose no party with which to side, but in that they actively turn their backs on Roman civic institutions. In this incarnation, oratory, born in the courts, assemblies, and other public places of the Roman Republic, appears to have been quietly 'domesticated'—both literally resituated in its performance space from the Forum to the home, and refocused on the functioning of a fantasy private sphere rather than that of public life.[69]

---

[68] There has been no definitive answer offered for why the declamations which are preserved focus so exclusively on 'personal' or private matters rather than civic life. Recent scholarship, however, has emphasized the need for Roman orators under the early Empire to construct their own (free, masculine) identity against the servility and femininity of those who populate their declamations: Richlin (1996) and (1997); Connolly (1998). Fitzgerald (2000) does not discuss declamation, but does offer a compelling analysis of how and why 'other' identities (like that of the slave) both fascinate and repel Roman authors.

[69] Dupont (1997) makes this point about literary production more generally under the early Empire.

The extent to which the declamations insist on concerning themselves with 'trivialities' rather than the 'real' questions of early imperial politics has traditionally led scholars to dismiss them as sources
for the history of the early Empire. More recently, however, there
have been some attempts to recoup their reputation, as critics such as
Mary Beard have argued for reading through the fantastic narratives
to the cultural anxieties they reveal: 'we are (again) being wilfully
blind to the historical importance of the most basic social rules if we
write off as "trivial" stories which... negotiate the problems of
transgressive sexuality, legitimate and illegitimate succession, marriage and its subversions, and the fragile boundaries of the family.
One of the social functions of declamations was precisely to provide
a mytho-fictional framework within which to debate and re-debate
those human problems which lay at the heart of Roman (or any)
society.'[70] It is tempting, of course, to see the absence of 'politics'
from the declamations as a manifestation of the stifling of free
expression under the Empire,[71] but such a conclusion would be to
overread our evidence: Seneca actually praises the liberality with
which Augustus treated the declaimers (*Controv.* 2. 4. 13). Indeed,
the only instance of even indirect censorship which we are offered in
the *Controversiae* is the time Porcius Latro was declaiming before
Augustus and Agrippa, on a grandfather's adoption of a child which
his son had fathered with a prostitute. In the course of his speech,
Latro remarked of the grandson, 'taken from the depths, that one is
now grafted onto the nobility by means of adoption' (*iam iste ex imo
per adoptionem nobilitati inseritur.* 2. 4. 13), a statement apparently
taken by Agrippa as a reference to himself and his sons Gaius and
Lucius, whom the princeps was in the process of adopting. Seneca
tells us that Agrippa signalled Latro to wind up the performance,
since Augustus was in a hurry—hardly the most severe reaction
imaginable, although there might have been other consequences

[70] Beard (1993) 59–60. Cf. Gunderson (2003) 1–25.
[71] As is suggested in G. A. Kennedy (1994: 172). Fantham (1997*b*) discusses the shift
of emphasis in where and how speeches were produced, but notes that oratory was still
important in the 'public' context of addressing the emperor.

for the speaker which Seneca does not record. What is interesting about the story, however, is the fact that Agrippa is here provoked by an oration on a purely domestic issue, one of the classically fantastic and overblown family dramas which appear to have formed the substance of the vast majority of practice declamations. Especially in the context of the difficult succession issue, separating political from domestic concerns was by no means easy.

If, however, the story of Latro and Agrippa represents the ways in which declamations on private themes might be understood as political statements, Seneca's collections also provide illustrations of political acts construed as private dramas. Thus, for instance, the death of Cicero in the triumviral proscriptions is remarkably prominent, the subject of two *suasoriae* and a *controversia*. Especially given the fact that this was an event through which many of the speakers had lived, and given also the at least possible complicity of Octavian in the crime, here would seem to be an instance where some rather delicate civic issues might come to the fore. Yet the speakers are persistent in making the critical points of the case personal rather than political. Thus, in *Controversiae* 7. 2, the topic is the 'misbehaviour' of the reputed killer sent by Antony, a certain Popillius, whom Cicero had defended and who owed the orator, in consequence, a debt of gratitude. The law to be applied is the vague *de moribus sit actio*, a statute of which, curiously, we only hear otherwise in cases of divorce, when a wife is accused of violating her vows to her husband.[72] The case against Popillius, therefore, is argued in explicitly familial terms, a situation heightened by the rhetorical fiction that the earlier charge against which Cicero had defended his client was parricide. The declaimers, as Seneca tells us, invented this fact, presumably in order to draw comparisons between the first and second of Popillius' victims. The violation is thus represented in the context of two different domestic relationships, that between husband and wife and that between father and son.

---

[72] Bonner (1949) 124.

In fact, Seneca's hero Latro insists that it is only on the basis of the personal relationship between Cicero and Popillius that the latter may be successfully tried. To the traditional charge that the assassin killed 'a human being, a citizen, a senator, a former consul, Cicero, [and] your patron',[73] Latro retorts that this smothers the act of which the accused is guilty with those of which he is innocent: 'For during the war it was permitted to kill a human being and a citizen and a senator and a former consul, nor is there even a crime in the fact that it was Cicero, but only in that the victim was his patron' (*Controv.* 7. 2. 8).[74] Seneca goes on to indicate that Latro had some doubt as to whether someone might be held accountable for *any* act committed during civil war, and quotes with approval the epigram of Varius Geminus, *si illa... tempora in crimen vocas, dicis non de hominis sed de rei publicae moribus* ('if you are calling those times to account, you are talking about the character not of a man but of the Republic': 7. 2. 9)—the implication being that there is no case to be argued since one man cannot be tried for the crimes of a whole nation. The circumstance of civil war, therefore, is important as the historical context for the act, but only insofar as it renders null and void its civic implications; Popillius may only be convincingly argued as violating the particular individual bond between himself and his victim.

Indeed, putting Cicero aside for the moment, if we look to the other times in Seneca's collections that the recent civil war surfaces as a theme, we may be struck by the refusal of the speakers to consider it in any way other than as a context for the negotiation of personal relationships: thus, in *Controversiae* 4. 8, a nobleman attempts to reclaim from a freedman services which he had renounced in return for sanctuary during the triumviral proscriptions, leading to a discussion of friendship and fidelity between superior and subordinate; in 6. 4, a proscribed husband 'accidentally' poisons his wife who has

---

[73] *obicio tibi quod occidisti hominem, quod civem, quod senatorem, quod consularem, quod Ciceronem, quod patronum tuum* (*Controv.* 7. 2. 8).

[74] *licuit enim in bello et hominem et civem et senatorem et consularem occidere, ne in hoc quidem crimen est, quod Ciceronem, sed quod patronum.*

chosen to go into exile with him, a case which turns on the question
of whether the accused only loved the victim for her money. Whereas
the declamatory perspective on Popillius' assassination of Cicero
attempts to personalize a political act, these others make politics
the backdrop for defining the boundaries of personal loyalty. The
point remains, however, that the war is only presented through such
individual human dramas; late republican history has been reduced
to a series of domestic crises within elite families. The underlying
question which informs those domestic crises is perhaps most clearly
articulated in *Controversiae* 10. 3, the most complex and extensive of
Seneca's scenarios in which the civil war is a factor. Here, a father is
charged by his son with insanity over the death of his daughter, who,
during a civil war, had refused to desert her husband when he joined
the opposite side from her natal family; after the war was over and
her husband killed, the daughter went to her father and asked what
she might do to make amends. He responded 'die!', whereupon she
killed herself before his door.

　　None of the speakers in *Controversiae* 10. 3 attempts to play down
the intersection between the imagined situation and the historical
reality which many of them had experienced. In fact, Seneca explicitly tells us that one of the orators extensively quoted in 10. 3,
Clodius Turrinus, came from a family which had suffered greatly in
the recent conflicts (10. pref. 16). None of those whose words are
adduced, however, seems particularly anxious to mask the parallel
with contemporary history, as two cite the story of Caesar's sympathetic reaction to the death of *his* son-in-law (10. 3. 1 and 5), one
offers the example of Cicero's defence of Ligarius (10. 3. 3), and
another brings up the suicide of the younger Cato (10. 3. 5).
Clodius Turrinus, in fact, actually addresses the *imperator* in his
response,[75] favourably comparing the mercy which he displayed
after the end of the war with the harshness of the father under
consideration. Indeed, the actions of the 'victor' in the civil war are

---

[75] It is not clear whether this is supposed to be Julius Caesar or Augustus, although it
would no doubt be the Augustan wars which would be foremost in the participants'
minds.

the rhetorical touchstone to which the speakers continually return. Latro, the first to be quoted, remarks, *sic sibi satis fieri ne victor quidem voluit:... nullum fuit in proscriptione mulierculae caput* ('not even the victor wanted to be given satisfaction like this:... no woman lost her life in the proscriptions': 10. 3. 1); Clodius Turrinus says, *hoc quod ignovisti, victor, ad viros pertinet:... nam feminas ne si irascereris quidem proscripsisses* ('the pardon that you gave, victor, was meant for men:... for even if you were angry, you would not have proscribed women': 3. 2); Marullus offers the epigram, *O novum monstrum! irato victore vivendum est, exorato patre moriendum est* ('What a strange thing! When she provoked the victor, she might live; when she appealed to her father, she had to die': 3. 4). A certain Cornelius Hispanus even makes the point that either the victor was wrong to overlook the part played by women or the father was wrong to condemn his daughter, and notes on behalf of the accusing son, *aut pater noster aut victor insanit* ('either our father or the victor is out of his mind': 3. 6).

What is particularly interesting about this section in the *Controversiae* is the extent to which it addresses itself to the very question raised in, for instance, the debate around Cicero and Popillius: what, after all, is the relationship between private and public values in the case of a civil war? One implication of the comparisons made between the accused and the 'victor' is that, in forcing her to die, the father treated his daughter like a political enemy, like someone who should be proscribed as the victor proscribed his foes. But unlike the father, it is argued, the victor recognized that women do not have political identities, and thus did not include them on the lists of those to be killed. Correspondingly, however, by comparing the father's treatment of his daughter with the victor's treatment of his subjects, the speakers wilfully ignore the distinction between the relationships within a household and those within a state—a paradox picked up by a number of those who speak in favour of the father. As Labienius retorts, it was all very well for the victor to be merciful, since, after all, 'it is easier to pardon war than parricide'.[76] In a

---

[76] *facilius est ignoscere bello quam parricidio* (10. 3. 15).

similar vein, the two sides of the case differ in their answer to what seems to be a critical question raised early by Turrinus: *quare secuta est virum?* ('why did [the daughter] follow her husband?': 10. 3. 2). The speeches for the prosecution argue that she was simply acting as a virtuous wife, remaining loyal to her husband and emulating, as one puts it, examples such as Alcestis with which the accused himself used to exhort her (3. 2). It is the son-in-law who made the political choice; the daughter merely adhered to ideals of feminine domestic virtue. As one speaker says, most tellingly, *secutus est gener diversas partes, uxor suas* ('your son-in-law followed the opposite party, his wife followed her own': 3. 4). On the other hand, one of the major lines of argumentation pursued in defence of the father was that the daughter deserved to die because her choice *was* political: 'here is the accusation that the daughter followed the opposite party from her father and her brother, even though her sex exempted her from political vicissitudes.'[77] The father, therefore, had as much right to ask for the suicide of his daughter as Manlius and Brutus to execute their sons (3. 8). By allying with her father's enemies, she has entered the realm of politics and removed herself from the protection which her gender might have afforded her.[78]

Under the circumstance of civil conflict, is the relationship between father and daughter 'political' or not? As always in the practice declamations, there is no final answer offered to this question. But the point remains that Seneca's speakers are emerging from an environment in which the same action may be considered either the pinnacle of idealized domesticity or the worst kind of political treason—or perhaps most disturbingly, both at once. Whether the father acted rightly or wrongly in the case depends on locating the daughter's actions on one side or the other of the public/private dichotomy, an issue which reveals the cultural anxieties brought up by the topic of civil war. Those anxieties not coincidentally coalesce

---

[77] *Hic accusatio filiae contarias partes et patri <et fratri> sequentis, cum illam ipsa natura publicis excepisset malis* (3. 8).

[78] For a more detailed discussion of the familial relationships in *Controv.* 10. 3, see Gunderson (2003) 132–5.

around the figure of the daughter: as a woman, she represents the domestic sphere, yet her actions and those of her father seem to 'place' her in the realm of politics and public life. Indeed, this anxiety may also explain the concern which Seneca's speakers seem to have for the literal place of the daughter's death. It is repeatedly emphasized that she died on her father's threshold, rather than within his house; that he will not let her enter underscores the fact that he does not treat her as a member of his household, but as an enemy. Moschus accuses the father, *inquinasti filiae sanguine penates. quamquam quid ego dico penates, tamquam in domo perierit?* ('you have stained the penates with the blood of your daughter. But why do I say penates, as though she had died within the house?': *Controv.* 10. 3. 1). And another speaker argues, *hoc obsequio consequatur denique ut intra domum moriatur* ('this act of obedience should have allowed her at least to die inside the house': 3. 5).[79] Had the father accepted her back into his home before ordering her death, the act, it appears, would not be so shocking. As it is, she died where she had lived, on the threshold between public and private life.

Those moments in Seneca's text where the recent civil conflicts, and especially the triumviral proscriptions, surface are striking, particularly because along with real cases, real defendants, and real law, the absence of real Roman history in the *Controversiae* is almost total. Although a few instances of what we might call historical myth do appear (L. Quinctius Flaminius, proconsul in 184 BCE, appears in *Controversiae* 9. 2, and 4. 2 features L. Caecilius Metellus, who famously rescued the Palladium from a fire in 241), Seneca's collection has almost nothing to say about the last two hundred years of events in Rome. This may well be because Seneca's speakers generally agreed with the epigram offered by Labienus in 10. 3. 5, *optima civilis belli defensio oblivio est* ('the best defence against civil war is to forget it'). But in that case, why bring civic discord into it at all? The answer would seem to lie in the extent to which the recent civil wars, and in particular the triumviral proscriptions, are used in Seneca's

---

[79] Cf. 10. 3. 3 and 10. 3. 4.

catalogue of declamations to express the same kind of paradox expressed above by the proscription stories in the *Facta et Dicta Memorabilia*: the recent period of conflict is imagined to have been a time when Roman politics came 'home', compromising the right and privilege of certain people to be beyond the reach of public life. If the functioning of the household is the 'real' subject of a history of the triumviral proscriptions, they form the perfect backdrop for the delicate balancing act between public discourse and private life which consumes the rhetoricians—an opportunity to talk about the tribulations of late republican society without talking about politics. Domestic values such as kindness, loyalty, even love between the members of a household, have taken the place of civic ones as the declaimers seek a way of both remembering and forgetting the trials of civil war.

Let me end, as I began, with Appian's catalogue of proscription tales. One of the final stories which the historian includes in his list may be seen as an exception which proves the rule, a tale placed in this emphatic position because of the ways in which it makes an ironic counterpoint to the actions of wives, children, elderly parents, and slaves which precede it. At *Bellum Civile* 4. 50, Appian remarks that, after the third triumvir was deposed from his position, the family of Lepidus, although not the man himself, came under fire from those now serving Octavian: 'Maecenas accused Lepidus' son of plotting against Caesar, and accused the boy's mother of being in collusion with him; Lepidus himself he overlooked as insignificant.'[80] The irony to a certain extent lies in Lepidus' fall from grace, as he moves from perpetrator to victim—indeed, not even sufficiently important to be a victim himself, but forced to stand by and watch as his family is accused. This point is underscored by the fact that, when bail is demanded to guarantee that the wife will appear before Octavian, Lepidus is forced to beg mercy from the consul Balbinus, incidentally a man earlier proscribed for siding with

---

[80] Μαικήνας ἐδίωκε τὸν Λεπίδου παῖδα βουλεύσεως ἐπὶ Καίσαρι, ἐδίωκε δὲ καὶ τὴν μητέρα τῷ παιδὶ συνεγνωκέναι· Λεπίδου γὰρ αὐτοῦ ἄρα ὡς ἀσθενοῦς ὑπερεώρα.

Pompey while Caesar was still alive. Lepidus' appeal, however, bears the hallmarks not simply of a reversal of fortune, but of a reversal of roles, and not just between accuser and victim, but within the typology of victimage itself.

οὐδενὸς δὲ τὴν ἐγγύην ὑφισταμένου, ὁ Λέπιδος ἀμφὶ τὰς Βαλβίνου θύρας ἐτρίβετο πολλάκις καὶ δικάζοντι παρίστατο καὶ διωθουμένων αὐτὸν ἐς πολὺ τῶν ὑπηρετῶν μόλις εἶπεν· "ἐμοὶ μὲν καὶ οἱ κατήγοροι μαρτυροῦσιν ἐπιείκειαν, οὐδὲ γυναικί με ἢ παιδὶ συγγνῶναι λέγοντες· σὲ δὲ οὐκ ἐγὼ μὲν προέγραψα, κάτω δέ εἰμι τῶν προγραφέντων ... χάρισαί μοι τὴν γυναῖκα ἀπαντήσειν ἐς Καίσαρα ἐγγυωμένῳ ἢ μετ' ἐκείνης ἀπελθεῖν δεομένῳ." (BC 4. 50)

Since no one came forward to stand surety, Lepidus hammered on Balbinus' door many times and presented himself at the court and, although the servants continuously pushed him away, he managed to say with difficulty: 'The informers testify that I am blameless—they say that I was not in collusion with my wife or my son. On the one hand, it was not I who proscribed you; on the other, I am now lower than those who were proscribed ... Grant that I may stand surety for my wife's appearance before Caesar, or that I may be allowed to go along with her.'

Coming as it does at the end of a catalogue in which wives frequently attempt to intercede for their husbands, this representation of Lepidus' words and actions depicts him not only as disempowered, but as ironically feminized; it is he who is now excluded from public life and he attempts to parlay his innocence of political machinations into safety for the members of his family. Moreover, the kind of personal appeal to which Lepidus resorts had long been one of the informal strategies which women used to influence the conduct of public matters in Rome, as seen in Livy's narrative of the repeal of the *lex Oppia*, in Fulvia's actions on behalf of Antony, and in Appian's own description of Hortensia's response to the triumviral tax. The point is that Lepidus has been thrust into a female position, not simply in being ignored as an appropriate object of politically motivated prosecution, but in the means by which he is able to respond to such an attack.

The story of Lepidus and his family makes a fitting end to Appian's catalogue, both because its ironic reversals underscore the norm of the triumviral proscriptions—in which personal relationships affect the outcome of political events—and because it represents the ultimate point of the kind of 'domestic politics' enacted in this age of civil discord. As husband and wife switch roles, we see the ways in which the public and private spheres have become thoroughly indistinguishable from one another. Whether or not the story is historically accurate is beside the point: the idea which it expresses has come to be an accepted truth about the age of the triumvirs, a truth which both proves and is proven by the return to correctly constituted domestic life under the Principate. The historical fact of crisis is constituted by its solution. While it is unquestionable that terrible things happened in Rome during the triumviral proscriptions, it is the terms in which those terrible things were remembered and circulated that I have tried to outline here. And although the tales of domestic crisis were certainly not the only form in which the story of the end of the Republic was communicated to the early Empire, nevertheless it is clear that those tales occupied a significant place in the popular and historiographical imagination. In this sense, they should be understood as both evidence of and a contribution to the ways in which Augustus was celebrated as the saviour of the Roman home.

5

Natural Urges: Marriage, Philosophy, and the Work of the House

IN this book I have discussed the role of gender and domesticity in constructing the relationship between Augustus and the Roman public, between Roman imperialism and its subjects, between morality and law, and between the imperial present and the republican past. I have thus been arguing for a very broad view of the way in which the domestic functioned as ideology and symbol in early imperial culture. In the present chapter, however, I would like to look at the one relationship which has before been seen as constructed through a vision of household life, namely the relationship of the Roman citizen to himself. Michel Foucault, in *The Care of the Self*, famously and controversially argued that early imperial Stoic writers reveal an important shift in thinking about the role of a 'home life' in constituting the adult male citizen's sense of who he ought to be, as being a good husband somehow became an ethical project distinct from being a good citizen, magistrate, or statesman: 'it appears that marriage became more general as a practice, more public as an institution, more private as a mode of existence—a stronger force for binding conjugal partners and hence a more effective one for isolating the couple in a field of other social relations.'[1] Foucault's argument has been attacked by classical scholars from many different angles, for a number of legitimate

---

[1] Foucault (1986) 77.

reasons.[2] Yet I think Foucault does deserve credit for drawing our attention to early imperial reflections on the 'science' of domestic life as one way of imagining what it meant to be an early imperial citizen. In general terms, the idea that certain kinds of domestic lifestyle either promote or disrupt the pursuit of the good life does indeed suggest, as Foucault would have it, an imagined continuity between the 'private' world of the household and the 'private' state of a man's soul. What is not clear, however, is that this goes along with an isolation of the domestic sphere—and relations within it—from the wider world of social interaction.

In the pages which follow, then, I briefly discuss the philosophical treatises of Musonius Rufus on marriage and domestic life, in order to show how Foucault's reading of Stoicism offers only a partial view of a more complicated philosophical position. Yet, as has frequently been noted about Foucault's study, high-level 'Greek' philosophizing such as is represented by Musonius was not the only theory of good household life which was circulating under the early Empire. In the latter part of this chapter, therefore, I turn to a very different kind of text, the agricultural handbook of L. Junius Moderatus Columella, in order to examine how he frames the issue of female domesticity in a different generic and cultural context. Although Columella, like Musonius, understands the question to be a 'philosophical' one, the former author is careful to situate his argument both within a particular vision of Roman history and as part of a particularly Roman discourse about gender and society. Ultimately, both Musonius and Columella understand the quality and patterns of domestic life to be a way of reading both the ethical state of an individual and

---

[2] These critiques have come especially from feminists in classics, who worry both about the absence of women from Foucault's 'history' generally and his reluctance to cite earlier feminist work on his topic. See Richlin (1991) and (1998) and Foxhall (1998). Foucault has also come under fire from social historians, for errors in both fact and interpretation: Cohen and Saller (1994). Goldhill (1995) criticizes *The History of Sexuality* for taking too little account of genre and narrative in its interpretations of ancient texts, and attempts to fill in some of the gaps by looking at sex in the Greek novel. See the essays in Larmour, Miller, and Platter (1998) and Nussbaum and Sihvola (2002) for other attempts by classicists to find useful points of intersection with Foucault's work.

the moral level of society generally; far from the 'isolation' of the couple from civic concerns within their domestic environment, the maintenance of a good household becomes for both authors the ultimate expression of a healthy society.

It may be legitimately objected that the texts which I consider in this chapter are not, strictly speaking, 'Augustan'—in the sense that they were not written during the life of the first of the Julio-Claudian emperors—and that this is a book which has proposed to identify a strand of 'Augustan' ideology. Indeed, such an objection might have also been raised for the last chapter, many of whose central texts were Tiberian, although all were similarly concerned with representing the beginning of the Empire. As I suggested in the Introduction, however, I would prefer to see the 'age of Augustus' as a set of ideas and ideals which came to be associated with the advent of imperial governance, but which continued to be refined and renegotiated throughout the rule of the Julio-Claudian dynasty—even, as I will discuss in the Epilogue, after that dynasty was a thing of the past. Because Columella (true to his Neronian moment) understands himself to be the natural heir to both Ciceronian prose eloquence and Virgilian poetics, he is deeply concerned with the meaning of late republican and early imperial literature, and the truths which it expressed. This is not to say that, had Columella written under Augustus, his book would have looked the same as it does. Far from it: there is a reason why it is the bizarre and brilliant oddity of Virgil's *Georgics* that represents the Roman tradition of agricultural writing for the Augustan period,[3] rather than Columella's stolid and sober *de Re Rustica*. Fifty years after the death of the first princeps, getting Augustanism right in the Neronian period had a different kind of urgency from that which it manifested in its own time. To the extent that he is concerned to represent and repair early imperial society in exactly the terms outlined at the beginning of Julio-Claudian rule, Columella is more 'Augustan' than Ovid.

---

[3] For a discussion of how Virgil transformed 'subjects completely alien to the higher literary tradition' into poetry, see Thomas (1987).

I would thus argue that the visions of the domestic sphere as an aspect of public life which I discuss below would not have been produced without the authors' knowledge that the house was a political structure, an idea which could not be separated from the fact of the 'house' which was currently ruling Rome. In this sense, both Musonius and Columella reflect the later, and in some ways more refined, stages of Augustan ideology.

STOICISM ON HOUSE AND HOUSEHOLD

felix illud saeculum ante architectos fuit.
Happy was the age which came before architects.

Seneca, *Epistulae Morales* 90. 8

In the ninetieth moral epistle, Seneca the Younger dismisses architecture in response to a statement made by the Hellenistic philosopher Posidonius, who represented house-building as the first of the civilized arts invented by the wise man.[4] Seneca scoffs at this idea, remarking with heavy sarcasm that the wise man will soon be credited with the discovery of shoemaking: *non multum afuit, quin sutrinum quoque inventum a sapientibus diceret.*[5] In fact, such cultivated skills—building, weaving, baking, and the like—are more likely to imperil the pursuit of the good life than to promote it, Seneca insists, as they lead to the desire for greater and greater refinement and thence inexorably to *luxuria.* These sentiments have, over the years, got Rome's best-known philosopher into some trouble with critics: as notable a personage as Macaulay gave the verdict, 'if we are forced to make our choice between the first shoemaker and the author of the three books *On Anger*, we pro-

---

[4] '*illa [sc. philosophia]' inquit 'sparsos et aut casis tectos aut aliqua rupe suffossa aut exesae arboris trunco docuit tecta moliri*' (' "That thing (i.e. philosophy)", he said, "taught human beings to build houses when they were scattered and sheltered by huts or a hole in some cliff or the trunk of a hollow tree" ': *Ep.* 90. 7).

[5] *Ep.* 90. 23.

nounce for the shoemaker... [S]hoes have kept millions from being wet; and we doubt whether Seneca ever kept anybody from being angry.'[6] What has not seen much comment, however, is the particular primacy which domestic architecture is given in *Epistle* 90 and the place which it is assigned in the rise and fall of humankind. As I noted, it is Posidonius' praise of the first shelters which marks the beginning of Seneca's disagreement with him in section 7; architecture returns as a useless skill in comparison with the ability to live in accordance with nature (§15); nature provides perfectly adequate houses without the assistance of architecture (§17); many techniques of house-building are recent inventions, not ennobled by a long history (§§23, 32). Along the way, *Epistle* 90 takes in, and dismisses as 'unnatural', other arts associated with domestic life: weaving, cooking, the milling of grain to make bread. Finally, just as the invention of house-building began the critique of technical skills, it also ends it, as the letter's peroration contrasts the anxiety created by the modern house with the peace available to those who used to live in harmony and company with the natural world (§43):

at vos ad omnem tectorum pavetis sonum et inter picturas vestras, si quid increpuit, fugitis attoniti. non habebant domos instar urbium: spiritus ac liber inter aperta perflatus et levis umbra rupis aut arboris et perlucidi fontes rivique non opere nec fistula nec ullo coacto itinere obsolefacti... haec erat secundum naturam domus, in qua libebat habitare nec ipsam nec pro ipsa timentem: nunc magna pars nostri metus tecta sunt.

But *you* start at every sound of the roof and, if you hear a creak, you flee in panic between your paintings. *They* did not have houses to equal cities: the breath and free breezes through open spaces, the soft shade of rock and tree, the crystal-clear fountains and rivers, not degraded by gadget or pipe or any constriction to their flow... these formed a house in accord with nature, in which it was permitted to live without fearing either it or on behalf of it: now the great part of our anxiety is the house.

Far from being a refuge from the outside world, the domestic structure serves as both the symbol of the wealthy man's burdens

[6] Macaulay (1880) 411.

(which he fears, lest they overwhelm and crush him) and the material repository of his riches (which he fears for, lest something happen to them): rather than an element in human progress, contemporary domestic architecture is imagined as a threat to wisdom, happiness, and peace of mind.

It is clear, of course, that Seneca's criticism of 'unnatural' domestic lifestyles in *Epistle* 90 reflects the language of earlier critiques of luxurious building; thus, for instance, Seneca the Elder records a speech by Papirius Fabianus in which he laments, *adeo nullis gaudere veris sciunt, sed aversum naturam alieno loco aut terra aut mare mentita aegris oblectamenta sunt* ('(sc. those with large country houses) actually do not know how to enjoy things that are real, but in their sickness they only find amusement in falsehoods on land and sea, [constructed] against nature and out of their correct place': *Controv.* 2. 1. 13).[7] Within the context of the *Epistulae Morales*, however, the phrase *secundum naturam domus* also evokes a grander ideal, namely the Stoic principle of a life 'in accordance with nature'. In general, the natural law of the Stoics has been understood as a kind of universal humanism, the idea that there was a state of being which transcended the interests of self, family, or nation and which, if its call was heeded, allowed the wise man to live in perfect harmony with the governing principle of the universe.[8] In Seneca's *Epistle* 90, however, the Stoic ideal seems to be taken much more literally, as the philosopher expresses concern not just about having too grand a house, but about having a house at all; his objection to the over-construction of domestic space is broadened to include the general practice of domestic architecture. In the utopian time before the advent of luxury and excess, human beings needed neither houses nor philosophy, but the kind of 'progress' represented by the invention of the former necessitated the creation of the latter as protection

---

[7] Cf. Cicero, *de Leg.* 2. 2; Seneca the Younger, *Ep.* 86. 6–7, 89. 21, 122. 5. For a comprehensive discussion, see Edwards (1993) 137–72. Henderson (2004) discusses the image and idea of the villa and its relationship to Seneca's ethical programme in the *Epistulae Morales*.

[8] See Schofield (1991) 93–103, and Long (1996) 156–78.

for the wise man's soul. The original 'life in accord with nature', however, was one in which no boundary (literal or figurative) existed between human beings and the world around them. It is a curiously extreme position, especially since one of the aspects of Stoicism which appealed to the Romans was that it did not, unlike its rival Epicureanism, insist that a truly virtuous adherent would withdraw from politics and society. In dismissing the house, however, Seneca is also dismissing one of the traditional sites of Roman civic life.[9]

On the other hand, it is clear that it is not the house as civic space to which Seneca is objecting, but rather the house as anti-civic, as the originary site of the kind of self-serving greed which actually first disrupted humankind's ability to live together in peace: 'there followed a fortunate time, when the blessings of nature lay available for use in the open, before greed and dissipation divided mortals and caused them to run from harmony to plunder.'[10] Ironically, however, the possession of private property led not to greater liberty and self-determination but to oppression and the tyranny of wealth. Seneca here uses language which seems deliberately to evoke one dichotomy which had long structured Roman civic identity: *culmus liberos texit, sub marmore atque auro servitus habitat* ('straw [once] covered free men; slavery [now] lives under marble and gold': *Ep.* 90. 10). Indeed, Seneca's philosophical view of houses and their meaning in *Epistle* 90 seems to have been fairly standard in Stoic thought of the time; at any rate, it is echoed closely in the writings of his, in some ways, more influential younger contemporary Musonius Rufus.[11] Like Seneca, Musonius recommends maintaining as little a house as can be possibly managed, and contrasts the selfish life of luxury

---

[9] Such moments in Seneca's work may serve to remind us that the Stoic school was founded by Zeno, who studied at the feet of Crates the Cynic, a figure whose ideas may have shaped his student's writings more than later adherents were willing to admit. For a discussion, see Schofield (1991) 3–13, 119–27.

[10] *secutast fortunata tempora, cum in medio iacerent beneficia naturae promiscue utenda, antequam avaritia atque luxuria dissociavere mortales et ad rapinam ex consortio discurrere* (*Ep.* 90. 36).

[11] On Musonius' biography, see Lutz (1947) 14–18. Whitmarsh (2001: 141–56) discusses the ways in which Musonius situates himself between Greek and Roman culture.

which a large dwelling represents with the civic-minded generosity of one who spends on maintaining the community ('On Clothing and Shelter' (19)):

καθόλου δὲ ὅπερ ἂν παρέχοι σπήλαιον αὐτοφυές, ἔχον μετρίαν ὑπόδυσιν ἀνθρώπῳ, τοῦτο χρὴ παρέχειν ἡμῖν τὴν οἰκίαν, τοσοῦτον εἴπερ ἄρα περιττεύουσαν, ὅσον καὶ ἀπόθεσιν τροφῆς ἀνθρωπίνης ἐπιτηδείαν ἔχειν ...καί τοι πόσῳ μὲν εὐκλεέστερον τοῦ πολυτελῶς οἰκεῖν τὸ πολλοὺς εὐεργετεῖν; πόσῳ δὲ καλοκἀγαθικώτερον τοῦ ἀναλίσκειν εἰς ξύλα καὶ λίθους τὸ εἰς ἀνθρώπους ἀναλίσκειν; πόσῳ δὲ ὠφελιμώτερον τοῦ περιβεβλῆσθαι μεγάλην οἰκίαν τὸ κεκτῆσθαι φίλους πολλούς, ὃ περιγίνεται τῷ προθύμως εὐεργετοῦντι; τί δ' ἂν ὄναιτό τις τηλικοῦτον ἀπ' οἰκίας μεγέθους τε καὶ κάλλους, ἡλίκον ἀπὸ τοῦ χαρίζεσθαι πόλει καὶ πολίταις ἐκ τῶν ἑαυτοῦ;

On the whole, whatever is provided by a natural cavern, which offers a moderate covering for a person, ought to be given to us by a house, such that, if there should be a surplus, [the house] should provide a fit place of storage for human food...And how much more glorious is it to do good for many people than to live in luxury? How much more noble to spend on human beings rather than on wood and stone? How much more helpful to acquire many friends—which comes from actively doing good—than to build a great house around oneself? What advantage does someone gain from a large and lovely house which is as great as that which he achieves by using his wealth to provide generously for his city and fellow citizens?

Like Seneca's, Musonius' Stoicism expresses itself in a rejection of the house as a locus of private consumption in favour of the greater community and its values; the adjectives which he uses above in the comparative (εὐκλεής, καλοκἀγαθός, ὠφέλιμος) seem deliberately drawn from the list of traditional civic virtues.

Musonius' ambivalent feelings about domestic space are particularly worth noting because he and his fellow Stoics have become famous in recent years as champions of a particular kind of what we might call philosophical domesticity. As I noted above, the third volume of Michel Foucault's work on 'the history of sexuality' offers a particular reading of early imperial Stoicism, in which he sees a shift toward marriage as a unique and mutually dependent bond between a man and a woman: 'one sees the relation between husband and wife detach itself from matrimonial functions, from the status-determined authority of the husband and the reasonable government of the household, and take on the character of a singular relation having its own force, its own difficulties, obligations, benefits, and pleasures'.[12] In other words, Foucault argues, a new emphasis on the intimate relation of the couple and their mutual obligations to one another took the place of the earlier model of matrimony, which had insisted on the husband's duty to rule his wife.[13] The need and desire to create an affective bond within the marriage, moreover, supersedes the need to create an effective household, so that '[early imperial philosophical texts] show that marriage was interrogated as a mode of life whose value was not exclusively, nor perhaps even essentially, linked to the functioning of the oikos, but rather to a mode of relation between two partners'.[14] Musonius Rufus, and his pupil Epictetus, play an important role in Foucault's argument here, in part because their work explicitly addresses itself to the relationship between marriage and the good life, expressed by Musonius in the question 'Is Marriage an Impediment to Philosophy?'(Τι ἐμπόδιον τῷ φιλοσοφεῖν γάμος; (14)). The answer is no; in fact, Musonius argues that marriage is one of the things most in accord with nature, which is proven by the 'natural' desire of human beings to unite themselves in a male/female couple, both for the purpose of procreation and for the formation of an intimate bond. Foucault draws attention to this aspect of Musonius' thought, noting that here 'Nature is not content to make allowance for marriage; she incites individuals to marry through a primordial inclination; she urges each of them to do so, including the philosopher himself. Nature and reason coincide in the movement that conduces to marriage.'[15] It is this idea of the 'natural urge' to marry, he maintains, which is new in the writings of the early imperial Stoic philosophers.

---

[12] Foucault (1986) 79.   [13] Ibid. 148.   [14] Ibid. 80.
[15] Ibid. 153.

Indeed, it would seem to be true that this argument in Musonius marks a departure from earlier philosophical discussions of the same question, which tend to focus on reproduction as the primary goal of the union between a man and a woman. Thus, for instance, in Aristotle's *Politics* the production of children is listed as the first and most important reason for marriage.[16] Despite his desire to represent marriage as one of the most 'natural' acts, however, Musonius explicitly dismisses reproduction as its primary goal, noting that the birth of a human being is a great thing, but that it can result from any sexual joining between a man and a woman, just as it does in animals.[17] What makes marriage different, and significant, is that it represents the joining of two people in a union which creates not only offspring, but also a kind of commonality which depends on the dismantling of all barriers between them as individuals: 'The husband and wife, he used to say, should come together for the purpose of making a life in common and of procreating children, and furthermore of regarding all things in common between them, and nothing peculiar or private to one or the other, not even their own bodies.'[18]

Whereas in modern parlance, then, we think of natural urges as being the most basic, biological kind, it is clear that Musonius is here celebrating Nature in its Stoic sense: the guiding physical and rational principle of the universe, in accordance with which the wise man seeks to live his life. That physical and rational principle,

[16] 1252^a, 24–7, and Pomeroy (1994) 35: 'most Greek thought tended to reduce the value of a wife to the primary function of sexual reproduction.' See, however, her comments on the more 'progressive' views expressed in Xenophon's *Oeconomicus* (pp. 34–9).

[17] In 'What is the Primary Goal of Marriage?' (*Τι κεφάλαιον γάμου*; (13A)). This is not to say, I hasten to add, that Musonius does not see reproduction as significant, but only that it is not by itself the point of marriage. Elsewhere he juxtaposes sex which is pursued for pleasure with that which has reproduction as its goal: see Hauser (2002: 338–42) for a discussion. But the emphasis in those passages is the dismissal of pleasure as a good, and not the explanation of the married state.

[18] τὸν γὰρ γαμοῦντα, ἔφη, καὶ τὴν γαμουμένην ἐπὶ τούτῳ συνιέναι χρὴ ἑκάτερον θατέρῳ, ὥσθ᾽ ἅμα μὲν ἀλλήλοις βιοῦν, ἅμα δὲ⟨παιδο⟩ποιεῖσθαι, καὶ κοινὰ δὲ ἡγεῖσθαι πάντα καὶ μηδὲν ἴδιον, μηδ᾽ αὐτὸ τὸ σῶμα ('What is the Primary Goal of Marriage?' (13A)).

moreover, is what drives the philosopher to seek the best, most unified fashion of living together with his fellow human beings; for, as Musonius notes in 'Is Marriage an Impediment to Philosophy?', his nature (φύσις) is not that of the wolf, which lives in isolation without any notion of community (κοινωνίας), but is closest to that of the bee, which is not able to live if left on its own (ἣ μὴ δύναται μόνη ζῆν) and by necessity throws itself into working with its fellows toward a common goal (πρὸς ἓν δὲ καὶ κοινὸν ἔργον τῶν ὁμοφύλων συνένευκε). It follows, then, that it is most natural for human beings to live in companionship with one another, a companionship which finds its most profound expression in the union between a man and a woman in marriage: 'For it is clear that both the home and the city are composed not from the woman alone or the man alone, but from their communion with one another; and no one could find a communion more necessary or more pleasant than that between men and women.'[19]

Musonius' focus on this perfect joining of the married couple has been seen as a significant milestone in both the history of marriage and of gender relations in the ancient world.[20] As I noted above, Michel Foucault has argued that we may see here a shift under the early Roman Empire toward 'companionate marriage', in which the wife is considered an equal partner to her husband rather than his subject. Foucault would make this a general cultural trend, which seems unlikely; more probably we should see the Stoic view as coexisting with other, less egalitarian, attitudes toward relations between the sexes.[21] Indeed, even at the same time that he argues that women too should study philosophy—since they are the moral equals of men—Musonius continues to emphasize the separate spheres of male and female, and the necessity for the wife to

---

[19] ὅτι μὲν γὰρ οἶκος ἢ πόλις οὔτ᾽ ἐκ γυναικῶν συνίσταται μόνον οὔτ᾽ ἐξ ἀνδρῶν μόνον, ἀλλ᾽ ἐκ τῆς πρὸς ἀλλήλους κοινωνίας· δῆλον ἀνδρῶν δὲ καὶ γυναικῶν κοινωνίας ἄλλην οὐκ ἂν εὕροι τις οὔτ᾽ ἀναγκαιοτέραν οὔτε προσφιλεστέραν.

[20] See, in addition to Foucault, Veyne (1987*a*); Dixon (1992: 83–90) is unusual in arguing that romantic love was always an aspect of Roman marriage.

[21] A point made most strongly by Cohen and Saller (1994: 44–55), but also illustrated in Treggiari (1991: esp. 215–28).

subordinate herself to her husband's needs.²² But perhaps most critical for my purposes is the fact that Musonius' arguments in favour of companionate marriage must be seen to spring directly from his focus on the communal nature of human beings; the philosopher's point that there should be nothing private between the couple reflects an ideal society where private needs and desires are subordinate to the greater good. While it is true, then, that Musonius and his fellow Stoics certainly seem to accord women greater credit as fellow human beings to men, the notion that marriage should be a mutually satisfying partnership is based on a more general drive toward a more collective, 'natural', and mutually satisfying community. Far from being a 'privatization' of the couple, then, companionate marriage in Musonius' thought is actually inextricably connected to his distrust of private or individual drives within human society.

This contrast, between marriage and privacy, becomes particularly evident when we contrast what Musonius has to say about the naturalness of domestic life with the profound *un*naturalness of domestic space. For instance, Musonius' section 14 on 'Is Marriage an Impediment to Philosophy?' opens by citing the examples of Pythagoras, Socrates, and Crates, all of whom were married and the most philosophical of men. Musonius then elaborates on the life of Crates:

καίτοι γε Κράτης ἄοικός τε καὶ ἀσκευὴς καὶ ἀκτήμων τέλεον ἦν, ἀλλ' ὅμως ἔγημεν· εἶτα μηδ' ὑπόδυσιν ἔχων ἰδίαν ἐν ταῖς δημοσίαις Ἀθήνησι στοαῖς διημέρευε καὶ διενυκτέρευε μετὰ τῆς γυναικός· ἡμεῖς δὲ ἀπ' οἰκίας ὁρμώμενοι, καὶ οἰκέτας τοὺς ὑπηρετοῦντας ἔχοντες ἔνιοι, τολμῶμεν ὅμως λέγειν, ἐμπόδιον εἶναι φιλοσοφίᾳ γάμον;

Furthermore, Crates was without a home, without furniture, without property entirely, and all the same he was married. In fact, since he did not have a private dwelling, he spent his days and nights in the public

---

²² See Nussbaum (2002: 300–13) for a discussion of Musonius' feminist failings, and Whitmarsh (2001: 112–13) for a description of 'Musonius' strongly normative model' of female education.

porticoes of Athens together with his wife. But we, who have houses to start with, and some of us even have house-slaves to serve us, nevertheless dare to say that marriage is an impediment to philosophy?

Crates' homeless state is held up as an example of someone who held nothing back in the pursuit of a natural life. In spite of his lack of a private house, however, Crates nevertheless maintained what we in the modern day would call a private life, enjoying his relationship with his wife in the open colonnades of Athens. On the other hand, Musonius insists, those who not only have houses but slaves to go with them are much more in danger of losing their grip on a life in accord with nature—and yet they have the gall to ask if marriage will prevent them from pursuing a philosophical existence? In fact, Musonius continues, 'if anything is in accord with nature, it would seem to be marriage' (κατὰ φύσιν δ', εἴ τι ἄλλο, καὶ τὸ γαμεῖν φαίνεται ὄν). As the depiction of Crates and his wife indicates, however, this is not a vision of the married couple as cut off from the rest of the community, alone together in their own private home. Instead, Musonius goes on to offer a striking image of how the house-as-home should be imagined in relation to the city: οὕτω καὶ πόλεως ἑκάστῳ τῆς αὑτοῦ φροντιστέον καὶ τῇ πόλει οἶκον περιβλητέον. ἀρχὴ δὲ οἴκου περιβολῆς γάμος ('Thus it is necessary for each man to give thought to his community and to make his home into a protective wall around the city. And the starting point of this protective home is marriage.'). The image evoked by περιβλητέον and περιβολῆς is as strange in Greek as in English and seems deliberately provocative: instead of the community as protection for the home, here we have the home as protection for the community; instead of the city physically enclosing the house, the house encloses the city. When Musonius later turns to his critique of private architecture and dismisses the practice of τοῦ περιβεβλῆσθαι μεγάλην οἰκίαν ('building a great house as a protective wall around oneself'), the middle voice has particular force, emphasizing the mistake of using the home to protect private, personal interests instead of the community as a whole.

In short, despite his positive feelings about marriage, Musonius continues to have mixed feelings about the house—a curious separation, since traditionally in Greek philosophy the two had been understood as going hand-in-hand. Again, in Xenophon's *Oeconomicus*, the mutual dependence of man and woman in marriage is linked to the mutual dependence of 'inside' and 'outside' tasks (7. 22). I will have more to say about Xenophon's formulation of this point below, but for the moment I would simply like to underscore the point made by Foucault about Musonius: it is significant that marriage is represented as a natural state, toward which both bodily desires and rational thought compel human beings. But while Foucault would take this as evidence that early imperial Stoicism was driving toward 'isolating the couple in a field of other social relations', I think we need to take seriously Musonius' simultaneous rejection of the house as an aspect of his understanding of the correct relationship between domestic and civic life. It is more natural to get married than to build a house—indeed, the two actions almost exist at opposite ends of the natural/unnatural spectrum—because the relationship between man and woman in the conjugal couple exists as an originary paradigm for other social interactions. The desire for a house, on the other hand, represents the worst kind of selfish and anti-communal impulses to which contemporary human beings are inclined: the desire to live in isolation, free of responsibility for others, serving only one's own needs and not those of the social world to which the citizen ought to belong. Domestic relations between man and woman, then, function for Musonius as the redemption of private life, the thing which makes the household a worthwhile enterprise even though the house itself is imagined to be a danger to a truly philosophical existence.

As I noted above, Musonius was clearly an influential figure in elite Roman culture and politics from the end of Nero's reign through to that of Titus: we hear of him being exiled by Nero after the Pisonian conspiracy,[23] attempting unsuccessfully to intercede

---

[23] Tac. *Ann.* 15. 71; Cass. Dio 62. 27. 4.

between the armies of Vitellius and Vespasian,[24] being exempted by imperial order from the general banishment of philosophers from Rome under Vespasian,[25] and befriending Pliny the Younger during a sojourn in Syria. Indeed, Pliny speaks of him in the warmest terms, although he also notes that their intimacy could only progress so far due to the difference in their ages.[26] The fact that Musonius' surviving work is written in Greek, however, and certainly springs out of the Greek intellectual tradition, has led some scholars to dismiss him as a source for imperial Roman ideas about domestic life. It is a pity that we have lost Seneca's *de Matrimonio*, although we have evidence elsewhere in his writings that it put forward a position similar to Musonius'.[27] Stoic philosophy, of course, represents only one strand of the complex fabric of Roman thinking on the question of marriage, women, and private life, but it is worth noting that it was clearly still a live issue towards the end of the first century CE. The solution at which Musonius arrives, moreover, prioritizes the role of a wife in rescuing domestic life from private interests; simply by marrying, a man may show his desire and intent to work for the good of the community rather than his own personal pleasures. The Stoic philosopher thus advocates a kind of domesticity which depends on the presence of a wife but is abstracted from the house, the wife's traditional place in the map of Roman society. The place which he finds for the couple, however, as a model for other, more communal, relations, situates them at the centre of his vision of the ideal Stoic state.

---

[24] Tac. *Hist.* 3. 81; Cass. Dio 65. 18. 19.   [25] Cass. Dio 65. 13. 2.

[26] *Ep.* 3. 11. 4.

[27] It used to be thought that Seneca's work was opposed to matrimony, due to the fact that Jerome's *adversus Jovinianum* (which criticizes marriage) used it extensively. Torre (2000), however, carefully analyses Jerome's use of Seneca and concludes that the latter had a much more complex view of marriage, which distinguished between bad, excessive wives and good philosophical ones. Cf. Trillitzsch (1965). Although Seneca once speaks negatively about matrimony, as something which gives only fleeting pleasure (*Ep.* 59. 2), he suggests elsewhere that it is a natural impulse (with all of the positive Stoic connotations of the word 'natural'): *Ep.* 9. 17. He also describes it as one of the matters on which the philosopher should be prepared to give advice: *Ep.* 94. 15.

SHOULD THE BAILIFF MARRY? GENDER, DOMESTICITY, AND THE FARM IN COLUMELLA

It appears, in short, that Foucault misreads his Stoic sources at a critical point: it is the privacy of private life which Musonius distrusts; marriage is embraced by the philosopher because it represents a relationship within the domestic sphere which creates a link to the community beyond the walls of the house. It is clear, however, that it was not only in such rarefied philosophical contexts that questions about the relationship between men, women, the home, and society were being addressed under the early Empire. Nor were they the only places in which good domesticity—the 'work' of the woman within the home—was represented as the most important goal of both individual and community. The *de Re Rustica* of L. Junius Moderatus Columella is a book which has long lurked on the edges of literary study in classics. It has the misfortune not only of falling into the despised category of 'Roman technical writing' but of competing in its genre with two considerably more famous predecessors: the agricultural treatises of Cato the Elder and Marcus Terentius Varro. Like those earlier texts, however, the *de Re Rustica* understands the farm not just as a site of agricultural work, but as a place of moral and ethical rectitude where, if they so chose, contemporary Romans could reclaim the ancient values which had made their state great. In this sense, its imaginative project is similar to the essays of Musonius Rufus: to map out a lifestyle for the adult male citizen which will benefit not only him but also the wider community. Moreover, like Musonius Rufus, and *unlike* his generic predecessors, Columella sees domesticity and the correctly constituted bond between a man and a woman as perhaps the most important element in constructing his ideal society.

Columella's place as the third and least famous of the (prose) Roman agricultural writers has generally led scholars to ignore the ways in which his book makes a rather peculiar addition to the genre. To begin with, it is excessively long: nine books of technical prose which cover everything from the gastro-intestinal diseases of cattle to the pickling of onions, a tenth book on gardening which suddenly explodes into Virgilian hexameters, and two more books of prose tacked rather haphazardly onto the end.[28] This quantity of verbiage contrasts with the concise volumes of Cato and Varro, who covered the knowledge needed to run a farm in one book and three respectively. Yet when I label the *de Re Rustica* 'excessively long', I do not mean to judge the text as much as to echo it. It is clear that Columella did not mean to write the twelve (or, depending on how you count, thirteen) books of which the manuscripts consist. In the introduction to book 10, the author indicates that this was supposed to be the final book: he refers to it as *faenoris . . . reliquam pensiunculam* ('the remaining payment on what is owed': 10. 1. 1). He goes on, however, to remark in the preface to book 11 that 'since my friend the priest of Augustus kept on pestering me, I went beyond the number of books which I had already almost completed and put together this eleventh section of agricultural wisdom'.[29] Columella puts particular stress on this explanation since, he notes with some exasperation, he has actually already covered the subject of book 11—the duties of the *vilicus* or 'bailiff'—in book 1. Book 11 thus appears as a piece of text which has exceeded the natural boundary of the book, a rather superfluous return to and expansion of an earlier section of the work. Book 12, then, is excessively excessive, more than more than enough, a viewpoint which is not mitigated by the fact that book 11 ends with Columella's curious

---

[28] Although Columella has been out of fashion until very recently, histories of Latin literature usually give him a few pages, some more grudgingly than others—but even a comparative fan such as F. R. D. Goodyear remarks in Kenney and Clausen's *Cambridge History of Classical Literature*, '[Columella's] *enthusiasm* for his theme is evident . . . today he might be a *professor of agriculture*': Goodyear (1982) 669 (emphasis mine).

[29] *quoniam . . . noster Augustalis saepius flagitabat, numerum, quem iam quasi consummaveram, voluminum excessi et hoc undecimum praeceptum rusticationis memoriae tradidi* (11. 1. 2).

statement that he has appended a table of contents to the current volume in order to facilitate consultation of the whole work (11. 3. 65). This seems like a concluding remark, or, at the very least, leads the reader to expect that the final book will consist of the kind of book-by-book summary represented in the opening chapters of Pliny the Elder. The surprise, therefore, comes when we discover that book 12 is nothing of the sort, but rather introduces an entirely new subject, one which, unlike that of book 11, has not hitherto made any appearance in the text.[30]

There is, of course, a natural symmetry between the *de Re Rustica's* eleventh and twelfth books: where book 11 outlines the duties of the *vilicus*, book 12 turns to those of the *vilica*. The latter word in Latin is usually translated into English as 'bailiff's wife', but it is important to keep an eye on the original term: whereas the English would render her primary relationship to the bailiff, both her and her 'husband's' names in Latin prioritize their connection to the villa, the civilized centre of the farm. They thus appear as something like Adam and Eve figures, the human faces of the space they inhabit and the embodiment of its labour—so that, for instance, in book 1, Columella's preliminary remarks progress naturally and sequentially from the purchase of a farm (*fundus*: 1. 2. 1–1. 4. 5) to the construction of farm buildings (*villa*: 1. 4. 6–1. 6. 24) to the appointment of a farmer (*vilicus*: 1. 7. 1–1. 8. 14). In this context, then, the relationship of books 11 and 12, *vilicus* and *vilica*, to the rest of the work seems much less tangential, and it is a little surprising to discover that they were not part of its original plan. Moreover, as John Henderson has recently pointed out, the overriding theme of book 12 is that of preservation: the main task of the bailiff's wife is to collect, conserve, and maintain for the future the food produced on the farm.[31] Thus, book 12 is mainly taken up with the mechanisms of storage, from the pickling of fennel to the drying of raisins, the

---

[30] It is worth noting that the word *vilica*, whose duties are the subject of book 12, does not appear in Columella's text until book 11, whereas the masculine *vilicus* is found prominently in book 1 and throughout the intervening books.

[31] Henderson (2002) 122–5.

mixing of fig-paste to the bottling of wine. The farm's agricultural produce, whose cultivation has been so lovingly detailed in the first eleven books, is safely tucked away in the twelfth; the *vilica* makes a perfect end point for Columella's text in that she stabilizes and guarantees its contents, a sort of bucolic prose version of Horace's poetic *monumentum aere perennius* ('monument more lasting than bronze': *Odes* 3. 30. 7).[32] In this sense, book 12 appears as anything but excessive; indeed, it looks like the point towards which the text was naturally progressing, an almost eerily tidy conclusion for a work not especially noted for its tight and coherent structure.

Part of the point here is that there seems to be a powerful contrast between the intended and the actual conclusions of Columella's book, between, that is, the exuberant verses on gardening which comprise book 10 and the sensible prose describing the bailiff's wife in book 12. Indeed, if one were to take a bird's-eye view of the text and ask which book seems to merit the description 'excessive', it would be book 10 which would probably emerge. Of course, on one level, Columella offers us in the preface to book 10 a clear and coherent explanation for the intrusion of these 439 hexameters into the middle of his text: he always intended to write a final book on gardens; his friends Silvinus and Gallio suggested that it might profitably be done in verse in the manner of the *Georgics*; an examination reveals that Virgil himself ran out of space to include the *hortus* in his poem and explicitly leaves the task to others to complete.[33] Columella, in true Neronian fashion, seized the opportunity. The 439-line hexameter poem which resulted is, let us say, unique and has been variously described by modern critics as

---

[32] The *vilica* thus represents a very different kind of 'feminine ending' from that outlined by Dietrich (1999) for the *Thebaid*, in which femininity is made to represent the text's desire to remain open to proliferation and continuation.

[33] *pinguis hortos quae cura colendi / ornaret canarem . . . verum haec ipse equidem spatiis exclusus iniquis / praetereo atque aliis post me memoranda relinquo* ('I would sing how the careful tending of rich gardens makes them lovely . . . but indeed I for my part am prevented from going through such things further by the lack of space, and I leave them to others who come after me to describe': *Georgics* 4. 118–19, 147–8).

'uninspired,'[34] 'respectable,'[35] 'very respectable,'[36] 'gallant but ill-fated',[37] and (worst of all) 'somewhat on the level of a university prize poem'.[38] Such tepid responses, as Emily Gowers has noted, may do justice to the quality of the verses but rather undersell their content: Columella's garden is a space of abundance, fertility, and luxurious excess.[39] If the purpose of an agricultural manual is to give the farmer control over nature, or at the very least bring the labour of farmer and nature into harmony, Columella's book 10 appears to dramatize the instability of the project, as the rampant production and reproduction of the *hortus* threatens to outstrip the ability of both gardener and text to contain it.

In contrast with the neatly contained and virtuous world of the bailiff's wife in book 12, then, the verses of *de Re Rustica* book 10 give us excess, intemperance, and dissipation. Indeed, Columella may here reflect a general cultural ambivalence about the role of the garden and its relation to the world of 'real' agriculture. Whereas the kitchen garden once had symbolized the self-sufficiency and humble goals of the small farmer, by Columella's time the word *hortus* had come to be more associated with the great luxurious gardens of the wealthy urban elite.[40] This trend is reflected in the particular plantings described in *de Re Rustica* 10: Gowers notes the large number of plants 'grown to restore senses numbed by life indoors', and the many different kinds of vegetables from all over the Empire, apparently included merely for the sake of novelty.[41] Like the language and form of the book, the content also exceeds the alimentary needs of the humble farmer who is the hero of the rest of the text.[42] The point is that, far from growing organically out of the preceding nine books of technical prose, book 10 leaves the reader

---

[34] Howatson (1989) 147.   [35] Grant (1980) 108.
[36] Rose (1936) 429.   [37] Goodyear (1982) 669.
[38] Cruttwell (1970) 393.   [39] Gowers (2000).
[40] Purcell (1996); Beard (1998); Boatwright (1998).
[41] Gowers (2000) 127.
[42] It is worth noting that, if the description of the *hortus* in Columella's book 10 does not fit neatly into the didactic project of books 1–9, it does have a certain affinity with its literary model, Virgil's description of the old man of Tarentum and his garden in book 4

with the impression of having stumbled into an entirely different text, one which has very little to do with the realities of agricultural life so carefully orchestrated in books 1–9. It would have made a strange and unsatisfactory end to the *de Re Rustica*. Fortunately or unfortunately, however, book 11 returns us comfortably to the world we left behind in book 9, as Columella returns to prose to add the human overseer to the descriptions previously provided of the land, crops, and animals which make up the rest of the farm. When the bailiff's wife appears in book 12, then, she offers a comfortable supplement to her mate as well as a reassuringly final and contained end to the text.

Here again, however, it is important to recognize the extent to which Columella appears to have deviated from, or rather added to, the generic tropes of Latin agricultural prose. The prominence which domestic femininity as a principle is given at the end of the *de Re Rustica* is completely at odds with its representation in both Cato and Varro. In Cato, the vast majority of the text is taken up with the mechanics of farm work, because, as he says at the outset, his hope is to return society to the days when 'good farmer' was synonymous with 'good man'.[43] Although he includes a section on the duties of the *vilica* (143), it is clear that she holds no more or less significance for the text's overall project than the olive-gatherers whose employment is described at much greater length in the following section. And, indeed, although Columella uses Cato's book extensively elsewhere, he does not cite him on the duties of the *vilica*. The case of

of the *Georgics* (lines 125–48). It has been noted that there too the bizarre collection of plants in the old man's garden conform neither to nature nor to any kind of realistically sustainable agriculture: he mixes cabbages with lilies, verbena, and poppies; his winter crop appears to be hyacinths; he has a few fruit trees but has spent a lot of effort to transplant fully grown elms and planes which don't actually do anything at all. In short, the landscape of his garden is such that, as D. O. Ross (1987: 201) remarks, 'one can wonder whether his solitary existence hasn't addled his brains'. Cossarini (1977) argues that Columella generally sees Virgil's *Georgics* primarily as a technical handbook and is thus not fully aware of its literary investments. If, however, Columella was indeed the expert farmer that most scholars (including Cossarini) seem to think he was, the horticultural difficulties of the old man's garden can hardly have escaped him.

[43] *de Agricultura* 1. 2.

Varro is somewhat more complex, as gender is actually foregrounded by the fact that the author dedicates the first book of his *de Re Rustica* to his wife, Fundania (1. 1. 1). He notes that, since she has bought a farm, she ought to know how to run it, and for this reason he has written down the conversations—all of which are among men— which make up the three books which follow. Fundania's female presence here is curious and not easy to explain, especially because gender does not play much of a role in the rest of the text. Most significantly for my purposes, moreover, it is only the first book which is ultimately dedicated to her: Varro, like Columella, pro- gresses from the tending of plants (*agri cultura*, the subject of the first book), to that of animals (*pecuaria*, the second), to what he calls *villaticae fruges* or 'the fruits of the homestead' (the final book).[44] Although he originally promised all three books to Fundania, by the time he reaches the 'homestead' book he has turned to another addressee, a certain Pinnius,[45] who is imagined to need the advice because he already has an elaborate house (3. 1. 10). My point is that Varro's Fundania, whatever her function in the text as a whole, is explicitly not associated by him with householding, and cannot therefore be considered a model for Columella's *vilica*.

Indeed, the actual model for the *vilica* comes from further afield, so much so that her appearance at first seems like something of a red herring. Whereas the other books in Columella's text tend to open with fairly unambiguous statements of intended content—e.g. book 3, *Sequitur arborum cura quae pars rei rusticae vel maxima est*,[46] or book 7, *De minore pecore dicturis, P. Silvine, principium tenebit minor* [47]—book 12 commences on a loftier note: *Xenophon Athenien- sis eo libro, P. Silvine, qui Oeconomicus inscribitur, prodidit maritale*

---

[44] This is the outline of the three books as it is represented in Varro, *RR* 3. 1. 9.

[45] Whose name, like Fundania's, seems to be a pun on one of the central themes of his/her particular book. 'Fundania' seems to derive from *fundus*, 'a country estate', while Pinnius, who owns a substantial aviary, may take his name from *pinna*, 'feather'.

[46] 'What follows is the care of trees, which is perhaps the most important part of agriculture' (3. 1. 1).

[47] 'Since we are going to speak about the lesser farm animals, Publius Silvinus, a lesser [animal] will take the first place [in the book]' (7. 1. 1).

coniugium sic comparatum esse natura, ut non solum iucundissima, verum etiam utilissima, vitae societas iniretur ('Xenophon the Athenian, Publius Silvinus, in that book which is entitled the *Oeconomicus*, asserted that the marital relationship was established by nature so that not only the most pleasant, but also the most useful, partnership in life might be undertaken': 12. 1. 1). This rather surprising opening is followed by an extended quotation of one of the most famous passages in Xenophon's text, the story which the gentleman Ischomachos tells his wife about the invention of gendered domesticity: when the god created the two sexes, he saw that the labour of living must be divided between them, since it was necessary for someone to go out into the world to hunt and farm and for someone else to stay inside to perform the household tasks. For this reason, he made men powerful and brave, in order that they should be physically and mentally suited to the outside world, and women more fearful and weaker, in order that they should be fit for a life indoors. Thus, the two sexes are natural complements of one another and together form a unit around and on top of which all society is built (*Oeconomicus* 7. 18–28).

The appearance of Xenophon's domestic cosmology at the opening of *de Re Rustica* book 12 certainly helps to give Columella's text 'a sense of an ending', as the author pulls back to offer a philosophical overview of the agricultural world he has built. On the other hand, the extended quotation, placed at the very beginning of the book, calls attention to itself, especially because it is almost unprecedented in the preceding eleven books. The only other place in the *de Re Rustica* where we see such extensive ventriloquization is with Virgil in book 10. In book 12, moreover, Xenophon's name (*Xenophon Atheniensis*) is also quite noticeably the first word of the text, contrasting with the emphatically Roman *Claudius Augustalis* which opens book 11. But the *Oeconomicus*' appearance here is not, it should be said, a total surprise. Xenophon surfaces in Columella's list of sources in book 1 among the Greek philosophers who have turned their attention to farming (1. 1. 7), although the author does not here cite the *Oeconomicus* by name and the text does not show up again overtly until book 11. More generally, however, Columella's interest in Xenophon, like his interest in Virgil, is perfectly in keeping with his place in the history of Latin literature. One of the curious, and under-discussed, issues around the *Oeconomicus* is that it appears to have enjoyed rather more popularity in late republican and imperial Rome than in classical Greece:[48] Varro (*RR* 1. 1. 8) and Pliny the Elder (*NH* 18. 22) mention it with admiration; Servius tells us that Virgil used it as a source for the *Georgics*; the famously elusive Epicurean Philodemus, resident of the bay of Naples and friend to Virgil, wrote a treatise which critiques Xenophon's views on women and marriage.[49] Moreover, although *Xenophon Atheniensis* is given top billing in Columella's book 12, he is quickly followed by another, equally illustrious and this time Roman, author: the second sentence of the book reads, *nam primum, quod etiam Cicero ait, ne genus humanum temporis longinquitate occideret, propter hoc marem cum femina esse coniunctum* ('for in the beginning, as Cicero also says, the male was joined together with woman for this reason, so that the human race might not die out in the fullness of time'). The reference is to Cicero's translation of Xenophon (the line is a Latin version of a sentence in *Oeconomicus* 7. 19[50]) a work which may be dated from comments in the *de Officiis* to the mid-80s BCE, or when the orator was about 21.[51] It is from this text, rather than Xenophon's Greek, that Columella has drawn the passages which he quotes from the *Oeconomicus*.[52]

---

[48] Pomeroy (1994) 68–90.

[49] Though its substance has unfortunately perished: the papyrus of Philodemus' *Oeconomicus* frustratingly breaks off just at the beginning of his discussion of Xenophon. See Laurenti (1973) 21–53.

[50] πρῶτον μὲν γὰρ τοῦ μὴ ἐκλιπεῖν ζῴων γένη τοῦτο τὸ ζεῦγος κεῖται.

[51] *res autem familiaris quaeri debet iis rebus a quibus abest turpitudo, conservari autem diligentia et parsimonia eisdem etiam rebus augeri. has res commodissime Xenophon Socraticus persecutus est in eo libro qui Oeconomicus inscribitur, quem nos, ista fere aetate cum essemus, qua es tu nunc, e Graeco in Latinum convertimus* ('But personal wealth ought to be gained by means of those businesses in which there is no shame, and also conserved and augmented with care and thrift. Xenophon, the student of Socrates, argued these things very well in the book which is called the *Oeconomicus*, which I translated from Greek into Latin when I was around the age that you [sc. Cicero's student son] are now': *de Off.* 2. 87).

[52] For fragments and a discussion of the text, see Garbarino (1984) 15–18.

In other words, book 12's use of the *Oeconomicus* may be seen to arise naturally from the *de Re Rustica*'s interest in that most Roman of literary themes, the praise of the countryside. Yet the *Oeconomicus* does not fit entirely comfortably into Columella's technical treatise. Although it is certainly true that Xenophon includes a few suggestions about the practicalities of land management in the final section of the book, it is clear that his primary interest is in the management of human beings: thus, Ischomachos is made to introduce certain facts about farm life in sections 16 to 19, not because they are especially significant in and of themselves, but in order to illustrate that agriculture is so commonsensical that it needs little teaching. In fact, in a neat reversal of the Socratic norm, much of the 'information' which is produced in these sections is elicited by Ischomachos from Socrates, who begins by insisting that he knows absolutely nothing about farming. By the end, however, the philosopher is able to say, 'I had no idea that I knew any of these things. But now I wonder if perhaps I might not know that I know how to smelt gold, or play the flute, or paint. For no one taught me any of these things, just as no one taught me how to farm' (*Oec.* 18. 9). The point is that agriculture does not require a vast store of knowledge but rather an inherent virtue: anyone can farm, as long as he is willing to work at it. As Ischomachos says in his concluding remarks, 'it is not the knowledge of farmers, or the lack of it, which makes some successful and some poor... as it is with generals, some are better and some worse, not because they differ from one another in their knowledge of military matters, but clearly in the amount of effort they put in' (*Oec.* 20. 2–6). Xenophon's *Oeconomicus*, therefore, is almost anti-technical, in the sense that its goal is not to offer specific precepts but to illustrate the kind of virtuous character which will guarantee success. Columella's text and Xenophon's could not, in certain aspects, be more different; the vast majority of the *de Re Rustica* is taken up with providing exactly the sort of didactic detail which the *Oeconomicus* would set aside.

Columella, therefore, appears to have embraced a text which, if examined closely, would deconstruct his carefully assembled didactic project as fast as it builds it up. But perhaps our mistake lies in imagining that we know what that project actually is. Certainly, from the preface to book 1, it is clear that Columella takes as his primary goal education of a practical sort. He complains that, whereas those who would learn oratory, or music, or architecture will be sure to select a wise man to teach them the fundamentals of their chosen pursuit, agriculture alone lacks not only teachers but students (*sola res rustica... tam discentibus egeat quam magistris*: 1. pref. 4). This is the gap into which, presumably, he sees himself as stepping. But in the same sense that Vitruvius' *de Architectura* proposes to explain not simply the art of building but the meaning which lies behind what is built—as he puts it, *quod significat et quod significatur* (1. 1. 3)— Columella understands agriculture to have meaning beyond the purely practical. This is clear in his lament over the decline of country life in the preface to book 1, as he catalogues the less worthy means by which people in his own day make a living: warfare, trade, usury, oratory, sycophancy, and public office (1. pref. 7–10). Only agriculture, the author proclaims, is left as *unum genus liberale et ingenuum rei familiaris augendae* ('the one manner of increasing the family's property which is fit for a free man and a gentleman': 1. pref. 10). He backs up this point by reference to the grand old days of Italian agriculture, the days of Quinctius Cincinnatus, Gaius Fabricius, Curius Dentatus, and 'so many other famous leaders of the Roman people' (*tot alios Romani generis... memorabiles duces*: 1. pref. 14), each of whom came from the field of his farm to the field of battle. Columella notes that these would now be shocked to see their descendants, who have moved to the city and lost their connection to the land (1. pref. 15–17):

omnes enim ... patres familiae falce et aratro relictis intra murum correpsimus et in circis potius ac theatris quam in segetibus ac vinetis manus movemus; attonitique miramur gestus effeminatorum, quod a natura sexum viris denegatum muliebri motu mentiantur decipiantque oculos spectantium ... dies ludo vel somno consumimus, ac nosmet ipsos ducimus fortunatos, quod 'nec orientem solem videmus nec occidentem'. itaque istam vitam socordem persequitur valetudo. nam sic iuvenum corpora fluxa et resoluta sunt, ut nihil mors mutatura videatur. at mehercules vera illa Romuli proles assiduis venatibus nec minus agrestibus operibus exercitata firmissimis praevaluit corporibus ac militiam belli, cum res postulavit, facile sustinuit...

For all of us who are heads of families have left behind the sickle and the plough, and we have crept inside the wall where we make use of our hands in the circuses and theatres rather than in cornfields and vineyards; we marvel, astonished, at the mannerisms of effeminate men, as they counterfeit by female movements a sex which is denied to men by nature and capture the eyes of the spectators... We eat up our days in play and sleep, and we count ourselves lucky that 'we see the sun neither as it rises nor as it sets'. Accordingly, strength does not attend such an indolent life. For the bodies of young men are so soft and loose that death would seem to make no change in them at all. But, by Hercules, those true offspring of Romulus, trained by continuous hunting no less than by work in the fields, were distinguished by rock-hard bodies and, when circumstances demanded it, easily endured service in war...

In other words, agriculture is both symptomatic of, and a cure for, what ails the Roman people; Columella's book, then, does not propose simply to teach the principles of farming, but to offer an alternative way of life, one which will restore Rome to a morally (and physically) superior state of being.[53]

Of course, such romanticization of farm life is nothing new in Roman literature.[54] But the point is that from the beginning Columella's text sets up the idea that his project has an ethical dimension, something to say, not just about farm management but also about Roman society generally. In the same way that Virgilian hexameters give us the over-cultivated flowers of the garden, Greek philosophy serves to introduce the human element to the farm. Indeed, it is

---

[53] See Cossarini (1978) and (1980) for the argument that the 'agricultural crisis' which supposedly provoked Columella to compose the text is not real but ideological, i.e. an attempt by the author to speak specifically to the land-owning aristocracy whose connection to their farms had been attenuated by increasing urbanization.

[54] Indeed, the first sentence in the passage above from Columella includes a close paraphrase of a passage in Varro's *RR*, book 2 (pref. 3). Varro, however, does not include the subsequent lament about urban effeminacy.

worth noting that, in book 12, all of the quotations from the *Oeconomicus* appear at the beginning of the book, in the section which concerns *in universum administranda* ('overall administration': 12. 3. 11). This section takes the reader from a general description of the relations of men and women, to a comparison of the wife's role in the household with that of a good city's νομοφύλαξ ('guardian of laws'), a simile imported directly from the *Oeconomicus* (9. 14).[55] But when he makes his transition to more mundane advice such as the best vessels for storing wine, Columella makes explicit his change of sources: he gives a list of agricultural writers whose work he will now be using and notes that they are useful here because 'tradition shows that attention to details was not lacking in the Carthaginian and Greek authors, or even among the Romans'.[56] In other words, it was not for the 'details' (*parvae res*) that Columella valued the *Oeconomicus*; rather it was useful because it could be marshalled to explain the human structure of the world about which the *de Re Rustica* was written.[57]

The fact that that human structure is, on the one hand, intimately connected with the places it inhabits and, on the other, finds its primary expression in the marital bond, is the point of Xenophon's domestic cosmology, quoted at the beginning of Columella's book 12. Indeed, it seems likely that the introductory material in book 1 about space and its effect on physical character was also, on some level, influenced by Xenophon's *Oeconomicus*: at 4. 2–3, as a part of his support of farming as the noblest occupation for a gentleman, Socrates remarks on men employed in the 'banausic' occupations, understood to be craftsmen who work indoors.[58] States which excel

---

[55] In fact, though he freely uses the comparison as found in Xenophon, Columella feels bound to explain to his Roman audience what a νομοφύλαξ is, and to add that these days magistrates are used for this function.

[56] *parvarum rerum curam non defuisse Poenis Graecisque auctoribus atque etiam Romanis, memoria tradidit* (12. 4. 2).

[57] On Columella's (underappreciated) sensitivity to his sources, see Baldwin (1963).

[58] Xenophon seems to mean all indoor craftsmen, although the term βαναυσικός may derive from βαῦνος, or furnace, and thus at some point signified only those who worked with fire: Pomeroy (1994) 235–6.

in war particularly frown on the participation of citizens in such jobs, he explains, since they require the worker to sit inside all day and 'as [the workers'] bodies are effeminized,[59] so too do their spirits become terribly weak'.[60] As a result, 'they are thought bad both at being useful to their friends and at being defenders of their country'.[61] The terminal lassitude and softness which in Xenophon is imagined to afflict the bodies of men who sit inside a workshop all day is translated by Columella to the city, depicted as a kind of inside space in the phrase *intra murum correpsimus*. Ironically, of course, Xenophon's primary concern is with men's fitness to serve the society of the *polis*, not simply in the military but in the sphere of civic life: the assembly, the law courts, the theatre, the agora. Indeed, it has been persuasively argued that Xenophon's rejection of inside space is rooted in a fear of the isolation and individuality which the house may produce in a man, as he is separated from the company of his fellow citizens and put with those domestic inhabitants (slaves, women) whose private interests do not necessarily coincide with those of the state.[62] But it is exactly the kind of communal activities and 'urban' pursuits so prized by Xenophon which are rejected by Columella as both corrupted and corrupting: the communal and equalizing spaces of democratic Athens have been replaced by Rome as—to borrow a phrase from Judith Walkowitz on Victorian London—the 'city of dreadful delight'. The physical rigours of farm work, the wholesome and uncomplicated hierarchy of life in the country, and the neat symmetry of the relationship between villa, *vilicus*, and *vilica*, have stepped into the gap as Columella's version of 'public life'.

---

[59] The verb which Socrates uses, θηλύνω, is cognate with the word for female, θῆλυς.

[60] τῶν δὲ σωμάτων θηλυνομένων καὶ αἱ ψυχαὶ πολὺ ἀρρωστότεραι γίγνονται (4. 2).

[61] οἱ τοιοῦτοι δοκοῦσι κακοὶ καὶ φίλοις χρῆσθαι καὶ ταῖς πατρίσιν ἀλεξητῆρες εἶναι (4. 3).

[62] Humphreys (1983) and Murnaghan (1988) 17–18.

XENOPHON, CICERO, AND THE BAILIFF'S WIFE: GENRES OF FEMININITY IN THE *DE RE RUSTICA*

In the *de Re Rustica*, then, feminine domesticity serves two complementary functions. First, it serves to bring the text to a neat and contained conclusion, as the bailiff's wife stores away what has been produced in the earlier books, stabilizing and guaranteeing the continued prosperity of the farm. Secondly, it serves as the moral counterpoint to the city so vividly described in book 1, where masculinity is compromised by modern living. Urban effeminacy is thus juxtaposed to domestic femininity, represented in the household tasks so lovingly managed by the bailiff's wife in book 12. Like Musonius Rufus, therefore, Columella sees the 'work' of the household to be both practical and symbolic: the good woman in the good home serves to rescue contemporary culture from the luxurious living which afflicts it. In this sense, it is clear both why and how Columella's attention was attracted to Xenophon's *Oeconomicus*, even though (as I noted) it does not on the surface seem to fit neatly into a didactic technical treatise. Not only is the *Oeconomicus* generally a text which, like Virgil's *Georgics*, serves to lend the *de Re Rustica* a certain level of cultural legitimacy, it also accords the domestic a significant place in society, offering the agricultural writer a way to explain his final book about femininity and the home. Yet Columella's use of Xenophon is not entirely unmediated. This is clear not just from the fact that he chooses to quote from Cicero's Latin translation rather than directly from the original Greek (about which I will speak more below), but also in how and where Columella chooses to locate Xenophon's *Oeconomicus* and its defence of domestic life. As we saw above in Musonius Rufus and Seneca, an emphatically Roman sensitivity to *luxuria* and its deleterious effects on society leads Columella to a very different conclusion from his Greek source about what should be done in, and by, the world of the house.

This shift in culture and values is evident when we consider the explicit reference to, and quotation of, the *Oeconomicus* at the beginning of *de Re Rustica* book 12, most notably when we consider the function which the domestic cosmology serves in the original text, and the different use to which it is put by Columella. Although Xenophon's text divides itself neatly into sections, there is still a clear overall coherence and narrative progression to the dialogue: it begins with a conversation between Socrates and a young man named Kritoboulos about the definition of prosperity and how best to attain it; Socrates then offers to repeat to Kritoboulos a conversation which he had with Ischomachos about how and why the latter came to be called a 'gentleman'; Ischomachos, in turn, repeats a series of conversations which he had with his wife, including the domestic cosmology, in order to illustrate her role in caring for the household so that he might be free to occupy himself with the matters appropriate to a well-born Athenian man. He goes on to outline his daily activities and then to his dialogue with Socrates on the sociocultural merits of farming, i.e. the ways in which agriculture is not only the easiest of arts to learn but the most efficient in creating a virtuous character. Although the *Oeconomicus* is frequently taken as a dialogue 'about' domesticity, therefore, such a reading does not really do justice to the text, since less than a fifth of its total length (4 out of 21 chapters) directly concerns the house. It is certainly true that the embedded description of and by Ischomachos begins with his description of his wife, and that the amount of attention paid here to household affairs is extremely unusual in a classical Greek text. But the point is that domesticity is introduced, explained, and contained in order to give Ischomachos (thematically and actually) the freedom to pursue the life of an Athenian citizen outside the home. The stable world of the *oikos*, although an essential building block for the stable city, is only the beginning of the *Oeconomicus'* description of how a good man lives, the springboard, if you will, for a larger discussion of the ways in which the correct management of resources may lead to a just society. It is this narrative that the domestic cosmology in Xenophon inaugurates, and it is no accident that

Ischomachos' version of the story starts with the generation of the two sexes and ends by noting that 'the law designates as correct the things in which the god made each [sex] naturally superior'.[63] Like any good creation story, it begins with undifferentiated chaos and ends with human society.

But if the domestic cosmology specifically, and the description of the wife's role in the household more generally, serve Xenophon's purpose by containing and (on some level) dismissing the functioning of the home as a matter of concern for the good citizen, they are given a much more important place in Columella's version of the ideal society. As I have already noted, the placement and particular tasks assigned to the book on the bailiff's wife cannot be accidental, as she is given the job of preserving the contents of the farm whose production was so carefully described in the *de Re Rustica*'s first books, from the general introduction in book 1, to ploughing and planting in book 2, to the management of trees and vines in books 3–6, to the care of farm animals in books 7–9. Indeed, by way of contrast with book 12, we may note that the introduction to the *vilicus* in book 11 is concerned with finding a way for a single person to embody all the knowledge described thus far. In an echo of book 1's lament over the state of agricultural teaching and learning, Columella notes, 'Nevertheless, even though you will scarcely find any single person learned in the whole discipline, you will find many teachers of parts of it, through whom you should be able to create a complete bailiff. For someone may be found who is a good plough-man, and [one who is] the best digger, or reaper, and certainly [can be found] an expert in trees and a good vineyard worker, and also a veterinarian and a sturdy shepherd ...'[64] In other words, the creation of a good *vilicus* involves finding a series of individual teachers who can communicate the contents of books 1–9, in exactly the

---

[63] καὶ καλὰ δὲ εἶναι ὁ νόμος ἀποδείκνυσιν ἃ ὁ θεὸς ἔφυσεν ἑκάτερον μᾶλλον δύνασθαι. (*Oec.* 7. 30).

[64] *verumtamen ut universae disciplinae vix aliquem consultum, sic plurimos partium eius invenies magistros, per quos efficere queas perfectum villicum. nam et arator reperiatur aliquis bonus, et optimus fossor, aut faeni sector, nec minus arborator et vinitor, tum etiam veterinarius et probus pastor ...* (11. 1. 12).

order that Columella himself does (ploughing, planting, and harvesting; trees and vines; care of farm animals). In fact, I would argue that book 11's focus on summing up and the efficient communication of the totality of agricultural knowledge explains why the index was placed at the end of this book rather than at the conclusion of the work as a whole.

But if the *vilicus* is supposed to embody the learning of the text, the *vilica* is supposed to manage, control, and preserve it. As Columella says, 'she ought to have in mind what things are brought in [from the farm], so that they may remain in their own particular and safe places, set aside without damage. For there is nothing more worthy of concern than to have a plan of where each thing should go, so that, when it is needed, it may be produced. . . . For who would think that there is anything more beautiful in every aspect of living than regulation and order?'.[65] This is, of course, a powerful echo of Xenophon, who has Ischomachos proclaim to his wife in a similar context, 'everything appears more beautiful when it is set out in order'.[66] But the point is that whereas Ischomachos is establishing a principle which will then be expanded to encompass good management in many different aspects and areas of social life, Columella treats the stability of the household as the goal towards which the knowledge of the text is striving. In other words, Columella's text ends where Xenophon's begins.[67] This shift in order has a profound effect on the ways in which we read the *Oeconomicus* within the *de Re Rustica*, even when the latter text is quoting the former almost

[65] *meminisse debebit, quae inferantur, ut idoneis et salubribus locis recondita sine noxa permaneant. nihil enim magis curandum est, quam praeparare, ubi quidque reponatur, ut, cum opus sit, promatur. . . . quis enim dubitet nihil esse pulchrius in omni ratione vitae dispositione atque ordine?* (12. 2. 1, 4).

[66] ἅπαντα καλλίω φαίνεται κατὰ κόσμον κείμενα (8. 20).

[67] It is clear, moreover, that this shift in structure was not drawn from Cicero's translation of the *Oeconomicus*. Servius, who says that Cicero's text was used by Virgil as a source for the *Georgics* (Serv. *Georg.* 1. 43 = Garbarino (1984) fr. 1), notes that in his time the translation was divided into three books: the first covered the duties of the *materfamilias*, the second the *pater*, and the last was a guide to farming. Like Xenophon's original, this structure is the exact reverse of Columella's, which proceeds from farm to farmer to farmer's wife. Macrobius also mentions the 'third book' of Cicero's *Oeconomicus* (*Sat.* 3. 20. 4).

verbatim. Thus, for instance, following the rhetorical question above, Columella offers a series of comparisons: order is necessary and beautiful in theatrical performances (*ludicris spectaculis*), since a harmonized chorus 'seduces those watching and listening with most delightful pleasure' (*spectantes audientesque laetissima voluptate permulcentur* 12. 2. 4); it is necessary in an army, to prevent the individual divisions from impeding one another; it is necessary on board a ship, so that, in an emergency, the required equipment may be produced on demand. Each of these examples is imported directly from the *Oeconomicus*, as is the final comparison of the bailiff's wife with a Greek city's νομοφύλαξ, whose duty it was 'to give praise, and honours as well, to those who obey the laws, but to punish those who do not'.[68] For Xenophon, such illustrations drawn from the sphere of public life serve to represent the household as a microcosm of the larger social world, that world which the rest of his text will go on to explore. For Columella, however, who has already in book 1 explicitly rejected the pursuits of the city, from the viewing of theatrical performances to the holding of magistracies, the terms of the comparisons seem to work the other way: it is *only* within the sphere of the household that Roman society can be made to work; it is only by separating the home from the city, and reducing public life to the status of metaphor, that the individual morality of *vilicus* and *vilica* may triumph over communal vice.

In this sense, I would argue that the inclusion of the *Oeconomicus* in the last book of the *de Re Rustica* is more than a simple citation of the *locus classicus* for a discussion of ancient domesticity. Rather, it serves to recast the *de Re Rustica*'s programmatic rejection of the city in favour of the farm in a more universal mould: it is no longer merely a question of sophisticated urban degeneracy versus simple countryside virtue, but of the 'private' world of the household versus the communal activities of public life. This is not, however, the only way in which Columella deploys and redeploys the earlier text. As

---

[68] *horum erat officium, eos qui legibus parerent, laudibus prosequi nec minus honoribus: eos autem qui non parerent, poena multare* (12. 3. 11).

I have noted, the *de Re Rustica* does not actually quote from Xeno-phon's Greek directly, but rather chooses to offer passages from Cicero's Latin translation. Of course, it is natural that Columella should wish to offer an extended quotation, such as the one which opens book 12, in the language of the majority of the rest of the text. But at the same time, it is clear that the author was capable of both reading and writing Greek, and so could presumably have provided his own translation. The prominence of Cicero's name in the second sentence of the book, moreover, seems to foreground the illustrious orator: like the citation and elaboration of Virgil in book 10, the passages quoted here clearly have a role to play beyond the merely ornamental. Indeed, it has been argued that Ciceronian rhetorical style generally, throughout the entire *de Re Rustica*, is used by Columella to legitimate and elevate his prosaic subject beyond the rather rough *Romanitas* for which it was known from Varro and Cato the Elder.[69]

When we come to the end of the extended quotation from the *Oeconomicus* in *de Re Rustica* 12, however, Columella offers some commentary of his own which suggests a further reason for the prominent citation of Cicero (12, pref. 7–10).

haec in Oeconomico Xenophon, et deinde Cicero, qui eum Latinae con-suetudini tradidit, non inutiliter disseruerunt. nam et apud Graecos, et mox apud Romanos usque in patrum nostrorum memoriam fere domesticus labor matronalis fuit, tamquam ad requiem forensium exercitationum omni cura deposita patribusfamilias intra domesticos penates se recipienti-bus. erat enim summa reverentia cum concordia et diligentia mixta, flagra-batque mulier pulcherrima aemulatione, studens negotia viri cura sua maiora atque meliora reddere. nihil conspiciebatur in domo dividuum, nihil quod aut maritus, aut femina proprium esse iuris sui diceret: sed in commune conspirabatur ab utroque, ut cum forensibus negotiis matronalis industria rationem parem faceret. itaque nec vilici quidem aut vilicae magna erat opera, cum ipsi domini quotidie negotia sua reviserent atque administrarent.... quam ob causam cum in totum non solum exoleverit,

---

[69] André (1994).

sed etiam occiderit vetus ille matrumfamiliarum mos Sabinarum atque Romanarum, necessaria irrepsit vilicae cura, quae tueretur officia matronae.

So wrote Xenophon quite usefully in his *Oeconomicus*, and then Cicero, who put it into Latin idiom. For both among the Greeks, and then among the Romans almost down to the time that our fathers can remember, domestic labour belonged to the wife, so that the father of the household only withdrew to his home for rest, with every care set aside, from his work in the outside world. For then there was the highest respect [for them] mixed with harmony and diligence, and the wife was fired up to imitate [him] in the loveliest way, eager to repay her husband's work with her own greater and better care. There was nothing evident in the house which was divided up, nothing which either the husband or the wife could claim was their own by law: but they conspired together for their common welfare, so that the woman's work balanced equally with the external business. Therefore there was no great need for the *vilicus* or *vilica*, since the masters themselves on a daily basis looked after and managed their own business.... And for this reason, since that old custom of Sabine and Roman 'mothers of the household' has not only faded but died away completely, the care of the *vilica* has necessarily crept in, so that she may look after the duties of the matron.

Domestic labour used to be the responsibility of Roman women, before luxury and lassitude (*luxu et inertia*: pref. 9) stole away the will to work; there used to be a neat parallel between the work of the household and that of the city, between the world of men and that of women. In the modern day, however, fashionable women do not even weave, nor would they be caught dead on a farm, so that the *vilica* must take over the tasks which used to be done by the master's wife. It is for this reason, Columella adds, that he has felt it necessary to provide a final book on the duties of the 'bailiff's wife'.

In a certain sense, Columella here is engaging in a standard kind of moralizing and romanticization of the past.[70] His lament over present-day mores, moreover, echoes that found in book 1 and not infrequently in the intervening pages. Yet the citation of Cicero here, as well as the phrase *mox apud Romanos usque in patrum nostrorum*

---

[70] On the use of this trope in Columella, see Noé (2001), esp. 327–35.

memoriam fere, serve to make this a more chronologically particular complaint than those which precede it. The decline in domestic life is a recent phenomenon, associated for Columella (writing in the 50s or 60s CE) with the mid-to-late first century BCE ('almost down to the time our fathers can remember'). In other words, implicitly, the end of the Republic marked the end of good domesticity; Cicero is significant not just to prove that the world described in Xenophon once did exist among the Romans, but also to mark the *terminus post quem* of its demise. It was the period of the rise and triumph of Augustus which saw the disintegration of the old Roman home, of Roman women's ability and desire to match within the walls of their houses the work which their husbands did in the public sphere. While on the one hand, therefore, *de Re Rustica* 12 reuses standard moralizing language to describe present-day excesses, his implicit chronology adds a particular—and peculiar—historicizing element. In its own day, the Augustan age may have managed to convince writers that it represented a return to good domesticity after the excesses of the civil wars. Half a century later, however, Columella associates imperial governance with the birth of luxury and the demise of women's labour on behalf of the household. Moreover, adding to the contrast which we have already seen being drawn between book 10 (where the text was meant to end) and book 12 (where it actually does), we may see a further contrast between the presiding authorial presences in each book: as Virgilian hexameters give a generic shape and texture to the excessive garden in book 10, so does Ciceronian philosophical prose provide a staunch overlay of traditional Roman republican virtue to book 12.

In fact, the contrast between books 10 and 12 is carried through even further in the use and abuse of Xenophon's *Oeconomicus* in *de Re Rustica* 12. Unfortunately, we have no way of knowing whether, or to what extent, Columella modified Cicero's translation to suit his own needs when he quotes it in the *de Re Rustica*. But no matter whose Latin it is that we are reading at the beginning of book 12, a comparison between it and Xenophon's Greek original yields some striking results. For instance, we may note that the second sentence of book 12, the one which introduces Cicero, is, as I said, a translation of a line in Xenophon—with the notable omission or mistranslation of the last words, κεῖται μετ' ἀλλήλων τεκνοποιούμενον. Whereas Xenophon says, 'first of all, lest the race of living beings should cease to be, the married couple *lies down together to have children*' (*Oec.* 7. 19), Columella offers only 'for in the beginning, lest the race of human beings should die out in the fullness of time, the male was joined together with the female'. *Esse coiunctum* may do for τὸ ζεῦγος, and possibly for κεῖται μετ' ἀλλήλων, but it does not give us τεκνοποιούμενον, which is the point, really, of Xenophon's sentence. Reproduction may be implied in Columella, but, especially given what follows, we are free to interpret the female's role as caring for the current generation rather than producing the next. Again, in the list of activities which require shelter, Xenophon lists the nursing of newborn children as the primary concern, along with making food and clothing from raw materials (7. 21): στεγνῶν δὲ δεῖται καὶ ἡ τῶν νεογνῶν τέκνων παιδοτροφία, στεγνῶν δὲ καὶ αἱ ἐκ τοῦ καρποῦ σιτοποιίαι δέονται· ('The nursing of newborn children requires shelter, and so also does the preparation of food from crops'). Columella, on the other hand, says *nam et fruges ceteraque alimenta terrestria indigebant tecto, et ovium ceterarumque pecudum fetus, atque fructus clauso custodiendi erant* ('for corn and other products of the earth require shelter, and the young of sheep and other kinds of livestock, and fruits need to be preserved in an enclosure': 12. pref. 3).

Similarly, Xenophon notes in his list of traits apportioned by gender that the god made woman emotionally, as well as physically, suited to her proper role (*Oec.* 7. 23–5):

τῇ δὲ γυναικὶ ἧττον τὸ σῶμα δυνατὸν πρὸς ταῦτα φύσας τὰ ἔνδον ἔργα αὐτῇ... προστάξαι μοι δοκεῖ ὁ θεός. εἰδὼς δέ, ὅτι τῇ γυναικὶ καὶ ἐνέφυσε καὶ προσέταξε τὴν τῶν νεογνῶν τέκνων τροφήν, καὶ τοῦ στέργειν τὰ νεο γνὰ βρέφη πλεῖον αὐτῇ ἐδάσατο ἢ τῷ ἀνδρί. ἐπεὶ δὲ καὶ τὸ φυλάττειν τὰ εἰσενεχθέντα τῇ γυναικὶ προσέταξε, γιγνώσκων ὁ θεὸς ὅτι πρὸς τὸ φυλάττ ειν οὐ κάκιόν ἐστι φοβερὰν εἶναι τὴν ψυχὴν πλεῖον μέρος καὶ τοῦ φόβου ἐδάσατο τῇ γυναικὶ ἢ τῷ ἀνδρί. εἰδὼς δέ ὅτι καὶ ἀρήγειν αὖ δεήσει, ἐάν τις ἀδικῇ, τὸν τὰ ἔξω ἔργα ἔχοντα, τούτῳ αὖ πλεῖον μέρος τοῦ θράσους ἐδάσατο.

It seems to me that the god, having created for the woman a body weaker in power for such things [outdoor tasks], assigned to her the indoor work. *But also knowing that he had constructed in the woman and assigned to her the nourishing of new-born children, he gave a greater share of love for babies to her than to the man.* In addition, since he had allotted to the woman the job of guarding that which was brought into the house, and knowing that—for the purpose of guarding things—it is not a bad thing for the soul to be timid, he also gave a greater share of fear to the woman than to the man. And knowing that it would furthermore be necessary, if a criminal should come along, for the one performing the outside tasks to fight him off, he gave a greater share of bravery to the male.

But although Columella provides a close translation of the sentences which introduce the section, concerning the assignment of domestic duties to women, he proceeds directly from there to the following discussion of fear. He thus omits entirely the sentence about the love of newborns (12. pref. 5–6):

mulieri deinceps, quod omnibus his rebus eam fecerat inhabilem, domestica negotia curanda tradidit, et quoniam hunc sexum custodiae et diligentiae assignaverat, idcirco timidiorem reddidit quam virilem. nam metus plurimum confert ad diligentiam custodiendi. quod autem necesse erat foris et in aperto victum quaerentibus nonnumquam iniuriam propulsare, idcirco virum quam mulierem fecit audaciorem.

To the woman, in turn, because he had made her physically unsuited for all such things, he turned over the responsibility for household business. And since he had assigned this sex to caretaking and management, for this reason he made the female sex more timid than the male. For fear is most conducive to diligence in caring for things. Because, however, it was sometimes necessary for those seeking nourishment outside and in the open to ward off an attack, for this reason he made the male braver than the female.

In other words, reproduction, in many senses and quite logically the linchpin of Xenophon's cosmological narrative, has entirely fallen out of the quotation in *de Re Rustica* 12.

At this point, it is worth noting one major difference between Columella's ideal household and his Xenophontic model: where Ischomachos' wife is a freeborn woman, the counterpart to a citizen husband, the *vilica* is only an employee, or even (potentially) a slave.[71] In this sense, it is logical that the wife's role in reproducing the next generation should have been left out of Columella's description. But we should not miss the central paradox expressed here in the *de Re Rustica*. Certainly, it is true that the *vilica* does not, for Columella, really exist separate from the work (both symbolic and actual) which she does, and thus occupies the place which slaves often hold in Roman literature. At the same time, however, if the *de Re Rustica* is in fact going to have the salutary effect on social mores which Columella claims, it makes little sense to deflect the responsibility for domestic management onto a slave woman; Columella is not arguing that elite Romans should feel free to live as they like because their slaves will pick up the slack. Rather, the *de Re Rustica*'s *vilica* performs a more symbolic function, both within the text as a text and as a part of the ideal society which it imagines: she is present to embody domesticity, which, as a virtue separate from other feminine virtues like good motherhood, is the *sine qua non* both of Columella's book and of his utopian agricultural vision. In this sense, she is at once the actual person conjured up by the author, whose social position might be of some interest to the reader, and a kind of personification, whose 'status' is entirely abstract.

Indeed, it is as an abstraction, rather than a real woman with a real—and potentially reproductive—body, that the *vilica* performs her textual function most efficiently. After all, her role is to put a neat and contained end on Columella's text, and her task, as the overdue culminating point of the book, is to encapsulate and preserve, not to proliferate and extend. It is striking, however, that a book on the natural world, or the human relationship with the natural world,

---

[71] In fact, it is never made clear in Columella exactly what social position the *vilica* is imagined to have, except that she is to be selected by the farm's owner for the job (*RR* 12. 1. 1–6). This is in contrast with Cato, whose remarks at *de Agricultura* 143 make her servile status clear.

should end by suppressing one of the most paradigmatic aspects of human 'nature', namely female fertility. This is particularly evident in the *de Re Rustica* because, in fact, Columella has already done reproduction, on a sufficiently grand and glorious scale to suit the most voyeuristic agriculturalist, back in book 10. In that book, moreover, fertility is celebrated not simply in the superabundance of the garden plot but specifically and repeatedly through the image of the human body. Thus, for instance, as prosaic an activity as hoeing (the preparation of the earth for planting) is described as rape (10. 68–73):[72]

>   eia age segnes
> pellite nunc somnos, et curvi vomere dentis
> iam virides lacerate comas, iam scindite amictus.
> tu gravibus rastris cunctantia perfode terga,
> tu penitus latis eradere viscera marris
> ne dubita ...

>   Come now!
> Drive away slow dreams, and now let curved teeth
> tear her green hair with the ploughshare, now rip her mantle.
> You, dig into her resisting back with a heavy drag-hoe;
> do not hesitate to scrape deep inside her belly
> with broad mattocks ...

From this assault, the earth ends up pregnant: *assiduo gravidam cultu curaque fovemus* ('we tend her, pregnant, with assiduous attention and care': 141); *sitis exurat concepto semine partum* ('thirst may burn up the offspring once the seed has been fertilized': 144); *soboles materno pullulat arvo* ('young burst forth from the maternal field': 146). But don't worry, Columella cheerfully reassures the reader, since the race of men born from the earth perished in the great flood and *we* were created by Deucalion, this isn't incest. For that, we have to wait for spring, as earth meets Zeus in the form of rain and sparks occur: 'The greatest of the gods himself... flows down into

---

[72] Gowers (2000) 137–8.

the lap of his mother in a drenching rain. Nor does the parent reject the love of her son, but the earth, fired with desire, allows the embrace.'[73] Soon everyone is in on the act: 'From here the seas, the mountains, finally the whole world is "doing" spring: from here [arises] the lust of men, beasts, and birds, and love kindles in the mind, burns in the marrow, until Venus, satiated, finishes off fertile limbs.'[74]

Yet it is not simply 'mother earth' who is assigned a reproductive body in book 10. The products of the garden, most notably the gourd and the cucumber, appear as both monstrous and sexual (10. 381–95):[75]

> nam si tibi cordi
> longior est, gracili capitis quae vertice pendet,
> e tenui collo semen lege: sive globosi
> corporis, atque utero nimium quae vasta tumescit,
> ventre leges medio. . . .
> lividus at cucumis, gravida qui nascitur alvo,
> hirtus, et ut coluber nodoso gramine tectus
> ventre cubat flexo. . . .
> at qui sub trichila manantem repit ad undam,
> labentemque sequens nimium tenuatur amore. . . .

> For if you want
> a longer [gourd], which hangs from the slender tip of its head,
> take the seed from the soft neck: if you would like a rounded
> body, and one which swells out with an enormous womb,
> choose from the middle of the belly. . . .
> But the dusky cucumber is born with a pregnant stomach
> and hairy, and, like a snake covered in textured grass,

---

[73] *Maximus ipse deum . . . inque sinus matris violento defluit imbre. Nec genetrix nati nunc aspernatur amorem, sed patitur nexus flammata cupidine tellus* (204–8).

[74] *Hinc maria, hinc montes, hinc totus denique mundus / ver agit: hinc hominum pecudum volucrumque cupido, / atque amor ignescit menti, saevitque medullis, / dum satiata Venus fecundos compleat artus* (209–12).

[75] Gowers (2000) 139–40.

lies on its bending belly. . . .
And under the summer house creeps toward the dripping water,
and pursuing too far as it slips by is worn thin by love . . .

Even when things in the garden take a turn for the worse, as in the
catalogue of plant illnesses at lines 311–68, it is the female body
rather than the gardener's skill which wins out in the end: the last
resort against a plague of caterpillars turns out to be a naked woman,
who walks three times around the field, spattering the ground with
menstrual blood (357–68).

Columella, therefore, can hardly be accused of leaving reproduction out of the *de Re Rustica*; what he has done, however, is to split it
off from the text's final book, to isolate it away from the domestic
duties of the *vilica*. Indeed, in case we have forgotten one of the more
striking images from book 10, one which connects the fertility of the
human female body with the successful production of the earth's
fruits, the close of book 11 takes the trouble to remind us in prose
what we last saw fleshed out in hexameter verse: 'but Democritus, in
that book which is called in Greek "On Oppositions", states that
these little pests are killed if a woman, who is in her period of
menstruation, walks with bare feet and hair unbound three times
around each garden plot: for after this all the little worms will fall
down and then die.'[76] When, then, Columella turns immediately
afterwards to the task of adding the *vilica's* Eve to the *vilicus'* Adam,
the omission of the reproductive role of the wife is all the more
noticeable. I am unwilling to ascribe a purely structural explanation
to this phenomenon, i.e. that Columella must metaphorically and
actually close down his already hypertrophic text by refusing the
possibility of further proliferation. Instead, I think that we have to
understand the extent to which the structure of the *de Re Rustica*, like
its use and misuse of the *Oeconomicus*, also works to communicate its
message: not just that having a woman around the farm is a good

---

[76] *sed Democritus in eo libro, qui Graece inscribitur* Περὶ ἀντιπαθῶν, *affirmat has ipsas
bestiolas enecari, si mulier, quae in menstruis est, solutis crinibus et nudo pede unamquamque
aream ter circumeat: post hic enim decidere omnes vermiculos, et ita emori* (11. 3. 64).

idea, but that the kind of civilized domesticity which she embodies is the natural goal of the wisdom laid out in the book. Her sterile, sober, and morally unimpeachable body is the 'solution' to the fertile free-for-all represented in book 10, in the same way that her job is to stabilize and contain the agricultural products of the farm. Columella's ideal world cannot exist without the house, its domestic values, and the female guardian who gives them a human face.

That Columella's vision of the correctly constituted household is built on the basis of a Greek philosophical work gives book 12 a kind of grand universality which marks it out from the rest of the didactic text. But it also provides the agricultural writer with the means to explore the relationship between his own world and that of a morally superior time, which he uses Cicero to locate in the prelapsarian age of the late Republic. The generic, chronological, and moral counterpoint to book 12 has already been established in book 10, with the sensual excess of the garden represented in Virgilian hexameters. Columella's innovations in the genre of agricultural handbook, the inclusion of the hexameter *hortus* in book 10 and the domestic *vilica* in book 12, work together and against one another. This is not to say that Columella is seeking to undermine the authority of Virgil, who has clearly been canonized in his own way as much as Cicero. It is, however, to underscore the ways in which we should see the different genres included in the *de Re Rustica*—as well as Columella's moral 'history' of domesticity—as driving toward an idea of the good home as something more than simply the site of child-rearing and food preparation. Rather, the housekeeping represented in book 12 is simultaneously the natural endstage of the *de Re Rustica*'s construction of the perfect farm, and a significant aspect of the 'productive' life.

Should the bailiff marry? Like the philosopher, yes. But Columella's text, like Musonius Rufus', engages the question on a very particular level. What is significant about marriage for both authors is the extent to which it makes society a fit place for human beings to live, whether that place be the ideal Stoic city in which private needs have become subordinated to the communal good, or the imaginary

Roman farm in which luxury and effeminacy have given way to the values of hard work and traditional gender roles. The point, however, is that Columella and Musonius each in his own way seeks to isolate and celebrate domestic life as good in and of itself; the 'work' which the home does is not simply the pragmatic and prosaic tasks of daily life, but a grander and more symbolic labour, namely to serve as the moral and ethical linchpin of human society. The absence of reproduction as a priority in both authors' visions of the ideal home is a significant case in point: while Musonius has no objection to children as such, in themselves they are not sufficient to motivate marriage, and in the *de Re Rustica*, reproduction becomes associated—through the rampant overproduction of the garden—with sexuality and luxurious excess. In the case of Columella, furthermore, this isolation of domesticity is profoundly symbolized in the fact that his book on the running of the house is not directly aimed at the elite women whose luxurious lives he criticizes in the preface of book 12. Rather, he creates an abstract entity, the *vilica*, to serve as household manager and create the domestic world which contains, controls, and guarantees the continued existence of the farm.

Perhaps the most significant difference between the two authors' perspectives lies in their implied audience: whereas Musonius' precepts are aimed at the man who wishes to live as a Stoic philosopher, in harmony with Nature, Columella's ideals spring more from the Roman tradition of moral writing rather than Greek philosophy—despite Xenophon's prominence in book 12. For this reason, the *de Re Rustica*'s ideal community is not a city-state where all men live in harmony and equality with one another, but rather a farm with a strictly controlled hierarchy of master, servants, and slaves. In neither author, however, is the house a 'private' institution, nor can what happens there be understood as simply an aspect of 'private life'. Rather, the home is where a healthy society finds both its natural beginning and its most productive end, so that female domesticity appears not just as a traditional Roman virtue but as an almost transcendentally significant value, needing to be of concern to philosophers, farmers, and all those, men and women, who wish to live a responsible life. This is, as I have argued, the point towards which a certain strand of imperial ideology had been striving since the beginning: the idea that the citizen owes it not just to himself but to his fellow citizens to construct a virtuous and happy household around a virtuous and happy woman. The distance between the image of Livia propagated by her husband, the more abstract good wife recommended to the philosopher by Musonius, and the perfect *vilica* described by Columella, is not great. All three, however, serve a particular model of 'domestic politics' which would place the world of the *domus* at the heart of public life. In this sense, both Columella and Musonius must be seen to have consumed and reproduced the ideological vision of the age of Augustus.

Epilogue
Burning Down the House:
Nero and the End of Julio-Claudian Rule

> Someone, he added, ought to draw up a catalogue of types
> of buildings listed in order of size, and it would be imme-
> diately obvious that domestic buildings of *less* than normal
> size—the little cottage in the fields, the hermitage, the
> lockkeeper's lodge, the pavilion for viewing the landscape,
> the children's bothy in the garden—are those that offer us at
> least a semblance of peace, whereas no one in his right mind
> could truthfully say that he liked a vast edifice such as the
> Palace of Justice on the old Gallows Hill in Brussels. At the
> most we gaze at it in wonder, a kind of wonder which in
> itself is a form of dawning horror, for somehow we know by
> instinct that outsize buildings cast the shadow of their own
> destruction before them, and are designed from the first
> with an eye to their later existence as ruins.
>
> W. G. Sebald, *Austerlitz*[1]

I END, as I began, with the imperial house. In the last chapter,
I discussed two texts, or sets of texts, which do *not* associate the
advent of imperial rule with the return of good domestic life—
although, as I argued, they still reflect an Augustan sense of the
household as the most important site of social life. Nevertheless,
unlike most of the authors in previous chapters, both the Stoic
philosophers Seneca and Musonius Rufus and the agriculturalist
Columella see 'bad domesticity' as a particular problem in their

---

[1] Sebald (2001) 18–19.

own historical moment. The fact that that moment happens to have been the age of Nero is not, I would argue, coincidental. From his supposed murder of his adoptive father and brother to that of his second wife and unborn child, from his two 'marriages' with male freedmen to his forced prostitution of respectable senators' wives, from his dependent, perhaps incestuous, relationship with his mother to his three different attempts to murder her, Nero seems to embody the very worst kinds of disrespect for, and violation of, the patterns of good household life. Add to this his luxurious spending habits, on ridiculously lavish entertainments for himself and the people of Rome, his refusal to attend to the defence of the Empire's borders, and his notorious inaction during the great fire which consumed a third of the capital city, and he emerges as the paradigm of the evil emperor—corrupt both in person and in policy, equally bad in public and private life.

Of course, it is clear that the image of Nero which is handed down to us by later historians is influenced by, or even predicated on, the fact that his reign marks the end of the Julio-Claudian dynasty at Rome. There is thus a natural impulse to contrast him with the 'good' beginning of imperial rule. Although his predecessors had shared many of his faults, Nero's villainy looms largest in the historical record, and the year 69 ('the year of the four emperors') which followed Nero's death marked the first wide-scale civil conflict which had afflicted Rome since that between Octavian and Antony. The idea of Nero as both the culmination and the nadir of the first *domus Caesarum* is underscored by later authors in different ways: Tacitus brings his *Annals* to an end with Nero, whom he has Galba describe at the beginning of the *Histories* as *longa Caesarum serie tumentem* ('swollen with the long succession of Caesars': *Hist.* 1. 16); Suetonius offers two omens, including one in which a grove of laurel, sprung from the sprig which had long before predicted Octavian's triumph over Antony, died completely away in Nero's last year (*Galba* 1). In the anonymous play *Octavia*, probably written soon after Nero's death, a conversation between the late emperor and Seneca is depicted in which the philosopher is made to plead for moderation, holding up the example of Augustus, in much the same terms that he had actually used in the *de Clementia*. The character Nero, however, will have none of it, and counters his tutor's representation of the modest and gentle elder statesman Augustus with a description of the crimes of the youthful Octavian.[2] Nero is thus made to appear the natural end point for the Julio-Claudians in Rome, ending the dynasty where it began, in murder, betrayal, and civil war.

As the end to Augustus' beginning, therefore, Nero is imagined both to reflect and refract the qualities of the founder of his dynasty. Although he may, as in the *Octavia*, be seen as representing the early negative traits of the first princeps, he never managed to achieve the later wisdom and moderation of the man who founded the imperial system. Indeed, the contrast between the two figures is and was heightened by the fact that Neronian ideology—to the extent that it can be separated out from later revisions—seems to have used the image of Augustus and the ideals of Augustanism extensively. Writers seeking to flatter Nero appreciated, and therefore attempted to reuse, the Augustan language of rebirth, renewal, and regeneration. Although not as insistently moralizing as the original, parts of Neronian literature sound eerily, and deliberately, like certain texts written three-quarters of a century earlier, at a very different historical moment. Thus, for instance, one of the *Einsiedeln Eclogues* (fragmentary anonymous pastorals from the reign of Nero[3]) proclaims (2. 21–9):

> ergo num dubio pugnant discrimine nati
> et negat huic aevo stolidum pecus aurea regna?
> Saturni rediere dies Astraeaque virgo

---

[2] *Octavia* 363–592. For a discussion, see G. D. Williams (1994*b*).

[3] There is almost universal agreement that the *Einsiedeln Eclogues* should be dated to Nero's reign, on the basis of the reference in the first of the two to an emperor as beautiful as Apollo (ll. 32–5) who composed an epic poem on the fall of Troy (36–49). See Cizek (1972) 379–81. There is some difficulty, however, in establishing their relationship to the work of Calpurnius Siculus who either quotes, or is quoted, in the opening line of the second Einsiedeln fragment. See Courtney (1987) 156–7.

tutaque in antiquos redierunt saecula mores.
condit secura totas spe messor aristas,
languescit senio Bacchus, pecus errat in herba,
nec gladio metimus nec clausis oppida muris
bella tacenda parant; nullo iam noxia partu
femina quaecumque est hostem parit.

Surely, therefore, no young men fight in an uncertain struggle
and no foolish flock denies that to this age belong the
    golden realms?
The Saturnian days, and maidenly Justice, have returned,
and safely has our age come back to ancient customs.
The reaper takes in his entire crop of corn with firm confidence,
Bacchus is lazy with old age, the flock wanders among the
    greenery;
we do not reap with the sword, nor do cities with
    tight-closed walls
make unspeakable war; nor now does any woman,
harmful because of her young, give birth to an enemy.

The sentiments are so familiar from Augustan literature as to be
almost cliché, from the *antiquos... mores* and the golden age to final
image of the reproductive female body which serves to guarantee the
whole enterprise. Indeed lines 23–4 clearly imitate Virgil's fourth
Eclogue: iam redit et Virgo, redeunt Saturnia regna (6). In retrospect,
of course, the idea that Nero's reign ushered in a new era of peace,
prosperity, and the rule of law seems a little strange, and it is at least
possible that the Einsiedeln fragments are actually meant to be
parodic.[4] Yet the terms of praise here are found elsewhere in Neronian literature as well,[5] and thus may be seen to reflect the new
regime's preferred language of self-representation.[6]

Augustus was a model for Nero in other, more overt, ways as well.
Suetonius says that upon becoming emperor he 'proclaimed that he

---

[4] As suggested by Korzeniewski (1966).
[5] For instance, in the younger Seneca's *Apocolocyntosis* (4. 23–4) and Calpurnius
Siculus 1. 71–2.
[6] Momigliano (1944) 99–100; Wiseman (1982) 66–7.

would rule following the model of Augustus' (*ex Augusti praescripto imperaturum se professus*: Nero 10. 1), which in context seems to refer particularly to the displays of *liberalitas, clementia,* and *comitas* that the historian goes on to describe. Miriam Griffin calls this list 'moral, rather than political',[7] a distinction which, as we have seen in the case of Augustus himself, is really without difference. The examples which Suetonius goes on to describe might certainly be construed to be as much political as personal: the distribution of money to the people, the senate, and the Praetorian Guard; the reduction of rewards for informers against violators of the *lex Papia Poppaea*; even the new emperor's ability to greet people of every rank by memory. This last was, in fact, also one of Augustus personal skills (Suet. *Div. Aug.* 53. 3), although in his case he confined himself to remembering the names of the senate. In Tacitus' more detailed summary of Nero's first speech, he does not mention Augustus by name, but does allude to the 'models for taking up imperial rule exceptionally well' (*exempla capessendi egregie imperii*). He also adds the codicil that, unlike some, he managed to have 'a youth unstained by civil war and domestic disputes' (*iuventam armis civilibus aut domesticis discordiis inbutam*: *Ann.* 13. 4). As in Seneca's *de Clementia*, the point seems to be both to create a link between Augustus and Nero and to indicate how much more promising were the auspices for the latter's rule.

It was not, however, only Nero who seems to have had an eye on his illustrious ancestor. Tacitus states explicitly that the younger Agrippina, Nero's mother, made Claudius' funeral as grand an occasion as Augustus', 'copying the magnificence of her great-grandmother Livia' (*aemulante Agrippina proaviae Liviae magnificentiam*: *Ann.* 12. 69. 2). Indeed, the role which she plays in Claudius' final illness, regulating the flow of information from the palace in order to orchestrate the smooth succession of her son, clearly reflects Livia's actions while Augustus was on his deathbed. In this, Nero appears less as Augustus than as Tiberius, and, indeed, some of the similarities between

---

[7] Griffin (1984) 63.

Agrippina and her great-grandmother may well be emphasized by
Tacitus in order to create ring composition over the course of
the *Annals*: the text moves from one emperor with a domineering
mother to another. But while Livia was only married to Augustus,
Agrippina is actually descended from him, a point which is repeatedly
emphasized in Tacitus. At *Annals* 13. 14, for instance, she reacts
to Nero's removal of Pallas by threatening to ally herself with Britannicus, a move which would have power because 'on the one side
would be heard the daughter of Germanicus, on the other the cripple
Burrus and exiled Seneca'.[8] The extent to which she is able to marshal
the support of the military solely on the basis of being of the Julio-
Claudian house is illustrated when Nero's praetorian commander
Burrus, having been asked to execute her, refuses on those grounds
alone: 'he responded that the praetorians were under obligation to the
entire house of the Caesars, and that, remembering Germanicus, they
would not dare any savage deed against his offspring.'[9] Later, when
Nero is excusing himself to the senate for Agrippina's assassination, he
charges 'that she had expected to share in the imperial power, to have
the praetorians swear themselves to a woman, and create a like disgrace
for the Senate and people'.[10]

The younger Agrippina's popularity with the military may serve to
remind us not just of her father and grandfather, but of her mother,
the elder Agrippina, who famously won the soldiers' admiration and
loyalty while on campaign with her husband Germanicus (*Ann.* 1.
69). Like her daughter, moreover, she could claim a closer blood
relationship with the divine Augustus than the man currently holding the Principate, so that, for instance, popular sentiment held her
up as *decus patriae, solum Augusti sanguinem* ('the pride of the
country, the last of Augustus' blood': *Ann.* 3. 4). Later, during a
dramatic episode in her ongoing conflict with Tiberius, Tacitus has

---

[8] *audiretur hinc Germanici filia, inde debilis rursus Burrus et exul Seneca.*
[9] *ille praetorianos toti Caesarum domui obstrictos memoresque Germanici nihil adversus
progeniem eius atrox ausuros respondit* (*Ann.* 14. 7).
[10] *quod consortium imperii iuraturasque in feminae verba praetorias cohortes idemque
dedecus senatus et populi speravisset* (*Ann.* 14. 11).

her deliver a stinging rebuke to him which underscores the point that Augustus lives on, not in the memory of his power or position, but in his blood relations. Having sought out Tiberius to confront him over the prosecution of her cousin Claudia Pulchra, Agrippina discovers him in the act of sacrificing to his divine stepfather: 'Provoked by this to anger, she said that it was not for the same man both to cut open sacrifices to the holy Augustus and to cut down his descendants. The divine spirit had not been poured into speechless statues: she her-self—the true representation, sprung from the blood of heaven—perceived her hazard and took up the mourning garments.'[11] Tiber-ius responds with a tag line in Greek, and (according to Suetonius) never spoke to her again.[12]

Indeed, it is one of the significant accidents of history that Augustus only left a single biological child, his daughter Julia, through whom all subsequent descendants would be forced to trace their lineage. In addition to this, the hazards of being a male scion of the imperial house meant that sometimes only the daughters of a given family survived to produce their own children.[13] This is true of the children of the elder Julia by Agrippa, whose sons Gaius, Lucius, and Agrippa Postumus all died young, but whose daughters Julia and the elder Agrippina carried on the line. Similarly, of the six children of the elder Agrippina, only her namesake produced sig-nificant offspring, Caligula's baby daughter and wife having perished along with him. Thus, in a very real sense, the Julio-Claudian women bore the burden of continuing the house of Augustus, and this debt became more and more visible as the dynasty grew older. Caligula's intimacy with his sisters passes into the historical record as unnatural, but even so the coin which he struck depicting Agrippina, Drusilla, and Julia gives them a remarkable prominence.[14] In a similar vein is his memorial coin of the elder Agrippina which

[11] *quo initio invidiae non eiusdem ait mactare divo Augusto victimas et posteros eius insectari. non in effigies mutas divinum spiritum transfusum: se imaginem veram, caelesti sanguine ortam, intellegere discrimen, suscipere sordes* (*Ann.* 4. 52).
[12] Suet. *Tib.* 4. 53.   [13] Discussed by Corbier (1995) 181–2.
[14] *RIC*[2] Gaius 33. Barrett (1996) 53.

proclaims her MAT[ER] CAESARIS AUGUSTI.[15] Claudius was faced with the problem that he was the first emperor not to be directly related to Augustus in any way, a difficulty which he partially addressed through his marriage with Agrippina.[16] Tacitus has Pallas argue for the marriage by noting that Agrippina, 'a woman of proven fertility, still in the prime of life, should not carry away the glory of the Caesars into another house'.[17] The later prominence of Agrippina in Nero's propaganda, then, may at least partially be due to his desire to underscore the fact that he was actually a blood relation of the divine Augustus, unlike his adoptive father and predecessor. Ironically, moreover, several times over the course of his rule Nero is forced to suppress popular sentiment which has arisen in favour of another person related to the Julian *gens*, always through the female line.[18]

In fact, the succession of Nero comes to be understood as the triumph of—to coin a phrase—the fundamental femininity of Julio-Claudian rule. This is true in both practical and symbolic terms. For the first, as I noted above, it was at least partially Agrippina's biological relation to the Julian *gens* which made her appealing as a wife to Claudius, and Nero appealing as an adoptive son and heir. If the Julio-Claudian dynasty was, as it is often described, akin to a hereditary monarchy, nothing should have stood in the way of Britannicus, Claudius' biological son by Messalina.[19] Yet it is clear that, following the emperor's marriage with Agrippina, Nero quickly became his designated successor. In part, this may have been because Nero was older than his stepbrother by three years, and the 59-year-old emperor and his advisers were concerned to ensure the

[15] *RIC*[2] Gaius 55. Trillmich (1978) 33–6.

[16] Wiseman (1982) 59–63. Whereas Tiberius was directly adopted by Augustus and was thus a legitimate member of the *gens Iulia*, Claudius' only real connection to the family was through his grandmother Livia. Wiseman notes that 'Claudius' use of the name "Caesar" was presumably based on the adoption of his grandmother Livia into the *gens Iulia* ... but her adoption did not, of course, affect *his* position' (59 n. 7).

[17] *ne femina expertae fecunditatis, integra iuventa, claritudinem Caesarum aliam in domum ferret* (*Ann.* 12. 2).

[18] e.g. Junius Silanus (Tac. *Ann.* 13. 1); Rubellius Plautus (*Ann.* 13. 19); Rubellius Blandus (*Ann.* 14. 22).

[19] As noted in Cass. Dio 61. 1. 1.

succession with an heir closer to manhood. On the other hand, as was apparently noted at the time, adoption may have been an imperial tradition but it was not one among the patrician Claudii, who had been able to trace an unbroken line of biological succession back to Attus Clausus. Britannicus' eclipse was thus viewed by many as shameful and unfortunate, as it became increasingly evident that it was more significant to be Agrippina's son than Claudius'.[20] Even before the old emperor's death, in fact, Nero's maternal descent was celebrated as much as that through his adopted father.[21] In one particularly striking version of imperial propaganda, in the sculpted reliefs which decorate the Sebasteion in Aphrodisias, Agrippina is clearly represented as the agent of her son's acquisition of imperial power. While she appears beside Claudius simply in the guise of a good wife, grasping his hand in a traditional display of *concordia*, she is shown crowning Nero with a laurel wreath, interpreted by R. R. R. Smith as a reference to his accession to the Principate.[22] This would seem to be the visual version of the claim attributed to Agrippina in the later historical tradition: 'it was I who made you [Nero] emperor' (Cass. Dio 61. 7. 3).

In symbolic terms, moreover, the 'femininity' of the last Julio-Claudian's reign is equally pronounced. Nero quickly passed into the historical record as the least masculine of emperors, and not simply because, like his adoptive father, he surrounded himself with freed-men and women. Rather, Nero's inability or refusal to conform to traditional ideals of Roman masculinity is understood as functioning on a grander scale than that of his, in some ways equally problematic, predecessors. On the most simplistic level, this may be seen in his portraiture, which grows increasingly fleshy and elaborately coiffed as the reign goes on.[23] It is presumably partially these later portraits

---

[20] Tac. *Ann.* 12. 25–6, 41; Griffin (1984) 29.

[21] As, for instance, in the *Acta Fratrum Arvalium* from CE 50–4 (Smallwood (1967), no. 14). See also Barrett (1996) 152: '[Nero] is in fact the first princeps who does not limit himself in his inscriptions to his paternal descent.'

[22] Smith (1987) 129.

[23] For the chronology of the portraits, see Hiesinger (1975).

which are reflected in Suetonius' description:[24] 'he was of a fair size, with a spotted and smelly body, blondish hair, a face pretty rather than attractive, eyes blue and somewhat dull, a fat neck, a protruding belly, and very delicate legs.... He was so shameless about his appearance and clothing that, during his travels in Greece, he even grew his hair (which was always fixed in waves) long at the back. ...'[25] His habits of dress are reported to have tended toward the Hellenic and therefore seemed rather effeminate: Suetonius makes reference to an ungirt *synthesina* or dinner robe (*Nero* 51), and Cassius Dio speaks of a 'flowered tunic' (63. 13. 3). More generally, in a telling if imaginary episode, Dio has Boudicca speak contemptuously of Nero in explicitly gendered terms, citing his personal appearance as part of the evidence for his effeminacy: 'I give thanks to you, Andraste,... that I do not rule over burden-bearing Egyptians like Nitocris... nor over the Romans themselves as did once Messalina and then Agrippina and now Nero (who, even though he has the name of a man is in fact a woman; this is illustrated by his singing and lyre-playing and self-beautification).... So let this Nero-Domitia rule me and you [Britons] no more, but let her, as she sings, dominate the Romans (for they are worthy to serve such a woman, since they have already borne her tyranny for so long).'[26]

---

[24] It is difficult to tell whether Suetonius reflects just the representation of Nero in the textual tradition or has also seen some images of the emperor, who suffered *damnatio memoriae* (erasure of his name and images) after his suicide (Bradley (1978) 281–2). Nevertheless, some portraits did survive: Varner (2000) 17.

[25] *statura fuit prope iusta, corpore maculoso et fetido, subflavo capillo, vultu pulchro magis quam venusto, oculis caesis et hebetioribus, cervice obesa, ventre poiecto, gracillimis cruribus.... circa cultum habitumque adeo pudendus, ut comam semper in gradus formatam peregrinatione Achaica etiam pone verticem summiserit...* (Suet. *Nero* 51). On the ways in which this passage uses the tropes of physiognomy, see T. Barton (1994) 57–8.

[26] "χάριν τέ σοι ἔχω, ὦ Ἀνδράστη,... οὐκ Αἰγυπτίων ἀχθοφόρων ἄρχουσα ὡς Νίτωκρις,... οὐ μὴν οὐδὲ Ῥωμαίων αὐτῶν ὡς πρότερον μὲν Μεσσαλῖνα ἔπειτ' Ἀγριππῖνα νῦν δὲ καὶ Νέρων (ὄνομα μὲν γὰρ ἀνδρὸς ἔχει, ἔργῳ δὲ γυνή ἐστι· σημεῖον δέ, ᾄδει καὶ κιθαρίζει καὶ καλλωπίζεται),... τοι μήτ' ἐμοῦ μήθ' ὑμῶν ἔτι βασιλεύσειεν ἡ Νερωνὶς ἡ Δομιτία, ἀλλ' ἐκείνη μὲν Ῥωμαίων ᾄδουσα δεσποζέτω (καὶ γὰρ ἄξιοι τοιαύτῃ γυναικὶ δουλεύειν, ἧς τοσοῦτον ἤδη χρόνον ἀνέχονται τυραννούσης)..." (Cass. Dio 62. 6. 2–5).

As Boudicca's speech indicates, Nero's theatrical pretensions also compromised his ability to appear fully masculine in the eyes of later commentators. The Romans always had mixed feelings about actors, as men who notionally sold their speech, lied about their identities, and seduced their audiences.[27] Valerius Maximus attests that permission was refused for the building of a permanent theatre in Rome in 154 BCE because such a structure was incompatible with *virilitas propria Romanae gentis nota* ('the famous distinct manliness of the Roman people': 2. 4. 2).[28] Nero did not assist his critics in looking past this already ingrained cultural prejudice by playing female roles on the public stage, Niobe and 'Canace giving birth' to name only two.[29] His inability to measure up to the good Roman masculinity displayed by his predecessors—especially the divine Augustus—is additionally articulated through the contrast between their concern with military achievement and his with the theatre. Suetonius reports that, when he finally was forced into doing something about growing restlessness on the frontiers, 'in putting together his campaign he considered it of primary concern to set aside carts to carry his theatrical materials, to cut short the hair of his concubines (whom he planned to take with him), and to outfit them with the shields and axes of Amazons'.[30] He also celebrated his artistic victories upon returning from Greece, where he had won numerous crowns in festival competitions, by riding through Rome in the chariot used by Augustus in his military triumphs. The scene is vividly depicted in Suetonius: the hero of the day dressed in a purple gown and a Greek *chlamys* covered in golden stars, wearing his Olympic crown and bearing the Pythian in his hand, with all the other prizes carried before him like the booty from a foreign war. His group of hired audience members followed along behind like soldiers once did in

---

[27] Edwards (1993) 98–136.   [28] Edwards (1994) 86.

[29] Suet. *Nero* 21. 3. Cf. Juvenal 8. 227–30. Suetonius also notes that he played other heroines and goddesses, having masks for these roles fashioned to look like his own face or those of women with whom he was enamoured.

[30] *in praeparanda expeditione primam curam habuit deligendi vehicula portandis scaenicis organis concubinasque, quas secum educeret, tondendi ad virilem modum et securibus peltisque Amazonicis instruendi* (*Nero* 44. 1).

the triumphs of Augustus.[31] Again, Nero appears as the debased echo of his illustrious ancestor, transforming the first emperor's celebrations of military success into an empty performance, and his populism into an appeal to the plebs' most base desires.

Nero's interest in theatrical performance thus comes to be read as an aspect of his effeminacy and moral corruption, which is measured against the solid masculine *Romanitas* of his illustrious ancestors. It is also represented in the ancient sources, however, as arising out of a more general impulse toward 'publication'—that is, the desire to share with the populace at large what ought to have been kept private. Tacitus describes a gradual degeneration after the death of Agrippina, as Nero's taste for public display grew more and more pronounced: first he performed songs at dinner, then was given an enclosed space 'in which he could drive his horses without it becoming a public spectacle' (*in quo equos regeret haud promisco spectaculo*), but undid the good intentions of his advisers by inviting the populace, who 'exalted him with their praises'.[32] He then instituted the Juvenalia Games in Rome, 'since he still was not yet at the point of disgracing himself in a public theatre' (*ne tamen adhuc publico theatro dehonestaretur*), and joined a number of his fellow aristocrats performing on stage.[33] Subsequently, he wished for a wider audience: 'During the consulship of C. Laecanius and M. Licinius, Nero was seized by a growing desire for performing on the public stage: for up until this point he had sung at home or in his garden or in the Juvenalia—venues he thought too little frequented and too small for his great voice.'[34] Reluctant to begin in the capital, however, he performs in Neapolis—to great local acclaim—leaving his Rome debut for the next year at the Neronia festival. According to Tacitus,

---

[31] *Nero* 25. The attendants explicitly identify themselves as *Augustianos militesque.* Cf. Dio 63. 8. 2, where the historian compares Nero's trip through Greece to win festival crowns with the journeys of Augustus and Agrippa who went there to fight. On the triumph, see also Dio 63. 20.

[32] *laudibus . . . extollere* (*Ann.* 14. 14).   [33] *Ann.* 14. 15.

[34] *C. Laecanio M. Licinio consulibus acriore in dies cupidine adigebatur Nero promiscas scaenas frequentandi: nam adhuc per domum aut hortos cecinerat Iuvenalibus lucis, quos ut parum celebris et tantae voci angustos spernebat* (*Ann.* 15. 33).

the senate attempted to forestall the 'shame' (*dedecus*) of having the emperor perform publicly, and offered him the victory crowns before the competition, 'by which the hideous performance might be veiled' (*qua ludicra deformitas velaretur*). But Nero and the populace at large are insistent: 'first he recited a poem on stage; then, as the crowd demanded that he make public all of his passions (these were their words), he came into the theatre, obeying all of the rules for playing the lyre.'[35] Suetonius too reports that, at this first Roman performance, 'when everyone was demanding his heavenly voice, he responded that he would fulfil their desires in his gardens; but when the military guard which was then on duty added to the prayers of the crowd, he willingly promised to appear.'[36]

Nero's theatricality, then, passes into the historical record not just as effeminate and decadent, but as a kind of prostitution: he and his audience appear as co-conspirators, mutually destructive of each other's morals.[37] The emperor's taste for public display both exacerbates and is exacerbated by the crowd's desire to see him on stage. In this sense, Nero's descent into the theatrical is inscribed on the historical tradition as both a transgression of gender norms and a confusion of the public/private dichotomy.[38] Tacitus reports an episode after the performance in Neapolis in which Nero puts off a trip to Greece, claiming that he did so because of his affection for the people of Rome: '[he said that] he had seen the sad faces of the citizens, heard their quiet complaints that he whose short excursions they could not bear was about to make so great a trip, when they were accustomed to revive themselves in adverse circumstances by

[35] *primo carmen in scaena recitat; mox flagitante vulgo ut omnia studia sua publicaret (haec enim verba dixere) ingreditur theatrum, cunctis citharae legibus obtemperans* (*Ann.* 16. 4).

[36] *flagitantibus... cunctis caelestem vocem respondit quidem in hortis se copiam volentibus facturum, sed adiuvante vulgi preces etiam statione militum, quae tunc excubabat, repraesentaturum se pollicitus est libens* (*Nero* 21).

[37] Cf. Dio 61. 5. 2, 62. 20. 5. For a discussion of theatricality and popularism under Nero, see Bartsch (1994) 1–35.

[38] See Edwards (1997) for a discussion of the general Roman prejudice against actors and prostitutes, who present 'bodies [which] are the objects of uninhibited public gaze' (p. 85).

looking on the face of the emperor. As in personal relationships, therefore, the nearest ties are the dearest, and thus the Roman populace had the greatest power and he, held back from his journey, ought to obey them.'[39] Although this might be taken as one more instance of Nero's egomania, Tacitus does go on to report that the populace was indeed relieved that the emperor would be staying at home—because they became bored and hungry when he did not. The terms in which Nero is made to express his relationship with the populace, however, are significant: their intimacy is like that between the closest of friends or family members. Indeed, in order to prove his affection, Tacitus reports, the emperor went on to stage a series of debauched escapades to entertain the people of the capital: 'in order that he should credibly appear to delight in nothing so much as [being in Rome], Nero held dinner parties in public places and used the whole city as though it was his house... he [even] wed one of that noxious crowd (his name was Pythagoras), in the ritual manner of marriage. The bridal veil was put over the emperor, witnesses were provided, the dowry and the marriage bed and the nuptial torches [were all present]—everything, in short, was seen which, even when it is a woman getting married, is covered in darkness.'[40]

The import of this passage in Tacitus is not simply to underscore Nero's love of performance and his adoption of a feminine persona. The theme is display, and the destruction of the barrier between

---

[39] *vidisse maestos civium vultus, audire secretas querimonias, quod tantum itineris aditurus esset, cuius ne modicos quidem egressus tolerarent, sueti adversum fortuita aspectu principis refoveri. ergo ut in privatis neccessitudinibus proxima pignora praevalerent, ita populum Romanum vim plurimam habere parendumque retinenti* (*Ann.* 15. 36).

[40] *ipse quo fidem adquireret nihil usquam perinde laetum sibi, publicis locis struere convivia totaque urbe quasi domo uti... uni ex illo contaminatorum grege (nomen Pythagorae fuit) in modum sollemnium coniugorum denupsisset. inditum imperatori flammeum, missi auspices, dos et genialis torus et faces nuptiales, cuncta denique spectata quae etiam in femina nox operit* (*Ann.* 15. 37). Suetonius contains similar stories, that he dined sometimes in public spaces such as the Campus Martius or the Circus Maximus (*cenitabatque nonnumquam et in publico, ... vel Martio campo vel Circo Maximo*: *Nero* 27) and that he married his freedman Doryphorus, afterwards imitating the screams of girls being raped (*cui* [sc. *Doryphoro] etiam, ... ita ipse denupsit, voces quoque et heiulatus vim patientium virginum imitatus*: 29). Dio also reports marriages to Sporus (with Nero as the husband) and Pythagoras (with Nero as wife): 62. 28. 2–3, 63. 13. 1–2.

public and private: Nero uses the whole city as a house, putting on dinner parties in public places and opening up to general view even those parts of domestic life which are normally shielded from the community's gaze. The emperor's 'love' for his people is expressed as a need to include them in his private life. In this sense, the last Julio-Claudian again emerges as the dark reflection of the first, whose openness about and investment in the functioning of his own house was one of the things which distinguished him as a different kind of civic leader. But whereas Augustus' allegiance to domestic life represented his ability to transcend the messy politics of the late Republic, the later incarnations of the imperial house have become a burden to the state, consuming Roman government in a miasma of petty jealousies, personal betrayals, and infantile bids for attention. This irony is the subtext of much of the later historiographical tradition. Thus, for instance, Tacitus offers a précis of the first speech which Nero delivered upon succeeding to the Principate, in which he attempts to assure the senate that he will be different from his predecessors (*Ann.* 13. 4):

tum formam futuri principatus praescripsit, ea maxime declinans, quorum recens flagrabat invidia. non enim se negotiorum omnium ludicem fore, ut clausis unam intra domum accusatoribus et reis paucorum potentia grassaretur; nihil in penatibus suis venale aut ambitioni pervium; discretam domum et rem publicam.

Then he outlined the shape of his future government, steering particularly clear of those things which had recently inflamed resentment. For [he said that] he would not be the judge of every matter, so that—with prosecutors and defendants shut up in a single house—the power of a few should roam free; nothing in his own dwelling was open to bribery or ambition; there would be a firm distinction between his house and the state.

The terms of the speech, at least as they are represented in Tacitus, seem carefully calculated to reassure the audience of aristocrats[41]—and singularly ironic in the light of Nero's later behaviour. The ideal

---

[41] Indeed, Dio reports that the speech was so popular that the senate ordered it engraved on a silver column and recited again every year thereafter: 61. 3. 1.

of a strongly articulated boundary between civic institutions and the world of the imperial *domus* is one which the last Julio-Claudian emperor never even attempted to achieve, a circumstance which is highlighted in Tacitus' narrative by the empty promises made in the lines quoted above.

Understood in this context it seems hardly accidental that the most potent and memorable symbol of Nero's reign was, and would continue to be, the so-called Golden House or Domus Aurea, the great palace which he built between the Palatine and Esquiline hills and which would become the most hated emblem of him as debauchee, egomaniac, and greedy tyrant. The vastness of the House quickly became proverbial, so that Nero was supposed to have started the great fire of Rome in order to clear space for it, and it was remembered as having almost taken over the entire city. Suetonius quotes a popular epigram which advises Romans to migrate to Veii if they are looking for somewhere to live: *Roma domus fiet; Veios migrate, Quirites, / si non et Veios occupat ista domus* ('Rome is becoming a house; translocate to Veii, citizens—as long as that house has not also taken over Veii').[42] The sense of competition between Nero and the people over who would be able or allowed to claim Rome as a home is a commonplace of the later writings about the Golden House, from Pliny the Elder to Martial to Tacitus, all of whom make reference to (in Tacitus' words) 'the house built out of plunder from the people'.[43] Indeed, it has long been argued that later rebuilding of the area under the Flavians was meant as a propagandistic gesture, reclaiming for the people land which had been appropriated for the private use of the emperor.[44] Thus, for instance, the Flavian Colosseum is built on the site of Nero's artificial lake, the baths of Titus over part of the House's Oppian wing, and the temple of the Divine Claudius, begun by Agrippina but made into a nymphaeum by Nero, was completed by Vespasian. The point, as

[42] Suet. *Nero* 39. 2.
[43] *spoliis civium exstructa domo* (*Ann.* 15. 52). Cf. Pliny the Elder, *NH* 33. 54, 34. 111–13.
[44] See, for instance, Darwall-Smith (1996) 36–8, 72–4.

Martial neatly puts it, is that 'Rome has been returned to herself, and under your rule, Caesar [Domitian], what was once the playground of a tyrant now is one for the people'.[45]

Recently, however, critics have questioned the vision of the Golden House and its builder which have come down to us in later historiography. While it is true that the Neronian palace seems to have been built on a grand scale, it is not at all clear that the idea behind it was to create a 'private' dwelling in the sense of excluding the populace from it. After all, the House seems to have included at least one public temple,[46] and two major thoroughfares, including part of the via Triumphalis which Nero himself used in 67 for the mock triumph described above.[47] Systematic analyses of what had previously occupied the space which was incorporated into the new palace reveal that very little of it had actually belonged to individual citizens; although the land occupied by a few wealthy families on the Velia and the Caelian hill may have been appropriated by the emperor, 'much of the area enclosed within the Domus Aurea was already imperial property'.[48] Poorer citizens who may have inhabited *insulae* (apartment buildings) in the Colosseum valley were actually already scheduled to be rehoused in safer and more aesthetically pleasing dwellings, subsidized by the emperor.[49] They had in fact been temporarily housed in the imperial gardens, as well as the Campus Martius, after the devastation of the fire.[50] When the emperor had fastened upon the Christians as scapegoats for starting the fire, he opened up the gardens of the Golden House to the public in order to display their punishments.[51] In general, moreover, imperial palaces had not since Augustus been 'private' structures, but instead served a multitude of public functions, from

[45] *reddita Roma sibi est et sunt te praeside, Caesar, / deliciae populi, quae fuerant domini* (*de Spectaculis* 2. 11–12).

[46] That of Fortuna, which he rebuilt lavishly in translucent marble: Pliny, *NH* 36. 162. Griffin (1984) 139–40.

[47] From the descriptions, hardly a 'private' affair. Champlin (1998) 334–5; Davies (2000) 41.

[48] Morford (1968) 160.   [49] Tac. *Ann.* 15. 43; Morford (1968) 161–2.

[50] Tac. *Ann.* 15. 39.   [51] Tac. *Ann.* 15. 44.

meeting places for the senate, to libraries, to courts—as, indeed, is noted in Nero's first speech to the senate quoted above.[52] The last Julio-Claudian, even more than his predecessors, was nothing without his audience, and seems therefore unlikely to have excluded them from his most lavish performance of luxury and excess.

In short, although later authors certainly attempt to cast the Golden House as a representation of Nero's greedy private consumption of Rome's landscape and resources, the palace also seems to illustrate the opposite problem: the publication of the emperor's privacy, the demise of the boundary between the imperial house and the imperial state. This is emphasized in Suetonius' description of the House's gardens, located in what would become the Colosseum valley (*Nero* 31. 1):

non in alia re tamen damnosior quam in aedificando domum a Palatio Esquilias usque fecit.... de cuius spatio atque cultu suffecerit haec rettulisse:... item stagnum maris instar, circumsaeptum aedificiis ad urbium speciem; rura insuper arvis atque vinetis et pascuis silvisque varia, cum multitudine omnis generis pecudum ac ferarum.

Since he was more harmful in nothing else as in building, he made a house which stretched between the Palatine and the Esquiline.... The following should suffice to illustrate [the House's] extent and decoration:... there was also a lake like the sea, ringed by buildings made to look like cities; there was countryside besides, made up of fields and vineyards and pastures and forests, with a host of different kinds of domesticated and wild animals.

Tacitus too emphasizes the naturalized landscape of the House: 'and he built a house, in which the gems and gold—to which we were long ago accustomed and which have been made common by [the spread of] luxury—were scarcely as amazing as the fields and lakes and, closer in, forests [laid out] in the manner of a wilderness, and, further out, open spaces and vistas.'[53] Scholars have generally seen in these descriptions an expression of the traditional moralizing

---

[52] Elsner (1994) 121; McGinn (1998a) 100–4.

[53] *exstruxitque domum, in qua haud proinde gemmae et aurum miraculo essent, solita pridem et luxu vulgata, quam arva et stagna et in modum solitudinum hinc silvae, inde aperta spatia et prospectus* (*Ann.* 15. 42. 1).

critiques of *rus in urbe*, which focus on the unnaturalness of building a country villa in the midst of a city.[54] At the same time, however, it is also clear that these authors are attempting to represent the gardens of the Golden House as offering a view of the world in miniature, as the lake becomes a sea, the buildings around it are made to look like cities, and the rest of the environment is transformed into a microcosm of the Roman countryside. The House thus becomes a grand symbol of how Nero wished to treat the entire Empire, as an extension of his personal space, an enormous playground in which he might indulge his egomania and idiosyncratic whims. The problem with the House was in this sense as much the extent to which 'the public', both space and people, was included within it as excluded from it; Nero goes down in Roman history as the emperor whose inability to maintain the boundary between private and public, between *domus* and *res publica*, brought down both his own reign and that of the Julio-Claudian house.

I opened this Epilogue with a quotation from *Austerlitz*, W. G. Sebald's lyrical novel about memory, architecture, and identity in the aftermath of devastating loss. Sebald here notes the power which buildings can have, both as representations of the comfortable stability of home and family, and as emblems of the restless, relentless instability of power and time: 'domestic buildings of *less* than normal size . . . are those that offer us at least a semblance of peace . . . outsize buildings cast the shadow of their own destruction before them, and are designed from the first with an eye to their later existence as ruins.' One of the things which I have tried to delineate in this book is how the architectural metaphors which appear with such frequency to describe early imperial governance manage to gesture to both tropes at once: both to the private, particular world of the family and to the cold, disinterested march of Roman history. This, I believe, is one of the things which made the Roman Empire work in its first inception: the ability of the Augustan age to represent itself as a different kind of answer to the problems which had long beset

---

[54] Purcell (1987) 198–9.

the *res publica*, constructing a new system which transcended the divide between public and private life. This construct, however, both created and was created by an understanding of the *domus* as one of the most important sites of politics—not just, as it had been under the Republic, one more location where the business of civic life might be done, but as the place where politics was felt most deeply, expressed most profoundly, and played out on an emotive and moral level not achieved in the more formal sphere of the state. It is this sense of the home as both entirely different from and intimately connected with the vicissitudes of civic life which is the 'invention' of the Augustan age.

In this sense, Nero (or, at any rate, the idea of Nero which is communicated to us by later historians) was almost inevitable. The last Julio-Claudian comes across in the historiography as almost a parody of the first, as Augustus' use of his female relatives as public symbols becomes the unnatural dominance of Agrippina over her son; the self-advertisement of Augustus as a domestic figure becomes Nero's performative intimacy with the theatre-going populace; the carefully constructed public/private dwelling on the Augustan Palatine becomes Nero's attempt to incorporate all of Rome into the Golden House. It is, of course, difficult to know how much of what is remembered of Nero achieves prominence in the historical record simply because of the neat symmetry between him and the founder of his dynasty. But my point is that the terms in which that memory is recorded are testimony to the power of domesticity as a way of reading the Julio-Claudians and what they had made of Rome. On both material and symbolic levels, the fact of the imperial *domus* transformed how Rome thought about the 'correct' relationship between public and private life, and how the work of the one influenced the construction of the other. This was the legacy of the first dynasty, and despite Nero's fall, that legacy would continue to have power and consequence, as the emperors who followed would be forced to position themselves in relation to it—to find a way, that is, of inhabiting the ruins of the house that Augustus built.

References

ABE, H., SATO, H., and KITAGAWA OTSURU, C. (1999) (eds.), *The Public and the Private in the United States: International Area Studies Conference* V (Osaka: Japan Center for Area Studies, National Museum of Ethnology).

ALCOCK, S. E., CHERRY, J. F., and ELSNER, J. (2001), *Pausanias: Travel and Memory in Roman Greece* (Oxford and New York: Oxford University Press).

ALFÖLDI, A. (1971), *Der Vater des Vaterlandes im römischen Denken* (Darmstadt: Wissenschaftliche Buchgesellschaft).

ALLISON, P. (1997), 'Artefact Distribution and Spatial Function in Pompeian Houses' in Rawson and Weaver (1997) 321–54.

ALONSO-NÚÑEZ, J. M. (1987), 'An Augustan World History: The *Historiae Philippicae* of Pompeius Trogus', *G&R* 34/1: 56–72.

ANDERSON, B. (1991), *Imagined Communities*, 2nd edn. (London and New York: Verso).

ANDERSON, J. C., Jr. (1997), *Roman Architecture and Society* (Baltimore: Johns Hopkins University Press).

ANDO, C. (2000), *Imperial Ideology and Provincial Loyalty in the Roman Empire* (Berkeley, Calif.: University of California Press).

ANDRÉ, J.-M. (1994), 'Littérature technique et héritage de la rhétorique cicéronienne chez Columelle', in J. Dangel, ed., *Grammaire et rhétorique: Notion de Romanité* (Strasbourg: Université des sciences humaines de Strasbourg), 179–96.

ANTONACCIO, C. M. (2000), 'Architecture and Behavior: Building Gender into Greek Houses', *CW* 93: 517–33.

ARCHER, L. J., FISCHLER, S., and WYKE, M. (1994) (eds.), *Women in Ancient Societies: 'An illusion of the night'* (Houndmills, Basingstoke, Hants: Macmillan).

ARENDT, H. (1958), *The Human Condition* (Chicago: University of Chicago Press).

ARIETI, J. A. (1997), 'Rape and Livy's View of Roman History,' in S. Deacy and K. F. Pierce, *Rape in Antiquity: Sexual Violence in the Greek and*

Roman Worlds (London and Swansea: Duckworth/The Classical Press of Wales), 209–29.

ARMSTRONG, N. (1987), *Desire and Domestic Fiction* (Oxford and New York: Oxford University Press).

ASTIN, A. A. (1988), 'Regimen Morum', *JRS* 78: 14–34.

BADIAN, E. (1985), 'A Phantom Marriage Law', *Philologus*, 129: 82–98.

BALDWIN, B. (1963), 'Columella's Sources and How he Used them', *Latomus*, 22/4: 785–91.

—— (1972), 'Women in Tacitus', *Prudentia*, 4: 83–101.

BALSDON, J. P. V. D. (1971), 'Dionysius on Romulus: A Political Pamphlet?', *JRS* 61: 18–27.

BALTRUSCH, E. (1989), *Regimen Morum* (*Vestigia*, 41; Munich: C. H. Beck).

BARCHIESI, A. (1993), 'Insegnare ad Augusto: Orazio, *Epistole* 2,1 e Ovidio, *Tristia* II', *MD* 31: 149–84.

BARRETT, A. A. (1996), *Agrippina: Mother of Nero* (London: Batsford).

—— (2002), *Livia: First Lady of Imperial Rome* (New Haven: Yale University Press).

BARTON, I. M. (1996*a*), 'Palaces', in I. M. Barton (1996*b*) 91–120.

—— (1996*b*), *Roman Domestic Buildings* (Exeter: University of Exeter Press).

BARTON, T. (1994), 'The *inventio* of Nero: Suetonius', in Elsner and Masters (1994) 48–63.

BARTSCH, S. (1994), *Actors in the Audience: Theatricality and Doublespeak from Nero to Hadrian* (Cambridge, Mass.: Harvard University Press).

BEARD, M. (1993), 'Looking (Harder) for Roman Myth: Dumézil, Declamation and the Problems of Definition', in F. Graf, ed., *Mythos in mythenloser Gesellschaft: das Paradigma Roms* (Stuttgart: B. G. Teubner), 44–64.

—— (1998), 'Imaginary *horti*: or Up the Garden Path', in Cima and la Rocca (1998) 23–32.

BELLEMORE, J. (1984), *Nicolaus of Damascus: Life of Augustus* (Bristol: Bristol Classical Press).

BELLEN, H. (1987), '*Novus Status—Novae Leges*: Kaiser Augustus als Gesetzgeber', in G. Binder, ed., *Saeculum Augustum*, i: *Herrschaft und Gesellschaft* (Darmstadt: Wissenschaftliche Buchgesellschaft), 308–48.

BENHABIB, S. (1998), 'Models of Public Space: Hannah Arendt, the Liberal Tradition, and Jürgen Habermas', in Landes (1998*b*) 65–99.

BÉRANGER, J. (1958), 'L'Accession d'Auguste et l'idéologie du "privatus" ', *Palaeologia*, 7: 1–11.

BERG, B. (1997), 'Cicero's Palatine Home and Clodius' Shrine of Liberty: Alternative Emblems of the Republic in Cicero's *De domo sua*', in Carl Deroux, ed., *Studies in Latin Literature and Roman History*, 8 (Collection Latomus, 239; Brussels: Latomus), 122–43.

BERGMANN, B. (1994), 'The Roman House as Memory Theater: the House of the Tragic Poet in Pompeii', *Art Bulletin*, 76/2: 225–56.

—— (1996), 'The Pregnant Moment: Tragic Wives in the Roman Interior', in Kampen (1996), 199–218.

BERRY, J. (1997), 'Household Artifacts: Re-interpreting Roman Domestic Space', in Laurence and Wallace-Hadrill (1997), 183–95.

BINDER, G. (1971), *Aeneas und Augustus: Interpretationen zum 8. Buch der Aeneis* (Meisenheim am Glan: A. Hain).

BLOK, J. (1987), 'Sexual Asymmetry: A Historiographical Essay', in J. Blok and P. Mason, eds., *Sexual Assymmetry: Studies in Ancient Society* (Amsterdam: J. C. Gieben), 1–57.

BLOOMER, W. M. (1992), *Valerius Maximus & the Rhetoric of the New Nobility* (Chapel Hill, NC: University of North Carolina Press).

—— (1997), 'A Preface to the History of Declamation: Whose Speech? Whose History?', in Habinek and Schiesaro (1997), 199–215.

BLUMENTHAL, F. (1913), 'Die Autobiographie des Augustus I', *WS* 35: 113–30, 267–88.

—— (1914), 'Die Autobiographie des Augustus II', *WS* 36: 84–103.

BOATWRIGHT, M. T. (1998), 'Luxuriant Gardens and Extravagant Women: The *horti* of Rome between Republic and Empire', in Cima and la Rocca (1998), 71–82.

BONNER, S. F. (1949), *Roman Declamation in the Late Republic and Early Empire* (Liverpool: University Press of Liverpool).

DE BOUVRIE, S. (1984), 'Augustus' Legislation on Morals—Which Morals and What Aims?', *Symbolae Osloenses*, 59: 93–113.

BOYLE, A. J. (1999), '*Aeneid* 8: Images of Rome', in C. Perkell, ed., *Reading Vergil's Aeneid* (Norman, Okla.: University of Oklahoma Press), 148–61.

BRADLEY, K. R. (1978), *Suetonius' Life of Nero: An Historical Commentary* (Collection Latomus, 157; Brussels: Latomus).

BRADLEY K. R., (1991), *Discovering the Roman Family* (Oxford and New York: Oxford University Press).

BRIDGE, R. T., and LAKE, E. D. C. (1908) (eds.), *Select Epigrams of Martial, Books I–VI* (Oxford: Clarendon Press).

BRISCOE, J. (1981), *A Commentary on Livy, Books XXXIV–XXXVII* (Oxford: Clarendon Press).

BROTHERS, A. J. (1996), 'Urban Housing', in I. M. Barton, ed., (1996*b*) 33–63.

BRUNT, P. A. (1971), *Italian Manpower 225 BC–AD 14* (Oxford: Clarendon Press).

BUTLER, S. (1998), 'Notes on a *Membrum Disiectum*', in Murnaghan and Joshel (1998), 236–55.

CALLEBAT, L. (1989), 'Organisation et structures du *De Architectura* de Vitruve', in Geertman and de Jong (1989), 34–8.

CANFORA, L. (1980), 'Proscrizioni e dissesto sociale nella repubblica Romana', *Klio*, 62/2: 425–37.

CAPE, R. W. Jr. (1997), 'Persuasive History: Roman Rhetoric and Historiography', in Dominik (1997), 212–60.

CARETTONI, G. (1983), *Das Haus des Augustus auf dem Palatin* (Mainz am Rhein: P. von Zabern).

CARRATELLI, G. P., *et al.* (1990–9), *Pompeii: Pitture e Mosaici*, i–x (Rome: Istituto dell'Enciclopedia Italiana).

CARTER, C. J. (1975), 'Valerius Maximus', in T. A. Dorey, ed., *Empire and Aftermath: Silver Latin*, ii (London and Boston: Routledge and Kegan Paul), 26–56.

CASEVITZ, M. (1998), 'Note sur le vocabulaire du privé et du public', *Ktema*, 23: 39–46.

DE CERTEAU, M. (1984), *The Practice of Everyday Life*, trans. Steven Rendall (Berkeley, Calif.: University of California Press).

CERUTTI, S. M. (1997), 'The Location of the Houses of Cicero and Clodius and the Porticus Catuli on the Palatine Hill in Rome', *AJP* 118: 417–26.

CHAMPLIN, E. (1998), 'God and Man in the Golden House', in Cima and La Rocca (1998), 333–44.

CHAPLIN, J. D. (2000), *Livy's Exemplary History* (Oxford and New York: Oxford University Press).

CHASE, K., and LEVENSON, M. (2000), *The Spectacle of Intimacy* (Princeton: Princeton University Press).

CHUNN, D. E., and LACOMBE, D. (2000) (eds.), 'Introduction', in *Law as a Gendering Practice* (Oxford and New York: Oxford University Press).

CIMA, M., and LA ROCCA, E. (1998) (eds.), *Horti Romani* (Rome: L'Erma di Bretschneider).

CIZEK, E. (1972), *L'Époque de Néron et ses controverses idéologiques* (Leiden: Brill).

CLAASSEN, J. M. (1998), 'The Familiar Other: The Pivotal Role of Women in Livy's Narrative of Political Development in Early Rome', *Acta Classica*, 41: 71–104.

CLARKE, J. R. (1991), *The Houses of Roman Italy, 100 BC–AD 250: Ritual, Space, and Decoration* (Berkeley, Calif.: University of California Press).

—— (2003), *Art in the Lives of Ordinary Romans* (Berkeley, Calif.: University of California Press).

CLUETT, R. G. (1998), 'Roman Women and Triumviral Politics, 43–37 B.C.', *Échos du Monde Classique/Classical Views*, 42/NS17: 67–84.

COARELLI, F. (1972), 'Il Complesso Pompeiano del Campo Marzio e la sua Decorazione Scultorea', *Rendiconti della Pontificia Accademia Romana di Archeologia* 44: 99–122.

—— (1989), 'La casa dell'aristocrazia romana secondo Vitruvio', in Geertman and de Jong (1989), 178–87.

COHEN, D. (1991), 'The Augustan Law on Adultery: The Social and Cultural Context', in David I. Kertizer and Richard P. Saller, eds., *The Family in Italy from Antiquity to the Present* (New Haven: Yale University Press), 109–26.

—— and SALLER, R. (1994), 'Foucault on Sexuality in Greco-Roman Antiquity', in J. Goldstein, ed., *Foucault and the Writing of History* (Cambridge, Mass.: Blackwell), 35–59.

CONNOLLY, J. (1998), 'Mastering Corruption: Constructions of Identity in Roman Oratory', in Joshel and Murnaghan (1998*b*), 130–51.

CORBEILL, A. (1996), *Controlling Laughter: Political Humor in the Late Roman Republic* (Princeton: Princeton University Press).

—— (2002), 'Political Movement: Walking and Ideology in Republican Rome', in Fredrick (2002*b*), 182–215.

CORBIER, M. (1995), 'Male Power and Legitimacy through Women: The *Domus Augusta* under the Julio-Claudians', in Hawley and Levick (1995), 178–93.

CORNELL, T. (1995), *The Beginnings of Rome: Italy and Rome from the Bronze Age to the Punic Wars* (London and New York: Routledge).

COSSARINI, A. (1977), 'Aspetti di Virgilio in Columella', *Prometheus*, 3: 225–40.

—— (1978), 'Columella: Ideologia della terra', *Giornale Filologico Ferrarese*, 1/1: 35–47.

—— (1980). 'Columella interprete del suo tempo: alcune considerazioni', *Giornale Filologico Ferrarese*, 3: 97–108.

COUDRY, M. (1998), 'Conclusion générale: Valère Maxime au cœur de la vie politique des débuts de l'Empire', in David (1998), 183–92.

COURTNEY, E. (1987), 'Imitation, chronologie littéraire et Calpurnius Siculus', *Revue des Études Latines*, 65: 148–57.

—— (1993), *The Fragmentary Latin Poets* (Oxford: Clarendon Press).

CRAWFORD, O. C. (1941/2), 'Laudatio Funebris', *CJ* 37: 17–27.

CRUTTWELL, C. T. (1910), *A History of Roman Literature: From the Earliest Period to the Death of Marcus Aurelius* (London: C. Griffin and Co.).

CSILLAG, P. (1976), *The Augustan Laws on Family Relations* (Budapest: Akademiai Kiadó).

CULHAM, P. (1982), 'The *Lex Oppia*', *Latomus* 41: 786–93.

—— (1987), 'Ten Years After Pomeroy: Studies of the Image and Reality of Women in Antiquity', *Helios*, 13/2: 9–30.

—— (1997), 'Did Roman Women Have an Empire?', in M. Golden and P. Toohey, eds., *Inventing Ancient Culture: Historicism, Periodization, and the Ancient World* (London and New York: Routledge), 192–204.

CUTOLO, P. (1983/4), 'Sugli aspetti letterari poetici e culturali della cosidetta *Laudatio Turiae*', *Annali della Facoltà di Lettere e Filosofia dell'Università di Napoli*, 26: 33–65.

D'AMBRA, E. (1993), *Private Lives, Imperial Virtues* (Princeton: Princeton University Press).

D'ARMS, J. H. (1998), 'Between Public and Private: the *Epulum Publicum* and Caesar's *Horti trans Tiberim*', in Cima and La Rocca (1998), 33–44.

DARWALL-SMITH, R. H. (1996), *Emperors and Architecture: A Study of Flavian Rome* (Collection Latomus, 231; Brussels: Latomus).

DAUBE, D. (1972), *Civil Disobedience in Antiquity* (Edinburgh: Edinburgh University Press).

DAVID, J.-M. (1998) (ed.), *Valeurs et mémoire à Rome: Valère Maxime ou la vertu recomposée* (Paris: De Boccard).

DAVIDOFF, L. (1998), 'Regarding Some "Old Husbands' Tales": Public and Private in Feminist History', in Landes (1998*b*), 164–94.

DAVIES, P. J. E. (2000), ' "What Worse than Nero, What Better than his Baths?": *"Damnatio Memoriae"* and Roman Architecture', in Varner (2000), 27–44.

DAVIS, P. J. (1995), 'Praeceptor Amoris: Ovid's *Ars Amatoria* and the Augustan Idea of Rome', *Ramus*, 24: 181–95.

DEONNA, W. (1954), 'La Légende de Pero et de Micon et l'allaitement symbolique', *Latomus*, 13: 140–66, 356–75.

—— (1956), 'Les Thèmes symboliques de la légende de Pero et de Micon', *Latomus*, 15: 489–511.

DESIDERI, P. (1984), 'Catone e le Donne (il Dibattito Liviano sull'Abrogazione della *Lex Oppia*)', *Opus*, 3: 63–73.

DESSAU, H. (1903), 'Die Vorrede des Livius', in *Festschrift zu Otto Hirschfelds sechzigstem Geburtstage* (Berlin: Weidmannsche Buchhandlung), 461–6.

DETTENHOFER, M. H. (2000), *Herrschaft und Widerstand im augusteischen Prinzipat: Die Konkurrenz zwischen res publica und domus Augusta* (*Historia* Einzelschr. 140, Stuttgart: F. Steiner).

DIETRICH, J. S. (1999), '*Thebaid*'s Feminine Ending', *Ramus*, 28/1: 40–53.

DIONISOTTI, A. C. (1988), 'Nepos and the Generals', *JRS* 78: 35–49.

DIXON, S. (1983), 'A Family Business: Women's Role in Patronage and Politics at Rome 80–44 B.C.', *Classica et Mediaevalia*, 34: 91–112.

—— (1991), 'The Sentimental Ideal of the Roman Family', in B. Rawson, ed., *Marriage, Divorce, and Children in Ancient Rome* (Oxford and New York: Oxford University Press), 99–113.

—— (1992), *The Roman Family* (Baltimore: Johns Hopkins University Press).

—— (2001*a*), *Reading Roman Women: Sources, Genres, and Real Life* (London: Duckworth).

—— (2001*b*), 'The "Other" Romans and their Family Values', in S. Dixon, ed., *Childhood, Class and Kin in the Roman World* (London and New York: Routledge), 1–17.

DOBESCH, G. (1978), 'Nikolaos von Damaskos und die Selbstbiographie des Augustus', *Grazer Beiträge. Zeitschrift für die Klassische Altertumswissenschaft*, 7: 91–174.

Dominik, W. J. (1997) (ed.), *Roman Eloquence: Rhetoric in Society and Literature* (London and New York: Routledge).

Dover, K. (1978), *Greek Homosexuality* (Cambridge, Mass.: Harvard University Press).

Dupont, F. (1997), 'Recitatio and the Reorganization of the Space of Public Discourse', in Habinek and Schiesaro (1997), 44–60.

Durry, M. (1950), *Éloge funèbre d'une matrone Romaine* (Paris: Belles Lettres).

Dwyer, E. (1991), 'The Pompeian House in Theory and in Practice', in E. K. Gazda, ed., *Roman Art in the Private Sphere* (Ann Arbor: University of Michigan Press), 25–48.

Earl, D. (1967), *The Moral and Political Tradition of Rome* (London: Thames and Hudson).

Eck, W. (1997), '*Cum dignitate otium*: Senatorial domus in Imperial Rome', *Scripta Classica Israelica*, 16: 162–90.

Edmondson, J. C. (1996), 'Dynamic Arenas: Gladiatorial Presentations in the City of Rome and the Construction of Roman Society during the Early Empire', in W. J. Slater, ed., *Roman Theater and Society* (Ann Arbor: University of Michigan Press), 69–112.

Edwards, C. (1993), *The Politics of Immorality in Ancient Rome* (Cambridge and New York: Cambridge University Press).

—— (1994), 'Beware of Imitations: Theatre and the Subversion of Imperial Identity', in Elsner and Masters (1994), 83–97.

—— (1996), *Writing Rome: Textual Approaches to the City* (Cambridge and New York: Cambridge University Press).

—— (1997), 'Unspeakable Professions: Public Performance and Prostitution in Ancient Rome', in Hallett and Skinner (1997) 66–95.

Ellis, S. P. (2000), *Roman Housing* (London: Duckworth).

Elsner, J. (1994), 'Constructing Decadence: The Representation of Nero as Imperial Builder', in Elsner and Masters (1994), 112–27.

—— and Masters, J. (1994) (eds.), *Reflections of Nero: Culture, History, and Representation* (Chapel Hill, NC: University of North Carolina Press).

Fantham, E. (1986), 'Ovid, Germanicus and the Composition of the *Fasti*', *Papers of the Liverpool Latin Seminar*, 5: 243–81.

—— (1997*a*), 'Images of the City: Propertius' New-old Rome', in Habinek and Schiesaro (1997), 122–35.

—— (1997*b*), 'The Contexts and Occasions of Roman Public Rhetoric', in Dominik, ed., (1997), 111–28.

FAVRO, D. (1996), *The Urban Image of Augustan Rome* (Cambridge and New York: Cambridge University Press).

FEENEY, D. C. (1992), '*Si licet et fas est*: Ovid's Fasti and the Problem of Free Speech under the Principate', in Powell (1992), 1–25.

FELDHERR, A. (1997), 'Livy's Revolution: Civic Identity and the Creation of the *res publica*', in Habinek and Schiesaro (1997), 136–57.

—— (1998), *Spectacle and Society in Livy's History* (Berkeley, Calif.: University of California Press).

FIELD, J. A. (1945), 'The Purpose of the *Lex Julia et Papia Poppaea*', *CJ* 40/7: 398–416.

FISCHLER, S. (1994), 'Social Stereotypes and Historical Analysis: The Case of the Imperial Women at Rome', in Archer *et al.* (1994), 115–33.

FITZGERALD, W. (2000), *Slavery and the Roman Literary Imagination* (Cambridge and New York: Cambridge University Press).

FLACH, D. (1991), *Die sogenannte Laudatio Turiae* (Darmstadt: Wissenschaftliche Buchgesellschaft).

FLANNERY, H. W. (1920), 'Roman Women and the Vote', *CJ* 16: 103–7.

FLORY, M. B. (1984), '*Sic Exempla Parantur*: Livia's Shrine to Concordia and the Porticus Liviae', *Historia*, 33: 309–30.

—— (1993), 'Livia and the History of Public Honorific Statues for Women in Rome', *TAPA* 123: 287–308.

—— (1995), 'The Deification of Roman Women', *Ancient History Bulletin*, 9/3–4: 127–34.

—— (1996), 'Dynastic Ideology, the Domus Augusta, and Imperial Women: A Lost Statuary Group in the Circus Flaminius', *TAPA* 126: 287–306.

FOGAZZA, D. (1981), *Domiti Marsi Testimonia et Fragmenta* (Rome: Edizioni di storia e letteratura).

FORBIS, E. P. (1990), 'Women's Public Image in Italian Honorary Inscriptions', *AJP* 111: 493–512.

FORSYTHE, G. (1999), *Livy and Early Rome: A Study in Historical Method and Judgment* (Stuttgart: F. Steiner).

FOUCAULT, M. (1978), *The History of Sexuality*, i: *An Introduction*, trans. R. Hurley (New York: Random House).

FOUCAULT, M. (1986), *The History of Sexuality*, iii: *The Care of the Self*, trans. Robert Hurley (New York: Random House).

FOWLER, W. W. (1917), *Aeneas at the Site of Rome* (Oxford: B. H. Blackwell).

FOXHALL, L. (1998), 'Pandora Unbound: A Feminist Critique of Foucault's *History of Sexuality*', in Larmour, Miller, and Platter (1998), 122–37.

FRANK, R. I. (1976), 'Augustus' Legislation on Marriage and Children', *California Studies in Classical Antiquity*, 8: 41–52.

FREDRICK, D. (1995), 'Beyond the Atrium to Ariadne: Erotic Painting and Visual Pleasure in the Roman House', *Classical Antiquity*, 14: 266–88.

—— (2002*a*), 'Mapping Penetrability in Late Republican and Early Imperial Rome', in Fredrick (2002*b*) 236–64.

—— (2002*b*) (ed.), *The Roman Gaze: Vision, Power, and the Body* (Baltimore: Johns Hopkins University Press).

FREYBURGER, M.-L. (1998), 'Valère Maxime et les Guerres Civiles', in David (1998), 111–17.

FRÉZOULS, E. (1989), 'Fondements scientifiques, armature conceptuelle et praxis dans le *De Architectura*', in Geertman and de Jong (1989), 39–48.

FULLERTON, M. D. (1985), 'The Domus Augusti in Imperial Iconography of 13–12 B.C.', *AJA* 89: 473–83.

GABBA, E. (1956), *Appiano e la storia delle guerre civili* (Florence: La Nuova Italia).

—— (1960), 'Studi su Dionigi da Halicarnasso I: la Costituzione di Romolo', *Athenaeum*, 38: 175–225.

—— (1984), 'The Historians and Augustus', in F. Millar and E. Segal, eds., *Caesar Augustus: Seven Aspects* (Oxford: Clarendon Press), 61–88.

—— (1991), *Dionysius and the History of Archaic Rome* (Berkeley, Calif.: University of California Press).

GALINSKY, K. (1981), 'Augustus' Legislation on Morals and Marriage', *Philologus*, 125/1: 126–44.

—— (1996), *Augustan Culture* (Princeton: Princeton University Press).

GANZERT, J., and KOCKEL, V. (1988), 'Augustusforum and Mars-Ultor-Tempel', in M. Hofter, ed., *Kaiser augustus und die verlorene Republik* (Mainz am Rhein: Ph. von Zabern), 149–99.

GARBARINO, J. (1984) (ed.), *M. Tulli Ciceronis Fragmenta ex libris philosophicis, ex aliis libris deperditis, ex scriptis incertis* (Milan: A. Monodori).

GARDNER, J. F. (1986), *Women in Roman Law and Society* (Bloomington, Ind.: Indiana University Press).

GEERTMAN, H. (1994), 'Teoria e Attualità della Progettistica Architettonica di Vitruvio', in Gros (1994), 7–30.

—— and DE JONG, J. J. (1989) (eds.), *Munus non Ingratum: Proceedings of the International Symposium on Vitruvius' De architectura and the Hellenistic and Republican Architecture, Leiden, 20–23 January 1987* (Leiden: Babesch).

GEORGE, M. (1997), 'Repopulating the Roman House', in Rawson and Weaver (1997) 299–319.

GINSBURG, J. (1993), '*In Maiores Certamina*: Past and Present in the *Annals*', in T. J. Luce and A. J. Woodman, eds., *Tacitus and the Tacitean Tradition* (Princeton: Princeton University Press), 86–103.

GLEASON, M. W. (1995), *Making Men: Sophists and Self-Presentation in Ancient Rome* (Princeton: Princeton University Press).

GOLD, B. K. (1993), ' "But Ariadne Was Never There in the First Place": Finding the Female in Roman Poetry', in N. S. Rabinowitz and A. Richlin, eds., *Feminist Theory and the Classics* (New York: Routledge), 75–101.

GOLDBERG, M. Y. (1999), 'Spatial and Behavioural Negotiation in Classical Athenian City Houses', in P. M. Allison, ed., *The Archaeology of Household Activities* (London and New York: Routledge), 142–61.

GOLDHILL, S. (1995), *Foucault's Virginity: Ancient Erotic Fiction and the History of Sexuality* (Cambridge and New York: Cambridge University Press).

GOODYEAR, F. R. D. (1982), 'Technical Writing', in E. J. Kenney, ed., *Cambridge History of Classical Literature*, ii (Cambridge and New York: Cambridge University Press), 667–73.

GOW, A. S. E., and PAGE, D. L. (1968), *The Garland of Philip*, 2 vols. (Cambridge and New York: Cambridge University Press).

GOWERS, E. (2000), 'Vegetable Love: Virgil, Columella, and Garden Poetry', *Ramus*, 29/2: 127–48.

GOWING, A. M. (1992), *The Triumviral Narratives of Appian and Cassius Dio* (Ann Arbor: University of Michigan Press).

GRAHAME, M. (1998), 'Material Culture and Roman Identity: The Spatial Layout of Pompeian Houses and the Problem of Ethnicity', in R. Laurence and J. Berry, eds., *Cultural Identity in the Roman Empire* (London and New York: Routledge), 156–78.

GRANSDEN, K. W. (1976), *Virgil: Aeneid VIII* (Cambridge and New York: Cambridge University Press).

GRANT, M. (1980), *Greek and Latin Authors, 800 BC–AD 1000* (New York: H. W. Wilson Co.).

GRIFFIN, M. (1984), *Nero: The End of a Dynasty* (London: B. T. Batsford).

GRIMAL, P. (1943), *Les Jardins romains a la fin de la république et aux deux premiers siècles de l'empire: Essai sur la naturalisme romain* (Paris: De Boccard).

GROS, P. (1976), *Aurea Templa: Recherches sur l'architecture religieuse de Rome à l'époque d'Auguste* (Bibliothèque des Écoles françaises d'Athènes et de Rome, 231; Rome: École française de Rome).

—— (1987), 'La Fonction symbolique des édifices théâtraux dans le paysage urbain de la Rome Augustéenne', in *L'Urbs: Espace urbain et histoire* (Collection de l'École française de Rome, 98; Rome: École française de Rome), 319–46.

—— (1989), 'L'auctoritas chez Vitruve', in H. Geertman and J. J. de Jong (1989), 126–33.

—— (1994), '*Munus non ingratum*: Le Traité Vitruvien et la notion de service', in *Projet de Vitruve* (1994), 75–90.

—— (1997) (ed.), *Vitruvio: de Architectura*, trans. and comment. A. Corso and E. Romano (Turin: Giulio Einaudi).

GROSS, W. H. (1981), 'Augustus als Vorbild', *ANRW* 2. 12. 2: 599–611.

GUNDERSON, E. (1998), 'Discovering the Body in Roman Oratory', in M. Wyke, ed., *Parchments of Gender: Deciphering the Bodies of Antiquity* (Oxford and New York: Oxford University Press).

—— (2000), *Staging Masculinity: The Rhetoric of Performance in the Roman World* (Ann Arbor: University of Michigan Press).

—— (2003), *Declamation, Paternity, and Roman Identity: Authority and the Rhetorical Self* (Cambridge and New York: Cambridge University Press).

GURVAL, R. A. (1995), *Actium and Augustus: The Politics and Emotions of Civil War* (Ann Arbor: University of Michigan Press).

HABERMAS, J. (1989), *The Structural Transformation of the Public Sphere*, trans. Thomas Burger (Cambridge, Mass.: MIT Press).

HABINEK, T. N. (1998), *The Politics of Latin Literature: Writing, Identity, and Empire in Ancient Rome* (Princeton: Princeton University Press).

—— and SCHIESARO, A. (1997) (eds.), *The Roman Cultural Revolution* (Cambridge and New York: Cambridge University Press).

HAHN, E. (1933), *Die Exkurse in den Annalen des Tacitus* (Borna-Leipzig, R. Noske).

HALES, S. (2000), 'At Home with Cicero', *G&R* 47/1: 44–55.

HALLETT, J. P. (1984*a*), *Fathers and Daughters in Roman Society* (Princeton: Princeton University Press).

—— (1984*b*), 'The Role of Women in Roman Elegy: Counter-Cultural Feminism', in J. Peradotto and J. P. Sullivan, eds., *Women in the Ancient World* (Albany, NY: State University of New York Press), 241–62.

—— (1989), 'Women as *Same* and *Other* in Classical Roman Elite', *Helios*, 16/1: 59–78.

—— and SKINNER, M. B. (1997) (eds.), *Roman Sexualities* (Princeton: Princeton University Press).

HARDIE, P. (1986), *Virgil's Aeneid: Cosmos and Imperium* (Oxford: Clarendon Press).

—— (1992), 'Augustan Poets and the Mutability of Rome', in Powell (1992) 59–82.

HARRISON, S. (1998), 'The Sword-belt of Pallas: Moral Symbolism and Political Ideology (*Aeneid* 10. 495–505)', in Stahl (1998), 223–42.

HAUSER, J. S. (2002), '*Eros* and *Aphrodisia* in the Works of Dio Chrysostom', in Nussbaum and Sihvola (2002), 327–53.

HAWLEY, R., and LEVICK, B. (1995) (eds.), *Women in Antiquity: New Assessments* (London and New York: Routledge).

HEMELRIJK, E. A. (1987), 'Women's Demonstrations in Republican Rome', in J. Blok and P. Mason, eds., *Sexual Asymmetry* (Amsterdam: J. C. Gieben), 217–40.

—— (1999), *Matrona Docta: Educated Women in the Roman Élite from Cornelia to Julia Domna* (London and New York: Routledge).

HEMKER, J. (1985), 'Rape and the Founding of Rome', *Helios*, 12: 41–8.

HENDERSON, J. (1989), 'Satire Writes "Woman": Gendersong', *PCPS* 215: 50–80.

—— (1998), 'Three Men in a Vote: Proscription (Appian, Civil Wars 4. 1–6)', in *Fighting for Rome* (Cambridge: Cambridge University Press), 11–36.

—— (2002), 'Columella's Living Hedge: The Roman Gardening Book', *JRS* 92: 110–33.

—— (2004), *Morals and Villas in Seneca's Letters* (Cambridge: Cambridge University Press).

HERRMANN, C. (1964), *Le Rôle judiciaire et politique des femmes sous la République romaine* (Collection Latomus, 67; Brussels: Latomus).

HIESINGER, U. W. (1975), 'The Portraits of Nero', *AJA* 79: 113–24.

HILLARD, T. (1989), 'Republican Politics, Women, and the Evidence', *Helios*, 16/2: 165–82.

—— (1992), 'On the Stage, Behind the Curtain: Images of Politically Active Women in the Late Roman Republic', in B. Garlick, S. Dixon, and P. Allen, eds., *Stereotypes of Women in Power: Historical Perspectives and Revisionist Views* (New York: Greenwood Press), 37–64.

HINARD, F. (1985), *Les Proscriptions de la Rome Républicaine* (Collection de l'École française de Rome, 83; Rome: École française de Rome).

HONIG, B. (1998), 'Toward an Agonistic Feminism: Hannah Arendt and the Politics of Identity', in Landes (1998*b*) 100–134.

HORSFALL, N. (1983), 'Some Problems in the "Laudatio Turiae" ', *Bulletin of the Institute of Classical Studies*, 30: 85–98.

—— (1989), *Cornelius Nepos: A Selection* (Oxford and New York: Oxford University Press).

HOWATSON, M. C. (1989), *The Oxford Companion to Classical Literature* (Oxford and New York: Oxford University Press).

HUMPHREYS, S. C. (1983), 'Public and Private Interests in Classical Athens', in *The Family, Women, and Death* (London and Boston, Mass.: Routledge and Kegan Paul), 22–32.

HUNT, L. (1992), *The Family Romance of the French Revolution* (Berkeley, Calif.: University of California Press).

JACQUEMIN, A. (1998), 'Valère Maxime et Velleius Paterculus: Deux façons d'utiliser l'histoire', in David (1998), 147–56.

JAEGER, M. (1997), *Livy's Written Rome* (Ann Arbor: University of Michigan Press).

JAMESON, M. H. (1990), 'Domestic Space in the Greek City-State', in Susan Kent, ed., *Domestic Architecture and the Use of Space* (Cambridge and New York: Cambridge University Press), 92–113.

JOSHEL, S. R. (1992*a*), *Work, Identity, and Social Status at Rome: A Study of the Occupational Inscriptions* (Norman, Okla.: University of Oklahoma Press).

—— (1992*b*). 'The Body Female and the Body Politic: Livy's Lucretia and Verginia', in A. Richlin, ed., *Pornography and Representation in Greece and Rome* (Oxford and New York: Oxford University Press), 112–30.

—— and Murnaghan, S. (1998*a*) (eds.), 'Introduction', in Joshel and Murnaghan (1998*b*), 1–21.

—— —— (1998*b*) (eds.), *Women and Slaves in Greco-Roman Culture* (London and New York: Routledge).

Kampen, N. B. (1981), *Image and Status: Roman Working Women in Ostia* (Berlin: G. Mann).

—— (1991), 'Between Public and Private: Women as Historical Subjects in Roman Art', in Sarah B. Pomeroy, ed., *Women's History and Ancient History* (Chapel Hill, NC: University of North Carolina Press), 218–48.

—— (1996) (ed.), *Sexuality in Ancient Art* (Cambridge and New York: Cambridge University Press).

Kaster, R. A. (1997), 'The Shame of the Romans', *TAPA* 127: 1–19.

Katz, M. A. (1995), 'Ideology and "The Status of Women" in Ancient Greece', in Hawley and Levick (1995), 21–43.

—— (1998), 'Did the Women of Ancient Athens Attend the Theater in the Eighteenth Century?', *CP* 93/2: 105–24.

Keith, A. M. (2000), *Engendering Rome: Women in Latin Epic* (Cambridge and New York: Cambridge University Press).

Kellum, B. (1990), 'Display at the Aedes Concordiae Augustae', in Raaflaub and Toher (1990), 276–307.

—— (1993), 'Sculptural Programs and Propaganda in Augustan Rome: The Temple of Apollo on the Palatine', in Eve D'Ambra, ed., *Roman Art in Context: An Anthology* (Englewood Cliffs, NJ: Prentice Hall), 75–83.

—— (1996), 'The Phallus as Signifier: the Forum of Augustus and Rituals of Masculinity', in Kampen (1996), 170–83.

—— (1997), 'Concealing/Revealing: Gender and the Play of Meaning in the Monuments of Augustan Rome', in Habinek and Schiesaro (1997), 158–81.

Kelly, J. (1984), 'Did Women Have a Renaissance?', in *Women, History, and Theory: The Essays of Joan Kelly* (Chicago: University of Chicago Press), 19–50.

Kennedy, D. F. (1992), ' "Augustan" and "Anti-Augustan": Reflections on Terms of Reference', in Powell (1992), 26–58.

Kennedy, G. A. (1994), *A New History of Classical Rhetoric* (Princeton: Princeton University Press).

Keuls, E. (1974), *The Water Carriers in Hades* (Amsterdam: A. M. Hakkert).

KING, D. (1998), 'Figured Supports: Vitruvius' Caryatids and Atlantes', *Numismatica e Antichità Classiche*, 27: 275–305.

KLEINER, D. E. E. (1978), 'The Great Friezes of the Ara Pacis Augustae: Greek Sources, Roman Derivatives, and Augustan Social Policy', *Mélanges de l'École française de Rome, Antiquité*, 90: 753–85.

—— (1996), 'Imperial Women as Patrons of the Arts in the Early Empire', in D. E. E. Kleiner and S. B. Matheson, eds., *I Claudia: Women in Ancient Rome* (New Haven: Yale University Press), 28–41.

KOLENDO, J. (1981), 'La Réparition des places aux spectacles et la stratification sociale dans l'Empire Romain', *Ktema*, 6: 301–15.

KOLOSKI-OSTROW, A. O. (1997), 'Violent Stages in Two Pompeian Houses: Imperial Taste, Aristocratic Response, and Messages of Male Control', in A. O. Koloski-Ostrow and C. L. Lyons, eds., *Naked Truths: Women, Sexuality and Gender in Classical Art and Archaeology* (London and New York: Routledge), 243–66.

KONSTAN, D. (1986), 'Narrative and Ideology in Livy: Book I', *Classical Antiquity*, 5: 198–215.

KORZENIEWSKI, D. (1966), 'Die "Panegyrische Tendenz" in den *Carmina Einsidlensia*', *Hermes*, 94: 344–60.

KRAUS, C. S. (1994*a*), *Livy: Ab Urbe Condita, Book VI* (Cambridge and New York: Cambridge University Press).

—— (1994*b*), ' "No Second Troy": Topoi and Refoundation in Livy, Book V', *TAPA* 124: 267–89.

LANDES, J. B. (1998*a*), 'Introduction', in Landes (1998*b*) 1–17.

—— (1998*b*) (ed.), *Feminism, the Public and the Private* (Oxford and New York: Oxford University Press).

LARMOUR, D. H. J., MILLER, P. A., and PLATTER, C. (1998) (eds.), *Rethinking Sexuality: Foucault and Classical Antiquity* (Princeton: Princeton University Press).

LATTIMORE, R. (1942), *Themes in Greek and Latin Epitaphs* (Urbana, Ill.: University of Illinois Press).

LAURENCE, R. (1994), *Roman Pompeii: Space and Society* (London and New York: Routledge).

—— (1997), 'Space and Text', in Laurence and Wallace-Hadrill (1997), 7–14.

—— and WALLACE-HADRILL, A. (1997) (eds.), *Domestic Space in the Roman World: Pompeii and Beyond* (*JRA* suppl. 22; Portsmouth, RI: JRA).

LAURENTI, R. (1973), *Filodemo e il pensiero economico degli Epicurei* (Milan: La Goliardica).

LEACH, E. W. (1997), 'Horace and the Material Culture of Augustan Rome: A Revisionary Reading', in Habinek and Schiesaro (1997), 105–21.

LEFÈVRE, E. (1989), *Das Bild-Programm des Apollo-Tempels auf dem Palatin* (*Xenia*, 24; Konstanz: Universitätsverlag Konstanz).

LEFKOWITZ, M. R. (1983), 'Wives and Husbands', *G&R* 30/1: 31–47.

LEHMANN, Y. (1998), 'Les Revendications morales et politiques de Valère Maxime', in David (1998) 19–26.

LEWIS, R. G. (1993), 'Imperial Autobiography, Augustus to Hadrian', *ANRW* 2. 34. 1: 629–706.

L'HOIR, F. S. (1994), 'Tacitus and Women's Usurpation of Power', *CW* 88/1: 5–25.

LINDERSKI, J. (1990), 'Mommsen and Syme: Law and Power in the Principate of Augustus', in Raaflaub and Toher (1990), 42–53.

LINTOTT, A. W. (1972), 'Imperial Expansion and Moral Decline in the Roman Empire', *Historia*, 31: 626–38.

LONG, A. A. (1996), *Stoic Studies* (Cambridge and New York: Cambridge University Press).

LOUTSCH, C. (1998), 'Procédés rhétoriques de la légitimation des exemples chez Valère Maxime', in David (1998), 27–42.

LUCE, T. J. (1965), 'The Dating of Livy's First Decade', *TAPA* 96: 209–17.

—— (1977), *Livy: The Composition of his History* (Princeton: Princeton University Press).

—— (1990), 'Livy, Augustus, and the Forum Augustum', in Raaflaub and Toher (1990), 123–38.

LUTZ, C. E. (1947), 'Musonius Rufus, "The Roman Socrates" ', *Yale Classical Studies* 10: 3–147.

MACAULAY, T. B. (1880), 'Lord Bacon', repr. in *Miscellaneous Works of Lord Macaulay, edited by his sister Lady Trevelyan*, ii. (New York: Harper and Brothers), 330–458.

McDowell, L. (1996), 'Spatializing Feminism: Geographic Perspectives', in Nancy Duncan, ed., *BodySpace: Destabilizing Geographies of Gender and Sexuality* (London and New York: Routledge), 28–44.

McEwen, I. K. (2003), *Vitruvius: Writing the Body of Architecture* (Cambridge, Mass.: MIT Press).

McGinn, T. A. J. (1998*a*), 'Caligula's Brothel on the Palatine', *Échos du Monde Classique/Classical Views*, 42: 95–107.

—— (1998*b*), *Prostitution, Sexuality, and the Law in Ancient Rome* (Oxford and New York: Oxford University Press).

—— (2002), 'The Augustan Marriage Legislation and Social Practice: Elite Endogamy versus Male "Marrying Down" ', in Jean-Jacques Aubert and Boudewijn Sirks, eds., *Speculum Iuris: Roman Law as a Reflection of Social and Economic Life in Antiquity* (Ann Arbor: University of Michigan Press), 46–93.

McKay, A. G. (1998), '*Non enarrabile textum*? The Shield of Aeneas and the Triple Triumph of 29 BC (*Aeneid* 8. 630–728)', in Stahl (1998), 199–221.

Magnino, D. (1998), *Appiani Bellorum Civilium Liber Quartus* (Como: Edizioni New Press).

Malcovati, H. (1928) (ed.), *Caesaris Augusti Imperatoris Operum Fragmenta* (Turin: in aedibus Io. Bapt. Paraviae et sociorum).

—— (1955), (ed.), *Oratorum Romanorum Fragmenta* (Turin: in aedibus Io. Bapt. Paraviae et sociorum).

Maltby, R. (1991), *A Lexicon of Ancient Latin Etymologies* (Leeds: F. Cairns).

Marshall, A. J. (1975), 'Tacitus and the Governor's Lady: A Note on *Annals* iii. 33–4', *G&R* 22/1: 11–18.

—— (1989), 'Ladies at Law: The Role of Women in the Roman Civil Courts', in Carl Deroux, ed., *Studies in Latin Literature and Roman History*, 5 (Collection Latomus, 206; Brussels: Latomus), 35–54.

—— (1990*a*), 'Roman Ladies on Trial: The Case of Maesia of Sentinum', *Phoenix*, 44/1: 46–59.

—— (1990*b*), 'Women on Trial Before the Roman Senate', *Échos du Monde Classique/Classical Views*, 34: 333–66.

Maslakov, G. (1984), 'Valerius Maximus and Roman Historiography: A Study of the *exempla* Tradition', *ANRW* 2. 32. 1: 437–96.

MENSCHING, E. (1967), 'Livius, Cossus und Augustus', *Museum Helveticum*, 24: 12–32.

MILES, G. B. (1995), *Livy: Reconstructing Early Rome* (Ithaca, NY: Cornell University Press).

MILLAR, F. G. B. (1973), 'Triumvirate and Principate', *JRS* 53: 50–67.

—— (1977), *The Emperor in the Roman World* (Ithaca, NY: Cornell University Press).

—— (1988), 'Cornelius Nepos, "Atticus" and the Roman Revolution', *G&R* 35/1: 40–55.

—— (1993), 'Ovid and the Domus Augusta: Rome Seen from Tomoi', *JRS* 83: 1–17.

MILNOR, K. (2002), 'Playing House: Stage, Space, and Domesticity in Plautus' *Mostellaria*', *Helios*, 29/1: 3–25.

MOMIGLIANO, A. (1944), 'Literary Chronology of the Neronian Age', *CQ* 38: 96–100.

MOMMSEN, T. (1899), *Römisches Strafrecht* (Leipzig: Duncker and Humblot).

MORELAND, J. (2001), *Archaeology and Text* (London: Duckworth).

MORFORD, M. P. O. (1968), 'The Distortion of the *Domus Aurea* tradition', *Eranos*, 66: 158–79.

MORGAN, L. (2000), 'The Autopsy of C. Asinius Pollio', *JRS* 90: 51–69.

MURNAGHAN, S. (1988), 'How a Woman Can Be More like a Man: The Dialogue between Ischomachus and his Wife in Xenophon's *Oeconomicus*', *Helios*, 15: 9–22.

MYEROWITZ, M. (1992), 'The Domestication of Desire: Ovid's Parva Tabella and the Theater of Love', in A. Richlin, ed., *Pornography and Representation in Greece and Rome* (Oxford and New York: Oxford University Press), 131–57.

NELIS, D. (2001), *Vergil's Aeneid and the Argonautica of Apollonius Rhodius* (*Arca*, 39; Leeds: F. Cairns).

NÉRAUDAU, J. P. (1985), 'Rome dans l'Art d'Aimer', in Jean Marc Frécaut and Danielle Porte, eds., *Journées Ovidiennes de Parménie* (Collection Latomus, 189; Bruxelles: Latomus), 25–39.

NEVETT, L. (1994), 'Separation or Seclusion? Towards an Archaeological Approach to Investigating Women in the Greek Household in the Fifth to Third Centuries BC', in Pearson and Richards (1994), 98–112.

NEVETT, L. (1997), 'Perceptions of Domestic Space in Roman Italy', in Rawson and Weaver (1997) 281–98.

—— (1999), *House and Society in the Ancient Greek World* (Cambridge and New York: Cambridge University Press).

NICOLET, C. (1991), *Space, Geography, and the Politics of the Early Roman Empire* (Ann Arbor: University of Michigan Press).

NIPPEL, W. (1998), 'Von den "Altertümen" zur "Kukturgeschicte" ', *Ktema*, 23: 17–24.

NISBET, R. G. M. (1939), *De domo sua ad pontifices oratio* (Oxford: Clarendon Press).

—— (1995), 'The Survivors: Old-Style Literary Men in the Triumviral Period', in *Collected Papers on Latin Literature* (Oxford and New York: Oxford University Press), 390–413.

—— and HUBBARD, M. (1978), *Commentary on Horace: Odes II* (Oxford: Clarendon Press).

NOÉ, E. (2001), 'La memoria dell'antico in Columella: Continuità, distanza, conoscenza', *Athenaeum*, 89: 319–43.

NOVARA, A. (1994), 'Faire œuvre utile: la mesure de l'ambition chez Vitruve', in *Projet de Vitruve* (1994), 47–61.

NUGENT, S. G. (1990), '*Tristia* 2: Ovid and Augustus', in Raaflaub and Toher (1990), 239–57.

NUSSBAUM, M. C. (2002), 'The Incomplete Feminism of Musonius Rufus, Platonist, Stoic, and Roman', in Nussbaum and Sihvola (2002), 283–326.

—— and SIHVOLA, J. (2002), (eds.), *The Sleep of Reason: Erotic Experience and Sexual Ethics in Ancient Greece and Rome* (Chicago: University of Chicago Press).

OGILVIE, R. M. (1970), *A Commentary on Livy, Books 1–5* (Oxford: Clarendon Press).

O'GORMAN, E. (1997), 'Love and the Family: Augustus and Ovidian Elegy', *Arethusa*, 30/1: 103–23.

O'HIGGINS, D. (1995), 'The Emperor's New Clothes: Unseen Images on Pallas' Baldric', *Hermathena*, 158: 61–72.

OLIENSIS, E. (1997), 'Sons and Lovers: Sexuality and Gender in Virgil's Poetry', in C. Martindale, ed., *The Cambridge Companion to Virgil* (Cambridge and New York: Cambridge University Press), 294–311.

ORTNER, S. B. (1998), 'Is Female to Male as Nature is to Culture?', repr. in Landes (1998*b*) 21–44.

OSBORNE, R. (1997), 'Law, the Democratic Citizen and the Representation of Women in Classical Athens', *Past and Present*, 155: 3–33.

OTIS, B. (1963), *Virgil: A Study in Civilized Poetry* (Oxford: Clarendon Press).

PAIS, E. (1910), 'L'orazione di Catone a favore della Lex Oppia', *Atti dell'Accademia di Scienze morali e politiche della Società nazionale di Scienze, Lettere ed Arti di Napoli*, 1: 123–9.

PAPI, E. (1998), ' "Domus est quae nulli villarum mearum cedat"(Cic., *fam.* 6.18.5): Osservazioni sulle residenze del Palatino alla metà del I secolo a.C.', in Cima and La Rocca (1998), 45–70.

PARKER, H. (1998), 'Loyal Slaves and Loyal Wives: The Crisis of the Outsider-within and Roman exemplum literature', in Joshel and Murnaghan (1998*b*), 152–73.

PAUL, G. M. (1982), 'Urbs capta: Sketch of an Ancient Literary Motif', *Phoenix*, 36: 144–55.

PEARSON, M. P., and RICHARDS, C. (1994), *Architecture and Order: Approaches to Social Space* (London and New York: Routledge).

PELLECCHIA, L. (1992), 'Architects Read Vitruvius: Renaissance Interpretations of the Atrium of the Ancient House', *Journal of the Society of Architectural Historians*, 51: 377–416.

PERL, G. (2002), 'Zur Problematik der Lex Oppia (215/195 v. Chr.)', *Klio*, 84/2: 414–39.

PESKOWITZ, M. B. (1997), *Spinning Fantasies: Rabbis, Gender, and History* (Berkeley, Calif.: University of California Press).

PETERS, W. J. T. (1993), (ed.), *La casa di Marcus Lucretius Fronto a Pompei e le sue pitture* (Amsterdam: Thesis).

PLOMMER, H. (1979), 'Vitruvius and the Origin of the Caryatids', *Journal of Hellenic Studies* 99: 97–102.

POHLENZ, M. (1924), 'Eine politische Tendenzschrift aus Caesars Zeit', *Hermes*, 59: 157–89.

POLLITT, J. J. (1978), 'The Impact of Greek Art on Rome', *TAPA* 108: 155–74.

POMEROY, S. B. (1975), *Goddesses, Whores, Wives, and Slaves: Women in Classical Antiquity* (New York: Schocken Books).

POMEROY, S. B. (1994), *Xenophon Oeconomicus: A Social and Historical Commentary* (Oxford and New York: Oxford University Press).

POOVEY, M. (1988), *Uneven Developments: The Ideological Work of Gender in Mid-Victorian England* (Chicago: Chicago University Press).

PÖSCHL, V. (1962), *The Art of Vergil*, trans. G. Seligson (Ann Arbor: University of Michigan Press).

POWELL, A. (1992) (ed.), *Roman Poetry and Propaganda in the Age of Augustus* (Bristol: Bristol Classical Press).

Projet de Vitruve (1994), *Le Projet de Vitruve: Objet, Destinataires et Réception du* De Architectura (Collection de l'École française de Rome, 192; Rome: École française de Rome).

PURCELL, N. (1986), 'Livia and the Womanhood of Rome', *PCPS* 32: 78–105.

—— (1987), 'Town in Country and Country in Town', in E. B. MacDougall, ed., *Ancient Roman Villa Gardens* (Washington: Dumbarton Oaks Research Library and Collection), 187–203.

—— (1996), 'The Roman Garden as a Domestic Building', in I. M. Barton (1996*b*), 121–51.

PUTNAM, M. C. J. (1965), *The Poetry of the Aeneid* (Cambridge, Mass.: Harvard University Press).

RAAFLAUB, K. A., and TOHER, M. (1990), *Between Republic and Empire: Interpretations of Augustus and his Principate* (Berkeley, Calif.: University of California Press).

RADITSA, L. F. (1980), 'Augustus' Legislation Concerning Marriage', *ANRW* 2. 13: 278–339.

RAMAGE, E. S. (1987), *The Nature and Purpose of Augustus' 'Res Gestae'*, (*Historia* Einzelschr. 54; Stuttgart: F. Steiner).

RAWSON, B. (1986), 'The Roman Family', in B. Rawson, ed., *The Family in Ancient Rome: New Perspectives* (Ithaca, NY: Cornell University Press), 1–57.

—— and WEAVER, P. (1997) (eds.), *The Roman Family in Italy: Status, Sentiment, Space* (Oxford and New York: Oxford University Press).

RAWSON, E. (1985), *Intellectual Life in the Late Roman Republic* (Baltimore: Johns Hopkins University Press).

—— (1987), '*Discrimina Ordinum*: the Lex Julia Theatralis', *Papers of the British School at Rome*, 55: 83–114.

RICHLIN, A. (1983), *The Garden of Priapus: Sexuality and Aggression in Roman Humor* (New Haven: Yale University Press).

—— (1991), 'Zeus and Metis: Foucault, Feminism, Classics', *Helios*, 18/2: 160–80.

—— (1996), 'How Putting the Man in Roman Put the Roman in Romance', in N. Hewitt, J. O'Barr, and N. Rosebaugh, eds., *Talking Gender: Public Images, Personal Journeys, and Political Critiques* (Chapel Hill, NC: University of North Carolina Press), 14–35.

—— (1997), 'Gender and Rhetoric: Producing Manhood in the Schools', in Dominik (1997) 90–110.

—— (1998), 'Foucault's *History of Sexuality*: A Useful Theory for Women?', in Larmour, Miller, and Platter (1998), 138–170.

—— (1999), 'Cicero's Head', in J. Porter, ed., *Constructions of the Classical Body* (Ann Arbor: University of Michigan Press), 190–211.

RIDGWAY, B. (1999), *Prayers in Stone: Greek Architectural Sculpture Ca. 600-100 BCE* (Berkeley, Calif.: University of California Press).

RIGGSBY, A. M. (1997), ' "Public" and "Private" in Roman Culture: The Case of the *cubiculum*', *JRA* 10: 36–56.

—— (1999), 'Integrating Public and Private', *JRA* 12: 555–8.

ROLLER, M. B. (2001), *Constructing Autocracy: Aristocrats and Emperors in Julio-Claudian Rome* (Princeton: Princeton University Press).

ROMANO, E. (1994), 'Dal *De Officiis* a Vitruvio, da Vitruvio a Orazio. Il dibattito sul lusso edilizio', in *Projet de Vitruve* (1994), 63–73.

ROSALDO, M. Z. (1974), 'Woman, Culture and Society: A Theoretical Overview', in M. Z. Rosaldo and L. Lamphere, eds., *Woman, Culture and Society* (Stanford, Calif.: Stanford University Press), 17–42.

ROSE, H. J. (1936), *A Handbook of Latin Literature, from the Earliest Times to the Death of St. Augustine* (London: Methuen and Co.).

ROSS, D. O., Jr. (1987), *Virgil's Elements* (Princeton: Princeton University Press).

ROSSI, A. (2002), 'The Fall of Troy: Between Tradition and Genre', in D. S. Levene and D. P. Nelis, eds., *Clio and the Poets* (*Mnemosyne* suppl. 224; Leiden: Brill), 231–51.

ROYO, M. (1999), *Domus Imperatoriae: Topographie, Formation et Imaginaire des Palais Impériaux du Palatin* (Bibliothèque des Écoles Françaises d'Athènes et de Rome, 303; Rome: École française de Rome).

Ruggini, L. C. (1989), 'Juridical Status and Historical Role of Women in Roman Patriarchal Society', *Klio*, 71: 604–19.

Ruggiu, A. Z. (1995), *Spazio Privato e Spazio Pubblico nella Città Romana* (Collection de l'École française de Rome, 210; Rome: École française de Rome).

Rykwert, J. (1996), *The Dancing Column: On Order in Architecture* (Cambridge, Mass.: MIT Press).

—— Leach, N., and Tavernor, R. (1988) (trans.), *On the Art of Building in Ten Books / Leon Battista Alberti* (Cambridge, Mass.: MIT Press).

Saller, R. P. (1984), '*Familia, Domus*, and the Roman Conception of the Family', *Phoenix*, 38/4: 336–55.

—— (1994), *Patriarchy, Property and Death in the Roman Family* (Cambridge and New York: Cambridge University Press).

—— (1997), 'Roman Kinship: Structure and Sentiment', in Rawson and Weaver (1997), 7–34.

—— (2001), 'The Family and Society', in J. Bodel, ed., *Epigraphic Evidence: Ancient History from Inscriptions* (London and New York: Routledge), 95–117.

Schofield, M. (1991), *The Stoic Idea of the City* (Cambridge and New York, Cambridge University Press).

Schrijvers, P. H. (1989), 'Vitruve et la vie intellectuelle de son temps', in Geertman and de Jong (1989), 13–21.

Scott, J. W. (1999), *Gender and the Politics of History*, rev. edn. (New York: Columbia University Press).

Scullard, H. H. (1951), *Roman Politics 220–150 BC* (Oxford: Clarendon Press).

Seager, R. (2002), *Pompey the Great: A Political Biography*, 2nd edn. (Oxford and New York: Oxford University Press).

Sebald, W. G. (2001), *Austerlitz*, trans. A. Bell (New York: Random House).

Sebasta, J. L. (1998), 'Women's Costume and Feminine Civic Morality in Augustan Rome', in Maria Wyke, ed., *Gender and the Body in the Ancient Mediterranean* (Oxford and Malden, Mass.: Blackwell), 105–17.

Severy, B. (2000), 'Family and State in the Early Imperial Monarchy', *CP* 95: 318–37.

—— (2003), *Augustus and the Family at the Birth of the Roman Empire* (London and New York: Routledge).

SHARROCK, A. R. (1991), 'Womanufacture', *JRS* 81: 36–49.

—— (1994), 'Ovid and the Politics of Reading', *MD* 33: 97–122.

SHIPLEY, G. (1996), 'Ancient History and Landscape Histories', in G. Shipley and J. Salmon, eds., *Human Landscapes in Classical Antiquity* (London and New York: Routledge), 1–15.

SIEBERT, G. (1998), 'Vie publique et vie privée dans les maisons hellénistiques de Délos', *Ktema*, 23: 171–80.

SIMON, E. (1986), *Augustus: Kunst und Leben in Rom um die Zeitenwende* (Munich: Hirmer).

SKIDMORE, C. (1996), *Practical Ethics for Roman Gentlemen: The Work of Valerius Maximus* (Exeter: University of Exeter Press).

SKINNER, M. (1993), 'Ego Mulier: The Construction of Male Sexuality in Catullus', *Helios*, 20: 107–30 (repr. in Hallett and Skinner (1997), 129–50).

SKUTSCH, O. (1985), *The Annals of Q. Ennius* (Oxford and New York: Oxford University Press).

SMALLWOOD, E. M. (1967), *Documents Illustrating the Principates of Gaius, Claudius and Nero* (Cambridge and New York: Cambridge University Press).

SMART, C. (1995), *Law, Crime, and Sexuality: Essays in Feminism* (London and Thousand Oaks, Calif.: Sage Publications).

—— (1992), *Regulating Womanhood: Historical Essays On Marriage, Motherhood, and Sexuality* (London and New York: Routledge).

SMITH, R. R. R. (1987), 'The Imperial Reliefs from the Sebasteion at Aphrodisias', *JRS* 77: 88–138.

—— (1988), '*Simulacra gentium*: the *ethne* from the Sebasteion at Aphrodisias', *JRS* 78: 50–77.

SPAETH, B. S. (1996), *The Roman Goddess Ceres* (Austin, Tex.: University of Texas Press).

SPENCE, S. (1991), 'The Danaids and the End of the *Aeneid*', *Vergilius*, 37: 11–19.

STAHL, H.-P. (1998) (ed.), *Vergil's Aeneid: Augustan Epic and Political Context* (London: Duckworth).

STROTHMANN, M. (2000), *Augustus—Vater der res publica: Zur Funktion der drei Begriffe restitutio—saeculum—pater patriae im augusteischen Principat* (Stuttgart: F. Steiner).

STRUENING, K. (2002), *New Family Values* (Lanham, Md.: Rowman and Littlefield Publishers).

SWANSON, J. A. (1992), *The Public and the Private in Aristotle's Political Philosophy* (Ithaca, NY: Cornell University Press).

SYME, R. (1939), *The Roman Revolution* (Oxford: Clarendon Press).

—— (1959), 'Livy and Augustus', *HSCP* 64: 27–87

TAYLOR, L. R. (1966), *Roman Voting Assemblies* (Ann Arbor: University of Michigan Press).

THÉBERT, Y. (1987), 'Private and Public Spaces: the Components of the Domus', in Veyne, (1987*b*), 213–37.

THOMAS, R. F. (1987), 'Prose into Poetry: Tradition and Meaning in Virgil's *Georgics*', *HSCP* 91: 229–60.

THOMPSON, D. L. (1981), 'The Meetings of the Roman Senate on the Palatine', *AJA* 85: 335–9.

TOMEI, M. A. (1990), 'Le tre "Danaidi" in Nero Antico dal Palatino', *Bollettino di Archeologia*, 5/6: 35–48.

—— (1997), *Museo Palatino* (Rome: Electa).

TORRE, C. (2000), *Il Matrimonio del Sapiens: Ricerche sul de Matrimonio di Seneca* (Genoa: Università di Genova, Facoltà di Lettere e Filosofia).

TREGGIARI, S. (1991), *Roman Marriage* (Oxford and New York: Oxford University Press).

—— (1994), 'Putting the Bride to Bed', *Échos du Monde Classique/Classical Views* 38/3: 311–31.

—— (1998), 'Home and Forum: Cicero between "Public" and "Private" ', *TAPA* 128: 1–23.

—— (1999), 'The Upper-class House as Symbol and Focus of Emotion in Cicero', *JRA* 12: 33–56.

TRILLITZSCH, W. (1965), 'Hieronymus und Seneca', *Mittellateinisches Jahrbuch*, 2: 42–54.

TRILLMICH, W. (1978), *Familienpropaganda der Kaiser Caligula und Claudius: Agippina Maior und Antonia Augusta auf Münzen* (Berlin: Walter de Gruyter).

VARNER, E. R. (2000) (ed.), *From Caligula to Constantine: Tyranny and Transformation in Roman Portraiture* (Atlanta: Michael C. Carlos Museum).

VASALY, A. (1993), *Representations: Images of the World in Ciceronian Oratory* (Berkeley, Calif.: University of California Press).

VERMEULE, E. (1996), 'Archaeology and Philology: The Dirt and the Word', *TAPA* 126: 1–10.

VERNANT, J.-P. (1989), *L'Individu, la mort, l'amour: Soi-même et l'autre en Grèce ancienne* (Paris: Gallimard).

VEYNE, P. (1987*a*), 'Marriage', in Veyne (1987*b*) 33–49.

—— (1987*b*) (ed.), *A History of Private Life*, i: *From Pagan Rome to Byzantium* (Cambridge, Mass.: Harvard University Press).

WAGNER, B. (1998), ' "Le Privé n'existe pas": Quelques remarques sur la construction du privé par l'Altertumswissenschaft au xix siècle'. *Ktema*, 23: 25–38.

WALKER, S. (1983), 'Women and Housing in Classical Greece: The Archaeological Evidence', in A. Cameron and A. Kuhrt, eds., *Images of Women in Antiquity* (Detroit: Wayne State University Press), 81–91.

WALLACE-HADRILL, A. (1981), 'Family and Inheritance in the Augustan Marriage Laws', *PCPS* NS 27: 58–80.

—— (1982*a*), 'The Golden Age and Sin in Augustan Ideology', *Past and Present*, 95: 19–36.

—— (1982*b*), 'Civilis Princeps: Between Citizen and King', *JRS* 72 (1982) 32–48.

—— (1994*a*), 'Public Honor and Private Shame: The Urban Texture of Pompeii', in T. Cornell and K. Lomas, eds., *Urban Society in Roman Italy* (London and New York. St Martin's Press), 39–62.

—— (1994*b*), *Houses and Society in Pompeii and Herculaneum* (Princeton: Princeton University Press).

—— (1996), 'Engendering the Roman House', in D. E. E. Kleiner and S. B. Matherson, eds., *I Claudia: Women in Ancient Rome* (New Haven: Yale University Art Gallery), 104–15.

—— (1997), '*Mutatio Morum*: The Idea of a Cultural Revolution', in Habinek and Schiesaro (1997), 3–22.

WALSH, P. G. (1961*a*), 'Livy and Augustus', *Proceedings of the African Classical Association*, 4: 26–37.

—— (1961*b*), *Livy: His Historical Aims and Methods* (Cambridge: Cambridge University Press).

WALTERS, J. (1998), 'Juvenal, *Satire* 2: Putting Male Sexual Deviants on Show', in L. Foxhall and J. Salmon, eds., *Thinking Men: Masculinity and its Self-Representation in the Classical Tradition* (London and New York: Routledge).

WARDLE, D. (1997), ' "The Sainted Julius": Valerius Maximus and the Dictator', *CP* 92: 323–45.

—— (2000), 'Valerius Maximus on the *Domus Augusta*, Augustus, and Tiberius', *CQ* 50/2: 479–93.

WEILEDER, A. (1998), *Valerius Maximus: Spiegel Kaiserlicher Selbstdarstellung* (Munich: Ed. Maris).

WEINSTOCK, S. (1971), *Divus Julius* (Oxford: Clarendon Press).

WESENBERG, B. (1984), 'Die Kopien der Erechteionkoren und die Frauen von Karyai', *Jahrbuch des deutschen Archäologischen Instituts*, 99: 172–85.

WEST, D. (1998), *Horace Odes II* (Oxford and New York: Oxford University Press).

WHITE, H. (1978), *Tropics of Discourse: Essays in Cultural Criticism* (Baltimore: Johns Hopkins University Press).

WHITE, J. B. (1985), *Heracles' Bow: Essays on the Rhetoric and Poetics of Law* (Madison: University of Wisconsin Press).

WHITMARSH, T. (2001), *Greek Literature and the Roman Empire* (Oxford: Oxford University Press).

WIEDEMANN, T. E. J. (1983), 'ἐλάχιστον ... ἐν τοῖς ἄρσεσι κλέος: Thucydides, Women, and the Limits of Rational Analysis', *G&R* 30/2: 163–70.

WILLIAMS, G. (1962), 'Poetry in the Moral Climate of Augustan Rome', *JRS* 52: 28–46.

WILLIAMS, G. D. (1994*a*), *Banished Voices: Readings in Ovid's Exile Poetry* (Cambridge and New York: Cambridge University Press).

—— (1994*b*), 'Nero, Seneca and Stoicism in the *Octavia*', in Elsner and Masters (1994), 178–95.

WILLIAMS, R. D. (1973), *The Aeneid of Virgil, Books 7–12* (London: Macmillan).

WILSON JONES, M. (2000), *Principles of Roman Architecture* (New Haven: Yale University Press).

WILTSHIRE, S. F. (1989), *Public and Private in Vergil's Aeneid* (Amherst, Mass.: University of Massachusetts Press).

WISEMAN, T. P. (1982), 'Calpurnius Siculus and the Claudian Civil War', *JRS* 72: 57–67.

—— (1987), '*Conspicui Postes Tectaque Digna Deo*: The Public Image of Aristocratic and Imperial Houses in the Late Republic and Early

Empire', in *L'Urbs: Espace Urbain et Histoire* (Collection de l'École française de Rome, 98; Rome: École française de Rome), 393–413.

WISTRAND, E. (1976), *The So-Called Laudatio Turiae* (Göteborg: Acta Universitatis Gothoburgensis).

Women and Geography Study Group (1997), *Feminist Geographies: Explorations in Diversity and Difference* (Harlow, Essex: Addison, Wesley, Longman).

WOODMAN, A. J., and MARTIN, R. H. (1996), *The Annals of Tacitus, Book 3* (Cambridge and New York: Cambridge University Press).

WYKE, M. (1994), 'Woman in the Mirror: The Rhetoric of Adornment in the Roman World', in Archer *et al.* (1994), 134–51.

—— (2002), *The Roman Mistress: Ancient and Modern Representations* (Oxford and New York: Oxford University Press).

YAVETZ, Z. (1984), 'The *Res Gestae* and Augustus' Public Image', in F. Millar and E. Segal, eds., *Caesar Augustus: Seven Aspects* (Oxford: Clarendon Press), 1–36.

ZANKER, P. (1968), *Forum Augustum: Das Bildprogram* (Tübingen: Wasmuth).

—— (1983), 'Der Apollontempel auf dem Palatin: Ausstattung und politische Sinnbezüge nach de Schlact von Actium', in *Città e Architettura nella Roma Imperiale* (Analecta Romana Instituti Danici, suppl. 10; Copenhagen: Odense University Press), 21–40.

—— (1988), *The Power of Images in the Age of Augustus*, trans. A. Shapiro (Ann Arbor: University of Michigan Press).

ZETZEL, J. E. G. (1995), *Cicero: de Re Publica* (Cambridge and New York: Cambridge University Press).

—— (1997), 'Rome and its Traditions', in C. Martindale, ed., *The Cambridge Companion to Virgil* (Cambridge and New York: Cambridge University Press), 188–203.

Index Locorum

General Index

Swiss Banks
AND
Jewish Souls

Swiss Banks

AND
Jewish
Souls

Gregg J. Rickman

Transaction Publishers
New Brunswick (U.S.A.) and London (U.K.)

Second printing 1999

Copyright © 1999 by Transaction Publishers, New Brunswick, New Jersey.

Library of Congress Catalog Number: 99-17332
ISBN: 1-56000-426-6
Printed in the United States of America

Library of Congress Cataloging-in-Publication Data

Rickman, Gregg J.
    Swiss banks and Jewish souls / Gregg J. Rickman.
        p. cm.
    Includes bibliographical references and index.
    ISBN 1-56000-426-6 (alk. paper)
    1. Banks and banking—Corrupt practices—Switzerland—History—20th century.   2. Foreign bank accounts—Switzerland—History—20th century.
3. Holocaust, Jewish (1939–1945)   4. Jewish property—Switzerland.
5. Jews—Europe—Claims.   I. Title.
HG3204.R53   1999
940.53'494—dc21

HG
3204
R53
1999

99-17332
CIP

To Ira, Sam & Rachel.
May they know only happiness
and fun throughout their lives.

Contents

Illustrations following page 137

Acknowledgements

The idea for this book took shape just as the Swiss bank drama began to develop into a full-blown scandal. Along the way there was much that occured due to the many who joined this effort simply out of a belief in the cause. It was these people who provided me with the input, advice, and encouragement that carried me through to the end.

In this vein, I would especially like to thank former United States Senator Alfonse M. D'Amato, for whom I have had the pleasure and honor not only to work for, but work with, for seven years. His trust in me and his encouragement to do this book is greatly appreciated.

Numerous others must be mentioned as well. Stan Turesky has been a quiet, yet guiding force not only in the ongoing investigations of the Swiss banks, but in support and help to me during the entire process of this book. Miriam Kleiman, for whom two weeks' work has turned into a vocation, encouraged, cheered, and helped me along with important materials. Her investigative work and committment to this cause is heroic. Willi Korte, quiet and unyielding, has stuck by me as well as the rest of us throughout this long process, long after his assignment to the cause was to have ended. B.J. Moravek was something akin to a bull in a china shop. He never stopped the search and his interest continued well beyond his reassignment in the Secret Service. Brian Hufker, also reassigned to the Pentagon, still calls to check on the issue. His hard work and long hours provided us with information we could never have gotten without his understanding. Marc Isser, our first intern at the National Archives also went on to work for us and deservedly so for all of his fine research efforts.

I also want to thank Phil Bechtel of the Senator's staff on the Banking Committee for his concern, dedication and help over the years as well as his help to me during the writing of this book.

At the National Archives, Dr. Greg Bradsher, whose name I have finally learned to spell correctly, found documents and sources there no one else could have found and assembled a finding guide for documents in the Archives second to none. He also was of immeasurable help in the finishing process of this book. Along with Greg, others from the National Archives deserving of thanks are Calvin Jefferson who has provided us with every appropriate extension of help with regard to use of the Textual Reference Room, Clarence Lyons for his help in the overall effort, Cary Conn for his help in declassifying hundreds of boxes of documents, and John Taylor for his wisdom and guidance. In addition to these fine and dedicated people, I would like to thank the following for their help: Rich Boylan, Rebecca Collier, David Giordano, Milt Gustafson, Ken Heger, Marty McGann, Wil Mahoney, William Deutscher, Robert Coren, Tim Nenninger, David Pfieiffer, Fred Ramanski, Ken Schlessinger, Amy Schmidt, Donald Singer, Marilyn Stachelczyk, Carolyn Powell, Dr. Michael Kurz, R. Michael McReynolds, Peter Jefferies, and Lee Rose.

No acknowledgment can be complete without mentioning the role of the World Jewish Congress, particularly Edgar Bronfman, WJC Secretary General Israel Singer, Elan Steinberg, and Doug Bloomfield. Despite some disputes, they made this all an amazing experience.

I cannot ignore the help and kindness of Ambassador Stuart Eizenstat as well as his staff, Bennet Freeman and Judith Barnett. Others helping in the State Department were Vic Comras, Dan Nehr, and Felix Hernandez. In the Justice Department, Eli Rosenbaum and Barry White played an important role as did Francine Barber and David Joy of the Treasury Department.

There were also a great number of researchers without whom the banks would have escaped justice. I would like to thank Charles Borden, Rick Crowley, Polly Crozier, Joshua Cypress, Mary Helen Dupree, Ben Fallon, Aaron Field, David Ganz, Avi Glazer, Jessica Hammer, Anantha Hans, Miriam Haus, Olivia Joly, Mary McCleery, Daniel Renna, Adam Sonfield, Hannah Trooboff, Kevin Vinger, and Brian Wahl. Hannah Trooboff especially, did excellent work with her research at the various research archives in and around New York City, all while attending Columbia University. She now works for the Bergier Commission.

Marc Mazurovsky has been an inspiration and supplier of useful hints and direction in the research, as was Sid Zabludoff. Cees Wiebus of Holland provided hints as well to unknown sources.

Michael Hausfeld and Marty Mendelsohn were of special help both in their guidance and their undying devotion to truth and justice. They fought and won a battle of historic proportion.

Lord Greville Janner and Janice Lopatkin, Tom Bower, Helen Junz, Gisela Blau, Rico Carish, Sharon White of the British Embassy, and Christoph Meili whose courage has become legendary, were all my "foreign" contacts. They were indispensable to the inquiry and to me personally. I also benefitted greatly from the help of Sybil Milton, Irwin Nack, Neil Levin, Greg Wierzynsky, and Bob Fink.

I cannot forget my late grandfather Isadore Levinsky who instilled in me the thirst for knowledge, a sense of history, and unfortunately a sense of tragedy as well. His experiences in the pogroms of 1920s in Ukraine, in which he lost nearly his entire family, scarred him in untold ways but impressed upon me the need to try to right a wrong, in whatever fashion or degree possible.

Finally, I want to thank my dear wife Sonia. She endured the endless days on the computer, the same computer she wished to use to pay the bills, and she graced me with time to write while entertaining the kids for a few hours out of the house. She is my best friend, my partner, and my lifelong companion.

Preface: The Devil's Bridge
and Other Swiss Myths

There were six shipments of gold worth $19,441,233. Sent from Switzerland to New York during February and March 1940, they came from the Swiss Bank Corporation in Zurich raising the suspicions of L.W. Knoke, Vice President of the New York Federal Reserve. By this time the Federal Reserve was tracking the flow of gold into the New York branches of the Swiss Bank Corporation. They were suspicious of the gold's origin and suspicious of the intent of the Swiss bankers for whom secrecy was as important as their jobs.

On April 23, Knoke telephoned Mr. Lichtensteiger of the Swiss Bank Corporation to ask the origin of the gold. Knoke, thinking out loud, wondered if the gold had come from Germany or Russia. If it came from Germany, Knoke feared, it may well have been looted from the countries the Nazis had recently conquered. Lichtensteiger, however, pleaded ignorance saying that he had no idea from where the gold came. His denials, however, betrayed a deeper feeling within.

In an exchange of letters with the Manager of the Swiss Bank Corporation's London Office, S. Lorsignol, some weeks before, Lichtensteiger confided that "[w]hat the origin of the 'stuff' is, I can only surmise, preferring not to ask...but somehow, I have an uneasy suspicion which makes me think, at times of the monument below the Devil's Bridge in the Reuss Valley."

This allusion to eleventh- and twelfth-century Swiss folklore was lost on the Treasury Department officials who examined this letter after finding it in the files of the New York branch of the Swiss Bank Corporation. Only a year after this episode, President Roosevelt froze the assets of the remaining, unoccupied European nations, on June 14, 1941. The irony of this ancient Swiss fable was not lost on either of the Swiss bankers. Clearly, they knew more than they were telling.

The tale involves the desire of the townspeople of a Swiss alpine village to build a bridge across two very rocky and treacherous mountain peaks. When they are unable to build the bridge, the Devil appears and offers the townspeople his assistance in exchange for the first soul that crosses the bridge. Once the bridge is built, the townspeople try to trick the Devil by sending a goat across the bridge first instead of one of the townspeople. The Devil becomes infuriated and hurls the goat off the bridge, turning it to stone as it falls. This is how the stone in the Reuss Valley came to be called the Devil's Bridge Monument. The moral of the story is quite simple, the Swiss are special and they will be spared. Someone else will pay for the deal they made with the devil. What the two Swiss bankers feared most, had indeed happened, they made a deal with the devil. But what makes this true life version of the Devil's Bridge different from the fable is the simple fact that the Swiss are no longer spared. Now they will have to pay for their deal with the devil.

In the time between the December 1995 meeting of Edgar Bronfman and United States Senator Alfonse M. D'Amato and the settlement of multibillion dollar class action lawsuits against the Swiss banks on August 12, 1998, a great number of myths would be shattered. This unlikely alliance would spurn a total reevaluation of Swiss wartime history brought on by an onslaught of revelations that changed the way the people of Switzerland, and indeed the world looks at this supposedly neutral nation.

Where once the world thought Switzerland could do nothing wrong, it now thinks it can do nothing right. With the release of hundreds of historically damaging documents, in the world's eyes, Switzerland has become a nation of greedy bankers, collaborators with the Nazis, and robbers of the wealth of the victims of the Holocaust. Shocked by the torrent of damaging press, the Swiss reaction was just as uncharacteristic to them as the charges they faced. They panicked and froze, and then more damaging to them, they lost their composure. It would be this response that would cost an Ambassador his job, an outgoing President his reputation, and in the end, the Swiss people their innocence.

The Truth Beckons

"The Swiss, who are the most respectable of peoples, found themselves in a shocking pedicament today," wrote Wallace R. Deuel. "Their government," he wrote, "and some of their most prominent citizens were accused of acting as receivers of stolen goods."[1] Owing to the vast extent of negative press coverage the Swiss banks received during the long term of the scandal, this comment was not unlike many others we had read. Yet, it was different because it was printed in the *Chicago Daily News* on May 6, 1946.

Indeed, the Swiss had seen accusations of malfeasance before, in fact on and off since the end of World War II. Accusations like this followed them like a pesky bee that would not go away. In each instance, they managed to avoid the sting. Like the moral of the tale of the Devil's Bridge, the Swiss thought themselves to be special. They were unique. They would find a way out of their problems.

The accusations Deuel directed at the Swiss, at the time, were swatted away. Again in the late 1950s, talk of a genuine search through the banks' records sputtered on and off. By the early 1960s with the endorsement of the government, a plan came into being, but again petered out in the early 1970s with slightly more than one thousand people actually obtaining justice. And through the rest of the decade and into the 1980s, talk of accounts missed in the efforts of the 1960s popped up now and again, but only as faint rumors.

With each mention of the problem, the Swiss bankers shooed the whispers away with little effort. They never feared the sting of being caught because they knew their opponents were divided and without support. They were special, they thought. They would be spared.

Spared they would remain until the end of the Cold War. Now all the factors that had worked in their favor, indifference, neglect, and disunity, would evaporate. As the world shook off the chill of a fifty-year-long dark night, the sunlight of the new day would bring freedom for people as well as truth. This same sunlight opened countries as well as archives. Finally, the Swiss were unable to dodge that pesky little bee known as history. Now, after so long they would finally be stung.

The Truth Speaks

This is an account of how a small and determined group of people from divergent backgrounds took on and humbled the legendary Swiss financial empire achieving a measure of justice for Holocaust survivors and their heirs while shattering the myth of Swiss wartime neutrality. Through the laborious task of pouring over millions of archival documents from five countries, this group debunked the myth of Swiss innocence and victimization, shedding light on Swiss collaboration and illicit deals during and after the darkest chapter in human history.

Just as our two Swiss banking friends felt, the Bronfman-D'Amato alliance showed that the Swiss bankers were in fact doing business with the devil. It was proven and the Swiss acknowledged that they accepted gold looted from the central banks of the conquered nations of Europe, and most disturbing of all, gold taken from the mouths of concentration camp victims and melted down into ingot by the Nazis. Swiss bankers accepted gold from the Nazis regardless of their suspicions.

Yet, gold was gold. It mattered little to the Swiss. In the words of Emil Puhl, the Vice President of the German Reichsbank and a frequent visitor to Switzerland during the war, "gold is fungible, one bar is the same as the other." Their intentions, like the gold they so readily accepted, the Swiss pretended, were pure.

More deceitfully, the Swiss bankers denied Holocaust survivors and the heirs to the victims, access to accounts that they placed in trust with the "inviolable" Swiss banks. Untold numbers of European Jews and others placed their funds in Swiss banks because they offered a safe haven for funds of which the Nazis were trying to gain control. What better place to put their money than in Switzerland. "It will be safe there," the depositors told their wives and children. The Swiss banks were always known to be safe. What reason did these people have to doubt the legendary Swiss banks? Before the war they didn't. After the war, doubt became commonplace.

When claimants came back after the war to claim the accounts, the bankers did whatever they could to keep them from what was rightfully theirs. Sometimes, they simply denied an account existed. Other times they demanded an account number, something concentration camp victims, newly freed from the hell of the camps clearly could not produce. More disgracefully, they would request a death certificate to prove that the original account holder was no longer alive, knowing full well that at Auschwitz, Maidanek, and the other Nazi death camps, the issuance of death certificates certainly did not occur. In the end, successfully filled claims were as hard to find as the information to substantiate them.

As the Swiss banks and their protectors in the Swiss government maintained, there were little or no Jewish assets to turn over. Swiss diplomats committed to the Allies in 1946 in the Washington Accord on German External Assets, and again in 1952, that Switzerland "would look sympathetically to turning over any heirless assets to refugee agencies. These were hollow promises.

In a conference of Swiss diplomats and politicians on February 14, 1946, Walter Stucki the veteran Swiss diplomat who was the lead negotiator for the Swiss with the Allies in the negotiations for the Washington Accord, pointedly stated that a large part of the foreign assets brought to Switzerland were those of the enemies of Nazi Germany and were brought there as a result of opposition to the Nazis. Seeking to exclude as many categories of foreign assets from the calculation to determine the amount to satisfy Allied claims on German external assets, Stucki urged his colleagues to "exclude other categories of assets based on their source. Property of emigrants, Jews and political foes," he declared, "are of no significance to the financing of another war."[2] One of the main goals of the Allies at the end of World War II was the prevention of a resurgence of German militarism, and the Swiss steadfastly denied any role in this effort.

The Swiss government, while perhaps not knowing exactly how much Jewish money was in their banks, fought and won the right to keep these assets in 1946, as well as in an associated agreement with the Allies in 1952. After a poorly planned, poorly implemented, and half-hearted search through their banks starting in 1962, the Swiss again managed to elude the depositors and continued to hold on to what did not belong to them.

Maintenance of the myth was a must. Like the mantra of "we took no Nazi gold, we have no Jewish money," when it came to confronting charges of collaboration with the Nazis, the Swiss government maintained another: "we had no choice, we were surrounded." This was plain to see in what ordinary Swiss soldiers, like Fridolin Wuthrich-Stieger, were told for all these years, it was only because of their courage, while Switzerland was surrounded on all sides and under threat of invasion by the Nazis, that prevented the onslaught.[3] Because of their vigilance at the Swiss-German border, Switzerland was safe. "The situation was clear," wrote Andreas Munger, "Switzerland was surrounded by Germany, Austria, Italy and France. All of these countries were allies of Hitler. So Switzerland was surrounded by the biggest Nazi-Deutschland you've ever seen in worlds [sic] history."[4] What were the Swiss people to do. Surrounded, outnumbered, and outgunned, the Swiss, as the myth went, had no choice. Switzerland, wrote Emil Abegg, "had no option in regard to trading with the Hitler Regime."[5] In the words of the Swiss Foreign Ministry, "Switzerland constantly held to its basic principles toward the German Reich: noninvolvement and independence."[6] What they did not know then, and are having great trouble understanding to this day, is that it was not their vigilance that saved Switzerland, but the collaboration of the Swiss banks with the Nazis that saved Switzerland in World War II.

What bothers the Swiss people is that they were the inheritors of a rich legend. To them Switzerland has always been a place of benevolence and humanitarianism. These kinds of charges were unthinkable.

In 1995, in a foreshadowing of things to come, former Swiss President Kaspar Villiger apologized to the Jewish people on the fiftieth anniversary of the end of World War II, when he stated, "We can only bow our heads in silence before those who experience suffering and imprisonment or even death because of us; and bow our heads also to their kin and heirs." He apologized for Switzerland's treatment of some 1,400 Jewish refugees during World War II. What he did not know, was that this number would soon change.

The Swiss people continue to believe that Switzerland, in the view of Eugen Gachter, "was protecting a lot of refugees of all kinds and of many nationalities, also of many Jewish people."[7] As a "neutral" state in the middle of wartorn Europe, Switzerland was a beacon of hope for many people seeking to escape the grasp of the Gestapo. Swiss humanitarianism and benevolence, though only went so far. In 1996, Swiss archivists disclosed that 30,000, not 1,400 Jews were turned back at the border. With future historical research, this number might well rise again.[8]

What Switzerland and its people have endured these last few years is of their own doing. Those that committed theses crimes and perpetuated them and those that hid them from history for half a century are indeed the Swiss people. It has been said that individual Swiss had some idea of what happened, but only as rumors. Why did they not act on them, why did they not seek to correct the wrongdoings?

Swiss historian Jacques Picard told me clearly, that without outside intervention, these revelations would not have come out. Without being pushed, the Swiss government, the banks, or industry would not have stepped forward to offer compensation. Is the money too little, too late? The answer to both questions is yes. While important to claimants and Holocaust survivors, what is more important than the money is that history is finally beginning to be served.

For the first time since the war ended fifty years ago, the truth is finally coming out, not only about Switzerland, but about all the other neutrals and even non-neutrals, Sweden, Spain, Portugal, Argentina, Turkey, France, Great Britain, Poland, Hungary, and even the United States. Each of these countries was either a victim, participant, or bystander to these horrible events. Each has a record that has yet to be fully written and explained.

This book relates how a small group of people, by no means professional historians, pieced together a puzzle of unknown proportions and proceeded to dismantle the myth of Swiss wartime neutrality and expose a fifty-year coverup. What they did was to lay out the premise: Switzerland stole the money of the Jews and helped the Nazis do the same. No one had any proof and no one had a source of knowledge upon which to fall back. All they had was an instinct, a feeling that something was terribly wrong and that a great injustice had occurred. What they produced was amazing. In more than two years of research, former U.S. Senator Alfonse M. D'Amato, the World Jewish Congress, the Simon Wiesenthal Center, Lord Greville Janner of Britain, Alan Hevesi, and a handful of Holocaust survivors with claims against Swiss banks accomplished what the Allies and a handful of feuding Jewish organizations could not or would not do in fifty years.

This effort has resulted in a reexamination of how the world views Switzerland, and how Switzerland views itself and in fact, how we view ourselves. Most important of all, those who survived the Nazi horrors, only to be victimized again by the Swiss bankers, have now achieved a measure of justice after more than fifty years.

Notes

1. Wallace R. Deuel, "Swiss Called 'Fence' for Nazis," *Chicago Daily News*, 6 May 1946.
2. Transcript from the Conference of the Finance and Commerce Delegation of the Federal Council, February 14, 1946, Swiss Federal Archive, E 2801, 1968/84B1 29.
3. Letter from Fridolin Wuthrich-Stieger to U.S. Senator Alfonse M. D'Amato, 5 March 1997.
4. Letter from Andreas Munger to U.S. Senator Alfonse M. D'Amato, 28 February 1997.
5. Letter from Emil Abegg to U.S. Senator Alfonse M. D'Amato, 16 January 1997.
6. "Swiss Behavior Toward the Warring Countries," Foreign Ministry Task Force, Internet page, www.eda-tf.ethz.ch/topics_e.htm, 1997.
7. Letter from Eugen Gachter to U.S. Senator Alfonse M. D'Amato, 12 November 1996.
8. This number would indeed rise again, now up to 51,000. See "Swiss to publish names of World War II refugees," Associated Press, 9 October 1998.

1

Justice Denied

Clearly no state would wish to benefit by reason of the slaughter of millions of helpless human beings. A most extraordinary situation arose as a result of the racial, religious and political persecutions of the Nazi regime, which demands, and in the main has received, unusual corrective measures. The justice of the position that heirless assets should be devoted to the relief of the miseries of persecutees falling in the same category as those who perished and who left these heirless assets can hardly be gainsaid.[1]

M. W. Beckelman of the American Joint Jewish Distribution Committee had penned an ironic statement. Unfortunately, there were in fact nations that did profit from the slaughter of millions. Switzerland, the land of cuckoo clocks and chocolate bars, was a nation of bankers providing a haven for "flight capital," for the Jews of Europe and the Germans who slaughtered them.

Because of the declassification and increased availability and accessibility to documents once locked away in boxes on dusty shelves all over the world, we have a greater understanding of how this misfortune occurred. Were it not for the intense work of the archivists and staff of the National Archives at College Park, Maryland, the details would have remained sketchy and the problem unresolved.

1937, Satu Mare, Romania

He was seventeen years old, a bit young to travel, but Jacob Friedman was on his way to Zurich to make bank deposits for his father Marton. While at the time, it was illegal for Romanians to have accounts outside the country, this would certainly not stop Jacob from making the trip. It was 1937 and people like the Friedmans could see the writing on the wall, they knew that perilous times were coming. Jacob would make this trip six more times in the next year, placing deposits in three Swiss banks. According to his memory, Jacob would go on to deposit slightly more than $5,500 in a now defunct bank called

1

Wohl and Landau in Zurich, $16,000 in the Union Bank of Switzerland, another $16,000 in the Swiss Bank Corporation, and $2,500 in another branch of the Swiss Bank Corporation in the small town of Le Loch, near the French border. Added to the amounts that his father placed in the bank accounts when he opened them, Jacob Friedman now estimates that these accounts totaled some $41,000.

Although he does not know the account numbers, he knows that they existed because he made deposits into them. His father knew the account numbers but he took them with him when the Nazis cleared out Satu Mare in spring 1944. Marton Friedman died after his deportation to Auschwitz, leaving his son Jacob with only memories.[2]

Marton Friedman was only one of thousands who sought to get their assets out of the reach of the authorities who made every attempt to gain control of the assets of Europe's Jews for their own use. This was true for Jews in Romania and was even more so for the Jews of Germany, who had the great misfortune to live directly under the boot of Nazi Germany. Freidman is one of many who came to the attention of the Senate Banking Committee. In telling us his story, we gained a greater appreciation for the suffering of the time and how Switzerland came to gain millions in Jewish flight capital.

The End of Liberty, the End of Life

Upon the ascendancy of Hitler to power, Germany's Jews were subjected to the *Reichsfluchtsteuer*, or Reich's flight tax. Begun in 1931, under the Bruning government, the law forbade the transfer of capital to prevent reichsmarks from leaving Depression-era Germany. Yet, the Nazis allowed exceptions to this law in order to facilitate the emigration of German Jews. For the next few years, it was still possible, even in a limited way, albeit covertly, to transfer funds out of Germany to places such as Switzerland.

It has been suggested that Swiss banks, sensing an influx of foreign flight capital, urged the Swiss Parliament to pass the November 8, 1934 Bank Secrecy Act to protect these funds. Motivation aside, Switzerland nevertheless became the first place of refuge, or "safe haven" for Jewish flight capital. Switzerland offered anonymity and ostensible security for the assets of European Jews seeking to provide for their families against some future dark event.

Increasingly, Jews were being disenfranchised by the Nazis, especially after the imposition of the Nuremberg Laws of September 15,

1935. Aryanization measures were imposed and the Jewish ownership of business was disappearing. On April 26, 1938, by decree, all Jewish property had to be registered. Hermann Göring, planning Nazi designs on Europe, was authorized to make provision for the utilization of Jewish property "in conformity with the interests of the German economy." Jews were denied entry into more and more professions, until November 12, 1938, a day after Kristallnacht, or "Night of Broken Glass," when all Jewish business activity was forbidden and a collective fine of one billion reichsmarks was imposed upon the Jewish community. Further decrees were imposed, and Jews throughout the expanding areas acquired by the Third Reich were denied rights of any kind, and according to Nazi ideology, subject to extermination.

Despite the imposition of Nazi decrees, both in Germany and the countries the Nazis came to occupy, refugee funds did in fact make their way into Switzerland and beyond. As France and the low countries fell to the blitzkreig, Switzerland feared invasion. With this, moderate amounts of assets were moved overseas by the Swiss banks to safeguard them against confiscation, were Switzerland to be invaded by the Nazis.

"Institutions in European financial centers, particularly in Switzerland," wrote W.H. Rozell of the Federal Reserve Bank of New York, in June 1940, "have for some time been engaging in an active and probably lucrative business of transferring European refugee funds to New York in accordance with a system devised by Swiss capitalists."[3] In many cases, Rozell wrote, the funds were transferred to the United States branches of the Swiss banks and commingled into a single account, therefore disguising the ownership of all the accounts. Moreover, the deposits were "no longer reported to us as foreign deposits despite the instructions on our report forms to that effect." Using the New York branches of the Swiss banks, "immediate transfer of the ownership of these funds to third parties under certain conditions, such as invasion or threat of invasion" were to take place.

Most importantly, these omnibus accounts were transferred to Swiss banks and American banks acting as correspondent banks for Swiss banks not present in the United States. A Swiss bank could simply open an account in its U.S. correspondent bank under the name of the bank and pour funds in from a variety of sources, all of it remaining anonymous, even to the bank holding the account. How much refugee money could have been transferred to American banks in this manner is impossible to guess.

The steady rise in the flow of capital into the Swiss banks in New York, in addition to the camouflaging of German industrial concerns became of interest to the FBI. B.E. Sackett, Special Agent in Charge of the FBI office in New York wrote Director J. Edgar Hoover, that in light of the increasing volume of transactions in the foreign departments of the various banks in New York City, it appears "extremely desirable to attempt to make contact with the officials of this corporation for the purpose of monitoring transactions passing through the institution."[4]

Having placed agents in the Swiss banks to monitor their actions, the FBI in coordination with the Treasury Department sought information on the dealings of the banks, as well as their personnel. The information they found convinced Treasury Secretary Henry Morgenthau to push for a freeze on the funds of these banks and a search through their records. Only in that way, could they get a better understanding of what these banks were doing, legally or illegally, on behalf of or in betrayal of their clients and for the enemy.

On June 14, 1941, President Roosevelt issued an executive order freezing the assets of the belligerent countries, all invaded or occupied countries, and the remaining unoccupied states of Europe, in order to prevent the forced transfer of funds and the manipulation of looted assets. With this order, Treasury Department auditors and investigators gained access to all the files, account information, secret account numbers, and ledger books of the three Swiss banks in New York. Credit Suisse, Swiss Bank Corporation, and the Swiss American Corporation files were now all available to Henry Morgenthau's enthusiastic Treasury Department investigators. What these files showed scared Morgenthau and his investigators, a closely knit team that would go on to hound the Swiss banks throughout the war. What these men saw in the New York files, convinced them that the Swiss bankers were not the wholesome, honest men the Swiss wanted the world to believe.

This much was conveyed to Morgenthau in an interoffice memorandum from Edward Foley, General Counsel at Treasury. After June 14, 1941, the banks had been operating under special license, with their actions proscribed. Now, Foley wrote seeking permission to place a group of investigators in the offices of the Swiss banks in New York on a permanent basis. Foley's concerns were many. Investigators had found documentary information on Swiss-German industrial concerns in the United States as well as the camouflaging of German concerns by Swiss companies and banks.

More ominously, Foley explained to Morgenthau that a former top executive of the Swiss Bank Corporation in Switzerland, who then moved to the United States, wrote to a colleague in a letter the Treasury obtained, that he resigned because of the fact that "certain high officials of the Swiss Bank Corporation were allowing themselves to be unduly influenced by Germany's apparent success in establishing a new European order."[5] This was all that Morgenthau needed to hear.

Foley was now free to act. Within days, Foley sent his investigators into the Swiss banks and immediately searched the files, even opening private files. This was clearly too much for George Ludwig of the Swiss American Corporation. Ludwig wrote to Foley, "while we have no idea as to what information is being sought, we notice that special attention is being paid to what might be described loosely as refugee accounts... we are being placed at a definite business disadvantage with respect to our foreign clients."[6]

In the files of the Swiss Bank Corporation, Foley's men found thousands of accounts, including a list of demand deposits totaling over $14.5 million from all over the world that the bank had transferred to the U.S. over fears of invasion. While blocked, most of these accounts represented capital that was successfully moved out of Europe. Were the owners so lucky?

Amorality: The Swiss Banks and the Looted Gold of Europe

"Since the outbreak of the war," wrote an American military attache in London, "Switzerland has played the role of international banker for Germany and her satellites. Swiss banks, the leading commercial and private banks as well as the Swiss National Bank, purchased gold from Germany to a value of several hundred million dollars." He continued,

> The proceeds obtained from the sale of gold provided Germany with the necessary Swiss francs (the only currency that is freely transferrable in the world today) to finance her purchases of critical war materials from the neutral countries outside the clearings and barter agreements; to pay for espionage and propaganda activities abroad; and to invest in neutral industries. The German Reichsbank and Swiss commercial banks did not hesitate to take part in transactions involving looted gold which was smuggled back and forth from other neutral countries in order to create an extra profit for the Nazi officials who handled the deals.[7]

For the Allies, it was already clear that Swiss bankers were the Nazis' bankers. To use a modern law enforcement term, they were "laundering" stolen Nazi gold. Exchanging gold taken from the vaults and bodies of Holocaust victims, for untainted gold, the Swiss bankers gave the Nazis the ability to continue the war by making their stolen gold, "clean" again. With the "clean gold," they could buy precision tools, small arms, artillery, and other vital equipment, to sustain their war effort. Sometimes they even did their shopping in Switzerland.

Allied intelligence was watching the Swiss banks. They knew how much gold was passing in and out of the Swiss banks on a weekly basis, from where it came, and to where it went. When it was added up, Morgenthau's men came to the conclusion that the Swiss banks had to be stopped. Failing this, they had to at least be put on warning that we knew what they were doing.

On January 5, 1943, eighteen nations, including the United States, issued a joint declaration warning the neutral nations they would not recognize the legality of their purchases of German looted gold. Not all the Allies, however, were unified behind this warning. The British, came to the conclusion "that it would be undesirable for His Majesty's Government to issue an official warning to neutrals about receiving Axis-owned gold, saying,

> We are assured that difficulties of identifying bar gold would be considerable. If therefore allied [sic] governments (who are parties primarily interested) were to ask our help in recovering looted gold we should probably be unable to do so directly nor of course should we be prepared to seize for their benefit other neutral gold of equivalent value within our jurisdiction.... On the other hand our belief is that existing German gold reserves have been looted from various European countries and Germany is certainly using gold as a means of payment in neutral countries.[8]

The gold warning had no effect. Swiss banks bought even more gold from the Nazis in 1943, and went right on laundering it through their banks and transferring it to other neutral countries, all the while benefitting the Nazi war effort.

The weakness of the Allied warning was made very clear in a November 6, 1943 memorandum of J.W. Pehle, Director of Foreign Funds Control, memo to Harry Dexter White, Assistant Secretary of the Treasury:

> Although our information is, of course incomplete, it is significant to note that transfers during the past six months total more than 100 million dollars and that such transfers have increased both in frequency and amount. It is evident that Germany is becoming more and more dependent upon sales of gold for the purpose of obtaining critical materials from European neutrals and that her credit position is growing progressively weaker. Accordingly, I believe that we should arrange for the issuance of our statement on gold as soon as possible in order to limit Germany's ability to dispose of her gold holdings in the future.[9]

As the months proceeded Treasury officials convinced Morgenthau that a second warning was needed. On February 22, 1944, Morgenthau issued the second declaration, this time in cooperation with the British and the Soviets:

> On January 5, 1943 the United States and certain others of the United Nations issued a warning to all concerned, and in particular to persons in neutral countries, that they intend to do their utmost to defeat the methods of dispossession practiced by the governments with which they are at war against the countries and peoples who have been so wantonly assaulted and despoiled. Furthermore, it has been announced many times that one of the purposes of the financial and property controls of the United States Government is to prevent the liquidation in the United States of assets looted by the Axis through duress and conquest.
>
> One of the particular methods of dispossession practiced by the Axis powers has been the illegal seizure of large amounts of gold belonging to the nations they have occupied and plundered. The Axis powers have purported to sell such looted gold to various countries which continue to maintain diplomatic and commercial relations with the Axis, such gold thereby providing an important source of foreign exchange to the Axis and enabling the Axis to obtain much-needed imports from these countries.
>
> The United States Treasury has already taken measures designed to protect the assets of the invaded countries and to prevent the Axis from disposing of looted currencies, securities, and other looted assets on the world market. Similarly, the United States Government cannot in any way condone the policy of systematic plundering adopted by the Axis or participate in any way directly or indirectly in the unlawful disposition of looted gold.
>
> In view of the forgoing facts and considerations, the United States Government formally declares that it does not and will not recognize the transference of title to the looted gold which the Axis at any time holds or has disposed of in world markets. It further declares that it will be the policy of the United States Treasury not to buy any gold presently located outside of the territorial limits of the United States from any country which has not broken relations with the Axis, or from any country which after the date of this announcement acquires gold from any country which has not broken relations with the Axis, unless and until the United States Treasury is fully satisfied that such gold is not gold which was acquired directly or indirectly from the Axis powers or is not gold which any such country has been or is enabled to release as a result of the acquisition of gold directly or indirectly from the Axis powers.[10]

Within months, the Allies began a concerted effort to force an acceptance of the policy on nonrecognition of looted gold, or the "gold clause." They had been partly successful, the year before with the Swedes, whose banks were also accepting gold in vast quantities. Sweden ceased accepting Nazi gold, within defined parameters, as of July 1, 1943.[11]

While the Swedes accepted the gold clause, the Swiss did not. When the Nazis tried to sell some 110 tons of gold to Sweden, they rightly refused the gold. Soon afterward, however, the Nazis offered this same gold to the Swiss, who gladly accepted.[12]

We would learn later through the release of a document to us by the Central Intelligence Agency and subsequent documents found in the National Archives, that Switzerland accepted gold from the Nazis after the Spanish government, owing to high German debt, refused the gold. The Swiss National Bank accepted the gold, laundered it, and then exported it to Spanish and Portuguese banks.

In one of numerous meetings held on the gold clause, Treasury and State Department officials discussed the wording of a statement they would try to induce the Swiss government to sign foreswearing the acceptance of looted gold from the Nazis. The U.S. was desperate. They knew what the Nazis were buying with the stolen gold, and they knew that with every purchase, more weapons were available to be used against our troops. They wanted the Swiss to accept some kind of clause along the lines the February 22 statement. Many were despondent, feeling "it was quite doubtful whether the Swiss could be induced to accept the statement."[13]

Despite everything, the warning failed and the gold transfers continued. Most worrisome was that the transfers continued coming but through a variety of routes. One route was through the German diplomatic pouch directly into the German Embassy in Bern or to the personal homes of Swiss citizens. One notorious case involved Baron von der Heydt, a onetime German national who acquired Swiss citizenship and was very friendly to the Nazi cause. According to a Polish intelligence source, quoted by the Assistant U.S. Military Attache in London, Captain Paul M. Birkeland, the gold was brought by "diplomatic couriers during 1944 and buried in the cellars of the estate," of von der Heydt.[14] According to the declaration under given under oath after the war by Hans Schroeder, former Chief of the Personnel Department of the German Foreign Office, the gold was taken into Switzerland by a courier by the name of Edward Voerckel.[15] According to a report by the American Legation in Bern of August 23, 1946,

[T]he Swiss Federal Political Department presently is conducting an inquiry into the affairs of a certain Baron von der Heydt, one time German national who obtained Swiss citizenship in 1937 nad [sic] has resided in Ascona, Switzerland since that date. Allegations received by this Legation are that Baron von der Heydt was formerly on intimate terms with many high German officials and businessmen. He was reported to have served as financial adviser to the former German Kaiser and during 1944 to have assisted in the concealment of large quantities of gold brought from Germany by diplomatic bag. He is further alleged to have registered in his own name in Switzerland bank accounts beneficially owned by former German diplomats...The Federal Political Department has advised the Legation that during a recent interrogation of von der Heydt the latter declared that in 1944 he was approached by an agent of Schroder [sic], Chief of Personnel, of the German Minisrty [sic] of Foreign Affairs. This agent asked von der Heydt whether he was disposed to handle gold which was to be intoduced [sic] into Switzerland by the German diplomatic courier service. Von der Heydt allegedly rejected the proposal.[16]

Both men claim to have never met, but were to have been in contact through the former German Ambassador to Spain, von Stohrer, who was a friend of von der Heydt. The sum of gold the Legation in Bern, as well as Office of the Military Government of the United States (OMGUS) authorities were investigating amounted to 1.5 million reichsmarks.

Despite his denials, von der Heydt was tried at the end of the war for "conducting military intelligence for one foreign state directed against another foreign state" and was stripped of his Swiss citizenship. In January 1946, however, he "donated" the bulk of his vast art collection to the Rietberg Museum in Zurich. A year later, the charges against him were dismissed and his citizenship was restored.[17]

The von der Heydt case could not have been an isolated one. One can surely guess that gold was sent to Switzerland through the diplomatic pouch on other occasions as well, perhaps even through the German Embassy. Emil Puhl, the former Vice-President of the Reichsbank, captured after the war testified to this much when answering questions posed to him by Allied investigators. "Do you know these cases where gold was kept by your embassies if it was held on the premises or deposited in banks?" Puhl's answer: "I suppose on the premises of our embassies. In Switzerland I am rather sure."[18]

By the beginning of 1945, the U.S. had had enough. With the end of the war in sight, the goal of stopping looted gold and other resources from being taken into Germany and laundered through Switzerland was changed. Now, the Allies had to try and prevent these assets from being sent out of Europe, again with the help of Swiss banks. The one goal was to prevent a continuation of the Nazi party after the war ended. In a series of interrogations after the war, as well as in letters during March and April 1945 from Emil Puhl to Dr. Walther Funk, President of the Reichsbank and Nazi Minister of Economics, Puhl wrote of the continued willingness of Swiss officials to help the Nazi cause:

President [Hans] Weber repeatedly and strongly advised me to continue in my endeavours made a forceful impression [sic]. He pointed out that under the given present day conditions an agreement between the Nationalbank [sic] and the Reichsbank would be of far reaching importance beyond the present day.[19]

It was in this vein, that Lauchlin Currie, Deputy Administrator of the Foreign Economic Administration and close friend of President Roosevelt, was sent to try and convince the Swiss, once and for all, to stop buying Nazi gold. On February 12, 1945 Currie, led a delegation to Switzerland to negotiate the recovery of Germany's legal and looted assets including looted gold. Currie asked first for a census of all Swiss banks and Swiss industry in order to identify German assets and finally a freeze of these assets in order to turn them over to the Allies as reparations.

Finally, on February 16, the Swiss Federal Council bowed to U.S. pressure and froze all German assets. On March 8, 1945, the Swiss Federal Council agreed to conduct a census of all German assets in Switzerland as part of the agreement. Currie was thrilled and the U.S. felt that at long last the Swiss had seen the light.

Yet, only one week after this agreement, on March 15, 1945, Puhl, traveled to Switzerland to negotiate the unblocking of the Reichsbank assets frozen only one month before. Less than three weeks before the surrender of Nazi Germany, on April 19, Puhl departed Switzerland having succeeded in getting the Swiss to lift the freezing order imposed at the behest of the United States.

Puhl, in a statement at Frankfurt on November 17, 1945, declared

The Swiss people realized that the February 16 decree blocking German assets, was written with a hot pen and involved Switzerland in a type of control which was not in the best interests of Switzerland.... I was assisted in attaining the desired results by the interests of certain Swiss circles in obtaining a resumption of payments.[20]

With the formal occupation of Germany, Military Intelligence, Treasury and State Department, and Office of Special Services (OSS) investigators finally had access to the German archives, gaining much greater knowledge of the financial dealings of the Third Reich. Great amounts of information were gathered and the puzzle was beginning to come together. The more U.S. investigators discovered, the more their initial fears were verified. In an extraordinary memorandum from Donald R. Heath, Director, Office of the Political Director, OMGUS, of February 1, 1946, Swiss good faith was strongly questioned:

It was known to monetary statisticians everywhere that at the start of the war the Germans possessed monetary gold reserves of about $70,000,000 in gold which had been spent by Germany at the latest by 1943 in her war effort. If the Swiss accepted the 100 tons of gold offered them by the Germans in 1943 which was worth $123,000,000, how can it be conceded by the Swiss that they acted in good faith? Moreover, how can the Swiss claim they acted in good faith when this gold was acquired at the time they knew that it had been refused for those very reasons by the Swedes? (Documents found in Germany by the United States military forces indicate this; in the meantime it has been established that the aforementioned gold in fact was gold looted from the Belgians.) In connection with the above facts the January 1943 declaration must have been known in part at least to the Swiss; this constitutes a strong argument in our opinion against the Swiss bona fides.[21]

Project Safehaven

Allen Dulles, the OSS Station Chief in Bern, had just sent a report explaining his views on Swiss-Nazi economic relations and the monthly quota of gold that Emil Puhl was arranging with his personal friend Hans Weber for the Swiss to buy yet more gold from the Nazis. OSS Director "Wild" Bill Donovan, sent the report on to the President. Roosevelt asked Donovan to discuss the report with the Secretary of State "right away." In his short memo to Donovan, FDR concluded, "We ought to block the Swiss participation in saving the skins of rich or prominent Germans."[22]

While FDR had expressed the need for a program to prevent the Nazis from benefitting personally as well as nationally from the spoils of the war, an effort was already under way by Morgenthau's men at Treasury to do just that. On May 11, 1944, Samuel Klaus, a Special Assistant to the General Counsel at Treasury, wrote a memo to the Assistant Administrator of the Foreign Economic Administration, Frank Coe, outlining the basic principles of a program that would come to be known as "Operation Safehaven" or "The Safehaven Project."[23]

Treasury officials, then were of course quite willing to facilitate expressions like those issued by FDR. Following Klaus' lead, in meeting after meeting they formulated complicated plans, with carefully defined categories of assets to uncover and differing strategies, based on the country targeted, in which to gain control over these assets. In order to be thorough, investigators suggested that no distinction be made between looted and nonlooted assets.[24] They were mindful that none of their plans would be easy, much less enforceable, especially in the neutral countries. Without the backing of sanctions or the continued holding of blocked property as leverage against the neutrals, Treasury officials were sure that public opinion would not be enough to convince them of the necessity of surrendering German assets.[25] Fifty years later, we would conclude this as well, with regard to Jewish assets.

The various departments had their orders. They were to uncover the extent of German assets abroad and do all they could to prevent them from being transferred to the neutrals and on to the Western Hemisphere. Whereas, there was great interest and enthusiasm for the concept of the Safehaven program, in reality the practice would be much more difficult than the program's creators imagined. Tracing the assets of the Nazis and their accomplices in wartime was one thing. After the war, with the complexities of rebuilding Europe; the transitioning of wartime economies to peacetime economies took loans, credits, and trade to accomplish. Once the common enemy was defeated, self-interest took over, within governments and between them.

The formal notification of the beginning of Safehaven was issued to all U.S. diplomatic posts on January 16, 1945. This circular signed by Assistant Secretary of State, William Clayton, stated

> This Government is attempting through all available means to obtain information concerning enemy investments and plans, and the activities of persons which could be employed as a means of preserving the enemy's economic, political and military potential abroad after the cessation of hostilities.[26]

While Safehaven had its successes in a variety of areas, it could be said that with regard to Switzerland, the program was stillborn. Treasury officials, wound up and excited about the chance to chase down and retrieve the assets the Nazis hid away all over Europe, had to deal with the State Department whose turf-conscience officers, sticklers for protocol, "worked at keeping business within the closed corporation of the State Department." The various State Department officers in the Legation in Bern, did all they could to place "every obstacle that can be put in the way of any other agency." James H. Mann, U.S. Treasury Representative in Bern, lamented,

> My principal difficulty in the Safehaven field thus far is the fact that the Legation is determined to prevent outside agencies, such as Treasury, from actively participating in this work. This failure to work closely with the other "outside" agencies has resulted in little if any progress being made on this project.[27]

Mann was not alone with his complaints. Walter Ostrow, another Treasury Department Representative in Bern echoed Mann's concerns about the State Department officers who were systematically "sabotaging our efforts to look after the Treasury's interests."[28]

Mann was recalled to Washington for briefings with the new Secretary of the Treasury, Fred Vinson, in September. If the problems he and the other serious-minded Treasury representatives were having with their own ostensible partners in the State Department were not bad

enough, he had to turn his attention to the disparity developing between the U.S. and British on the implementation of Safehaven.

"The British are attempting to obtain a loan from the Swiss," wrote
Mann. "With the thought of a loan in mind they apparently are of the
opinion that they should not take a strong stand on anything which
might antagonize the Swiss."[29] Mann warned of British trade consciousness so serious that it was harming the Safehaven program itself.

Mann seemed to be fighting a one-man battle. He consistently reported to Washington complaining that the State Department officers
in the Legation made it impossible to operate Safehaven according to
the way he envisioned. Soon the State Department officers with whom
he quarreled incessantly were being transferred to other posts and their
replacements were, according to the reputations that preceded them,
worse for Mann's tastes than those who preceded them. With the transfer of new State Department personnel to Bern by November, the "trade
conscious" British Embassy officers would be joined by the "old line
trade promoters" of the State Department. Mann was further isolated
and so was the Safehaven program about which he cared so much.

By November, Mann in despair, reported to Washington that
Safehaven was deteriorating and that origin of the problem lay directly
within the State Department. While urging the transfer of control of the
program to the Treasury Department, he held out little hope of this
happening.

Bernard Feig, in the American Embassy in London, was even
gloomier about Safehaven's future. "It seems eminently clear that not
only have the Safehaven people 'lost heart' but it cannot be expected
that any effective pressure can be placed on the British throughout he
Embassy here in London."[30] The program was collapsing from within.

"It was the best we could do"

What the Allies "really want," said Swiss officials "is to cash in on
the money under the pretext that they are doing so to avoid a third
war."[31] It was this belief that guided the fifteen members of the Swiss
Finance and Commerce Delegation of the Federal Council as they debated the formulation of their strategy for the upcoming negotiations
with the Allies in Washington over German assets in Switzerland. The
Allies wanted to get the Swiss to return the assets and at the first of two
meetings held on that day, the Swiss debated the strategies to avoid
returning these assets. Arrogant and resentful of the American and Al-

lied demands, this high-level meeting displayed deep Swiss distrust of the motives of the Allies, whom they felt were only trying to take from the Swiss what they felt was rightfully theirs. As it would turn out, the Swiss prevailed with their arguments, thus fulfilling their goal. The Allies, in retrospect, allowed this to happen simply because they failed to push any harder.

Seymour Rubin, a negotiator for the United States claimed in a 1997 interview, "everybody was anxious to get rid of the proclaimed list and controls."[32] The proclaimed list, irritated the Swiss. Being placed on it meant that the one was formally accused of trading with the Nazis and was forbidden to conduct business with the Allies. The Swiss government wanted to get their companies off the list so that they could reestablish trade. During the war, this list was maintained and updated continuously. After the war, maintenance of the list became a barrier to trade. The British objected to continuation of the list, arguing for wholesale deletions and even an end to the list altogether. It would be easier for the British to trade in Switzerland if the list of Swiss companies, whose factories were undamaged and hungry for business after years of war, could be thinned or even eliminated.

With this as a background, U.S. and Allied negotiators sat down with the Swiss to address these questions, in a protracted and unfriendly atmosphere. The Allies sought to wrest control of assets looted by the Germans and deposited in Swiss banks and wanted the Swiss to return the gold they accepted from the Nazis, all with the goal of preventing the financing of a rebirth of Nazism. Moreover, the Allies wanted the return of "heirless," or dormant bank accounts of Holocaust victims held in Swiss banks. These assets were to be put toward the benefit of the millions of displaced across Europe. For the Swiss, the issue was simply one of getting rid of the proclaimed list and getting the Americans to leave them alone.

On all counts though, the Swiss were not interested in negotiating away their rights to assets which they k ept and truly believed were theirs by virtue of their mere possession. The official excuse was that German assets in Switzerland, negotiators argued, were barely enough to cover the amount of money the Swiss were owed by Germany from before and during the war. What legal right did the Allies have in attempting to seize control of all German assets in Switzerland, they asked? For the Swiss it was certainly without precedent in international law, for this to happen. According to Seymour Rubin, they took the line "that there was no entitlement on the part of the Allies to any of these

German assets in Switzerland, let alone the heirless assets."[33] Steadfastly they denied the legality of the Allies' Potsdam agreements which claimed all German assets as their own.

As for the gold, the Swiss argued that it was received "in a standard transaction from the Reichsbank and the Vice President of the Reichsbank Puhl has always maintained that the gold stems from before the war."[34] It was a legalistic interpretation, taking as a given that Puhl was telling the truth, much less that the Swiss National Bank accepted the gold with no questions asked.

Heirless assets, too, would be pushed aside. They had no interest in discussing how much flight capital was deposited into Swiss banks. The banks would be no party to looking for such funds and the negotiators shared this feeling. Walter Stucki, the stern and "stiff" former Swiss Ambassador to Vichy France told the Swiss Federal Council, "we now will need to attempt a further limitation of the topic of discussion, as it relates to Flight Capital of Nazi enemies."[35] While Swiss negotiators in Washington were trying to avoid discussing with the Allies, the topic of Jewish assets in their banks, the Swiss government took steps at home to restrict access to these assets from the people who rightly claimed them. In December 1945 the Swiss government issued an administrative order blocking German-Jewish Holocaust survivors and the victims' heirs access to their accounts. Never published, the order was transmitted orally to Jewish organizations. Secretly, the Swiss government amended a law by decree that was originally designed to permit German Jews access to their accounts and to deny Nazi Germans access to theirs. With the issuance of this secret decree, all Germans, including Jews, lost access to their accounts. The Swiss began treating Holocaust survivors and their families like the Nazis who persecuted them.

Jewish service organizations seized upon this, among other restitution issues and presented forceful, yet futile claims to the Swiss government. Devastated by the destruction they saw in Europe at the end of the war, representatives of these groups sought to influence the Swiss and were convinced that through persuasion and a tug at their heartstrings, the Swiss would open up and provide the funding they so badly needed to care for the displaced in Europe. As they found to their dismay, their approach failed to work with the Swiss.

In constant contact with the U.S. State Department and the American Legation in Bern, groups such as the American Jewish Committee, the American Joint Jewish Distribution Committee, the American Federation of Jews from Central Europe, and the World Jewish Congress, sought help with their efforts. In response, the State Department representatives tried their best. Toward the end of the negotiations for the Washington Accord, in early May 1946, Seymour Rubin, on behalf of Acting Secretary of State Dean Acheson, cabled the American Minister in Bern John Carter Vincent, authorizing him to approach Max Petitpierre, the Swiss Foreign Minister, with a request for the Swiss to contribute $25 million out of German assets to a fund for refugee purposes. Rubin's cable ended by telling Vincent that "prospects for settlement on basis of proposal of Swiss would be substantially enhanced if Petitpierre were to clarify this ambiguous point of Swiss proposals along lines of willingness to make available contribution."[36]

Following months of discussion, sometimes heated, the Allies and the Swiss signed the Washington Accord of May 25, 1946, whereby the Swiss agreed to turn over some $58 million in gold, or Sfr.250 million, payable in New York at the Federal Reserve, and Sfr. 250 million, evenly split between the Swiss and the Allies. On the issue of heirless assets, Walter Stucki signed a letter to the Chiefs of the Allied Delegation stating that his government

> will examine sympathetically the question of seeking means whereby they might put at the disposal of the three Allied Governments, for the purposes of relief and rehabilitation, the proceeds of property found in Switzerland which belonged to victims of recent acts of violence of the late Government of Germany, who have died without heirs.[37]

The Swiss were neither sympathetic nor willing to look for heirless assets. As the Federal Council decided, they had no intention discussing the issue. They stalled, dodged, and did everything they could to gloss over the subject. Only fifty years later would they begin to face the issue of heirless assets in a serious manner, albeit under severe worldwide pressure.

Upon examination of the documents, one conclusion is inescapable: U.S. negotiators settled for a much lesser amount of gold and German assets than they knew the Swiss had accepted from the Nazis. This fact became readily apparent and was not lost on other Allied negotiators, members of Congress, Safehaven people at State, or even private citizens.

A French negotiator, complained that the settlement was inadequate. As relayed back to the State Department in a telegram a year later from the American Embassy in Paris, the French diplomat protested,

During negotiations in Washington with the Swiss regarding liquidation German assets, [sic] we were induced under American pressure, to accept the forteitary transfer of 25,000,000 [sic, a typo in the document that should read 250,000,000] Swiss francs of gold as restitution, although the French delegation had in its possession information to prove that the Swiss National Bank had received from the Reich approximately twice that amount of looted gold.[38]

Only a few months after the signing of the Washington Accord, Representative Joseph Clark Baldwin, Republican of New York, sent a telegram to the President, expressing his profound disappointment with the agreement. Agreeing to the terms of the Washington Accord on "58 millions out of a reliably estimated 300 millions of gold looted by Germany from our Allies seems completely inadequate. I earnestly urge halting the Swedish negotiations [going on at the time]," he wrote angrily, "until the whole problem can be reexamined and more forceful directives given our negotiators."[39]

Seymour Rubin, well aware of the available information during the negotiations, was responsible for the Department's answer to Representative Baldwin's letter. Yet, despite his intimate knowledge of the true nature of Swiss actions, Rubin agreed to the text of the response that went out under Acting Secretary Dean Acheson's signature stating, "there was no reasonable evidence that Switzerland had purchased $300,000,000 worth of gold looted by Germany."[40] Rubin knew better, yet strongly denies it today.

Within the State Department, the very department designated to negotiate the treaty with the Swiss, two of Seymour Rubin's deputies, Walter S. Surrey and Otto F. Fletcher, accepted a decision beyond their control, when they wrote in a memo, declassified only in December 1996,

We were compelled to strike a bargain with the Swiss for reasons which are known to you, in spite of the fact that we knew that figure reached with them was far below the figure of looted gold acquired by them—far below even the Belgian looted gold acquired by them, the amount of which was exactly known at the time. So far there is in the drafts no legal ground on which to fight the Swiss and the appeal to their "morality and justice" was made in an exhaustive manner at the time of the negotiations, the results of which are known to you.[41]

Disparaging as their tone is, Surrey and Fletcher, hit upon the very problem of the Allied strategy to negotiate with the Swiss. During the entire negotiations, the Allies obsessed about the legality of their case, worrying, like Surrey and Fletcher, about the legal approaches available under international law at the time. They felt their only recourse was moral suasion to push the Swiss towards the surrender of the German assets they held.

Individuals fared no better under the Washington Accord. Freiderick Weissmann, owner of the aryanized Berlin shoe store Emil Jacoby in 1938, wrote Randolf Paul, head of the American Delegation negotiating with the Swiss, complaining that the Bally Footware Company offered him no relief for their undervalued purchase of his store and that situations like this were not being properly addressed by the negotiators. Weissman concluded his telegram by asking Paul, "pray help us in our distress."[42] There is no evidence that Weissman, or anyone else in his position ever received compensation for their losses.

Try to Survive

It was 1942, and through the fence at the camp Rivesaltes, outside Perpignon in southern France that Joseph Sapir, once a successful businessman in Warsaw, reached for the hands of his daughter Estelle. He implored her, "try to survive, you'll be taken care of, there is money for you in England, France, and Switzerland. Go back to the house and find the ledger books. Try to survive."[43]

Joseph Sapir died at Maidanek, outside of Lublin, Poland, in 1943. Three years later, and two since the end of her time in hiding from the Nazis, Estelle Sapir traveled to Paris and later London. Finding the locations of the banks her father's ledger books provided, she obtained money from both cities. From the British bank alone, she withdrew $10,000 from her father's account.

Next, as her father's ledger books indicated, she traveled to Credit Suisse in Geneva. When she arrived at the bank she was greeted graciously and told in fact, her father did have an account. Could she show him, she was then asked, a death certificate? She ran out crying, "Who am I supposed to ask for a death certificate, Hitler, Himmler, or Mengele?" Sapir was one of many who came forward to volunteer their stories in the hope that we could help. This is how we came to learn her story.

Thus the broken, shattered remnants of the Jews of Europe began to return home or sought refuge in other lands. Like Estelle Sapir, some sought money left for them in Switzerland so that they could rebuild their lives. Where individuals could not, or would not seek their funds, Jewish service organizations seeking to ensure a life for the displaced of Europe began a long and bitter fight to gain reparations throughout

Europe for them. While successful in some European countries, Jewish groups lacking real support from the U.S. and Allied governments and unity among them, failed in Switzerland and like Estelle Sapir, were unable to reason with the cold-hearted Swiss bankers.

The reasons why Jewish groups failed to convince the Swiss banks to return Jewish assets were many, but none were very different from the reasons why the Allies failed as well. Both the Jewish groups and the Allies were at odds with their partners and both had their responsibilities multiplied by pressing and emerging threats. Jewish groups were trying to deal with the resettlement of hundreds of thousands of Jewish refugees as well as rebuilding the Jewish community in Europe. For the Allies it was the Cold War and rebuilding Germany that preoccupied their time. Inherently, the exigencies of the times dictated how far either could go towards pressing the Swiss to return Jewish wealth entrusted to them.

It was clear by the aide memoire of the Swiss Legation to Washington, of April 25, 1947, that trying to retrieve Jewish assets from Swiss banks would be next to impossible. "It would be helpful to the Swiss authorities," wrote the Swiss Legation "to know the basis for the allegation of the Allied Governments that a considerable number of the victims had their estates in Switzerland."[44] The Swiss were playing dumb. They pleaded innocence, hoping that the Allies would grow tired of pleading for Jewish assets or simply move on to something else. Max Isenburg of the American Jewish Congress understood this tactic when he wrote in an internal memorandum in 1948, "Thus far, the Swiss have used the difficulties of defining heirless property as a pretext for doing nothing."[45]

If requesting death certificates from claimants to a prove relationship to their deceased relatives was not enough of an indignity, the attitude afforded these people could only be described as arrogant and condescending. One opposition Swiss Parliamentarian, Gottlieb Duttweiler in a meeting with the U.S. State Department, blithely referred to the claimants as "little people" who were not considered "politically interesting" and therefore unable to convince the Swiss government to work on their behalf.[46] Duttweiler explained to his hosts that the Swiss government preferred to settle the larger outstanding cases between the two countries first.

One such case concerned Interhandel, otherwise known as I.G. Chemie. This case represented a real barrier to clear relations between Switzerland and the U.S., not the heirless assets issue. I.G. Chemie's

U.S. operation was closed early on in the war because it was in reality, the camouflaged Swiss branch of I.G. Farben, the massive German chemical concern that was the largest chemical company in the world and the creator of Zyklon B. To Treasury officials, the matter was simple, the American branch was providing the parent company with supplies vital to the Nazi war effort. The case would drag on until the Kennedy administration when it was finally settled, but not before it went all the way to the U.S. Supreme Court.

Duttweiler, despite his lack of finesse, was nevertheless correct. With the onset of the Cold War, the "little people" had no chance for justice. Jewish organizations fighting on their behalf had few resources and were not privy to the vast amount of information about the Swiss banks and their behavior that has only now become available to the public, but at the time was certainly available to the U.S. government. They were left to negotiate directly with the Swiss government on a variety of Jewish restitution issues with only a modicum of support from the Allies. This was painfully evident when the American Jewish Joint Distribution Committee in New York was alerted to the existence of large warehouses full of unclaimed baggage that German Jews had sent before the war to Switzerland in anticipation of reaching that country, they pondered whether they would ever be able to gain custody of this property without paying the storage costs for the time it sat there.[47]

Jewish groups nevertheless pressed on. The American Jewish Committee, the American Jewish Congress, the American Jewish Joint Distribution Committee, the Jewish Agency, the World Jewish Congress, all held meetings and corresponded with Swiss government officials, in Washington and in Switzerland. The various archives are full of correspondence and memoranda of meetings between the various groups and Swiss ministers. The groups also wrote to each other begging for a word to be said on their behalf, the ones with lesser influence wrote the ones with the greater influence. Regardless of the size, all had little leverage. All pleaded and tried to play to the mercy of the Swiss government or the U.S. authorities for some acceptance of their requests.

Dr. Rudolf Behr, a New York attorney representing the World Jewish Congress, explained to the State Department that the Swiss approach to the release of the property of "persecutees" had to change. If it did not, "additional pressure on the part of the World Jewish Congress and influential citizens of Switzerland" would be brought to bear in order to change the Swiss policy.[48] While the threat was duly reported to the American Legation in Bern, it was not real. Neither the World Jewish

Congress nor any other Jewish organization could apply pressure, political or otherwise, on Switzerland to release the property of the refugees. It would be five decades later before this kind of threat would have real meaning. But in 1948, threats rang hollow, devoid of any danger for the Swiss government or its newly rich banks. These deficiencies would become abundantly clear within a short time with the signing of the Swiss-Polish Treaty of Indemnification of 1949.

Stealing According to the Law

Walter Loery had sent his niece Hilde Sorkin a congratulatory telegram from Danzig, Poland, on the occasion of her wedding in 1937. Two years later, Loery was among those taken off by the Nazis to Stutthof concentration camp outside of Danzig. Before the invasion, he left an account at a Swiss bank in Zurich. The balance was 3,378 Swiss francs. After Loery's death at the hands of the Nazis, his Swiss bank account remained in Zurich, untouched until 1949. That year, the proceeds from his account would be transferred, not to Hilde Sorkin, his listed beneficiary, but the Polish government. Forty-six years later, with the exposure of the agreement that sanctioned this transfer, Hilde Sorkin would finally begin the process toward receiving the funds her uncle left her.

In January of that year, Gaston Jaccard took up his new post as Swiss Ambassador to Poland. On January 25, 1949, American Ambassador Waldemar J. Gallman and Cecil B. Lyon, Counselor of the American Embassy paid a call to Jaccard at the Swiss embassy. The men discussed the presence, in Warsaw, of a Swiss finance and trade delegation to restart negotiations begun in June 1948. Jaccard informed Gallman that the delegation was trying to tie up a trade agreement that included compensation for Swiss property nationalized by the Polish Communist government a year before. According to Jaccard, the properties included chemical, pharmaceutical and hospital instrument concerns.[49]

The number of these properties, however, was in dispute. Lucien Horowitz, the Polish Director of Planning and Coordination of the Ministry of Foreign Trade, told U.S. embassy officers of the disingenuous attitude taken by the Swiss delegation. According Horowitz, some of the properties in Silesia claimed by Switzerland for compensation, had previously been sold to the Nazis during the war. [50] According to Gallman, the negotiations had broken down and the Swiss delegation had left for Switzerland.

By June the delegation was back and on the 25th an agreement had been reached. In an exchange of letters between Max Troendle of the Swiss Trade Ministry and head of the Swiss delegation and Leon Kurowski, Chairman of the Polish Financial Delegation, the agreement was laid out. Troendle wrote Kurowski that after a lapse of five years from the implementation of the agreement, Swiss banks would close the accounts and liquidate the insurance policies of Polish citizens missing since May 9, 1945. The balance of these accounts and the proceeds from the liquidation of the policies would then be deposited in the Swiss National Bank under the control of the National Bank of Poland.

The treaty between Switzerland and Poland had satisfied Jaccard, who nevertheless complained that the negotiations had been "sharp, hard, and good."[51] The agreement may have been good for Switzerland and Poland, but it was not good for the heirs of those whose accounts were destined for liquidation. Jewish groups now feared the precedent this treaty might set because Switzerland would now feel free to treat heirless assets in terms of the nationality of the account holder, as opposed to the location of the assets. The difference between the two mattered. Like the Polish treaty, the Swiss followed the principle that the assets belonged to Polish citizens, therefore Poland was entitled to them. If the Swiss merely considered the assets on the territorial basis, they could then take control of the assets, and in the minds of the Jewish groups, apply them to the displaced refugees in Europe. This, however, would not be the case.

The State Department, the only real resort for the Jewish groups, seemed to be more concerned about the timing of the treaty owing to Poland's increasing dependence on the Soviet Union. They seemed less concerned about the legality or long-term effect on the heirless asset problem. They wanted to know how Poland's economy would benefit by deals like this and in turn to what extent Poland's actions were dictated by the Soviets. This much was made clear in a memo to Minister Vincent in a Legation memo of August 8, 1949:

> It appears that for almost two years there has been complete apathy on the part of the Department with respect to heirless assets in Switzerland. It also appears that since July 1946 it has been aware of the Polish claim to heirless assets in Switzerland but preferred to treat it at a "later stage."[52]

On July 8, a meeting on the heirless assets question was held in Geneva, at the behest of the Frank Bienenfeld of the World Jewish Congress, S. Adler-Rudel of the Jewish Agency, Max Isenburgh and

Seymour Rubin, no longer with the State Department and now representing the American Jewish Committee, and Jerome Jacobson of the
Joint Distribution Committee. All five met with Federal Councillor and
Minister of Justice Eduard von Steiger. Yet, going into the meeting,
none of the four knew of the existence of the Swiss-Polish Accord which
was not publicized until two weeks after this meeting.

Von Steiger was, to say the least, bureaucratic. He and his aides
went through the exhaustive legal measures that the Swiss government
would need to take in order to solve the overall issue of heirless assets.
Von Steiger listed the obstacles to an immediate resolution: a census of
heirless assets in all the banks in Switzerland would have to be undertaken; once found, the assets would have to be blocked; legal successors would have to be found and the process to certify them would have
to be created; death certificates issued to avoid wrongful confiscation
of the assets; and finally, a legal examination of whether Switzerland
or the country of origin of the former account holder could be the recipient of the assets.

In his memo on the meeting, Bienenfeld came out flatly against this
complicated and bureaucratic list of procedures:

> The intentions or the last wills of the missing persons are not known, however, the
> Swiss authorities and everybody know exactly, that all the missing persons, who
> deposited flight money in Switzerland for an emergency, foresaw the dangerous
> situation in their countries of origin, which was later realised [sic]. Their intention
> cannot be doubted, that the assets concerned should never fall in the hands of
> their governments, moreover, the Swiss authorities recognised [sic], their desire
> by favouring the deposits of those assets with Swiss banks and bankers by taxation
> laws and other measures. It would be against good faith, now to surrender those
> assets against the intention of the former owners to the countries of persecution.[53]

While correct for Bienenfeld to argue the injustices of such treatment of heirless assets, it was disingenuous, and even callous, for von
Steiger to argue whether Switzerland can or should treat the assets in
this matter. During their meeting, von Steiger stated that any such transfer to another nation would require legislation. After all, it was less
than two weeks before this meeting that his government had done just
that, committing to turn over Polish assets to Poland by a treaty, and
not legislation, that would need to be ratified by the Swiss Parliament,
just as would legislation.

Having committed to this treaty, the Swiss government knew that by
treating unclaimed assets according to the national theory, Switzerland
would not have to surrender the assets to the Allies, as called for in the

Five Power Conference in Paris in June 1946, a month after the signing of the Washington Accord. By offering the assets as an exchange, they could bargain for trade and other benefits. Although not binding, the Paris conference set the parameters by which restitution for Jewish refugees could and would later be made.

Max Isenburgh's conversation with the Legation staff on the meeting was detailed in a lengthy report back to the State Department three weeks later. Isenburgh reported that the Swiss-Polish agreement would create a precedent thereby depriving all Jewish organizations of ever recovering Polish Jewish assets, not to mention "the proceeds of 'heirless assets formerly belonging to nationals of countries other than Poland."[54]

Jewish organizations continued to press for a reversal of the Swiss-Polish treaty. In letters, meetings, and in any forum possible, they tried to persuade the Swiss authorities of the precedent-setting nature of their actions and the harm it would bring. In one such meeting Max Isenburgh held with Felix Schnyder, of the Swiss Political Department of the Foreign Ministry, Schnyder resisted his arguments toward canceling the treaty. Isenburgh explained that he thought, quite prophetically, that "Switzerland would be regarded by world public opinion as falling short of her usual standards of public morality in this incident." With this, Schnyder informed Isenburgh that nothing was to be gained from public opinion except for moral satisfaction. He had been working on a plan to contain the Polish situation within its own limits and would work toward a general solution, he told Isenburgh "along the lines of what we wanted." He said that if the agreement were publicized other countries would learn of it and ask for the same treatment and the Swiss government would be forced to defend it.[55] At a any rate, Schnyder said, the Swiss Parliament would ratify the treaty with or without publicity.

Isenburgh responded that Schnyder's remarks were simply a confirmation that the Swiss were using heirless assets belonging to victims of persecution for their own purposes. These same accusations would be heard again by the Swiss almost five decades later. Only after public disclosure by Senator D'Amato in October 1996, did the Swiss affirm this claim. Isenburgh, continued to hold onto the belief well into November that "blocking of the Swiss-Polish Accord is decisive, if any of the heirless assets in Switzerland are to be salvaged."[56]

By December, the groups felt their only recourse would be a public relations effort to stop the Swiss Parliament from ratifying the treaty. In this effort Michael Hoffman of the *New York Times* was recruited to write an article exposing the treaty. The article, appearing in the De-

cember 7, 1949 issue of the *Times*, quoted a Swiss government spokesman as saying that under Swiss law dating back to 1891, the property
of foreigners who die heirless, must be disposed of according to the
law of the foreign state from which the owner was a national. However,
a committee of jurists commissioned by the Swiss Jewish Community
stated that the 1891 law did not cover this case.

The article's last paragraph was the most important:

> The upshot is that if the Swiss Parliament ratifies the accord, the funds, whatever
> their size, will be used to settle claims of Swiss owners of property nationalized in
> Poland instead of for the benefit of refugees under the care of the International
> Refugee Organization.[57]

The groups refused to give up. With Rubin's help with his old friends
at the State Department and pressure applied to the Legation in Bern,
they tried to stop the impending vote on the treaty. Max Isenburgh was
sent to Bern, and arrived there on December 12 to talk to various officials and Parliamentarians in an effort to kill the treaty's ratification.

On December 20, after months of pressuring the State Department,
the groups got a jolt of much needed support when Minister Vincent
delivered an official American demarche to the Swiss Foreign Ministry
protesting the Swiss-Polish treaty. Within two days, the British Minister also delivered a demarche. Unfortunately, the demarches, the protests, the letters, and the meetings were of no help. On the same day as
the British demarche, the Swiss Nationalrat ratified the treaty by a vote
of 98 to 33. Twenty-six years later in 1975, Switzerland, fulfilled its
obligations under the treaty and transferred 480,000 Swiss francs to
Poland.

Recriminations

Frank Bienenfeld was still smarting from the news of the ratification of the Swiss-Polish Treaty of Indemnification, a treaty that he and
other American Jews fought so hard, but failed to prevent. He felt that
the Jewish service organizations had not done enough. The Vienna-
born Legal Advisor of the World Jewish Congress in London, was angry. Five years after the end of World War II and the Holocaust, the
campaign for restitution to the remnants of the Jewish people in Europe was not going well.

"[T]he failure of your organisation [sic]," he wrote to Max Isenberg,
Counsel for European Operations of the American Jewish Committee,

"and of the Jewish Agency in acting sufficiently and too late against my advice caused the disastrous failure in respect to the Jewish-Polish assets in Switzerland." Bienenfeld, added, "I am very sorry that under the circumstances collaboration appears to be very difficult."

Angered, but not shocked by the tone of Bienenfeld's accusations and finger-pointing, Max Isenberg, then a thirty-seven-year-old, Harvard-trained attorney and musician, wasted no time in answering the charges made against him and his organization. "I find it particularly difficult to excuse your irrelevant reference to the Swiss-Polish affair," he wrote to Bienenfeld, "and your suggestion, which I must admit seems to me to be intolerantly self-centered, that the failure of the Jewish Agency and our organization to take your advice 'caused the disastrous failure there.'"

Eugene Hevesi, back in the United States offices of the American Jewish Committee, was also angered by Bienenfeld's angry complaints about his organization. Hevesi wrote to Nehemiah Robinson of the World Jewish Congress that "what I deplore deeply is the attitude reflected, and the tone used in the Bienenfeld communication. This letter is a documentary proof of the fact that in the view of some of your people the only thing that counts is the hunting of organizational credit, and the envy over the accomplishments of others, rather than what is actually accomplished in the Jewish interest." Robinson, closed this extraordinary exchange of letters by answering Hevesi's letter claiming "I do not want to indulge in questions of 'organizational credit' because this is a very touchy topic to discuss and would lend itself to abuses on the part of everyone."[58]

Telling as these exchanges are, Robinson felt that there were other reasons, beyond the lack or possibility of progress with regard to Jewish assets in Switzerland. He wrote of the fear of antagonizing the Swiss who might, in his eyes, renege on their pledge to contribute an early amount of $5,000,000 for Jewish refugee relief in Europe. Despite the recriminations, Jewish groups hoped the Swiss-Polish experience would not be repeated. They were wrong.

The April 21, 1950 headline in the *London Jewish Chronicle*, Britain's oldest Jewish newspaper, read "Savings of Hungarian Jews in Switzerland." According to the *Chronicle*, "The Hungarian delegation to the Swiss-Hungarian commercial conference being held here is to ask Switzerland to transfer to Budapest the savings of Hungarian Jews who dies [sic] heirless in Switzerland, it is reported here. The sum involved is 15,000,000 Swiss francs (about £1,250,000)."[59]

Despite assurances from various Swiss officials that an agreement like that which they signed with Poland would not be repeated, the word quickly spread that another one was in the planning stages. Officials for the Joint Distribution Committee in Europe had reported back to New York that embassy officials in Bern told them that negotiations for such an agreement had been progressing for nearly six months in Budapest. The U.S. Legation in Bern was watching developments, but like the various groups concerned, they were largely powerless in preventing an agreement from happening. Far from being able to prevent an agreement, most parties were hard pressed even to get information. All they knew for certain was that the Swiss were at it again.

Israel Steps In

Having pursued discussions with Switzerland for more than four years, the Jewish organizations failed in numerous attempts to pry their share of the proceeds of heirless assets in Swiss banks to be turned over for refugee purposes as called for in the Five Power Agreement in Paris of June 1946. The Israeli government grew weary of the lack of success on the part of the Jewish groups. Due to the stubbornness of the Swiss, their lack of full support from the Allies and their sharp infighting, the groups were formally asked to turn over responsibility for seeking restitution from the Swiss to the State of Israel. At a meeting with the four Jewish organizations, Dr. Moshe Karen, Chargé d'Affairs in the Israeli Embassy in Washington along with First Secretary A. Liverhant, explained that the Israeli government felt the failures of the organizations had caused problems as well as delays in the entire matter with the Swiss. Time was running out and something had to be done. If the organizations would step aside, Karen told them, Israel would step in and take over the negotiations. The Jewish Agency, the Joint Distribution Committee, and the American Jewish Committee all agreed to Israel's approach. Only the World Jewish Congress, represented by Nehemiah Robinson, refused to give sanction to the plan. They feared, Robinson told Karen, that with Israel taking up the negotiations with Switzerland, the Jewish organizations would be cut out of the process irrevocably and the dispute would be reduced from the international to the national level, lessening the pressure on Switzerland.[60] Under pressure, the World Jewish Congress eventually agreed to the Israeli proposal, but left the door open for future talks with the Swiss, possibly through the ambiguous instructions the WJC sent to Frank

Bienenfeld loosely instructing him to stop his meetings with Swiss officials. The other organizations, aware of this, made every effort to follow what the WJC was doing, even to the point of keeping each other informed of Bienfeld's activities.[61]

Despite this fundamental break between the American Jewish leaders and the government of Israel, the Israelis prevailed. On June 15, 1950, Dr. Karen informed the Secretary of State of this arrangement and that preliminary discussions had already taken place with the International Refugee Organization.[62] For the State Department, essentially it would rid itself of an unsolvable problem. State no more wished to deal with Switzerland on an issue it could not prove with certainty and it would be rid of the Jewish organizations that had constantly sought U.S. help and guidance. On the same day, the Secretary of State responded to Dr. Karen, approving of the Israeli initiative. Now, the Jewish groups were left to pleading their case with the Israeli government.

Regardless of the change of responsibility for dealing with the Swiss, the agreements proceeded. There were reports that Switzerland was attempting to sign similar agreements with other Eastern European nations. Through the next four years, Switzerland would sign more agreements, but not deals of the magnitude or hypocrisy of the Polish or Hungarian treaties.[63] In none of these later agreements were there indemnification clauses for expropriated property or the surrender of Jewish assets.

Throughout the years following the 1946 Washington Accord, there were numerous issues which remained unresolved and unfulfilled by the Swiss. The Allies pressed the Swiss to agree to a conference to discuss these issues. Finally, on March 5, 1951, the Swiss began negotiations with the Allies in Bern in the "Four Powers Conference." The Swiss agreed to discuss three major issues in addition to the Swiss fulfillment of the 1946 Washington Accord: the rate of exchange for the German mark, compensation for Swiss losses in Germany during the war, and minimum exemptions and hardship cases. It was the latter that interested the Jewish groups the most and the one that in the end was never satisfactorily resolved leaving the individual claimants with nothing. As Estelle Sapir had been required to provide proof of death of the account holder in 1947, nothing had changed. The Swiss had still maintained that successful claimants provide this "in order to establish the interest and right of such parties to the possible estate." Moreover, according to Seymour Rubin who informed the American Legation in Bern of his difficulty in obtaining information on a specific account holder, he was required to provide either the name of the bank or the town in which the bank was located.[64] In the vast majority of cases, this was clearly impossible.

After more than a year of negotiations, the parties came to an agreement. On August 26, 1952, the government of Switzerland and the Federal Republic of Germany (FRG) concluded an agreement by which the Swiss government received 121,500,000 Swiss francs from the FRG. Two days later, on August 28, 1952, in another agreement, concluded between the U.S., U.K., France, acting on behalf of the Inter-Allied Reparation Agency, and Switzerland, the Swiss agreed essentially to turn over the 121,500,000 Swiss francs received from the FRG.

There were exemptions made for the unblocking of property below 10,000 Swiss francs and others for sums above this. While unable to get any admission out of the Swiss of the existence of any heirless assets, Allied negotiators were able to exact a promise, for what that was worth, from Walter Stucki, the same Swiss negotiator with whom they had dealt in 1946. Just as in 1946, the Swiss agreed to take "sympathetic consideration" of using any heirless assets found in the future, to be put towards the rehabilitation of victims of Nazi persecution. As would prove to be the case again, this was a hollow promise. Swiss bankers proved reluctant to search for the assets of Holocaust victims. Even when they did conduct a search, nothing was found.[65]

Again, the Swiss banks managed to elude justice. The 1952 treaty with the Allies, specified that all claims were final. The Allies, not wishing to pursue the matter any further, and the Swiss not wishing to discuss it any more were done negotiating. With the Americans now out of the way, the Swiss bankers could afford to ignore the pleas of the Israeli government and the Jewish groups. This was abundantly clear in the minutes to a meeting of the American Joint Jewish Distribution Committee of June 9, 1953, when it was reported that "the Swiss banks have refused to make their records available in order to determine which are Jewish accounts. When the question comes up for discussion, the Swiss always ask what the United States is doing in that connection."[66]

Confessions

It seemed safe now for the Swiss bankers to loosen their collars and confide in their friends that in reality, they had put one over on the Allies. There really was victims' money in the banks after all.

On May 27, 1957, Walter Stucki wrote,

From rather reliable French and Swiss sources I believe that I must accept that
very significant 'valuables' are located in the safes of West [sic] Swiss banks
which had been deposited by private French citizens shortly before the last war. It
is quite possible that the depositors died during the war without their families and
heirs being informed about the deposits and that since then in some cases nothing
more has been prescribed in any way. Would these valuables eventually go to the
concerned banks? If one wants to undertake something legislatively in the matter
to which I don't have anything to say, it would probably be good to also think
about such cases.[67]

Despite his startling admission, Stucki, addressed the issue of legislative relief, something with which the Swiss parliament would have to
handle, and had been discussed on and off in Switzerland since 1952.

In October 1958, anticipating Swiss action, Israel proposed its own
plan for relief. On October 16, the Israeli Embassy in Bern suggested
to the Swiss Federal Department of Justice and Police Affairs, that a
joint Israeli-Swiss committee be formed to discuss the heirless asset
problem. In a reply to the Embassy of December 16, 1958, the Swiss
rejected such an approach, claiming, "it is, of course, understood that
in the eventuality that any regulations might be adopted, the appropriate Swiss authorities would not fail in their search for unknown owners
of property located in Switzerland, or their heirs, to have recourse, in
individual cases, to the intervention of the foreign countries concerned."[68]

Others in Switzerland would suggest different courses for relief.
Harald Huber, a Socialist member of the Swiss Parliament invited the
Federal Council to suggest to Parliament a manner in which the funds
of Holocaust victims that remain in Swiss banks, could be utilized for
humanitarian use. During the debate in Parliament, Huber mentioned
that there remained large amounts of unclaimed funds in Swiss banks.
Something, he felt, must be done with these funds.

Two days after the American Embassy in Bern reported Huber's
speech of March 24, 1959, Huber wrote a letter to the Swiss Justice and
Police Department detailing further his motivations and information
behind his call for action in Parliament:

I took the view in my brief statement that the unclaimed assets amount to much
more than 1 million francs. This view has since been confirmed by a banker of
many years experience, a member of an old established Swiss family, who has
told me that he himself knows from his years in the big banks that hundreds of
millions [of francs] belonging to missing and presumed dead persons are still in

the banks. Indeed, the accounts in question have already been settled to some extent and the sums put into corporations which were established in an ad hoc fashion. The banks naturally are not interested in paying interest on these accounts to those who have a legal claim to the money—wanting to make use with the capital as along as possible for their own profit, even if they certainly don't intend to appropriate the money directly.[69]

Unfortunately this information only became available in 1996 due to the intense research of Tom Bower, author of the book, *Nazi Gold*.

Seymour Rubin, having fought long and hard over the previous twenty years on the problem, again approached the State Department for help. He sought a tripartite approach to the Swiss, involving the U.S., British, and French, in order that they carry out their promises made in 1946 and 1952 to look for heirless assets. The State Department, with no interest in reopening what they viewed as a closed chapter in the heirless assets saga, cabled the embassy in Bern declaring, "at this time the Department considers it premature to raise the matter on a tripartite basis."[70] Roughly two months later, at the end of January 1960, the embassy in Bern cabled back to the Department the same conclusion.

Over the next two years, debate went on. On May 4, 1962, the Federal Council prepared the bill, first proposed by Harald Huber, which came to be known as the Disclosure Decree, mandating a search for Holocaust victims assets in the banks and other fiduciaries, insurance companies, notaries and any other enterprise that would have or could have knowledge of the deposit of funds by people fleeing persecution on religious or political grounds. The goal of the Disclosure Decree was to find those accounts from which there had been no word from the depositors since May 9, 1945. The results of this search were to be reported to a central office. Claimants had five years to submit their claim and the entire process would last ten years. On December 20, 1962, the National Council, or lower house, approved the law, 130–0 and on the same date, the Council of States, or the upper house, approved the bill 36–0.

With the expiration of the Disclosure Decree, ten years later, Swiss authorities disclosed the finding of slightly more than 10.8 million Swiss francs, or slightly more than $2 million, belonging to 1,048 owners, yet close to 7,000 people had filed unsuccessful claims.[71] As the behavior and practices of the Swiss banks came under fire during the Senate Banking Committee inquiry twenty-six years after the decree's passage, criticism of the search would intensify and glaring mistakes, not to mention willful omissions and overlooked parties would come to light. Yet, even at the time and shortly thereafter, criticism arose as to the methods chosen to search for claimants.

In 1966, a claim surfaced from Israel for a Holocaust victim, Ernestine Steinhardt. An application was made on her behalf by an Israeli attorney, H.Z. Veigl, of Tel Aviv. Veigl applied on her behalf to the Swiss Bank Corporation who denied the claim because it was considered customer contact, thereby classifying Mrs. Steinhardt as being alive, and because her lawyer was inquiring and not her, information on the account was denied.[72] However ludicrous this might be, Veigl was never able to successfully fill the claim.

When I gave this document to Tom Bower, he then passed it on to his researchers in Switzerland for further research. They uncovered the full obstruction of the Swiss Bank Corporation regarding the Steinhardt case in the Swiss Federal Archives and it was detailed it in the highly embarrassing report commissioned by the Swiss Foreign Ministry.[73]

As demonstrated by the Steinhardt case, the Swiss looked for excuses to not fulfill the claims. The Swiss exploited loopholes and mixed interpretations to avoid providing the truth to claimants. They expressed a fear that through exposure of claimants in Eastern Europe, these people would be exposed to the wrath of xenophobic Communist governments. This soon became a convenient excuse to hang on to assets of Eastern European depositors. Owing to this, the search for these people was to say the least, lax. The searches were compromised by the fact that in some cases rabbis were brought in to search for Jewish names. Who was to say for sure what was a Jewish name or not. The accuracy was again hampered by the fact that deposits made by Polish and Hungarian nationals were returned to those countries in separate deals more than a decade before with the names of account holders withheld from the two governments.

In all, the 1962 search, was only a partial fulfillment of those looking for the true amount of Holocaust victims assets in Swiss banks. Hans Baer, representing the Swiss Bankers Association (SBA) in his testimony before the Banking Committee, even faulted the Disclosure Decree when he testified, "it is possible that the 1962 process did not identify absolutely all of the assets of Holocaust victims."[74] Mistakes would also be found by Paul Volcker and his auditors, upon the creation of his Commission in May 1996. Inquiries by reporters around the world would also expose the banks' errors in the 1962 search.

By the time the Disclosure Decree expired in 1973, there was very little interest remaining in the issue. Few articles appeared, and the few claimants that had been found in the search were compensated. In 1979, Jean Ziegler, a veteran member of the Swiss Parliament, and frequent critic of the Swiss banks, wrote an article in the *International Herald Tribune* on the subject in response to the television series "Holocaust." In 1986, Mark Talisman, then the Director of the Washington Office of the Council of Jewish Federations wrote the State Department for information on the problem. Little else was written or said about the problem.

At a the time of the debates in Switzerland surrounding the 1962 Disclosure Decree, there appeared a letter to the editor in the New York Times by Max Oetterli, then the Secretary of the SBA. His words at the time appeared to be simply in defense of the process in Switzerland. Today, they have an ironic tone that would, more than thirty years from their writing, be proven very wrong:

> In fact unclaimed assets are very rare in Swiss banks for at least two reasons: first, every bank keeps an accurate record of names and identity domicile of its clients, even of those who have a so-called "numbered account," so as to be able to contact them or their relatives at any time; secondly, it is very seldom that a person with an account in a Swiss bank does not leave some clue in his papers of the existence of that account or has not given to some trustworthy person indications as to the location of the assets. Swiss law obligates banks to furnish all information to the duly established heirs as to the assets of a deceased depositor.[75]

In 1962, Mr. Oetterli was doing what was expected of him. He was keeping up the facade. Unfortunately for the Swiss bankers, it would not last.

Notes

1. Letter of M.W. Beckelman, Director General of the American Joint Distribution Committee to Moshe Sharett, Minister of Foreign Affairs of Israel, 6 November 1953, pp. 2–3, Archives of the Jewish Agency in Israel.
2. Letter of Jacob Friedman to Gregg Rickman, Office of United States Senator Alfonse M. D'Amato, 19 August 1996.
3. W.H. Rozell, "Refugee Dollar Funds: Effect on Balance of Payments," Federal Reserve Board of New York, 7 June 1940, p.2. Only through the special declassification of hundreds of documents like this by the Federal Reserve in 1997 could we have discovered these transfers.
4. Letter from B.E. Sackett, Special Agent in Charge, New York Office of the Federal Bureau of Investigation to Director of the Federal Bureau of Investigation, J. Edgar Hoover, 10 February 1941. Like the Federal Reserve documents, this was one of several that was declassified at our request, more than fifty years after it was written.
5. Treasury Department Inter Office Communication from Edward Foley, General Counsel of the Treasury Department to Secretary of the Treasury Henry

Morgenthau, 2 June 1942, RG 131 Foreign Funds Control, National Archives and Records Administration (hereafter referred to as NARA).

6. Letter from George Ludwig, Swiss American Corporation to Edward Foley, General Counsel of the Treasury Department to Secretary of the Treasury Henry Morgenthau, 15 June 1942, RG 131 Foreign Funds Control, NARA.

7. "German Economic Assets and Activities Outside Germany," Inclosure #4 to Report RH511-45, Military Attache, London, n.d., Records of the Foreign Economic Administration, Records of the War Crimes Branch, RG 153, Entry 134, Box 8, NARA.

8. Memorandum from the Ministry of Economic Warfare to the British Embassy, Washington, D.C. June 3, 1943, Records of the Alien Property Custodian, RG 131, 1942–60, Box 51, NARA.

9. Memorandum from J.W. Pehle to Mr. White, "Treasury's Gold Statement," November 6, 1943, Foreign Funds Control, NARA.

10. Telegram to Certain American Diplomatic and Consular Officers," Records of the State Department, RG 59, the Legal Advisor, Box 13, pp.1–2, NARA.

11. Memorandum for the Files, "Meeting in Mr. Patten's Office, State Department, May 30, 1944," June 8, 1944, Foreign Funds Control, RG 131, 1942–60, p.1, NARA.

12. Telegram from Secretary of State to U.S. Embassy in London, December 20, 1945, Foreign Funds Control, RG 131, 1942–60, NARA.

13. Ibid.

14. "Transfer of German Gold to Switzerland," Military Intelligence Report Germany, May 1, 1945, Captain Paul M. Birkeland, NARA.

15. "Report of Schroeder, Hans, given as declaration on oath on 16 October 1946 at Darmstadt," Records of the Office of the Military Government of the United States, hereafter known as OMGUS, RG 260, Property-OMGUS, "German Intelligence and Investment," Box 653, NARA.

16. Report of the American Legation in Bern, August 23, 1946, OMGUS, RG 260, Property-OMGUS, "German Intelligence and Investment," Box 653, NARA.

17. Nicholas Faith, *Safety in Numbers: The Mysterious World of Swiss Banking*, London: Hamish Hamilton, 1982, pp.108–109.

18. "Emil Puhl Interrogation, August 6, 1945," OMGUS, RG 260, Office of Finance Adviser, General Records of Financial Intelligence Group, 1945–49, Box 204, p. 4, NARA.

19. Letter from Emil Puhl to Dr. Walther Funk, Bern, 6 April 1945, from "Elimination of German Resources for War, Hearings before a Subcommittee of the Committee on Military Affairs, United States Senate, 79th Congress, First Session, p. 936. This is one of four letters collectively known as the "Puhl Letters."

20. Ibid, pp. 3, 2.

21. Memorandum from Donald R. Heath, Director, Office of the Political Director, OMGUS, to Colonel D.L, Robinson, Acting Director, Finance Division, February 1, 1946, OMGUS, RG 260, Property, Box 654, NARA.

22. Memorandum from President Roosevelt to OSS Director William Donovan, 13 July 1944, RG 226, Microfilm Roll # M1642, Roll 30, Frames 865–9, NARA.

23. Margaret Clarke, *The Safehaven Project*, Foreign Economic Administration Study, #5, 1945, RG 169, Entry 170, NARA.

24. Letter from Sidney Homer, Jr., Chief, Enforcement Section, Blockade Division, Foreign Economic Administration to Orvis Schmidt, Director, Foreign Funds Control, Treasury Department, 13 June 1944, RG 131, Office of Alien Property Custodian, Foreign Funds Control, Box 27, NARA.

25. "Notes of July 5, 1944, Re: Enemy Assets in Neutral Countries: Portugal," RG

131, Office of Alien Property Custodian, Foreign Funds Control, Box 27, NARA.

26. "Safehaven Project," January 16, 1945, RG 59, Records of the Department of State, 800.515/1-1645, NARA.
27. "Memorandum For The Files: Re: Safehaven," by James H. Mann, U.S. Treasury Representative, Bern, 29 May 1945, U.S. Department of the Treasury. This was one of many documents that came to us directly from the Department and declassified at our request.
28. Letter from Walter Ostrow, U.S. Treasury Representative to Harry D. White, Assistant Secretary of the Treasury, 31, May 1945, U.S. Department of the Treasury.
29. Letter from James Mann to Harry D. White, Assistant Secretary of the Treasury, 10 October 1945.
30. Interoffice Communication to William H. Taylor from Bernard Feig, United States Embassy, London, 16 February 1946, United States Department of the Treasury.
31. "Transcript of the Finance and Commerce Delegation of the Federal Council, First Session," 14 February 1946, E 2801 1968/84 B 1 29, Swiss Federal Archives.
32. Interview with Seymour Rubin, 21 March 1997, Washington, D.C.
33. Interview with Seymour Rubin, 6 January 1997.
34. "Transcript of the Finance and Commerce Delegation of the Federal Council, First Session."
35. "Transcript of the Finance and Commerce Delegation of the Federal Council, Second Session,"14 February 1946, E 2801 1968/84 B1 29, Swiss Federal Archives.
36. Telegram from Acting Secretary of State Acheson to American Minister Vincent, 6 May 1946, RG 59, Records of the United States Department of State, 1945 49, Box 4205, NARA
37. Letter of Walter Stucki to the Chiefs of the Allies Delegations, 25 May 1946, RG 59, Records of the Department of State, NARA.
38. "Telegram from American Embassy in Paris to the Secretary of State," July 1, 1947, Records of the Department of State, RG 59, Entry 1945–49, Box 4231, NARA.
39. Telegram from Representative Joseph Clark Baldwin to President Truman, 13, July 1946, RG 59, 1945–49, Box 4211, NARA.
40. Response of Dean Acheson to Representative Joseph Clark Baldwin, 31 August 1946, RG 59, 1945–49, Box 4211, NARA.
41. Inter-Office Memorandum of W.S. Surrey and O.F. Fletcher, United States Department of State, 17 March 1947, RG 59, Department of State Office of Financial Operations, Entry NN3-59-69-59, Box 23, NARA.
42. Telegram of Frederick Weissman, Eden, Switzerland, 21 March 1946, RG 84, Post Files of the U.S. Legation in Bern, Switzerland, Box 6, NARA.
43. Interview with Estelle Sapir, conducted by B.J. Moravek, New York City, 17 June. It was at Perpignon that records of some 1,000 Jews deported from Rivesaltes were discovered after French City Hall workers dumped them in a garbage dump to make room for an art exhibition. See, "Death Camp Records Trashed," *Jerusalem Post*, 19 May 1997, p. 4.
44. Aide Memoire, Legation of Switzerland, Washington, D.C., 25 April 1947, RG 59, Records of the Department of State, Entry 1945–49, Box 4228.
45. Max Isenburgh, Memorandum to the Files, 17 November 1948, American Jewish Committee Records, RG 347.7.41-46.
46. "Memorandum of Conversation" between Gottlieb Duttweiler and Members of the State Department's Western European Bureau, 4 January 1951, Records of the Department of State, RG 59, Box 1013, 254.0041/1-451.
47. Letter from the AJDC, New York to the AJDC in Paris, Joel H. Fisher, General

36   Swiss Banks and Jewish Souls

Counsel, 26 January 1948, Records of the American Jewish Joint Distribution Committee, AR 45/64, #1207.

48. Letter from "Lovett" to the American Legation in Bern, 30 September 1948, RG 59, Records of the Department of State, Negotiations with Switzerland, 1943–57, Box 2, NARA.

49. Memorandum of Conversation, Polish-Swiss Trade Agreement, American Embassy, Warsaw, Poland, 25 January 1949, RG 84, Foreign Service Posts, General Records, 1945–49, Box 97, NARA.

50. Telegram from Ambassador Gallman to the Department of State, 15 February 1949, RG 59, 654.60C31/2-1549, Box 2850, NARA.

51. Conversation with Swiss Minister, Memorandum from Cecil Lyon to Ambassador Gallman, 30, June 1949, RG 84, Foreign Service Posts, General Records, 1945–49, Box 97, NARA.

52. Memorandum on Heirless property in Switzerland belonging to Nazi persecutees, 8 August 1949, American Legation in Bern, RG 84, American Legation, Bern Confidential File, 1940–49, 501.5–510.2, Box 80, NARA.

53. S. Adler-Rudel, Memorandum on the Conference with the Swiss Minister of Justice in respect of heirless and unclaimed Jewish assets in Switzerland, in a cover letter to the Executive of the Jewish Agency in Jerusalem, including Frank Bienenfeld, Note on the proceedings in Berne Concerning Heirless and Unclaimed Jewish Assets in Switzerland, 28 July 1949, Central Zionist Archives, Jerusalem, 557–242.

54. Representatives of Jewish committees express concern over clause in recent Swiss-Polish Agreement whereby Heirless Assets in Switzerland are to be turned over to Poland rather than to Jewish committees as was recommended by signatories to Five Power Conference of June 1946," Report of the American Legation in Bern to the Department of State, 27 July 1949, RG 84, American Legation, Bern Confidential File, 1940–49, 501.5–510.2, Box 80, NARA.

55. Memorandum of Conversation with Dr. Felix Schnyder of the Swiss Federal Political Department, Bern, 15 October 1949, YIVO Archives, RG 347.7.41-46, Box 47, Folder, "Switzerland, Heirless Property-FO-EUR 49."

56. Memorandum from Max Isenburgh to the Foreign Affairs Division of the American Jewish Committee, 7 November 1949, American Jewish Committee, RG 347, Box 295, Gen. 10, Folder 1.

57. Michael Hoffman, "Swiss Will Turn Over to Warsaw Property of Heirless Polish Jews," *New York Times*, 7 December 1949, p. 26.

58. Exchange of letters during February and March 1950, YIVO Institute, American Jewish Committee Records, RG 347, Box 276, Gen. 10. Hevesi was the father of New York City Comptroller Alan Hevesi, who would go on to play a role in pressuring the Swiss banks to come forward with information.

59. Letter from F.R. Bienenfeld to J.J. Jacobson, World Jewish Congress, London, England, 24 April 1950, American Jewish Joint Distribution Committee, AR 45/64, #1207.

60. "Minutes of Meeting between Four Organizations and Representatives of the Israeli Embassy regarding Question of Swiss Heirless Assets," 14, June 1950, American Jewish Joint Distribution Committee, AR 45/64, #1207.

61. Cable from Paris office of the Joint Jewish Distribution Committee to the New York office, 23 June 1950, American Jewish Joint Distribution Committee, AR 45/64, #1207; Letter from Eli Rock, American Joint Distribution Committee, New York to Jerome Jacobson, Paris, 23, June 1950, American Jewish Joint Distribution Committee, AR 45/64, #1207.

62. Memorandum of Conversation, "Heirless Funds in Switzerland," Department

of State, Near Eastern Affairs, RG 59, Department of State Decimal Files, 1950–54, Box 59; Note to the Secretary of State from the Israeli Charge d'Affairs, 15 June 1950, RG 59, Box 1013, 254.004/6-1-1550, NARA.

63. Switzerland would go on to sign trade deals with the following Eastern European nations: Yugoslavia, November 26, 1948; Czechoslovakia, December 22, 1949; Romania, August 3, 1951; and Bulgaria, November 26, 1954; see Peter Hug and Marc Perenoud, *Swiss Foreign Ministry Report on Unclaimed Assets of Victims of Nazis and Compensation Agreements with East European Countries, Swiss Foreign Ministry*, December 19, 1996, translated by the Foreign Broadcast Information Service, January 23, 1997, p. 21.

64. Memorandum of L. J. Daymont, American Consul, American Legation, Bern, to the Department of State, 21 March 1951, NARA.

65. In a report to the Secretary of State from a Legation counselor, Reams, of May 21, 1951, it was reported, the "Swiss have submitted a paper stating that investigation by Swiss Bankers Association and Swiss Association of Life Insurance Companies has revealed no (rpt. no) assets of heirless Ger [sic] victims of Nazi action."

66. Minutes of a meeting of the American Joint Jewish Distribution Committee, 9 June 1952, p.3, Archives of the American Joint Jewish Distribution Committee, New York City, AR45/64, #1207. As would be the case forty-three years later, Seymour Rubin would write Ambassador Stuart Eizenstat, leading the Clinton Administration's Interagency Taskforce on Holocaust Assets, complaining of the lack of U.S. effort to uncover the assets of Holocaust victims in U.S. banks.

67. Letter of Walter Stucki to Professor Rudolf Bindschedler, 27 May 1957, E 2001(E) 1972/33 Bd 280 (B.42.13), Swiss Federal Archives, translated by Brian Hufker and David Skelly.

68. Note from Swiss Federal Department of Justice and Police Affairs to the Israeli Embassy in Bern, 16 December 1958, Archives of the Jewish Agency for Israel, translated by David Skelly.

69. Letter of Harald Huber to the Dr. Fritz Wahlen, Minister of the Swiss Justice and Police Department, 31 March 1959, E 4110 (a) 1973/85, Bd.2, Swiss Federal Archives, translated by Brian Hufker and David Skelly, courtesy of Tom Bower.

70. Cable from the Department of State to the U.S. Embassy, 8 December 1959, U.S. Department of State.

71. Hug and Perenoud, *Swiss Foreign Ministry Report on Unclaimed Assets of Victims of Nazis and Compensation Agreements with East European Countries*, p. 59.

72. Memorandum of February 1, 1966, Jewish Agency for Israel, Archives of the Jewish Agency for Israel. Courtesy of Itamar Levin.

73. Hug and Perenoud, *Swiss Foreign Ministry Report on Unclaimed Assets of Victims of Nazis and Compensation Agreements with East European Countries*, pp. 49–50.

74. Testimony of Hans Baer before the Senate Committee on Banking, Housing, and Urban Affairs, 104th Congress, Second Session, 23 April 1996.

75. Max Oetterli, Letter to the Editor, *New York Times*, 6 February 1962.

2

Unfinished Business

"You must be aware of the fact, that Switzerland is still holding on to all the property incl.[sic] money in banks—left by Jews, who perished during World War Two thru [sic] the Nazis and their helpers. AMONG THE SIX MILLION VICTIMS, our Nation lost during the Nazi holocaust, are also the HEIRS of the depositors and this heirless property has not been released yet by Switzerland almost 25 years after the end of the terrible war. Does the American Government also intend to do something about it?"[1]

The honest answer to Liba Weingarten's question to New York Senator Jacob Javits was "no." In December 1969, there was no interest in dredging up the past. Weingarten, Vice President of the Jewish Nazi Victims Congregation of New York wrote to Javits because of his long interest in the subject.[2] Yet, for Javits's office, the letter seemed like just another constituent request. In order to handle it quickly, the office "bucked" the letter to the State Department as a quick way to get an answer to a constituent by having an administrative agency answer the letter. Weingarten, undeterred, would continue to correspond with Javits's office for some months, with little more than a polite exchange of letters to show for her efforts.

There were many others like Liba Weingarten who also wanted to know what happened to the Jewish assets in Swiss banks. Answers were hard to find because the search had long since ended. Twenty-seven years later, Ms. Weingarten's questions would be answered.

The Burden of Proof

In the years after the war, the Jews were saddled with the burden of proving to the Swiss that there were Jewish assets in their banks. Their position was weak. Jewish service organizations had to beg and scrap for whatever they could. Moreover, Allied governments, sympathetic as they were, nevertheless had other things on their minds. They did the best they could. This was the crux of the problem.

As Nehemiah Robinson of the World Jewish Congress wrote to Eugene Hevesi of the Joint Distribution Committee in March 1950 regarding their internal disputes as to who would claim credit for various achievements, "we have to make the best out of the limited existing cooperation." Jewish groups could only do so much. After so long, it was time for this burden to shift. Now, it would be time for the Swiss to prove that Jewish money was not in their banks.

December 7, 1995

The U.S. Congress, not often known for working into December, was running over this year. It was the first session of the first Republican Congress in forty years, and there was plenty of legislation to clear away and send to the President. Whereas, normally they would be home in their States, Senators were in Washington tending to the business of Congress.

The meeting was set. At 12:20 P.M. the President of Joseph E. Seagram & Sons, Inc. was to arrive at the U.S. Capitol and proceed to the Senate Dining Room where he would meet with the new Chairman of the Senate Banking, Housing, and Urban Affairs Committee. Bringing with him Israel Singer, the General Secretary of the World Jewish Congress and Steve Herbits of Seagrams, Edgar Bronfman, Sr., billionaire President of the World Jewish Congress was set to meet Alfonse M. D'Amato, Senator from New York.

Bronfman, came with the intent of recruiting D'Amato to join him in pressuring Swiss banks into providing an accounting of the assets belonging to the Jewish people, assets dating back to the end of World War II. They sat at a corner table, chatted, and ordered lunch.

Once into the conversation, Bronfman and Singer began to detail for D'Amato the events of that year, and what the World Jewish Congress had done to bring the banks around. While Bronfman was there to set the stage for the discussion, it was to be Singer who would explain what the controversy was all about.

Over a bowl of soup, D'Amato listened to Singer tell the story how the Swiss bankers had found 774 dormant accounts, opened between 1933 and 1945, and left unclaimed since that time. The Swiss banks, Singer said, were stalling. They were not providing the WJC the information that they had agreed to provide, on the schedule they had agreed to provide it. Singer detailed meticulously the steps of the negotiations and the preliminary finds the SBA had made. Yet, the SBA was taking its time, and Bronfman and Singer were getting nervous, after fifty years, they wanted news, more news, and faster.

"They're taking advantage of you," said D'Amato. "They think that they can wait you out. I wouldn't trust them." "That's why we're here," said Singer. "We want to ask you," Bronfman interrupted, "to help us. What can you do?" Without as much as a thought about its implications, D'Amato said quite simply, "we'll hold hearings. We'll research it and we'll look into the problem." Simple as this might seem, with this, Bronfman had found his man, only he did not really know the significance of his actions. Soon the Swiss bankers and the Swiss people would find out.

What made this new alliance different than most was that it involved two men who could not be more different, politically and personally. Bronfman, President of Seagrams and of the WJC, had come late to his religion, and late to his role as a man who could open doors to kings and presidents. He was also known as a big Democratic Party contributor. Bronfman became President of the WJC in 1981, after being recruited for the position by Nahum Goldman. His first victory as President was in the Kurt Waldheim affair. Waldheim, the Secretary General of the United Nations, was exposed by Bronfman's WJC as a Nazi officer who had committed war crimes in Salonika. It was Bronfman's staff, largely composed of Singer and WJC Executive Director Elan Steinberg who did Waldheim in, and these same two men were sharpening their knives for the Swiss bankers they, and now, D'Amato were about to take on.

D'Amato, two years into his third term as the Republican junior Senator from New York, took pride in his reputation as a pitbull, a tenacious street fighter who fought to the bitter end for his constituents. It was said that his constituents would go to him for a visa and to the state's senior Senator, Daniel Patrick Moynihan for a lecture. He brought home the bacon and he was proud of his moniker as the "pothole Senator."

October 26, 1992

Jacques Picard, a young historian with the Institute for Social Research in Bern, received a request to write a report for Lawrence Lever, the financial editor of the *Mail on Sunday* and a BBC film producer.

The result was a thirty-page paper entitled "Switzerland and the Assets of the Missing Victims of the Nazis." Picard, a curious, truth-seeking historian, then expanded his study into a book, *Switzerland and the Jews, 1933–1945*. While the book became popular in Switzerland, what Picard could not have known was that his book would be the beginning of the shattering of the myth of Swiss wartime history.

Two days after Kaspar Villiger's V-E day fiftieth anniversary apology to the Jewish people on May 7, 1995, the SBA announced that it would form a working group to examine dormant accounts. The working group would formulate policies for the handling of such assets and consider the creation of a central office to handle claims for such accounts. According to the late American Ambassador to Switzerland M. Larry Lawrence, the Commission was not directed exclusively at Holocaust victims nor "is it likely to address all of their concerns."[3] As would prove to be the case, whatever actions the Swiss bankers tried to pass off as proactive, in reality were mere half-measures, more damaging to their cause. They simply refused to face their problems head on. Throughout the affair, the Swiss government and the banks would consistently act in this manner.

Within two weeks the press began to pick up on the issue and soon there were stories in *Business Week* and later in the *Wall Street Journal*, propelling the issue from a Swiss internal problem to an international one. The Swiss government was then faced with a proposal by two Swiss parliamentarians, Verena Grendelmeir, a member of the Nationalrat or Lower House, and Otto Piller, a member of the Standerat or Upper House, both friendly to Jewish causes, who became interested in the problem. On June 12, the two introduced separate motions calling for the creation of a centralized agency to help claimants determine the location of their lost accounts. While including other provisions, the legislation had little chance of passage. Yet, in an interview in the *Wall Street Journal*, Piller explained his action was no ploy when he stated, "for me, its a question of Switzerland's standing. We can't be indifferent to our reputation."

Ambassador Lawrence, while suggesting to his DCM to look into the matter in early July, nevertheless, thought that this latest talk of dormant Swiss bank accounts was "nothing more than unsubstantiated allegations, and the source of the articles [discussing the matter] may be suspect." Recommending against a visit by Presidential Envoy for restitution issues, then Undersecretary of Commerce Stuart Eizenstat, Lawrence expressed his belief that the SBA was satisfactorily addressing the issue. Moreover, he discounted any thoughts that the government of Switzerland was "stonewalling."[4]

While Lawrence may have discounted the new talk of dormant bank accounts, the Swiss Jewish community was not. By this time, the Swiss Federation of Jewish Communities (SFJC) made an approach to the Swiss Bankers Association and began a dialogue with them as to what could be done. Michael Kohn, Vice President of the European Jewish Congress, asked Rolf Bloch, Swiss chocolate magnate and leader of the Swiss Jewish community, to contact Edgar Bronfman and Israel Singer to inform them of their progress. In doing so, they set in motion the opportunity for the World Jewish Congress to become involved. This would occur in Brussels when they would meet on September 12, 1995 for the upcoming Brussels meeting of the World Jewish Restitution Organization.

Close to a month before the Brussels meeting, on August 14 the United States embassy in Brussels cabled the Secretary of State dismissing the growing problem. The embassy continued to disregard the press reports, maintaining "they are replete with falsehoods." And they urged, "USG officials not to lend respectability or weight" to them. "More importantly, we hope that the facts below will disabuse any USG officials of the notion that there are significant amounts of money to be recovered here..."[5] The cable went on to recite their belief in the reassurances of the senior officials of the Swiss Banking Association, with whom they had recently met that everything was being handled in a correct and just manner.

While U.S. diplomats may have believed the Swiss bankers, Edgar Bronfman did not. Just days before the convening of the Brussels conferences, Bronfman sought and obtained a letter from the late Israeli Prime Minister Yitzhak Rabin, declaring that he as President of the World Jewish Restitution Organization as well as the WJC, represented "the Jewish people and the State of Israel" in negotiations with the Swiss banks. Bronfman felt proud of his official sanction from Rabin and carried it to Switzerland for a meeting with the SBA on September 14, 1995 and later to Brussels.

It was on the 14th, that Bronfman, along with Israel Singer, Avraham Burg, President of the Jewish Agency, and Rolf Bloch, leader of the Swiss Jewish community met with the SBA and the two sides announced the creation of a working dialogue as well as a central office with a Swiss Banking Ombudsman, as called for in the May 9th SBA decision creating the working group on missing assets. Announcing that the banks had found nearly $32,000,000 in dormant assets, George Kreyer, head of the SBA, stated quite clearly that there was no intention of performing this service "free of charge."[6] Kreyer maintained that the SBA and the Swiss banks have always "proceeded correctly with requests for the search of dormant accounts by relatives who had little or no information as to where these assets could have been." Kreyer's statement went on to list the litany of "correct" procedures that Swiss banks followed to settle the problem, throughout the past decades. A repetition of the 1962 decree, in which the Swiss banks were to have searched for dormant accounts, was "not warranted." Kreyer appeared as clearly willing to do only the bare minimum to settle the problem.

Later Bronfman would travel to Brussels to attend the WJRO conference on the various restitution issues that he and the other leading Jewish groups had been pursuing throughout Europe. According to Maram Stern of the Brussels office of the WJC, as told to the American embassy in Brussels attending the conference, the Swiss were under the misapprehension that Bronfman was simply in this for the money. The Swiss, Stern told the embassy official, asked Bronfman to "name a price" in order to negotiate a lump sum payment. According to Israel Singer, the Swiss suggested that $32 million was a workable number with which to start. Bronfman, held out, as he would later tell D'Amato, for a full accounting of the assets in Swiss banks.

But what angered Bronfman the most was their arrogance. In what would become symbolic of the Swiss bankers, Bronfman related the story many times that when he walked into the room with the Swiss, he was not even offered a chair. The Swiss simply made him an ultimatum, "take it or leave it." However, simple, the Swiss would live to regret their callous ommission of such a common courtesy.

Between the September meeting with the Swiss and the December one with D'Amato, the Swiss had been silent. Promising some word on the assets and the search for their owners, Bronfman and Singer became impatient. As D'Amato warned, they were trying to stall them. Yet, at a meeting on December 12 in Bern, between the WJRO and the SBA, the two sides agreed to a six-point plan calling for, among other things, secrecy in their dealings. It was the violation of this point by the Swiss that would signal the descent of Swiss fortunes and the beginning of the search for the truth about Swiss activities in World War II.

February 6, 1996

On February 6, 1996, the WJC was notified that the SBA was going to hold a press conference the following day to announce the final results from their search through the banks. Considering this a "blatant disregard" of their agreement, the WJC condemned the coming announcement.[7] The next day, the WJC went even further in denouncing the Swiss move and declared it to be unilateral and unacceptable. Having read of the Swiss announcement, I contacted the WJC asking for an update on the situation and asked what should be done. Singer explained that he would be in Washington on February 14th and he would give me a full briefing.

Over lunch at the Capitol Hill restaurant, La Colline, Singer, Elan Steinberg, Executive Director of the WJC, Eli Rosenbaum, former Counsel of the WJC and head of the Justice Department's Nazi-hunting Office of Special Investigations, and Doug Bloomfield, Washington lobbyist and the WJC representative in Washington, presented their case. That same day, Steinberg had faxed to our office a document found by the United States Holocaust Museum detailing the attempted raiding of a Swiss bank account by Radu Lecca, a high-ranking official of Romania's wartime government. Apparently, in 1963, Lecca had tried to gain access to an account, with the requisite account number, but was told that documents from all accounts from 1944 were destroyed. Steinberg, during the lunchtime meeting conveyed the importance of this document, explaining that the Swiss bank had already begun destroying documents at that time. Steinberg smelled corruption and the "Lecca document" as it became known, was the source.

Later that afternoon, Howard Menell, the Staff Director for the Banking Committee, as well as Phil Bechtel, the Deputy Staff Director, and I met with lawyers for the SBA. C. Boyden Gray and Marc Cohen, representing the powerful and well-connected Washington law firm of Wilmer, Cutler, and Pickering, as well as Bob Dinerstein, representing the Union Bank of Switzerland, came to downplay the simmering dispute. In choosing this prestigious Washington law firm, the SBA hoped that its two most prominent members, Gray and Lloyd Cutler would easily be able to rein in any trouble simply by using their Washington contacts. Gray was President Bush's White House Counsel and Cutler had held the same post under President Clinton. The SBA hoped that Cutler could even stroll into the White House and obtain the President's help in quieting this whole affair. The SBA could certainly afford this caliber of representation and money was of course no concern. As Andreas Hubschmid, the First Secretary and Chief of the Legal Office of the SBA would later tell the SBA's former Washington attorney Bob

Royer, the SBA spent $1–2,000,000 per month over the entire episode for representation. Gray and Dinerstein tried desperately to get the Banking Committee inquiry stopped before it had really begun. They tried to reassure us that the SBA was doing all that it could to search its records and was even willing to allow its methodology for such a search audited. Their line simply was not believable. Menell explained to them that the Senator was committed and informed Gray that the inquiry would proceed.

When presented with the Lecca document, which the WJC had released earlier to the press, they downplayed it, and Gray expressed deep doubt that a Swiss bank would dare destroy documents. When I asked if it was possible for a Swiss banker to have closed an account and pocketed the proceeds when he knew the owner was not coming back, surprisingly Gray, in a very relaxed way, said "why sure."

Meanwhile in Switzerland, SBA officials were meeting with American Embassy officials to downplay the role of Swiss banks and their attractiveness as a haven for refugee flight capital during the war. Very little Jewish money, they said, could have been deposited in Swiss banks. They maintained Swiss innocence for any wrongdoing and declared that all the money was returned after the 1962 mandated search.

By the end of February, the Banking Committee had begun its inquiry and we were sending out letters seeking the help of any federal agency that might possibly help with documents. In the last two weeks of the month, seeking documents, we sent letters to the United States Holocaust Memorial Museum, the State Department, the National Archives, the CIA, the Army Intelligence Archives in Fort Meade, Maryland, the Treasury Department, the embassies of Poland, Hungary, Italy, Holland, France, England, and Germany which steadfastly denied retaining any records having anything to do with the matter. The Germans were quite happy to see someone else, for a change, get in trouble for their actions during World War II, and they were not the least bit cautious about making this joy known.

Two days before the briefing by Singer and Steinberg, Swiss Ambassador to the United States Carlo Jagmetti met with us in the Senator's office. Jagmetti, an attorney graduated from the University of Zurich and a career diplomat, had served as Swiss Ambassador to South Korea, the European Community, and France before being posted to Washington in 1993.

Even without D'Amato present in the city that day, Jagmetti, and Embassy Counselor Christopher Bubb, felt it important enough to come in to quell the controversy. In what might well prove to be some of the most ironic words he would utter in his tenure as Ambassador, Jagmetti begged for calm and serenity and asked that "the situation not be allowed to deteriorate." Jagmetti himself would contribute to this deterioration nearly a year later with a career ending memo leaked to the press by someone in his own Foreign Ministry.

He, like Gray and Dinerstein proceeding him, explained that the SBA was doing all that it could to solve the problems posed by this situation and he asked for patience. He also explained that it was only reasonable that the Swiss bank Ombudsman charged a "nominal" fee to search for accounts so as to discourage false claims. This aspect had proven to be a real point of contention because claimants have been charged several hundred dollars for the Swiss Ombudsman to search the Swiss banks for dormant accounts. Many of those claiming lost assets were very much in need of these funds and could barely scrape together the money to pay for the search.

Soon responses began to arrive from the various agencies to which D'Amato had written. Only the National Archives offered any real help in providing records, and it became obvious that we needed researchers. I called Elan Steinberg and asked for help. In turn, he asked Doug Bloomfield to find us two Washington area researchers who could help us, as long as whatever they found for the Banking Committee was shared with the WJC. Miriam Kleiman, a University of Michigan graduate and former Clevelander who had worked for a number of Jewish organizations in Washington, was between jobs and was told by Bloomfield, that "it would be only a few days work."

To direct the research, Bloomfield found Willi Korte, a German-born attorney, turned researcher and tracker of Nazi looted artwork to help locate the appropriate records. Korte had previously worked with the WJC on the Waldheim case and understood what it would take to pursue this kind of research, even if Steinberg and Bloomfield underestimated it.

As Kleiman and Korte settled down in the Archives II building in suburban College Park, Maryland, it did not take very long at all for them to find pertinent records. Korte found 2,100 boxes of documents from the "Economic Intelligence Division" of the Treasury Department. Archivists at College Park had not even recalled receiving the boxes months before from the document warehouse in Suitland, Maryland. Then after only a few days sifting through the dusty brown boxes of onion-skinned papers, with the original rubber bands and paper clips, last seen decades before, Kleiman found records relating to "Operation Safehaven." Up until this time, no one really knew much about this wartime operation, but soon the world would come to learn a great deal about this effort by the U.S. government to track German external assets in Europe and elsewhere during and after the war.

Kleiman then found a single document dated July 12, 1945, detailing a list of 182 separate account balances held by the Societe General de Surveillance S.A. of Geneva (SGS). The account holders were from Romania, Hungary, Bulgaria, Croatia, Moravia, Slovakia, France, Holland, and Denmark. According to the Congressional Research Service, which did the necessary conversions and factored in a rough estimate of inflation and a nominal interest rate over five decades, these accounts conservatively equalled $20 million at today's rates. Shortly after the discovery of this document, D'Amato wrote to SGS requesting information on the accounts. Nearly six months later, after hiring a top-flight auditing firm, SGS reported that they could trace postwar account activity for all but four of the accounts. The names of these four have been withheld from us for reasons of confidentiality.

Almost immediately after finding the SGS document, the WJC released the document to the press declaring that it was proof of Swiss criminality. The WJC released the document before we could, and the WJC proudly stated that it had turned it over the Committee for further investigation. This pattern would repeat itself dozens of times over the next few months, turning into a race for press between the WJC staff and us.

Within a few weeks documents began to pour in detailing Nazi gold shipments, stolen securities, looted artwork, stolen jewelry, and Swiss collaboration with the Nazis. All the horrors and misdeeds of the past were being brought back to life in the pages of the documents Kleiman and Korte were finding and copying. Within a very short time, it became readily apparent that this project was bigger than the two, now weary researchers could handle, and it was obvious that Doug Bloomfield's "few days work" would turn into weeks and perhaps months.

On March 18, as the research in the Archives was beginning, Singer and Steinberg again came to Washington and met with us. Joining the meeting was Dr. Walter Reich, the former Director of the Holocaust Museum who would later provide the resources of the Museum for us to expand the inquiry. Singer and Steinberg wanted to share with us their views on the evolving project and how it should proceed. They explained that they knew of archives all over Europe and even in the former Soviet Union that contained records the Committee could use. They declared they would use their connections established over the years, in Singer's words, to "liberate" these documents for the Committee.

They requested that the research be comprehensive and cover all different types of assets and the study should be broadened to cover the other neutral countries as well. We disagreed as to the scope fearing that we were not ready to move that fast. We felt we should stick to Switzerland and establish the facts before we could examine other countries' roles in the war. This point of contention would be one that would continue throughout the year long process with the WJC preferring to "attack" along a broad front while we tried to remain focused on attacking Switzerland alone.

With the release of the SGS document, the world slowly began to focus on large sums of money that were being discovered. Quickly, Avraham Burg, head of the Jewish Agency in Jerusalem was declaring to Israeli television that there was much more money in the Swiss banks than anyone ever thought. After all, did not the Swiss banks claim only $32,000,000 was found? The SGS document amounted to $20,000,000 alone. Where did all the money go? Burg wanted to know. While the document did not appear to be wholly substantiated, its release did achieve one purpose, proving for the Swiss banks that this inquiry was not going to stand still. If anything, it was moving forward and the banks were beginning to look bad in the process.

As news of this and other documents released by both the Committee and the WJC spread, people around the world began to offer help, and more importantly, access to documents from other countries. In Israel, Itamar Levin, Deputy Editor of the Israeli business paper *Globes* began to scour the Central Zionist Archives in Jerusalem. Although he was using them for his reporting on the issue in Israel, he gladly supplied copies to the Committee. After a request from D'Amato to the British Embassy in Washington, the embassy supplied hundreds of British Foreign Office documents brought over from the Public Records Office in London.

Soon, I felt that we needed to send help out to Kleiman and Korte. I sent out my intern Marc Isser and a legislative fellow assigned to the office from the United States Secret Service, B.J. Moravek. Moravek, a former Green Beret and experienced financial crimes investigator, was just who we needed to examine what we quickly began to see as a massive money laundering operation.

Volunteers, needed and unneeded, also began to come forward. Marc Masurovsky, owner of a translation service in Washington and the author of a master's thesis on Operation Safehaven for American University, volunteered his services as well as documents and reference sites in the National Archives. Letters and phone calls from people all over the world came in as well, with people volunteering information or offering help. One call came from a World War II vet who phoned claiming he heard from another vet where millions of dollars of gold bullion was buried in Turkey. If I called this man, he would provide me with the location, on the proviso that I fly to Florida to meet him..

By March, we were prepared to put together the first Congressional hearing on the role of Swiss banks in fifty years. The last hearings were under the leadership of Senator Harley Kilgore, Democrat of West Virginia and Chairman of the War Preparedness Subcommittee of the Senate Military Affairs Committee. Kilgore was very critical of the Swiss banks accusing them of laundering Nazi gold and extending aid and comfort to the enemy. Kilgore's hearings took place in an entirely different atmosphere. His accusations, while new then, never really made an impact because of the onset of the Cold War made Switzerland a necessary tool for the Allies. In 1996, the Cold War was over and the Swiss were not so necessary anymore.

Trial by Public Opinion

Throughout the 1940s and 1950s during the long and fruitless negotiations with the Swiss, American diplomats and negotiators dealt with the Swiss bankers and diplomats on legal terms. At each session with their Swiss counterparts, they laid out their arguments in a legalistic and methodical manner trying to convince them of the merits of their case. Each time the Swiss would listen and argue back as if they were in a court of law. The mistake our diplomats made then was that they played by the Swiss agenda. This is where they made their fatal error and is one of the main reasons the problem was not solved back then.

By the sheer weight of the information we gathered in less than a month of research, it became clear that we could not, and most assuredly would not refight the battles our diplomats lost fifty years ago. Our goal was simple. We would bring the Swiss bankers into a court, but not one in which they were used to dealing. In the court of public opinion we controlled the agenda. The bankers were on our turf and conveniently, we were judge, jury, and executioner. Like it or not the

Swiss bankers would have to play by our rules. As it turned out, they were not very good at this game.

On April 23, 1996, the hearing was set. Senator D'Amato had assembled a prestigious group of witnesses for the hearing. Under secretary of Commerce and Presidential Envoy for Property Restitution Stuart Eizenstat, WJC President Edgar Bronfman, claimant Greta Beer, and Hans Baer, Chairman of Julius Baer Bank and a member of the Executive Board of the SBA would testify before the packed audience in the Banking Committee Hearing room in the Senate Dirksen Office Building.

Convening the hearing, D'Amato opened by stating that the issue at hand was about the "systematic victimization of people." He explained that the victims had placed their trust with the Swiss banks and that trust was broken. The evidence, D'Amato stated, although early in the inquiry, was troubling. He commented on the irony that the very bank secrecy laws enacted in Switzerland to attract Jewish funds, were now being used against the families of the claimants to keep them from their assets.

Speaking for a short time, he painted a picture of Swiss greed and exploitation of Holocaust victims that everyone, but the Swiss and their lawyers in the audience, seemed to understand very clearly. After D'Amato, Senator Christopher J. Dodd, then General Chairman of the Democratic National Committee and son of Thomas Dodd, a former prosecutor at the Nuremberg War Crimes trials, took the microphone. After his brief statement, Senator Barbara Boxer, another Democrat on the Committee delivered her opening statement. What Hans Baer and his "handlers" from Wilmer, Cutler, and Pickering could not understand was that there would be no partisan bickering from the members of the Committee. Despite the ongoing Whitewater hearings D'Amato was chairing at the time and the presence of Senator Dodd, there was absolutely no difference of opinion on this matter. The issue was black and white. Add to the fact that in New York State and California combined, there were more Jews than in Israel, the Swiss banks were in trouble.

When Greta Beer spoke she put down her prepared remarks and laid out her story of her travels to Switzerland in the 1940s with her mother to try to get the money back that her father, Siegfried Deligdisch had placed there for her and her brother Otto. Her father, she explained, crying at times while she told the story, had owned textile mills in Romania before the war. Traveling all over Europe to sell his products, he would stop in Switzerland to make deposits to his accounts. With her father's death in Vienna in 1940, she and her family had to fend for themselves in war-torn Europe. After the war, she went to Switzerland several times trying in vain to get her father's accounts. There was near silence in the room while she told her story, her voice cracking throughout her testimony.

Following Greta was Edgar Bronfman. His message was simple, representing the six million who could not represent themselves, he sought justice and closure of "the last chapter of World War II." He mocked the Swiss bankers for declaring "trust us, this was all we could find."

Following Bronfman came Stuart Eizenstat to tell the U.S. Government's actions to date. Left for the end, purposely so, was Hans Baer. He was to speak last so that he would have to respond to all that he heard, with the help of the attorneys from Wilmer and Cutler, who during the testimony of the other witnesses, chatted among themselves like fidgety children in a movie theater.

Baer, while a prominent member of the banking elite in Switzerland, was known as the industry's token Jew. It could not have been a mistake then that C. Boyden Gray picked him to testify before the Committee. How could anyone question the integrity of a Jewish banker testifying on behalf of the Swiss banks?

Although he was not sworn in to testify, Baer nevertheless had Wilmer, Cutler and Pickering partner Daniel K. Mayers sitting beside him throughout his testimony. With wavy grayish-white hair and thick black rimmed glasses, Baer bore a striking resemblance to the wheelchair-bound rocket scientist character played by Peter Sellers in the classic movie *Dr. Strangelove*. Listening to his testimony delivered in a thick German accent, staffers behind the dais commented that they expected him, like the movie's character, to "Seig Heil," at any moment.

Baer tried the best he could to defend the banks and their misdeeds, but, he said, these actions occurred a long time ago. At any rate, he said, the real mistakes that were made resulted from a faulty search conducted in 1962 in Switzerland, and that now, all of the dormant accounts had been found. The inaccurate search of 1962 was to blame.

Baer also proudly detailed the coming formation of a joint commission with the WJC to study the dormant accounts in a detailed way. Independent accounting firms would be appointed to audit the methodology the banks used to arrive at the sum of $32,000,000, not one penny of which, the Swiss bankers wanted to keep as their own. He declared the money would go to Eastern European Jews, not granted restitution before due to the Cold War.

Although weak in defense, Baer tried a move on the offensive by offering to bring Greta Beer to Switzerland, all expenses paid, to help her look for her father's account. This sounded nice and conciliatory and won him a few compliments from the Senators, yet the cheer did not last very long. Boxer, knowing a good issue when she had one, lit in to him and persisted in questioning him about the deposits of Nazis in the banks. Boxer was following up on the lead of D'Amato who had earlier taken up a line of questioning about Nazi looted gold passing through Swiss banks into Portugal. Boxer extended her line of questioning to include individual deposits of Nazis. Baer was at a loss for words.

I had suggested the subject of looted gold as the line of inquiry to the Senator because, quite frankly, despite just four weeks of research by Kleiman and Korte, it was clear we were not going to find much on individual accounts except for the information gleaned from the claimants. What we were finding, however, in great amounts was information on the vast sums of looted gold laundered through Swiss banks as well as the Swiss National Bank by the Nazis. Our figuring was that if we were unable to find evidence of Swiss bank accounts of Jews, we might well look for Nazi activity with the banks. We felt that if we could prove the banks accepted the looted valuables and gold the Nazis stole from all over Europe, then it would be easier to show complicity on their part in withholding the Jewish accounts. As the evidence would later bear out, this would be the case.

After the close of the hearing, Singer approached Baer to talk about the formulation of the commission Baer discussed in his testimony. Unresponsive, Singer felt slighted and exchanged words with him until the two were quickly separated. Baer went out into the hall to talk with reporters and Singer joined Bronfman for a trip down Pennsylvania Avenue were the two would meet with President Clinton to discuss, among other things, the Swiss banking issue. While we would not find this out for another six months, Bronfman had met the day before with Hilary Clinton in New York and mentioned the issue to her. He asked her to pass on to the President an article in *New York* magazine on the banks that featured Greta Beer's story. He also asked the First Lady to seek a meeting for him with the President the next day.

We would come to learn later as well, that Marc Cohen, the day-to-day attorney on this matter with Wilmer for the SBA, was said to have told Baer that if this was the "best they could throw at them," they had nothing to worry about. This attitude at least seems to have been verified by Swiss journalist Patrick Cabot-Martin, who passed along information that the Swiss felt they got off lightly. After the hearing, the SBA seemed, according to Cabot-Martin, to be proud of the way they seemed to have escaped relatively unscathed. These pleasant thoughts might have made them feel better, but this was only the first skirmish of the war.

The following day, among the many clips reporting the events of the previous day, we found one in the *New York Post*, quoting President Clinton as saying that at Bronfman's suggestion, he would even work together with Senator D'Amato to solve the problem. Owing to the events of the time, this was quite a statement.

Within two weeks, the commission Hans Baer talked about in the hearing was coming into being. On May 1st, Israel Singer called to tell us that they were on the verge of signing an agreement with the SBA to form the commission. After reading a faxed copy of the draft, we were shocked that the WJC would agree to all that was included in the agreement. The WJC was ready to agree to a secrecy clause that would bind them to silence and prevent them from calling attention to violations the SBA might commit. After discussing the issue with Singer, he agreed to seek this change.

There were other sections which we felt were overly gracious to the SBA, and despite this, the WJC agreed to them. For one, the SBA became the arbiter of what files the commission would see. The audit would be conducted by firms licensed to operate in Switzerland and we feared that the firms would most certainly have been cognizant that they would need to gain other contracts from the Swiss banks once this search was over, perhaps causing them a bit of caution with respect to the establishment of results. The SBA would be the financing authority of the commission and that clause made us question how far the commission would go. Finally, the commission had no subpoena authority, no authority to punish parties in Switzerland for withholding information, destroying information, or simply lying. Despite these loopholes, the WJC signed the agreement the next day. In a letter informing the Senator of the pending agreement, Bronfman summed up his assessment of the chances of the commission by writing, "when one orders a bottle of wine, the sommelier presents it to you unopened. You examine it as to the shipper, the vintage and the label and then say 'so far so good.' The next step is to taste the wine. I am hopeful that the Swiss banks are operating with openness, but past performance doesn't hold much promise for total disclosure."

The media had played the importance of the agreement to a great extent as being of historic proportions. They explained that this was the beginning of the opening up of the Swiss banks and would lead to the solution of the problem. They were very, very wrong. It was not the Swiss banks that were opening up to provide a solution, it was the thousands of archival boxes at the National Archives.

Within weeks of the agreement, the WJC released a document detailing an August 1944 meeting in Strasbourg, France at a hotel, the Maison Rouge, where high-level Nazis and German industrialists met to discuss the lost cause of the German war effort. In the document, they discuss efforts to smuggle assets and equipment out of Europe in order to reestablish the Nazi order sometime after the war. This, like dozens of articles that would appear later originated on the Reuters wire under the byline of reporter Art Spiegelman to whom the WJC went first with documents.

Nevertheless, the story, was off target. It said nothing about the role of the Swiss banks, and most importantly, Spiegelman cited several historians that said, essentially, this was old news. It was known, and moreover, it was not fully established, that the meeting actually did take place. Yet, the WJC maintained its story, as well as its reasons for releasing the document.

A Call for Help

It was about this time that Mike Kinsella, our Chief of Staff and Administrative Assistant, at the suggestion of Bob Royer, gave British author Tom Bower a call to see what he was doing for the next six to eight months of his life. Bower, an award-winning author of several works on World War II, including "Operation Paperclip," the U.S. operation to bring the Nazi scientists to the United States for use in our missile and rocket program, was ideally suited to research this topic. Kinsella knew Bower from that time and felt that with Bower's connections and research ability he could help the Committee's inquiry as well as himself if he could put it together in a book. Bower agreed to fly to Washington and look at what we found in the Archives.

Bower arrived and I sat down with him to explain what we had found. I showed him the files detailing the vast amounts of gold and other valuables laundered through Switzerland. It did not take long for Bower to get hooked. He realized what we were on to and asked his researcher from New York, Bob Fink, to come to Washington to join the search.

Bower went back to London to begin research there and Fink came out to the Archives to start the search here. Leading us to the files on the Allied-Swiss negotiations, Fink opened up another avenue of research for us. The new areas they uncovered made it clear that we needed more researchers. If it was not abundantly clear after receiving almost daily, foot high stacks of documents from Miriam Kleiman and Willi Korte, it was now. I decided to call Stan Turesky at the Holocaust Memorial Museum to see if he could help us.

After explaining what we had found and how far we had progressed, Turesky seemed outrightly excited to help. We discussed the option of the Museum, as a federal agency, working with the Committee and providing us with interns to work with Kleiman and Korte. Although he himself could not guarantee it, he felt quite confident that Walter Reich would love the idea and would agree to help. After lunch we went back to the Museum and sat down for a meeting with Reich. I gave him the same briefing I gave Turesky and he agreed. The Museum would provide the Committee with college students from the very best schools to help us through the records at the Archives.

By the end of June, the Museum had followed through on its promise. We would have at first, ten and later twelve college interns at our disposal. They came from all over the country and some of the best schools in the U.S., two from Harvard, one from Yale, Columbia, Princeton, American, Georgetown, and other schools. They were smart, enthusiastic and honestly excited about being involved with a project like this. Once they settled in, my foot high stacks of documents doubled. Soon I was awash in paper.

While I had more documents than I knew what to do with, the SBA and the Swiss embassy began to complain that they were in a difficult position to respond to the stories that were to come out. They wanted the documents, or at least some of them. Every time I would talk with Marc Cohen or Tom Delaney from Wilmer, they would complain that we were not sharing our information. If we really wanted to do this inquiry correctly, they complained, we should provide them with copies of the documents in order to get the fullest amount of information possible. Oscar Knapp, formerly of the Swiss embassy, was also beating the same drum. We should share, he said, just for the principle of fairness. I could not help but think, just imagine, these guys are representing and defending Swiss bankers who aided and abetted the Nazis in carrying out the Holocaust by financing the German war effort and they were complaining about a lack of fairness. To hell with them, I thought. If they wanted documents, I told them, the National Archives are free and open to the public. Go and get them for their own use.

To their credit, they did. Within a few weeks, Cohen assembled a team of college interns like we put together. We sat in a glass-encased room, they sat at a group of tables. We were able to take out more boxes of documents at a time than they were. And we had our own set of copy machines reserved for us and they did not. These things irked Cohen. He wanted and felt that his interns deserved the same treatment as ours. He complained heartily but the Archives staff put aside his complaints, saying that as a matter of practice, federal government research teams generally were given these perks.

Despite their having to live through the "indignities" of these "discriminatory practices," we did not feel to bad for them. First, we could not care less if they saw documents or not, but the fact that Wilmer, according to information gained by Willi Korte, was billing these interns out to the SBA at $75 per hour, and paying them $10, made us feel even less bothered by it all.

Complaints aside, Cohen's team really was at a disadvantage. They had fewer people. Half the time they were not there for a full week, sometimes the team was absent for an entire week. Moreover, they changed researchers often, depriving themselves of any institutional knowledge, albeit short, for what they were researching. Their biggest disadvantage, though was Cohen plan of research. Cohen's stated goal, made in an interview, according to Korte, was to find the good things Switzerland did during the war. While we were admittedly looking for the bad things and it was not that hard to find bad things about the Swiss banks, Cohen's research task was immensely more difficult, and if I must say, wrong. If he wanted to find the good that Switzerland did, all the power to him. In the course of our research we found few good things about the Swiss during the war. But if he was, as he explained, trying to set up a proper defense for his client, his few "good" documents could not possible compare with our thousands of "bad" ones.

By June, we were beginning to really put the picture together. We understood the greater part of the story. Documents were plenty, we had by far enough researchers, yet we continued to deal with the WJC in a race to disclose documents. They were clearly benefitting from our improved resources because it got copies of everything that was found. As the document flow increased, so did Art Spiegelman's stories. The WJC was shooting in all directions. One day there was a story about Portugal's role, the next day it was the International Red Cross. What made it more difficult was the fact that every time they released a document, we received press calls for comment. While I had the documents the press inquired about, I wanted, as we agreed to do, impose some sort of order to it all, not just to take in the documents and then send them right back out attached to press releases. As the joke goes, this was no way to run a war.

I complained often and loudly to the WJC. First of all, stay on message. Second, please tell me when you are going to send something out. They said they would. This would last for while, then I would get another surprise press call.

At the same time, both Miriam Kleiman and Willi Korte were encountering demands from the WJC for more documents. Korte kept telling them that there was more to this inquiry than churning out document after document. What they did not understand, or want to hear, was that each document led us to another one, and another one. Korte correctly treated his end of the investigation like a jigsaw puzzle. The only thing being that we had no idea of the proportion of the picture. Korte genuinely wanted to get the Swiss banks after they had gotten away with this crime for so long. Because of this, he refused to send the WJC all the documents until he could put them all together. He wanted to complete the picture and do it right for the sake of not only us, but for that of the WJC. Korte, knew the WJC very well from his work with them on the Waldheim case. He knew how they thought, and how they operated. For Korte, they acted the same then as they were acting now. The only difference was that this investigation was not about Kurt Waldheim, one man in one German Army unit. This was the entire Swiss banking industry, and increasingly, the Swiss nation itself that was coming under increasingly hostile fire. Korte believed that there had to be a plan, a method of research or there would be chaos.

For the WJC, the matter was simple. No documents, no check. Korte, while not wholly dependent upon the WJC for a living continued helping us. Just as they pressed Korte, they pressed Kleiman. Just as committed, Kleiman did what was requested of her, but was justifiably concerned with job stability and only requested to know just how long the job would last. To this question, Doug Bloomfield could not provide a committment.

Singer and Steinberg traveled to Washington at the end of July to meet with me. Again, I tried to impress upon Singer the need for conformity and working together. He assured us that the across-the-board release of documents would end. Singer also informed me that he was in Washington to ask Paul Volcker, the former Chairman of the Board of Governors from 1979–87, to head the WJC-SBA commission. Volcker agreed.

While Singer and Steinberg were in my office, they also had an opportunity to meet in person with Korte who tried, in vain, to explain how the investigation should proceed. They were unable to work out the problem. Yet, the WJC had their problems with Korte for a time before this, when Korte agreed to travel to Switzerland with Greta Beer, invited there at the courtesy of Hans Baer. We were greatly concerned that the Swiss bankers, who were beginning to feel the heat over this affair, would use Beer to create a press extravaganza. Frail and emotional, we felt they might try to provide her with some token settlement to buy her off and score some badly needed public relations points. We needed an attorney and someone who was knowledgeable about the history of the times. It took us a while, but Korte and I found the perfect candidate, Korte himself. He was able to arrange travel and went to Switzerland with her.

She met with Baer, held a press conference, visited the Swiss banking Ombudsman, and a few banks and found nothing. Korte made a few important contacts and they both came home after a week. Beer received a great deal of European press attention, but contrary to our fears, not even the hint of a settlement.

Before they left, staff from the WJC, having been alerted to Korte's role in accompanying Beer to Switzerland, called to ask me how Korte had managed to get there. I told him that he found a way to get there and I knew nothing more. He could not believe it. He said, "we didn't pay for him to go. You didn't pay for him to go. How did he get there. The only thing I can think is that the Swiss paid for him." Shocked by what he said, I could only reassure him this was not the case.

Opening a Third Front

Greville Janner had long been active in Jewish affairs. In Britain, he was active in Soviet Jewry, and fundraising for Israel. He has also been the Chairman of the Holocaust Education Trust in London. As a Labor member of Parliament, he had a podium from which press his agenda. As a Vice President of the World Jewish Congress in Britain, Janner was uniquely positioned to open up yet another front from which to attack the Swiss banks.

In June, Janner wrote then British Foreign Secretary Malcolm Rifkind and Defense Secretary Michael Portillo asking them to do a search for intelligence documents relating to the Swiss banks. Armed with documents from the WJC, Janner began the campaign in Britain. He had information that led him to believe that the British knew more than they admitted. At the end of July, Rifkind ordered a search through the Foreign Office, Treasury, and Defence Ministry archives, which were still closed due to the Official Secrets Act.[8]

Meanwhile, we had finally received our answer from the Swiss archives to a letter the Senator sent to the Interior Minister of Switzerland, Ruth Dreifus. While we had sent a great many letters to the SBA and Marc Cohen at Wilmer, until this time, we refrained from sending letters to the Swiss government. Our letters to Cohen had been largely based on documents about particular banks and were designed to keep them on their toes. A standard practice on Capitol Hill, and perhaps at not a few law firms was to, as it is called, "paper them with requests." We papered Cohen and others to let them know we were still digging. But the letter to Dreifus was more serious. Dreifus was the only Jewish member of the Swiss Federal Council and we figured she might well be particularly sensitive to this issue. As one of seven members, largely of an oligarchy, she had immense power, not the least of which was vested in the Interior Ministry, which in Switzerland, among other departments, controlled the Archives, obviously of immense interest to us. The Senator's letter to Dreifus was a request for both a list of the roughly 1,000 successful claims from the 1962 search through the Swiss banks, and the roughly 7,000 unsuccessful claims from the time. We wanted to have this to see who filed claims and failed back then, so that if we could not search for them, someone else could. Andreas Kellerhalz, the Deputy Director of the Swiss Federal Archives answered on Minister Dreifus's behalf promising a microfilming of the index cards for the files. Several months later, four rolls of microfilm arrived, courtesy of Mr. Kellerhalz. Thanks to the American Jewish Genealogy Society, and its former President Sally Ann Sack and Mike Radel, these lists will soon be available on the Internet.

By the end of August, things had simmered down a bit and we were reviewing what we found. The WJC was still leaking documents like a sieve, and they were still pressing Kleiman and Korte for more. Korte, who had essentially been working without pay for three months finally sent two large boxes of documents to Steinberg and included a detailed report on what had been found in the Archives up until that time.

In September, the world was told that the Union Bank of Switzerland might hold accounts opened for Adolf Hitler into which he put his royalties from *Mein Kampf*. Reported in the *London Jewish Chronicle*, the document was given to Janner by the WJC so that it could be published in London. The story received wide coverage in the European and American press. It was one thing for a reporter to get a document from either the WJC or from us that gave information on Swiss bank accounts for Hermann Göring, but to have found one for Hitler was an entirely different story. It was so fantastic that it led the reporting on Swiss television on September 6. The drip, drip, drip approach of documents was beginning to take its toll on the Swiss, but things would get worse, and soon.

Three days later, the Foreign Office released its report, "Nazi Gold: Information from the British Archives," instigated by letters to the government from Janner and commissioned by the Foreign Secretary. The report consisting of sixteen pages was a well-written, well-documented narrative of the problem. Yet, the entirety of the report was summed up in the first paragraph of the forward, written by Ian Soutar, of the Library and Records Department.

> During the Second World War Nazi Germany acquired over $550 m of gold by seizing the national reserves of Occupied countries and the assets of organisations and individuals. The Jewish community was a particular target. Much of the gold looted by Germany-whether gold bullion, coins or jewellery-was melted down and resmelted into ingots marked with the Reichsbank stamp, concealing its origins [sic].[9]

To make matters worse, Soutar, stated that Britain and the Allies knew that this gold was going to Switzerland and other countries and did nothing about it. Now Switzerland was reeling. For the first time in this campaign against Switzerland and its banks, an officially sanctioned governmental study called them collaborators with the Nazis. Moreover, the amount of money allegedly accepted by the Swiss banks, according to the report, $550,000,000, was a higher figure than we had seen. As it later turned out, the historians writing this report made a miscalculation in the exchange rate, but the damage had already been done.

Three days later, the WJC released a report from the American embassy in Paris from 1946 that stated that American troops had found a massive horde of treasure and gold in a salt mine in southern Germany, called the Merkers Mine. Towards the end of the war, the Nazis realizing they were going to lose, buried vast amounts of loot in the salt mines in the south of Germany, for retrieval at a later date. Unfortunately for them, the Allies got to the mines first. In the log of what they found, the embassy reported that there were 8,307 gold bars, the origin of which no one could ascertain. Immediately, the WJC seized upon this document as being of monumental importance.

They decided to make a leap in logic. Owing to the fact that the gold was viewed by Allied investigators as being of questionable origin, it might as well have come from the victims of the concentration camps. After fifty years, certainly no one could disprove this theory and quite honestly, who would try. This gold, once catalogued and repacked, was sent to the newly created Tripartite Commission for the Restitution of Monetary gold (TGC), created in the 1946 Paris Agreement. The TGC was created to adjudicate the claims from the central banks of the occupied countries of Europe whose entire gold reserves were stolen by the Nazis. After the war, the gold was split up and sent for safekeeping, first to the Allied-run Reichsbank in Frankfurt, and then, in parts, to the Bank of England, the Bank of France, and most importantly for the case the WJC was assembling, the Federal Reserve Bank in New York.

According to their line of reasoning, the gold that was sent there could well have been tainted with gold from the concentration camps. To add another factor to the mix, the TGC gold pot, as it was called, over the years had paid out millions of dollars in claims to the formerly occupied countries of Europe. Now, fifty years after the creation of the TGC, there was only $68,000,000 in gold left. This amount has come to be called the "residual gold." The beauty of this line of argument is that by alleging the gold pot was tainted, coupled with the fact that it could be neither proven nor disproven in fact or as to which bars were tainted, the sanctity of the entire gold pot was called into question. Certainly then, the residual gold could have been tainted. It was, therefore, this gold the WJC was after and they wasted no time in calling for the freezing of any further distribution of the gold until its origin could be determined.

As per Rabin's, later Peres's, and then Benjamin Netanyahu's letters to Bronfman attesting to the fact that the WJRO represented Israel and the Jewish people in these ongoing negotiations and exchanges with the Swiss, the WJC would lay claim to the $68,000,000 worth of gold and the right to distribute it.

While we felt they were again going off on a tangent by alleging that tainted gold was in the vaults of the Federal Reserve Bank in New York, their motives did not become immediately clear until some time later.

While the WJC had played a prime role in the drama thus far, now it was D'Amato's turn. His actions and their incredibly debilitating psychological and cultural effects on Switzerland, and the Swiss response to his accusations will take decades to heal. With D'Amato on the attack, for the Swiss, their troubles were only beginning.

Notes

1. Letter from Liba Weingarten to Senator Jacob Javits, 16 December 1969, United States Department of State.
2. Javits was defeated in 1980 in the Republican primary for reelection to the Senate by the Hempstead, New York Town Supervisor by the name of Alfonse M. D'Amato who would go on to be elected Senator that year.
3. Cable from the American Ambassador M. Larry Lawrence in Bern to the Secretary of State, 5 July 1995, United States Department of State.
4. Letter from Ralph Grunewald, Director of External Affairs, United States Holocaust Memorial Museum to Ambassador M. Larry Lawrence, 22 June 1995; Cable from Ambassador M. Larry Lawrence to the Secretary of State, 7 July 1995, U.S. Department of State.
5. Cable from the United States Embassy in Brussels to the Secretary of State, 14 August 1995, U.S. Department of State.
6. Press Release of the Swiss Bankers Association, 12 September 1995.
7. Letter from Maram Stern to the SBA, Brussels, 6 February 1996.
8. Letter from Foreign Secretary Malcolm Rifkind to Greville Janner, QC MP, London, 5 September 1996.
9. Foreign Office Report , "Nazi Gold: Information from the British Archives," 9 September 1996.

3

Exposed

"We live on this myth of neutrality," responded Fritz Gysin, a professor of American literature at Bern University to *New York Times* reporter Alan Cowell's questions.[1] During the course of the next four months this myth, long held in Swiss society, would be shattered. Through an intense, daily release of damaging documents, the Swiss people themselves would come to understand that this campaign, begun by the WJC, was now shifting in intensity and responsibility to a much tougher foe. Up until September, the affair was viewed simply as an irritant. WJC press releases bothered some in Switzerland, but the banks could muddle through. In a manner that only a Brooklyn-born politician could, Alfonse D'Amato, however, would teach the country and its prestigious banks, a lesson they would not soon forget. Through another much publicized Congressional hearing coupled with a series of devastating disclosures directed towards the Swiss banks, and even the Swiss government, Switzerland would fall into its worst foreign policy crisis since WWII. For D'Amato, his name would become a household word in Switzerland and himself a hated man there. In the U.S., even those who did not like him, however grudgingly, had to admit he had done something very good.

Freezing the Gold

In a conference in Jerusalem, at the beginning of August, Stuart Eizenstat confessed that there might have been looted gold turned over to the United States by the Swiss, after the war. At the time, we thought that Eizenstat might have hurt the effort, by diverting the attention we were trying to keep on the Swiss, and on to the United States. If the United States could be drawn into a defense for its past historical mistakes, then the Swiss could point the finger at us. Yet, at the time we had no idea that the WJC was "going for the gold," as it was, and

Eizenstat, bent on collecting the truth was, albeit unknowingly, aiding their effort.

Eizenstat, the former domestic policy advisor in President Jimmy Carter's White House, was a Harvard-educated attorney who earnestly sought the truth. Long active in Jewish causes, Eizenstat was appointed by President Clinton to be the Department of States Special Envoy for Property Claims in Central and Eastern Europe in early 1995 at the suggestion of Ambassador Richard Holbrooke and the WTC, while still the U.S. Ambassador to the European Union. He would continue to hold this title after moving to the Commerce Department. He traveled widely throughout Western and Eastern Europe urging leniency in these countries to the fulfillment of claims by the dispossessed of property taken from their families by the Nazis and the various Communist regimes over the last fifty years. He knew well the mind-set of the countries there, as well as the difficulty after so many years, of the ability to still obtain just restitution for the claimants.

The WJC, after declaring that Nazi-looted gold could perhaps still be located in the Federal Reserve in New York, initiated its legal claim to it in the name of the World Jewish Restitution Organization, as the representative of the Jewish people. On September 16, Edgar Bronfman and Greville Janner wrote then Secretary of State Warren Christopher, Foreign Secretary Malcolm Rifkind, and French Foreign Minister Herve de Charette, stating that in regard to the gold from the Tripartite Commission Gold Pot, the WJRO "is available to receive the residue as may be decided on behalf of the Jewish people."[2]

For our part, we needed to know what happened to the gold. The Federal Reserve fell under the jurisdiction of the Banking Committee, so it was D'Amato's prerogative to find the truth about the gold's origin.

D'Amato initiated a series of letters to the Federal Reserve Bank in New York, as well as to the Tripartite Gold Commission (TGC) in Brussels, to discover the actual content of the gold in New York. The TGC refused to answer our questions for reasons of confidentiality. Without the consent of our partners in the TGC, the British and French, information on each of the shipments to and from the TGC and the Federal Reserve that we sought, could not be released.[3] The Federal Reserve maintained the same general policy but would confirm the existence of 162 bars of TGC gold in its stocks, worth $24.9 million.[4]

On May 7, 1997, the Federal Reserve simultaneously released documentation to the National Archives, but also to us, though thankfully in annotated form, that for the first time confirmed that looted gold, in "chips, sheets, and button," making up four bars, was of that date, still in the bank. The gold had been sent to New York in February 1952, and was resmelted from 17 boxes of assorted gold and then stored in the bank's vaults.[5]

On February 3, 1997, the Allies agreed to freeze this gold, along with that in London, but this was done only after the TGC commissioners tried in the previous December to order a final disbursement of the $68 million in residual gold and vote itself out of existence. Eizenstat put a stop to this. He had been very concerned over the content of the gold. He feared that the gold in New York was in fact "tainted" with victims' gold. Moreover, he was afraid to test the gold for fear of it either being tainted, or that it was not. Either way, he preferred to not know, saying, as they taught him at Law School, "never ask a question you can't answer."[6]

Coming to Terms

With the release of the British report, stories increased appearing like scattershot, telling the story of the stolen Belgian gold and the circuitous route it made through Africa and back to Europe; analyses of how the Swiss were able to keep the gold for fifty years; and even how Nazi gold made its way into the Bank of England.

As if things were not bad enough for the Swiss, four days after the terribly damaging British report, the Swiss National Bank issued a statement that "in its transactions with the German Reichsbank, the SNB board manifested considerable credulousness."[7] Only days after being labeled as collaborationists by the British government report, the SNB confession of naiveté was something akin to pouring salt on an open wound.

There was more salt to pour with anther revelation by the SNB detailing an argument, in 1946, between two bank officers, General Director Alfred Hirs and Vice President Paul Rossy. In a secret memo, Hirs, with whom the Allies negotiated in 1946, accused Rossy of knowingly accepting gold from the Germans that was looted.

"They are paying the price now for not coming to terms in the years after 1945 with World War Two," wrote Swiss historian Gian Trepp.[8] The Swiss had no idea what was happening to them. Every day their newspapers were filled with stories from overseas relating to another wartime scandal for the banks or Switzerland itself. The government was confused, unable to respond. All they could do was to sit back and absorb the attacks. About all that they could muster was an anemic statement by Foreign Minister Flavio Cotti that "we take these heavy attacks from abroad very seriously."[9]

Cotti, in an interview with the *London Jewish Chronicle*, complained of the situation in which his nation was being placed. "Switzerland," he said, "is accused by the public of having received the stolen property of the Nazi Reich. We are asked to prove our innocence or to admit our moral guilt, which to some is already established in any event. There is no doubt that these accusations have seriously damaged Switzerland's reputation."[10]

By September 16, the Swiss took one of their first concrete actions to stem the tide of bad press. The government formally announced that it would support legislation in the Parliament to establish a commission of historians to examine Switzerland's wartime conduct. Positive as it was, Swiss actions were always half-steps. Flavio Cotti, while announcing support for the bill, nevertheless qualified his government's statement by saying that it was important to examine the issue, but his government had already done so thoroughly in 1946. Simply put, whatever information was found, the issue remained settled and a renegotiation of the 1946 treaty was out of the question.

Reopen the Negotiations

Within a week, Cotti's refusal would come back to haunt him. D'Amato, who had held back while the WJC laid claim to the gold in the Federal Reserve in New York, decided to counter Cotti's claim.

The weight of the evidence since we began searching in March came to be overwhelming. Clearly, while circumstantial, it was obvious that the Swiss were at the least, guilty of massive diversions of funds, both Jewish and Nazi. From the documents we had seen by this time, we were convinced that, at the least, Switzerland had failed to live up to its obligations under the 1946 Washington Accord. Document after document laid out a story of greed and deceit, gold bar after gold bar. They had accepted so much gold and returned so little. The numbers just did not add up.

On September 24, D'Amato sent his second letter to Secretary of State Warren Christopher on the subject, the first letter being one of a general indictment of the Swiss as crooks and informing him of the results from our investigation thus far. Now, according to D'Amato, the Swiss were being dishonest with us and worse yet, we allowed ourselves to be shortchanged in 1946. The U.S. had to get to the truth and the Swiss had to "make amends" for their sins. After fifty years of stonewalling the truth, D'Amato asked Christopher to seek a renegotiation of the treaty. We knew this would not be an easy request to fulfill, much less a politically viable one owing to the Clinton-D'Amato relationship at the time. Nevertheless, owing to the kinds of documents we were finding, the request was the least we could do. Renegotiation, or at least getting the administration moving on this subject was absolutely necessary in order to move ahead on the issue. Besides, the WJC was busy chasing the gold in the Federal Reserve, calling for a renegotiation would clearly put the game back on track and swing the story back to us.

As we suspected, the Swiss were not amused. Defiant, the next day, Jean-Philippe Tissieres, a spokesman for the Foreign Ministry declared the 1946 treaty to be nonnegotiable. For the Swiss, the treaty was signed, ratified, and legal, moreover it was finished fifty years ago. "We have nothing more to say about it," snapped Tissieres.[11]

As for the State Department, the request placed them in a difficult position. Our relationship with Switzerland was not as important to us as that of the other European countries, yet no one in the building wanted the U.S. to be seen as bullying little Switzerland. On the other hand, it was clear that the revelations coming from us, the WJC, and Europe showed that there was a real problem developing and the Swiss were not helping themselves any with their lack of honesty or their less than sparkling public relations campaign.

Two days after D'Amato's request to Christopher, citing a snowballing press campaign, including requests from *60 Minutes* to interview Ambassador Eizenstat and the new U.S. Ambassador to Switzerland Madeleine Kunin, E. Anthony Wayne, Acting Assistant Secretary of State for European and Canadian Affairs sent an action memo to Deputy Secretary of State Strobe Talbott offering him options to handle the growing problem. Owing to the avalanche of documents, press stories, and letters from D'Amato to the various agencies throughout the preceding months, the general feeling in the halls of the State Department was that the administration had to do something. In the preceding months, there were a series of meetings within the administration, between members of Eizenstat's staff at the Commerce Department, Treasury, and State, from the European Bureau, as well as from the Holocaust Museum, all trying to get a handle on this burgeoning story.

Wayne suggested to Talbott that the NSC conduct an interagency review of the U.S. role in disbursing Nazi gold and other assets after the war, as well as tasking the State Department Historian to conduct a study of the documents to determine just what happened.

Wayne told Talbott of our meetings with Ruth van Heuven, Director of the Bureau of Austrian, German, and Swiss Affairs of the European Desk at State, as well as the Department's search for documents. The Holocaust Museum, too, was looking for documents and had specifically been tasked to do so in their funding bill (a provision we requested and obtained from the Interior Appropriations subcommittee). Wayne, as any good aide would, laid out the entire story for Talbott, with all the options and all the pitfalls. He concluded his memo by stating, "As we urge the Swiss to conduct a review of their role in handling Nazi assets, it is imperative that we too engage in a thorough and transparent review of our role in retrieving and disbursing Nazi gold and other assets."[12] Within a very short time, the State Department proposal was approved.

In Bern, the new U.S. Ambassador to Switzerland, Madeleine Kunin, who herself emigrated to the United States from Switzerland with her family in 1940 fleeing the Germans, very publicly pressed the Swiss to thoroughly examine their history and uncover all dormant accounts. In a Swiss newspaper interview, she refused publicly to endorse D'Amato's request to reopen the 1946 treaty, but within a few days she would play a role in influencing the administration's evolving position on the question.

The same day Kunin's interview appeared, Glyn Davies, a spokesman for the State Department held the daily briefing for the press. When asked to respond to D'Amato's letter, he indicated that the administration would not seek a renegotiation of the treaty with the Swiss. Saying that State was confident that the Swiss would conduct an adequate search, Davies complimented the Swiss for the actions taken by the Swiss government and the banks' decision to form committees to handle claims and that the U.S. would "look to that process to play out."

We were surprised to hear a response so quickly from the administration, yet not surprised to hear a negative one. After all, we thought, the administration was just paying us back for Whitewater and the State Department was just being the same old State Department, stubborn and bureaucratic. We expected to be turned down so we were not disappointed. When I spoke with Stan Turesky about the rejection, he was more reassuring. "Don't be so sure," he said, "there's more going on here than you think." What Turesky meant was that in the meetings that were held over the summer, there were very serious discussions about history and heritage, the heritage of the people involved. For a great number of people in the administration, the fact that they were Jewish had some input. As Turesky asked, would they really be able to live with a rejection of D'Amato's entreaties toward the administration? Would they, in their heart, turn their backs on their heritage for the sake of political expediency. Turesky knew the answer. Soon, we would too.

On October 1, I picked up a fax sent to us directly from the U.S. Embassy in Bern. Contrary to Davies' rebuff of four days earlier, the Embassy statement began with the word "correction" in bold type. "The U.S. has not taken a position on reopening discussions concerning the 1946 Washington Agreement," read the release. In Davies' briefing, the release read, he "did not address this issue in either a formal briefing or a background briefing." The U.S., "is reviewing the whole issue of Nazi plundered gold in Switzerland and Swiss dormant financial accounts of Holocaust victims."[13]

We were surprised and excited that the correction came from the Embassy in Bern and not directly from the State Department in Washington. It meant that Kunin had actually reversed the situation. It was Kunin who through Eizenstat sought and obtained a change. On the same day, in the Swiss Parliament, Foreign Minister Cotti had proudly declared that D'Amato's request had been declined, no doubt feeling very happy that Switzerland's growing nemesis had not succeeded in his quest to embarrass Switzerland. Kunin's intervention now made this possible.

Recriminations

"Certain circles," editorialized the Swiss business paper *Finanz und Wirtschaft*, "are using the tragic fate of Holocaust victims to discredit the extant advantage Switzerland as a financial centre and its banks have in global competition."[14] Individual Swiss citizens also took offense at D'Amato's seeming interference. "Sir, nobody likes the clever tactics of a foreign Senator attacking authorities for their behaviour [sic] fifty years ago," Sepp Haener of Laufen, Switzerland wrote D'Amato.[15] Marc Suter, a deputy from the Swiss Radical Democratic Party charged "one reason this storm of indignation is roaring through the Anglo-Saxon newspapers may be to weaken Switzerland as a financial centre, to undermine Swiss banking secrecy or to deflect attention from their own shortcomings [sic]."[16]

Switzerland was in an uproar. Two governments, first the British and now the American, had come out against them. They felt besieged. Many were outraged that D'Amato would even suggest that the Swiss could have possibly violated an international treaty, and that now, fifty years after the fact he was calling for its reopening.

How could D'Amato do this? It could only be that the "certain circles," the *Finanz und Wirtschaft* mentioned, doubtlessly code for influential Jews, were pressing American and British politicians and their own governments for action against the Swiss or D'Amato was simply doing this for Jewish votes. "I served," wrote Eugen Fink of Basel, "as a Private in the Swiss Army where Jews, as far as I could make out, were conspicuously absent." Fink continued, "Rocking the boat unilaterally is unlikely to secure for you jewish [sic] votes in New York as long as this exercise is carried out with no regard to accepted standards of decency and accuracy."[17]

After nearly six months of steadily worsening press, the Swiss bankers began to worry. Their carefully pruned and molded image was coming apart before their eyes. "This is a story touching the reputation of the whole financial sector. Perhaps the private banks are less touched than the larger banks," said Matthieu Bauer, a private banker in Geneva, in an interview with the *Christian Science Monitor*, "but the whole industry is concerned now because its a question of image."[18]

It was precisely that image that the Swiss bankers as well as the Swiss government itself reacted too late to protect. Had they been more forthcoming earlier on they could have forestalled what was happening to them now and what would happen later. Yet, the Swiss system was not built for speed. Precisely the opposite was to occur. As a confederation, Switzerland is supposed to move slowly and precisely, like the Swiss watches the country is known for. If the federal government moved precipitously, direct democracy would be threatened and the national consensus would be shattered. Jan Marejko, a professor at the Institut Florimont and a municipal councillor for the City of Geneva provided a speculative example to understand the paralyzed state of Swiss politics:

> To move in one direction or another, they wait until some expert tells them what to do or count votes to know whether or not they can proceed. If Pearl Harbour [sic] had happened to Switzerland, there would have been a committee made up of experts in international law, then a vote on war or peace, and then a six-month delay on a possible referendum against this vote. Something like two years would have elapsed between the event and the reaction to it.[19]

The voice of each of the twenty-six cantons had to be heard, but moreover, the important thoughts and views of each Association, especially the Bankers Association, must be taken into account. For their part, the Bankers Association felt contrite. George Kreyer, in an interview in Switzerland, admitted that the SBA could have started the search sooner. Moreover, he offered the view that Swiss banks acted with "not enough understanding in too many cases" in dealing with Holocaust survivors claiming funds after the war. Even Hans Baer, testifying before the Banking Committee almost six months before commented "this could have been handled earlier with greater charm and delicacy."[20]

Brian Brown of the *Wall Street Journal European* wrote in the beginning there was no one in charge. "No one seemed able to answer simple questions."[21] This was plain to see. At any given time, we could find no one to answer our questions. First, I would call Marc Cohen at Wilmer, Cutler & Pickering. Usually unable to speak for the government, Cohen would put me off and tell me he would get back to me and I should continue to wait.

Even the Swiss Embassy in Washington was unable to help, either us, or their own government. Former Swiss Ambassador Carlo Jagmetti confided in me before a television interview with the CBC, in November, that the Embassy was left out in the cold. "They don't even listen to us," he quipped. Pietro Gerosa, of Swiss television, told me how he had been the first to interview Jagmetti, in May, when Jagmetti told him that he and the Embassy had been frozen out even by that time. The government in Bern would not listen to him and went about the "fight" their own way.

Accounts in New York

While evidence against Swiss banks in Switzerland mounted, we realized that there were Swiss banks in places other than Switzerland and that there could be a great amount of information available there. From the Swiss banks in New York came records originally obtained by Henry Morgenthau's Treasury investigators and now in the National Archives. In 1941, the Swiss Bank Corporation in New York was one of the banks to receive a visit from Morgenthau's investigators. When the records were found, there were hundreds of deposits found with their origin in the bank's branches overseas.

We decided to take this list and see how many of the 1,500 or so names appeared to be Jewish. While it appeared ironic to us that we were using the same methods the Swiss bankers used in 1962 to identify Jewish names on their accounts, we had little choice. Having identified 298 seemingly Jewish names, the Senator wrote a letter to the President of the Swiss Bank Corporation, however, not in Switzerland, but in New York. We figured that we might as well "paper" the New York banks a bit to let them know they would come under scrutiny right along with their parent company in Switzerland. It would be good for them to receive a little flak so that they could tell headquarters back in Switzerland that they too were targets in the expanding search.

In a letter to Simon Canning, President and CEO of the bank in New York, D'Amato wrote asking whether these accounts, whose owners appeared to be Jewish, were opened overseas and then moved to New York. We wanted to know, if after their freezing and "defrosting" as it was termed after the war, did the accounts escheat to the bank in either New York or Switzerland. We also asked, if after the war, the owners died in the Holocaust what happened to the accounts and what efforts were made to locate the heirs. I realized that these were questions about events that occurred fifty years ago and were difficult to answer, much less the responsibility of Simon Canning. Yet, not only did these questions need to be answered, Canning had to understand that we were serious. If we were to have any leverage against the Swiss banks in general, it would be against their branches in the United States which, we were told, amounted to at least 25 percent of their overall business. This was not an insignificant factor in our thinking and we hoped it would not be for them either.

"The accounts you have singled out," wrote Canning, in his August 20 response, are worth "only about $500,000 (approximately 25%) of the accounts you identified belonged to residents of Germany or countries occupied by the Nazis...moreover, such deposits constituted less than 4% of the agency's total frozen demand and time deposits due to foreign individuals." Canning concluded by stating

pursuant to U.S. law, the frozen funds you have identified would have been either returned to the account holders (or their rightful heirs) or, in the case of funds that were classified as 'enemy' assets, turned over to the U.S. government. It is possible that some accounts of less than $5,000 and a small number of the non-Swiss, non-enemy accounts may not have been claimed and were not required to have been turned over to the U.S. government.[22]

While Canning was unsure of the exact disposition of the accounts, New York State was also unable to determine their fate. *New York Jewish Week* reporter Stuart Ain, who went on to write a series of probing articles on the subject that were later picked up by the national press, told me that he was unable to follow the accounts beyond the Swiss

Bank Corporation. Ain wrote of our findings on October 11 and continued to follow up on the subject.

Meanwhile, the WJC released the full document from which the Jewish names were pulled, but released the list to the European press four days after the *Jewish Week* article was published. "We have the specific names and records," Elan Steinberg was quoted by the *Agence France-Presse,* "we have hundreds and hundreds of names. Of those we estimate several hundred represent the Jews and those who died in the Holocaust."[23] This was easy enough to do for Steinberg, yet we were aiming at a different audience with this effort. Edgar Bronfman would later use this list in discussions with the Swiss to drive home the point that there were more accounts than they were claiming.

The list was also deftly used by the Simon Wiesenthal Center in Los Angeles, which was given the list by Miriam Kleiman. Kleiman had since gone to work for the law firm Cohen, Milstein, Hausfeld & Toll which instituted a class-action lawsuit against the banks and was supported by the Center. Today, the list is an important feature on the Center's homepage on the Internet, with a search feature included.

What the WJC, the Wiesenthal Center, nor I could have known was that the list would end up being more than mere fodder with which to attack the Swiss banks, Stuart Ain would find a claimant from the list which was published in its entirety in the *Jewish Week* in December. Rudolfine Schlinger, through her attorney Edward Fagan, came forward to claim $3,717.75 in an account of her husband William's name that was opened in Versoix, Switzerland by the wealthy furrier before he left Europe in 1939. William Schlinger's name appeared on an attached list of frozen Hungarian accounts held by the bank and frozen in 1941. Once the accounts were defrosted in 1946, Schlinger tried to obtain the funds in the account but was turned down repeatedly. According to Schlinger's wife, William died heartbroken in 1985, never having been able to retrieve his funds from the bank.[24]

Canning, no doubt was disturbed by the revelations that the Swiss Bank Corporation was in fact holding onto accounts, yet his fellow Swiss bankers in New York would get another black eye when we disclosed that Credit Suisse in New York held an account of $5,000 for Benito Mussolini. The document, released more for fun than anything else only worsened the case for the banks, in that once again they were shown to be bankers for the dregs of humanity. I released the document to Gabe Kahn of the *Jewish Forward* on a lark. He asked me if I had anything new, and looking at what was now drawers and drawers of documents, I responded "sure, how would you like Mussolini's bank account in New York." Kahn dutifully printed it. The WJC, after its staff read the article when it appeared in the October 4 edition of the *Forward*, released it again to Art Spiegleman of Reuters who reported it on October 10.

Spiegleman's article was overlooked that day because of the announcement of the Senate Banking Committee that it would hold a field hearing in New York into the Swiss banks' behavior, with special attention to the heirs. By the time this hearing was over, the Swiss bankers, and the Swiss government itself would have wished that it would not have taken place.

"They wanted Jewish money"

In July, we began planning for another hearing. Owing to scheduling difficulties and the coming August Congressional recess, we put off these plans until the fall. By September, we had sent B.J. Moravek and Holidae Hayes, from the Banking Committee, to our New York City office to conduct interviews with potential claimants for the upcoming hearings. They interviewed dozens of claimants in order to get a few credible and solid ones for the hearing.

Moravek had been searching for claimants with solid stories all through the summer and had real success in doing so. Early on, after joining Kleiman and Korte at the archives, they had found a file on a young girl, Elizabeth Trilling, whose mother Rosa and father Roman Trilling, were killed in Poland by the Germans. Roman's brother Max, wrote to the State Department on behalf of his niece Elizabeth, then only twelve, claiming funds in a Swiss bank. The State Department, then swamped with letters seeking help from claimants to lost property and funds, directed them to the Swiss Compensation Office, set up after the war to adjudicate claims to property in Switzerland. History has proven this office to have largely been a black hole for most refugee requests, and Trilling's case was no different.

The file was one of many that we found but it seemed promising because of its unfulfilled status and its poignancy. Trilling had been rescued from the Warsaw ghetto and hidden during the war by her Polish Catholic nanny, Jania Zlow, at her residence in Lublin until 1945. After the war, Zlow took Trilling with her to Sweden, on to Cuba, and eventually to the United States in 1950.[25]

As soon as we gathered enough files, Moravek, in a way that only a good investigator could, started to work. Very quickly, Moravek found Trilling in El Cerito, California and interviewed her. When asked if her name and number could be given out to the press, she agreed. We felt this was important because we could then put a face onto the nameless claimants for whom we were fighting. This was vital for us and for the overall effort. By now, journalists had become interested in talking with and doing stories on claimants. Finally, we had a real, documented claimant that we had found, not one from the WJC, but a claimant who could tell her story and back it up with documents we found about her. *Newsweek* was the first to do a story on Elizabeth Trilling.[26] More stories would follow. Trilling would go on to be interviewed for a PBS/BBC joint production that aired on the series *Frontline*, the following summer.

After finding Trilling, Moravek, worked tirelessly for the next few weeks searching for others. The hard work paid off. Between the files from the Archives and the personal interviews, we had a half a dozen good, well-documented stories.

While we had a good collection of claimants we needed more. We needed to do more than show victims, we needed a startling revelation, one that would knock the socks off the Swiss and create a firestorm. While this might have been a tall order, we found one.

When the Swiss government signed the treaty of indemnification with Poland in 1949, the Jewish world was incensed that such a hypocritical agreement could come about. Soon, however, like the effort to retrieve Jewish assets from Swiss banks in general, the treaty and all the greed and deception it stood for, was forgotten. During our research, we found evidence of this agreement in American Joint Jewish Distribution Committee documents. We found related information in the National Archives. Notwithstanding what we found, we were missing one crucial part of the story, how and why the deal was really implemented.

A few days before the second hearing, Tom Bower came over from London to conduct more research and interviews for his book. He was looking through my files for more evidence, and we began to talk about how important the Swiss-Polish treaty really was. He had told me by phone some weeks before about the complicated financial relationship created by this treaty, but it really did not sink in. He had the great fortune, having in his possession documents from his researchers in Switzerland who provided him with clear evidence of the agreement.

I told him that I wanted to send a letter from the Senator to Swiss President Jean Pascal Delamuraz posing questions regarding the treaty.

Tom had told me that Swiss citizens had directly benefitted from the treaty, but exactly how this occurred was still a bit muddled to me. I gave him a copy of the draft letter I wanted to send and he worked on it overnight.

Once it was rewritten, I felt that I now understood the agreement they made and I felt that it was outrageous that they could do this. Once I understood what had taken place, it became obvious that this was too good to simply put in a letter to the Swiss President. After all, he would not answer it directly anyway. I decided to put it into the Senator's statement for the hearing in New York. Only the Senator could do this story justice and a field hearing in New York, of all places, was just the place to break it.

We were ready. It was a clear morning on October 16. Tom and I took the shuttle up to New York in the morning and walked to the United States Courthouse on Pearl Street in Manhattan. Our witnesses were there, all six of them, five women and one man, all lived in the New York area, as well as Leon Levy, then President of the Conference of Presidents of Major Jewish Organizations, and Nobel Laureate Elie Wiesel.

Although he had read the statement I wrote for him the weekend before, he still did not completely comprehend how serious was the offense the Swiss had committed and what its impact would be. And there we sat, in the courthouse anteroom, D'Amato, Elie Wiesel, and me. With only ten minutes remaining, he just could not believe that the Swiss would do such a thing. Even weeks later, he told me that it just all made no sense. I told him that Tom had gone over it with me and that it was real, they did sign this kind of deal and if he only read it as I wrote it, it would be fine. He agreed and went before the fifty or so people in the room and the dozen or so cameras and read the statement.

D'Amato explained that the Swiss government, in 1949, signed a treaty with the Communist government of Poland to transfer the assets of Polish Holocaust victims in the Swiss banks to the Swiss National Bank, in an account under the control of the Polish National Bank. From this fund, the Poles then compensated Swiss citizens whose property was confiscated and nationalized by the Communists the year before. Most importantly, D'Amato stated, was that the deal was kept secret for all these years and that there might well have been more deals like the Polish one, with other East European Communist countries. The crowd was stunned. They could not believe that this could have happened, much less how, but it did.

Following his opening statement, Elie Wiesel, who had heard my explanation of this agreement before the hearing, thanked D'Amato for his courageous leadership on the subject and continued by expressing his shock of hearing of this agreement:

> Now we know that they didn't simply want to kill Jews, as horrible as this may sound; they wanted Jewish money. It came down to money. Now we know, and I'm sure that your investigation will uncover even more aspects, more details about that scandal on universal scales…Senator, each day we learn so much about that tragedy. Is there no limit to pain? Is there no limit to outrage?

After Wiesel, we heard poignant, often tearful testimony from Estelle Sapir, seventy, whose father died in Maidanek and who was refused access to her funds from Credit Suisse, even after being told that her father's money was there. We heard from Rose Spitz, seventy-three, who was born in Czechoslovakia, and whose father's lumber mills were taken from him and the family deported first to Auschwitz, and then to Buchenwald where her brothers were executed. Trudy Sommer, eighty-two, born in Munich, Germany, told of her family's dispossession and of her mother's execution by the Nazis and of her own emigration to the U.S. in 1938. Zenta Birkmanis, seventy-three, born in Riga, Latvia, was the only non-Jew to testify, but we chose her because her story was concrete but also because of the very fact that she was not Jewish, so as to show that Jews and non-Jews alike were victims of the Swiss bankers. Birkmanis told of the confiscation of her father's properties in Riga by the Bolsheviks and that she was pursuing the legacy left for her in an unknown bank in Switzerland. Veronica Braun-Katz, sixty-seven, told of her life in Budapest and of only partial success in getting her legacy from banks in France in 1960, yet her inability to retrieve them from Switzerland. Finally, we heard from Lewis Salton, eighty-five, the creator of the Salton hot plate, and a man Moravek had tracked down in New York from a document we found about his attempts to claim his father's funds in 1954.[27] The testimony was gripping. All had come from wealthy backgrounds, all were well-provided for, and all were victimized, first by the Nazis, and then by the Swiss bankers.

Throughout the testimony, Marc Cohen and his associates talked back and forth and moved about, at times quietly mocking the statements of D'Amato and even the witnesses, just as he had done during the first hearing in April. His disregard for the sincerity of the event showed a still present feature of the Swiss overall game plan. Monitor

D'Amato, attend his hearings, but do not treat him seriously. In their minds and their words to match, this was all electioneering.

Others in the crowd were busy taking notes and this included a great number of lawyers for the opposing sides of the law suits that had just been filed in the federal court in New York. Still more, were reporters, who flooded us at the front table at the end of the hearing to clarify D'Amato's opening statement about the Swiss-Polish treaty. Just as D'Amato at first could not understand the complexity of the deal, neither could they. Unfortunately for the Swiss government, the reporters all gathered around us quickly came to understand the importance of D'Amato's disclosure.

It did not take long for the news to hit the wires. By that afternoon, there were multiple stories of this illicit deal. By the next day, newspapers around the world, from New York, to Los Angeles, to London, and most importantly to Zurich, were full of stories explaining this secret and unholy deal to cover the bad debts of a Communist state with the assets of Holocaust victims in Swiss banks. It was as if Switzerland had been hit by an all-out nuclear strike. Simply put there was chaos in the country. What happened next was a series of denials, half-hearted admissions, and then finally, a full disclosure.

The next day, Swiss Foreign Ministry spokesman Jean-Philippe Tissieres denied any secret deals were made. He told Reuters, "we had agreements with all countries after the war. None of those is secret. Our archives are open and none are related to the subject Mr. D'Amato was speaking about yesterday."[28] Tissieres, was simply wrong. While he could not have known, the archives did have information on such a treaty, and we knew that because Tom's researchers told him as much.

Swiss banks too, reacted to the hearing. The Swiss Bankers Association demanded more time to investigate these new charges. A spokesperson for Credit Suisse apologized for any mistreatment Estelle Sapir might have endured, but stubbornly added that "Swiss bank secrecy prevented her from confirming or denying the incident ever took place."[29]

To add insult to injury, D'Amato, granted the Swiss paper *Journal de Geneve*, an interview, probably for the first and only time, and declared that the Swiss were too biased to lead an impartial probe of their own behavior during and after the war. He expressed a lack of confidence in the Swiss banking Ombudsman, searching for accounts in Swiss banks, and even charged that the time period set by the newly formed international commission to probe the entirety of Swiss history at the time, was too long. "Five years is too long," he said, "how many claimants will be alive by then to see the results?"

On October 18, the Swiss story began to crack. After two harried days of searching the archives in Bern, government researchers were forced to tell their superiors in the Foreign Ministry, that in fact Switzerland had signed an agreement with Poland in 1949. The next day, the Foreign Ministry announced the existence of the agreement, but denied that Swiss citizens had benefitted by the deal. On the same day, Kalman Sultanik, a Vice President of the WJC declared the Swiss admission proved that they had "immorally transferred Jewish assets to Poland," and on behalf of the WJC he demanded that the Swiss government pay compensation for having conducted the illicit deal.[30]

To counter the Swiss denials, we released a March 22, 1950, a translation of a transcript of a Swiss Parliamentary session where then-Swiss President Max Petitpierre, under questioning from Swiss Parliamentarian Werner Schmid, acknowledged that such a deal took place and was done so to compensate Swiss citizens. Petitpierre, in a detailed narrative explained that funds from bank accounts and insurance policies of Holocaust victims would be used to pay Swiss citizens for their losses. This only made life worse for the Swiss government. This document, coupled with the original revelation, and complicated by calls for compensation by the WJC, sent Switzerland reeling. News that Poland, too, was looking into their archives for information on the treaty added to Switzerland's woes.

Finally, on October 22, almost a week from the day of the New York hearing, Swiss Foreign Ministry spokesman Hans-Ruedi Bortis, held a press conference in Zurich and admitted "Jewish money was used to compensate Swiss citizens."[31] Bortis continued by stating that researchers were looking for further documentation on any other possible deals with other nations.

The next day, Swiss historian Peter Hug, writing in an article in the Swiss daily, *Neue Zürcher Zeitung*, wrote that the assets of Polish Holocaust victims

> were to be paid into an account in the name of the Polish National Bank at the Swiss National Bank. The Swiss Political Department did not publish the correspondence at the time, but did indicate briefly in a press release that the agreement had been made. However, the Political Department did not make the text available to any attorneys, bank, or others who inquired about it.[32]

That same morning an article based on Hug's research, written by

Mark Shields of *Reuters* in Zurich, appeared detailing exactly how the deal was done. When he saw this interview, D'Amato suggested that I call Hug directly. I called him in Bern to verify the wire stories in which he was quoted. I asked him directly, "did Swiss citizens benefit from these accounts?" He said yes. He complained about "stupidities of D'Amato," imagined mistakes that he said D'Amato had made, which were not the case, but he did confirm the story. Yet, the Swiss he declared, had every right under private international law to do what they did. They transferred the money soon after the treaty was signed. Yet, while only partially fulfilling their promise to pay the Poles the funds of their own Holocaust victims, Hug explained initially that the sum to be paid was 2,000,000 Swiss francs. They paid only 16,347 francs.

Despite Hug's article, the next day Flavio Cotti, with much audacity, held a news conference in Bern denying any misuse of the victim's money, claiming D'Amato's charge was "without foundation." By this time, however, the damage was done. Editorial writers and journalists across the country and around the world were wholly convinced that the Swiss had been caught in a very big lie. Even the editors at the *Times Union*, in Albany, New York, doubted the story. When they ran a story in their October 24th edition on the subject, the headlines read, "Swiss deny misuses of Holocaust money, Foreign minister disputes D'Amato's claim, despite evidence of deals made after World War II."[33]

Despite the denial, at the same time Cotti announced the Swiss government was forming a task force to look into the questions D'Amato raised. In reality, Cotti was doing what Ambassador Jagmetti had suggested to Swiss reporter Pietro Gerosa, was six months overdue, namely to centralize the Swiss response and provide some damage control. For the Swiss though, the damage clearly had already been done.

In the course of less than a week, the Swiss had first denied any deal was made. Then they admitted there might have been a deal, but it was certainly not done secretly. Then they admitted that the deal did occur, but that Swiss citizens did not benefit from the assets. Finally, after admitting that their own citizens did benefit from the treaty, their Foreign Minister turned the story around completely and denied it. The absurdity and total confusion of it all was clear. They were like a top, spinning out of control. This was quite clear by the remarks of an unidentified Swiss diplomat from Jagmetti's embassy staff, quoted in the *Washington Times*, who admitted, "we're having a terrible week."[34]

David Vogelsanger, the former Political Affairs Officer at the Swiss Embassy in Washington, would later be unable to hide his disgust over his government's embarrassing reaction to D'Amato's revelations. "A total screw-up," cried Vogelsanger, almost angrily, "their reaction should have been 'no comment.'" Even Linus von Castelmur, a Swiss historian who has written on the period and would soon be appointed to the Swiss Historical Commission investigating Swiss wartime behavior, admitted that the agreement did occur and that he would follow up my meeting with him, with more information on the subject, including a list of the names of those whose accounts were returned to Poland, and even those from a similar deal with Hungary.[35]

On the same day the Swiss came clean and admitted the full story, D'Amato wrote a letter to Swiss President Jean-Pascal Delamuraz, concerning the "series of astonishing and inexplicable developments" since he disclosed the secret agreement. "What I find particularly galling," wrote D'Amato, "is that these agreements are being referred to as 'secret.' It strains credibility to expect anyone to believe that the Swiss Government did not have knowledge of such agreements since the end of World War II." D'Amato continued,

The head in the sand attitude of the Swiss Government raises serious questions about the intentions and credibility of officials charged with responsibility for rectifying the injustices of the past perpetrated against innocent Jews who died in the Holocaust and their survivors. These most recent revelations illustrate that the problem in Switzerland is far more serious than anyone could have imagined. These documents make clear why the Swiss banks and their Government would not cooperate with previous efforts to identify and return assets. The reason is very simple. The Swiss Government was actually part of a conspiracy with the Communist Government of Poland to confiscate these assets and use them to compensate Swiss citizens. This dishonesty and deception by any Government would be offensive against the background of one of the saddest chapters in human history. It is especially disturbing given Switzerland's reputation for neutrality and compassion.[36]

Hug, while confirming the story to Sheilds as well as me, and duly reported by D'Amato, was in the middle and not pleased by his situation. He had confirmed what the Swiss government did not want confirmed. Moreover, the day after the Foreign Ministry admitted to the full story and D'Amato sent his blistering letter, in a front-page story in the *New York Times*, Allan Cowell detailed his extensive interview with Hug and told the same story. Hug was in trouble. He was cornered and had told this story to too many people and to an audience far too wide for Swiss comfort. Because of this, the Swiss had evidently gotten to him. There was the suggestion that he was perhaps advised of a downgraded future earnings potential were he to continue his campaign of truth.

Now Hug had to recant his story. A few weeks later, at a press conference held at the Swiss Embassy with Ambassador Jagmetti, the Swiss released the text of his unpublished letter to the editor of the *New York Times*. "Paul [sic] Cowell," wrote Hug, "*New York Times* correspondent in Bonn, makes the monstrous assertion: 'Swiss Used Nazi Victims' Money for War Payments, Files Reveal' in an article which appeared on 24 October 1996. This accusation is false," continued Hug. "The same holds true for the majority of other comments which Mr. Cowell has attributed to me, a historian at Berne University in the abovementioned article."[37] Hug concluded his mea culpa piece to the *Times* by writing,

> Polemics, speculation, and incorrect reports such as those of Paul Cowell and Senator d'Amato [sic] are not appropriate ways to support this task. Quite the contrary. They threaten to demolish the positive attitude which exists today in probing as required this complicated chapter of Swiss history.[38]

When I met with Jagmetti and Vogelsanger, in November, the two entertained me with the party line that Hug was, quite inappropriately, "misquoted." I could not hold back and I said to Jagmetti, "with all due respect sir, do you expect me to believe that Hug was misquoted some 15 times by Allan Cowell in a front-page story in the *New York Times*, misquoted by Reuters, and that he lied to me. I find that very hard to believe." Together, they continued the argument, but there was not a thread of conviction in anything they said.

Switzerland had now received its first strong dose of Alfonse M. D'Amato. Most in that country had not seen anything like him. Amusement grew into irritation. Soon irritation would grow into disgust.

Esther Mamarbachi, writing in a special series on the Swiss bank affair for the *Journal de Geneve*, commented on the methods and the man that was quickly becoming public enemy number one in Switzerland:

> [T]he Senator is dispensing genuine or alleged revelations to the international media editors, one by one and drop by drop, thus manipulating everyone's historical recall. The example of the 1949 agreement between Switzerland and Poland, authorizing the use of orphaned Polish funds as compensation for Swiss subjects despoiled by the Warsaw communist regime, is a very eloquent case-in-point; reputedly secret, it ultimately turned out to be known since 1950 and quite within the law.[39]

D'Amato, while sinking in the popularity polls in Switzerland by this time, conversely, was being touted, albeit grudgingly by newspapers around the country. *Newsday*, while critical at times of D'Amato, could not help but grant him credit for touching an "exquisitely sensitive nerve."[40] The *Chicago Tribune* commented that Swiss critics of D'Amato accused him of playing politics, politics the *Tribune* declared "in pursuit of a good end."[41] Deroy Murdock, writing in the *Washington Times*, asserted that D'Amato's allegations, along with others that had come out by that time placed "Switzerland among the ashes of history."[42]

Damage Control

The fallout from D'Amato's revelations and the subsequent botched response of a paralyzed Swiss system, caused shockwaves throughout Switzerland. Cotti and the Federal Council saw the dire need to stop the hemorrhaging and Cotti announced on October 24 that a Commission would be formed out of the Foreign Ministry to "research the issues" surrounding D'Amato's revelations. In reality, what Cotti needed to create was a rapid response team, with a single voice that could appear before Switzerland's accusers and provide a defense. The man chosen, two days later, to lead the "charm offensive," was a young Foreign Ministry diplomat by the name of Thomas Borer, a Cotti ally and rising star in the Swiss Foreign Ministry. At thirty-nine, Borer had a fine curriculum vitae for the role. As an international lawyer, he had held the post of Deputy Chief of the International Law Division of the Foreign Ministry from 1989–1993, and then was posted to the embassy in Washington, returning to the Ministry a year later when he became the Deputy Secretary General there.

Borer, some argued, was not the man for the job. They said he was too dry, too German. On the contrary, Borer was everything that the Swiss were looking for.[43] He was tall, he dressed like he stepped off the pages of *GQ Magazine*, and smiled a lot. He was young, outgoing, and approachable. He was not the staid and stiff banker type of a Swiss diplomat that the others were. Moreover, he had a girlfriend who was a former Miss Texas, Shawn Fielding, a blonde, who would quite intentionally showcase herself walking back and forth during a Senate hearing D'Amato held in May 1997, and shown live in Switzerland. He represented the "new Swiss."

Unfortunately for the "new Swiss," they were forced to try to explain the sins of the old Swiss. Back in September, I received a call from Rico Carish, of *Stern TV*, in Germany. He had heard the many press stories resulting from documents we sent to European newspaper and television reporters and he wanted to do a story himself. He would not be discriminating he said. He just wanted a story and wanted to know what I could give him. By chance, I had just been looking through the growing number of documents we had gathered and I came across two lists of Swiss attorneys who, according to the OSS, were working on behalf of the Nazis in Switzerland hiding funds for them. The lists were so detailed that the attorney's addresses and telephone numbers were included.[44] I asked him if he wanted these lists to do a story on them. Perhaps he said, "we could look up some of the names and see what they would get us." Little did I know, or even did he guess, that his story would have lasting impact and bring the story home to the Swiss in a very personal way.

Carish and *Stern* printed their story. Playing in Switzerland as well as Germany, the story gave the names of the attorneys, especially that of Alois Grendelmeier of Zurich. As the father of Verena Grendelmeier, Swiss Parliamentarian, this represented a great embarrassment for her in Switzerland. She had cared greatly about the effect of Switzerland's wartime history would have on the nation as well as the people, and she wanted to make amends for it. In 1995, she had tried to expose the truth and seek a greater understanding of the period. Little did she know that she would become a victim of what she helped start. According to U.S. Ambassador Madeleine Kunin, Grendelmeier was greatly embarrassed by the story.[45] She went on Swiss television to refute any connection to anything her father might, or might not have done. The story might well have remained only an embarrassment for her in Switzerland. After Kunin told me about the story, I relayed it, only as a casual aside to Patty Cohen formerly of the *Washington Post*, who was trying to gather information on a story on Washington-area claimants. In turn, Cohen, unknown to me, passed it on to a *Post* reporter overseas, William Drozdiak, who parlayed it into a story that ran on the front page of the *Post* at the end of October.

"The Grendelmeier saga," Drozdiak wrote, "illustrates the kind of wrenching emotions that have jolted this proud, affluent country as growing international pressure to determine the fate of assets of Holocaust victims held in Swiss banks has prompted a fresh wave of soul-searching about secret deals with the Nazis."[46] Grendelmeier told Drozdiak, "I threw a small stone because I wanted to know the truth, and an entire wall came tumbling down. But catharsis is always painful."[47] Painful as it was, as many would soon come to realize, it would be a scandal that would be troublesome for the mind and stature of

Switzerland as a whole. While I had no intention of embarrassing Grendelmeier, I found it ironic that even her father was on this list. It seemed by now, that the story of Swiss collaboration with the Nazis was so pervasive that no one in that country would escape attack.

Borer, after his appointment, announced that a separate commission would be formed to look into D'Amato's allegations and that the report answering these charges would be released within the next month. We had struck a chord in the Swiss psyche. Borer's call for a commission to examine the allegations D'Amato leveled at his country, while important, would come back to haunt Borer and Switzerland. Hug, the man who confirmed the agreements to the world would lead the study. Based on what he had already said, the outcome, despite his government-imposed reluctance, was already cast.

By now, Swiss newspapers were running stories calling Swiss jewelry dealers, "fences of the Holocaust." Soon reporters all over the world were looking for stories on what other misdeeds the Swiss might have committed during the war. "Were, they, or their forebears,"asked Alan Cowell in the *New York Times*, of the ever growing stories of wartime deceit in Switzerland, "the Holocaust's greatest profiteers, trading not just in stolen bullion but also in gold, jewelry, paintings and other assets belonging to Hitler's victims?"[48]

This was all clearly getting to the Swiss and it was too much for them to swallow. Their politicians were sitting back and taking these accusations but were not responding. Their only answer was that "we will leave it to the historians" to decide how bad they were. D'Amato's comments in the interview with the *Journal de Geneve*, illustrated that we could not trust them after fifty years of obfuscation to investigate themselves. This was too much for Cotti, who called D'Amato's remarks "offensive and totally unacceptable." Swiss President Delamuraz called him arrogant and other Swiss officials complained that he should have tried to settle things quietly. Even Borer, writing to D'Amato in November questioned D'Amato's intention to play by the "general rules of fair play."[49] The point was inescapable though, Switzerland was in trouble and Thomas Borer's appointment came not a minute too soon.

As the accusations against Switzerland grew, the number of parties making them grew as well. The government of Poland, drawn into the scandal, by virtue of D'Amato's exposure of the Swiss-Polish agreement, wasted no time in distancing itself from the actions of the Communist government that had concluded the treaty with Switzerland. Within days of the accusation, the government formed a committee of legal and historical experts to determine the legality and status of the agreement upon Poland and perhaps saw it as another chance to show the wrongs of the Communist system. Within days of the Swiss admission of the transfer of funds, the Polish Foreign Ministry declared the deal to have been illegal.

In a report issued on December 10, the Interministerial Fact-Finding Commission on the Negotiation and Implementation of the Polish-Swiss Agreements of 1949, issued its report. The Commission found that the treaty was never ratified by the Polish Parliament, only by a resolution of the Government Cabinet; that due to this, Switzerland acquiesced to a procedure of exchange of ratification documents which did not comply with international law; that contrary to Swiss claims, the Polish government in 1949, was not authorized to legally take over the accounts of those people not heard from since 1945, mainly because it was not in power in 1945; additionally, the Swiss refusal to turn over the names of the account holders and their heirs, made it impossible for the Polish government to implement procedures, even if it was legally authorized to do so, to find the heirs or claimants to the bank accounts or insurance policies. The damning report concluded,

> The Treaty of June 25, 1949 between the Republic of Poland and the Swiss Confederation on compensation for Swiss property in Poland was negotiated in violation of the interests of Polish citizens, the owners or their heirs, of accounts and deposits in Swiss banks, and policies in Swiss insurance companies.
> Pursuant to the Treaty, the Swiss banks and insurance companies are the first to be liable to qualified persons for using account (deposit, policy) moneys without an owner's consent. This is because there were no contractual relationships of the Polish State Treasury with accounts (deposit, policy) owners.... Issues settled in the Treaty of June 25, 1949, on compensation for Swiss Property in Poland, so far as they concern "dead accounts," cannot be acknowledged as finally closed, despite that almost fifty years have passed since the treaty was negotiated.[50]

All that remained to be seen was the list of the account holders. Borer, in a meeting with D'Amato, in New York on December 12, committed to providing us with this list. On January 20, 1997, Borer transmitted the list of fifty-three Jewish names to us by facsimile. A month later, Borer turned over the list of thirty-three Hungarian Jewish accounts that suffered the same fate. This list, was never turned over to us by the Swiss government because of privacy requests by the Hungarian government, which itself later complained about the low number of names on the list. The WJC, which did receive the list, to their credit gave it to Stuart Ain who promptly published it in the *Jewish Week* on February 27, 1997.[51]

At the same time that we received the Polish list, the WJC and Greville Janner got it as well. As such, it would be Janner's staff in London, which would be the first to locate an heir, and they had to go no further than the telephone book where they found the name of Hilde Sorkin. It was Sorkin, whose uncle, Walter Loery, had listed his niece Hilde as a contact person in 1937 for his account of 3,378 Swiss francs in a Zurich bank.

Growing Accusations

Following the New York City hearing, and the disastrous Swiss re-action that accompanied it, groups all over the world, Jewish and non-Jewish, began to see that we had actually discovered gaping holes in the Swiss story. As with a dying animal in the field, Switzerland began to see birds of prey circling overhead. By the end of October, the Wiesenthal Center in Los Angeles joined the fight in earnest. Rabbis Marvin Hier and Abraham Cooper, the Dean and Associate Dean of the Center, wrote Ambassador Jagmetti with seven recommendations for action in an effort to both tighten the screws on the Swiss, but to also obtain information. One recommendation was for the convening of a "truth commission" to offer immunity to potential witnesses who might come forward with information on the Swiss banks.[52] To add to this, D'Amato joined the call in a letter to Ambassador Jagmetti on the same day. Following the angry reaction in Switzerland to D'Amato's revela-tions, Borer, now in charge of officially responding to accusations made against Switzerland, swiftly rejected the joint call, saying "comparing Switzerland to South Africa is absurd."[53] We knew that the request car-ried great connotations. South Africa, after all, was and still is, going through the painful task of examining its own history of apartheid to uncover the misdeeds and crimes of the past. To have associated Swit-zerland with South Africa was insulting to the Swiss and we knew it. What we were telling them was that if their response to the Swiss-Polish agreement was a sign of their commitment to honesty and to finding the truth, they were in trouble.

At the same time, the first signs occurred that the tremors from the document disclosures and letters were having their effect. When the Swiss franc dropped, albeit slightly against the dollar on the world market on November 1, rumors of the possibility of the lifting of bank secrecy were blamed. The franc also was forecast to fall against the mark in the longer term, due in part to the fallout from the scandal.[54]

The call for a truth commission, however, was nevertheless criticized and no doubt contributed to the instability.

While insulting to the Swiss, the parallel between Switzerland and South Africa disturbed many there, not so much because of the implication of historical misdeeds, but of historical punishment. Just as South Africa faced a sustained campaign of boycotts and international isolation, Switzerland too was vulnerable to the same fate. This subtle message was not lost on the industry in Switzerland with the most to lose, the banks. Apartheid was brought to its knees by disinvestment and sanctions. Could not their banks, feared the Swiss, suffer the same fate?[55]

Great sums were invested in the banks, with thirteen branches in the United States, the Swiss banks were exposed. D'Amato, as Chairman of the Senate Banking Committee, could effect their business in the U.S. Falling as they were onto the black side of this clearly black and white issue, the Swiss banks had no friends and no supporters. D'Amato was on the side of the just, the banks on the side of the Nazis. This is what we tried to portray and what we achieved. The world now began to see the Swiss as the bad guys as the charges took their toll. They were becoming daily more susceptible to what they feared the most, a boycott. While calls for embargoes would come later, the comparisons with South Africa, proved to be chilling for the Swiss. In the coming weeks, further disclosures and weak showings by the Swiss government and banks would only hasten calls for such actions. In another year and a half, these fears would become a reality.

Meager Results

Since the campaign against Switzerland began, the WJC had claimed that Swiss banks were holding as much as $7 billion in Jewish assets. They maintained this figure, adding in looted artwork, jewelry, securities, bonds, and, of course, bank accounts. Many in Switzerland doubted this figure and attacked the WJC for estimating such a high number. The SBA insisted that the sum was $31.9 million and no more. After exhaustive searches, they maintained they could find no other assets.

Following the creation of the Banking Ombudsman's office to investigate claims against the banks, the Ombudsman Hans Peter Haeni, received thousands of claims from all over the world. On November 12, Haeni held a press conference in Zurich to deflect criticism that his office was doing little to help claimants. In announcing the findings,

Haeni criticized the WJC claims to $7 billion in Jewish funds in Swiss banks as "unrealistic to an unprejudiced eye."[56] Haeni's press conference, while much anticipated, was disappointing. He pronounced findings of only $1.3 million, belonging to only eleven claimants, with only $9,000 belonging to five deceased Jewish claimants. One account was worth over $1 million. The WJC found these results to be "pathetic." Others criticized Haeni's methods and correctly described the meager results as adding to the growing mistrust of the banks and Switzerland as a whole. Paul Volcker, leading the commission to investigate the dormant accounts, was himself so bothered by Haeni's results that he announced the next day that he would examine Haeni's methodology to determine why more money was not found.

As we later discovered, there were instances of accounts remaining dormant, yet drained monthly for lack of transaction activity. In one particular case, an account opened in the 1940s, was drained in this manner for fifty years, well into the 1990s. Could it not have been the same for countless other accounts? It had been nearly a year before we came to learn of this travesty. This could be an answer to why all the searches have turned up accounts with such small sums of money.

Nevertheless, Haeni's meager showing, was part of the problem the Swiss now faced. Due to the sometimes competing, sometimes equal claims of D'Amato and the WJC, the bar was set too high. Expectations were too great and whatever the Swiss found in any search, would not be enough to satisfy its critics.

The Counteroffensive Begins

Within weeks of his appointment, Thomas Borer set about to change the perception of Switzerland in the world from one of robbers of Jewish wealth and Nazi collaborators, to one of a sympathetic and caring people willing to admit the mistakes of the past and make amends for it. His first step in this effort was to call back to Switzerland, its Ambassadors to twelve European nations, as well as the United States and Israel, to confer on strategy and options for the future. He sought to coordinate the message that Switzerland was doing all that it could to correct the problem and that the world should not judge the country before all the facts were in. Following his consultations with his Ambassadors, Borer then met with executives from the banks and industry in Switzerland. At the same time, Foreign Minister Cotti also met with the banks and insurance companies to coordinate strategy.

As part of this effort, the banks too, felt the need to combat the squeeze of the public relations nightmare that was descending upon them. Richard C. Capone, Executive Vice President and Chief Executive Officer of UBS's North American Division, a recipient as well, of several letters from D'Amato on behalf of claimants, released a memo to all staff in the North American region concerning the allegations leveled at UBS as well as the other Swiss banks. Regarding the media reports that had filled the news, Capone in his October 25 cover memorandum to the October 9 memo from the parent company, wrote "these reports are a matter of deep concern to me and the other members of UBS senior management because of the distorted view they represent and the erroneous impression they leave of the seriousness with which we view these matters."[57] In the underlying memo, the implicit goal was to educate staff on how to counter the avalanche of information coming out in the documents. "Aware that the discussions and accusations have had a negative impact on our image," the memo read, staff, with this memo in hand, could then respond with the "party line" to clients in an effort to prevent any more harm from occuring to the bank.[58] On the whole the memo was a whitewash of the facts as borne out by the documents we had at the time, and especially by those we have found since then. The memo alleges that further searches will not turn up any further funds, which has since proven to not be the case. The memo said categorically that private banks such as UBS had no connection to the gold issue at all. This too, was inaccurate. Documents clearly indicate that UBS, along with the other banks, transferred funds as well as proceeds from gold, possibly even looted gold, out of Switzerland for the Nazis. Clearly, the memo sent out by Capone, was lacking in facts and in veracity. Nevertheless it was necessary for UBS to circulate. Whether Capone wanted its existence publicized in papers like the *Financial Times* in London, is another question.

While Borer was reaching out at home, he was also carrying his campaign to Britain and the United States, where his ambassadors told him he should concentrate his efforts and charm.[59] Realizing that the "issue is more pressing in some countries than in others, most of all in the United States but also in Britain," Borer began writing to D'Amato and Congressman Jim Leach, Chairman of the House Banking Committee, as well as Greville Janner, with whom he met on November 18, seeking meetings with them in order to calm the waters. Moreover, Borer sought a dialogue with the leaders of the major Jewish organizations in the United States, particularly in New York. In letters to the individual groups, Borer expressed an interest in establishing a "frank and open communication" with them.[60]

Janner's trip to Switzerland was productive, if not important for uncovering the mood there. While there, Janner inquired whether the Swiss had made good on their promise to pay reparations following former Swiss President Kaspar Villiger's apology for Switzerland's role in turning over to the Nazis, thousands of Jews during the war. According to Janice Lopatkin, the Director of Janner's Holocaust Educational Trust, they got testy and angrily asked Janner if he wanted to see the check. At the end of the day, George Kreyer, President of the SBA gave them a photo copy of the $800,000 check that was given to the AMCHAM Jewish charity in Israel.[61] Moreover, Janner would suggest the creation of an interim fund, with contributions from the major Swiss banks, from which elderly Holocaust survivors could receive however modest, a pension to alleviate their suffering. This suggestion, while turned down flatly at the time, would grow in appeal to both Bronfman and D'Amato, and to a great deal of antipathy in Switzerland until calls for such a fund would boil over into an international uproar due to the unfortunate remarks of an outgoing Swiss President.

A December Switzerland Wishes to Forget

December would bring more revelations and unexpected actions that would be described by the London *Daily Telegraph* as bringing Swiss banks descending from "peak to valley."[62] As if the months of revelations, accusations, and negative press had not done enough damage for the once vaunted Swiss banks, Standard & Poor's, officially put UBS on warning that its AAA rating was in danger of being withdrawn. This review came after UBS announced that the bank would suffer a $400 million loss in 1996. These two factors, coupled with the ongoing banking scandal created market worries for UBS that would contribute to a Swiss siege mind set in the following months and would help blow the Swiss banking scandal wide open.

Within days, of UBS's threatened downgrading by Standard & Poor's, Jean Ziegler, a Socialist member of the Swiss Parliament, offered a motion to abolish the core essence of the Swiss banking system, the holy clause of bank secrecy. Arguing that Switzerland, by ridding itself of this practice, would also rid itself of the opportunity to be accused of improprieties such as the issue of Holocaust accounts. As expected, the Swiss cabinet unanimously rejected Ziegler's motion.

On December 4, the head of the Roma, or Gypsy community in Switzerland, wrote to Foreign Minister Cotti, demanding that the community receive compensation for the gold taken from individual Gypsies and diverted to Switzerland by the Nazis. Building on Janner's call for compensation to be paid to Jewish survivors of the Holocaust, the Roma felt they were no less deserving because they were no less persecuted.

On the same day as the Roma's request, the Swiss Federal Archives issued a statement declaring that after months of research into the question of Swiss refugee policy during the war, more than 30,000 people, fleeing the Nazis were turned back either at the border with Germany, or after being turned down for asylum. This number was almost thirty times the number Kaspar Villager had acknowledged in his May 7, 1995 address to the Swiss people when he apologized for the policy of turning back refugees.

As the line goes, if things could get worse, they probably will. On that same day, D'Amato released a letter to Ambassador Jagmetti with questions about a document we had found some time earlier in the year. The document, a March 23, 1945 State Department transcript, for radio broadcast presumably to South America, detailed allegations of Swiss bankers being entrusted with the diplomatic pouch, in this case, to South America. Nazis leaders such as Hermann Göring, Joseph Goebbels, and others were said to have transferred fortunes from the proceeds of looted properties and other assets into Swiss banks, and with direct Swiss aid, onto Buenos Aires. Worse yet, Göring was said to have used German submarines to transfer as much as $20 million in funds to Argentina.[63]

The following day's cover of the *New York Post*, featured a cover-sized photo of Herman Göring, with the headline, "Secret Nazi Cash Stash." Inside, under the title, "Swiss Sneaks Smuggled Nazi Loot: Al," the story was told. In New York City, important for D'Amato, this was front page news in the other papers as well. Across the world, the story ran, seemingly verifying the writings of Frederick Forsyth on the conspiracy behind the illegal transit of Nazis to South America, yet now with ostensible proof that their money was sent out ahead of them. The story dropped like a bomb in Switzerland. By linking Switzerland with the Nazis and their escape from justice, the story took on a new and sinister odor, one which the Swiss government would find difficult to shed.

Yet, there were more devastating documents that we had found only days before and released immediately after the Göring document. Now, there were documents from the American military attache in The Hague, who in 1948 expressed concern over reports that the Swiss government, in its rush to expel Nazis from its territory was, through Swiss Air agents, arranging flights aboard KLM Royal Dutch Airlines, Air France, and Swedish Air, for Nazis fleeing Europe. For 200,000 Swiss francs, some $50,000 at the time, a residency permit or "Ersatzpass," could be obtained for the fleeing German in order to stay in Switzerland. As soon as an Argentine visa was obtained, the Germans were booked on the airlines and flown to either Argentina or Brazil.[64]

Coming one after the other, in the course of two days, the Swiss were livid. "Mr. D'Amato," said Lukas Beglinger, deputy head of Borer's Task Force, "is not very cooperative, which reinforces the suspicion that he is pursuing tactical objectives in making his revelations."[65] Beglinger questioned the historical accuracy of the documents and failed to see why we were releasing them one at a time. They just did not get the concept. They could not understand our approach.

Pietro Gerosa of Swiss television, commented that the government was shocked by the tone of our approach to them. The letters D'Amato sent Swiss government leaders baffled them. They were flabbergasted at the sharpness and the barefisted nature of these attacks. Tom Bower, explained it better to me. "They are not thinking like you. They are in a different world."

Borer complained bitterly that there was no context to the documents. "What I once again regret," Borer said, "is that Mr. D'Amato is presenting obvious allegations as proven facts and basing himself solely on sources that have not been checked."[66] Borer, trying since his appointment in October to meet with D'Amato, was frustrated that his entreaties to him went unanswered. In this respect, Jagmetti, too, was upset that he was also unable to obtain an appointment with the Senator. The requests came almost exclusively through me and I admittedly sat on them. I stalled the requests believing that not only did they not deserve an audience, but that D'Amato should be viewed as obstinate, stubborn, and unwilling to grant them an audience with which the Swiss envoys could use to beg for mercy. They should be left, I felt, to stew over the matter. It would only make them more desperate.

From the *New York Times* to the *London Times*, newspapers were filled with stories of direct Swiss complicity in helping Nazis escape to South America. The press for the Swiss was getting uncontrollable and the situation was coming to a boiling point. Responding to accusations that his inquiry was self-serving, D'Amato responded, "My job is not to hide this embarrassment the Swiss may suffer...I didn't make these charges up, shocking as they are."[67]

"It cannot be excluded," Borer admitted, "at some time a diplomatic pouch was misused."[68] All Borer could do, aside from complaining over the pace of the disclosures, was to announce the formation of yet another panel to examine them. A week later, though, Borer would get his first exposure to the American media, before the House Banking Committee, whose Chairman, Jim Leach (R-IA) which called a hearing into the matter on December 11.

Mr. Borer Comes to Washington

It was approaching dusk and a long black limousine pulled up to the United States Holocaust Memorial Museum on Raoul Wallenberg Place, just off the mall in Washington. Out popped a Swiss television film crew. It was December 10 and Thomas Borer was visiting the museum and the crew was there to film his visit. The visit would be portrayed as a pilgrimage to a holy site by a repentant Swiss official. In reality, according to a museum official, the visit was a canned shot that lasted no longer than fifteen minutes, where Borer was repeatedly filmed walking in, and walking out of the museum. Owing to the shortness of the days of December, it would not be long before the sun would go down, and dwindling sunlight would be an accomplice in the ruse. According to Lanny Griffith, of Barbour, Griffith & Rogers, a Washington law firm ostensibly hired to prepare Borer for the upcoming hearing, contrary to the museum's interpretation, Borer spent "a good hour-and-a-half" in the museum taking a sympathetic look at one of Washington's biggest attraction.[69] This view was not supported by the museum staff which forbids such events, or even the Swiss Embassy. According to my conversation with Christopher Bubb, a member of the Swiss embassy staff the next day, the Ambassador had a busy schedule that day and "would perhaps really need more time to visit the museum in the future."[70]

Borer's mission to Washington, aside from testifying before Leach's committee, was to carry on the charm offensive, however clumsily it began. He was to meet U.S. officials to try and persuade them that Switzerland was really trying to discover the truth. They were looking at all areas of their history, they said, and they would make good on their promises.

Before Leach and the other members of the House Banking Committee, Borer was to testify on Switzerland's actions to that date. Before him, however, D'Amato would testify for an hour and a half on his Committee's findings. He would detail the recent disclosures regarding the transfer of Nazi assets by Swiss diplomatic pouch to South America, the Swiss-Polish treaty, and other revelations we made in the previous months. He was truly captivating. Committee members, Democrat and Republican alike, commended him and expressed their approval of his work. He led off the hearing and stole the show. Yet, there were other witnesses, aside from Borer, including Edgar Bronfman, Stuart Eizenstat, Chairman of the Swiss Bankers Association, George Kreyer, leader of the Swiss Jewish Community, Rolf Bloch, Paul Volcker, and two claimants.

Borer, the most anticipated person at the hearing, carried himself well. He appeared as sensitive to the issue and promised results as well as an investigation that would "go beyond the narrow legalistic path onto the broader avenue of a higher morality and legitimacy."[71] He also asked for time.

> Mr. Chairman, Switzerland is deeply aware of the pain, mistrust, and confusion that surrounds this issue. With this in mind, you can rest assured that this committee will receive full and unfettered cooperation from all quarters of my government. We are not afraid of the truth. In fact, we consider it essential to reach it as quickly as possible. Yet to do so, we must all rise above the speculations, hasty conclusions, and unsubstantiated claims without substance that further rob the process of the compassion, tact, and empathy it so rightly deserves.[72]

No doubt aiming his remarks at D'Amato, Borer's testimony ironically foreshadowed the opposite. In the very near future, the actions of the Swiss officials and bankers would betray the cooperative tone of his testimony. Their actions convinced the world that Switzerland cared more about shredding the truth then in exposing it.

In the four months since the World Jewish Congress had been joined by D'Amato, and for that matter Janner, they were no longer alone. For his part, D'Amato became the most hated man in Switzerland. According to then Swiss Counsel General in New York, Alfred DeFago, D'Amato embodied "the never-ending bashing from New York."[73] As *Vanity Fair* editor Ann Bardach told me, this was "Alfonse's finest moment." D'Amato, only recently a thorn in Bill Clinton's side, was now described by the former State Department spokesman Nicholas Burns, as doing "the Lord's work."[74] For D'Amato the Swiss bank affair would become a crusade. For the Swiss, it would become a time of national shame.

In the coming weeks, the Swiss, clearly rattled by the events of the past year, lashed out in anger at its critics. One embarrassment bred another. If the autumn was bad for Switzerland, the winter would be much worse. Soon they would have wished that they settled with Edgar Bronfman when they had the chance.

Notes

1. Alan Cowell, "Self-Doubt at Last for the Swiss," *New York Times*, 6 October 1996.
2. Letter from Edgar Bronfman and Greville Janner to former British Foreign Secretary Malcolm Rifkind, 16 September 1996.
3. Letter of E.T. Davies, Secretary General, Tripartite Commission for the Restitution of Monetary Gold to United States Senator Alfonse M. D'Amato, 7 October 1996.
4. Letter of William J. McDonough, President, Federal Reserve Bank of New York, to United States Senator Alfonse M. D'Amato, 11 October 1996.
5. Letter of William J. McDonough, President, Federal Reserve Bank of New York, to United States Senator Alfonse M. D'Amato, Summary of Attachments, 7 May 1997, p.4.
6. Discussion with Ambassador Stuart Eizenstat, Washington, D.C., 13 January 1997.
7. Marcus Kabel, "Swiss National Bank says it trusted Nazis on gold," Reuters, 13 September 1996.
8. Marcus Kabel, "Swiss hounded for Nazi loot after ignoring past," Reuters, 12 September 1996.
9. Carolyn Henson, "Swiss Embarrassed Over Wartime Dealings," Associated Press, 16 September 1996.
10. Jenni Frazer, "Nazi Loot in Switzerland could be worth £65 billion," *Jewish Chronicle*, 20 September 1996.
11. Marcus Kabel, "Swiss say 1946 Nazi wealth accord remains valid," Reuters, 25 September 1946.
12. Action Memorandum from Acting Secretary of State for European and Canadian Affairs, E. Anthony Wayne to Deputy Secretary of State Strobe Talbott, 26 September 1996, p. 2.
13. "Nazi Gold and the Washington Agreement of 1946," Press Release, United States Information Service, Embassy of the United States, Bern, 1 October 1996.
14. Michael Shields, "Swiss suspect foreign agenda for wartime review," Reuters, 1 October 1996.
15. Letter of Sepp Haener to Senator Alfonse M. D'Amato, 9 January 1997.
16. Shields, "Swiss suspect foreign agenda for wartime review."
17. Letter of Eugen Fink to United States Senator Alfonse M. D'Amato, 28 February 1997.
18. Cathryn J. Prince, "Gold Rush on Swiss Banks: Story of Nazi Loot Unfolds Past Dealings with Hitler's Germany come under Renewed Scrutiny," *Christian Science Monitor*, 27 September 1996.
19. Jan Marejko, "Protracted Decisions Hamper the Swiss," *European*, 16 January 1997.
20. Alan Cowell, "Self-Doubt At Last for the Swiss," *New York Times*, 6 October 1997.

21. Brian A. Brown, "Why Switzerland Bungled Jewish Claims," *Wall Street Journal Europe*, 2 September 1997.
22. Letter from Simon Canning to United States Senator Alfonse M. D'Amato, 20 August 1996.
23. "Holocaust Victims' Bank Records Identified: World Jewish Congress," Agence France-Presse, 16 October 1996.
24. Stuart Ain, "Victim of Swiss Banks Steps Forward," *New York Jewish Week*, 3 January 1997, p.8; James Rutenberg, "Bucking Swiss Bank, Queens Widow Demands Funds," *New York Daily News*, 4 January 1997.
25. Letter of Max Trilling to the United States Department of State, 12 March 1950, RG 59, Central Files of the Department of State, 254.4851, 1950–54, Box 1017, NARA; Letter from Roswell H. Whitman, Office of Western European Affairs, United States Department of State, to Max Trilling, 23 March 1950, RG 59, Central Files of the Department of State, 254.4851, 1950–54, Box 1017, NARA; Letter of Leland Harrison, United States Legation, Bern, Switzerland, to the Secretary of State, 28 July 1947, RG 84, Records of the Consular Posts, United States Department of State, 850.3, Economic Section, Box 104, NARA; Letter of Daniel J. Reagan, Counselor, United States Legation, Bern, Switzerland, to the Joint Commission, Bern, 29 January 1947, RG 84, Records of the Consular Posts, United States Department of State, 850.3, Economic Section, Box 104, NARA; Interview with Elizabeth Trilling by B.J. Moravek, 10 June 1996.
26. Michael Hirsh and Mark Frankel, "Switzerland, Secret Bankers for the Nazis," *Newsweek*, 24 June 1996.
27. Letter from Douglas Henderson, Secretary of the American Embassy in Bern, to the Department of State, concerning Lewis Salton, 23 December 1954, RG 59, Central Files of the Department of State, 254.1151, 1950–54, Box 1017, NARA.
28. Michael Shields, "Swiss deny secret deals on Jewish funds," Reuters, 17 October 1996.
29. Ibid.
30. Arthur Spiegelman, "Jewish group demands restitution from Swiss," Reuters, 18 October 1996.
31. Felix Bauer, "Swiss admit Polish Jews' funds compensated Swiss," Reuters, 22 October 1996.
32. Peter Hug, "Haggling at the Conference Table Over Dormant Assets, Swiss-Polish Correspondence not an Isolated Case," *Neue Zürcher Zeitung*, no. 247, 23 October 1996, pp. 2–3, translated by David Skelly.
33. Balz Bruppacher, "Swiss deny misuse of Holocaust money, Foreign minister disputes D'Amato's claim, despite evidence of deals made after World War II," *Times Union*, 24 October 1996.
34. James Morrison, "Swiss Gold Standard," *Washington Times*, 25 October 1996, p. A 18.
35. Discussion with David Vogelsanger, Public Affairs Officer, Swiss Embassy in Washington, and Linus von Castelmur, Task Force-World War II, 12 December 1996.
36. Letter from United States Senator Alfonse M. D'Amato to Swiss President Jean-Pascal Delamuraz, 22 October 1996.
37. Peter Hug, "Rectification, Paul Cowell: "Swiss Used Nazi Victims' Money for War Payments, Files Reveal," Unpublished letter to the editor of the *New York Times*, released by the Swiss embassy to the United States, 30 October 1996.
38. Ibid.
39. Esther Mamarbachi, "Forum: Switzerland Stung by Lack of Political Sensitiv-

ity," *Journal de Geneve*, Internet Edition in English, http://geneva-international.org/
Forum/Dossier/Piege.E.html, p. 2.

40. "Did Swiss Profit From the Holocaust?" Editorial, *Newsday*, 3 November 1996.
41. "Switzerland's Holocaust Profiteers," Editorial, *Chicago Tribune*, 8 November 1996.
42. Deroy Murdock, "Switzerland among the ashes of history," *Washington Times*, 17 December 1996.
43. See, "Full Borer Response," *Financial Times*, 28 October 1996.
44. "List of Swiss Lawyers in Zurich Said to be Hiding German Assets," RG 226, Records of the Office of Strategic Services, Washington SI, Special Funds Records, Box 22, NARA.
45. Discussion with Madeleine Kunin, United States Ambassador to Switzerland, Washington, D.C.,17 October 1996.
46. William Drozdiak, "Swiss Forced to Face Troubled Past of Wartime Dealings With Nazis," *Washington Post*, 26 October 1996, p. 1.
47. Ibid.
48. Alan Cowell, "How Much did the Swiss Profit from the Holocaust," syndicated in *Ottawa Citizen*, 27 October 1996.
49. Letter from Ambassador Thomas Borer to United States Senator Alfonse M. D'Amato, 7 November 1996, p. 1.
50. Marek Grela, Commission Chairman, Jan Ciszewski, Krzysztof Majczuk, Janusz Stanczyk, and Wieslaw Szczuka, "Determinations of the Interministerial Fact-Finding Commission on the Negotiation and Implementation of the Polish-Swiss Agreements of 1949," Warsaw, 10 December 1996, translated by Congressional Research Service.
51. "Hungarian Account Holders," *Long Island Jewish Week*, 27 February 1997.
52. Letter from Rabbis Marvin Hier and Abraham Cooper to Swiss Ambassador to the United States, Carlo Jagmetti, 30 October 1996.
53. Felix Bauer, "Swiss reject calls for 'truth commission' on Nazi gold," Reuters, 1 November 1996.
54. Peter Semler, "Focus: Swiss franc to weaken on fading safe-haven role, sterling EMU hedging," *AFX News*, 11 November 1996.
55. See Charles Fleming, "The South Africa Scenario," *Wall Street Journal*, 11 November 1996.
56. William Drozdiak, "Lost Assets Found in Swiss Accounts," *Washington Post*, 13 November 1996, p. A 17.
57. Richard C. Capone, Memorandum, "Recent Media Coverage of Holocaust Victims' Assets," UBS North American Region, 15 October 1996, p. 1.
58. Ibid, p. 7.
59. Marcus Kabel, "Swiss envoy targets U.S., U.K. on Holocaust funds," Reuters, 15 November 1996.
60. Letter from Ambassador Thomas Borer to Phil Baum, Executive Director, American Jewish Congress, 28 November 1996.
61. Discussion with Janice Lopatkin, Director, Holocaust Educational Trust, London, 25 November 1996.
62. "European Business: Swiss banks descend from peak to valley, European Notebook," *Daily Telegraph*, 27 November 1996.
63. "Nazi and Fascist Capital in Latin America," Memo from H.J. Cummings to Lt. Karasik, for radio broadcast, United States Department of State, 23 March 1945, RG 59, Records of the United States Department of State, NARA.
64. Report of Philip W. Bonsal, Counselor to the Embassy, The Hague, "Illegal Movement of German Citizens to Argentina," with enclosures, to the Secretary

of State, 1 March 1948, RG 319, Records of the Army Intelligence File, ID 446231-ID 446282, Entry 85, Box 2882, NARA.

65. "Memo: Swiss Made Phony Documents for Germans," Associated Press, 6 December 1996.
66. Marcus Kabel, "Swiss say claims they hid Nazi wealth unverified," Reuters, 5 December 1996.
67. Larry McShane, "D'Amato, Swiss Officials Swap Barbs Over Nazis," Associated Press, 6 December 1996.
68. "Swiss to Investigate possible Nazi Smuggling," *Asbury Park Press*, 13 December 1996.
69. Telephone conversation with Lanny Griffith, 12 December 1996.
70. Telephone Conversation with Christopher Bubb, 12 December 1996.
71. Statement of Ambassador Thomas Borer before the House Committee on Banking and Financial Services hearing, "The Disposition of Assets Deposited in Swiss Banks by Missing Nazi Victims," 104th Congress, Second Session, 11 December 1996, Serial Number 104–76, p. 34.
72. Ibid.
73. Peter Gorner, "Alfred DeFago, Swiss Ambassador to the United States," *Chicago Tribune*, 14 September 1997.
74. State Department Briefing by Nicholas Burns, 27 January 1997.

4

"Bern, We Have a Problem"

"If this was [the] case as is also believed by us those whom we owe unmerited insult of [an] American Senator and those who through their inadmissable attitude make believe that we have something [to] hide and fear light should be pilloried before public opinion."[1] So wrote the editors of the *Tribune de Geneve*. The editorial is fitting, in light of the worldwide condemnation of Switzerland had been receiving during the previous year, yet it was written not in 1996 but in 1945. Switzerland, criticized by Harley Kilgore, had lashed out with violent rhetoric against the Democratic Senator from West Virginia. Now, they had another Senator to worry about, but this time the normally placid Swiss would react very differently to the "unmerited insult" of an American Senator.

"Psychological errors were made"

"Finally, one is speechless," wrote a Swiss reader to the *Neue Zürcher Zeitung*, "at the excessiveness of the arrogant attacks of D'Amato and pals who don't shy away from putting 'Switzerland' in the vicinity of responsibility for the Holocaust."[2]

By this time, the Swiss people were fed up with the external attacks on their country. They were fed up with D'Amato, the WJC and the entire process by which they were being picked apart on a daily basis. The Swiss people were not alone in their disgust with their situation. The Swiss government itself would not be spared grief either. The Swiss Ambassador to the United States, Carlo Jagmetti, knew well of our campaign because he was in the middle of the storm in Washington. We wrote Jagmetti routinely, both for answers and to convey our displeasure with the lack of Swiss response to a variety of questions and problems. Between May and December, Jagmetti received no less than eight separate letters from D'Amato. Questions ranging from complaints about a lack of cooperation by the SBA, to newly discovered documents, to outright accusations against his government, were all directed to the beleaguered Ambassador. It got to the point that he would respond to our letters not individually, but in pairs to save time and aggravation. The communication for Jagmetti was only one way. While continually receiving letters from D'Amato, he was unable to receive an appointment to meet him in person. In the end, he never did get to meet the Senator. Perhaps in retrospect this was wrong, but I felt that when he and his government were more forthcoming, so would be an appointment with the Senator.

Early on, this agitation showed very clearly when, Jagmetti, disturbed at the tone of a letter from D'Amato on May 16, retorted "the Swiss government and the Swiss people must have the primary responsibility for the resolution of these issues, just as other countries, including the United States, have to examine difficult episodes in their own history."[3] Normally a calm, measured and straightforward man, Jagmetti came to understand all too well that the last year of his service in Washington was not going to be an easy one.

Perhaps more cognizant of the threat facing his country than any other member of the Swiss government, Jagmetti understood the climate he was in and the quickly souring view of Switzerland steadily forming in the U.S. With this in mind, he held a press conference in the embassy in Washington on October 30. Although he could not have done so without the permission of the Federal Council in Bern, in light of the recent events, it was necessary, Jagmetti felt, for a representative of the government of Switzerland to stand before the press and appear, of all things human, perhaps even repentant.

"From a human point of view," he conceded, "some real mistakes were made. He admitted before a packed room of journalists in the Swiss embassy that Switzerland had indeed stonewalled Holocaust survivors and that "psychological errors were made."[4] Progress was being made, however, but Switzerland still needed time. Mistakes too, were made by claimants, said Jagmetti. In this vein, he centered on the case of Greta Beer, the claimant who testified before D'Amato and the Senate Banking Committee in April.

Beer, he said, had gotten her information all wrong. According to Jagmetti, the account about which Beer had testified was opened by her father and in her reckoning had been one of those lost over the past half-century by the Swiss bankers. Not so, said Jagmetti, as he proudly, yet apologetically explained to the reporters. Beer's uncle, Jagmetti reported, had long since closed the account and this was proof that mistakes, too, were made by claimants.[5] The next day, Greta Beer called me strenuously denying the story. "It is not true," cried Beer over the phone to me. She had remained in close contact with the office since her testimony before the Committee in April and her trip to Switzerland. It was not possible, in her words for this to have happened.

For Jagmetti, the source of the story was Edgar Bronfman, who spoke in New York with D'Amato on the latest findings of the ongoing investigation on October 23. Having heard Bronfman relay this story to the packed crowd, D'Amato asked me to check out the story. I assured him that I had never heard of such a thing.

Having spoken to Willi Korte, he informed me that during her time in Switzerland, she had met with Hans Baer, her sponsor for the visit. While talking, she conveyed to him the possibility that her uncle, her father's brother, might also have had an account in Switzerland as well. For Bronfman, as we later found out, the source of the story was, as Korte said, Hans Baer.[6] Baer, either confused or purposely spreading a tale, passed the story on to Bronfman who, believing it, announced the news in New York. Jagmetti then, was only repeating what Bronfman heard from Baer. Unfortunately for Jagmetti it was not true and it was to him D'Amato would write complaining of the "callous manner" in which "Greta's case could be thrown around like it has."[7] Not only did Jagmetti hear loudly from D'Amato, but the left-wing press in Switzerland, David Vogelsanger was quoted as having said, "made a huge fuss" over Jagmetti's remarks. According to Vogelsanger, headlines appeared in Switzerland like "Swiss ambassador insults Nazi victim."[8] While he later apologized personally to Beer for his remarks, for Jagmetti, this was only the beginning of his troubles.[9]

"Rivers of blood...into lakes of gold"

While Jagmetti was trying to dig himself out of the pit he dug for himself, Greville Janner and his fellow Parliamentarian David Hunt, were in Switzerland seeking a preliminary, or interim fund, as it became known, to provide compensation to those survivors of the Holocaust who had yet to receive compensation for their suffering. "Those rivers of blood from the concentration camps came into lakes of gold," said Hunt who traveled to Bern with Janner.[10] Janner, complaining to the Swiss that five years to examine Swiss wartime history was, as D'Amato expressed, was too long a period to wait, pushed for the interim payment to provide some relief to the survivors. Thus, the idea for an interim fund was born yet the gestation period would be long and painful.

The Swiss, while not entirely cold to the idea, nevertheless made it contingent upon the results of the Volcker Commission study, still in its infancy. They felt that only then would there be any idea of how much Jewish wealth had been deposited in Switzerland. More importantly for the Swiss however, as cited by Marcus Kabel of *Reuters,* was the question if the fund were to be set up, would it quiet Switzerland's critics, the WJC and D'Amato.[11]

One idea circulating in Switzerland was to take the $31.9 million from the dormant accounts and donate it to charity on behalf of survivors, not unlike what was done after the 1962 process. This was criticized as being a rush to judgment and it was too early to make such a move before all of the claimants could be found. As events of the next year would show, simply donating the funds would prove premature as the accounts would be made public only causing a greater firestorm for the Swiss.

Yet, Janner's idea picked up momentum. At a breakfast meeting with reporters in New York on December 10, D'Amato endorsed the idea of an interim payment saying, "they'd be happy to buy us out. We should not take $31 million and go away." Yet, for D'Amato, it was "a very good idea, provided we state very clearly that this in no way closes the books."[12] The same day, Bronfman, meeting with Borer in New York would make the same pitch, but for Borer and Cotti alike, it was too soon to start talking about money.[13] As Swiss President Jean Pascal-Delamuraz would soon discover, it would also be too early to talk about.

"Nothing less than extortion and blackmail"

If there was ever a more an unfortunate slip of the tongue, Jean Pascal-Delamuraz could not have made it. The outgoing President of the Swiss Confederation, in a year-end interview with the *Tribune de Geneve*, likened calls for an interim compensation fund to "blackmail and extortion." "Such a fund," Delamuraz snapped, "would be considered an admission of guilt." For him, like the derisive articles appearing earlier in the Swiss press, such calls were nothing more than an attempt to destabilize the Swiss financial system.

The sixty-year-old President and Minister of Economics, was known for having "loose lips" and his outspoken nature sometimes got the better of him. This time he made the worst of an already bad situation. Now came the recriminations.

For Elan Steinberg of the WJC, Delamuraz's remarks were shocking, representing an assault and challenge to the very soul of Switzerland." Kalman Sultanik, a Vice President of the WJC, said Delamuraz's comments showed "shocking insensitivity to the moral concerns of the Jewish people..."[14] The spokesman of the Swiss Jewish Community, Martin Rosenfeld, who weeks later told me how isolated and alone the community felt, was compelled to comment that "the Jewish community feels deeply hurt and finds the remarks are an insult to the victims of the Holocaust."[15] Even the Israeli Foreign Ministry formally expressed "regret" about his statements.

Without any thought, and only a few words, Delamuraz did more damage to his country's effort to stem the tide of adverse public opinion than anything we had yet been able to throw at them. In an instant, he managed to characterized Jews and their allies as blackmailers and extortionists, bringing along all the canards of past accusations, including those of the Nazis. His comments reeked of an anti-Semitism reminiscent of a not too distant past. For anyone who doubted our claims that the Swiss were hiding something, their doubts were swept away.

The Swiss government only made matters worse the next day when a spokesman, Yves Seydoux, declared that "the statements of Mr. Delamuraz clearly reflected the view of the Cabinet. He merely expressed in stronger terms what has already been said." The new Swiss President, Arnold Koller was also said to have backed Delamuraz's remarks and indicated that he would resist the creation of an interim fund as well.[16] With government backing, Delamuraz stood his ground. Within a short time, he apologized for any hurt his remarks might have caused, but maintained there would be no interim fund until the results of the Volcker Commission were available.

The State Department reacted with surprise at Delamuraz's remarks including those which accused the U.S. as being behind a move to destabilize Switzerland's banking system. State Department Spokesman Nicholas Burns commented, "frankly to make a charge that somehow an agency of the United States government is attempting to destabilize the Swiss banking system, or is blackmailing the Swiss government, is ludicrous."[17]

Sensing that the Swiss were not about to budge, Israel Singer of the WJC along with Jewish Agency Chairman Avraham Burg, declared that normal discussions with the Swiss would be impossible as long as the

Swiss government continued to refuse to denounce Delamuraz and his remarks. Until this was done, his remarks would be viewed as official policy. More importantly, Singer and Burg declared, unless the Swiss government acted, a boycott would be called over all Swiss business worldwide. They would give the Swiss several weeks to make up their minds. Swiss banks rejected the call, yet George Kreyer, admitted on Swiss radio, the losses could be considerable."[18]

Calls for a boycott had their intended effect within the Swiss political system, albeit through a sympathetic party. The Social Democrats, part of the ruling coalition, joined the WJC's call for the Cabinet to denounce Delamuraz, and days later even demanded Delamuraz's resignation. The party expressed fears that the views, expressed by Delamuraz showed Switzerland in an even worse light and asked that the Cabinet distance itself from the former President's remarks. The Social Democrats, while complaining about the effect of the remarks, could not have been ignorant of their widespread support among the Swiss people.

On January 6, the Federal Council held another meeting to discuss the remarks. Again, Delamuraz "deplored his remarks and the misunderstandings and bad feelings it created."[19] Yet, this time, perhaps reflecting some fear of the calls for boycotts, the Council statement included a willingness to pay damages, should any wrongdoing be found in any of the various investigations going on. The Council confirmed,

> Should substantiated facts be found which require immediate action, even while the investigation process is under way, the Federal Council will immediately take the necessary steps. This also applies to different demands regarding damage payments which have recently become ever more vocal.[20]

For Burg and Singer, these words rang hollow. They felt the Swiss were, in Burg's words, "trying to buy them off with money that was not theirs," a reference to the offer to donate the $31.9 million to charity. For the new President, Arnold Koller, this was all that was to be offered. Furthermore, Koller categorically refused to apologize for the remarks. "A further distancing is not being discussed," Koller stated on Swiss television.

Inaccurate Information

On January 14, Delamuraz put his apology on paper to Edgar Bronfman. "I am very sorry that I offended your feelings as well as those of many other people concerned," wrote Delamuraz, "particularly those of the Jewish community at large. I assure you this was not my intention. The information on which I had based my statement regarding the fund was inaccurate."[21] With this short note, Delamuraz defused an ominous threat to his country. In response, Bronfman, without any more chance for an official Swiss government apology, promptly wrote back to Delamuraz, "I look forward to return to constructive work together with the Swiss authorities and the Swiss banks…"[22]

Thus, with the exchange of simple apologies, the threat of a boycott, which the Swiss and even D'Amato and the Foreign Minister of Israel did not support, evaporated and the "constructive work" Bronfman sought would return. Yet, the confusing line in Delamuraz's note to Bronfman conveyed a curious question. Was he misinformed? Was Delamuraz fed the wrong information?

The source of Delamuraz's facts came in a memo from Thomas Borer to only four of his closest confidants on his Foreign Ministry Task Force. Somehow, the memo was given to the entire Federal Council. Borer wrote the memo after a meeting he requested with Bronfman in New York, on December 9, before testifying before the House Banking Committee. The meeting according to Elan Steinberg was congenial and this view was agreed upon by others who attended. Yet, according to Borer's memo, dire action was threatened by the WJC if the interim fund was not set up by the Swiss and done so quickly. The WJC was said to have warned Borer's colleagues of boycotts, protests, and other threatening actions if concrete actions by the Swiss were not forthcoming.[23] Steinberg denied Borer's allegation. The cable, now in the hands of unintended recipients, made its way to Delamuraz, who now feared the worst. The suggestion of an interim fund, with a price tag of $250 million was suggested, according to published reports, by Borer himself, although he steadfastly denied it.[24] According to Greville Janner, during his meetings with the Swiss in November, no number was mentioned only the idea of the fund.[25] According to Elan Steinberg, a Swiss diplomat, although not necessarily Borer, was the source.[26] Either way, Delamuraz now understood that threats were made against his country, and that exorbitant amounts of money were being demanded in return for calling a stop to them. This lethal mix resulted in his outburst.

A more interesting question, however, is how the document got to the former President, when it was only intended for Borer's aides on the Task Force. As Carlo Jagmetti would soon learn, Borer's leaked cable would not be the only confidential communication to make its way into the wrong hands. For Jagmetti, however, the damage would be much worse, and impossible for the Swiss to contain.

Twenty-Six of Five Hundred

While the intrigue of leaked documents and mixed signals filled the news, the Swiss banks received another jolt, although it only confirmed what many had long thought. In a press conference at the airport in Zurich, on January 29, Paul Volcker confirmed that his auditors, although in a preliminary fashion had discovered that the Swiss banks had not been totally truthful with Swiss government investigators during the 1962 search. According to Volcker, only twenty-six of 500 banks responded to the search. "That raises questions as to how diligent everybody was in responding, and how much follow-up there was by whoever authorized the investigation in the first place,"[27] said Volcker.

This revelation only added to the problems the Swiss banks and Switzerland were facing. Now, the one investigative committee in which the Swiss placed so much hope, was now criticizing their past performance. In further questioning, Volcker promised a thorough search through the banks, one which would go "beyond 26 banks."[28] In light of this, Volcker received permission from the Swiss Federal Banking Commission to treat his auditors' searches as binding under Swiss banking law. Now, his auditors would, in the words of Kurt Hauri and Daniel Zuberbüler, Chairman and Director of the Banking Commission, "have full and unfettered access to all relevant files in the banks including customer files protected by bank secrecy legislation."[29]

Volcker also took the important step of creating a separate study of Jewish wealth in Europe before the war. In February, he announced the Commission was hiring Helen Junz, a former IMF, OECD, and Federal Reserve economist to write a study of the extent of Jewish wealth so that the Commission might have a better idea of what kind of wealth and how much they might find in the banks. Junz, began her study by examining the situation in Holland, Belgium, and France, and will move on to Eastern Europe, examining the situation in Poland, the former Czechoslovakia, and Hungary.[30]

D'Amato's Numbers are Inflated

Sing a song of golden bars,
Pockets bulging wide—
Little Bo Peep is much concerned
Her innocence may slide.

With years of practiced arrogance,
Nourished well by greed,
Little Bo Peep is losing some sleep—
For abetting a very dark deed.
　　　　　　　　　—Richard Hoyt [31]

The total value of gold shipped from Switzerland to banks in Spain and Portugal, between May 1943 and February 1944, stated the informant to his OSS interviewers, was estimated between 1,000,000,000 and 2,000,000,000 Swiss francs. The investigation of these gold transfers, codenamed "Operation Laura," found 280 truckloads were sent during these critical ten months across the French frontier into Spain and Portugal, all arriving with little trouble. In today's figures, this gold would be worth $2.5 to $5 billion.

At first glance, this document appeared like many of the thousands of documents on the gold trade found during the course of our research. With amounts of money staggering in any context, this remarkable document turned out to be nearly as damaging to Switzerland's denials of misdeeds as anything else we had found previously about Swiss actions during or after the war, perhaps with the exception of the Swiss-Polish treaty.

Formally classified as "Top Secret" by the OSS, and specifically directed to Director "Wild" Bill Donovan himself, this January 12, 1946 document detailed the transfer of vast sums of gold, in the middle of the war, not from Germany to Switzerland, but from Switzerland to Spain and Portugal, on Germany's behalf. For the first time, we had found evidence that Switzerland not only accepted gold looted by the Nazis, but in fact, laundered it for them as well.[32] Historically, it is interesting that January 12 was chosen as the day to release the document, fifty-one years, to the day after it was written. It was symbolic in that like all of the details from this investigation, they had unfortunately been released fifty years too late.

What was critical for the Swiss in this disclosure was that the facts were laid out quite neatly and were undeniable. We had more documents about these shipments and they fully supported the original. It was clear from the information we found about these shipments, this time, the Swiss National Bank, agent for the Germans in these transfers, had been cornered. Yet, we could not have judged how stupid they would be in answering the charge D'Amato made.

"D'Amato's numbers are inflated," asserted Swiss National Bank Vice President, Jean Pierre Roth. "We shipped only 70 truckloads."[33]
"It concerns gold bought by Switzerland from Germany and resold to

Portugal," stated Gabriel Juri, a Swiss National Bank spokesman, "If one omits the moral aspect, its' about a technical exchange: a purchase and a transport."[34]

If anything confirmed to us that they had no idea what was happening to them and that their credibility was evaporating by the second, it was this response. They just did not get it. They looked foolish. Had they been smart they would have denied the charge and attacked D'Amato. Instead, they admitted to accepting gold from the Nazis and then shipping it into other countries for them. For the editorial writers and average reader anywhere in the world, it made no difference whether it was seventy truckloads or 280. "It undermines," wrote the *Guardian* reporter Ed Vulliamy, " Swiss pleas that the country is being 'blackmailed' and that its own banking inquiry is adequate to the task of locating the Nazi gold."[35] Vulliamy was right. Coming on the heels of Delamuraz's remarks, the Swiss were greatly embarrassed.

The same day as news of the document hit the papers, a Portuguese freight company Arnaud, acknowledged that it had participated in the shipping. "We didn't know it was Nazi gold," stated director Ricardo Fernandes. Had it been known that the gold was looted German gold, the company would have never participated in the shipments.[36]

The only Swiss defense to these charges was that they did not know that the gold was looted. While this excuse fell on deaf ears, we knew that we had to hit them again to quash this pathetic defense.

We released a document explaining the Swiss acceptance of $123 million in Belgian gold looted by the Germans. In this document, the Swiss defense, as it was in the case of Spain, was that they had no idea it was looted. While showing that the Swiss had accepted vast amounts of gold, now we had to show that they had to know it was looted.

"It was known to monetary statisticians everywhere," wrote Donald R. Heath, Director of the Office of Political Affairs of the Office of Military Government for Germany, "that at the start of the war the Germans possessed monetary gold reserves of about $70,000,000 in gold which had been spent by Germany at the latest by 1943 in her war effort." Heath as previously sated, questioned Swiss credibility on the gold issue:

> If the Swiss accepted the 100 tons of gold offered them by the Germans in 1943 which was worth $123,000,000, how can it be conceded to the Swiss that they acted in good faith? Moreover, how can the Swiss claim they acted in good faith when this gold was acquired at the time they knew that it had been refused for those very reasons by the Swedes? (Documents found in Germany by the United States military forces indicate this; in the meantime it has been established that the aforementioned gold in fact was gold looted from the Belgians.) In connec-

tion with the above facts the January 1943 declaration must have been known in part at least to the Swiss; this constitutes a strong argument in our opinion against the Swiss bona fides.[37]

Heath's questions were exactly what we wanted to ask and by releasing his memorandum from 1946, we could let his words do our talking for us. Faced with questions first posed about their behavior fifty years later, the Swiss were left without a defense. Having just been battered by the accusations against them for sending gold to Spain and Portugal for the Nazis, now CNN and the print media were reporting still another gold scandal and more Swiss denials.

In the course of these denials, UCLA historian Arthur L. Smith complained to the press that we were using the same documents that he used for his 1989 book, *Hitler's Gold*. For Smith, D'Amato's release of the 1946 Heath memo was unjust because he featured it in his book. When he used it, in the words of the Syracuse *Post Standard*, "few outside of academic circles paid attention."[38] When we released it, the imprimatur of a Senate committee went along with it. While I knew about Smith's book, I made a point of not reading it so that I could not be accused of using "his" documents.

The Belgian gold documents had their intended effect. The Swiss were confronted with clear evidence that not only did they take the gold sent to them by the Nazis, but they knew that it was stolen gold. The Belgians, now dragged into the fray, felt obliged to comment. In a Parliamentary debate, Belgian Finance Minister Philippe Maystadt, answered questions about the looted gold. The Central Bank gold was returned. When it came to the gold taken from private citizens, especially Jews he said, "so far no traces of these assets have been found in the (central bank's) capital."[39] Borer pleaded with D'Amato that the charges were old. Once again, the Swiss were challenged by a new revelation.[40]

The Lone CIA Document

Throughout the course of the document hunt, we had made several requests of the CIA for documents that we could not get. As we expected, we got nothing. We asked for Allen Dulles's papers from his time as OSS Chief in Bern during the war, we asked about individual OSS agents in Switzerland, and we asked about "Operation Laura." In August 1997, nearly eight months after we released the documents detailing the 280 truckloads of gold, we received a document, declared by

CIA Congressional Affairs to have been misfiled for fifty years, explaining the source for the information in the documents we released in January.

Johannes Bernhardt, a key Nazi economic figure in Spain during the war, was the man, who after the war, explained the rationale behind the massive gold sales to Spain. The document capsulized what the OSS came to learn about the shipments and explained that the Nazis had tried to send large sums of gold to Spain directly, but were refused due to credit difficulties with the Spanish government. They then turned to the Swiss who willingly accepted the gold, laundered it, and then sent it on, as we had disclosed, to Spain and Portugal.[41]

Once we had the CIA document, I was able to go back into the Archives and find the Bernhardt interviews which explained in great detail, how the Nazis shipped the gold to Switzerland and then laundered it.[42] Once again, we found the Swiss, like with the case of the Belgian gold, gladly accepted gold refused by another nation.

On March 6, Jean Pierre Roth and Peter Klauser of the Swiss National Bank, wrote D'Amato, confirming the existence of 126 truck transports of gold to Spain and Portugal, not seventy as they previously had claimed. They also admitted that the transports we listed appeared in their documents as well.[43]

"In addition to having to deal with the uncertianties of the present and future, the Swiss now have to deal with the past."

"Just as Mr. Jagmetti was preparing to retire after 35 years as a diplomat," wrote David Sanger of the *New York Times*, "he suddenly finds his days filled explaining what a leading Swiss official meant when he said that American Jewish groups were trying to 'blackmail' Switzerland's banks and that Washington and London were intent on 'demolishing the Swiss financial system.'"[44]

As of the date of Sanger's article, Jagmetti's days were in fact, filled with defending Delamuraz's unfortunate remarks. Soon he would have to defend his own, only for not nearly as long as Delamuraz did.

In December 1996, events had flown so fast around the Swiss government and the banks, they could hardly come up for air before they were pulled down again by events well beyond their control. On December 19, Ambassador Jagmetti sent a classified fax memorandum to Borer in Bern. In this memo, Jagmetti outlined his views of how the campaign against Switzerland was carrying on and how it should be countered.

"This is a war that must be fought and won by Switzerland on the inside and on the outside," wrote Jagmetti. "Most of the enemies" he wrote, "cannot be trusted."[45] The enemies to whom Jagmetti referred were, as explained earlier in his memo, "Jewish circles as well as senator [sic] D'Amato."[46] Yet, the real enemies were in his own Foreign Ministry.

This shocking strategy memo was private and addressed to Ambassador Borer, and as in the previous month, a document available to Borer's staff made its way to unintended recipients. Many in the embassy in Washington would later state, off the record to a Swiss reporter, that this leak was no mistake, but a deliberate conspiracy against Jagmetti.[47] This deliberate conspiracy was played out through the willing services of a prominent Swiss newspaper.

On January 26, shocked readers of the *Tages-Anzeiger* read that their Ambassador in Washington had urged war against the Jews and a United States Senator. The reactions were immediate.

D'Amato expressed anger at Jagmetti's reported comments. "These words are all too reminiscent of words we have heard before," wrote D'Amato to Jagmetti.[48] Avraham Burg, boldly proclaimed "if we are the enemies, then he truly has a war on his hands."[49] Both while decrying Jagmetti's remarks, also asked for an immediate apology from the Swiss government.[50]

Unlike Delamuraz before him, Jagmetti had a greater sense of honor and perhaps grace. It took only a day for him to realize that his position was untenable. On January 27, he resigned his post in a letter to Swiss President Arnold Koller, "In view of the situation created by violating traditional and legally protected confidentiality and without wanting to anticipate the reactions in the U.S., I no longer consider it proper to carry out my function as Ambassador in this country."[51]

The U.S. official reaction was swift. Nicholas Burns at the State Department stated that "we would have hoped that those quotes were inaccurate." Yet, the remarks betrayed a "fundamental lack of understanding of the commitment the United States government has to its own citizens and of the search for justice for people who had their human rights fundamentally violated during the Second World War."[52] Swiss Foreign Minister Cotti, although unwilling to bow to requests for a governmental denunciation of Jagmetti, nevertheless regretted that "a truly successful and conscientious diplomatic career should end in such a way only a few months before planned retirement."[53] For Edgar Bronfman, the sentiment was not as gracious. "I have never seen a country," said Bronfman, "[whose envoys] go out of [their] way to do stupid things, like ex-president Delamuraz and this Washington ambassador [sic]."[54]

Despite the recriminations, Jagmetti, of all the Swiss we dealt with, was clearly the most placid, the most respectable of representatives. Of the contact I had with him, he seemed honorable. The passages in his memo belied a calming presence. Members of the Washington diplomatic corps, Jewish and non-Jewish complimented him on his civility and apparent inoffensive manner. Yet, as I was told by a State Department official he was warned when this all began, it would not be right to let this "get personal." Seemingly he understood this sentiment when we spoke in March 1996, and he told me that "we should operate out of mutual respect." Yet, it did get personal, and by this time, the respect was gone.

Jagmetti commented felt he was misunderstood. While not denying what his memo said, Jagmetti reflected on the damage caused by the leak of his memo. "I am fully aware that because of the targeted, selective and ill-intentioned leak in Switzerland of my confidential memo," he sighed, "a slanted perception of me in the public eye has already become a reality. Correcting a wrong in these circumstances, is a task too often beyond redemption."[55]

His remarks could not be more prescient. Jagmetti had said, perhaps what most in Switzerland could not or would not come to terms with. His country had been devastated now with its second international blunder in less than one month. Instead of being viewed merely as a nation refusing to come to terms with a problematic history, Jagmetti's Switzerland was viewed as anti-Semitic and meanspirited. Yet, Jagmetti's himself was said by U.S. officials to have made the remark that Nicholas Burns's comments on D'Amato "doing the Lord's work," had "Jewish overtones to it." Had this been made public at the time, his exit from public life would have been even bumpier and perhaps even swifter.

When the Swiss government appointed Alfred Defago, the Swiss Consul General in New York, as its Ambassador in Washington, they had hoped that things would change. Defago would make things better, clean house, and work to improve Switzerland's image. One step he would take was to inform one of Borer's confidants and a close aide of Jagmetti, David Vogelsanger, that he would no longer be needed in Washington. Vogelsanger, an acerbic and caustic spokesman for the Embassy, said upon his departure from Washington for the Chargé d'Affaires post in Sofia, Bulgaria, that he was leaving "the America of

Jefferson and Lee, of Lincoln and Roosevelt.... not that of D'Amato and Bronfman and TV sound bites."[56] Over a year-and-a-half later, we would learn from Swiss sources that Vogelsanger had a role in drafting Jagmetti's offending memo.

Jagmetti's remarks that correcting the misperceptions of his country was a "task too often beyond redemption," would become ever more real in the next and perhaps most harmful scandal to hit Switzerland.

While most of the world now felt quite sure that there was something terribly wrong in Switzerland, they could not have known that the discovery of hundreds of pages from assorted record books stacked in carts in the basement of the Union Bank of Switzerland's branch in Zurich by a simple, caring night watchman would provide the final blow to a teetering Swiss claim of victimization at the hands of D'Amato and the WJC. Now, what little that had remained of their credibility, would be blown apart by the discovery of shredded materials by a simple bank guard.

Notes

1. Press Report, American Legation in Bern, Switzerland, 21 November 1945, RG 56, Records of the Department of Treasury, 66A-1039, Box 33, NARA.
2. Letter to the Editor, *Neue Zürcher Zeitung*, "Shadows of the Second World War," provided by Elaine Povich, *Newsday*.
3. Letter of Carlo Jagmetti, Swiss Ambassador to the United States, to United States Senator Alfonse M. D'Amato, 28 June 1996.
4. "Envoy concedes Swiss banks mistreated Holocaust Survivors," *New York Post*, 31 October 1996.
5. Discussion with Miriam Kleiman, 1 November 1996.
6. Telephone discussion with Elan Steinberg, 2 November 1996.
7. Letter from United States Senator Alfonse M. D'Amato to Swiss Ambassador to the United States Carlo Jagmetti, 5 November 1996.
8. "D'Amato's Swiss Hit," Embassy Row Column, *Washington Times*, 18 November 1996, p.A 14.
9. Letter from Swiss Ambassador to the United States Carlo Jagmetti to Greta Beer, 23 December 1996.
10. Matthais Bruellmann, "British Parliament Push for Speedy Gesture to Holocaust Victims," Associated Press, 18 November 1996.
11. Marcus Kabel, "Swiss to consider compensating victims of Nazis," Reuters, 20 November 1996.
12. "Senator wants immediate relief for surviving Holocaust claimants," Associated Press, 10 December 1996.
13. "D'Amato insists on gesture," *Tages Anzeiger*, 12 December 1996, translated by Brian Hufker.
14. "Swiss President Denounces Calls for Holocaust Fund," *Toronto Star*, 1 January 1997, p. A 2.
15. Clare Nullis, "Swiss Jews 'deeply hurt' by government response to compensation fund," Associated Press, 2 January 1997.

16. Ibid.
17. State Department Briefing of Nicholas Burns, Reuters, 3 January 1997.
18. Marcus Kabel, "Swiss banks reject Holocaust boycott threat," Reuters, 6 January 1997.
19. Letter from Christophe Bubb, Swiss Embassy to Gregg Rickman, 7 January 1997.
20. Statement by the Federal Council, Bern, Switzerland, 7 January 1997.
21. Letter of Jean Pascal-Delamuraz to Edgar Bronfman, 14 January 1997.
22. Letter of Edgar Bronfman to Jean-Pascal Delamuraz, 14 January 1997.
23. See Alan Cowell, "How Swiss Strategy on Holocaust Fund Unraveled," *New York Times*, 26 January 1997, p. A 6.
24. Ibid; Stuart Ain, "Blackmail Charge by Swiss Untrue," *New York Jewish Week*, 10 January 1997; Discussion between Thomas Borer with United States Senator Alfonse M. D'Amato, New York City, 12 December 1996.
25. Discussion with Greville Janner, London, 28 October 1996.
26. Telephone discussion with Elan Steinberg, 13 January 1996.
27. Transcript of the Press Conference of Paul Volcker, Zurich Airport, 31 January 1997.
28. Ibid.
29. Letter of Chairman Kurt Hauri and Director Daniel Zuberbohler, Swiss Federal Banking Commission to Paul Volcker, Chairman of the Independent Committee of Eminent Persons, 29 January 1997.
30. Discussion with Helen Junz, Washington D.C., 13 May 1997.
31. Letter from Richard Hoyt to United States Senator Alfonse M. D'Amato, 9 May 1997.
32. Top Secret Document, Untitled, from War Department, Strategic Services Unit, to Director of the OSS, 12 January 1946, RG 226, Office of Strategic Services, Washington Office, Entry 190, Box 94, NARA.
33. "Swiss banker calls D'Amato's assertion inflated," Associated Press, 13 January 1946.
34. Tani Freedman, "Swiss National Bank Admits Senator D'Amato's Nazi-Gold Charges," Paris AFP in English, 13 January 1997, *FBIS-WEU-97-008, Daily Report*.
35. Ed Vulliamy, "Portugal on Nazi gold trail," *Guardian*, 14 January 1997.
36. Tani Freedman, untitled, Agence France Presse, 13 January 1997.
37. Memorandum from Donald R. Heath, Director of the Office of Political Affairs of the Office of Military Government for Germany to Colonel D.L. Robinson, acting Director, Finance Division, Office of Military Government for Germany, 1 February 1946, RG 260, Office of Military Government for Germany, Property, Box 654, NARA.
38. "Documents Spur Search for Nazi Gold," *Post Standard* (Syracuse, New York), 24 February 1997, p. A 4.
39. "Belgium says not traced all gold stolen by Nazis," Reuters, 10 February 1997.
40. Letter of Thomas Borer to United States Senator Alfonse M. D'Amato, 30 January 1997.
41. Untitled War Department-Strategic Services document, 13 April 1946, declassified by the CIA on 13 August 1997.
42. Interviews with Johannes Bernhardt of March 12 and March 21, 1946, Central Files of the Department of State, RG 59, 1945–49, 800.515/3-2146-800.515/3-2846, Box 4202; Interviews with Johannes Bernhardt of March 27, 1946, Central Files of the Department of State, RG 59, 1945–49, 800.515/3-2945-800.515/4-1446, Box 4203; Interviews with Johannes Bernhardt of April 3 and June 7,

1946, Central Files of the Department of State, RG 59, 1945–49, 800.515/6-146-800.515/6-1946, Box 4209.

43. Letter of Jean Pierre Roth and Peter Klauser to United States Senator Alfonse M. D'Amato, 6 March 1997.

44. David Sanger, "Swiss Envoy in U.S. in Midst of a Squall," *New York Times*, 20 Januaary 1997.

45. Memorandum of a letter from Swiss Ambassador to the United States Carlo Jagmetti to Ambassador Thomas Borer, Task Force of the Swiss Foreign Ministry, 19 December 1996, as it appeared in the 27 January 1997 edition of *Tages-Anzeiger*, translated by Brian Hufker.

46. Ibid.

47. Thomas Rust, "Victim of a Conspiracy," *Tages-Anzeiger*, 28 January 1997, translated by Brian Hufker.

48. Letter of United States Senator Alfonse M. D'Amato to Swiss Ambassador to the United States Carlo Jagmetti, 27 January 1997.

49. Onna Corray, "Swiss ambassador describes crisis over Nazi dealings as 'war,'" Associated Press, 26 January 1997.

50. Letter of United States Senator Alfonse M. D'Amato to Swiss President Arnold Koller, 27 January 1997.

51. Letter of Resignation of Swiss Ambassador to the United States Carlo Jagmetti to Swiss President Arnold Koller, 27 January 1997, translation from the Swiss Embassy in a facsimile letter to United States Senator Alfonse M. D'Amato, 27 January 1997.

52. State Department Briefing by Nicholas Burns, 27 January 1997.

53. Balz Bruppacher, "Ambassador resigns amid new Nazi gold controversy," Associated Press, 27 January 1997.

54. Arthur Spiegelman, "Swiss try to smooth relations with Jews," Reuters, 27 January 1997.

55. Prepared Remarks of Ambassador Carlo Jagmetti's address to the National Press Club, 31 January 1997, p. 4.

56. "Proud Swiss Diplomat," *Washington Times*, 11 April 1997, p. A 16.

5

The Righteous and the Persecuted

"The examiner, who has a personal knowledge concerning the background of the trust as a result of his many years residence in Germany before the war, described the Gustloff Stifftung as a "fund" in which were placed the assets and titles of property taken by the Nazis from Jewish businessmen in Germany and the occupied territories."[1] This Nazi-created fund held in a Swiss bank in the 1940s was the byproduct of Nazi evil and Swiss indifference. More than fifty years later, very little had changed.

A Violation of Bank Secrecy

"The office of the district attorney number 4 for the district of Zurich (BAK IV), based on information received from the Israeli Cultural Society on 10 January 1997," wrote Peter Cossandey, District Attorney for Zurich, "has intimated [the need for] a criminal investigation of a possible violation of the 'federal resolution regarding the historical and legal examination of the fate of assets which ended up in Switzerland as a result of national socialist rule' as well as possible violation of bank secrecy."[2]

The violation Cossandey was to investigate was the shredding of holocaust-era documents by the Union Bank of Switzerland (UBS), discovered at its Zurich branch on the night of January 8, 1997 by an unassuming bank guard named Christoph Meili. At first, we thought it impossible this could have happened. We believed that the Swiss bankers were deceitful and immoral, but we did not think that they would stoop to destroying documents or at least be stupid enough to get caught doing it. We were wrong.

Immediately, after learning of the shredding, we established contact with Meili. B.J. Moravek, usually resourceful, quickly tracked down his number and Brian Hufker, a thirty-nine-year-old diligent and deeply committed Defense Department analyst and linguist detailed to our office as a Legislative Fellow, and I called Meili in Zurich on January 14. The story of Meili's discovery broke that day and was the talk of Switzerland and soon the world. When we finally reached him, he already had a good number of reporters interviewing him in his home. With Hufker translating, we learned the background of his story.

On the night of January 8, he was conducting his rounds in the basement of the bank when he came upon the shredding room. When he looked in, he saw two huge carts stacked with bank book ledgers dating back to 1875 from one of Switzerland's formally largest banks, the Eidgenossiche Bank, bought after the war by UBS. According to UBS, the material that had already been shredded, filled three large packing crates, each roughly three feet square and two feet deep, as well as two plastic garbage bags four to five feet high.[3] One of the books Meili saved contained documents relating to bankruptcy proceedings and forced property sales by Jews from the 1930–1940 period. Meili felt it was wrong, in light of all he had read regarding the banks and Jewish assets, that books like this should be shredded. He had read of D'Amato's investigation and of the WJC and he could not let these records remain in the shredding room.[4] Over the next two nights he continued to examine the books, eventually taking two back with him under his coat and storing them in his locker in the bank until he could take them home.[5]

At first, he took the books home and reviewed them with his wife Giusippina. Then he showed them to Gisela Blau, a Swiss journalist who wrote for a Swiss publication *Cash* as well as the *London Jewish Chronicle*. Fearing, in his words, "police officers that work in the banks," he decided to turn the books over to the Jewish community.[6] Before doing so, he tried to give the books to the Israeli embassy in Bern. Speaking with an unidentified embassy officer, Meili was instructed, that while he did not know exactly what Meili had, if he was interested he could mail the books in a package to the embassy. Surprised at the apparent lack of interest, Meili then turned to the Zurich Jewish Community for help.

Werner Rom, head of the Israeli Cultural Center in Zurich was much more receptive of Meili's entreaties than was the Israeli embassy. Rom saw what Meili had saved from the shredder. Rom felt the best thing for him to do was to turn the records over to the Zurich Police so that Meili would not be seen as being in continued possession of material in violation of Switzerland's bank secrecy laws. After turning the records over to the police on January 10, Rom and Meili received a surprise when Peter Cossandey announced on January 14, that not only was

UBS being investigated for violating the new law forbidding the destruction of documents, passed only one month before, but that Meili was himself under investigation for removing the documents from the bank. Meili was now in the classic "Catch 22." He had protected historically important documents the destruction of which is against Swiss law, yet he was accused of violating bank secrecy for doing so.

While the ensuing press conferences brought the world the news, it was the Swiss police that first announced the discovery of the shredding, not Meili. Only after the police department's press conference did Rom bring Meili before the press to explain his side of the story. Soon afterward, Robert Studer, President of the UBS Executive Board, appeared on Swiss television to confirm what the world already knew, namely that UBS had "regrettably" shredded documents.

UBS claimed that the bank's archivist and a UBS Vice President, Erwin Hagenmuller, was unaware of the ban on Holocaust-era documents' destruction because, in their words, his superiors failed to inform him. This flew in the face of testimony by Ambassador Borer before the House Banking Committee on December 11, 1996, that every precaution would be taken to prevent documents from being destroyed. At the time, we thought news of the law and its implications would have been extended to all in the banks.

Gertrude Erismann, a UBS spokesman, nevertheless declared quite confidently that Hagenmuller assured the bank's directors that the "bottom line is that he is 100 per cent confident that no material that he sent to be shredded related to the Holocaust."[7] Hagenmuller, however, was soon suspended pending an investigation into his role in ordering the shredding.

Ulterior Motives?

"What I currently know," answered Studer in a television interview days later, "allows me to assume that the motives Meili has stated for his actions aren't the only ones."[8] In questioning Meili's motives, Studer only made matters worse. This accusation appeared to Meili to intimate that he was an "agent provocateur," or without actually saying so, for Studer, Meili was working for the Jews. Studer's remarks reverberated throughout Switzerland. Even the Swiss paper *Blick*, a conservative daily, ran the headline, "That was low, Herr Studer."[9] Meili, now with the support of a lawyer, Marcel Bossonet, supplied by Rom and the Zurich Jewish Community, initiated a lawsuit against Studer for slander for these remarks.

Despite their admissions and assurances, once again the Swiss created a situation that its critics could not avoid. D'Amato commented, "When you think about all of the publicity this issue has had in Switzerland, it seems remarkable that they let this stuff sit around for 50 years and then start shredding this month."[10] Elan Steinberg declared the shredding to be morally obscene."[11]

D'Amato, on the day Meili exposed the shredding, wrote Ambassador Borer, demanding information as to Meili's status following the disclosure of the shredding at UBS. While Meili had reported being fired for his actions, Borer denied this in a phone conversation with D'Amato the next day. "He was only suspended," Borer told D'Amato from Bern. "I will work to make sure that he is rehired."

Almost comically, this new scandal, we commented was too good to believe. We could not imagine that one, they would shred documents; two, get caught doing it; and three, fire the one who uncovered the plot. No one, we thought, could write something better. The Swiss bankers were now caught red-handed.

During the next three weeks, we spoke by phone with Meili or his lawyer no less than nine separate times, gathering details of his growing troubles in Switzerland and the progress of the scandal there. Early on we had conveyed to Meili that Senator D'Amato wanted him to come to the United States and testify before the Banking Committee. More than willing, Meili proudly told every reporter that interviewed him, and there were many, that he was being invited to the United States to tell his story. One Swiss reporter would go too far with his reporting and at the same time infuriate D'Amato and implicate Meili in further crimes in the same story, both charges having no basis in fact.

It became obvious that we needed to keep an eye on the Swiss press, simply to have an idea what they were up to and what they were finding. With Hufker "surfing" the Internet, we did not have to wait long. On January 19, in the *Sonntags Zeitung,* he found an article warning of an impending prosecution of Meili for economic espionage, not for taking the documents from UBS, but for talking to us by phone. More surprisingly, the reporter, Barbara Ritschard, suggested that even D'Amato, contrary to what she knew to be the story, could be charged under Article 271 of the Swiss Penal Code, "Actions of a Foreign State," for talking to Meili.[12] When D'Amato heard he could be charged with economic espionage, in Switzerland, he flipped. While he knew nothing of the kind would ever happen, he was nevertheless angry that it could even be suggested.

D'Amato wrote Borer on January 22, enraged that having spoken to him by phone only a week earlier, he now read that not only could Meili be prosecuted, but that he could as well. While he knew that he could not be touched, he was concerned about the suggestion and in fact, threat communicated to us by Bossonet the day before, that the situation was worsening for Meili and that prosecution of Meili was imminent.

The next day, Daniel B. Smith, of the American Embassy in Bern, assured Ruth van Heuven of the State Department that neither D'Amato or Meili would be charged for economic espionage under Swiss law.[13] Borer confirmed the same in a letter to D'Amato on January 29. This was of no real comfort to Meili, however, because he was still under investigation for taking the records from the bank.

The Third Strike

The discovery of UBS's document shredding was the third strike against Switzerland in January alone. First Delamuraz's miscue, then Jagmetti's memo and resignation, and now the unfolding shredding scandal caused utter shock throughout Switzerland and the world.

"The uproar that followed Meili's find," wrote Bill Schiller of the *Toronto Star*," appears to have driven yet another nail into the flagging credibility of Swiss banking and government, as both institutions continue to grapple with a troubling history come back to haunt them."[14] For the *Financial Times* of London, "the mishap could not have come at a worse time."[15]

Despite the severe international fallout in Switzerland from the disclosure of the shredding, Meili was left in limbo. At the center of an international scandal, he was suspended without pay from his job. Without the security provided to him and his family by his job, he had only savings upon which to depend. Soon, though Meili received relief in the form of a $36,000 donation from the Anti-Defamation League, headed by Abe Foxman. Yet, Foxman had trouble even opening up the account at a Swiss bank to deposit the money for Meili. "We went to several banks who refused to take the account saying that they don't want this type of problem," said Foxman.[16]

Finally, six weeks after his fateful discovery, Meili received a letter from Wache AG, the Security firm which had employed and then suspended him. "Although your conduct was classified as ethical and moral in certain circles," wrote H. De Capitain and Christian Tschopp of Wache AG, "this is unjustifiable from the perspective of labor law." The firm suggested that Meili should have reported any irregularities to his superiors. Failure to have done so, in their words was "a basic breach of trust."[17]

Meili notified Hufker of the firing by phone on the same day and agreed to come to Washington to testify before the Banking Committee. Bossonet, however, now in the process of carrying out Meili's lawsuit against Studer, was less willing to allow him to speak in the U.S. or for that matter anywhere but in a courtroom trial against Studer for slander. Moravek and Hufker spoke with Bossonet several times, but with no success. D'Amato very much wanted Meili to appear before the Committee, but Bossonet blocked each attempt.

At UBS, Mathis Cabiallavetta, Chief Executive Officer of UBS, ensured reporters that there would be no more shredding. At the same time, Cabiallavetta announced that effective May 1, the Union Bank of Switzerland, known by the German-language initials of SBG (Schweizerische Banksgesellschaft) would simply be known as UBS. Clearly this was seen as an attempt to hide the word Switzerland from the title of the bank, even though it was not officially removed. Most observers saw this as a result of the heavy criticism UBS suffered from this growing scandal.

Missing from all of this flurry, was any word on Erwin Hagenmuller. As a Vice President of the Zurich branch, it was Hagenmuller that authorized the shredding. Nevertheless, while Meili was fired, Hagenmuller still had his job. He suffered no penalties for his actions, save a temporary suspension. This fact only fueled criticism of UBS's actions and to many portrayed the bank as a willing partner in the event.

Desperately Seeking Meili

By now, Christoph Meili was both a victim and a hero. He had taken on the aura of a selfless hero, who without regard for his personal well-being sacrificed himself for the greater good and exposed the evil corporate accomplices of the Nazis. The press had seized upon him and portrayed him as a tragic figure. Meili, for his part, was somewhat reticent about the matter. "It's not easy for me at the moment," he told *USA Today*, "I may be a hero in the USA, but here I'm not perceived as such."[18] Yet, now he would be sought out to tell his story.

At the end of February, Avraham Hirschson, a member of the Israeli Knesset, cabled the Speaker of the Swiss Parliament, imploring him to prevent Meili's dismissal. Hirschson, Chairman of the Knesset committee on the restoration of Jewish property, jumped into the fray. He invited him to speak before his Knesset committee as soon as possible, suggesting early March, coincidently the same time we were trying to bring him to Washington.

After hearing the news of the Hirschson invitation to Meili, we called him and told him that it would not be right for him to testify in Israel first before coming to the U.S. first, where he would get a greater reception. If Meili went to Israel first, we felt, it would be a betrayal of the support D'Amato had already shown him. Hufker tried to present this view to him diplomatically, and he agreed. He even commented that Borer, had tried to convince him that coming to the United States was the best move. Borer, however, had less than altruistic reasons for his decision. According to Meili, Borer wanted him to testify to the good works of the task force he was leading. Meili commented, "it was easy for Borer to talk, he had a job."[19]

With Meili's approval, we arranged for flights for him, his wife, and kids to fly to New York on February 26 and on to Washington to testify before the Banking Committee. We had the entire itinerary worked out. We even arranged for him to be met at the gate at JFK in New York and escorted to a waiting area for his flight to Washington later in the day. Everything proceeded just fine, until he got to New York.

Once in New York, he was greeted as we had arranged. However, his children were tired, and according to Meili, he would spend the night with friends and call us in the morning. He refused to tell us where or with whom he was staying. This, we felt, was the first sign of trouble. By the next day, it was clear that he would not be flying on to Washington. That morning he left a message on Hufker's voice mail that he was advised that it was not in his best interests now to testify owing to his ongoing slander case against Studer in Switzerland and that he would be returning to Zurich that afternoon.

Later we found the truth about his decision to return to Switzerland. Meili, insecure and overwhelmed by all that he had endured to this point, began almost immediately to regret his trip to the U.S., especially to testify before D'Amato's committee. While originally arriving at the decision to travel to the U.S. on his own, he contacted Gisela Blau, the Swiss journalist, and quite possibly even Bossonet before he left Zurich. It might have been too late for Bossonet to have stopped him once he left, nevertheless, he convinced him to call him once he got to New York. Once there, Meili did call him and Bossonet managed to talk Meili into returning immediately.

D'Amato was disappointed but felt that perhaps that this was the best outcome for the moment. If he could act so abruptly and return after just flying here, who knew what he would say before the Committee.

"Please protect me"

We had all but given up hope of having Meili testify before the Committee. Throughout March and April, we were preoccupied with other details of the inquiry and Meili had seemed already to be part of the past. As it turned out, this would not be the case.

Meili had made contact with several organizations including Boys Town Jerusalem, in New York, as well as New York attorney Edward Fagan. Rabbi Ronald Gray of Boys Town quietly brought Meili to New York in late April. They told all that it was just for a short time and that Meili and his family would be returning. Gray's story, while necessary, was only a cover for Meili who had no intention of returning to Switzerland. After the disclosure of the shredding, Meili was persona non grata in his native country. He received threats and lived, quite literally, in fear for his life.

D'Amato, while in New York, was invited to participate with Meili on a local television news shown on Friday, May 2. Impressed with his calm and quiet bearing, D'Amato was honestly taken with Meili. Immediately he invited him to come down to Washington to testify. Meili agreed.

On Tuesday, May 6, Meili, his family, and Fagan walked down the hall to the Banking Committee's hearing room in the Dirksen Building into a throng of reporters. D'Amato, carrying Meili's then two-year-old boy David, entered the packed hearing room and posed for pictures.

D'Amato opened the hearing by calling Meili a hero and his actions courageous. "Instead of being viewed as a hero," D'Amato declared, "he is being treated as a criminal. I am privileged to sit here in front a good and decent man."[20]

Meili was unassuming. "I was convinced that the documents were being destroyed illegally," testified Meili through an interpreter. "I wished to prevent the Swiss people from suffering harm," continued Meili, "and to make the documents and actions known to the public. I also wanted the oppressed Jewish population—the Holocaust victims— to not again be left behind in their search for documentation at the Swiss banks and to get justice."[21]

Meili was careful throughout his testimony. Never did he slip or appear confused at the questions he faced. Senators Dodd, Boxer, and

Bryan, were exceedingly respectful toward him and harshly critical of UBS, both for shredding and for having him dismissed. While D'Amato had finally succeeded in getting Meili before the Committee, he could not have imagined what he would hear from Meili at the conclusion of the hearing.

When D'Amato asked Meili what made him think the records he saved were important, Meili responded, "a few months before, I had seen the movie 'Schindler's List.' And that's how, when I saw these documents, I realized I must take responsibility; I must do something."[22] When D'Amato asked Meili, as well as Israel Singer if they had any further remarks to make before the hearing concluded, Meili responded,

> Please protect me in the U.S.A. and in Switzerland. I think I become [sic] a great problem in Switzerland. I have a woman, two little children, and no future. I must see what goes on in the next days for me. Please protect me. That is all.[23]

Never before had I seen D'Amato so taken by a witness' testimony before him. He was truly touched and vowed right there to work to fulfill Meili's request.

The next day, the papers in New York were filled with stories of Meili's "pleas" before the Committee, that he was "inspired to act" and of the threats he had received. Christoph Meili was now, in the words of the *Guardian*, a "flesh-and-blood hero."[24] We even received offers from constituents in New York to provide help for a man whom they termed a "true hero."

There was a lot of truth behind Meili's fears. He faced death threats to himself and his children. "Meili, you bastard," read one delivered directly to his home in Zurich, "the secret numbered account won't do you any good. You are a sonofabitch, a traitor to your country. It will cost you your life. Your children are in danger. We will kidnap them and make sure that you have to pay the ransom with your Jew money. We'll finish you off."[25]

Meili's family too, was bothered by their son's actions. "My mother doesn't understand the situation," Meili told the *New York Jewish Week*. "My father understands. He did not like what I did. He makes bad words, saying that Jewish people only want money. He's a typical Swiss businessman."[26]

A Man Without a Country

"I now ask you to end your harassment of Mr. Meili. You do both your office, Mr. Meili and the citizens of Switzerland a great injustice in continuing your present course of action," wrote D'Amato to Peter Cossandey, the Zurich District Attorney, on May 12. D'Amato was now determined to act on Meili's plea during his testimony before the Committee. In writing Cossandey, he expressed his anger at the treatment of Meili, his unresolved status and the lack of investigation of the UBS executive that ordered the shredding.

In carrying out this strategy, we felt one clear way to allow the Meilis to stay in the United States was to get them permanent residency in a Private Relief bill. The one drawback was that Private Relief bills historically can take years to pass. D'Amato agreed to this choice and on May 14, filed legislation to do just that. D'Amato wanted and got bipartisan support for the bill. On May 20, the Senate Judiciary Committee's Immigration subcommittee held a hearing in which Meili and D'Amato both testified. The subcommittee, sensitive to Meili's plight and D'Amato's commitment to see the bill through to passage, voted the bill out of the subcommittee the same day and sent it to the full Senate for consideration. Three days later, with intense lobbying by D'Amato, the Senate passed the bill without opposition, in what some said was record time for such legislation.[27]

While the House had to pass the bill, Congressman James Sensenbrenner (R-WI) was in no rush to see the legislation pass. Sensenbrenner objected to the bill being considered on the floor immediately after it passed the Senate, going down there himself to block it. Meili had to wait three more weeks. Seemingly trivial, the three weeks mattered greatly to him, in that he had no funds of his own upon which to live. He depended on the goodwill of those in the Jewish community to sustain him and his family. Because he did not yet have permanent residency status, he could not work in this country. He was stranded and he told this much to D'Amato on several occasions.

D'Amato, not about to give up the fight, carried on the campaign to the House, where he met with Speaker Newt Gingrich on June 4, seeking his support. "a thick veil of Swiss bank secrecy has covered this entire affair for too long," stated Gingrich. "The heroic efforts of this young man deserve commendation, not prosecution, and I will do everything in my power to ensure that this legislation is quickly brought to the House floor and approved."[28]

D'Amato's sense of urgency was based not only on Meili's financial situation, but also continued threats by Swiss prosecutor Cossandey to prosecute Meili in Switzerland, regardless of the political uproar swirling about. D'Amato feared that Meili, who under U.S. law could only stay in the U.S. for ninety days, was running out of time. The longer Sensenbrenner stalled the bill, the closer the deadline got and the more nervous Meili became.

The Swiss for their part were disbelieving. Borer could not believe Meili's claims saying, perhaps "he likes the media interest." Borer even made light of Meili's complaints: "He takes himself a little bit too important. Death threats and kidnaping, give me a break."[29] Cotti complained that the treatment Meili received both in Congress and in the press was grossly out of proportion to the threat he, in Cotti's estimation, really faced in Switzerland. "In this way," snapped Cotti, "the grotesque impression was created that Switzerland is a country in which human rights and basic freedoms aren't respected."[30]

Sanctuary, Notoriety, and Vindication

On July 15, the House passed the "Meili" bill without dissent. Two weeks later, President Clinton signed the bill into law, making Meili, his wife Giussippina, his children Mirijam and David, permanent residents of the United States. Finally, after six months of worry, threats, and intimidation by the Swiss authorities, Christoph Meili had obtained sanctuary. He now had a place to live, work and provide for his family. He no longer faced the fear of being forced back to Switzerland. All that he had to deal with now was a new status; a celebrity status.

Meili soon went onto the speakers circuit. He was speaking and honored in synagogues from Chicago to Boca Raton. He was now viewed as a "Righteous Gentile," held up with the likes of Oskar Schindler, the man about whose film portrayal enticed him to act. He received a great deal of mail, even some sent to him through our office. Churches, synagogues, and universities called to invite him for speeches, all wanting to hear his story and to convey their thanks for his courageous act.

Meili, a quiet man, just trying to make his way in the world, stumbled onto something he had not expected and became a kind of folk hero. Despite the failure of the Swiss government or UBS to provide him an official apology, he did receive an unofficial one from Manuel Sager, Deputy Consul General in New York. According to Meili's version of the story, as told to Brian Hufker, he was approached by Sager in New York City, shortly before the President signed his relief bill into law, telling him that "he was sorry for what had happened."

However much Sager sympathized with Meili's plight, it mattered little to the executives at UBS who stubbornly maintained their insistence that whatever Meili had found was irrelevant and unimportant for the historical record. They continued to hold this view until Swiss historians testified to the contrary two days after the President signed his bill. On July 17, Linus von Castelmur, speaking for the Independent Commission of Historians, established on December 13, 1996 in the law passed by the Swiss Parliament, asserted that "we are talking here about documents, some of which are crucial to the investigation."[31]

While this decision vindicated Meili, it did not however, restore his reputation in Switzerland, nor did it end the threat of prosecution by the Swiss authorities. Meili expressed satisfaction over the announcement, yet he still felt betrayed.

> UBS hurt my life and my family. UBS drove me from my country. UBS turned my country against me. UBS turned my friends against me. UBS made my family afraid. UBS destroyed my name. UBS hurt my future. Why?[32]

Despite Sager's off-the-record apology, Meili sought a genuine one and would enlist D'Amato's help. Meili, his wife, and Fagan, again came to Washington on July 30 for a press conference with D'Amato. Before the press, D'Amato announced that he was tired of the way Meili had been treated. After all he had been put through, after the threats, the harassment, and finally vindication by Swiss historians, Meili still could not obtain the one thing he wanted most, an apology. For D'Amato, the matter was clear. If UBS refused to apologize, perhaps legislative action to restrict UBS's business in the United States would make them understand.

In a letter to Swiss President Arnold Koller, D'Amato threatened UBS with series of legislative and legal measures, ranging from requests to the Justice and State Departments to determine whether UBS violated the terms of the 1946 and 1952 Washington Accords, to a review of UBS's behavior to determine whether the bank should be banned from or limited in doing business in the U.S.[33] In response to D'Amato's threats, UBS issued a simple response, saying there would be no need for D'Amato to carry out these threats because the issues revolving around Meili's find would be resolved "in a fair and just manner."[34]

Two days after the D'Amato-Meili press conference, citing a clear separation of powers in Switzerland, Koller responded that no apology would be forthcoming. Borer, echoed these sentiments in a letter to D'Amato dated September 9. "We cannot interfere with the normal course of justice," Borer wrote. "You seem to be unaware of the fact that the

Swiss widely share the US [sic] public sentiment on the merits of Mr. Meili's conduct. Your assertion according to which Mr. Meili has been labeled a traitor and was chased from his country is groundless and preposterous." For Borer, the entire matter came down to his belief that the Meilis were becoming targets, not of death threats, but "an over-blown media exposure that appear [sic] to be a self-serving campaign for their alleged benefactors."[35] What Borer's letter did not convey was the contents of a telephone conversation with D'Amato, the day before. Despite claims to the separation of powers in Switzerland, Borer claimed to have had "a few friends talk to Cossandey," and Meili, Borer ensured D'Amato, would not be prosecuted. While this was good news, Meili would have to wait until October until receiving it officially.

Safe and secure in the United States, vindicated and nearly exonerated, Meili now traveled to Israel where he visited Boystown Jerusalem and was greeted like a conquering hero. Some five hundred people greeted the shy bank guard who had once worked on a kibbutz there. Meili, quite overcome by his reception, was carried atop the shoulders of students in Jerusalem and honored for his efforts.

Mysterious Fires

UBS's attempt at record destruction was not an isolated event. Documents were being destroyed all over, not only in Switzerland, but in the United States as well. On March 20, South Brunswick, New Jersey saw a three-story warehouse belonging to the Iron Mountain Records Management Company burn to the ground. This fire, the third in two weeks at the facility, engulfed some 800,000 boxes of records, including some belonging to U.S. branches of Swiss banks in the United States. Previous fires in other buildings at the same site destroyed over 1,200,000 additional boxes of records.

On May 5, over 800,000 more boxes burned at a Diversified Records Management facility in West Pittston, Pennsylvania. State Police Sgt. Al Della Fave commented, "they found some similarities between the fire last week and the one in South Brunswick."[36]

Iron Mountain said they had never had a fire in any of their twenty facilities since the company's creation in 1951. Yet, there were worries, still unresolved, that the fires, seemingly intentional, were planned to destroy important financial records, other than those of the Swiss banks, stored in the facilities. Rewards were offered and the FBI was forwarded information allowing them to profile a potential arsonist.

According to the South Brunswick Police Department, the fires there clearly were arson, and as far as they were concerned, so was the one in South Pittston. Still unresolved, however, is the interesting notion that the fires in New Jersey occurred just three weeks after the New York State Banking Department's request to the American branches of the Swiss banks that all their records in storage be put under the control of their auditors. Whether the fires were aimed at the Swiss banks' records or not, they raise the specter of further acts by the banks to destroy records to bury their sordid past.

It should be mentioned, however, that suspicious fires also took place involving bank records in a warehouse in Normandy, France in 1997 and in 1996 at the Paris headquarters of Credit Lyonnais, itself a party to a lawsuit filed in New York in December 1997.[37] Additionally, in 1991, the Dutch Finance Ministry deliberately destroyed entire archives detailing the liquidation of Jewish companies by the Nazis.[38] In this sense then, the Swiss by no means were alone, yet the question of the persistent destruction of documents is an important one that must be answered.

During the course of the inquiry, information also came to light that the banks might have shredded large amounts of documents, intentionally or otherwise earlier, perhaps before 1996. These suggestions remain open, awaiting further investigation.

"Lex Meili"

Swiss academics complained on September 9, that the treatment of Meili was not only wrong but was counterproductive to those with information to provide. "The long-running persecution by the Zurich judiciary," stated the Democratic Swiss Jurists in a statement, "has not only punished Christoph Meili for his courage, but it has also sent signals to other witnesses…that they may meet the same fate if they release their knowledge publicly."[39] If other cases were to arise like this, the jurists announced, they would provide free legal advise.

With the fallout from Meili's actions, Swiss legislators felt compelled to close the loophole that existed in Swiss law that made shredding of historically important bank documents illegal, yet the disclosure of the same documents, illegal as well. On September 24, the National Council decided that those who came forth with information as did Meili, could not be charged with civil or penal charges for breaking the sacred laws of bank secrecy. Nicknamed the "lex Meili," it would be of no value to Meili, for it would be prospective and not retroactive.

While the Swiss parliament took the necessary moves to absolve any future Christoph Meilis, the Zurich prosecutor, Peter Cossandey, made official what Borer had told D'Amato three weeks before, but with a twist. On October 1, Cossandey announced, and rather proudly, that further investigation of Meili was not necessary, and for that matter an investigation of Erwin Hagenmuller was also being dropped. To make matters worse, the timing of the announcement was not lost on a great number of observers, in that Cossandey's press conference would be held in Zurich on Yom Kippur, the holiest day of the Jewish calendar. In this way, criticism would be blunted. Nevertheless, Caroline Heimo, a spokeswoman for the Swiss Embassy in Washington lauded the decision, saying "we welcome the withdrawal of this burden placed on the Meili family and expect that this decision will have a positive effect on our work."[40]

Just as Meili had feared, the connection between the banks and the Swiss government was too much to overcome. While now free to live without the fear of death threats and prosecution, Meili had nevertheless become a victim. He sought to do as his conscience had guided him, yet he was, Borer's denials to the contrary, chased from the land of his birth, the land where his larger family remained, and forced to seek the help of the American political system. Never before had the world heard of a Swiss citizen seeking political protection like Meili was forced to do.

In the end, Meili was immensely grateful. All he wanted to do was help a people with whom he sympathized but he was up against forces far greater than him. "The greatest thing what you did to us, was that you believed us from the very beginning," wrote Meili to D'Amato when the story was over. "You never questioned if we are real or not, you just believed [sic]."

In one respect, Cotti's interpretation of Meili's treatment was actually right, Meili's case was unique. It did give a warped, although well-earned and deserved impression of Switzerland. Before this campaign began, a case like Meili's would indeed never have happened. Yet, now with Switzerland under the microscope, watched for its every move in reaction to the barrage of revelations, cases of a magnitude like this now were not surprising.

When Cossandey dropped the case against Meili, the fact that he dropped the one against Hagenmuller, as well, caused an uproar. Swiss historians even protested the dismissal, yet the protests had no effect.

There was some chance for a payback for Meili if the $2.65 billion lawsuit filed on his behalf by Ed Fagan in Federal Court in January 1998 against UBS had been allowed to proceed. If he won, he said he would have donated much of the award to the Swiss people, who he said were as much a victim of the banks as he was. Yet, Meili, just as he had sacrificed his security and that of his family that January night in Zurich, did so again in August 1998. As part of the settlement with the Swiss banks, Meili agreed to drop his lawsuit. Once again, he let his conscience guide him. Once again, he did something selfless.

* * *

The damage though had already been done. Meili's disclosures added to the misstatements of Jean-Pascal Delamuraz and Carlo Jagmetti and were the final blows against the Swiss defense of their innocence. Never would that country be the same. Never would the world look at them and think innocent thoughts of Heidi and Swiss chocolates. Now, the world would view Switzerland as a nation of evil, greedy, and anti-Semitic bankers. The Swiss, by now also knew the damage they caused and clearly understood that they had to begin to change this view. As has been said, reputation is hard to achieve; it takes years to form and can be shattered in a moment. Faced with no choice, the attempt at mending that reputation was about to begin for Switzerland, its people, and its now utterly dishonored banks.

Notes

1. "Interim Report on Johann Wehrli & Co., Zurich," p. 2, RG 407, Records of the Adjutant General's Office, War Department, Entry 368, Box 1033, NARA.
2. "Announcement to the Media regarding 'regrettable mistake at the Union Bank of Switzerland," Peter Cossandey, District Attorney, Zurich, 14 January 1997, translated by Brian Hufker.
3. Edmund L. Andrews, "Bank Says Shredded Papers May Not Have Involved Nazis," *New York Times*, 16 January 1997.
4. Telephone Conversation with Christoph Meili, 14 January 1997.
5. Conversation with Christoph Meili, Washington, D.C., 1 August 1997.
6. Telephone Conversation with Christoph Meili, 14 January 1997.
7. Christopher Francescani, "Fury over new twist in Swiss scandal," *New York Post*, 15 January 1997.
8. Quoted in Alexander G. Higgins, "Whistleblower's lawyer demands explanation from bank chief," Associated Press, 19 January 1997.
9. "UBS Head Asked to Explain Remark Over Watchman," *Wall Street Journal Europe*, 21 January 1997.
10. David Sanger, "Swiss Bank 'Regrets' Destroying Documents of World War II Era," *New York Times*, 15 January 1997, p. 1 A.

11. Francescani, "Fury over new twist in Swiss scandal."
12. Barbara Ritschard, "Telephone Conversation with Consequences," *Sonntags Zeitung*, 19 January 1997, translated by Brian Hufker.
13. Memorandum to Ruth van Heuven and Mark Fry from Daniel B. Smith, American Embassy in Bern, 23 January 1997.
14. Bill Schiller, "Meili's find rocks secretive banks," *Toronto Star*, 2 February 1997, p. F 6.
15. William Hall, "UBS mishap leaves image in shreds," *Financial Times*, 11 February 1997.
16. Telephone discussion with Jess Hordes, Washington Director of the Anti-Defamanation League, 30 January 1997; "Swiss Bankers Shut the Door on ADL," *Forward*, 24 January 1997, p. 4.
17. Letter of Termination of Employment to Christopher Meili from Wache AG, 18 February 1997, translated by Brian Hufker.
18. "Swiss Hailed," *USA Today*, 25 February 1997.
19. Telephone conversation with Christoph Meili, 22 February 1997.
20. Testimony of Christoph Meili before the Senate Committee on Banking, Housing, and Urban Affairs, 105th Congress, 1st Session, 6 May 1997, p. 4.
21. Ibid.
22. Ibid, p. 14.
23. Ibid, p. 16.
24. Alex Duval Smith, "Guard who Found Hitler's Gold," *Guardian*, 14 May 1997.
25. Death threat received by Christoph Meili, 2 April 1997, translated by Brian Hufker.
26. Stuart Ain, "Hard Times for a 'Hero," *New York Jewish Week*, 9 May 1997, p. 17.
27. "Recent Private Relief Bills, Unusual for Today," *St. Louis Post Dispatch*, 20 July 1997.
28. Press Release of Speaker Newt Gingrich, 4 June 1997.
29. Stuart Ain, "Swiss Envoy: Meili Exaggerating," *Long Island Jewish Week*, 23 May 1997, p. 8.
30. "Swiss official says U.S. view of whistelblower is 'grotesque,'" Associated Press, 9 June 1997.
31. Georges Wuthrich and Patricia Diermier, "Meili's Documents are Historically Important After All," *Blick*, 17 July 1997, translated by Brian Hufker.
32. Statement of Christoph Meili, New York City press conference, 29 July 1997.
33. Letter of United States Senator Alfonse M. D'Amato to Swiss President Arnold Koller, 30 July 1997.
34. David Sanger, "D'Amato Threatens Action Against Swiss Bank in Shredding Case," *New York Times*, 31 July 1997.
35. Letter of Ambassador Thomas Borer to United States Senator Alfonse M. D'Amato, 9 September 1997.
36. Sue Epstein and Tom Haydon, "Arson authorities look to Pennsy for clues, West Pittston warehouse blaze resembles fire that gutted South Brunswick storage facility," *Newark Star Ledger*, 11 May 1997.
37. Lee Yanowitch, "Report: French banks dumped Jewish-owned stocks during the war," Jewish Telegraph Agency, 22 January 1998.
38. Elise Friedman, "Holland destroyed records listing stolen Jewish assets," Jewish Telegraph Agency, 21 January 1998.
39. "Swiss academics defend watchman who rescued Holocaust documents," Associated Press, 9 September 1997.
40. "Meili Case Dropped, Embassy of Switzerland Welcomes Decision," Press Release of the Embassy of Switzerland, 1 October 1997.

Estelle Sapir (center), Senator Alfonse M. D'Amato (right), Jeanette Bernstein, Sapir's niece (left).   Courtesy of the office of Senator Alfonse M. D'Amato

Senator Alfonse M. D'Amato testifying before the House Banking Committee hearing on the Swiss banks, December 11, 1996. Behind D'Amato to the left are former Ambassador Carlo Jagmetti and Ambassador Thomas Borer; to D'Amato's right are Michael D. Hausfeld, claimant Alice Fisher, and claimant Gizella Weisshaus.

Courtesy of the Office of Senator Alfonse M. D'Amato

In the cellar of the Race Institute in Frankfurt, Chaplain Samuel Blinder examines captured Torah scrolls.   Courtesy of the National Archives and Records Administration

American soldier of the 86th Division inspects German loot stored in a church at Ellingen, Germany, April 24, 1945.   Courtesy National Archives and Records Administration

Caps and teeth in dentures found at Buchenwald by U.S. First Army, May 5, 1945.

Merckers Mine, Germany, 90th Division, Third Army, April 15, 1945.

Elan Steinberg, Executive Director, World Jewish Congress.

Courtesy of the *Jewish Week*

Stuart Eizenstat, Under Secretary of State for Economic, Business, and Agricultural Affairs.

Courtesy of the United States Department of State

Christoph Meili, Giussippina Meili, and Ed Fagan, Washington, D.C.

Courtesy of the Office of Senator Alfonse M. D'Amato

Israel Singer, Secretary General, World
Jewish Congress.

Ambassador Thomas Borer.

Courtesy of the *Jewish Week*

Courtesy of the Swiss Embassy, Washington, D.C.

Lord Greville Janner.

Courtesy of the Holocaust
Educational Trust, London, U.K.

6

Writing the Check

"There was a line of about 60 people waiting with cash, jewelry, old pictures, securities and other valuables," wrote C.E. Freyvogel in August 1937 on his tour of the Societe De Banque Suisse, in Basel. "It would appear" he continued, "this is going on all along and the Swiss Bank has reached the point where they do not know how they can continue to handle French customers, owing to the physical shortage of space for safe custody. Whereas before it was the big fellows who ran across the frontier, today it is the small people who export their capital."[1] Sixty years later, the heirs of these unfortunate people would begin to see justice, but it certainly would not be easy. After a disasterous beginning for Switzerland in the new year, a lot would have to happen before justice would begin to be served.

By now, there were few who actually believed the Swiss banks and the Swiss government were innocent of the charges made against them. What had become painfully clear was that finally after fifty years, something was going to be done to establish justice for the survivors and heirs of the Holocaust.

"It is going to cost us"

The late Franz Leuteneger, who had previously served as head of the Swiss National Bank, and a well-respected member of the Swiss banking community was said to have urged settling now, rather than later. "Let's get it over," he was said to have commented.[2] Yet, getting over it would not be that easy and would prove to be quite an unpopular idea to sell in Switzerland.

The December 16, 1996 issue of *U.S. News & World Report*, featured a small story in its "Washington Whispers" column illustrating how difficult it would be to fulfill Leuteneger's recommendations. Entitled "Not So Fast," the report detailed concern by the Swiss government and Swiss financial officials, according to Norwegian sources, who expressed to Norway that it should not act too hastily in providing compensation to 1,600 Norwegian Jews whose possessions were confiscated during the war by the Quisling regime. Norwegian officials were urged by their Swiss counterparts to proceed with "restraint."[3]

The Swiss bankers, while not in lock step with Leuteneger, first cracked on January 7, 1997, following the Delamuraz affair, when Swiss Radio International announced that the Swiss government was ready to enter into immediate talks with world Jewish groups and the Swiss banks to create a compensation fund.[4] The fund, though, would be based on the original sum of money said to be found in the search through the banks in 1995 and amounted to slightly more than $31 million.

D'Amato, responding to questions about the announcement on CNN, scoffed at the Swiss offer:

> The $31 million that they're talking about is nothing new. These are moneys which the Swiss banks admitted do not belong to them, and this does not take into consideration the hundreds of millions of dollars we believe are unaccounted for.... It is absolutely insufficient.[5]

Despite the criticism from D'Amato, and Avraham Burg as well, the Swiss Bankers Association spokeswoman Silvia Matile told reporters on January 8, "we are open to discussions with the Federal government and will examine any proposals they put forward and see what we can do."[6] The next day, Borer, also commenting to the press, obliquely referred to the idea that the Swiss government would add to the fund in a "gesture of goodwill," yet continued to deny rumors circulating that he had been the one that had offered the sum of $250 million for an interim fund for survivors.

Political Realities

On the same day as the Borer offer of a "gesture of goodwill," Swiss Jewish Community leader Rolf Bloch met with Cotti and proposed the Swiss government repay, with interest, the money, totaling some $55 million collected from the international Jewish community to support Jewish refugees afforded haven in Switzerland during the war. Bloch was trying to bridge the gap between the requests for payment by Janner, Bronfman, and D'Amato, and the refusals of the Swiss government and banks to consider anything that resembled or was termed "compensation." If it was compensation, this implied guilt or complicity and this was out of the question. Bloch interceded because as the leader of a small Jewish community of 18,000 people, he was in no place to play stubborn or difficult. He had to be constructive because he was in a bad place and he knew it. He even admitted this much to me both in New York several weeks later and again still months later in London.

This sentiment was echoed by Werner Rom, who had helped Meili in the beginning with legal and political help in Switzerland, when he complained in an interview of the lack of consultation by the WJC and others with the Swiss Jewish community. "Action should be co-ordinated," he protested, "between world Jewish communities. Whoever calls for a boycott of Swiss banks is not familiar with political realities here."[7]

Yet, the political realities in Switzerland were clear. In polls taken in the German and French-speaking regions of Switzerland by the Swiss daily *Blick*, 44 percent or respondents replied there was no basis to Jewish demands for immediate compensation. As for the government standing by Delamuraz's remarks, 45 percent backed the government's stand.[8] In a similar poll by DRS, Swiss Radio, 60 percent of the respon dents felt the accusations from abroad were exaggerated, with 38 per-cent blaming foreign politicians, 35 percent blaming foreign media, and 26 percent blaming Jewish circles.[9]

At the same time, newspapers printed full pages of letters praising Delamuraz and demonizing D'Amato, the "foreign politician," most associated with the issue. "When will this Jewish wailing stop which was cleverly staged by this demagogue and egotist D'Amato?" read one printed in the *Neue Zürcher Zeitung* on January 13.[10]

While the poll numbers were convincing that the Swiss people as a whole were resentful of the attacks from abroad, there were those in Switzerland, such as Federal Councillor Ruth Dreifus, the only woman and only Jew on the Swiss Federal Council was more reticent and un-derstood that "something had to be done fast." We can't wait for years and accept," she said, "that people who are already 80-years old are suspended between poverty and hope."[11] While she was only one per-son, albeit a Federal Councillor, there were others who were more sym-pathetic, if not embarrassed by what this international scandal was do-ing to the Swiss people. On January 21, over 100 of Switzerland's most prominent personalities signed a manifesto in their words "free of any pressure of any kind from any Jewish organization, but discredited by the behavior of our country's banks and Federal Council."[12]

The signatories berated the Swiss banks, whose directors they decried for agreeing to inspection by independent experts only after fifty years. They complained as well about "massive international pressure" and for continuing to behave as if "the role of the Swiss financial marketplace as a willing helper of the Nazis and recipient of their stolen goods were not already well and widely known." Finally, they castigated the Swiss government for not distancing itself and denouncing former President Delamuraz for the "wave of anti-Semitic sentiment triggered by his remarks."[13]

The Reputation of Swiss Banks

On March 24, 1948, Walter Stucki, negotiating then the follow-up treaty to the 1946 Washington Accords, told his State Department hosts that "the Swiss did not care to have history brand them as 'thieves.'"[14] Nearly forty-nine years later, Rainer Gut, Chairman of Credit Suisse, made the same declaration. Both men were trying to salvage a bad situation for the Swiss banks. Stucki was thinking about history and perhaps a point of honor, Gut was much more interested in the bottom line, money. In an interview with the *Neue Zürcher Zeitung* on January 22, that Switzerland and its bankers had just about run out of time to defuse the public relations crisis in Switzerland.[15] He feared, the longer he waited, the more his bank would lose.

Gut, a realist, with the interests of his stockholders in mind, saw the situation was only getting worse. Each day brought new revelations and the press, Bronfman, D'Amato, and the growing army of critics at home and abroad were becoming too much for them to handle. Gut immediately approached the other two big Swiss banks, Swiss Bank Corporation (SBC) and UBS, with a proposal to contribute, independent of the government, to a fund to offer, in Borer's words, "a gesture of goodwill." What Gut and the others were doing would cost them little. In what began as a fund comprising some $70 million, was in essence a mere pittance, split by the three banks it amounted to a little more than $23 million a piece. In reality, a point missed by no one, the banks were buying a temporary peace. Within hours of the publication of Gut's proposal, SBC agreed to contribute funds. On February 6, Borer announced the creation of the fund, that now even UBS, in the heat of the controversy over Meili's exposure of the bank's document shredding, had no choice but to contribute to as well.

A year to the day the Swiss Banker's Association unilaterally announced the results of its survey into the Swiss banks' dormant accounts, an act that enraged Bronfman, the Swiss banks had finally agreed to put money on the table that did not belong to the claimants or victims of the Holocaust, but was their own. While a small sum, considering the weight of the evidence mounting against the banks, the gesture by Gut was a credible move. After so many months of horrible press, embarrassing disclosures, and pathetic reactions and overreactions by Swiss officials, Gut had managed to push through a gesture that was seen even by Switzerland's critics as a positive act deserving of praise.

Borer announced that the Swiss government would administer the fund, a decision that would not only be criticized but later reversed, and pronounced himself "very happy," the fund was created. "It should take the pressure off Switzerland," he said, "and show our good faith to do what's necessary."[16] Happy he most certainly was. Now, finally, he had something to offer his critics, instead of apologies for the many miscues his government and banks committed. He had been hoping for such a move by the banks, and as such had already begun the process of locating survivors with the help of many including the Holocaust Memorial Museum, from whom he requested information at the end of January.[17]

Switzerland's critics praised the move. D'Amato now could say something positive about what the Swiss were doing, after all the fund was what he and others were asking for, and these funds were separate from the money already found. "It is a breakthrough," said D'Amato, "it was a good first step." The WJC felt vindicated and proclaimed that the Swiss had fulfilled their goal of making moral and material restitution. Sam Bloch, the Vice President of the American Gathering of Holocaust Survivors made an emotional assessment of the fund, claiming "I can see here the wings of history and the wings of justice. I see here the shadows of the souls of the millions who were lost, whose gold rings and teeth were melted down…and found in the stairways to the vaults of the Swiss banks."[18]

While the Swiss finally were receiving positive press for creating the fund, their decision to allow the Swiss government to administer it drew criticism from D'Amato. Enraged at the Swiss decision to administer the funds, he complained loudly that they had no place in managing private funds and when they did so in the 1960s, the entire process proved to be a sham, resulting in the present scandal. At any rate, how, he asked could they agree to do so when the government has refused to contribute to the fund? D'Amato's sharp criticism of the plan even caused the Swiss banks to lose several points on the Swiss stock exchange.[19] D'Amato had a point. Now the government faced a problem.

While they were benefitting from the glow of praise for the banks' plan, Bern now came under pressure to contribute to the fund as well. In its defense, Borer claimed the government was working as fast as it could to form the guidelines for the "Humanitarian Fund for Victims of the Holocaust," but added that the decision on the government's contribution could not be made until the results of the historical study initiated by the December 13, 1996 law could be made. This would not be good enough for either D'Amato, or for that matter critics in Switzerland. "The government," wrote Zurich's *Tages-Anzeiger*, "is therefore going to have to act faster than it wants to." Swiss public radio, *RSR* concluded, "the political authorities today must resign themselves to jump on the train that is already in motion and cooperate."[20] Cotti for his part, was resolute. "But let's not forget: banks and businesses can do what they want with their money. The Federal Council has to answer to the taxpayer."[21]

Cotti was right, banks and businesses could do what they wanted with their money and they did. After a meeting with Swiss business executives on February 9, Cotti's Foreign Ministry announced that the executives were ready to make a contribution to the Humanitarian Fund. At the same time, the Swiss Insurance Association announced that its members would soon contribute to the fund as well.

On February 11, the chemical and packaging group, Alusuisse-Lonza said it would contribute "generously" to the fund. Administrative Council President, Hans Jucker, declaring "We are today's generation. We feel morally, but not personally responsible," and announced the company was ready to contribute and that the amount would be disclosed later. Alusuisse's German plant in Singen used forced labor from Ukraine during the war, a fact that had only recently come to light.[22]

Three days before, at a rally in Bern, a Swiss organization, Judeo-Christian Friendship, collected more than 120,000 Swiss francs, or $85,000 to aid Holocaust victims. The money the group collected would later be deposited into the Humanitarian Fund.[23]

Over the following months, sixteen other Swiss firms, including Nestlé, Swissair, Novartis International, Roche, Schindler Holding Group, and Zurich Insurance Company contributed to the Humanitarian Fund. According to New York City Comptroller, Alan G. Hevesi, one company preferred that its contribution remain silent, other companies including Société Generale de Surveillance, about whom the first document Miriam Kleiman discovered in April 1996, refused to contribute to the fund when asked.[24]

"Healing the remaining wounds"

"Our reputation has suffered," stated Borer at the gathering of the World Jewish Restitution Organization at the Seagrams Building in New York on February 14. Borer, Bronfman, D'Amato, Eizenstat, and thirty-nine Jewish leaders met under the auspices of the WJRO to discuss the case of Switzerland and its new fund.

The delegates gathered to discuss the disbursement mechanism under which the Swiss Humanitarian Fund would operate. Bronfman, Singer, and Eizenstat spoke of the urgency to bring to a close the Swiss fund and get it working and providing aid to those survivors in Eastern Europe, the "double victims" as Eizenstat called them, before it was too late. The double victims were those who survived the war and the Holocaust, but then were stranded in Eastern Europe behind the Iron Curtain under Communism, whose fall made the Swiss banking scandal a reality. Eizenstat warned against sanctions which were then being discussed by the New York State legislature and updated the meeting on the progress toward getting the gold sitting in the Federal Reserve and the Bank of England consigned to a fund to benefit Holocaust survivors. He also praised D'Amato for being the "lone voice in the wilderness for a very long time," on the issue.

Borer, who came to the meeting more at ease than his trip to the U.S. in December before the Congress, nevertheless was repentant and remorseful. "We are deeply aware of the mistrust, pain and confusion surrounding this issue," he confided to the Jewish leaders.

Jean François Bergier, the Chairman of the Historical Commission, also offered apologies seeking mercy from the leaders. "We have to restitute our past to face the present," Bergier declared. On his visit to the National Archives in Maryland the day before, he commented that he saw the various tables where the opposing teams of researchers sat each researching a different aspect of the growing problem. In a hope for the future, he wished for the day that "all the researchers will be at one table working together."

Finally, explaining what was obvious to the world by Swiss actions and miscues, Paul Volcker, during his statement, concluded that a few weeks prior to this meeting, "the situation was getting dangerous." As for Swiss handling of the crisis, "it was uncoordinated...with a lot of accusations going on."[25]

Aside from the formalities of it all, the meeting was a useful one, if only for the fact that all the leaders on the issue were meeting in the same place at the same time. Yet, this was more than a gathering of all the central players in the Swiss story. It was a coming-out party for Borer. On previous occasions, Borer came to meetings with trepidation, fearful of the assault he would face from hostile Congressmen and Senators, or distrusting Jewish leaders. This time, however, Borer had progress to report. Yes, there was mention of the shredding, the "blackmail," and the leaked memo, but he was treated more as an equal than as a target suitable for pummeling. At the news conference that followed the principals' speeches, Borer sat at the conference table along with Bronfman and Eizenstat as an equal. He answered questions along with them and was even complimented by them.

In impromptu meetings in the hallway before and after the meetings, many of the participants talked of the situation in Switzerland. Rolf Bloch and Martin Rosenfeld warned of the effect the Senator's campaign was having on the Jewish community there. Alfred Defago, the incoming Ambassador, told me very defensively, we "are going to have to start going after other countries." He added, "we weren't the only ones."

Swiss diplomats, while sounding defensive at times, apologetic at others, felt as if the bad times were coming to a close and that a constructive period, after such a brutal and embarrassing one was approaching. In general, news stories reporting on the meeting supported this theory. *Newsday* described the event as "a cease-fire between D'Amato and the Swiss government..."[26] For his part, D'Amato came away reassured that the Swiss were actually moving in the right direction. Swiss insistence on administering the Humanitarian Fund, D'Amato was reassured by Defago, would ease and the fund would eventually be turned over to the control of a private Swiss-WJC committee to be formed in the coming weeks. Even Bronfman reported that the mood had brightened.

"The world has given its verdict. The Swiss were guilty"

As the saying goes, no good deed ever goes unpunished. Maram Stern, Assistant Secretary General of the WJC, declared "this is only the beginning," and he was right. The fund would bring out all those who had yet to receive compensation for their suffering fifty years after the war's end. Now that the Swiss had agreed to create a fund, whether it was for compensation or not, groups from all over the world would treat it as such. Representatives for the Pink Cross, a homosexual group, met with Swiss officials in Bern on February 27, seeking compensation for homosexual victims of the Nazis. Ten days before that meeting, the Romani Union, the association of Roma and Sinti gypsies met with Foreign Minister Cotti seeking compensation for the half-million gypsies murdered by the Nazis.

The Swiss, finally with something to offer its critics did not object to payments being made to non-Jews, and neither did the WJC. Yet, there was the fear of every group now seeking money from the fund. The only way that this could be alleviated would be through a board set up by the Swiss and the WJC. In two days of meetings between Cotti and Israel Singer, on February 24–25, an agreement was reached whereby there would be created a Fund Executive composed of seven members, four Swiss and three recommended by the WJC. The Executive would decide upon the Fund's use and the procedures and regulations by which recipients could qualify for funding. Below the Executive would sit the Fund Council, composed of eighteen members, nine chosen by each party. The Council was simply to attend to the needs of and make arrangements for the receipt by the beneficiaries of the grants from the Fund.[27]

With the formal announcement of the Fund, a nationalist, right-wing industrialist and member of the Swiss parliament, Christoph Blocher, issued threats to block the government's contribution to the Fund, declaring that it would be an unwarranted and unapproved use of public funds for a purpose with which he disagreed. While Blocher did not object to the banks contributing to the Fund, the government was a different matter. For Blocher, the banks were the ones that got Switzerland into the mess it was in, therefore they should be the ones who paid to get Switzerland out of it. Blocher defiantly asserted that Switzerland had no need to apologize for its role in aiding the Nazis during the war. Reparations or an apology, for Blocher, would be out of the question.

Blocher threatened to call for a public referendum, a move quite achievable in Switzerland, one of the last bastions of near direct and popular democracy that exists in the world today. A referendum, according to the public opinion polls he read, overwhelmingly supported his objections.

With the Fund established, Blocher's call for resistance provided a bit of comfort, in that now domestic opposition to the onslaught Switzerland was facing was surfacing publicly. While the opposition centered on D'Amato, until now it was the sheer weight of all that he had said and done and the documents we threw at them that formed their hatred of the man. Now, D'Amato's public statement in reaction to the establishment of the Fund would demonize him more than anything else done previously in the eyes of the Swiss people.

"The world has already rendered its verdict," D'Amato's press statement read. "The Swiss were guilty. We're now debating the penalty, and the penalty should fit the crime."[28] While the statement presumed guilt from the start, it was really nothing harsher than anything he said previously. The Swiss daily *Blick*, however, did not play the statement this way. In a front page headline, "D'Amato, That's Enough!," *Blick* complained "he's going too far: D'Amato insults the Swiss as being criminals." *Blick*'s George Wuthrich editorializing, asked "what is the man really after?" Wuthrich claimed that D'Amato had gone overboard and to justify this belief, he quoted Rolf Bloch as saying "it was too much," and Borer expressing the belief that statements like this "were hurting Switzerland at home."

He had skillfully managed to turn D'Amato's statement into a first rate scandal by twisting his words into an insult against the entire Swiss people. Concluding his story, Wuthrich wrote, "Dear BLICK reader: If you want to write your opinion to D'Amato, here is his address…" Blick readers were encouraged to write D'Amato and complain. Wuthrich, added, "please provide a copy to BLICK."[29]

This was all that the Swiss people needed to launch a letter-writing campaign, leaving us with scores of letters, mostly in German or French, as well as a good number in English, vilifying D'Amato and his motivation for his campaign and complaining of the multitudes of wrongs the United States had committed around the world over the past two hundred years.

"What we and a large majority of the swiss [sic] population resent greatly," wrote Margrit and Franz Stutz-Laube, "is the fact that now you Senator D'Amato, seeking reelection into the Senate, are literally misusing this issue to gain votes!!"[30] "The Americans drove the Indians off their land," wrote Jean Marc-Pochon, "killing their wives and children so that they could no longer reproduce. Those were the heroic deeds of the American cavalry. The Americans then went on to procure slaves in Africa, who they treated like animals and put to work for them."[31] Ernst Kurth of Oltigen, was more succinct in his criticism of D'Amato, calling him the "biggest scoundrel in history."[32] Some letters were filled with expletives, others while quite respectful, were nevertheless angry and questioning why D'Amato had called the Swiss people criminals, insults like this in practice he took great pains to avoid doing.

Wuthrich had succeeded in his goal. If D'Amato had not been public enemy number one in Switzerland before, he was now. Unpleasant letters were not only what D'Amato would receive from the Swiss people. Death threats were now a common occurrence. Two came in one day to the American Embassy in Bern, several came in the mail directly.

Cotti, too, reacted harshly to D'Amato's remarks. "This man is manifestly not interested in either the facts or a reasonable dialogue," proclaimed Cotti. For the beleaguered Swiss Foreign Minister, D'Amato was creating "the worst conditions imaginable for a minimal dialogue."[33]

Despite D'Amato's vehement attacks against the Swiss banks, the common thread in each response by the Swiss was that D'Amato had ulterior motives for his actions. If it was not the Jewish vote, it was that he was out to hurt the Swiss banking industry to the advantage of the American. On March 7, this last theory took a good dent when *Newsday* reported that over past few years, D'Amato had received campaign contributions from none other than employees of the American branches of Credit Suisse, UBS, Swiss Bank Corporation, and Bank Julius Baer. Contributions are, in one form, of course a sign of support. If the banks did not like D'Amato, the thought went, why then would they contribute to him.

"Of course we are embarrassed," admitted Gertrud Erismann of UBS in Zurich. All told, as far back as 1995, employees of the banks contributed $12,000 to D'Amato. In response, D'Amato confidently asserted, it "goes to show you that I don't determine policy and actions on the basis of who has contributed to me." He added, and quite ironically, "For anybody to assume now that the Swiss banks got any preferential treatment would be absurd."[34]

Admitting the Obvious

In the annual board meeting of UBS, in the first week of April, Robert Studer, addressed his stockholders on the financial shape of UBS and his view of the future. Concerning UBS's contribution to the Humanitarian Fund, to no one's surprise, Studer confessed it was "strongly motivated by our business activities in the US, which are important for the overall performance of the UBS."[35]

Studer's statement was a realization of the situation the banks and Switzerland itself were in. Facing an economic downturn that included massive bank layoffs and attempted bank takeovers, the banks faced court battles in the U.S., a sanctions drive by state and local institutions in the U.S., and D'Amato's and the WJC's continued drive against the banks. They realized they had to turn things around and begin to direct the press stories in their favor.

Outgunned

"Spearheaded by New York Republican Senator Alfonse D'Amato," wrote Andrew McCathie of the Australian *Financial Review*, "the normally staid world of Swiss banking in Zurich has also clearly been outgunned by New York's more street-wise politicians..."[36] Clearly the Swiss bankers had a problem. They had to act.

One of the first moves made was to invite an international group of reporters to Switzerland on a press junket to Bern to speak with and interview people like Borer and Jean-Pierre Roth of the Swiss National Bank, Bank CEOs and others. Moreover, they would all be there to cover the announcement of the Swiss government's creation of the Humanitarian Fund. The Foreign Ministry invited reporters from the British newspapers, the *Jewish Chronicle*, the *Daily Telegraph*, the *Guardian*, the *Independent*, and the *Financial Times*; the Israeli papers, *Ha'aretz*, *Ma'ariv*, *Yediot Aharonot*, *Jerusalem Post*, and *Globes*; and the U.S. papers, the *Chicago Tribune* and the *Forward*.[37]

The reporters all filed their reports based upon their impressions gained while there. One reporter, Gabe Kahn formerly of the *Forward*, portrayed the Swiss people as old fashioned and reserved, resentful of what was being done to them by the press and D'Amato. In general, the will to say "I'm sorry" simply was not there. Like others that had visited Switzerland "under siege," Kahn concluded the Swiss people, government, and bankers, "just don't get it."[38]

A Certain Degree of Incompetence

While they "didn't get it," public relations firms the Swiss government finally agreed to hire clearly did. Cotti had long been reluctant to seek help from outside sources, but he realized the only way to handle the wave of bad press from the U.S., was to adopt U.S. methods.

Margaret Studer explained the problem in the *Wall Street Journal Europe*. Studer quoted Nicholas Hayek, chairman of SMH Societe Suisse de Microelectronique et d'Horlogerie SA, Switzerland's leading watchmaker, as saying "the Swiss government has shown a certain degree of incompetence" in communication.[39] It became clear to the

Swiss, something more had to be done, legally and on the public relations front as well.

Since Borer's appearance before the House Banking Committee, the firm of Barbour, Griffith and Rogers, of Washington, had already been on retainer. To compliment former RNC boss Haley Barbour's legal help, Ruder Finn of New York, was enlisted to handle media relations. Between the two firms, the Swiss government would reportedly pay $50,000 per month to learn the ways of the U.S. media.

Ruder Finn hired President Clinton's former Jewish Affairs advisor, Jay Footlick, to join the firm and handle the Swiss case. Footlick, a former actor and political activist, began a drive to get the new Swiss Ambassador to the United States, Alfred Defago "on the road," to both soften the message given, and to explain just what the Swiss people and government were doing to alleviate the problem. One of the first places Footlick took Defago was Chicago, where there was a sizeable and influential Jewish community. After Chicago, Footlick took Defago to his hometown, Skokie, the cite of the infamous neo-Nazi march. In Skokie, Defago spoke before the Chicago Board of Rabbis, seeking *Tshuvah*, Hebrew for repentance, for the upcoming Jewish New Year.[40]

Help was also brought in to join Borer's Task Force. Corinne Goetschel, owner of a Swiss media firm, a dual U.S.-Swiss national, and a Jew, a point very much emphasized, was signed to get "the message across in a sensitive manner," as she declared in her interview with *USA Today*.[41]

The Swiss clearly had problems handling infighting on their side. Now, the groups who fought so hard for compensation from the Swiss, and had finally obtained it, would also have to handle their own internal problems.

Infighting

Trying to force the Swiss to create a fund, seemingly difficult, "that was the easy part. Now someone has to decide who gets it.... This is where it gets nasty," wrote Marilyn Henry of the *Jerusalem Post*.[42] Henry, writing from New Jersey for the *Post* from the early days of the inquiry had gotten the story right this time. To many, she seemed too willing to accept Swiss explanations for the accusations they faced. Now, though she had the story right.

Throughout the then, year-long inquiry, the most that had been discussed focused on gold, so felt many Jewish leaders. While other revelations were made, gold seemed to be the issue at hand, how much the Nazis had looted, how much the Swiss bankers accepted, how much was still in the Federal Reserve or Bank of England, and which pot of gold was tainted with victims' gold. Many Jewish leaders, including Ben Meed of the American Gathering of Holocaust Survivors and Abe Foxman of the Anti-Defamation League, feared that the search for gold, in fact tainted the Jews themselves.[43] This point had repeatedly come up in our own internal discussions. Could Jews, rightly pursuing the wealth stolen from the Jews of Europe be accused of fulfilling the stereotype of Jews seeking only money? Despite the dictum that "Jews don't create anti-Semitism, anti-Semites do," we feared this would fuel criticism of the entire effort. While it did not hinder us, it did cause consternation on the part of those who headed some of the Jewish organizations.

Many groups sought a seat at the table in deciding who would divide up the money. After all, until this time, it was the Germans who were the only ones who provided compensation for the crimes of the Nazis. The Claims Conference administering the payments, had always been a point of criticism from survivors who claimed it was too bureaucratic and too tight with releasing payments.[44] Now, with the Swiss beginning to make payments, disagreements as to the composition of the WJRO's constituent members on the new Humanitarian Fund Executive, as well as the allotment and destination of the funds, began to emerge.

Meed suggested that all survivors should be eligible for compensation, because the sums of the payments would be small, those not in need should be presented with the option of returning their portion for allotment to the needy of the survivor population. Simon Wiesenthal, the famed Nazi hunter felt the funds should go to survivors in Eastern Europe. Eizenstat agreed with him, stating there were survivors that never did get compensation, those in the former Eastern bloc, and they should be the first to receive the Swiss funds that would "help them live out their declining years in dignity."[45]

Eligibility for the fund was debated, but membership for the Fund caused a greater stir. In April, just two weeks after the WJRO made its recommendations, the Swiss made theirs. The disagreement came with the proposal to appoint Elie Wiesel as the President of the Fund. When this did not work out, the next dispute arose over the appointment of Rolf Bloch to the position. Ruth Dreifus, the only Jewish Federal Councillor made her objections to Bloch's appointment known privately to Cotti by letter, which was subsequently leaked to the press, to Dreifus's great consternation. Dreifus and others had opposed Bloch because they saw a conflict in Bloch assuming the position, due to his leadership of the Swiss Jewish community.[46]

Moreover, a deep public dispute between the WJC and Borer developed as to the Jewish composition of the Executive, even resulting in the trading of accusations between Borer and Elan Steinberg, with Borer decrying the "false accusations and outrageous calumny on the part of Mr. Steinberg" as to promises made by Borer to the WJC.[47] The President of the Board, was supposed to be Swiss, but according to Borer, the WJC had demanded their choice for the position. In retaliation, the Swiss Federal Council delayed the concluding appointments to the Executive Fund on April 23. As a result of the WJC-Borer dispute, the Council refused to confirm the WJC's candidates for the Executive but did agree, despite Dreifus' opposition, to appoint Bloch as the President of the Fund's Board. On May 2, the two sides worked out their disagreements and named a reluctant Wiesel to the position of Honorary Chairman of the Executive Fund. Four days later, Wiesel, claiming he never asked for the position, nor really wanted it owing to the controversy that preceded it, resigned the post in a letter to Cotti.

In an interview with the *Jerusalem Post* two weeks later, Wiesel elaborated more on his reasons for resigning. Just as Meed and Foxman had voiced concern over the money issue, Wiesel explained his discomfort with handing money out to survivors and having to choose who was more deserving of compensation. "I don't need titles," he added. "The World Jewish Congress wanted the title. First they wanted me to be president [sic] Switzerland said no, the president must be Swiss. So they began speaking about titles, which made the whole thing silly."[48] To take Wiesel's place, the Executive named Bronfman. In September, Bronfman gave up the position in favor of Ben Meed.

More Disagreement

By June, seemingly with the composition of the Executive Fund behind them, the members were free to begin to act. This would not be the case. Disputes lingered. Now the timing of the payouts became the issue.

By September, meetings of the Executive had already begun. On July 7, the Executive decided to release close to $11.6 million as the first tranche of payments that would go, as Wiesenthal, Eizenstat and others had suggested, to the "double victims" of Eastern Europe. Yet, other groups, such as the Gypsies who felt closed out, demanded to be included in the payouts, as did homosexual survivor groups and Red Army veterans.[49]

While the disputes dragged on, former U.S. Envoy to Bosnia, Richard Holbrooke, now and executive at Credit Suisse/First Boston, urged speedier action. He was not the only one. Sigi Feigel, the honorary head of the Israeli community in Zurich, denounced the Executive, saying "although 170 million Swiss francs have been available since March, the [directors of the fund] have not yet received requests or distributed money."[50]

The criticism fell on deaf ears. Weeks went by and nothing happened. Accusations were traded back and forth. The Swiss members of the Executive, as well as the Swiss press, accused the WJRO of missing meetings of the Executive and for not submitting aid proposals. "In the worst case," wrote the Zurich daily *Tages-Anzeiger*, "rivalries among competing organisations and attempts by their supporters to gain influence might be behind this."[51] The WJRO threatened to pull out of the Humanitarian Fund agreement due to their view of the failure of the Fund's administration. Avraham Burg, complaining of the inaction of the Executive, wrote Bloch seeking to move the Fund's operation out of Switzerland to the WJRO in New York. Bloch dismissed the suggestion out of hand.

This bickering, while not a real threat to the existence of the Fund, nevertheless showed the bitter feelings and the residual lack of trust from the months of attacks upon Switzerland. Despite the positive acts taken, Swiss politicians and the public alike, continued to express harsh views of their critics. Anti-Semitic remarks and actions became commonplace in Switzerland. On the trains, Swiss citizens were overheard making negative remarks about the Jews and mail to the newspapers and to Jewish organizations was increasingly harsh in its anti-Semitic tone.

As for views of D'Amato, by August, Swiss opinion was worse than ever. Meili had been granted the right to stay in the United States, and D'Amato had demanded an apology from UBS for him. To this demand, the leader of the Free Democratic party, Franz Steinegger, compared D'Amato's tactics as being "in no way different from the tactics the Nazis used."[52]

The Logjam Breaks

By the end of August, the Swiss Parliament's Legal Committee voted 12–5 to bypass Parliamentary approval for a 100 million Swiss franc contribution to the Humanitarian Fund. The Central Bank "did not ask for parliamentary approval when they did their questionable business with the Nazis," asserted Committee Chairwoman Lily Nabholz, "so why do they need our approval now?"[53]

By the middle of September, the WJC and the Swiss Government had reached a truce. While all the problems were not solved, by this time the WJC was in the position to submit names of needy Holocaust survivors to the Swiss government and in turn the Humanitarian Fund. On September 17, the WJC submitted the names of close to 14,000 survivors in Eastern Europe to Defago in New York. A day later, Hungary's Jewish community submitted a list of over 16,000 names to the Swiss embassy in Budapest. Together, the 30,000 names would form the beginning traunche of payouts from the Humanitarian Fund. Each of the survivors would receive payments of $1,000. While not a great amount of money, the sum would equal perhaps a year's worth of pension for the recipients who had never before received compensation for their suffering.

On November 7, 1997, in a much-publicized ceremony in Riga, Latvia, Riva Sefere, a seventy-five-year-old Holocaust survivor was the first to receive a check from the Fund. Along with seventy-nine other survivors, Sefere received a check for $400. The recipients did not receive the full sum, according to Rolf Bloch, because "the local Jewish organization was afraid to give it all to them at one time."[54] Sefere, would later complain that the amount was too small and that she would have preferred to have received a washing machine so she would not have to wash her clothes by hand, something she had done for more than fifty years.

In December, twenty-three survivors in Albania, Muslim and Christian, ages sixty-seven to eighty, each received $1000 payments from the Fund. The group was all that was left of 500 that were survivors of Mauthausen concentration camp in Austria. In January 1998, the Fund Executive announced that within three to four months, needy survivors in the United States would begin receiving payments.

"Were there in Switzerland possibly any fundamentally dubious operations"

"Unexpectedly, our country finds itself exposed to sharp international criticism. In the past few months," Swiss President Arnold Koller explained live on Swiss television to the Swiss Parliament and the nation, "we have been harshly reproached, suspected and accused, and sweeping statements have been made about our behavior before, during and after World War II." Koller, addressing a special joint meeting of the Swiss Federal Assembly on the subject of Switzerland and World War II, asked the Assembly, "were there in Switzerland possibly any fundamentally dubious operations?"[55]

To come to terms with Switzerland's past, Koller shocked the Assembly with a solution to Switzerland's problems no one present expected to hear:

> It is in this spirit that the Federal Council, in agreement with the National Bank and with regard to the national celebration of 1998, has developed the idea of the "Swiss Foundation for Solidarity." The object of the Foundation would be the lindering [sic] of pressing human needs in Switzerland and abroad. The Foundation is to be funded by the returns from the management of those parts of the goldstock of the National Bank made available for other public purposes following the necessary reform of the money and currency constitution. The total assets of the Foundation would probably amount to about seven billion Swiss francs. The Foundation would manage the respective goldstock according to open market rules. With careful management the average return per year would result in the long run to several hundreds of millions of Swiss francs, which would have to be used half in Switzerland half abroad. Such money is then to be destined to victims of poverty and catastrophes, of genocide and other severe breaches of human rights, such as of course victims of the Holocaust and of Shoa.[56]

What Koller suggested to a stunned Assembly was to endow a fund with which to make amends for the sins of the past, that were only just coming to light, albeit forcibly. The offer, complicated and not quite as achievable and realistic as he explained, amounted to a sell-off of some of the 2,590 tons of Swiss gold reserves at the market price instead of the below market book price held by the Swiss National Bank. The difference, would be put to an account for the benefit of the Foundation.

The "Solidarity Fund," as it has come to be called, sounded despite the flaws, long-term and quite positive. It accounted for Holocaust victims' interests, the ostensible reason for the plan in the first place, and it seemed to bring back an era of Swiss selflessness in the wake of the international outcry over Swiss misdeeds of the past fifty years. Other reasons for the plan however, came into play. Stuart Eizenstat's interagency team was finishing its work on its first report. This no doubt played on the Swiss leaders' minds. The severity and ongoing nature of the international criticism they faced also weighed heavily on the Swiss. It was clear, by this time that D'Amato was not going away anytime soon, and the same could be said of the WJC. Moreover, others including journalists, documentary producers, lawyers, and other governments were at their doorstep.

Also, with the European Union moving toward unity on a common currency, as well as other matters of integration, gold was becoming a liability. European governments, in order to meet budgetary goals for monetary unity by 1999 would have to sell off some of their gold holdings. Switzerland may have been neutral and independent of the E.U., but it still had to survive and deal with the same economies.

Hans Meyer, Chairman of the Swiss National Bank, who could be considered as the "spiritual father" of the Solidarity Fund was no doubt considering these matters as well. "I got the ball rolling and acted as an advisor to the Bundesrat in the political discourse," answered Meyer in an interview with the daily *Tages-Anzeiger*.[57] According to the paper, the Fund came "not a minute too soon."[58]

Although many questioned the real motive behind the Fund, the fact that its mere announcement received almost universal applause, proved its value. Journalists around the world declared that the Fund could probably bring an end to the damaging crisis for Switzerland. *Blick*, confidently declared, "the good Swiss are to be resurrected."[59] Switzerland's toughest critics agreed. The deal was a "breakthrough declaration," said D'Amato. Edgar Bronfman termed the Fund, "a victory for the Jewish and Swiss peoples."

"I would like to see if they can blackmail an entire people at the ballot box"

The Fund, bringing acclaim and finally positive reviews for Swiss actions, also effected the world's gold markets. Within hours of the announcement, gold futures contracts in New York began to fall, and by the next day gold had taken its biggest one-day drop in nearly two years, falling $6.10 an ounce to $354.

More importantly, the Fund brought Conservative Parliamentarian Christoph Blocher fully into the open, with promises of referendums and claims that the Cabinet had "lost its head." Only a week before the announcement of the Fund, in a well-publicized address at the Hotel International in Zurich, Blocher declared "our government and well-known representatives of industry are lacking in any kind of clear concept, acting—or rather reacting—in an extremely contradictory and unfortunate manner. With their attitude," Blocher continued, "they are continually encouraging those groups which are attacking us incessantly."[60] Blocher clearly set the tone for his actions and history showed he could not be ignored. In 1992, backed by the support he gained in the rural, more conservative areas of Switzerland, Blocher defeated efforts by the Swiss government to join the European Union: "They could blackmail banks, you can blackmail governments, you can blackmail national banks, you can force them to give in. (But) I would like to see if they can blackmail an entire people at the ballot box."[61]

Blocher had some following (his party polls 15 percent of the Swiss vote), but he was not without critics. There were those who objected to his strident and arguably anti-Semitic views and statements. In an editorial in *Tages-Anzeiger*, Bruno Vanoni, detailed the stir Blocher was causing in Switzerland including the history of Ems-Chemie, the firm he took over in a management buy out. Blocher had consistently maintained the firm never did any business with the Nazis. Vanoni explained that Swiss historian Peter Kamber's research proved otherwise. According to Kamber, Ems-Chemie began production with a German license and was dependent upon the delivery of raw materials by Nazi firms. Blocher, when encountered with these charges, answered simply, shrugging his shoulders saying "nothing new, nothing disreputable."[62]

Within three months of Blocher's declared intention to block the Fund, polling numbers in Switzerland clearly showed the effect his campaign was having on support for the plan. Within days of the announcement of the Fund, polls in Switzerland showed the Fund receiving the support of 50–73 percent of the population, with opposition running at 19–33 percent.[63] By the middle of June those numbers fell to 48 percent supporting the Fund, to 35 percent against it.[64]

To the Fund, Blocher proposed an alternative. In June, he suggested the creation of the "1998 Jubilee Collect," a plan to request donations from 400–500 of Switzerland's wealthiest businessmen to endow a foundation instead of using public funds in the form of gold sales. Claiming "my million is ready," Blocher challenged the rich to donate the equivalent of a year's salary to his foundation.[65] After some time, he reduced the required sum to around $100,000 and said he would accept smaller donations. By the end of 1997, Blocher had managed to raise close to $10 million.

Christoph Blocher has proven to be a charismatic and demagogic opponent to the Solidarity Fund. He has come to symbolize all that was blocking the truth: a dogged denial of wrongdoing and a solid defense of the Swiss bankers acting as the bankers for the Nazis. At the end of 1997, arguably the worst for Switzerland in a great number of years, he had managed to cast serious doubt on the chances for success of the one plan the Swiss had managed to create that actually took the sting out of a now two-year campaign against them.

In a faxed letter to the U.S. Embassy in Bern on August 1, Blocher requested they transmit a message to D'Amato on the occasion of the Senator's sixtieth birthday. Blocher offered D'Amato best wishes for his future and offered his hope that it would bring him "deeper knowledge and respect for our small independent and peaceful country."[66] For Blocher, the Swiss government, and especially, the Swiss bankers, D'Amato, while a sincere threat to their interests, was no longer the only threat. Now, the biggest threat to the Swiss would be themselves and their careless mistakes—mistakes they could have easily avoided, but like most of the problems they encountered during this time, they failed to see the trees through the woods.

Notes

1. Memorandum for Credit File, C.E. Freyvogel, Swiss Bank Corporation, August 1937.
2. Telephone discussion with Swiss journalist Patrick Mann, 24 March 1997, William Hall, "Leutwiler Assails Gold Fund," *Financial Times*, 25 March 1997.
3. "Washington Whispers," *U.S. News & World Report*, 16 December 1997.
4. "Switzerland: Bern Ready to Discuss Holocaust Victims Compensation Fund," Swiss Radio International in English, 7 January 1997, FBIS-WEU-97-005.
5. United States Senator Alfonse M. D'Amato, CNN interview transcript, 7 January 1997.
6. Agence France-Press, 8 January 1997.
7. Gisela Blau, Hadas Altwarg and Stephanie Genkin, "Swiss Jews angered by WJC boycott threat, *London Jewish Chronicle*, 10 January 1997.
8. Claire Nullis, "Poll finds majority against immediate compensation to Jews," Associated Press, 11 January 1997.
9. Poll by DRS, Swiss Radio, 22 January 1997, courtesy of Elaine Povich, *New York Daily News*.
10. Letters to the Editor, *Neue Zürcher Zeitung*, 13 January 1997, courtesy of Elaine Povich, *New York Daily News*.
11. Peter Nielsen, "Swiss government ready to act on Holocaust fund," Associated Press, 12 January 1997; "Switzerland Sees Quick Action on Jewish Funds, *Dow Jones Service*, 12 January 1997.
12. "Manifesto of January 21, 1997," courtesy of the American Embassy in Bern.
13. Ibid.
14. Memorandum of Conversation, "Meeting with Mr. Walter Stucki, Swiss Foreign Office," RG 59, Entry 1945–49, Box 4243, Records of the United States Department of State, NARA, p.1.
15. William Hall, "Divided by Goodwill," *Financial Times*, 25 January 1997.
16. John-Thor Dahlburg, "Swiss Banks Set Up Holocaust Victims Fund," *Los Angeles Times*, 6 January 1997, p. 2 A.

17. Fax message from Dr. Claude Altermatt, Swiss Foreign Ministry Task Force to the Holocaust Memorial Institute, 31 January 1997.
18. Christopher Fancescani, "Jews hail Swiss decision to set up Holocaust fund," *New York Post*, 25 January 1997, p. 12.
19. "Swiss shares flat in heavy midday trading," *AFX News*, 13 February 1997.
20. Marcus Kabel, "Bern comes under pressure to join Holocaust fund," Reuters, 6 February 1997.
21. Michael Shields, "Swiss speed Holocaust fund, public money unsettled," Reuters, 12, February 1997.
22. "Alusuisse to contribute to Holocaust Fund," Reuters, 11 February 1997.
23. "Swiss charity given funds for Holocaust victims," Agence France-Presse, 10 February 1997.
24. Alan G. Hevesi, New York City Comptroller, "Swiss Monitor," November 1997.
25. Proceedings of the Meeting of the Council of the World Jewish Restitution Organization, New York City, 14 February 1997.
26. Elaine Povich, "Nazi Gold Accord," *Newsday*, 15 February 1997, p. A 8.
27. Executive Ordinance concerning the Special Fund for Needy Victims of the Holocaust/Shoah, The Swiss Federal Council, 26 February 1997.
28. Press Statement of United States Senator Alfonse M. D'Amato, 26 February 1997.
29. George Wuthrich, "D'Amato, That's Enough!," *Blick*, 28 February 1997, p. 1, translated by Brian Hufker.
30. Letter of Margrit and Franz Stutz-Laube to United States Senator Alfonse M. D'Amato, 28 February 1997.
31. Letter of Jean Marc-Pochon to United States Senator Alfonse M. D'Amato, 12 March 1997.
32. Letter of Ernst Kurth to United States Senator Alfonse M. D'Amato, 25 April 1997, translated by Brian Hufker.
33. "Swiss FM attacks US Senator over Holocaust compensation fund," Agence France-Presse, 1 March 1997.
34. Roy Gutman and Elaine Povich, "D'Amato's Swiss Connection," *Newsday*, 7 March 1997.
35. William Hall, "UBS comes clean on gift to Holocaust Fund, *Financial Times*, 18 April 1997.
36. Andrew McCathie, "Swiss besieged by Nazi claims," *Financial Review*, 4 March 1997.
37. Telephone interview with one of the press participants, Itamar Levin of *Globes* from Tel Aviv, 3 March 1997; "Programme organised in the scope of the Task Force for journalists from Great Britain, Israel and the United States, February 23 to February 28, 1997, Federal Department of Foreign Affairs, Information Office, Bern, 21 February 21, 1997.
38. Telephone conversation with Gabe Kahn, *Forward*, 10 March 1997.
39. Margaret Studer, Switzerland's Image Restoration Needs a Hand," *Wall Street Journal Europe*, 29 April 1997.
40. Adam Zagorin, "Switzerland, They're Yodeling to a Different Drummer," *Time Internet Edition*, 13 October 1997; Speech by Swiss Ambassador to the United States Alfred Defago before the Chicago Board of Rabbis, Skokie, Illinois, 9 September 1997.
41. Helenna Bachmann, "Swiss Image Effort has U.S. Touch," *USA Today*, 21 March 1997.
42. Marilyn Henry, "A Divisive Legacy," *Jerusalem Post*, 10 March 1997.
43. Discussion with Ben Meed, Washington D.C., 14 January 1998.

44. Lorraine Adams, "Paying for the Holocaust," *Washington Post Magazine*, 20 April 1997.

45. Stuart E. Eizenstat, Forward to *U.S. and Allied Efforts to Recover and Restore Gold and Other Assets Stolen or Hidden by Germany During WWII*, Interagency Report, United States Government, May 1997.

46. Fredy Rom, "New Snag in Swiss Fund," Jewish Telegraphic Agency, *MetroWest Jewish News*, New Jersey, 3 April 1997.

47. Personal declaration of Ambassador Thomas Borer, Head of the Task Force, to statements made to the media by Elan Steinberg, Executive Director of the World Jewish Congress, Bern 17 April 1997.

48. Cited in "Why Wiesel Dropped Out," *MetroWest Jewish News*, New Jersey, 22 May 1997.

49. Letter of Leonid Rosenberg, President American Association of Invalids & Veterans of World War II from former USSR, New York, Executive Board to United States Senator Alfonse M. D'Amato, 13 August 1997.

50. "Israeli community leader slams heads of Holocaust fund," Agence French-Presse, 31 August 1997.

51. "Jewish Leader Launches Sharp Attack on Swiss Holocaust Fund," Deutsche Presse-Agentur, 16 September 1997.

52. Phillip Burkhardt, "No Different From Nazi Tactics," *Sonntagszeitung*, 4 August 1997, translated by David Skelly.

53. Fredy Rom, Swiss legislators remove hurdle to central bank's donation to fund," *MetroWest Jewish News*, New Jersey, 11 September 1997.

54. Interview with Rolf Bloch, London, 3 December 1997.

55. "Switzerland and its Recent Contemporary History," Statement of Swiss President Arnold Koller before the Swiss Federal Assembly, 5 March 1997, p. 1, translated by the Swiss Embassy in Washington.

56. Ibid, p. 8.

57. "Den Stein ins Rollen gebracht [To get the Stone rolling]," an interview with Hans Meyer, by Walter Niederberger, *Tages-Anzeiger*, 6 March 1997, translated by Brian Hufker and Melanie Wagner.

58. Thomas Rust, "Good Timing for Koller's Initiative," *Tages-Anzeiger*, 6 March 1997, translated by Brian Hufker.

59. Marcus Kabel, "Swiss aid foundation may end Holocaust row," Reuters, 6 March 1997.

60. "Switzerland and the Second World War, A Clarification," Speech of Christoph Blocher, Hotel International, Zurich-Oerlikon, 1 March 1997.

61. Michael Shields, "Populist vows to fight Swiss gold foundation," Reuters, 18 March 1997.

62. "Commentary," by Bruno Vanoni, *Tages-Anzeiger*, 13 March 1997, translated by Brian Hufker, "A Man on a Crusade, Blocher's Nazi gold campaign," *Business Week*, 14 July 1997.

63. "Swiss polls show solid support for huge aid fund," Reuters, 9 March 1997.

64. Michael Shields, "Swiss support for humanitarian fund waning—survey," Reuters, 15 June 1997.

65. "Critics dismiss challenge to Swiss Holocaust fund," Reuters, 22 June 1997.

66. Letter of Christoph Blocher to U.S. Senator Alfonse M. D'Amato, 1 August 1997.

7

We Were Right

Since 1995, the Swiss Bankers Association maintained that in their searches through their records they had found only 774 dormant accounts. It was only reasonable then that they should publish these accounts for claimants around the world to see. For D'Amato, this was the only logical course to take. The survivors were not getting any younger and they needed, in his words, "to be made whole again."

On March 20, D'Amato wrote Borer asking him to seek permission from the SBA to publish the names in order to speed the return of the assets. "The failure of Mr. Hani's [sic] office," wrote D'Amato, "is but one indicator of the barriers set up by Swiss law which prevent an effective notification system to the owners of heirs of dormant accounts."[1] D'Amato, feeling that he had a fairly good working relationship with Borer, placed a call to Bern to discuss the matter with him before we released the letter. Borer pledged to do his best.

While Borer had felt confident of success, we had to wait over a month to receive news of the product of Borer's efforts. On April 28, Borer transmitted a copy of the letter George Kreyer, head of the SBA, and J.P. Chapuis, the Delegate, sent to the Swiss Federal Banking Commission. The two SBA officials expressed "the SBA's unequivocal support for the concept of public disclosure of the names of account holders in the very special and limited circumstances presented by Holocaust-related dormant assets."[2] D'Amato was elated. For once he had been able to work with, instead of against, the Swiss bankers and at the same time put the claimants closer to restitution of their money. The SBA decision was a very good outcome for D'Amato, but a frightfully bad one for the SBA, their member banks, and Switzerland overall.

After Volcker had been apraised of the decision by the Swiss Banking Commission, a process was created that would not only allow him to work with them to publish the accounts but to set up a claims process once they were published. In preparing lists for publication, the banks, working with Volcker's auditors began to find a disturbing trend: more and more accounts, many more than the 774 the SBA first had maintained, "dramatically higher" according to one source. A week later, the *New York Times* reported the same story, adding that there were an incredible 15,000 to 20,000 more accounts for which the banks could not account.[3]

At the end of June, following the preliminary audits of the banks done by Volcker's auditors, the SBA ordered its banks to report by July 7 the details of their search through the records for dormant accounts. On July 23, then, the SBA would publish the account list.[4] Ominously for the Swiss, a day after the banks were to report their findings, Haeni reported that an additional $12,100,000 was found by his office, $7,100,000 belonging to Holocaust victims.[5] It was on this note that the Swiss began what many described as one of the most colossul blunder in a long list of blunders. On July 23, the SBA spent over $5,000,000 to publish 1,756 accounts belonging to 1,872 account holders or those with powers of attorney in newspapers in 28 countries around the world.

Proudly announcing the publication of the list on the morning the advertisements appeared, Ambassador Alfred Defago called the move and "example of Swtizerland's determination to shed light on its World War II history."[6] While the list appearing, in one case, in the *New York Times,*[7] shed light, that light was a spotlight on everything bad we had said about the banks.

Many of the names that appeared on the list, at first blush, were not Jewish at all. But, once people around the world began to carefully scan the names disturbing results were found. By mid-afternoon, after some checking of files, the WJC, the Wiesenthal Center, and Willi Korte and I found names of major Nazi figures on the list. An amazing collection of undesirables ranging from Nazi hangers-on to outright war criminals such as Willy Bauer, an alias used by Anton Burger, an aide to Adolf Eichman and Deputy Commandant of Theresienstadt; Elisabeth Eder, wife of Ernst Kaltenbrunner, who was sentenced to death at Nuremburg for his role in the deaths of hundreds of thousands in the "Aktion Heydrich"; Hermann Esser, the Vice President of the Reichstag; Hermann Schmitz, Chairman of the Board of I.G. Farben, the company that created Zyklon B; Dr. Hans Wendland, the infamous Nazi looted art dealer; Heinrich Hoffman, Hitler's photographer; Karl Jäger, head of a branch of the Gestapo in Lithuania; Hans Eppinger, Austrian doctor who performed water injection tests at Auschwitz; Kurt Herrmann,

Göring's jeweller; and clothier Hugo Boss who was found to have been responsible for making Nazi uniforms.[8]

If this was not bad enough, three Imperial Japanese diplomats were on the list, along with Vojtech Tuka, the Slovakian Nazi puppet premier responsible for the deaths of more than 100,000 Jews; as well as Francisco Franco's brother-in-law and wartime Foreign Minister Ramon Serrano Suner.[9]

"Imagine the feelings of victims' families as they read the list and see the names of victims alongside those of their murderers," said Greville Janner in reaction to the disclosure of the Nazis' names.[10]

Janner could not have been alone in this feeling. There were many who expressed anger that Nazis, some of them the most hideous, were found to have had Swiss bank accounts. In what was supposed to have been the first comprehensive listing of Jewish-owned bank accounts in Switzerland, turned out to be a who's who of Nazis and fascist criminals.

All over the world, people scanned the thousands of names looking for their family names, some for real, others for mere chance or fancy. For Ambassador Kunin in Bern, her search through the list turned out to be more than mere chance. On that morning, she scanned the list and to her utter surprise, she found the name of her mother, Renee May on the list. Until then, she had no idea that her mother had an account.

For the Swiss banks, the revelation that they were found to have been concealing, willingly or otherwise, the dormant account of the mother of the American Ambassador, the country from which the heaviest criticism had come, would become the supreme embarassment. On top of the growing list of Nazis and fascists on the list, this was the worst outcome for the banks from what was supposed to be a cathartic and healing action. There was no hiding the embarassment. "No fig leaf is big enough to cover the negilgence,"expressed George Kreyer. He had been ashamed that account holders were not told earlier of their accounts.[11]

Soon the press was full of stories of those who had tried for years to get their account, and were rebuffed. From New York to Detroit, Cleveland, California, and West Virginia, came claimants. Around the world too, people appeared having found their family names on the list. Israelis, who long ago gave up hope of finding information on Swiss bank accounts surfaced, as did claimants to the Koh-i-noor diamond in Punjab, India.[12] In Britain, Hungary, Romania, and Australia as well, people found names and expressed anger at why it took more than fifty years to get to this point.

In France, Madeleine Moulierac was amazed that she or her husband were not found, despite the fact they have lived at the same address for the past sixty years. "What's shocking," Madame Moulierac was quoted as saying, "is that the pharmacy has been in the same place for 51 years. The name hasn't changed. Couldn't they have sent a letter sooner?"[13]

D'Amato, calling the disclosures like this, "the tip of the iceberg," wanted to know what the SBA would do to prevent descendants of war criminals from getting their hands on the newly discovered funds of Nazis. He was concerned about all the claimants, but it would have been entirely wrong for the families of war criminals from benifitting from the ill-gotten gains of their infamous family members.

The Swiss, defensive about these funds, claimed they would take action to prevent this. On July 27, D'Amato wrote Kreyer asking questions about the accounts. "I am sure that you share in my conviction," wrote D'Amato, "that no one should profit from the horrors of the Holocaust."[14] Kreyer, answering D'Amato a month later, agreed with D'Amato and informed him that the SBA had instructed its members to put these accounts on hold. They would be referred to the Volcker Commission to determine their origin and then the proper disposition.[15] One month later, the SBA announced that it would freeze the accounts as opposed to merely putting them on hold.

The only answer the SBA had to this horrendous debacle, was that it was due to poor accounting proceedures. Poor accounting proceedures, however was an inadequate explanation for the presence of so many war criminals on the list, the very charge we placed against them. They argued that it showed they were being honest in their efforts. Moreover, they argued, the list was proof that there was not the $7,000,000,000 in their banks that Bronfman and others had claimed. They made it be known that paucity of Jewish names on the list as proof of the lack of evidence of their critics.

There was a greater explanation for this fact and it lied in the fact that the SBA only printed those accounts with a minimum balance. Anything below that balance was set aside, presumably for charity, as they had done in 1962. Most importantly, however, the reason a good number of accounts in fact fell below their arbitrary minimum level was the fact that for years untold numbers of accounts were drained by negative interest long after the depositor was dead. This fact was proven by the New York State Banking Department when it found the case of a claimant whose family member's account was drained of fees well into the 1980s or perhaps 90s despite the fact he died in the Holocaust.[16]

Just as the Swiss had set minimal amounts for the listing of dormant account on the July listing, they did the same thing with dormant accounts for their own citizens. Not long after the publication of the list in July, it was disclosed that there were thousands, perhaps tens of thousands of dormant accounts belonging to Swiss citizens. Within only a few days, the SBA agreed to publish this list in October.

While examining the records for these accounts, the Swiss quickly found more foreign-owned dormant accounts left off the first list. The SBA agreed to publish this list as well. These omissions only added fuel to the fire.

With suggestions that the failure to find or disclose all these names was proof that the Swiss violated the 1946 Washington Accords in not disclosing the names as they agreed to do, the Swiss bankers by now had fallen to new depths.[17] The *Irish Times* described the situation as "Switzerland's Shame."[18] The *Washington Times*'s headline for July 29 read "Printing lists backfires on Swiss banks."[19] Roger Altman, the former Deputy Secretary of Treasury, wrote of Swiss credibility following the printing of the lists, "The carefully built image of a tiny defenseless nation cowering before the ferocious Third Reich is a fiction."[20]

The October List

Two weeks before the second set of lists were published, the SBA took out full page ads around the world congratulating themselves for their "leadership and seriousness" in publishing the lists, calling it "Fulfilling Our Commitment."[21] But before the lists could even be published, D'Amato fired a broadside at them, castigating them for finding even more accounts, first after finding close to 2,000 in July, and second after insisting for two years previously that there were only 774 dormant accounts. "I am mystified," wrote D'Amato, "at the constant 'finds' of the Swiss banks. The number of accounts keep growing and the amount of money paid out to claimants stays static." D'Amato continued,

> I would like to know how much the SBA spent to publicize its investigative efforts in the major newspapers of the world. It is truly amazing that the SBA is focusing on its public relations campaign while no claims have been paid out and more accounts are being found.[22]

Nevertheless, on October 29, the SBA published the names of over 10,000 Swiss-owned dormant accounts and 3,687 foreign-owned dormant accounts. The Swiss owned accounts were valued at close to

$7,000,000 and the foreign-owned accounts were valued at close to $4,100,000. This time, however, the SBA was more careful. They published the lists on the Internet along with the list from July, the only difference being that in July the lists were also printed in the newspapers around the world. Now, the names were only available through a searchable name basis on the Internet. Without an all inclusive list, it would be much harder to find undesirable names and a claimant could only look for their own family names. Moreover, according to various reports, people with possible claims were contacted beforehand in an effort to avoid the embarassment of stories like those of Madeleine Moulierac in France.[23] Two weeks later, after Jewish groups all over the world attacked the Swiss for appearing to again be hiding something, the SBA reversed itself and agreed to publish the foreign-owned dormant accounts as they did in July. On November 10, the names were published in the *New York Times*, the *Neue Zürcher Zeitung*, and four days later in the Israeli paper, *Yedioth Ahronoth*.[24]

Despite the second printing, Jewish groups were still outraged. The Swiss remained deeply mired in mess of their own making. A process, proposed to them by their arch-enemy, agreed to with unanimity, and carried out, quite with an eagerness to do something right for once, all went terribly wrong. The advance work done on the lists was especially poor, lacking any attention to detail. While names of some of the Nazis' worst criminals were included on the lists, many others, including Holocaust victims were discovered, lending further credence to Switzerland's critics' charges.

As a postscript, Swiss did not escape criticism on the second list. The name of Wladimir Ulianow from Zurich appeared at first glance to be rather innocent. Yet, one needs to remember that in Russian and other Slavic languages "v" is transliterated in German as a "w." With these substitutions, the name of Vladimir Ulianov, otherwise known as Vladimir Lenin, the leader of the October Revolution in Russia, is easily recognizable.

"They sewed fig-leaves together and made themselves aprons"

The Swiss banks were embarassed at first by the disclosures D'Amato had made both during hearings and between them. They were also embarassed by the attacks of the WJC throughout as well. But it was easy for the banks to counter us both with accusations of ulterior motives. When the attacks came from "official sources," Switzerland stood in a different light. With the release of the first Eizenstat Report, the light would be shown brightly by the U.S. Government. When the fallout from the report subsided, the fig leaf of which Kreyer had spoken, would not been enough to cover Switzerland's shame. To paraphrase the Bible, the fig leaves would have to have been sewn together in an "apron" to cover all of Switzerland.[25]

By March, the interagency process Eizenstat was leading to look into the role Swiss banks played during the war was set to release its report. Eizenstat's team, led by State Department Historian William Slany, had poured through millions of documents, many of which we had already looked at, as well as those declassified by the various agencies, including the CIA, for this report.[26]

In the days leading up to the report, however, two participating agencies in the study, the Holocaust Memorial Museum and the Department of Justice's Office of Special Investigations (OSI), differed on the amount of non-monetary or victims' gold that reached the Swiss National Bank. The OSI's Director, Eli Rosenbaum and his historians did yeoman's work in discovering and translating microfilmed records of the Precious Metals Department at the Reichsbank. They calculated amounts that had never been disclosed. Rosenbaum fought fiercely inside the interagency process, much to his own detriment, to push forward with these numbers, even while they were still being assembled. The Holocaust Museum's researchers however, felt that the numbers could not be sustained when held up to criticism.

The decision had been made by March to publish the study without the OSI's findings. This caused great controversy between the agencies involved. The OSI objected, but the study was scheduled to be released on March 27. On March 10, however, someone on the interagency team leaked word to the press that the study did not conclude that victims' gold had been transfered to Switzerland.[27] This story enraged the WJC as well as Eizenstat and the other agencies, one because of the reported finding, and the other because it was leaked while the study was still being concluded.

Because of the leak, the report was delayed. The informant had succeeded in preventing the report's release without the conclusion the WJC had wanted in order to cast even greater doubt on the origin and content of the gold in the Federal Reserve in New York. Now with the report delayed, there was more time to research the issue.

The gold leak would not be the only leak. Soon others, despite a complete embargo on the report would talk to the press. The longer the report was withheld from the public, the more time there was for leaks. Nearly two weeks after the gold leak, David Lee Preston of the *Philadelphia Inquirer* reported that the report would be a "clear indictment of Swiss wartime policies."[28] Eizenstat was not pleased.

In the April 21 edition of the "Periscope" column, or weekly news forecast of *Newsweek*, it was reported that the report would now "state conclusively," that victim gold was indeed transfered to Switzerland.[29] On the morning of May 2, five days before the report would finally be issued, the Swiss Embassy in Washington, issued an immediate denial of the report and enlisting Eizenstat's help, quoted him as declaring the *Newsweek* story repeated that morning by Reuters as "pure speculation."[30]

Despite the denials, the reports were correct, as was Preston's report. The first Eizenstat Report as it has come to be called, was in most ways, as harsh on the Swiss as we were. Rosenbaum's efforts on victims' gold paid off, as did the confirmation of Switzerland as the overall banker for the Nazis. While we had been tough and unrelenting on the Swiss from the start, this report was forthright in its denounciation of the Swiss wartime role as being one of a "business as usual attitude."[31] Most importantly for our cause, we had been vindicated. Now, no longer was it just us, and even the WJC criticizing the Swiss banks, it was the entire U.S. government calling the Swiss banks crooks.

"Let me say," proclaimed D'Amato, "that the Swiss owe the world a full accounting in regard to what's taking place."[32] D'Amato reacted out of vindication and also with the view that now that the U.S. government had verified his claims after so long, it was time for the Swiss to make the proper restitution.

What made us all feel as if we had finally found the truth was the severity of the report. While in some ways it could have gone further, it nevertheless laid out the entire story, from Swiss culpability during the war to Swiss intransigence after. For Eizenstat, Swiss behavior during the war, however wrong, had a partial explanation. Their behavior after the war, however, was less valid, motivated by profit and little else.

Most importantly for the Swiss however, Eizenstat's remarks during his presentation of the report were the most damning of all. "But without question," he admitted, "Switzerland and other neutral nations benefited from their trade and financial dealings with the Germans and helped prolong the war effort."[33]

Our claims regarding the 1946 Washington Accords were also verified. The report also called into question Swiss sincerity in negotiating the 1946 Washington Accords. D'Amato's claim of an abject violation of the Accords by Switzerland was certainly strengthened by these conclusions.

For the Swiss, revelations that they indeed accepted victims' gold, knowingly or not, was bad enough. But for a senior U.S. official to state publicly that Switzerland's financial dealings with the Nazis prolonged the war, was shocking and perhaps to some in Switzerland, insulting. The reaction was immediate. The Swiss reacted with horror to these comments as well as the confirmation of Swiss acceptance of victims' gold. Borer, in Washington especially to comment on the report, was stunned. While refusing comment on the suggestion of Swiss prolongation of the war, he promised more study. "Ladies and Gentlemen," said Borer, "if this is really true, it is grave news of the most shocking nature."[34]

The report called into question past efforts by the U.S. to bring this issue to light, including those immediately after the war. The State Department itself came under fire for its lax approach to the problem. The report also explained the lack of attention to the gold pool, the collection of gold found by the Allies at the end of the war whereby victims' gold was freely mixed in with the monetary gold the Nazis looted from all over Europe. Because of this mixing, it now became a real possibility that the content of the gold that was transferred after the war to Britain and the United States was tainted.

With this, Eizenstat issued a formal call to Britain and France to declassify the Tripartite Gold Commission files in order to make the $68,000,000 in gold available for the use of Holocaust survivors.

International Outcast

On May 15, D'Amato held his fourth hearing on the Swiss banks, this time concentrating on the report. Eizenstat, Borer, Tom Bower, Rabbi Marvin Hier, and others all testified about the results. Eizenstat largely reiterated his remarks of the previous week. Bower and Hier stated their agreement with the findings and expanded on them.

Borer, however, changed tone. Instead of his usual diplomatic approach, Borer went into great detail to explain all that his country was doing to settle the problem, historically and financially, but complained that all of this was not being acknowledged. "The Swiss, old and young alike," stated Borer, "including the high school children...are perplexed and wonder why, in spite of these efforts, they continue to be treated as an international outcast."[35]

The Swiss had heard enough. Now that Eizenstat had verified what the rest of Switzerland's critics had already said, and more, the Swiss could no longer withhold comment on the role in which Switzerland had now been cast. The Federal Council issued a statement on May 23 denouncing the report, mainly Eizenstat's foreward, as containing "political and moral values which go beyond the historic report."[36] Moreover, the Council called the accusation of Switzerland acting as the banker of the Nazis as "a one-sided package judgement."[37] Publicly, the Swiss were displeased. Privately, they were livid. For the Administration to issue a report castigating their country in such a public and, in their view, judgmental way, was inexcusable.

The State Department took note of this Swiss reaction and was worried about it. The feeling was that while the report could not be undone, it nevertheless could be viewed in many different fashions. For diplomats accustomed to avoiding international disputes like this, especially ones of a historical nature, this was all very unsettling. They had to do something. Six days after the official Swiss reaction was released, President Clinton talked by phone with President Koller and praised Switzerland for all it had done and declared the conclusions of the report to be open to interpretation.[38]

The Swiss reaction to the report would be long remembered in the State Department. When the second Eizenstat report was issued on June 2, 1998, the object of study was different, as was the tone.[39] Now, the report would concentrate on the role of the other neutrals, but would also avoid the harsh criticism of the Swiss, so evident in the first report. It was clear from reading the tone of Eizenstat's forward to the second report that the Swiss reaction to the first had great influence on the second.

A day before the report was issued, David Sanger of the *New York Times*, wrote a story, quoting unnamed sources that the State Department was pressured to refrain from criticizing the Swiss too hard. Only under pressure from members of the interagency participants, did parts of the study felt to be too complementary to Switzerland's present efforts, wrote Sanger, come out of the final draft.[40] This story was similar to that which we had been hearing for months prior to the reports' release.

There Were Others

Other nations, in addition to the Swiss, had to be held accountable for their actions during the war as well. This subject, however delicate, could no longer be ignored and the best manner to address the issue was in an international conference. This conference took place at the stately Lancaster House in London on December 2–4. Forty-one nations attended the conference, and each gave papers on the role their country played, or alternatively how it was victimized, during the war. The Swiss delegation led by Borer, were still attacked for Switzerland's wartime role, this time by the Israeli delegation. Bobby Brown, Advisor on Diaspora Affairs to Prime Minister Benjamin Netanyahu, criticized the Swiss for not doing enough to bring the issue to a close and summed up the Israeli delegation's presentation by holding up his mother's German passport that was stamped with the red "J." Angrily, Brown glaring at Borer, told the conference that it was this "J", the very one the Swiss police first conceived of and persuaded the Germans to use, that meant life and death for those fleeing persecution like his mother.[41] Borer was clearly taken aback, as were the other members of the delgation by this emotional statement by Brown.

There were similar stories by delegates, of a personal and national nature. Those nations victimized by the Nazis told how their countries were systematically robbed and destroyed by the Nazis. In the end, just as the Swiss had hoped for, they were no longer the only ones being questioned and blamed. They were now one of many.

The Tainted Gold

At the beginning of the conference, British Foreign Secretary Robin Cook announced the creation of the Nazi Persecutee Relief Fund. The fund, to be held at the Federal Reserve Bank in New York, under the nominal control of Great Britain, would hold the proceeds of the gold held in dispute at the Fed since the beginning of this scandal. The three Allied countries would forgo their right to claim the gold, donating it instead to the fund. Other nations could contribute to it as well.[42] By the end of the conference several nations in addition to the three allies announced contributions. As of August 1998, the account had received pledges of $57,000,000 from eleven countries and promises of more from others.[43] It was clear now, the gold that had been held in dispute for nearly two years would finally be returned to whom it belonged.

* * *

The Swiss government, and especially, the Swiss bankers, had for awhile, only D'Amato and the WJC as villans to play off their hatred. They could counter that they had ulterior motives. While the U.S. government had issued a scathing report about them, this was really never a threat because, as will be seen later, there was only so far the Administration could and would go in criticizing the Swiss. D'Amato and the WJC remained a problem the Swiss would have to endure. But while they remained a real threat to their interests, they were no longer the only threat. Now, the banks would have to deal with an entirely different force, lawyers filing multibillion dollar lawsuits against them in U.S. courts that threatened the banks' very existence. Soon the lawsuits would become the driving force against the banks. It would be through them and because of them, that the unfinished business of the Second World War would be brought to a close.

Notes

1. Letter of United States Senator Alfonse M. D'Amato to Thomas Borer, 20 March 1997.
2. Letter of George Kreyer and J.P. Chapuis of the Swiss Bankers Association to Dr. Kurt Hauri, Chairman of the Swiss Federal Banking Commission, 28 April 1997 as an enclosure to the letter of Thomas Borer to United States Senator Alfonse M. D'Amato of the same day.
3. Arthur Spiegelman, "Jewish acocunts in Swiss banks higher than thought—source," Reuters, 5 June 1997; David E. Sanger, "Swiss Find Funds That May Belong To Nazis' Victims," *New York Times*, p. 1, Section A.
4. Clare Nullis, "Swiss set policy on unclaimed accounts," *Philadelphia Inquirer*, 26 June 1997.
5. Alexander G. Higgins, "Swiss banks report millions more in assets of Holocaust victims," Associated Press, 8 July 1997.
6. "Swiss Govenrment Heralds Release of Names on Dormant WWII Accounts in Swiss Banks," Press Release of the Embassy of Switzerland in the United States, 23 July 1997.
7. "Swiss Banks Commence Global Claims Process to Identify Owners of Dormant World War II-Era Accounts," *New York Times*, 23 July 1997, pp. 12–13, Section A.
8. Letter of Rabbis Marvin Hier and Abraham Cooper, the Simon Wiesenthal Center to Christopher Meier, Swiss Bankers Association, 23 July 1997; Michael Hirsh, "At Last, a Tally of Pain, Nazi or Jew? It didn't matter to the Swiss," *Newsweek*, 4 August 1997, pp. 32–33; Richard Sisk, "Good, evil eyed on Swiss List," *Daily News*, 24 July 1997; Robin Givhan, "Fashion Firm Discovers Its Holocaust History,"*Washington Post*, 14 August 1997; and "Only 5 francs in suspected old Nazi account," Reuters, 28 July 1997.
9. "3 of 6 Japanese said diplomats of dormant Swiss accounts," *Japan Economic Newswire*, 31 July 1997; "60 million dollars dormant in Slovakian Nazi account," Agence France-Presse, 30 July 1997; "Former Franco Aide Has Dormant Swiss Bank Account," Reuters, 24 July 1997.
10. Alexander G. Higgins, "Possible Nazi names on list of Swiss bank accounts angers Jews," Associated Press, 24 July 1997.
11. Alan Cowell, "Swiss Bank Reports Finding $11 Million," *New York Times*, 24 July 1997.

12. Sujatha Shenoy, "Swiss list of dead accounts springs Indian surprises," *Business Standard*, 26 July 1998.
13. Arlene Levinson, "Holocaust victims' relatives angry after being told of dormant accounts," Associated Press, 24 July 1997.
14. Letter of United States Senator Alfonse M. D'Amato to George Kreyer, Swiss Bankers Association, 27 July 1997.
15. Letter of George Kreyer, Swiss Bankers Association, to United States Senator Alfonse M. D'Amato, 29 August 1997.
16. Letter of Acting Superintendent of Banking Elizabeth McCarl, New York State Banking Department to Alan Greenspan, Chairman of the Board of Governors of the Federal Reserve System, 19 March 1998, Attachment, as cited in Gregg Rickman, "Swiss Banks and the Name Lists," *Avotaynu, The International Review of Jewish Genealogy*, Volume XIV, Number 2 (Summer 1998), p. 5.
17. David E. Sanger, "Bankers and Broken Promises, List of Accounts Confirms That Swiss Ignored Pact," *New York Times*, 28 July 1997.
18. "Switzerland's Shame," *Irish Times*, 28 July 1997.
19. Andrew Borowiec, "Printing lists backfires on Swiss banks," *Washington Times*, 29 July 1997.
20. Roger Altman, "The Triumph of Morality in a world where commerce rules," *Los Angeles Times*, 3 August 1997.
21. "Progress Report, Fulfilling Our Commitment," Advertisement of the Swiss Bankers Association, *Washington Post*, 14 October 1997, p. 7, Section A.
22. Letter of United States Senator Alfonse M. D'Amato to George Kreyer, Swiss Bankers Association, 15 October 1997.
23. Tani Freedman, "Swiss banks to publish new accounts list amid ongoing attacks," Agence France-Presse, 28 October 1997; "Swiss Banks Said to Find 'Hundreds' of Possible Nazi Accounts," Dow Jones Service, 29 October 1997.
24. "Our Progess Continues," Advertisement of the Swiss Bankers Association, *New York Times*, 10 November 1997, p. 15, Section A.
25. Genesis: 3.7.
26. The agencies involved were the CIA, the Departments of Commerce, Defense, Justice, State, Treasury, the FBI, the Federal Reserve Board, National Archives, National Security Agency, and the United States Holocaust Memorial Museum.
27. Tom Topousis, "Stalemate in Probe to Track Nazi Gold," *New York Post*, 10 March 1997, p. 11.
28. David Lee Preston, "U.S. to criticize Switzerland for abetting Nazis," *Philadelphia Inquirer*, 23 March 1997.
29. "Nazi Gold," Periscope column, *Newsweek*, 21 April 1997.
30. "Swiss Government and Eizenstat's Office Respond to Reuters' Story," Press Release of the Swiss Embassy in Washington, 2 May 1997.
31. *U.S. and Allied Efforts To Recover and Restore Gold and Other Assets Stolen or Hidden by Germany During World War II, Preliminary Study*, Coordinated by Stuart E. Eizenstat, Under Secretary of Commerce for International Trade, May 1997, p. vii.
32. Transcript of a News Conference of United States Senator Alfonse M. D'Amato, United States Capitol, 7 May 1997.
33. Transcript of the "Special Briefing of Under Secretary Eizenstat on the release of *U.S. and Allied Efforts To Recover and Restore Gold and Other Assets Stolen or Hidden by Germany During World War II*," at the United States Department of State, 7 May 1997.
34. Transcript of the News Conference of Thomas Borer on the Release of *U.S. and*

Allied Efforts To Recover and Restore Gold and Other Assets Stolen or Hidden by Germany During World War II, 7 May 1997.

35. Statement of Ambassador Thomas Borer before the United States Senate Banking Committee, hearing *Swiss Banks and Attempts to Recover Assets Belonging to the Victims of the Holocaust,* 105th Congress, 1st Session, S.Hrg. 105–176, 15 May 1997.

36. Declaration of the Federal Council on the Eizenstat Report, 23 May 1997.

37. Ibid.

38. James D. Besser, "Clinton Call Soothes Swiss," Associated Press, 2 June 1997.

39. *U.S and Allied Wartime and Postwar Relations and Negotiations With Argentina, Portugal, Spain, Sweden, and Turkey on Looted Gold and German External Assets and U.S. Concerns About the Fate of the Wartime Ustasha Treasury, Supplement to U.S. and Allied Efforts To Recover and Restore Gold and Other Assets Stolen or Hidden by Germany During World War II, Preliminary Study,* Coordinated by Stuart E. Eizenstat, Under Secretary State for Economic, Business, and Agricultural Affairs.

40. David Sanger, "U.S. Traces Nazi Gold to Neutral Countries, *New York Times,* 1 June 1998.

41. Speech of Bobby Brown, "London Conference on Nazi Gold," Lancaster House, London, United Kingdom 4 December 1997.

42. Account Agreement between the Federal Reserve Bank of New York and the Government ofthe United Kingdom of Great Britain and Northern Ireland, 27 November 1997.

43. Edith M. Lederer, "Reprot on Nazi gold conference notes Vatican failure to open archives, Associated Press, 24 August 1998.

8

The Lawyers

Gizella Weisshaus was fourteen in 1944 when her father was arrested and separated from her mother and six brothers and sisters in Sighet, Romania. Put in a sealed railcar, the family was sent on to Auschwitz. At war's end, Gizella alone was left to pick up the pieces. Having been told that there was money waiting for her in Switzerland, she heeded her father's words and traveled there on three separate occasions seeking the assets, each time without success.

Like so many others we spoke with, Weisshaus' case was touching and unfortunate. What made her different from the others, however, was the fact she did not write a letter explaining her case, she contacted a lawyer.

"Somebody finally sued"

"At first, Jewish organizations were taken aback," explained Ed Fagan, "How is it that somebody filed this suit without their knowing. Not that they were angry, but that somebody finally did it, somebody finally sued."[1]

Ed Fagan, a forty-four-year-old Yeshiva University-trained attorney, was the lawyer Weisshaus first contacted. Fagan had an interesting and flamboyant past. Among other cases, he had represented a six-year-old victim stabbed by an escaped mental patient with a hypodermic needle while riding a Brooklyn-bound commuter train, and had been featured prominently for his two trips to Colombia immediately following an airline crash in December 1995 in which 160 people died. Regarding the trips, Fagan was quoted as having stated, "I did not go down there talking about lawsuit...if, after I helped someone said it might be nice to represent us" that would be fine.[2]

On October 4, Gizella Weisshaus took the matter to court. Fagan, Dan L. Johnston, Robert Swift, who previously had sued the Swiss banks over the Marcos estate, Martin J. D'Urso, and later joined by Bill Marks, who worked to get restitution for Hugo Prinz, the American survivor of Auschwitz, filed a lawsuit in the Eastern District of New York against UBS, SBC, Credit Suisse, and other Swiss banks on behalf of Gizella Weisshaus and "others similarly situated," for $20 billion.[3]

After hearings by D'Amato and the publicity behind a rash of documents on the misdeeds of the Swiss banks, Fagan saw his opportunity to embark on a landmark legal case: "I looked at it from a legal perspective, and said to myself, Holy God, there's a lawsuit here."[4] Now, after nearly a year of attacks from D'Amato and the WJC the banks now faced attacks from a third and potentially more damaging source.

Soon afterward, Fagan reached out to our office for recognition. Fagan wrote us a day before the October 16, 1996 hearing in New York to offer his services in whatever way possible. He claimed, at the time, to have been receiving some 200–300 additional claimants each day, and some 1,600 by October 15.[5] It was obvious, though, that these numbers were inflated and this number of claimants could not have surfaced so quickly. According to Fagan, who confirmed this to me later, not all of the names on his list were at all sure that accounts in their name. His numbers were padded, but this served a cause, namely that it raised the stakes for the banks.

The banks, UBS and SBC, were incensed. They vowed to fight an unjustified lawsuit and rattled off a list of things they were doing to resolve the Swiss bank affair. "We shall naturally be taking action," answered the banks. "An appropriate response is being prepared."

Fagan's case could not and would not remain as the sole legal initiative filed against the Swiss banks. Soon others would express interest in suing them as well.

"A me-too case"

"As you know, at some point," wrote Gary W. Becker, of the law firm of Messerli & Kramer, in Minneapolis, "it may make sense for one or more of the victims' heirs to bring a civil action against the Swiss banks.[6] Becker offered his assistance for any such potential action. He was, though, not the only one to offer help. We received letters offering help from attorneys in Arizona, California, Canada and even Britain. Yet, these were mere offers to help. Two weeks later, another lawsuit, a class-action, filed by a team of fifteen law firms, nationwide, supported by the Simon Wiesenthal Center in Los Angeles, and led by Michael D. Hausfeld, was brought against the Swiss banks.

Hausfeld, a partner in the Washington firm of Cohen, Milstein, Hausfeld, and Toll had a long history of class action suits dealing with consumer issues, environmental disasters, and civil rights. He successfully sued Texaco, twice, once for an environmental spill in Virginia, and more recently in the landmark case for race discrimination to the tune of $176 million in which Texaco executives were heard, on tape, voicing racial epithets. He also leads a consumer suit against the big compact disc makers for price fixing.[7]

The suit was an in-depth and historically detailed account of the role Swiss banks played in helping the Nazis by acting as their bankers and by accepting funds from companies using slave labor in the concentration camps. Hausfeld's 109-page complaint did not impress Fagan who called it a "me-too case," nevertheless in the view of many who saw it declared it to be the more intricate and threatening of the two.[8]

"Not everybody can play on the all-star team"

From here on, it would be Fagan vs. Hausfeld. Both sought maximum exposure for their respective cases and each sought to downplay the other. There was a competition for attention, with Fagan placing much greater focus on the press than did Hausfeld. Fagan felt that because his case was filed first he deserved the greater attention, and by connection, greater press. "He thinks he does everything first," commented Fagan to a Hausfeld initiative soon after the second case was filed. Soon Fagan would hold demonstrations in front of the Swiss banks, calling for a boycott. Hausfeld would file a brief with the New York Federal Reserve seeking the revocation of the Swiss banks' charters. For Fagan, Hausfeld was "a good lawyer, but not everybody can play on the all-star team."[9]

Fagan and Hausfeld differed also on their fees in the case. Hausfeld took the case pro bono, as did most but not all of the other attorneys on his team. Fagan, however, would not agree to this formula. He declared to Gabe Kahn of the *Forward*, that it was "precisely because his team had a financial stake in the outcome of the case, they will do a better job."[10] After the settlement the fee issue would be the chief topic of discord between the victorious attorneys.[11]

With the filing of a third class action suit by the World Council of Orthodox Jewish Communities in Brooklyn on January 30, 1997, the rivalry between the two attorneys became more complicated. The World Council, representing the Satmar sect of Hasidic Jews, was filed by attorney David Berger of Philadelphia, whom we had heard was interested early on in suing the Swiss banks. Berger essentially filed Hausfeld's claim but with the Council's chosen claimants. Now, there were three similar suits filed in the same court, against the same defendants, all before Judge Edward R. Korman, U.S. District Judge in Brooklyn. Something had to be done. As Gabe Kahn wrote before Berger filed his case, "neither legal team is willing to back down, a scenario which will likely force Judge Korman to choose who will be lead counsel on the case."[12]

On March 7, Judge Korman did just that. He consolidated all three cases, now to be coordinated by a ten-member executive committee. Swift, Fagan's partner, and Hausfeld each held four seats on the committee, Stan Wolf representing the Satmar suit and now allied with Hausfeld, and New York University Law professor Burt Neuborne, formally with Fagan, each held a single seat.[13] Fagan, while nominally still part of the case, was no longer leading it.

Conflicts of Interest

"A criminal has the right in a free society to an attorney but he has no inherent right to public relations counsel," wrote Charles J. Levine, the President of Charles Levine Communications, one of Israel's largest public relations firms, to his colleague Gershon Kekst the head of the New York-based Kekst and Company, the lead publicity firm representing the SBA.[14] Kekst, one of the most prominent New York publicists represented the SBA, much to Levine's consternation, so much so, Levine took the unusual step of publicly upbraiding him for it. For Kekst, this was unusual, for he was normally very much the back door operator, an important asset necessary to achieve a satisfactory outcome for his high-placed battle-hardened clients. The choice of Kekst to represent the SBA was an important yet expensive one. According to the journal *Institutional Investor*, Kekst insists his clients sign on for a minimum annual retainer of $100,000, plus a billing rate of $500 an hour. "When you think of Gershon Kekst," said a competitor, "think of the Wizard of Oz."[15] For Levine to have criticized Kekst was fascinating and perhaps even embarrassing for Kekst who did all he could to keep a low profile and in essence be the "hidden hand" behind his clients' actions.

While Kekst was publicly exposed and castigated for accepting the evil Swiss bankers as clients, another high-priced public relations consultant John Scanlon, was engaged by Kekst to "handle" the New York City Council then considering sanctions against the Swiss banks operating in the city. Jack Newfield, writing in the *New York Post*, detailed Scanlon's hiring by Kekst in a column on April 2, 1997, quoting Kekst associate Jeffrey Taufield as saying that Scanlon was hired several months before.[16] Scanlon, the $350 per hour public relations artist who practiced what *Crain's New York Business* termed "no-holds barred advocacy," carried a much-scarred reputation, especially in light of his role in defending the tobacco companies by smearing a whistle blower who exposed the Brown & Williamson Company over the addictiveness of nicotine.[17]

If Kekst had a moral conflict of interest in representing the Swiss banks, it did not show. For others, namely twelve attorneys at the respected New York law firm of Cravath, Swaine & Moore, the conflict ran deeper and pushed them to voice their dissent.

On February 3, Samuel Butler a senior partner at the firm, began his regularly scheduled partnership meeting with what he thought would be a brief discussion of his decision to represent Credit Suisse in its troubles over the dormant Holocaust accounts. The bank had chosen Cravath based upon a recommendation from a Salomon Brothers general counsel.[18] What he described as a normal thirty-second procedure turned into a thirty-minute discussion, with several Jewish partners voicing objections to the firm taking Credit Suisse as a client. Butler decided to hold a second meeting in two days time.[19]

Between sessions, Butler sought the advice of attorneys from the prestigious law firms in New York as well as leaders in the American Jewish community, including Robert Rifkind, president of the American Jewish Committee. All thought that Cravath should represent Credit Suisse if their representation would result in a positive and mutually beneficial resolution of the dispute between the banks and the claimants. Although the firm would not represent the bank in the court case brought against them, it would provide them with "strategic advice" to handle the allegations brought against them. "We're going to help them determine what the truth is what really happened," said Rifkind.[20]

On February 5, the second session took place. With the firm's seventy-two partners present, the decision was made to accept Credit Suisse as a client. The decision, however, was not unanimous. According to some who attended, the partners voted "strongly, but not unanimously, in favor of taking the case.[21] Following the meeting, Butler circulated a four-page, single-spaced memo explaining why the firm had decided to represent Credit Suisse. A number of associate lawyers at the firm, nevertheless remained angry over the decision, but fearing for their futures at the firm, remained quiet.[22]

A week later, twelve associates overcame their apprehensions and responded to Butler's memo with one of their own. "Normally, this type of dialogue about client representation does not occur," they wrote, "But this case obviously raises profound questions about whether one can justify representing an institution that collaborated with the Nazis and subsequently concealed that collaboration."[23]

These associate attorneys, were for the most part Jewish, but not all of them. They were angry and felt this form of response was absolutely necessary in order to express their extreme dissatisfaction with the decision taken by the partners. Their memo was an impassioned statement that Credit Suisse had willingly profited from the Holocaust and did not deserve the firm's representation. "Credit Suisse earns through the Firm's involvement," they wrote, "a legitimacy worth more to it than the wealth it has hoarded."[24] The twelve concluded their memo by declaring, "It is our conviction that one cannot represent Credit Suisse in its role as bankers to those who committed genocide and do the justice we are all obliged to do to the victims and survivors of the slaughter. The two are simply incompatible."

Two days after the memo was circulated, there was another meeting held to quiet the dissent. Thirty attorneys attended, but the decision would stand.

Nearly a year after the memo, the fear of reprisal was still strong when I spoke by phone with one of the signatories. She refused to discuss the matter. "Talk to somebody else," she advised me.[25] At least one other of the signatories, Craig Arnott, left the firm returning to his native Australia where he joined the law firm of Gilbert & Tobin, only three months after he signed the memo.[26]

The Cravath twelve, caused a stir. Their memo again raised the often asked question, should attorneys be judged by the clients they keep. "Whoever does Credit Suisse's bidding is, as the conscientious dissenters at Cravath complained," wrote attorney Ronald Goldfarb, "serving as the agent of bankers who abetted genocidal murderers."[27] Just as Gershon Kekst was before them, Cravath now would be tarred by its choice to represent a bank so clearly identified with the Nazis. Once again there was fallout from a scandal that had managed to spread to the courts and high-priced law firms of the United States.

The Adversarial Process of a Trial

Just as C. Boyden Gray and Marc Cohen had tried early on to persuade us from beginning to investigate the Swiss banks, now by circumstance, equally they tried to pressure Judge Korman to drop the case to obtain relief for their clients, as they termed it, from the "adversarial process of a trail." The banks' lawyers sought a dismissal of the suit on a variety of grounds, chief among them, jurisdiction. They picked away at the composition of the plaintiffs' citizenship as well as the venue of the case. They would, however, not be alone in their efforts to persuade Korman. Soon, Wilmer's legal arguments would be joined by those of the new Swiss Ambassador, Alfred Defago.

In an eight-page letter to Korman on June 3 laying out the arguments of the Swiss Government against the continuation of the case, Defago wrote, "The Government of Switzerland believes that continuation of these lawsuits would be inconsistent with proper respect for Swiss sovereignty under internationally recognized legal principles." Moreover, using the same explainations as Wilmer, argued the case would get in the way of all the ongoing efforts the SBA, the Government and others were taking on behalf of the pursuit of the truth.[28]

Two days later Defago wrote again, this time to Secretary of State Albright urging her to help in the case, wrote seeking State Department pressure on Korman to "apply moderation and restraint."[29] In response to questions concerning the letter, State Department spokesman Nicholas Burns steered clear of the intended response by the Department, but was quite clear on where the Department's and Administration's sympathy lied. "Clearly, justice has got to be done for those people," answered Burns, "many of them elderly in their 70s and 80s, who at the end of their lives want to see some of their families' financial assets restored to them properly after having been stolen by the Nazis."[30]

If Wilmer could get Defago's help for their cause, Hausfeld to, could get help. On June 20, D'Amato sent an amicus curiae, or "friend of the court" brief to Korman supporting Hausfeld's case. D'Amato wrote that only through a hearing in a United States Court would address the issue of "whether Swiss banks violated the laws of the United States and fundamental international human rights laws with regard to their banking activities between 1939 and 1945."[31] D'Amato was now squarely on Hausfeld's side.

Now, each side in the case had put their chosen allies up front for the coming court hearing before Korman on July 31. But before the hearing, an unlikely respondent appeared. Paul Volcker, the chairman of the Independent Committee of Eminent Persons through himself into the case, much to the consternation of Hausfeld and even the WJC. On July 24, only a week before the first court hearing on the case, Volcker sent a nine-page, single-spaced letter to Korman expressing his personal reservations about the effects of the case on his committee's work. Volcker expressed fears of "the real possibility that a parallel investigation will impair our work, potentially to the point of ineffectiveness."[32]

Volcker wrote Korman that he expressed his personal reservations regarding the effects of a lawsuit on the possible forced disclosure of documents provided by the Swiss banks, and how they would effect his committee's relationship with the banks. His letter to Korman was not supported by the other members of the committee, in that he had tried and failed in an attempt to send the letter in the full name of the committee. When this was found to have been impossible, he sent it under his own name. This forceful approach angered Avraham Burg, a member of the Volcker Commission.

Burg wrote to Volcker expressing shock at receiving his letter. He asked that Volcker "inform the judge immediately that this letter does not represent the opinion of all members of the committee, at least not mine." Unfortunately, Burg added, "this is not the first such incident. I have spoken out about things being done behind the backs of some of the members."[33]

On October 29, Volcker added to his opposition to the lawsuits by filing a motion with Korman to file an amicus statement. On February 20, 1998, he filed a letter updating Korman on the process of the audits being conducted in the Swiss banks.

"The number can't be too small"

On July 31, the banks' twenty-two lawyers filed into U.S. District Court in Brooklyn for a hearing before Judge Korman. Hausfeld, Fagan, and Swift were ready. Hausfeld brought with him Bert Neuborne and Harvard law professor Arthur Miller. The hearing which lasted almost ten hours, went back and forth between the two sides, each putting forth their arguments. Korman, was said to have repeatedly asked if would it be possible to come to some compromise concerning the seemingly parallel work of Volcker's Commission. To this, Miller argued that parallel proceedings could "provide a breath of fresh air" to the investigation.[34]

Roger Whitten for the banks argued that the venue was wrong and that the case should proceed in the Swiss courts. Korman responded, "Why reject an entire case?"[35] While Korman did not hand down a decision, he did not strike the case down either. The decision was left open. Both sides felt hopeful, but the momentum seemed to lie with Hausfeld.

Following the hearing, there was a period of calm. Both sides eagerly awaited the decision of the judge and could do nothing more. It was now that talk of settlement began to surface. The talk was from both sides, Fagan suggesting that a settlement was around the corner, and Whitten confirmed a number could be reached. UBS' Robert Studer had suggested as far back as April that any future settlement should be covered by the Humanitarian Fund. Hausfeld immediately shot this idea down as ridiculous.

The argument put forth by Hausfeld since the filing of his suit was that the best and most judicious way to solve the problem once and for all was to submit the case to a court. In that way, there could be no accusations of back room deals or deals made out of political expediency, such as the offer from Studer. For Hausfeld and the other lawyers, the case seemed to drag on. Month after month passed without a word from Korman.

By December, the WJC watching the process very carefully, concluded that a global settlement could be the way out of the stalemate. Bronfman, who as early as March had also suggested that a method of some sort could be found to settle this issue out of court, now moved forward with his idea.

Elan Steinberg, interviewed on Swiss television, suggested that the Swiss, who it had been suggested had already spent over $500,000,000 fighting this scandal, would be receptive to a settlement.[36] He said the banks had approached the WJC in an effort to seek a settlement and that if conditions were right, a settlement might be possible. Bronfman suggested that $1,000,000,000 would be a starting point. "If they want complete and honorable closure, then it's going to be a very expensive closure."[37] Within weeks, with public speculation, the number grew to $3,000,000,000.[38]

Credit Suisse' Rainer Gut, who had previously initiated the Humanitarian Fund and Mathis Cabiallavetta both suggested that a settlement was possible but it would have to be all inclusive. In other words, the lawsuits would have to be resolved in addition to any other claims that might be made upon the Swiss banks.

Quiet talks proceeded, yet a guiding hand was needed in order to bring the parties together. While the banks could in some form communicate with the WJC, quite expectedly their relationship with Hausfeld was much more complicated and difficult. Since the lawsuits hung heavily over the heads of the banks, they were reluctant to talk at all about any type of number, despite Bronfman's suggested price tag. Moreover, they faced a dilemma. The banks had consistently maintained that no payments would be made until the results of the Volcker Commission finished its work. Following Volcker's communications with Korman, however, his impartiality was questioned. The disclosure that he had sat for ten years as a member of the board of directors for Nestlé the Swiss chocolate company, only added to the growing mistrust of him in the eyes of many. Would they now forgo this principle, like they did with the Humanitarian Fund, or would they settle? They chose to talk. It was then that Ambassador Stuart Eizenstat, who had previously announced his opposition to the lawsuits, preferring instead to settle "this matter in a quiet and dignified way," stepped in and tried to bring the two disparate parties together.[39]

Negotiations

Going into the planned December 14 meeting, the bankers remained skeptical. Cabiallavetta and the other CEOs stuck to their guns. A global settlement, including the lawsuits was the only way out. "If we cannot capture everything in a potential solution that on balance settles all the claims in one financial package," said Cabiallavetta, "then I won't be a part of it."[40]

At the Savoy Hotel in Zurich, Hausfeld, Swift, the three bank CEOs, and Eizenstat, met for roughly three hours. In a tense meeting in which the CEOs barely uttered a word and refused to talk about anything approaching a number, only process, both sides met and adjourned without any conclusion. After the meeting, Eizenstat told reporters that the meeting was "purely an exploratory mission." Exploratory it was, but it would eventually form the basis of settlement to this fifty-year-old problem.

While the banks had endured two years of attacks by D'Amato, WJC, and even the press, the lawsuits presented them with the greatest challenge to date. They spent a great deal of money fighting the suits, both in fees and man-hours. In all, justice would have been more aptly served had they simply donated the estimated $500,000,000 they had spent through 1997 to the victims as part of an overall settlement. Yet, the Swiss bankers stubbornly hung on and refused to give in completely. Soon they would however, be faced with the threat they feared the most, boycotts and sanctions. It was one thing for politicians and Jewish groups to harass them. But it would be a wholly different thing for them to be closed out of the largest market in the world and banned from doing business in the United States.

State and local politicians could not help but see the potential for leverage they had in their hands to deal with the obstreperous Swiss banks. Once they reacted, the situation would become a full-blown crisis for Switzerland. No more would this crisis be restricted to the banks, but it would now be a problem for the nation itself.

Notes

1. Hanan Sher, "Counsel for the Dead," *Jerusalem Report*, 16 October 1997, p. 45.
2. "Judge seeks records of stabbing suspect," *Albany Times Union*, 21 December 1995; Henry Gottlieb, "Inviting Disaster," *New Jersey Law Journal*, 22 January 1996.
3. Gizella Weisshaus v. Union Bank of Switzerland, Swiss Bank Corporation, Credit Suisse and Swiss Banking Institutions #1-100, Civil Action No. 96-4849, Eastern District of New York.
4. Hanan Sher, "Counsel for the Dead," p. 45.
5. Letter of Edward Fagan to U.S. Senator Alfonse M. D'Amato, 15 October 1996.
6. Letter of Gary W. Becker to United States Senator Alfonse M. D'Amato and Edgar Bronfman President of the World Jewish Congress, 7 May 1996.
7. Gabriel Kahn, "Federal Judge Could Represent Bellwether on Swiss Restitution," *Forward*, 3 January 1997, p. 3; Allison Frankel, "Tale of the Tapes," *American Lawyer*, March 1997, pp. 65–75; David Segal, "A Class-Action Fight? That's Music to His Ears," *Washington Post*, 14 October 1996, "Texaco Settlement Outlined," *Milwaukee Journal Sentinel*, 11 January 1997; Allanna Sullivan, "The Attorney Behind Texaco's Big Settlement," *Wall Street Journal*, 26 November 1996.
8. Wendy R. Leibowitz, "Getting the Gnomes of Zurich to Cough Up, Lawyers Pursuing Holocaust Wealth Face Huge Evidentiary Obstacles, But They're Unfazed," *National Law Journal*, 27 January 1997.
9. Kahn, "Federal Judge Could Represent Bellwether on Swiss Restitution," p. 1.
10. Ibid, p. 3; Leibowitz, "Getting the Gnomes of Zurich to Cough Up, Lawyers Pursuing Holocaust Wealth Face Huge Evidentiary Obstacles, But They're Unfazed."
11. Ann Davis, "Holocaust Suit Settlement Spawns a Legal Fee Fight," *Wall Street Journal*, 2 September 1998; Susan Orenstein, "Gold Warriors," *American Lawyer*, September 1998, pp. 62–68.
12. Kahn, "Federal Judge Could Represent Bellwether on Swiss Restitution," p. 3.
13. Wendy Leibowitz, "Judge Forces Disputing Counsel to Work Together," *National Law Journal*, 24 March 1997.

14. "Israeli Publicist Appeals to U.S. Colleagues: Do Not Represent the Swiss Banks," *PR Newswire*, 13 February 1997.

15. Suzanna Andrews, "Gershon Kekst, the Hidden Persuader," *Institutional Investor*, Vol. 30, No. 3, 1 March 1996.

16. Jack Newfield, "Swiss bank's flack has bared dark soul," *New York Post*, 2 April 1997, p. 7.

17. Robin Kamen, "He's Still the Man," *Crain's New York Business*, Vol. 12, No. 8, 19 February 1996.

18. Edward A. Adams and Daniel Wise, "Cravath Controversy: Suisse Connection," *New York Law Journal*, Vol. 19, No. 29, 17 March 1997.

19. Edward A. Adams and Daniel Wise, "Controversy Ruffles Cravath over Representing Swiss Bank," *New York Law Journal*, Vol. 217, No. 40, 3 March 1997.

20. "Cravath to Advise Bank Over Nazi Fund Charges," *Wall Street Journal*, 4 March 1997.

21. "Controversy Ruffles Cravath over Representing Swiss Bank," *New York Law Journal*.

22. Telephone discussion with Blaine Harden, reporter for the *Washington Post* in New York, who disclosed the dispute in that paper, 13 March 1997.

23. "Memorandum for Partners, Representation of Credit Suisse," Associate Attorneys of Cravath, Swaine & Moore, 12 February 1997, p.1.

24. Ibid, p. 2.

25. Telephone discussion with an Associate Attorney at Cravath, Swaine & Moore, New York City, 10 February 1998.

26. Telephone discussion with associates at Cravath, Swaine & Moore, New York City, 10 February 1998.

27. Ronald Goldfarb, "Guilt by Association," *Washington Post*, 6 April 1997, p. C1.

28. Letter of Swiss Ambassador to the United States Alfred Defago to Judge Edward R. Korman, 3 June 1997.

29. Letter of Swiss Ambassador to the United States Alfred Defago to Secretary of State Madeleine K. Albright, 5 June 1997.

30. Nicholas Burns, State Department Briefing, 17 June 1997.

31. Brief Amicus Curiae of Senator Alfonse M. D'Amato in re Holocaust Victims' Assets Litigation, 20 June 1997, p. 7.

32. Letter of Paul Volcker, Chairman, Independent Committee of Eminent Persons to Judge Edward R. Korman, 24 July 1997, p. 9.

33. Letter of Avraham Burg, Chairman of the Jewish Agency Executive to Paul Volcker, Chairman, Independent Committee of Eminent Persons, 27 July 1997.

34. Catherine Crocker, "Judge Delays Decision on Swiss Bankers' bid to Dismiss Lawsuit," Associated Press, 1 August 1997.

35. David Rohde, "N.Y. Judge Weighs Swiss Bank Suit," *International Herald Tribune*, 2–3 August 1997, p. 2.

36. "Estimation of the Cost of the Crisis," *L'Hebdo*, Switzerland, 30 October 1997.

37. "Historians say Swiss Moved Most Nazi Gold," *San Antonio Express-News*, 2 December 1997; William Hall, "Swiss Banks Inching to Holocaust Settlement," *Financial Times*, 15 December 1997.

38. Stuart Ain, "Stage Set for $3 Billion Swiss Bank Settlement," *New York Jewish Week*, 12 December 1997.

39. Daniel Kurtzman, "Eizenstat Warns Against Suing Swiss Banks," *New Jersey Metro West Jewish News*, 17 April 1997, p. 33.

40. Michael Shields, "Swiss Banker Skeptical about Holocaust settlement," Reuters, 13 December 1997.

9

Boycotts and Diktats

"Other sanctions can be employed at the appropriate time, such as further tightening of our control over the United States' assets of these Swiss banks," wrote Deputy Secretary of the Treasury Harry Dexter White in a memorandum to Treasury Secretary Henry Morgenthau, shortly before the end of 1944.[1]

White very clearly knew what the Swiss banks were doing for the Germans during the war. He knew about the gold, the camouflaging of German assets, and the other misdeeds they committed. In this enlightening memo, classified and withheld for over fifty years by the Treasury Department, White even proposed to Morgenthau that the U.S. should covertly buy controlling interests in a few of the Swiss banks so as to put a curb on their actions. Yet, White's enthusiasm for sanctions, and that of his fellow Treasury Department investigators was not shared by others in the U.S. government. At the time, only the federal government was in the business of imposing sanctions on foreign states. Fifty years later, this situation has changed. With a new found sense of power, now cities and states would carry on the fight and seek to impose their own will on the Swiss banks.

The Vanguard of Disinvestment

"New York City was in the vanguard of the disinvestment effort that brought the racist regime of South Africa to its knees, and brought the outrage of apartheid to an end," proclaimed New York City Council Speaker Peter Vallone, "New York City threw its financial weight behind the McBride Principles and helped start a peace process in Northern Ireland that some told us could never happen." Vallone continued,

In the 1970s we helped to break the Arab boycott of Israel, and even now this Committee is proceeding with a disinvestment bill that will put our moral and financial pressure on the military dictatorship in Burma that has ignored free elections and imprisoned a heroic nobel [sic] peace prize winner. We can do no less on this moral issue. And we have moral force that we can bring to bear and that is why two weeks ago, together with my colleagues we introduced legislation barring the deposit or investment of any New York City funds in any Swiss Bank until this issue has been resolved to the satisfaction of the Holocaust survivors and those families of Holocaust victims who are seeking simple justice.[2]

Vallone was voicing the sentiments of countless state and local officials at the disclosures made in the press about the Swiss banks during World War II. This February 1997 hearing of the New York City Council represented the first hearing of the Swiss bank scandal on a nonfederal level. It centered on Vallone's Council resolution of two weeks earlier that would ban city investments in the Swiss banks. The resolution and the hearing proved an ominous sign for the banks of worse things to come. D'Amato, Defago, Singer, and Steinberg all attended the hearing and spoke. With them came Estelle Sapir and Gizella Weisshaus and the leaders of New York City's Jewish community, followed by the CEOs of the three big Swiss banks in New York, who were said to have been very uncomfortable in the presence of this group so inimical to their interests.

Vallone's hearing, however, was not the first action taken on the local level against the banks. As early as May 6, 1996, New York City Comptroller Alan G. Hevesi, son of American Jewish Committee representative Eugene Hevesi, who fought with the Swiss banks throughout the previous decades for justice, wrote to Robert Studer of UBS and the other leading bank heads asking them to begin an internal investigation into the dormant accounts. Expressing concern over the fate of the unclaimed assets, Hevesi did not shy away from reminding the CEOs that as Comptroller of the City of New York he had direct control over the investment of city pension funds invested with the banks. He also was responsible for controlling the city's other financial relations with their banks.[3] Following D'Amato's New York field hearing in October, Hevesi wrote in the *Jewish Press* of his disgust of Swiss actions and reminded readers of his financial role in New York and, without a clear explanation, what he could do to the Swiss banks.[4]

On October 23, 1996, New York Governor George Pataki issued a statement saying that he was prepared to "initiate whatever appropriate action he can take at the state level to generate prompt action on the part of the Swiss Government and banking authorities."[5] Pataki's promise would later be acted on.

Two months later, New Jersey State Assemblymen Joel Weingarten and Kevin O'Toole introduced two resolutions in the Assembly, the first calling on the Swiss government to fully disclose all information on dormant accounts. The second resolution encouraged the President and Congress to take all appropriate actions to spur Swiss action. David Mallach, Assistant Executive Director of the United Jewish Federation of New Jersey said the point of these nonbinding resolutions is to "make clear that people are watching."[6] One month later, the State Assembly of Rhode Island passed a nonbinding resolution, like New Jersey's, calling on Switzerland to end the fifty-year coverup and make all its information available.[7] David Mallach could not have been more right; people were watching and the list was growing.

When It Rains, It Pours

Within weeks of the New Jersey resolutions, Weingarten and O'Toole's fellow Assemblyman from New York got an idea of his own. New York Assemblyman Brian McLaughlin of Flushing introduced a bill on January 16 that would require the eight foreign banks licensed to operate in the State of New York to open their books, those of the subsidiary and even the foreign parent bank, for inspection by the State Banking Superintendent, if the bank wished to continue doing business in the state.

An aide to McLaughlin attributed the high visibility D'Amato gave the issue, both instigated and enlivened the bill's chances in the Assembly.[8] Just as McLaughlin saw the vulnerabilities faced by the banks in New York, those whose money was managed by the banks did as well. On January 30, Sheila Salenger, a member of the New York State Teachers' Retirement Board, called to tell me of the Board's concern for the banks' actions. Hevesi had also threatened the banks with divestiture, but he only controlled government funds. What Salenger discussed with me was something wholly different and potentially much more dangerous for the banks: teachers' retirement assets invested with SBC. Salenger and her fellow board members told Georges Blum, Chairman of SBC,

> Your subsidiary, Brinson Partners, manages approximately $800,000,000 of New York State Teachers' Retirement assets. We are also shareholders of your organization through our EAFE investments. We, therefore, urge you to take appropriate action. This will send a clear message to the world that Swiss Bank Corp. is concerned with concluding this great tragedy.[9]

Salenger's call to me came a day after Vallone called his hearing in the City Council. "In no event shall such moneys be deposited or invested in a Swiss bank doing business in New York City," read Intro-duction 905 of the New York City Council.[10] "We are sending a clear message," proclaimed Vallone, "that New York City funds will not be deposited or invested in Swiss banks until proper compensation is made to the families of Holocaust victims who had deposited their life savings for safekeeping during World War II."[11] A spokesman for Vallone told reporters that the city council would also consider citywide divestiture.

None of this what was what the banks needed or wanted to hear. Vallone's threat came just three days after the resignation of Carlo Jagmetti, two weeks after Christoph Meili's disclosure of UBS's shred-ding of documents, and a month after Delamuraz's cries of blackmail by the Jews. In response to Vallone's threat, about all the beleaguered Swiss government and banks could muster was the simple wish that the City Council would reject Vallone's proposal.[12]

While Vallone was announcing his intentions in New York, New York Assembly Speaker Sheldon Silver, together with Kalman Sultanik of the World Jewish Congress in Albany, announced that he was calling hearings by the State Banking Committee on the issue. "Our obligation clearly extends," said Silver, "to ensuring that all banking institutions operate in New York according to the highest ethical standards."[13] Two weeks later, D'Amato, Singer, Defago, and a host of Holocaust survi-vors with claims against the banks, gathered in the historic Bar Asso-ciation in Manhattan to again tell their story. Once more, the Swiss were on trial.

Cooperation not Confrontation

With two Swiss Parliamentarians at his side, D'Amato stood in front of half a dozen cameras and several dozen reporters and together they declared that sanctions would not be the best course. "Now is not the time for punitive actions," announced D'Amato. "I understand the frus-trations and I share the concerns."

Lily Nabholz, Chairperson of the Swiss Parliament's Legal Affairs Committee, and François Loeb, the Parliament's only Jewish member, met with D'Amato on February 6 and begged for his indulgence to ease his pressure on Switzerland. Their country, they said, was doing all it could to get to the truth, truth they believed should and would in the end come out.

Seemingly out of step with his intention to attack until the Swiss gave up, D'Amato had consistently said the Swiss had to at least be given a way out if anything was to be resolved. As long as momentum was occurring, D'Amato would not advocate more forceful action. He maintained this position at the New York City Council and the New York State Assembly Banking Committee hearing. It seemed odd, in a way, that the foremost critic of Switzerland and its banks would hold to such a position, but D'Amato had achieved a lot in his campaign against the banks and a bit of moderation did not harm his standing on the issue or slow his criticism in other areas of the ongoing inquiry.

While D'Amato was calling for restraint, New York's Governor, George Pataki, announced his intention to send state Banking Superintendent Neil Levin to Switzerland to discuss the role the banks played in the prewar and war years in New York. Pataki was rather blunt about the decision when he said at a press conference, "if banks do not want to cooperate this will be a criminal act and their license will be revoked."[14]

Five days after Pataki's announcement on February 11, Levin was in Bern meeting with Daniel Zuberbüler, Director of the Swiss Banking Commission. According to Levin, the meetings went well and a good working relationship was established. This was evident by the fact that less than ten days later, Zuberbüler wrote back to Levin informing him that the Banking Commission had "declared its willingness to cooperate fully" with the department and to exchange information according to the stipulations of the Swiss Banking Act of 1934. Zuberbüler agreed to cooperate with Levin as long as information was not given to third parties and that it would be used for supervisory purposes only.[15]

By any standard, this was a landmark agreement. Never before had the Swiss banks agreed to allow a U.S. regulatory body to examine its customer records of its banks inside or outside of Switzerland. Immediately after World War II, Treasury Department officials had begged for the opportunity to examine the banks' records in order to glean from them the information necessary to put all the pieces together. Levin gained access to information on all accounts moved from Switzerland to New York between 1933 and 1960. Moreover, Levin's investigators would look at the records of the Swiss banks' U.S. correspondent banks, including Chase Manhattan, Citicorp, Bankers Trust, Bank of New York, and J.P. Morgan.

The deal Levin negotiated with the Swiss was better than what the WJC and the SBA had worked out. While Volcker's auditors could see bank records, Levin's investigators could look at actual customer accounts. Volcker did not have this privilege. Whether this agreement stemmed from Swiss preoccupation at the time, Delamuraz, Jagmetti, and Meili included, or because of Pataki's threat to close the banks down in New York, Levin's agreement with the banks would pay serious dividends in the coming months.

With the agreement in hand, Levin began work on assembling records from the banks in Switzerland as well as New York. While information was not publicly disclosed, we found that Levin's aides and researchers were finding tantalizing information about the extent of information still available and the detailed nature of it. Soon, Levin had arrived at an agreement with Volcker to exchange information and records with him as well.

To add what Levin had already built on, Pataki in May issued an Executive Order authorizing various state agencies in New York to pool their resources in order to help Holocaust victims with their claims. Pataki appointed a State Commission on the Recovery of Holocaust Victims Assets, and made Levin, now Insurance Commissioner, its Chairman.

The State Commission was preparatory to Pataki's bigger announcement that the state would open a claims processing office in New York. On June 25, Pataki authorized the creation of the office to serve those who felt they had a claim to make on the Swiss banks. Later the Commission would grow to take on claims of those seeking to claim the proceeds from wartime insurance policies from European insurance companies.

The office, located in New York, was placed under the overall supervision of Levin, run by Alan Z. Goodman, and later Catherine Lille. The eight-person staff was composed of experts in the fields of finance and banking, were multilingual and could handle calls from a variety of claimants, not only from New York but around the world. They advertised this point in order to serve as a one-stop shop for claimants, including the free preparation of claims to be submitted to the Swiss banks.[16] Levin's established relationship with the banks and Volcker made this possible. Personally, I felt relieved by the creation of this office because now, I could refer the twenty or thirty calls and an equal number of letters I received each week to them. After receiving close to 500 calls and letters over the previous year, I had long before run out of personnel and time to try to work each and every claim.

The office was opened with great fanfare on September 15, with a ribbon-cutting ceremony in which D'Amato and Pataki both attended, along with Elan Steinberg, Ben Meed, Levin, and Alan Hecht, a New

Yorker who wrote to us seeking our help with the Swiss Ombudsman's office who had bungled his claim and took his money. We invited Hecht as a living example of why this office was needed. Hecht wrote to D'Amato in August seeking help in filing his claim with the Ombudsman, who until only recently had been responsible for handling the claims for dormant bank accounts in Switzerland. Hecht sent $300, as required by the SBA, but then received a letter telling him that the Ombudsman was no longer responsible for searching for the accounts and returned a check to him for $75, keeping the rest. They referred Hecht to the Volcker Commission and left it at that.[17] The Ombudsman gladly accepted Hecht's money and did nothing for him in return. For people like Hecht, the Claims Office was a welcome addition to the ever-growing effort to both search for assets of Holocaust victims and to connect the survivors with those assets.

Despite its value, the office was not without critics, foreign and domestic. George Kreyer, wrote to Pataki that the office could serve a more useful purpose by opening up its claims process to claims against other nations' banking systems, including the United States and Israel. From Ed Fagan came the other criticism, namely that it was, of all things political.

Soon after the office's creation, we came to learn that Fagan's staff was discouraging claimants from calling the Claims Office on the grounds that it was politically motivated. Claimants were told by Fagan's staff that under no uncertain terms if they filed with the Claims Office, they were unwelcome to join Fagan's suit. Fagan, slightly dismissive of the accusation, did not outwardly deny his staff's remarks.[18]

Hevesi, meanwhile pressed on with an attempt to get other officials to form a monitoring group on the state and local level to formally observe the banks' handling of the assets. "I believe that it is appropriate and prudent for us, as public finance officers," wrote Hevesi to one State Treasurer, Judith Baar Topinka of Illinois, "to monitor this issue, track the progress made by the Swiss bankers and government in their efforts to resolve this issue and to share information about local initiatives relating to the issue."[19] The group, according to Hevesi, would meet informally every few months to exchange information and to coordinate their actions. Hevesi had traveled to Switzerland, and during the course of his six days there met with the bankers and had also tried to rally Swiss companies to contribute more money to the Humanitarian Fund.

While still holding out the possibility of imposing sanctions, Hevesi endeavored to make public the amount of city investments he controlled in Swiss banks in New York. Of the five pension funds Hevesi controlled, he declared to the press that $47,572,000 was invested in 322,880 shares of the Swiss banks. He added, that a subsidiary of Credit Suisse managed $1,000,000,000 in investments for the pension funds and that the city usually put $150,000,000 in overnight investments in the banks.[20]

Hevesi's publication of New York City's numbers and his call for meetings of an Ad Hoc Monitoring Task Force enlivened public debate over a nationwide disinvestment campaign like that used against South Africa and its then-apartheid regime. Other state and local finance officials began to discuss the possibility of divestment as a tool to "get into the act," or more succinctly, to become involved either for their own good or that of their constituents. The fact is inescapable, politicians saw the interest in the issue and saw the concern their constituents expressed in the Swiss reaction to D'Amato's attacks. If it was good for D'Amato, it could be good for them too.

Joining the Battle

"I assure you that I will continue to do everything in my power— working with Senator D'Amato and our state banking superintendent, Neil Levin," wrote New York Assembly Speaker Sheldon Silver "— to hold those Swiss banks to their promises."[21]

Silver was not alone. New York State Comptroller H. Carl McCall maintained his ban on new investments with the Swiss banks in New York as a mirror to what Hevesi had done. Yet, most of the sanctions imposed on the banks had been done by New York politicians. Pataki, Hevesi, Vallone, Silver, and McCall all had, more or less the same constituents. New Jersey's actions, while still not complete, were viewed as interesting but because of New Jersey's proximity to New York it all seemed the same. Even to the Swiss it seemed as if all the criticism they received came from one geographic area: New York. Flavio Cotti, in his remarks as incoming President of Switzerland on December 31, pointed this out when he said criticism directed against Switzerland came mainly from "the east coast of the United States, and in particular New York."[22] Apparently Cotti was continuing the new tradition of Swiss Presidents' putting their foot in their mouth in their yearly speeches. Cotti was wrong though. New York may have begun the ground war in the states' attacks on the Swiss banks, but it soon had plenty of volunteers.

One by one, states joined Rhode Island in proposing or passing resolutions condemning the Swiss banks. In March, the Illinois General Assembly saw the introduction of one; in April, the Maryland General Assembly passed one; and a resolution was introduced in January 1998 in Alaska.[23] State Treasurers in Mississippi and Nebraska also offered their offices' assistance to any of their states' residents who might need help in retrieving assets from the Swiss banks.[24]

While resolutions expressed interest, they had no real effect. Others, however would come forth with legislative action that would do to the Swiss banks what they feared the most, stop their business here cold.

New Jersey

In December 1996, Neil Cohen had introduced resolutions in the New Jersey Assembly encouraging the Swiss banks to disclose information. This effort was nonbinding; it had no teeth. In March, however, Cohen and Assemblyman Jeffrey Moran introduced a bill along with fifty-eight of their colleagues in the Assembly, with a companion measure introduced in the State Senate by Senator Robert Singer, that would require the state to sever all financial and commercial transactions with the Swiss government and Swiss businesses. "This legislative crusade for fairness," wrote Cohen, "now has 60 votes signed on to the bill. That is 19 votes more than the 41 needed for passage, and six more than needed to overturn any threat of a gubernatorial veto." With these numbers, it was all but assured, that whenever they wished to close the banks down in New Jersey, they could do so. Cohen said this much, declaring that the bill would be held in reserve if negotiations with the Swiss faltered.

Cohen and Moran's bill would do more than hurt Swiss banks. Under the bill, the state could no longer purchase goods and services from any company owned in whole or in part by Swiss entities. Additionally, the bill would prohibit the state from investing pension or annuity funds in banks, stocks, or securities of any company conducting business in or with the Swiss confederation; would deny eligibility of any company engaged in business in or with the Swiss Confederation, for any loans from the New Jersey Economic Development Authority; prohibit investing assets in American subsidiaries of Swiss corporations, and to require the state to divest any assets currently held in Swiss banks, stocks or securities.[25] Cohen also made contacts in each of the other states promoting similar legislation.

A month later, the Whitman administration proposed that Credit Suisse/First Boston be given a $100,000 contract to examine the possibility of selling the state's Temporary Disability Insurance fund, thereby raising $200,000,000 for the state's budget. Democrats in the state made political hay of the issue, with Whitman's eventual 1997 gubernatorial opponent James McGreevey calling a news conference to denounce Whitman for the contract. "This is a great disrespect to New Jersey's Jewish community," said McGreevey.[26] A day after Assembly Democrats introduced legislation to block the contract, on April 18 Governor Whitman canceled it by deciding against the idea of selling the fund, making the study unnecessary.

While Whitman's plan was unpopular with Republicans in New Jersey, it was nevertheless obvious that Credit Suisse was targeted because of the scandal. Like Cravath, Whitman came under fire for dealing with a bank that was quickly becoming an untouchable.

By March 1998, with Cohen's bill held in reserve, Assemblyman, Joel Weingarten proposed a similar measure to punish the Swiss, but only the banks. "To attempt to punish all Swiss institutions," wrote Weingarten, "whether or not they acted with volition against Holocaust victims, would be to attempt to do to the Swiss people what representatives of Swiss financial institutions have done, and continue to do, to the Holocaust victims themselves."[27] Weingarten then, drew a line between his proposal and Cohen's, refusing to punish everything Swiss as would Cohen's widely supported bill.

Weingarten pushed his bill through the Assembly's Banking Committee on a 7–0 vote, after the Committee voted down an amendment 4–2 by Cohen, to add language to extend the ban to all Swiss institutions. Cohen was attempting to pair his earlier initiative to Weingarten's out of a belief that the proposal would only pull $80,000,000 out of one bank, UBS, and therefore prove ineffective. "Sometimes it takes that kind of action to change a social fabric," said Cohen. "The Swiss businesses that flourished have done so because of the Holocaust assets."[28] Now the Assembly faced two competing forms of sanctions to place upon the Swiss, either all Swiss companies, or just the banks.

Chicago

On February 7, Chicago Aldermen Burton Natarus and Bernard Stone proposed to the Chicago City Council legislation that would ban all city investments with any bank with loans outstanding to Switzerland, any Swiss company, including a Swiss bank, or any business assisting in operations in or trading with any private or public entity located in Switzerland.[29]

"We've got to put our foot down," said Natarus, "If we don't see some changes in the very near future, you're going to see Ald. Stone and I come right back with this ordinance."[30] Stone, like Vallone before him, compared the legislation to that imposed against South Africa. He added that the bill would certainly pass the City Council because it had the support of black aldermen who see the same parallel.[31] Natarus and Stone, while not having pushed the City Council to pass their ban, sat in waiting, "very itchy" in the words of some, to pursue the matter. Since the introduction of the ordinance, the two had been quite vocal about their effort.

Illinois

State Treasurer Judith Baar Topinka, one of many in receipt of a letter from Hevesi requesting her support for the Ad Hoc Group, responded to Hevesi in July that she was "startled, like most others...and then saddened by the news reports that there were possibly such accounts and that there had been no effort at restitution.... Altogether, this is reflective of a very dark and sordid chapter in world history."[32]

Topinka continued by informing Hevesi that her state did not invest in foreign banks, thus investments in Swiss banks would not occur. Yet, she continued by saying that "we do have a Swissotel in Chicago in which we have held events in the past. We have put any future dealings on hold pending a favorable outcome to the Holocaust accounts issue."[33] This statement apparently caused concern for Topinka and it was soon reversed. Topinka's press spokesman later made this point very clear in a phone conversation.[34] Following her July response to Hevesi, Topinka issued a statement declaring that while "the Illinois State Treasurer's Office has nearly 400 banking partners in the state...I have chosen not to conduct business with Swiss-owned financial institutions. This policy should not be viewed as a sanction, but rather as encouragement for both sides in this issue to continue their efforts."[35]

Sanctions that Bite

Until this time, the only actions against the Swiss banks were more symbolic than anything else. Whatever actions taken were either resolutions in the various state assemblies, or actions held in abeyance until a decision could be made to go further and actually implement the sanctions. Throughout this early period, caution was urged by all sides and everyone waited for someone else to jump first into the sanctions fight. On October 9, the man who had pressed hard for action, but remained one of the most cautious, made the first move.

At the suggestion of Alan Hevesi, the City of New York excluded UBS from a syndicate of banks participating in a billion-dollar transaction with city funds. The syndicate, led by UBS was a response to the city's bid for a letter of credit on a $1,075,000,000 Revenue Anticipation Note. The letter of credit would have backed money the city would borrow in anticipation of state and federal funding. As the winning bid, UBS stood to gain a $1,300,000 fee for the exchange. Hevesi felt "it would be sending the wrong message to accept the bid," and Mayor Rudolph Giuliani was in agreement with the action.[36] In the place of UBS, Morgan Guaranty Trust took over the consortium's leadership.

The State Department was now faced with the first concrete punitive action taken in the United States against any of the Swiss banks. It no doubt caused concern for them, especially Stuart Eizenstat, who from Cairo described the action as "understandable but counterproductive."[37]

The effect of Hevesi's action was to legitimize genuine sanctions against Swiss banks. While the State Department was clearly displeased by the diplomatic row Hevesi's action caused, their fear of further action would not have to wait very long to become reality.

Five days after Hevesi excluded UBS from the New York City consortium, California Treasurer Matt Fong, a Republican seeking the nomination to challenge Barbara Boxer for her Senate seat in the November 1998 elections, saw an opportunity to strike and wasted no time in doing so. Fong, overseeing California's investments with banks there, announced that he was imposing a moratorium on any further investments with the banks. According to Fong, from January 1996 to May 1997, the state had purchased certificates of deposits and bankers acceptances totaling $2,000,000,000 from UBS, SBC, and Credit Suisse. During the 1996–97 fiscal year, the state also invested $228,000,000 with Credit Suisse.[38] According to the Agence-French Presse, UBS lost $200,000,000 worth of business with this moratorium, SBC lost $400,000,000, and Credit Suisse, $1,200,000,000.[39] Fong had imposed the moratorium earlier in the summer, but had not made it public according to Fong spokesman Roger Wildermuth because, "we just didn't make enough of an event of it to make the media aware of it."[40]

During the summer, the banks apparently tried and failed to convince Fong to lift the moratorium. In August, Fong sought full disclosure from the banks to solve the problem of the dormant accounts, but the banks failed to satisfy his demands.

Irritated at Hevesi's sanctions, the banks vented their anger at Fong's actions. "We regret the announcement," declared a spokesman for Credit Suisse, "It is disconcerting considering all the measures that have already been taken." An SBC spokesman called Fong's move "regrettable behavior."[41]

A day after his announcement, Fong became a main attraction in the Swiss bank drama. Soon Swiss officials from the Embassy in Washington, as well as representatives from the banks were calling on him in an effort to convince him to lift the moratorium. Fong asserted his actions were designed to encourage action from the banks, not to punish them. While the Swiss sought to change his mind, so did the Stuart Eizenstat. In a letter of October 17, Eizenstat mentioned their telephone conversation two days earlier, and proceeded to list, point by point all the Swiss had committed to do to handle the problem of dormant accounts. "I believe that the Swiss Government and Swiss banks will honor all of these commitments," wrote Eizenstat. "We should also not forget that Switzerland remains an important economic partner." Eizenstat warned,

> boycotts and sanctions against Swiss banks could also run afoul of our efforts to maintain open world markets in financial services. Continuation of sanctions against Swiss banks would hamper our ability to successfully conclude a financial services agreement in the World Trade Organization. I ask therefore that the State of California lift its sanctions against Swiss financial institutions.[42]

Eizenstat was not alone in denouncing the sanctions. American Ambassador Madeleine Kunin in Switzerland also expressed her disagreement with "that strategy." In an interview in Bern, Kunin said she did not "question their motivation but I don't think it is a winning strategy because it just creates backlash in Switzerland."[43] This was the theme of the State Department approach to sanctions. Backlash, diplomats and regional experts maintained, would be the main reaction of the Swiss to the torrent of state initiatives which they felt created a "piling on" effect.

What were the Swiss or State Department officials to expect from a campaign that began at the federal level with revelations that filtered down through newspapers all over the country, not to mention the world? Each and every politician could not help but see a multitude of stories about the misdeeds of the Swiss. Moreover, the shrill Swiss reaction to each charge did not help matters either.

This fact was borne out on the afternoon of October 20, when I received a call from a member of the office of Massachusetts State Treasurer Joe Malone. The staffer was interested in whether I could send her any recent news clips on Christoph Meili or anything else on the banks. I sent a few clips and thought nothing more about it. Later in the afternoon, I checked the news wires and found that Malone had ended the state's $200 million line of credit with UBS for the state's commercial paper program which netted the bank a base fee of $120,000 annually.[44] "The bank's failure to understand the need for common decency and respect for the memories of these Holocaust victims," wrote Malone to Allyson D. Samson, a Managing Director at UBS, "compels our decision to no longer do business with you."[45]

This time, instead of simply issuing their normal regrets, the Swiss banks went further and hired a Boston consulting firm to work with Malone to try to lift the ban. The firm chosen was the Commonwealth Group, a firm run by Robert Crowe, Massachusetts Senator John Kerry's finance chairman. Crowe, retained at a hefty $10,000 per month, was enlisted to lobby Malone to lift the ban on State business with UBS.[46] But Kerry, a potential 2000 candidate for President, needed Crowe to help him toward his goal and news like this certainly was not welcome.

A day after this story appeared in the *Boston Herald*, Kerry tried to stem the damage from the story. The *Herald* ran a story in which Kerry, in Kyoto with Eizenstat at the time, defended his record on Holocaust issues, with a press aide declaring, "he would fight anyone who would oppose those efforts." Tovah Ravitz, defending Kerry's record said, "certainly the senator has been a strong advocate on this issue."[47]

Yet, the criticism from Crowe's hiring to lobby Malone hurt him, and by connection Kerry. In December, the State of Massachusetts fired Crowe and canceled its $3,750 a month contract with his company to lobby in Washington on behalf of the state's $10,800,000 Central Artery project, otherwise known as the "Big Dig." Since 1993, Crowe had earned $180,000 lobbying for this project on behalf of the state. State officials blamed the firing on a lack of response from Crowe or any of his associates as to questions from the state, a charge Crowe vehemently denied.[48]

Two weeks later, Crowe bowing to increasing pressure, resigned as chairman of Kerry's campaign finance committee. According to the *Boston Globe*, "the publicity was potentially damaging to Kerry, who is serving his third six-year term in the Senate after winning a bruising reelection battle last year and is considering a run for the presidency in 2000."[49] Clearly Kerry felt his interests threatened by Crowe's associations. While it might not have been the exact cause of the separation between the two, most thought it certainly contributed to it.

"It's not fair"

The Swiss were stung by this rapid succession of U.S. state- or locally imposed sanctions. Within less than a two-week period, three separate actions were taken against the Swiss banks and officials in other states echoed sentiments that sanctions could or would be imposed. "It's not fair," cried Swiss Finance Minister Kaspar Villiger, who only two years earlier reopened the wounds of Swiss wartime history by apologizing for Switzerland's ill treatment of Jewish refugees during the war.[50]

The Swiss felt besieged. At every step they were being attacked for actions for which they felt no responsibility. They had done much, they claimed, to identify and return Jewish assets. They had begun investigations, agreed to the Volcker Commission, and they had established humanitarian funds. What more did the world want from them? Individually, Swiss citizens while angry at D'Amato from the beginning, in their words, for his "over-reaction" to the problem, now had a cast of enemies at whom to scream their anger. Now the Swiss were unsure of who would attack them next. The atmosphere was becoming worse rather than better.

Eizenstat had much with which to concern himself. Representing the administration, he had to deal evenly with the domestic pressures of thousands of claimants pressing for justice, state and local officials responding to these claims with demands for action or sanctions in retaliation for a lack thereof, and the effect this all was having on U.S. relations with Switzerland.

What Eizenstat needed was a break and Abe Foxman of the Anti-Defamation League provided just that. On October 31, Foxman wrote to Fong that "such initiatives are unnecessary and, indeed, might prove to be detrimental."[51] Foxman explained his belief that the Swiss have finally, under great pressure, become engaged in a search for the truth and that the recent spate of sanctions imposed upon the banks has caused a defensive and reactive approach to the issue. Sanctions now, Foxman felt, would only exacerbate this reaction. Five days later, Fong issued a press release saying he was rethinking the moratorium.

While Fong's statement was a reprieve for Eizenstat, Seccretary of State Albright's impending trip to Switzerland could not have come at a more sensitive time. As the first U.S. Secretary of State to visit Switzerland since 1961, the visit would be important not only because of the long absence of such a visit, but more importantly because of the strain existing between the two countries at the time. While Albright complimented present Swiss efforts, she also criticized past Swiss actions: "Over the decades our two countries have developed a relationship that is strong, warm, multi-faceted and mature; a relationship strong enough to meet even very difficult challenges in a constructive and cooperative way," stated Albright before the Swiss Parliament. "That is fortunate because we face such a mutual challenge today in the issue of Nazi gold." She continued:

> But just as surely the Swiss National Bank accepted large amounts of looted gold from Nazi Germany that, together with trade and vital commodities from other neutral nations, helped sustain the German war effort; and the Swiss National Bank resisted efforts after the war for full restitution of the stolen assets as private Swiss banks failed to provide full openness with respect to dormant accounts. The financial benefits of these wartime transactions accrued to the Swiss and were passed along to subsequent generations and that is why the world now looks to the people of Switzerland, not to assume responsibility for actions taken by their forebears but to be generous in doing what can be done at this point to right past wrongs. And indeed, Switzerland has shown courage in confronting this challenge. Among all the neutral countries of World War II, Switzerland is setting the pace in the intensity of its national debate and the comprehensiveness of its approach.[52]

Albright made her point clear. Switzerland was wrong for its actions during the war but was correct now for all it was doing to alleviate the problem. Eizenstat, with Albright, pointed to the dual notion of criticism and compliment. He also took great pains to make clear the administration's unalterable "opposition to these punitive steps taken against the Swiss banks."

In light of the multiplication of sanctions, and the administration's clear opposition to them, Hevesi called for a conference to be convened in New York on the issue. The conference, to take place on December 8, would provide a forum in which the 100 public finance officials Hevesi invited could discuss the question of sanctions on Swiss banks and the effect they would have on the overall goal of justice for the claimants. For Eizenstat, this provided a venue to publicly argue against sanctions and to do so before the widest possible audience of those making these decisions on a local level.

Yet, before the conference convened in New York, bowing to pressure on all sides, on December 4, Fong lifted the moratorium. "It's time to trust and verify the actions of the Swiss banks," Fong said. "We will continue to monitor the banks closely to ensure that they are cooperating with investigations into this matter."[53] Now, with at least one set of sanctions against them lifted, the bankers, public finance officers, Eizenstat, Singer, and even D'Amato would now attend Hevesi's International Conference on the Recovery and Return of Dormant Holocaust-Related Swiss Bank Accounts and Hidden Assets.

On December 8, 306 people, public finance officers, leaders in the fight against the Swiss banks, press and claimants such as Estelle Sapir and Greta Beer gathered in the Plaza Hotel in New York to discuss whether sanctions were the wise approach to take against the Swiss banks. The audience heard from Alan Hevesi, Edgar Bronfman, Madeleine Kunin, and Bennet Freeman representing Eizenstat, Thomas Borer, the CEOs of the Swiss banks in New York, D'Amato, Carl McCall, Matt Fong, Mel Weiss, Neil Levin, Paul Volcker, and Avraham Hirchson. All had varied viewpoints on the subject, the likely sources favoring a tough stance against the banks, with Singer at one point even calling for the imposition of sanctions, and the bankers them selves clearly opposing sanctions.[54] Singer's call showed an impatience with the Swiss that would increase in the coming weeks.

What did become clear though from the proceedings was that while for two years the issue was at first discussed in terms of accusations, recriminations, and then threats, first in the courts then by economic sanctions, something else was needed. The cast of players against the banks had now become legion. Everyone was dancing to his own drumbeat and there was little if any coordination between the various parties to the dispute. Hevesi's conference focused everyone on the need to talk, to coordinate their actions, both against the Swiss banks and with each other so that there was no disunity in the ranks.

Whereas the forces allied against the Swiss banks had become unwieldy, Hevesi forced unity. He guided the finance officials to form a board consisting of Fong, McCall, Pennsylvania Treasurer Barbara Hafer, Denise Ducharme, President of the National Association of Unclaimed Property Administrators, and himself to formally monitor the efforts of the Swiss banks and to monitor the imposition of sanctions against them. To this end, the conference recommended a ninety-day moratorium on sanctions. The banks would have this time to clear the way towards a settlement of the issue.

Not everyone was happy with the decision. While on the face of it, this was a respite for the Swiss, they clearly did not see it that way. Immediately afterward, Borer showed displeasure with the conference's decision by saying "sanctions now or in the future against Switzerland are unfair and against international law. Setting deadlines is also counter-productive."[55] Others, including spokesmen for the banks voiced disappointment that sanctions were not lifted entirely.

Natarus and Stone from Chicago, vocal during several of the conference sessions, were unhappy because they had been asked to hold their Chicago City Council ordinance and were angry that it would again be postponed. Claimants too, were angry. Estelle Sapir wanted action and so did members of the World Council of Orthodox Jews. Nevertheless, the conference produced breathing space for the Swiss, whether they liked it or not, and for those wishing for sanctions, their wishes would go unfulfilled.

The World's Second Largest Bank

When the attendees to Hevesi's conference gathered in the Plaza, they read in their morning papers the news that SBC and UBS had agreed to a merger to form the world's second largest bank and Europe's largest. The new bank, to be named the United Bank of Switzerland, would have combined assets of $595,000,000,000. The two would create a behemoth second only to Japan's Bank of Tokyo-Mitsubishi.

The merger was a very real necessity for UBS and this showed by the fact that SBC, much smaller than UBS, was essentially taking over its bigger rival, with SBC executives grabbing all of the top jobs in the new company. Nevertheless, the deal was pitched as a merger. UBS shareholders were very unhappy with the company's performance and particularly that of Robert Studer. The Swiss banking scandal, certainly not the guiding reason for the merger, nevertheless had a hand in it, especially because of Studer's caustic and aggressive approach to the banks' defense against the various charges levied against UBS.

While it seemed like a fairly easy task for the two rivals, merging their companies would not go so easily in the place it needed to the most, New York State. New York is particular to banking operations, in that banks, foreign and domestic, need to get the approval to operate in the state not only from the Federal Reserve as they do in every other jurisdiction, but also of the New York State Banking Department.

Even before the announcement of the merger took place, however, it became evident that the emerging record of the partners to the merger would become a distinct liability. Both banks, because of their history, had been swept up into the scandal. UBS, with its shredding and the arrogant comments of Studer, did not endear itself to anyone in this country. SBC, implicated in numerous of instances of improprieties in hundreds of documents we found in the archives, was less then willing to answer these charges with their own records.

For the New York State Banking Department, it was SBC's lack of candor and unwillingness to turn over these records that was the most troublesome. On December 5, after months of wrangling over requests for documents, New York issued a Consent Decree against SBC, mandating the bank's compliance with requests made of it, specifically related to the surrender of Holocaust-era records and the correction of their procedures for dealing with them.[56] The announcement of the Consent Decree, interestingly was held back until Sunday, December 7, the day before the Hevesi conference and the announcement of the merger. This was a sign of things to come.

On April 6, 1998, Elizabeth McCaul, Acting Superintendent of the Department again entered into a Consent Decree, this time with UBS due to the bank's refusal to turn over records as well as its failure to disclose the existence of a subsidiary company, the Union American Corporation, operating in the U.S. at the time designed to safeguard bank customers' assets.[57]

While New York State had taken an enforcement action against SBC and later UBS, it was not clear what action the Department would take with regard to the merger. Many had voiced their concerns about this merger and the two logical places to submit their claims to were D'Amato and the State of New York.

Immediately, upon hearing of the merger, we began to look into the laws regarding bank mergers and just how approval for such actions was undertaken. While it was quickly established that the lead federal agency to approve the merger was the Federal Reserve, it was less clear on what grounds D'Amato could oppose it. Soon, however, we found our hook.

Within weeks, news spread about massive losses from investments made in Asia by the derivatives office of UBS in London. At first, the losses were estimated to be in the tens of millions. Soon the number grew to hundreds of millions.[58] One of the men responsible for the bad trades was Romy Goldstein, an Israeli. According to confidential calls I received from bank employees in New York, Goldstein was being called a "rogue trader" and was blamed for the losses. Worse yet UBS, while not wanting to make any of this public, made clear anti-Semitic accusations against Goldstein, whom they quickly fired along with at least one of his aides.

Putting these losses together with the accumulating evidence on both companies with regard to the dormant accounts and Nazi gold issues made for just cause, we felt, to oppose the merger.

On February 5, 1998, D'Amato wrote the Chairman of the Federal Reserve, Alan Greenspan, "it is clear these banks participated in an ongoing conspiracy to conceal and prevent the recovery of assets deposited in their banks by victims of the Nazi regime." Moreover, "the reported inadequate separation of risk taking activities and risk monitoring activities on the part of UBS's management" wrote D'Amato, "brings to mind the highly publicized collapse of Barings and the intolerable conduct of Daiwa Bank and Daiwa Trust Company that led to the unprecedented termination of their banking operations in the United States by our regulators."[59]

Despite a moratorium on sanctions against the banks, D'Amato viewed his opposition to the merger, not as a sanction, but on the fact that the right to operate a financial institution in this country was a privilege rather than a right. In any sense, it was clear that were it a right or a privilege, neither bank was entitled to it.

On the face of it the Swiss acted as if nothing so terrible happened. An SBC spokesman played down D'Amato's letter stating that "the Fed is an independent agency and we are confident its decision will be based on factual considerations."[60] A UBS spokesman, however, termed D'Amato's letter as "disconcerting." Of the two responses, it seems that UBS was the more truthful. Swiss banks do roughly 25 percent of their business in the United States. A denial to operate here would be devastating to their business and many investors in Switzerland saw the threat posed by D'Amato's letter in this way. Immediately after the letter became known, the shares of both banks' stocks fell on the Zurich market.

The Swiss press also expressed anger at D'Amato's letter when the *Neue Zürcher Zeitung* wrote in its "Week in Review" that,

> It was also his right to pop up suddenly after the special shareholder's meetings of the two banks and write a letter to the chairman of the Federal Reserve Board. And he had a perfect right to spout outrageous nonsense in that letter. Nor can one blame him for shifting his strategy, now that the painful claims for billions by his crown witness, former Swiss bank security guard Meili, and the class action law suit filed by bank claimants, have so far failed to have the desired effect.[61]

Borer's Task Force even criticized the letter as "unfair" and "counterproductive." According to Task Force spokeswoman Linda Shepard, "D'Amato's steps were legally and politically questionable."[62]

The banks made these same points in an eighty-five-page letter to Greenspan in response to D'Amato's letter. They argued that they were not conspiring to conceal Holocaust victims' assets. They denied mistreatment of Meili, a point D'Amato brought up to show ill-intent by shredding, and they denied hoarding gold, another charge leveled at them by D'Amato. This massive response was replete with statements by officials praising Switzerland for all it had done to search for assets, the full English-language translation of the dismissal of the case against Meili and Hagenmuller, and letters by Volcker to Judge Korman.[63] The banks' lawyers were pulling out all the stops to persuade Greenspan of their sincerity and goodwill.

It was one thing for D'Amato to oppose the merger. He had, after all become such a leader on the issue that this action was expected of him and the Swiss knew it. Yet, the Swiss were clearly unprepared for others, namely Governor Pataki and the New York State Banking Department, to oppose it.

Elizabeth McCaul wrote Greenspan on March 19, "it has become clear to my office that a large part of the delay in making repayments to the accountholders [sic] has been due to the lax and uncooperative and perhaps even fraudulent conduct in this matter by UBS and SBC." McCaul concluded, "this department has seen no real evidence on the part of UBS which would suggest commitment toward a just resolution of Holocaust victims' claims…I do not believe that the proposed merger should be approved unless and until both SBC and UBS give the deposits back to their rightful owners and heirs."[64] It was in part, UBS's poor cooperation detailed in this letter that lead to the Consent Decree entered into between the bank and the Department.

McCaul's action was important in that New York State was actively blocking the merger and doing so on the same grounds as D'Amato. Not only did it reinforce D'Amato's position, it had real force behind it because McCaul, as the state's bank regulator, could keep the new entity from operating in New York. Richard C. Capone, UBS's North American CEO objected to McCaul's letter explaining that his bank was indeed cooperating, contrary to what she explained.[65]

A Milestone in the Unified Pursuit of Justice

In the two months following the December 8 conference in New

York, the agreement Hevesi and the other financial officers worked out stuck. Despite a few flareups such as Cotti's geography lesson and the attendant anger exhibited at his insensitivity, mum was the word and the word sanctions never came up.

There were those, however, that were growing wary of the lack of progress. Swiss banks, despite their own trumpeting of their efforts, had yet to make any payouts, and became mired in their own bureaucracy when it came to reaching what we all thought would be the logical and only just conclusion to this saga: settlement.

Bronfman, who in December had begun to talk publicly about the terms of some future settlement started what lead to private discussions parallel with those Eizenstat had mediated in Zurich. Singer, meanwhile had declared both publicly and privately that the banks were not moving on the settlement issue. It was not a mistake that he had called for sanctions on December 8. He had real concerns. He feared the banks would have no real reason to move any further toward settlement if there was no alternative to the status quo.

By March, Hevesi's ninety-day moratorium on sanctions was approaching its expiration and many were beginning to question what the moratorium had actually elicited from the banks. Stone and Natarus in Chicago were growing impatient, new parties in Florida were also thinking of taking action, and Hausfeld was growing tired of a total lack of action and most importantly, not a word from Korman as to the next step in the lawsuit.

On February 27, 1998, Hausfeld and Wiesenthal Center attorney and advisor to the suit, Marty Mendelsohn, traveled to Costa Mesa, California for a one-day symposium at Whittier Law School on the Swiss bank and Nazi gold issue. While there, they met with Matt Fong and Rabbi Marvin Hier, Dean of the Simon Wiesenthal Center in Los Angeles. Their purpose was to convince Fong that the only option left for the greater good of the entire effort was for him to either reimpose sanctions because of a lack of progress by the banks, or to set a deadline for them to act. Whatever his action, it would be tied to the end of the moratorium.

Fong however was in this position before and it backfired on him. He took a strong lead in imposing sanctions, only to fail to receive the backing of the Jewish community in California. Moreover, Eizenstat representing the administration opposed his action and Abe Foxman of the ADL came out squarely against him. Many conservative Jewish groups failed to back him as well. He was fearful of upsetting the very group he needed in his attempt to win the Republican nomination to face Senator Barbara Boxer in the November election for the U.S. Senate. Now, he had to be assured history would not repeat itself.

Hausfeld and Mendelsohn assured Fong that this time would be different. They would get him the support he needed to go forward. By March 12, Fong was ready to act but not before a conference call between Hausfeld, Mendelsohn, Elan Steinberg, and himself took place, in which Steinberg giving his unqualified and unconditional support on behalf of the WJC clinched the matter for the once-reluctant Fong.

Hausfeld had gained for Fong the support of both the WJC and one of its main competitors, the Wiesenthal Center. Hausfeld had now achieved what he termed as a "milestone in the unified pursuit of justice."

Fong sent letters to each of the members of the Executive Monitoring Committee asking them to join him in sending "this strong signal to the banks that we take our oversight role seriously."[66] The "strong signal" Fong meant was a letter to the Swiss Bankers Association outlining a two-part plan for the Swiss to agree in writing to settle all claims against the banks, by the plaintiffs to the lawsuit and all others by March 31, and a resolution of the amount of that settlement as well as a timetable for the transfer of this sum by May 1. "Your endorsement of these two principles," wrote Fong, "will demonstrate to our constituents and all those who share our concerns that Swiss banks are committed to finding a settlement that is founded on fairness and justice." While Fong promised an indefinite suspension of sanctions if the banks were to agree, Fong concluded the letter with his alternative for the banks. "Failure to embrace these goals," he wrote, "will result in the reinstatement of investment restrictions."[67]

It was no surprise that the Swiss government, perhaps on behalf of the banks, rejected Fong's demands immediately, with spokesmen for one Swiss political party calling them blackmail, and the spokeswoman for Borer's Task Force, calling them "a wholly false way to bring this question to resolution."[68]

Five days later, Robert O'Brien of Credit Suisse, Simon Canning of SBC, and Richard Capone of UBS, responded in a joint letter to Fong complaining that he was acting unilaterally and ignoring all they had done to resolve the problem. "Our banks," they wrote, "have worked hard and constructively to resolve these important issues as others have recognized." Arrogantly, they concluded, "We have earned the right to fair treatment."[69]

The Swiss bank executives were not alone in their objection to Fong's proposal. On the same day Fong circulated the letter to the SBA among the members of the Executive Monitoring Committee, Hevesi responded to Fong that his proposal was "narrowly focused." Reminding Fong of the ongoing negotiations between the banks and the attorneys and the WJC, Hevesi declared to Fong "I believe that you would not want to do anything that might harm the negotiations which may lead to a settlement.... I believe it is important for our credibility that we maintain our commitment to that process and delay any decision until we have heard full reports from all sides. Therefore I must decline to sign your letter."[70]

In the past, the Swiss government had reacted with the usual condemnation of any sanctions threats, but now with Fong's ultimatum, Swiss politicians jumped into the fray by threatening sanctions of their own against American companies wishing to do business in Switzerland. Swiss Parliamentarian Dick Marty, backed by thirty-seven of the forty-six members of the state Council or upper house, threatened to take legislative action to prohibit American telecommunications companies from receiving a license to expand into Switzerland. "Apparently," declared Marty on Swiss television on March 19, "the US are more sensible to these kinds of arguments than to diplomatic discussions, and they should be aware that we will not sit back quietly."[71] Others in Switzerland suggested that Switzerland boycott California-grown asparagus in retaliation for Fong's actions. The Swiss government, now feeling the pressure from politicians like Marty, threatened to take the issue to the World Trade Organization, an international trade dispute resolution tribunal to which Switzerland had joined only one month before, if Fong's threats were carried out.

The issuance of threats now from both sides of the Atlantic were now growing dangerous. Eizenstat who had consistency opposed U.S. state-level sanctions, did all he could to lower the volume on the threats and counter-threats that were growing by the day. Within days, Fong softened his tone and declared his ultimatum was not a threat but an opportunity for the banks to put this issue to rest. His tone was less strident and confrontational. For the Swiss too, the talk of counter sanctions was calmed when the new Director of the SBA, Niklaus Blattner opposed Swiss retaliation in an interview in *Tages Anzeiger*.[72] When Swiss Transportation, Communications, and Energy Ministry spokesman Ulrich Sieber told reporters there were absolutely no plans to deny licenses to any American telecommunications companies in retaliation for Fong's ultimatum or for any other reason, threats of Swiss retaliation disappeared. The two American companies eventually won the contract.

An Honorable and Moral Conclusion through a Global Settlement

In a poll conducted by the *Neue Zürcher Zeitung* of some 16,000 from fifteen European nations in October 1997, 40 percent believed Switzerland had not done enough to restitute Holocaust victims' assets. Moreover, two-thirds believed that Swiss banks played a "dubious role" in international transactions."[73]

In March 1998, American Jews had similar views. In a poll conducted by the American Jewish Committee, as part of their "1998 Annual Survey of American Jewish Opinion," an overwhelming majority of 72 percent believed that Switzerland was uncooperative in providing a full accounting of its wartime dealings with the Nazis. When asked what actions they would support to obtain such an accounting, 86 percent supported quiet diplomacy by the United States, but interestingly, 53 percent supported "sanctions and boycotts against Swiss banks and companies." A further 55 percent supported "public demonstrations by Jews and others."[74]

These results leading up to the end of the moratorium on sanctions against Swiss banks was not surprising. After more than two years of embarrassing disclosures and public relations disasters, the poll results only convinced us that we had achieved what we had set out to do, namely ruin their reputation with facts undeniable to anyone in order to force them to finally commit to righting a terrible wrong after more than fifty years. While we destroyed their "favorable ratings," in the American political colloquial, the harder part had to be obtained: settlement.

Alan Hevesi, who had organized the December conference in New York, now called a hearing to take place again in New York on March 26, whereby he and the other members of the Executive Monitoring Committee would hear testimony from the numerous parties to the problem as to their opinion on the moratorium and the question of settlement.

In the days leading up to the hearing, there was talk of the possibility of reaching such a settlement, or "global settlement" as it came to be called. Elan Steinberg had held a dim view as to the chances for success. As late as only two days before, he concluded that Hevesi's committee might even decide on recommending the imposition of sanctions on a state by state basis. The WJC was genuinely concerned. Bronfman,

Singer, and Steinberg over the past months had been skeptical of Swiss intentions and began to think they were being had. The bankers, Singer felt, were only stalling for time.

Bronfman's patience had grown thin. In an interview with the *Jewish Bulletin of Northern California*, he expressed the feelings he and Singer had begun to hold. "If the Swiss are going to keep digging their heels in," said Bronfman, "then I'll have to ask all the U.S. shareholders to suspend their dealings with the Swiss. It's coming to a point where it has to resolve itself or it has to be total war."[75]

Others, though, felt that sanctions were wrong owing to the harm they would cause the fledgling negotiations, but also bilateral relations between the two countries. Now, after an agreement in December that produced a unified front against the banks, that front had broken in two. On the one side were Eizenstat and Hevesi opposing sanctions, and the WJC, Hausfeld, D'Amato, and Pataki willing in varying forms to impose sanctions or block the merger of UBS and SBC to operate as a united bank in the U.S. and in New York State.

After months of attempts to reach a common negotiating strategy, Hausfeld obtained the support of Singer and the WJC. The first real sign of this was their agreement to support Fong's ultimatum. Now, Hausfeld and the WJC would consult and negotiate together for the purpose of a global settlement.

On March 24, Singer came to Washington and met with D'Amato. Together they worked out a common strategy. For Hevesi's hearing in New York, at which D'Amato asked me to represent him, D'Amato would propose that the banks be given until April 23, 1998, Yom Hashoah, or Holocaust Rememberance Day, to come back to the Committee with "meaningful progress." "If this is done," the statement before Hevesi was to read, "then a further 30 days could be granted in order to establish a framework and a methodology toward a conclusion of this agreement. If the banks choose not meet this deadline, no longer should anyone feel bound by a moratorium on sanctions."[76]

During the meeting, D'Amato spoke to Robert O'Brien of Credit Suisse in an attempt to obtain a statement from him committing Credit Suisse, if not all the banks, to achieving a global settlement. Singer had told D'Amato that he had been trying for weeks to get them to commit these words to paper but they could not bring themselves to do it. Singer had tried through Eizenstat to coax a Swiss draft of a joint statement out to present at the hearing. Without such a statement, the WJC would have no choice but to conclude that sanctions were the only option left.

O'Brien faxed D'Amato a statement that served as his private thoughts, not those of his bank. "We believe," O'Brien wrote in his draft statement, "that the time has arrived for the banks to achieve a global settlement with Holocaust survivors on all claims involving the banks." O'Brien continued,

> It has been too long for these people not to have achieved justice. In this regard we acknowledge that progress made to date by the Volcker committee [sic] and others, but we expect the Swiss banks to continue to work expeditiously and in good faith towards this global resolution of claims involving the banks and to bring this to closure. We are scheduling a meeting for April 23rd to determine whether or not the parties are meeting the stated objectives and will act accordingly.[77]

When I arrived in Hevesi's office on the morning of March 26, I met briefly with Singer and Steinberg who informed me that the letter O'Brien had tried to supply had not yet arrived. Going into the meeting, there was still no commitment from the banks to negotiate the terms of a global settlement.

Singer and Steinberg testified first. They proceeded for over an hour. After them, it was my turn. I read my statement, which took all of five minutes. Hevesi, thanked me and expressed his interest in only one point: the April 23 deadline. Would this be the absolute cutoff date? I answered yes, and my testimony was over. I would be followed by Mike Bradfield, representing Paul Volcker, then Hausfeld, Elizabeth McCaul, Rolf Bloch, Avraham Hirchson, Stuart Eizenstat, Capone, Canning, and O'Brien of the Swiss banks in New York, and Borer. After that the Committee went into executive session to decide what to do.

Before the Committee could hear from Eizenstat, however, the banks finally delivered the letter for which Singer and in fact the world had been waiting. After two years of embarrassment for the Swiss banks, Marcel Ospel, Chairman of the Board of the SBC wrote Singer,

> On behalf of Mathis Cabiallavetta, Lukas Muehlemann and myself I confirm that we welcome the direct involvement of the WJC along with the plaintiffs' lawyers in the productive discussions that are proceeding under the aegis of Under Secretary of State Stuart Eizenstat relating to an honorable and moral conclusion through a global resolution of Holocaust-era issues directly related to our banks. We all support the mission of the ICEP, [the Volcker Commission] and continuation of its work is the cornerstone to a proper resolution.[78]

The banks had finally committed to a process by which a final settlement could be achieved. While no number had been mentioned, the mechanism was created whereby Hausfeld and Roger Whitten could sit across the table from each other and conclude the lawsuits and most if not all claims against the banks, as Bronfman had suggested earlier.

Moreover, this commitment was proof that the sanctions threat that became such a decisive issue between the U.S. and Switzerland, and the banks' worst fear, had been the one issue that convinced the banks to negotiate constructively. "Today is proof that sanctions work," said Hevesi in response to Eizenstat during his testimony later that afternoon.[79] For D'Amato, the sanctions threat "was the real force. It demonstrated to some, who would have never come to this realization, that they had to react to this horrible injustice that has continued for over 50 years."[80]

Finally, the commitment showed to be true what Stan Turesky and others had said right from the very beginning, but the Swiss bankers were unwilling to face up to. The only way the banks would be able to get themselves out of this mess would be to sign a check and buy their way out of this disaster.

Ospel had been finally able to do what he and the other bankers had not been able to for not only two years, but over fifty. They committed themselves to the word "settlement." While it remained to be seen what that settlement would encompass and how much the final figure would be, Ospel's letter represented not necessarily an end to the dispute, but a new beginning. Now, committed to end the scandal that grew like a cancer in their midst, the Swiss bankers could sit down and negotiate with both the WJC and Hausfeld jointly. While negotiations are often extremely difficult with the Swiss, both sides had everything to gain by a speedy conclusion and everything to lose by a prolonged stalemate.

Justice for Estelle

While the main parties to the dispute were aligning themselves for negotiations, there were those, while represented, who were in need of a speedier resolution than the new proceedures would allow. Estelle Sapir, sick and deeply depressed over the struggle of the past two years, needed help soon.

In late November, Fagan spoke with D'Amato and stressed her poor health and deteriorating condition. D'Amato then called Bob O'Brien of Credit Suisse to talk about Estelle. On December 8, after speaking at the Hevesi conference, D'Amato informed Sapir that O'Brien agreed that Credit Suisse could pay her as much as $500,000 for her father's account. Following the release of Josef Sapir's account card by Credit

Suisse a month before, proving the existence of the account, it became nearly impossible for the bank to hold back any longer.[81]

Based the ledger book pages she gave to Moravek over a year before, the simple extrapolation of numbers made it clear that $500,000 would be the bare minimum the bank owed her, with interest and inflation included.

On May 4, after several false starts due mainly to her deteriorating health, Sapir joined O'Brien and D'Amato in New York to announce a settlement for her half-century of struggle with the bank. Finally, she said, referring to her father "When I die and go to heaven, I will see him and say, 'I accomplished it.'"[82]

Caving In

The agreement with the WJC and Hausfeld was taken with cautious optimism in this country. Both Singer and Hausfeld were careful to not predict a speedy conclusion to the negotiations and both said there was still a long way to go before it would be all over.

The Swiss government would have no part of the settlement. Sensing the anger of the Swiss people thus far, government spokesmen declared it was the banks' decision and therefore up to them to conclude this agreement with the WJC and the lawyers. Having already gone through the fight over the SNB's contribution to the Humanitarian Fund as well as the very public bickering in Switzerland over the Solidarity Fund and the attendant public referendum, the government had little interest in going down this path again.

Within days of the announcement of the "settlement," rumors spread that Hausfeld would file a lawsuit in California against the SNB for its role in the acceptance of gold, as well as the admission by the bank that under a 1905 charter, it too was able to accept private individual accounts and that the SNB itself had eight dormant accounts from World War II.

Upon news of the rumored lawsuit, President Cotti erupted in anger and the nation joined him as well. This disclosure, coupled with the report issued weeks earlier by the Simon Wiesenthal Center accusing the Swiss government of running slave labor camps in Switzerland for Jewish refugees during the war, renewed the intense anger in Switzerland that had subsided a bit over the previous months.[83]

Now Swiss politicians, already angry over Fong's sanctions threats, had another reason to be outraged. Already back in January, in reaction to the Wiesenthal report, Borer himself could not resist expressing the growing anger in Switzerland. "I am convinced," he said on the *CBS Evening News*, "that behind a lot of this are American lawyers who want to make a lot of money on the back of the Jewish survivors of the Ho—[sic] of the Second World War."[84] In March, Borer again expressed the mood of the country when he said, "The Swiss are saying 'Yeah, it's not about money. It's about more money.'"[85]

For Hausfeld, including the SNB in the process was the path toward a true global settlement. Owing to the clear evidence that the SNB accepted looted gold and Eizenstat's team's findings to be detailed later that victims' gold had indeed made its way into SNB gold stocks, the conclusion was inescapable: the Swiss National Bank had to be included in the process. The SNB, however, saw it a different way and steadfastly refused, along with the government to play any part in the settlement talks.

With the confluence of the Wiesenthal Center report, the various sanctions threats, rumors and threats of more, and the ongoing settlement process, there was a backlash. Whereas previously the banks were held up by the Swiss people as responsible for the troubles Switzerland faced, now the fact they agreed to negotiate with Switzerland's "enemies" was the last straw. Now, they too were criticized, but this time by politicians and the press alike for "selling out" to Jews.

A week after the agreement to reopen settlement talks, Eric Wollman of Alan Hevesi's office related a story told to him by Manuel Sager, from the Swiss Consulate in New York. Apparently, an unnamed bank head was having dinner in a restaurant in Switzerland when he was verbally assaulted by his own waiter for "caving in" to the Jews. Sager, according to Wollman, sounded scared and was worried about further sanctions being imposed on Switzerland, in defiance of the continued moratorium agreed to on March 26.[86]

Sager's fears were all that could have been expected. Over the previous two years, he had seen his country and its prized banking industry, in the words of one Swiss banker, "torn limb from limb." The once-proud Swiss bankers were reduced to thieves and criminals, in the eyes of the world. One by one, survivors of the Holocaust surfaced to say that they too had an account in Switzerland and that the banks would not return their funds.

Sager, Borer, the bankers and all the others who endured this worldwide onslaught of negative and accusatory publicity had to sit back and, as they say, take it on the chin. They could not, however, avoid comment. These reactions, however, belied a deeper truth. Down deep, perhaps deeper than they thought, a latent arrogance about themselves and against others existed in their very makeup. Try as they did, they could not hide their upbringing. Borer's statements and those of others showed that the systematic destruction of the Swiss national myth was hard for them and the Swiss public to endure.

A Firm and Concrete Offer

On June 3, Eizenstat wrote Israel Singer informing him that he had received "a firm and concrete offer" from the banks, through Roger Witten. Eizenstat wrote that the offer afforded the parties a good chance to achieve a "prompt and just resolution" to the litigation.[87] It was under this pretext that the WJC stood back and allowed the merger to go forth. This assurance by Eizenstat was important because it cleared the way for UBS and SBC to merge. Had the WJC objected, New York State might well have declined to approve the merger, costing the banks precious time and money.

With Eizenstat's assurances the negotiations proceeded, albeit at a snail's pace. The Swiss, being extremely tough negotiators, were barely budging. In negotiations in New York, on June 5, the banks made a proposal to settle the lawsuits for $450,000,000. This offer was firmly rejected by Hausfeld and Singer as pitifully low. The Swiss, while coming to the table with a substantive number had at least tried to present a figure. Hausfeld, however, was clear in his demand that the number be in the billions. He had assembled a team of historians to determine exactly what the settlement figure should be, and that number far eclipsed the banks' offer.

On May 25, the Bergier Commission released its long-awaited report on the gold trade of the Swiss National Bank. In doing so, Hausfeld's arguments for a higher number were clearly bolstered. The report confirmed Switzerland's role as the recipient of 80 percent of all the gold the Nazis looted, just as we and Eizenstat's reports had disclosed. It revealed that "the SNB was aware of its role as a hub for gold from the Third Reich," and concluded that the President of the Bank, Hans Weber, knew since the beginning of 1941 that the gold it was accepting was in fact looted from all over Europe.[88]

Now, the report that Borer, Hans Meyer of the Swiss National Bank, and others had so confidently referred to as the final arbiter of the facts of the claims against Switzerland, in a manner, convicted them as charged. The SNB did in fact everything everyone said it did, and more. Yet, to the findings of the panel to which the Swiss government pinned so much hope, all they could offer was their "profound regret." They denied requests that the SNB, and by connection, the Swiss Government, make a contribution toward the settlement, despite its now well-proven wartime complicity with the Nazis.

This stubborness irritated Singer, Hausfeld, and now Alan Hevesi. It was Hevesi who had previously refused Fong's attempt at imposing further sanctions, now understood what the Swiss were doing. On June 11, Hevesi wrote Cotti asking him to seek a contribution by the SNB in a final settlement. He also criticized Cotti for his government's weak response to Bergier's findings, calling them "innappropriate and wrong."[89]

The Swiss, however, remained firmly planted in their view that the government would not contribute to a settlement. Hevesi's letter began an exchange of letters with the Swiss, with Borer answering for Cotti. Borer answered Hevesi by stating that the SNB was not a party to the lawsuits for dormant accounts and therefore would have nothing to do with a settlement.[90]

On the same day as Hevesi's letter to Cotti, Witten and the other attorneys for the banks participated in a conference call with Hausfeld and the others, moderated by Eizenstat and made an enhanced offer. They would give $530,000,000, a figure which was to include the $70,000,000 the banks contributed to the Humanitarian Fund. This figure, like the previous one was, in Hausfeld's view, pathetic. It was nothing new, in fact it was a step back because it included money that had already been contributed. Now, it provided ample reason for Hausfeld to boycott any further talks with the banks until a "real" offer was made. The situation was getting worse. In the next weeks, it would develop into another full-blown crisis.

On June 19, a Friday, the banks, angry at what they called "excessive demands" made a unilateral public statement that as their last offer they would provide $600,000,000, "a generous and fair sum" to settle the lawsuits. They said they did it publicly to express the finality of their intentions as well as in response to what they perceived as the plaintiffs' lawyers' continued leaks to the press. Privately, however, many viewed the act simply as one of disdain for the process.

For Switzerland's critics the offer, not to mention the very public breach of the confidentiality agreement the negotiators signed, was obscene. They viewed this ultimatum of "take it or leave it," as insulting and insincere. Jewish groups all over the country denounced the banks' actions as an affront. Moreover, the offer was neither generous nor fair. "This ultimatum," stated Abe Foxman, ADL National Director, " is an insult to the memory of the victims, their survivors and to those in the Jewish community who in good faith reached out to the Swiss to work together to resolve this most difficult matter."[91]

The response by the world to the Swiss ultimatum was universally as bad. Viewed as reprehensible for their history, the banks were now viewed as the main obstacle to the very resolution of the problem which they plead they wanted so badly. Four days later, D'Amato, with Singer and Steinberg at his side, vowed to hold hearings again in the Banking Committee to push for a reopening of the 1946 Washington Accords, the results of which set this entire fifty-year problem in motion. Among other things, D'Amato wanted to understand the failure of the Swiss to abide by a treaty they signed to ostensibly settle the problem fifty-two years earlier, as well as to obtain a review of what the situation was at this time, now that settlement talks were on the verge of a breakdown.

As things went from bad to worse for the banks, Hausfeld had seen enough. As he said, "the gloves were now coming off." If the banks could talk publicly about the settlement, so could the plaintiffs. In the *New York Times* on June 24, Burt Neuborne, a professor of law at New York University and a member of Hausfeld's team did so in an opinion piece in which he labeled the banks' offer as "a paltry sum," and asserted that "no settlement can possibly be defended if it allows the Holocaust to stand as a profit-making enterprise for the Swiss banks."[92]

In response to Neuborne's article, Richard Capone of UBS and Robert O'Brien of Credit Suisse accused the plaintiffs' attorneys of "repeatedly raising the stakes." They then proceeded to list all that the banks and the Swiss government had done in the previous two years to get to the heart of the problem, just as Borer and other Swiss representatives routinely did.[93]

Days before the banker's article appeared, Hausfeld and Mel Weiss privately let it be known that while the real number was significantly higher, they would accept a settlement of $1,500,000,000 from the banks. The banks were cool toward the offer, refusing to comment on it.

The banks took solace in the fact though that at least one of the plaintiffs' attorney was encountering problems with his clients. By the end of June, reports surfaced that Gizella Weisshaus had sought to replace Fagan as her attorney because as she stated in one of her two letters to Korman, "he's lying to us." She listed a long miriad of complaints against Fagan and others and wanted Korman to remove him from the case.[94] Soon, she would not be alone in her request.

Breakdown

On June 26, Eizenstat held another meeting with the attorneys for the plaintiffs, this time, with Hausfeld, Weiss and the others boycotting the meetings, only Bob Swift of Philadelphia, from Fagan's team, showed up at the meeting, without the consent or knowledge of Hausfeld or the others.

When Hausfeld found out about the meeting three days later, he fired off an angry letter to Eizenstat, writing, "[t]his is not the first time that you and your office have attempted to exploit perceived differences within the group by segregating its members. It is one thing for the banks to try to divide our interests. It is a disgrace for you to do so." Hausfeld signed the letter with Mel Weiss and Israel Singer.[95] If it was not evident by then, it soon became apparent that the mediating role of Stuart Eizenstat was quickly coming to an end.

When Hausfeld said he was "taking the gloves off," he meant it. On June 29, Mel Weiss, Hausfeld and fourteen other attorneys filed suit against the Swiss National Bank in U.S. District Court in the District of Columbia on behalf of five plaintiffs.[96] The following day, in San Francisco, Hausfeld, Weiss, Mendelsohn, and twelve other attorneys filed suit against SBC, UBS, and Credit Suisse in the Superior Court of the State of California, on behalf of four plaintiffs.[97] Hausfeld had seen enough. By filing suit against the SNB in Washington, D.C., he had done what he was threatening to do for months, namely bringing the real culprit, closer to justice. In filing suit in California, he was pushing Korman toward a judgement by using a precedent under relevant state law. Now the Swiss Government was faced with a lawsuit of its very own. The government was not pleased.

Immediately, the Swiss protested against the SNB suit declaring the bank to be the government's central bank and immune from lawsuit because of the Swiss Government's sovereignty. Hans Meyer vowed the SNB would never settle the suit out of court. The SNB suit only contributed to an already hardening position of the Swiss government, inflaming passions on both sides of the Atlantic, but nowhere more than in New York.

The next day in New York proved to crucial to not only Hausfeld's case, but moreover, the entire fifty-year struggle with the Swiss. With the moratorium on sanctions having expired from the March 26 extension, Hevesi and the Executive Monitoring Committee met again amidst shattered settlement talks. With the June 30 letter to Judge Korman from Hausfeld and the other attorneys declaring the negotiations under Eizenstat's aegis over, the talks were officially dead.[98] Because the SNB had refused to participate in the talks and the banks had issued their ultimatum, Hevesi and his fellow financial officers were faced with a bleak situation. There was little hope anymore of any kind of a settlement. Eizenstat had been unable to deliver the Swiss despite inching the settlement number closer to $1,000,000,000, and informed Korman in writing on July 8 that his role had ended.[99] Moreover, the WJC was no longer objecting to the imposition of sanctions. Faced with Swiss obstinancy and therefore no forward progress, there was little choice but to lift the moratorium and call for sanctions to be imposed upon the Swiss banks.[100]

The Swiss, by now, had really expected this. Robert O'Brien of Credit Suisse, the most reasonable of all of the Swiss representatives, chalked the impasse and lift of the moratorium on divisions among the plaintiffs' attorneys and overreaching politicians who "basically see this as an opportunity…[to] pursue their own ends for their own purposes."[101]

Hevesi had held the line since December. At Edgar Bronfman's request, he called for and monitored a moratorium on sanctions. Yet, the Swiss made it impossible for him to hold this line. In the end, the decision to lift the moratorium lied with the Swiss, not Hevesi. Had they not dug in and refused to end the problem that had plagued them for now over two years, sanctions would not have been needed. In fact, Hevesi openly stated that the Swiss government, through its refusal to join the talks had brought this upon themselves. "Particularly upsetting is the role," asserted Hevesi "not of the banks so much, but as the Swiss government and the Swiss National Bank, two-thirds of the problem is their problem and they refuse to acknowledge and sit down and particpate in, as I say, moral and material restitution."[102] Mel Weiss went even further in laying the blame on the Swiss. "There's a virulent cancer throughout the Swiss society. We gave them an opportunity to get rid of it with a massive dose of radiation at a cost that is very small and they've turned it down."[103]

With the decision to lift the moratorium, states and cities across the country were now free to impose sanctions against the Swiss banks. The next day Hevesi and McCall held a press conference to announce the schedule for sanctions from New York State and New York City to go into effect. By September 1, if there was no settlement the two would bar short term investments in the banks, stop the banks and investment firms from selling state and city debt, and disallow the banks from providing letters of credit. If there was no settlement by November 15, further financial bans would be extended. By January 1, 1999, if there was no settlement, the bans would be extended to all Swiss companies.[104]

The Swiss Federal Council reacted with dismay. How could Hevesi do this to the entire country they wondered? "Such sanctions are counterproductive, unjustified, and illegal," declared the Council.[105] As devestating as the sanctions might have been, they were ever more troublesome for the Swiss because they were outside of the control of the State Department, long an opponent of such sanctions. Eizenstat had argued strenuously against such penalties pleading that they would damage relations between the U.S. and Switzerland. The Swiss fearing damage to an already troubled economy again threatened action before the World Trade Organization in retaliation for any sanctions imposed against the country. Eizenstat's warnings and Switzerland's threats were now of little importance to state and local financial officers around the country. Within a day of New York's plans, the Swiss Government's worst fears of a total U.S. boycott began to take shape.

In New Jersey, Assembly Deputy Minority Leader Neil Cohen called for a boycott of all Swiss products and State divestiture of all Swiss-related business. Pennsylvania Treasurer Barbara Hafer called for capping of pension fund holdings in Swiss banks and no new business with them either. Maine promised to withhold business, as did Vermont, Connecticut, Florida, and even individual counties in Michigan and New York.[106] Many state and city officials responded to a joint letter to hundreds of their colleagues by the members of the Executive Monitoring Committee asking them to join their efforts.[107] In California, Matt Fong, the most steadfast in applying sanctions, immediately reimposed his ban on investment with the banks. The rush to punish had now begun.

The Swiss banks fearing sanctions would overwhelm the country claiming them as the first victims, nevertheless stood pat, insisting their offer of $600,000,000 was still good. They could say little else.

The Swiss Government was not as cautious and was clearly in the mood to fight. They along with Swiss businesses doing business in the United States were ready to retaliate for anything done to them. After two years of accusations and threats, they did not care any more. They would fight back. Cotti made it clear that he wanted signal from Washington that the Clinton Administration would stop the implementation of sanctions.

State Department Spokesman Jamie Rubin ostensibly answered Cotti's call by declaring the Administration was opposed to sanctions but was unclear as to what, if anything the Administration could or would do to stop states and cities from imposing them.[108]

Swiss businessmen such as Swatch Watch Company CEO Nicolas Hayek threatened retaliation against U.S. companies' parts for his watches and said he would urge others to do so as well, if U.S. sanctions went into effect. Denner Supermarkets, the third largest in Switzerland announced they would remove all U.S. products from their shelves in retaliation for the threats made against Switzerland.[109]

Echoing the eerie calls for Jewish boycotts in 1930s Germany, spokesmen for the Swiss Democrats, with three seats in the 200 seat lower house of the Swiss Parliament, threatened to call for a boycott of the products of foreign-owned Jewish and American businesses in Switzerland and stated its intention to publish a list of such businesses.[110]

The atmosphere was getting hotter and hotter by the day. In Switzerland, Borer was denying Hevesi's continued calls for the Swiss Government to join the talks, and the escalation of threats and counter threats was getting worse. Mathis Cabiallavetta, Chairman of the new UBS, again gave an interview in a major Swiss paper urging restraint. For Cabiallavetta and Ranier Gut, theirs was the worst of situations. While Swiss government and business were ready to fight, they wanted and urged peace. But to do so too loudly placed them in jeopardy in Switzerland. The banks needed the security of the government in order to make a deal, yet in making a deal they were afraid to be seen as betraying the nation as a whole. While not enviable, their position was of their own making and they had to live with it.

One Last Plea

D'Amato's hearing on the 1946 Accords was held on July 22. We tried hard to make this hearing, which we felt would be the last, one to remember. Despite the *Neue Zürcher Zeitung's* claim that we were conducting a "show trial," we wanted to examine the Accords to understand what the Swiss paid and what they did not pay.[111] We invited the heads of the banks in Switzerland, Marcel Ospel of UBS, and Ranier Gut of Credit Suisse; Hans Meyer of the Swiss National Bank; George Kreyer of the Swiss Bankers Association; Professor Bergier of the

Bergier Commission; Thomas Borer of the Swiss Task Force; and Roger Witten, the U.S. attorney for the banks.

All seven refused to testify, which in reality was just fine for us. Without them, we went ahead with Stuart Eizenstat; Carl McCall; Steve Newman of Hevesi's office; Israel Singer; Rabbi Hier of the Wiesenthal Center in Los Angeles; Michael Hausfeld; Mel Urbach, counsel for the World Orthodox Jewish Communities; Fredy Rom of the Jewish Telegraphic Agency in Switzerland; and Professor Jean Ziegler, a member of the Swiss Parliament and critic of the Swiss banks for some thirty years.

If there was any message that came from this hearing, it was that all the participants, with the exception of Eizenstat, explained that sanctions were the only way to achieve justice. They might not have wanted to impose sanctions, but if forced to do so, they would. It seemed as if those supporting sanctions were begging the Swiss to give them a reason to not impose them.

But Eizenstat kept up his staunch defense against sanctions, maintaining the line that the Swiss had done more than anyone else to address the wrongs of the past. He steadfastly refused to endorse any punitive measures. Although he did label the 1946 Accords, in hindsight, as unsatisfactory to American interests, he offered little else than to maintain the course. Looking back at the hearing, he seemed isolated. While all the other witnesses explained the need to sanction Switzerland, he would not even hint at the need for a firmer hand.

The other witnesses, were eloquent and firm that there was no other course. McCall, in defending his call for sanctions and rebuking Eizenstat was the most eloquent. He related his visit with Nelson Mandela in South Africa, who told him sanctions by the state and local officials in the U.S. during the Apartheid regime in South Africa, were instrumental to his freedom and that of the nation itself.[112]

Jean Ziegler, like McCall was passionate in his disdain for the banks saying they were responsible for the woes Switzerland faced today. Ziegler testified to the horrible effect sanctions would have on the Swiss economy and scolded the banks for not immediately repaying all they were holding back. Privately, after the hearing, he conveyed his belief that what we were doing was entirely just and was the only recourse. The banks deserved what they got and it was long overdue. Yet, Zeigler, warned repeatedly in Switzerland beforehand not to attend the hearing suffered for his candor, if not his willingness to testify. At the end of August, conservative Swiss businessmen brought suit against Zeigler in Swiss courts for violation of Article 266 of the Swiss penal code, "actions against the independence of Switzerland, harmful behavior against Swiss public interests, treason." According to Zeigler, the Swiss government took the charges seriously and threatened to lift his Parliamentary immunity for among other things, testifying before Switzerland's arch-enemy, Alfonse M. D'Amato.[113]

The Impending Trainwreck

The Swiss Government refused to join the talks. Hevesi and McCall were committed to their self-imposed deadline of September 1. Eizenstat was out of the negotiations and the WJC had seen enough of Swiss stalling tactics. This scenario had all the markings of the unavoidable, as they say in Washington, of an "impending trainwreck."

Meanwhile, within the disparate group of lawyers, a "trainwreck" was about to occur as well. A week before D'Amato's hearing, Fagan and Swift tried to wrest back the initiative they had previously lost to Hausfeld. On July 15, both men held a press conference in New York and declared themselves ready to resume talks with the banks. Calling both sides inflexible, the two proclaimed their willingness to "come off the $1.5 billion figure," if the Swiss government and banks came up with more money from their original offer.[114]

Although they received a great deal of press for their "stunt," Fagan and Swift were completely wrong in undercutting Hausfeld and the other attorneys. Not only were they undercutting their colleagues, but they were undercutting their own clients in deviating from the court-appointed Executive Committee's strategy. Mel Weiss, in a strongly worded memo could barely contain his anger.

> The conduct of Swift and Fagan is the most outrageous flaunting of a Court appointed Executive Committee mandate that I have ever encountered. This comes at a time when in the view of the World Jewish Congress and in my view, we are winning the fight hands down. In addition, showing weakness undermines the decision of Hevesi, et al. To impose sanctions. Even if that were not true, as members of the Executive Committee, holding such a press conference without the authority of the Executive Committee is a gross violation of the Court's Order. The Judge has now called for a court conference and I think we should make a motion to remove both Swift and Fagan from the Executive Committee. I think we should also consider the imposition of sanctions.[115]

The next day, Stephen Whinston, of Berger & Montague of Philadelphia, another attorney on the Executive Committee urged a timeout and called for a meeting, on neutral territory of the Committee's members. Hausfeld, however, was livid. He agreed totally with Weiss and felt that Fagan, who was causing them trouble from the very beginning, was disruptive and had no place in these talks.

For his part, Swift responding in writing to all the members of the Executive Committee. "Some of you may be so emotionally wound up that you cannot appreceiate that my statement gives the Swiss banks and government a graceful way to resume negotiations," wrote Swift, "Then you truly misunderstand the process. In any event, the Swiss banks have responded saying they are willing to resume negotiations. Finally, as to Mel's threat, Mike has been trying to eliminate me as co-lead counsel from the outset. If this is his best shot, bring on the motion. I enjoy a good fight."[116]

While the Swift-Fagan proposal caused a serious problem for the other attorneys, their goal seemed to have been accomplished. The day after their press conference, the banks declared themselves ready to resume negotiations. In doing so, they also dropped their previous insistence that the Swiss government give preliminary approval to any settlement to which they might conclude. While Hausfeld said he would not take part in any talks resumed under the guise of Swift and Fagan, the change in terms for the talks by the banks was a great step forward.

On the same day, there appeared a story in the German newspaper *Handelsblatt*, that quoted Swiss banking sources as saying the banks were willing to double their offer to $1,000,000,000. Spokesmen for the banks denied the story calling it totally false. Within weeks, the denial would ring hollow.

"Expecting decisive action"

On the afternoon of the Banking Committee hearing, the Ambassador Defago delivered a confidential letter from Cotti to President Clinton, in which Cotti stressed the importance of the U.S.-Swiss relationship and the threat sanctions would have on that relationship. The embassy's press release on the letter explained that Cotti "expected President Clinton and his administration to take decisive action against the sanctions."[117] While Cotti's letter to Clinton was considered diplomatic correspondence, the contents nevertheless were clear by the text of the press release alone: the Swiss were not asking for help, they were demanding it. Still, this far into the crisis in Switzerland, with their interests so severely threatened, the Swiss Government still thought it best to demand help, as opposed to humbly requesting it.

To Cotti's call came a White House plea to refrain from imposing sanctions. To this call, came letters from Hevesi and the Executive Monitoring Committee to over 800 U.S. state and city finance officers asking them to join their sanctions effort.[118] For the White House, this was a tough call, under seige in the Monica Lewinsky affair, they had more to concern themselves with than tiny Switzerland's problem that was of their own making. Amid calls by Jewish organizations to ignore Cotti's demands, White House spokesman Mike McCurry said simply, the President was opposed to sanctions and called for a return to the negotiations.

To answer Hevesi's letter, the Swiss countered with one of their own. Written to the Comptrollers of each of the fifty states and fifteen cities, Ambassadors Borer and Defago jointly wrote defending their nation and urging restraint in the sanctions battle taking shape in the country. "It is our hope," wrote the two Ambassadors, "that you will join with us in calling for an end to counterproductive rhetoric and misguided sanctions that will only serve to delay a just and lasting conclusion, in the interests of the survivors of the Holocaust."[119] In response again, Hevesi and McCall wrote the President urging him to tell Cotti to join the talks to settle the problem "so that there is finally justice and restitution for Holocaust victims and their heirs."[120]

After 50 Years, a Deal

On July 27, the attorneys appeared before Judge Korman for the purpose of arguing a motion for dismissal. Instead of dismissing the case as Witten and the banks' lawyers had hoped, Korman suggested that he would try to mediate a settlement between the two parties.

Korman ordered another hearing for July 30 for Hausfeld to present his numbers for settlement. On August 7, it was Witten's turn. On August 10 the attorneys appeared jointly before Korman who informed them he was ready to propose a number to both sides. That night at a restaurant in New York, both sides met with Korman and again presented their case, defending their position. According to one of the plaintiffs' attorneys, Korman proposed that the banks could pay slightly more than $1,000,000,000 immediately, a sum to not include any estimated amount that Paul Volcker would find in the end of his investigative audits; or $1,500,000,000 spread out over a several years to cover Volcker's findings. Witten had to confer with his clients and needed time to do so.

Days earlier, Singer was certain that this time chances for a settlement were very real. He spoke with D'Amato on August 6, requesting his help in order to pave the way for closure to the lawsuits. D'Amato committed to do all that he could.

On the night of August 11, D'Amato talked by phone with Singer, and O'Brien to discuss the structure of a settlement. It was during this conversation that the basics of a settlement plan were worked out. According to other attorneys in the case, during the discussions the sum of $1,250,000,000 was agreed to, with money to cover the future Volcker findings. The money would be made over four years.[121]

When the attorneys appeared before Korman the next day beginning at 10:30 A.M., they haggled back and forth over the spread of the payments, the total amount of the settlement, and the overall structure of the agreement. Singer was present and so was D'Amato. The debate over the settlement raged on all morning and into the afternoon. At several points Hausfeld and other members of his team threatened to walk out, but between D'Amato's cajoling and Korman's insistence that they come to an agreement, this was avoided.[122]

By mid-afternoon, reports began to appear on the news wires that something serious was taking place in the court in Brooklyn and reporters began to beseige our press office trying to find the details of what D'Amato was doing there. By 5:00 P.M., D'Amato called down to us to tell us to get ready for an announcement. At 7:00 P.M., D'Amato walked out onto the steps of the Brooklyn Court House. Surrounded by hordes of cameras, dozens of lawyers from both sides, Estelle Sapir and Christoph Meili, Israel Singer, and others, D'Amato announced what Estelle Sapir, Jacob Friedman, Elizabeth Trilling, Greta Beer, and thousands of survivors had waited to hear for over fifty years:

> I am tremendously pleased and gratified to announce that we've reached an historic agreement with the Swiss banks that will bring moral and material justice to those who have suffered for so long and bring closure on these issues around the world and in Switzerland.[123]

After more than fifty years of frustration, rejection, denial, and abhorant treatment at the hands of the "gnomes of Zurich," as they have come to be called, Holocaust survivors around the world achieved a strategic and moral victory with this single statement. Not one of us who worked to expose the bankers' actions believed this day would ever come. But after two-and-a-half years of "political war" with the Swiss, the fighting was over.

The bankers had given up. They finally realized that however they viewed this struggle, they had no choice but to face the inevitability of their fate and back down. Many of us had said from the beginning, the only way out for the Swiss was for them to sign a check. The only question for all this time was "how much?"

It was this question that proceeded to dominate the stories after the settlement. What price do you put on the Holocaust? Did the banks get off easy? If the truth be told, according to all the available evidence, and by now this is a great deal of it, the answer is clearly yes. Bronfman's estimation of $7,000,000,000 that the Swiss owed the Jewish people could not have been far off. Attempts were made to arrive at a sum. They might have been right, and they might have been wrong. But in the end, the true number really does not matter. What matters is that some measure of justice was achieved. It was not perfect justice, but then again nothing like this really ever is.

For the Swiss, as a great many people told us during the past few years, they never really did "get it." The Joint UBS-Credit Suisse press release announcing the settlement was indicative of this when their spokesmen wrote, "The aim of the additional payment by Credit Suisse Group and UBS is to avert the threat of sanctions as well as long and costly court proceedings."[124]

* * *

"You have been a true pioneer in this saga, and with persistence and resolve you broke a scandalous conspiracy of silence which lasted half a century. The result is not only an achievement in material terms, but a moral victory and a triumph of the spirit," wrote Benjamin Netanyahu to D'Amato on August 18, 1998. For D'Amato it was a time to rejoice and bask in the reflection of having ended the fifty-year coverup. While he had not directly started this struggle, he surely ended it and he did so on his terms.

While it was now over for Switzerland, others would not be so lucky. In due time the blame would spread. Soon the Swiss would be joined in facing accusations of wartime impropriety. Soon companies, museums, and nations beyond Switzerland would become engulfed in this maelstrom.

As the Swiss tried to tell the world what most historians by now already knew, they were not alone. As the then incoming Ambassador of Switzerland to the United States, Alfred Defago told me in February 1996, with a clear snarl on his face, "you better look at others, we weren't the only ones."

Soon, the world would heed Defago's advice.

Notes

1. Memorandum from Harry Dexter White to Secretary Morgenthau, n.d., United States Treasury Department, declassified October 1996.
2. Opening Statement of New York City Council Speaker Peter Vallone at the Hearing on the Swiss Banks before the New York City Council Committee on Governmental Operations, 10 February 1997, pp. 9–10.
3. Letter of Alan G. Hevesi, Comptroller of the City of New York to Robert Studer, Chairman of the Board, Union Bank of Switzerland, 6 May 1996.
4. Alan G. Hevesi, "The Shame of the Swiss Banks," *Jewish Press*, 22 November 1996.
5. Statement of Jeff Wiesenfeld, Executive Assistant to the Governor, New York City, 23 October 1996.
6. Ellen Friedland, "NJ resolutions would urge Swiss banks to return assets," *New Jersey Metrowest Jewish News*, 19 December 1996, pp. 8,14.
7. Rhode Island House Resolution 97-H 5196, 14 January 1997.
8. William Murphy, "Open Files," *Newsday*, 17 January 1997.
9. Letter of George M. Phillip, Executive Director New York State Teachers' Retirement System to Georges Blum, Chairman, Swiss Bank Corporation, 24 January 1997.
10. Peter Vallone, Speaker, New York City Council, Introduction 90529 January 1997, p. 1.
11. Liz Willen, "City Takes Aim at Swiss," *Newsday*, 30 January 1997.
12. "New York's Vallone proposes to bar city from using Swiss banks," *AFX News*, 30 January 1997.
13. Press Release of Assembly Speaker Sheldon Silver, 30 January 1997.
14. "New York State to investigate Swiss, U.S. banks in World War II," Agence-France-Presse, 6 February 1997.
15. Letter of Daniel Zuberbüler and Dr. Urs Zulauf of the Swiss Federal Banking Commission to New York State Banking Department, 21 February 1997.
16. "Frequently Asked Questions, The Mission of the Holocaust Claims Processing Office," New York State Banking Department. The languages spoken by staff in the office are French, German, Hebrew, Polish, Russian, Spanish and Yiddish).
17. Letter of George Oetterli, Contact Office for the Search of Dormant Accounts Administered by Swiss Banks, to Alan Hecht, New York, 4 August 1997.
18. Telephone Conversation with Ed Fagan, 13 February 1998.
19. Letter of Alan G. Hevesi, Comptroller City of New York, to Judith Baar Topinka, State Treasurer of Illinois, 11 June 1997.
20. Press Release of New York City Comptroller Alan G. Hevesi, 14 May 1998.
21. Sheldon Silver, "Truth and Justice Still Elusive in Swiss Banks Probe," *Jewish Press*, 20 November 1997.
22. "Jewish group criticizes new Swiss president," Reuters, 31 December 1997.
23. Senate Joint Resolution No. 1, Senator Dave Donely, Alaska State Senate, January 1998.
24. "Bennett joins effort to recover money of Holocaust victims," [Mississippi] Associated Press, 18 December 1997; "State treasurer offers help to those entitled to Nazi assets,"[Nebraska] Associated Press, 10 December 1997.
25. Press Release of Assemblymen Neil Cohen and State Senator Robert Singer, "Cohen/Singer Propose Switzerland Divestiture Bill,"12 March 1997; "An Act concerning the use of public funds and the conduct of business between the State and State authorities and the Swiss Confederation and Swiss-owned and

connected companies and supplementing Title 52 of the Revised Statues," New Jersey General Assembly and State Senate.

26. "Democrats say Swiss bank should not be used for proposed TDI sale," Associated Press, 16 April 1997.
27. Joel M. Weingarten, "Move ahead on sanctions against Swiss financial institutions," *New Jersey Metrowest Jewish News*, 19 February 1998.
28. Ralph Siegel, "Assembly panel approves ban on investments in Swiss banks," Associated Press, 3 March 1998.
29. Chicago City Council Document Number PO 97-314, Aldermen Burton Natarus and Bernard Stone, February 7, 1997.
30. "City Council Tables Swiss Bank Issue," *Chicago Tribune*, 10 may 1997.
31. Deborah Orin, "Chicago is mulling bill to boycott Swiss banks," *New York Post*, 13 May 1997.
32. Letter of Judy Baar Topinka, Treasurer of the State of Illinois to Alan G. Hevesi, Comptroller of the City of New York, 15 July 1997.
33. Ibid.
34. Telephone Conversation with Gregg Durham, Press Spokesman, Illinois State Treasurer Judy Baar Topinka, 20 November 1997.
35. Undated "Policy Statement on Swiss Banks," Illinois State Treasurer Judy Baar Topinka.
36. "Swiss Monitor," Office of the Comptroller of the City of New York, November 1997; David E. Sanger, "Swiss Bank Loses Role in Bond Deal," *New York Times*, 10 October 1997, p.A1
37. Sanger, "Swiss Bank Loses Role in Bond Deal."
38. Press Release of California State Treasurer Matt Fong, 14 October 1997.
39. Tani Freedman, "Swiss banks reeling from latest business blow in California," Agence France-Presse, 15 October 1997.
40. Greg Frost, "California Halts Dealings with Swiss Banks," Reuters, 14 October 1997.
41. "Swiss banks 'regret' California move to halt dealings," Deutsche Press Agentur, 15 October 1997.
42. Letter of Ambassador Stuart E. Eizenstat, Under Secretary of State for Economic, Business, and Agricultural Affairs, to California State Treasurer Matt Fong, 17 October 1997.
43. Alice Ratcliffe, "U.S. envoy sees Swiss bank bans as counterproductive," Reuters, 15 October 1997.
44. Press Release of Treasurer Joseph D. Malone, 20 October 1997.
45. Letter of Massachusetts Treasurer and Receiver-General Joseph D. Malone to Allyson D. Samson, Managing Director, Corporate and Institutional Banking UBS, 20 October 1997
46. Andrew Miga, "Banks in Nazi flap hire Kerry adviser's co." *Boston Herald*, 9 December 1997.
47. Andrew Miga, "Kerry cites efforts on behalf of Holocaust victims," *Boston Herald*, 10 December 1997.
48. Frank Phillips, "Galled Officials Fire Big Dig Lawyer," *Boston Globe*, 16 December 1997.
49. Chris Black, "Kerry's Fund Aide Resigns. Move Follows Spate of Critical Stories," *Boston Globe*, 31 December 1997.
50. "Swiss slams U.S. sanctions against banks for Nazi-era account errors," *Agence France-Presse*, 22 October 1997.
51. Letter of Abraham Foxman, National Director, Anti-Defamation League of B'nai B'rith, to Matt Fong, California State Treasurer, 31 October 1997.

52. Secretary of State Madeleine K. Albright, Remarks Before Members of the Swiss Parliament Bern, Switzerland, 15 November 1997.

53. "Fong to Suspend Swiss Investment Moratorium," Press Release of California Treasurer Matt Fong, 4 December 1997.

54. Caroline Goldrick, "Sanctions sought on Swiss banks," United Press International, 8 December 1997.

55. John Authers, "Moratorium urged on Swiss boycott," *Financial Times*, 9 December 1997.

56. State of New York, Banking Department Consent Decree with the Swiss Bank Corporation Basle, Switzerland and the Swiss Bank Corporation, New York Branch, 5 December 1997.

57. State of New York, Banking Department Consent Decree with the Union Bank of Switzerland, Zurich, Switzerland and the Union Bank of Switzerland, New York Branch, 6 April 1998.

58. "Is this marriage a mistake?" *Economist*, 31 January 1998, p. 75.

59. Letter of Alfonse M. D'Amato to Alan Greenspan, Chairman, Board of Governors of the Federal Reserve System, 5 February 1998.

60. "Swiss banker plays down D'Amato threat to merger," Reuters, 6 February 1998.

61. "D'Amato's True Face," NZZ Editorial, *Neue Zürcher Zeitung*, Week in Review, 2–8 February 1998.

62. "Swiss criticizes D'Amato bank merger interference," Agence France-Presse, 9 February 1998.

63. Response by Union Bank of Switzerland and Swiss Bank Corporation to the Letter, dated February 5, 1998 from Senator Alfonse M. D'Amato, Chairman of the United States Senate Committee on Banking, Housing and Urban Affairs, to The Honorable Alan Greenspan, Chairman of the Board of Governors of the Federal Reserve System, 27 February 1998.

64. Letter of Elizabeth McCaul, Acting Superintendent of Banks, New York State, to Alan Grenspan, Chairman, Board of Governors of the Federal Reserve System, 19 March 1998.

65. Letter of Richard C. Capone, Executive Vice President and Chief Operating Officer Americas, to Alan Grenspan, Chairman, Board of Governors of the Federal Reserve System, 3 April 1998.

66. Letter of Matt Fong, Treasurer of the State of California to Denise Ducharme, Abandoned Property Manager, Department of the Treasury, State of Maine, 12 March 1998.

67. Letter of Matt Fong, Treasurer of the State of California to the Swiss Bankers Association, 12 March 1998.

68. "Swiss Officials Angrily [sic] California Threat," Associated Press, 13 March 1998.

69. Letter of Robert O'Brien, Managing Director and Head of Corporate Banking, Credit Suisse; Simon Canning, President and Chief Executive Officer SBC Warburg Dillon Read, Inc.; and Richard Capone, Executive Vice President and Chief Executive Officer Americas, UBS, to Matt Fong, Treasurer of the State of California to the Swiss Bankers Association, 18 March 1998.

70. Letter of Alan G. Hevesi, Comptroller of the City of New York to Matt Fong, Treasurer of the State of California to the Swiss Bankers Association, 13 March 1998.

71. Cited in "Switzerland & the Holocaust Assets," an Internet web page of Swiss journalist Bruno Giussani, http://www.com/holocaust-assets/welcome.html .

72. Cited in "Swiss World War II Task Force-2: Settlement with Jewish Groups Seen," *Dow Jones News*, 24 March 1998.

73. Cited in Bruno Giussani, "Switzerland & the Holocaust Assets."
74. Press Release, "New American Jewish Committee-Sponsored Public Opinion Survey Reveals Over Two-Thirds of American Jews Maintain the Swiss Government is Being 'Uncooperative in Providing a Full Accounting of its Dealings with the Nazis...," American Jewish Committee, 24 March 1998.
75. Joshua Meckler, "Swiss restitution settlement forthcoming, Bronfman predicts," *Jewish Bulletin of Northern California*, 9 March 1998.
76. Prepared Statement of U.S. Senator Alfonse M. D'Amato (R-NY), Before the Executive Monitoring Committee on the Issue of Holocaust Assets and American Sanctions, Chaired by Alan G. Hevesi, New York City Comptroller, Delivered by Gregg Rickman, Legislative Director, Office of Senator Alfonse M. D'Amato, 26 March 1998.
77. Draft "Resolution" of Robert O'Brien, Managing Director and Head of Corporate Banking, Credit Suisse, to U.S. Senator Alfonse M. D'Amato, 24 March 1998.
78. Letter of Marcel Ospel, Chairman of the Board, Swiss Bank Corporation, to Israel Singer, Secretary General of the World Jewish Congress, 26 March 1998.
79. Conversation with Deputy New York City Comptroller Steve Newman, 26 March 1998.
80. Tim Whitmire, "Sanction threat credited with forcing settlement in Swiss banks dispute," Associated Press, 27 March 1998.
81. Letter of Edward Fagan to United States Senator Alfonse M. D'Amato, 7 November 1997, with copy of the account card included.
82. David E. Sanger, "Big Swiss Bank Settles With Daughter of Nazi Victim," *New York Times*, 5 May 1998.
83. Alan Morris Schom, "The Unwanted Guests, Swiss Forced Labor Camps 1940–1944," A Report Prepared for the Simon Wiesenthal Center, January 1998; and "Funds, refugees, and attacks against Switzerland: this is enough," *Tribune de Geneve*, 11–13 April 1998, summary translated by Abigail Schirmann.
84. "Newscast: New accusation by Jews that Switzerland abused and exploited Jewish refugees from Nazi Germany," Transcript of the *CBS Evening News*, 13 January 1998.
85. "Swiss Backlash," *Washington Times*, 23 March 1998.
86. Telephone conversation with Eric Wollman, Office of the Comptroller of the City of New, Alan G. Hevesi, 3 April 1998.
87. Letter of Under Secretary of State Stuart Eizenstat to Israel Singer, Secretary General, World Jewish Congress, 3 June 1998.
88. *Switzerland and Gold Transactions in the Second World War, Interim Report*, Independent Commission of Experts, Switzerland—Second World War, Jean-François Bergier, Chairman, 25 May 1998, pp. 63, 80.
89. Letter of Alan G. Hevesi, Comptroller City of New York to President Flavio Cotti of Switzerland, 11 June 1998.
90. Letter of Thomas Borer to Alan G. Hevesi, Comptroller City of New York, 1 July 1998.
91. Statement of the Anti-Defamation League, Abraham Foxman, National Director, 19 June 1998.
92. Burt Neuborn, "Totaling the Sum of Swiss Guilt," *New York Times*, 24 June 1998.
93. Richard Capone and Robert O'Brien, "What's Right With the Swiss Banks' Offer," *New York Times*, 30 June 1998.
94. Letter of Gizella Weisshaus to Judge Edward R. Korman, Eastern District of New York, 26 April 1998; Letter of Gizella Weisshaus to Judge Edward R. Korman, Eastern District of New York, 3 June 1998.

95. Letter of Michael D. Hausfeld, Melvyn Weiss, and Israel Singer to Under Secretary of State Stuart Eizenstat, 29 June 1998.

96. Freda Rosenberg, Gertrude Jorisch, Eva Garai, Andor Mittleman, and Ernest Knopfler v. The Swiss National Bank, No. 1:98CV01647, Judge June L. Green, United States District Court, District of Columbia, 29 June 1998.

97. Irene Markovicova, Dr. Barbara Schwartz-Lee, Lia Atschuld Fishman, and Liliane Schmidt-Escobar v. Swiss Bank Coporation, Credit Suisse, and Union Bank of Switzerland, No. 996160, Superior Court of the State of California, County of San Francisco, 30 June 1998.

98. "Plaintiffs' Status Report and Request for Status Conference," in re Holocaust Assets, United States District Court, Eastern District of New York, 30 June 1998.

99. Letter of Stuart Eizenstat, Under Secretary of State to Messrs. Singer, Hausfeld, Weiss, Swift and Witten, 22 July 1998.

100. See David E. Sanger, "How a Swiss Bank Gold Deal Eluded a U.S. Mediator," *New York Times*, 13 July 1998, p. 6.

101. John Authers, "Swiss banks expect sanctions this week," *Financial Times*, 29 June 1998.

102. Interview with Alan G. Hevesi, *Morning Edition*, National Public Radio, 2 July 1998.

103. Verena Dobnik, "Claimants' lawyer sees long conflict," Associated Press, 1 July 1998.

104. Announcement from the Offices of the New York State and City Comptrollers, "Hevesi and McAll Announce Plans to Act Against Swiss Banks & Other Companies," 2 July 1998.

105. "Declaration of the Federal Council on the Hevesi Committee's Conclusions," Swiss Federal Chancellery, 2 July 1998.

106. Resolution of Wayne County Commissioner Wayne Cushingberry, Wayne County Commission (Michigan), 16 July 1998; Letters of Jack Doyle, Monroe County Executive (New York) to Banks in the County, July 1998.

107. Letter of Denise C. Ducharme, Alan G. Hevesi, Matt Fong, H. Carl McCall, and Barbara Hafer to Mark Spennaccio, Comptroller, Monroe County, New York, 13 July 1998.

108. Briefing of State Department Spokesman Jamie Rubin, 6 July 1998.

109. Discussion with Fredy Rom, Swiss reporter for *Jewish Telegraphic Agency*, in Washington, 21 July 1998; Bruno Giussani, "Switzerland and the Holocaust Assets."

110. "Israel slams Swiss fringe call for Jewish boycott," Reuters, 7 July 1998.

111. "Misguided Hesitation," *Neue Zürcher Zeitung*, 15 July 1998, p. 23.

112. See David E. Sanger, "State Department is Criticized By New York Comptroller," *New York Times*, 23 July 1998.

113. Letter of Jean Zeigler, National Councillor to Gregg Rickman, Office of Senator Alfonse M. D'Amato, 5 October 1998.

114. Grant McCool, "Lawyers for Holocaust victims want talks resumed," Reuters, 15 July 1998.

115. Memorandum from Melvyn I. Weiss to the Swiss Banks Executive Committee, "Re: Swift-Fagan Press Conference," 15 July 1998.

116. Memorandum from Bob Swift, to the Plaintiffs Executive Committee Members, "Re: Holocaust Victims Assets Litigation," 16 July 1998.

117. Press Release, "Swiss President Cotti writes to President Clinton of the United States, Embassy of Switzerland in the United States, 22 July 1998.

118. Letter of Denise C. Ducharme, et al. to Mark Spennaccio.

119. Letter of Ambassadors Thomas Borer and Alfred Defago to Phoebe Selden, Comptroller of the City of Chicago, 24 July 1998.
120. Letter of Alan G. Hevesi and Carl McCall to President William J. Clinton, 28 July 1998.
121. Discussion with Marty Mendelsohn, 13 August 1998, and Miriam Kleiman, 12 August 1998.
122. Discussion with Israel Singer, 12 August 1998.
123. Transcript of *Morning Edition*, National Public Radio, 13 August 1998.
124. Media Release, "U.S. class actions: banks reach settlement," UBS and Credit Suisse Joint Release, 12 August 1998.

10

History's Vengeance

"Of the funds brought from the former Independent Croat State where Jews and Serbs were plundered to support the Ustascha organization in exile," wrote Emerson Bigelow of the OSS, "an estimated 150 million Swiss Francs were impounded by British authorities at the Austro-Swiss frontier; the balance of approximately 200 million Swiss Francs was originally held in the Vatican for safe-keeping. According to rumor [sic], a considerable portion of this latter amount has been sent to Spain and Argentina through the Vatican's 'pipeline'..."[1]

Just as the war had engulfed the world, so too would the search for the assets robbed from the victims of that war. Bigelow's letter to the Treasury Department highlighted the very problem that Morgenthau's Treasury Department investigators had faced, a worldwide spread of the spoils of Nazi looting.

Just as Defago had admonished me, others certainly were guilty of the same things the Swiss were. Very early on we found clear evidence that Switzerland was not alone in the world with its growing problem. Soon we found overwhelming evidence of wrongdoing by all the other nations of Europe, South America, and even the United States. As the Swiss were being torn apart in the world's press, soon other nations were being hit as well. Quickly, the search for assets spread beyond Swiss banks to European insurance companies and to art museums around the world. This reopening of the unfinished business of the Second World War aroused other revelations as well, in some ways more disturbing about the period and would prove even more embarrassing to the countries tagged with these accusations. In all, the revelations of the misdeeds of the Swiss banks unleashed an unparalleled exposure for many countries and institutions throughout the world.

Auguste Forel

His face adorns the 1,000 franc note in Switzerland. In 1928, he was a psychiatrist in Vaud, Switzerland who advocated the policy of eugenics, or the so-called science of racial cleansing. Forel introduced the practice of forced sterilization of supposed mentally ill women in the French-speaking section of Switzerland, according to the Swiss historian Hans Ulrich Jost, who disclosed the existence of the program in August 1997. Jost explained that the practice might well have continued on until 1985 in Switzerland. According to Jost, Hitler was so impressed with the eventual law that codified the practice that he asked for a copy of it in order to implement it in Germany.[2]

As shocking as this story was, within days of its appearance in the world's press, similar stories appeared of similar programs in Sweden, Austria, Belgium, and France. All these nations had sterilized female patients who, in some cases were mentally ill, but others for supposed misbehavior or in one case, even a girl who had trouble seeing a schoolroom blackboard.[3]

Horror stories like these were a by-product of past memories brought back to life across the newspapers of the world. Claimants and survivors alike were reported to have suffered from a form of post-traumatic syndrome, triggered by testimony, stories, documentaries, and the general debate surrounding Hitler's accomplices, the Swiss bankers.[4] Survivors I talked to at events around the country and in Canada and others by phone from all over the world, used their time to relive their experiences, not only of the horrors they survived, but of their families lost to the Nazis. Not all related bad events, but they related experiences long forgotten, brought to light again by the revelations of the Swiss role in World War II.

What survivors and claimants alike were reliving was symptomatic of what had grown into a worldwide debate about looted assets. Each nation now began to look into their past. Was their nation simply a bystander that just looked the other way? Was it a victim? Was it a perpetrator? One by one, nations, largely in Europe, but later in South America, formed commissions to examine their past. Journalists talked of a European continent "on the couch," in psychoanalysis, trying to come to grips with its history. Important too, was not only that they examined it, but that they came to grips with it. Switzerland for example was held out as the example of how not to psychologically deal with the revelations of the past. Antonio Oyarzabal, the Ambassador of

Spain to the United States, referring to his nation, told our Chief of Staff Michael Kinsella at a reception, "we are not the Swiss."

In a study, "Unmasking National Myths: European Challenge Their History," Avi Becker, director of the WJC's office in Jerusalem wrote,

> More than fifty years after the Holocaust, European and other countries are confronting newly-emerging memories and guild-filled ghosts from the past. The campaign for the restitution of Jewish property stolen during the Holocaust touched a raw nerve within European society and, together with the end of the Cold War and generational change, created a need to reevaluate conventional historical truths.[5]

Not only nations were looking at their past, but companies as well. If Swiss banks could be hit, why could not others as well. Soon banks like Barclays, Deutsche Bank, and Bank of International Settlements (BIS), were hiring archivists and historians to look through their records. As far as the BIS, or the Central Bank of the world's central banks, was concerned, D'Amato sought their voluntary cooperation early on because of documents we found heavily implicating them in wartime dealings with the Nazis. Later, European automobile manufacturers, metal smelting firms, and optical firms would face separate multibillion dollar lawsuits by Fagan, Weiss, and Hausfeld.

Insurance companies did not escape the wrath of criticism. Sixteen European insurance companies were the subject of a lawsuit filed against them in New York by Ed Fagan. Soon they, too became the subject of an congressional hearings, and talk of boycotts and international commissions.

Art museums too, long thought to have held looted artwork came under the magnifying glass for this possibility. They too, were subjected to legal action and congressional action.

Finally, the venerable International Red Cross came under fire for wartime dealings with the Nazis, based upon documents that we found in the archives. Before too long, they were forced to not only research their past, but confess both errors in judgment at the time and indiscretions they preferred kept secret.

For Once Its Not Us

Werner Sonne, of ARD German Television was interviewing me for a broadcast on German television in the summer of 1996. While walking with me down the stairs to the spot he would film the interview, he commented to me, "for once its not us." For Sonne, who had grown up in postwar Germany, he experienced from the beginning the legacy

Germany would spend decades living down, the guilt and responsibility for the Holocaust and the Second World War. As he explained, he like other Germans had to accept responsibility for the horrors of the time and for all these years, they did so alone. Now, they were joined by the Swiss. This was comforting to him. Yet, for us and others as well, we wondered how long it would take for the story to come back to its source: Germany.

With the onset of the lawsuits against the European insurance companies which will be detailed below, Germany's role as the perpetrator of the "greatest robbery in history," came back into focus. As Oliver August wrote in the *Times of London*, "thus the row over the Nazi past of financial institutions has now reached a stage where it can no longer be confined to Switzerland, which is actively pointing the finger at Germany."[6]

A few weeks after August's article appeared in London, Michel Friedman, a leading member of the Central Council of Jews in Germany made the same point when he declared "the German banks have to take the initiative in atoning for the moral burden. Those who do not lay open their past, will be overtaken by history." What Friedman wanted was for the German banks to come forward with answers to the same questions that were being asked of the Swiss. For him, the same moral rules applied.[7] Several days later, Friedman continued his fight to open up the banks. "For more than five decades," he asserted, "we've been waiting for the officials of the banks which worked, cooperated and collaborated during the Third Reich to speak."[8] Friedman's efforts soon began to pay off. After decades of disregard for the role German banks played at the time, more and more people began to pay attention to this all important but ignored part of the German war economy.

"The Federal Republic of Germany has spent considerable amounts as reparation payments during the last decades," wrote Professor Dr. Julius H. Schoeps, Director of the Moses Mendelssohn Zentrum, Europäisch Jüdische Studien, Universität Potsdam to D'Amato in August 1997. "However, the German banking-houses [sic]—especially the 'Deutsche Bank' and the 'Dresdner Bank'—have not considered it necessary so far to publish information on bank-accounts [sic] that belonged to Holocaust victims and were confiscated by the German Reich."[9]

As we found with the Swiss, banks did more than hold bank accounts in this period. They held gold as well. In this realm, journalist Peter Bild began the search for documents on the whereabouts of Jewish confiscated gold found in the Merckers mine hurriedly stashed there at the end of the war by the Nazis. Bild discovered that Albert Thoms, the wartime head of the Reichsbank's Precious Metals Department, was given access to and perhaps control of the documentation on the Merckers gold, stored in the postwar Bundesbank. Thoms, in his position during the war, oversaw the massive inflow of looted gold from the European treasuries and the mouths and bodies of Holocaust victims that formed the basis of the Melmer Account, after the SS Captain Bruno Melmer. Because of his knowledge of the operations of the bank, Thoms was restored to his position at the new German bank after the war in return for his cooperation in war crimes investigations against other Nazi officials. Thoms, who died in 1977, Bild theorized, had knowledge of "sticky-fingered Americans," or others whom he used to safeguard himself for postwar security and employment. After his death, it was reported that missing documents were found among his papers. Ulrich Benckert who died in 1975 at the age of eighty-six, was the last liquidator of the Reichsbank and apparently also was reported to have been in possession of papers. A year after his death, these papers were said to have disappeared.[10]

These "disappearances" lend credence to Bild's theory of a conspiracy. Moreover, the disappearance of twenty-four Melmer account files ostensibly returned to the Bank Deutsche Lander by the U.S. Army in 1948, only adds to more mystery to the story. The other files, sixty-seven of a total of ninety-one, were microfilmed and sent to the National Archives in Washington. To this day, the remaining files have not been found, nor any copies in either Washington or Germany. Bild's findings have prompted both German banks as well as the National Archives and the Department of Justice's Office of Special Investigations to search for the missing files.[11]

Bild's findings and Friedman's calls for further investigation prompted Deutsche Bank to search their record for the truth. That truth, however would be difficult for the banks to swallow. From the documents we found, and there were many, both banks were full participants in the absorption of banks in occupied lands, all over Europe. In detailed studies done during and after the war, Deutsche Bank and another large German bank, Dresdner Bank, were found to have absorbed banks in Austria, Serbia, Czechoslovakia, Bulgaria, Romania, Croatia, Greece, Holland, Luxembourg, Poland, Hungary, Belgium, France, and Yugoslavia.[12] The banks also distributed their securities around their newly enlarged empire. Essentially, wherever the Wehrmacht went, so did the German banks. Despite any doubts, German banks were active participants in the Nazi economic pillage of Europe.

The bank pledged to reexamine its history to find just how much gold it accepted during the war. As such, if any dubious accounts or dormant accounts would be found, they said would be returned to the appropriate authorities. But because of an announced sale of their Argentine banking subsidiary to the Bank of Boston, the bank was a bit more sensitive to the possibility of evidence of looted gold and other assets showing up in the files. To determine the bank's role, in December 1997 they hired historians including Gerald Feldman of the University of California at Berkeley to examine their records and those of other nations. Feldman had also been hired to compile a history of the Allianz Insurance Company, which later came under fire for its wartime role regarding the disposition of life insurance policies of European Jews.

The bank's fears came true in May 1998, when Jonathan Steinberg, another of Deutsche Bank's historians, disclosed on German television that some 600 kilos, or five tons of gold held by the bank came from the wartime Reichsbank. Upon hearing this news, independent historian Hersch Fischler came forward to explain that most if not all of this gold probably came from gold melted down from dental fillings taken from concentration camp victims. Fischler whom, I met in London in December 1997, claimed to have found portions of the documents Peter Bild said had been turned over to the Germans after the war, but not microfilmed. Fischler claimed the files were for some unexplainable reason in Vienna, and that these coupled with diaries purported to be those of Albert Thoms, prove the gold was victim's gold.

Even before Steinberg and Fischler's revelations were made, in March 1998, Deutsche Bank agreed to provide $3,100,000 to Jewish foundations based on fears of what their historians would find. The money, proceeds of 711 pounds of gold the bank sold in 1995, would be split between the WJRO and the March of the Living, a program to take Jewish school children from all over the world on trips to tour the concentration camps.

While Deutsche Bank has been forthcoming and willing to examine its past, Dresdner Bank has been less willing and has faced criticism for their reluctance. As with Deutsche Bank, we found compelling evidence to suggest that Dresdner was at least as guilty as Deutsche Bank. Thus far, the bank's management has refused to deal with the issue.

Deutsche Bank's history was further explained in the publication of the second Eizenstat report. The bank, along with Dresdner, was named as having been complicit in the sale of gold from the Melmer Account in the Reichsbank in Turkey to supply Germany with hard currency. Upon hearing of this report, Ed Fagan, and five other attorneys almost immediately filed a class action in the United States District Court in the Southern District of New York on behalf of three plaintiffs against both Deutsche and Dresdner Banks for $18,000,000,000, on June 3, 1998.[13]

In July 1998, historians Avraham Barakai, Gerald Feldman, Lothar Gall, Jonathan Steinberg, and Harold James (also a member of the Bergier Historical Commission) concluded definitive, amounts of gold, monetary and nonmonetary, were sent from the Reichsbank to the Deutsche Bank. The sums, smaller by comparison than that which were funelled through the Swiss banks, nevertheless contributed to the looting of Europe and the victims of the Holocaust by the Nazis.[14]

Kept in the Dark

Like Switzerland, Sweden before the Swiss scandal erupted, was viewed in a benign way. Like Switzerland too, there had always been much whispering about alleged misdeeds during the war years by the Swedish government. It appeared that soon Sweden too would be implicated in the ever-expanding scandal.

The WJC, by May 1996, while receiving the same documents we did from the archives, began to release several implicating the Enskilda Bank in Stockholm. Just as the Swiss banks had been accused of laundering looted gold and U.S. dollars, so too was Enskilda. Moreover, Enskilda was owned by the Wallenberg family whose loyalties were split between the Nazis and the Allies. Jacob Wallenberg, who directed the bank, clashed with his brother Marcus who supported the Allies. Both were uncles of Raoul Wallenberg who disappeared at the end of the war, some say for helping so many Jews to escape from Hungary, others attributing his disappearance to his uncles' divided loyalties.

Yet, Sweden was unlike Switzerland in one very important way. The present-day Swedish government had seen what was happening to Switzerland and was less cornered by its own pride. By November, Singer was in Stockholm meeting with the Swedish Foreign Minister seeking his help in creating a commission to look into the activities of Swedish financial institutions at the time. According to Singer, the Swedes were quite a bit more forthcoming than the Swiss have ever been. I witnessed this myself when dealing with both the Swedish Ambassador to the U.S. and most of his staff.

Soon, more and more documents were being found exposing the role of not only Enskilda, but of Swedish trading of its rich stocks of iron ore, so important to the Nazi war machine, for gold and other assets, that according to former Swedish Ambassador Sven Fredrik Hedin, who would later serve on the Swedish Commission, was looted. Hedin wrote, "The coalition government knew of suspicions that the Germans paid for the ore in war loot. But it preferred to be kept in the dark."[15]

Hedin, along with Swedish radio reporter Göran Elgemyr, began to probe the Swedish archives and soon began to publish articles in the largest Stockholm newspaper *Dagens Nyhter*. Soon, the paper picked up the chase and dug even deeper. Stories of Swedish wartime improprieties appeared all over Europe.

As accusations mounted against the Swiss banks, especially by D'Amato, the Swiss reacted harshly to charges that they knew the origin of the gold they freely accepted. In their defense, they lashed out at the Swedes. "It is incorrect that Switzerland was the only neutral country to take gold from the German Reichsbank," declared Werner Abegg, spokesman for the Swiss National Bank. Sweden, they charged, did so as well.[16]

Things got worse for the Swedes, and quickly. Within days of the harsh Swiss accusations, the WJC released documents accusing Swedish industry of making precision parts for German rockets launched against Belgium. Soon, more documents surfaced implicating the Swedish branch of the Red Cross with smuggling looted assets to Nazis in Sweden after World War II.

As Swedes struggled to come to grips with the mounting claims against their country, they were able to take solace in the fact that they were not the only ones under the microscope. They had the added benefit of being second in line behind the Swiss and had the luxury of knowing where they made mistakes and hopefully would not repeat them. But like Swiss, the Swedes were faced with an unhappy scenario of dealing with fifty-year old damning accusations, as Senior Vice President of Investor AB, the Wallenberg holding company declared, that are "difficult to defend yourself [against], because historical research takes time and it's not finished."[17]

"We are not the Swiss"

It was a Washington reception not unlike numerous others at any given time, but Spain's ambassador, Antonio Oyarzabal, was very worried as he walked about the room in March 1997. He had received two letters in rapid succession from D'Amato and had no real idea of when the next one was on its way. To his surprise and perhaps relief, Mike Kinsella was attending the same reception and met Oyarzabal who immediately introduced himself and pressed hard for Kinsella to set up a meeting with D'Amato to discuss his letters and what Spain was doing to answer D'Amato's questions.[18]

At the same time D'Amato wrote to Oyarzabal, he had also written to President Koller of Switzerland asking about the 280 truckloads of gold sent to Spain and Portugal from 1942 to 1944.[19] As with the case of Sweden, within days of a hint of a Spanish connection, the press turned its attention to Spain, with reporters in and out of the country digging for stories on Spanish complicity with the Nazis. The news spread fast. Quickly, an official from the Wiesenthal Center on February 12, traveled to Madrid to meet with the Governor of the Bank of Spain to discuss Spanish gold transactions.

Soon newspapers in Spain took up the cause and began to look into General Francisco Franco's role in the acceptance of gold from the Nazis. Spanish reporters began to call us for copies of the documents to compare with what they could find in their country. Once D'Amato released documents explaining in extreme detail, the shipments from Switzerland to Spain and Portugal, including the day of shipment, the trucking company, the bank the gold was destined for, and even the truck's license plates, there was no going back. Spain had a full-blown crisis, while not as large as Switzerland's, nevertheless, it was one they did not want to reach that proportion.[20]

Oyarzabal, like Jagmetti before him, had received the infamous D'Amato interrogations and did not want to suffer the same fate as his former fellow ambassador. He told a B'nai B'rith reception at the end of February, "Spain will go as far as necessary and do all it can to clarify and resolve this matter."[21]

Unlike Jagmetti however, Oyarzabal was granted a meeting with D'Amato on March 13. While in his office, Oyarzabal was very gracious and reiterated to D'Amato what he had told the B'nai B'rith. "We have in our soul," Oyarzabal told D'Amato, "a kind of Don Quixote. We want to fight for lost causes."[22]

Oyarzabal had good reason to achieve peace with D'Amato. As he said, his reasons were "selfish." King Juan Carlos and the Queen Sofia were traveling to New York to speak at Yeshiva University in just a few weeks and he did not want this issue to blow up now. He could not afford to have this happen. He promised results and promised them quickly.

Soon, there was a Spanish commission created under the leadership of former Minister of Justice Mugica-Herzog, a long-time member of Spain's Socialist party. At the same time as appointment of the commission, Professor Pablo Martin Acena, a professor of economic history at the Universidad Alcala de Henares in Madrid, was asked by the Governor of the Bank of Spain to come to the United States and research the issue in the National Archives, where he started his research at the end of February.

In his meeting with D'Amato, Oyarzabal promised a report would be delivered to D'Amato, as soon as it would assembled. Less than four weeks later, on April 3, Oyarzabal's report was hand delivered by the Ambassador himself. While apologizing for any confusion, Oyarzabal's letter to D'Amato denied any Spanish complicity in the acceptance of looted gold proclaimed "the ongoing investigations establish beyond any doubt that the gold from the Spanish reserves of the IEME (Spanish Institute of Foreign Currency) was legitimately acquired..."[23]

Despite hundreds of U.S. documents to the contrary, the Spanish Commission's final report, issued in April 1998, concluded, as did Oyarzabal's report, that Spain's gold purchases during the war were perfectly legal.

In Denial as Well

Just as Spain came under criticism for its role in accepting Nazi gold, so too did Portugal. The same trucks that took gold from the vaults of the Swiss National Bank from all over Switzerland and made deposits in Madrid, continued on to Portugal to make deposits in banks in Lisbon. While we had found numerous documents concerning Spain's role, we found a great many more implicating Portugal. Once exposed in October 1996 in documents released by the WJC, Portugal retreated into denial, first refusing comment then declaring all gold purchases were legal. The Bank of Portugal would have no part of such a scandal. There were "two or three gold bars stamped with swastikas," still in the vaults commented Nuno Jonet a Bank of Portugal official. "We kept them as a curiosity. We do not admit any wrongdoing."[24]

Soon, like Sweden and Spain, reporters in and out of Portugal jumped on the bandwagon and began the hunt for Nazi gold in Portugal. By February 1997, D'Amato had asked the Portuguese Ambassador to the United States, Fernando Andresen Guimarães, for information on the same documents we sent to Ambassador Oyarzabal. Within two days of that letter, either by coincidence or because of it, the Portuguese Central Bank announced plans to form a commission to look into its record. According to Ambassador Guimarães, the commission was to be headed by Professor Joaquim Costa Leite.[25]

The Swiss meanwhile, like they had done with the Swedes, took great pains to announce to the world that the Portuguese were not as clean themselves. If the Swiss banks were bad, they implied, the Portuguese were the next worse. "Besides the SNB, Portugal was the most important buyer of German gold," Jean Pierre Roth, SNB Vice President told a March 20, 1997 news conference.[26] Roth's point was confirmed by Professor Leite in March 1998 when he publicly stated the same, reporting that Portugal only returned four of 123 tons of gold accepted from the Nazis.

A Safe Haven

In 1944, when Samuel Klaus, in part conceived of the program that came to be known as "Operation Safehaven," his goal was to stop the flow of German external assets out of Germany to neutral sites away from the reach of the Allies.[27] The term "safe haven" could not have been more appropriate for a nation like Argentina. It became abundantly clear to Klaus and his fellow sleuths, that Argentina could be and was an invaluable haven for Nazi funds and Nazis themselves, as has now become the stuff of legend. As such, Argentina was an obvious place to look for what everyone already suspected would be a rich target for finding Nazi assets.

This unfortunate part of Argentine history was not overlooked there either and soon, as suspicions began to be voiced as to Argentina's role regarding Nazi looted assets, President Carlos Menem took proactive measures to forestall what would inevitably become a messy affair. Early on in September 1996, he invited Argentina's Jewish community to look through the Central Bank's archives in search of gold stolen by the Nazis. Later, he presented Sergio Widder, the local director of the Simon Wiesenthal Center, with copies of five volumes of Central Bank transactions with the Nazis. While important for the historical record, the books did not really provide much because as we found in the documents, much of the financial dealings between the two was done through branches of German banks and even German companies operating in South America.

Less than a year later, in April 1997, Menem went further by creating a government commission to examine the disposition of gold and any other assets that might have been sent to Argentina. On May 6, 1997, Menem signed an executive order to create the "Commission on Clarification of Nazi Activities in the Argentine Republic."[28]

Dirty Money

"To my mind," said Rabbi Henry I. Sobel of Brazil, "the money deposited by Nazis in Swiss bank accounts or in Brazilian banks, or in any other banks, is not inherently 'dirty,' because before having been looted it belonged to Jewish families. Its 'dirtiness' disappears as soon as it is returned to its legitimate owners."[29]

Rabbi Sobel has served as an articulate voice for Brazil's Jewish community. As the Senior Rabbi for the Congregaçâ Israelita Paulista, in Sâo Paulo, it was Sobel that first sought Brazilian governmental support, in November 1996, for a commission in that country to investigate whether Nazi looted assets were transferred there by 1,200–1,500 Nazis fleeing justice after the war, according to Sobel's estimate.[30]

Five months later, a Brazilian President Fernando Henrique Cardoso announced the creation of "The Special Commission for the Search of Nazi Monies in Brazil. The Commission, with a membership of seven, sits in Sâo Paulo and established an agreement with the University of Sâo Paulo to house a documentation center holding the Commission's findings.[31] Sobel won his campaign for as he called it "moral restitution."

The Commission did not have to wait very long to find its first case when it was reported that the Nazi Albert Blume, who had died in 1983, was really a Nazi courier sent to Brazil to set up a network of contacts, had died leaving a safe deposit box with $4,000,000 in jewels, gold bars, and gold teeth. An aged aunt had begun a court battle to claim the contents of the box which were held pending examination by the new Brazilian Commission.[32] In November 1997, the safe deposit box was opened and found to have included, in addition to the gold and jewels, Blume' diary. Upon examination by the Commission, the 1,064-page diary convinced the examiners that however unpleasant were the contents of the box, they most likely were accumulated by Blume after the war after becoming a pawnbroker.[33]

Relearning History

"The Jewish community in France, like many others, has helped to forge our common culture. It has suffered from it more than others," declared former French Prime Minister Alain Juppé on January 25, 1997.[34] In Juppé's speech, he announced the creation of a commission to evaluate the extent of the confiscations by Vichy authorities during the war. This commission, to be headed by former French resistance hero and concentration camp survivor Jean Matteoli, appointed in March 1997, would soon have its work cut out for it.

Three days later it was disclosed in *Le Monde*, that the Third Chamber of the Court of Auditors filed a report on December 7, 1995, which stated that the various national museums in France which were still in possession of close to 2,000 works of art, including Cezannes, Rodins, Renoirs, Monets, and Gauguins, all confiscated from Holocaust victims by the Vichy regime. Moreover, little or no effort was ever made to find the owners or heirs of the artwork and that the museum directors were extremely reluctant to return paintings they deemed important to their collections.[35] According to the French Government the Louvre continues to hold 678 pieces of artwork; the Musée d'Orsay, 130; the National Museum of Modern Art, 38; the National Museum of Ceramics at Sévres, 131; and ten at the National Museum of the Château de Versailles.[36]

Fifty years after the fact, the French were a bit more sensitive to this problem. This became very clear in their reaction to D'Amato's May 1, 1997 floor speech excoriating the museums for their fifty-year delay in returning paintings. "I found the tone you thought fit to adopt in such a solemn setting as the United States Senate deeply regrettable," wrote French Ambassador Bujon de l'Estang to D'Amato weeks later. "In doing so, you deliberately mock my country's efforts to address a highly complex situation."[37]

These revelations, coupled with the fact the government withheld the information for over a year, irritated an already bad situation in France, long known for the collaborationist history of the Vichy government in the war. Against the background of the Swiss banks scandal, as well as the other nations then coming under close scrutiny, the disclosure by *Le Monde*, provided an opening for others to start looking for other assets that might have been confiscated. Those looking for the dirty deeds of the Vichy needed little time to find what they were looking for.

As was proving to be the case with so many of the other countries, France too, now fell under suspicion for a host of other indecencies. Soon researchers and journalists alike began to find an infamous history of confiscations by the Vichy government. Reports surfaced in the French weekly, *Le Point*, that the government secretly held on to gold, jewels and other property looted and later abandoned by the Nazis after their defeat. According to the report, the magazine used documents obtained from the Finance Ministry.[38]

As if this was not bad enough, French banks, just like the Swiss banks before them came under attack for withholding Holocaust victims' assets. According to reports in French papers, quoted by the Associated Press, in 1951, French banks discovered thousands of accounts worth some $175,000,000 in today's terms, yet did nothing.[39] In response to the reports, the French Bankers Association took a page from the SBA playbook and defended their actions as legal, but nevertheless accepted that their member banks would in fact cull their records for the possibility of finding the account holders.

Before the FBA could act, they were beaten to the punch when the law firm of Goodkind Labaton, Rudoff & Sucharow representing Fernande Bodner and Anna Zajdenberg, both of New York, brought suit against seven French banks and one British bank that operated in Vichy, France during the war. The suit sought an unspecified amount of damages from the banks for conversion, unjust enrichment, and breach of contract and fiduciary responsibility.[40]

Whereas before, the French bankers plead ignorance of guilt, now they sung a different tune. The government issued statements disassociating themselves from the kind of behavior their Swiss counterparts exhibited, and took great pains to show sympathy for the survivors and claimants. Bill Bowden, an attorney for Société Generale in New York called me the day after the suit was filed to explain the difference between the French and the Swiss banks. French Banks he said, "are quite aware of what happened to their counterparts in Switzerland."[41]

In January 1998, the disclosures for the banks only got worse when a French daily *Liberation* reported that French banks holding Jewish confiscated stocks continued to sell them as late as two weeks after the Allied invasion of France on June 6, 1944.[42] While sympathetic to the claimants, the French banks were nevertheless now in the same boat as the Swiss.

At the end of December 1997, France was again hit, this time by the results of the Interim Report of the Matteoli Commission. Matteoli's report detailed the widespread robbery of French Jews by the Vichy regime and the clear pattern of the retention of Jewish assets in France.[43] There would later be a subcommittee of the Matteoli Commission, known as the Saint George Group, created to examine the role played by French banks during the war. According to Bowden and Barclays officials, there would clearly be facts for this subcommittee to examine.[44]

All these disclosures and admissions combined to make France, in the words of Avraham Burg, "our next target."[45] It remains to be seen thus far, whether Burg's threat will be carried out.

So Many Others

There were others. Countries otherwise thought of as innocent, unable to have participated in the robbery of Holocaust victims. It was impossible some believed that institutions in countries like Israel, Britain, Russia, the former Czechoslovakia, and even the Vatican could have done what the Swiss banks did. But they did, in varying degrees participate in the avarice of the times.

In Israel, of all places, banks that held money collected from Jews in the diaspora, fifty and sixty years after the fact denied holding the accounts. When pressed, they refused to provide the names of the accounts, until threatened with legislative action in the Knesset by Avraham Hirchson.

In Britain, 25,000 names of account holders whose assets were confiscated by British banks after the war were placed on a searchable index on the Internet.[46] Britain, too, was not the least helpful in the postwar efforts of Operation Safehaven. At every turn, the British, more concerned with rebuilding its economy forestalled American efforts, as divided as they were to obtain proper compensation from the Swiss banks. The British too had skeletons in their closets.

Russia, victimized by invading Nazi armies, having lost over 20,000,000 people, fought back and reversed the tide and conquered all of Eastern Europe and ended up as the occupying power of half of Germany. In formalizing this occupation, the Red Army came into thousands upon thousands of artifacts, records, books, and other assets amassing much more in addition to that which was taken from them. Recently, President Boris Yeltsin tried in vain to get the Russian Duma to pass legislation that would allow for the return of artwork which was not originally Russian. The Duma refused, insisting that the country be allowed to keep as booty all that it had recovered as well as what was originally taken from their country.[47]

The former Czechoslovakia, like all the other former East Bloc states imposed barriers to compensation and restitution of property, both real and personal to its former citizens. In some cases it was through rigid citizenship requirements normally impossible to meet, and others through a near total lack of access to its archives, records of which are vital to proving one's case for proper restitution.

Finally, the Vatican, seat of the Catholic Church also has been drawn into the discussion because of the role of certain papal institutions played in routing the funds of Croatian war criminals to South America, not to mention the war criminals themselves. Questions too, arose about the disposition of the assets of Gypsies and Jews that might have been funneled through Vatican institutions. Efforts have been made by both the U.S. Government as well as the WJC and other Jewish institutions to persuade the Vatican to open its archives from the period for historical research. This opening is quite well far off.

A Foremost Task

"The battle against Jews, Freemasons and other affiliated forces of opposite 'Weltanschauung', wrote Hermann Göring, "is a foremost task of National Socialism during the war." Göring continued,

> I therefore welcome the decision of Reichsleiter Rosenberg to form Staffs in all occupied territories for the purpose of safeguarding all research material and cultural goods of the above-mentioned groups, and transporting them to Germany.[48]

In Göring's words lie the key to the Nazi's campaign to rob Europe of its art and cultural treasures. As Lynn Nicholas called it, it was the *Rape of Europa*.[49] This is not to say that the artwork of Jews was the only target of the Nazis, it was however, a specific one. Artwork owned by other victims groups was certainly open to confiscation and was widely looted.

Some chosen artwork was destined for the Linz Library Hitler wished to build to house the great works of art pleasing to his tastes and those of the Nazi motif. This much was explained in a directive issued by Reichshleiter Martin Bormann to Alfred Rosenberg, chief of the Nazis' art looting taskforces, and the "Custodian of the Entire Intellectual and Spiritual Training and Education of the Party and of all Coordinated Associations" on April 21, 1943.[50]

What was termed as "degenerate," art that did not fit the qualifications of the Nazi ideology and culture was sold off in return for works deemed more appropriate. In a Europe dominated by the Nazis, there was never any problem finding galleries and agents willing and able to either trade or buy the art the Nazis did not like.

Whereas throughout the course of our research we were looking for information first on dormant accounts, then gold looted by the Nazis, the proliferation of art losses that we discovered was staggering. We could not help but find hundreds of documents of reported losses of looted artwork. While art restitution was not a new process, it quickly became swept up into the swirl and became energized by the attention given to the Swiss banks. More importantly, artwork as differentiated from money or gold, is not fungible. Art, by its very nature cannot be adulterated or its value is lost. Because of this, it is, despite the difficulty in tracing looted art, an easier claim to prove for a claimant than one against a bank.

Willi Korte, who had provided us crucial help in the beginning days of our research, had previously been in the business of art restitution and continued to take cases on, even while helping us. He accepted clients that had either personally been robbed of their artwork by the Nazis, or more commonly, were heirs to families that had been victimized. Korte meticulously researched and tracked the path of those artworks from the point of confiscation, all through archives in France, Switzerland, Germany, Austria, and through archives in other European nations. He was well-known in the business and had taken on clients from all over the U.S., Europe, and Israel.

Featured on *60 Minutes*, Korte explained one of his prime cases, the "Goodman Case."[51] Friedrich Gutman, whose family had been one of the original owners of the Dresdner Bank in Germany, was by this connection, a very wealthy Dutch businessman, who incidently was not Jewish, but his family had converted to Christianity in the nineteenth century. Once the war began, Gutman however, was nevertheless classified as a Jew and both he and his wife, separated from their children, were faced with a choice: surrender his art collection, or be deported to a concentration camp. He refused and was sent to Theresienstadt where he was beaten to death for once again refusing to surrender his collection. His wife Louise, later died at Auschwitz.

The Gutman's collection ended up being divided up and scattered across Europe. Fifty years later, the Gutman's son Simon found one painting belonging to his parents in a museum catalogue. Then they hired Korte. The painting Goodman found was *Landscape with Smokestacks*, by the impressionist Edgar Degas, which was found to have been hanging on the walls of the Art Institute of Chicago. What followed has resulted in a prolonged court battle between the Art Institute and the man who originally purchased the painting exhibited in Chicago, Daniel Searle on the one side, and the Goodmans and Korte on the other.[52] Finally, on August 13, 1998, the case was settled out of court, but not before Searle lost a motion for summary judgment. As part of the settlement, *Landscape with Smokestacks* would be donated to the Art Institute of Chicago by Searle and the Goodmans and the Institute would pay half of the value back to the family.[53]

What Korte knew and others would find out, was that while artwork is easier to claim, it is nevertheless a laborious task documenting the chain of custody of the particular piece. For this reason, Korte and Marc Masurovsky, another alumnus from our early research, working with the B'nai B'rith Klutznick National Jewish Museum in Washington, created the Holocaust Art Restitution Project (HARP) in September 1997.[54] HARP would scour the archives to develop databases on the disposition of looted art.

In less than a week of HARP's formation, the WJC would counter HARP's creation by naming Ronald Lauder, one of the heirs to the Lauder Cosmetics empire, to head its new looted art commission, the Commission for Art Recovery. Lauder, an art collector of some note, was, for the WJC, the perfect person to head the commission. A well-known Jewish philanthropist, Lauder was Chairman of the Modern Museum of Art and a former U.S. Ambassador to Austria, during the 1980s. Soon, Lauder's time in Austria would come back to haunt him.

By the end of the year, Lauder's Commission, HARP, along with the rest of the artworld as well as all those pursuing looted assets of any type would receive a lesson as to how complicated and political the return of looted art could actually get. Never could the Austrian Expressionist Egon Schiele (1890–1918) have ever guessed that two of his paintings would end up at the center of a transatlantic battle.

It all started out very innocently with the announcement of the opening of the exhibit, "Egon Schiele: The Leopold Collection," at Lauder's Museum of Modern Art (MoMA), running from the beginning of December 1997 through January 4, 1998. The Leopold Collection belongs to Dr. Rudolf Leopold, an Austrian opthalmologist and art collector and owner of some 5,400 works of art.[55]

The normal buzz in the artworld concerning a new exhibit was increased by several decibles when Judith Dobrzynski's *New York Times* article appeared on December 24, 1997 about Dr. Leopold and the exhibit disclosing the claims of the Reigers and the Bondis to two separate paintings in the Leopold exhibition.[56]

A week later, Henry S. Bondi, a nephew of the late Lea Bondi wrote to Glenn Lowry, Director of the MoMA explaining his family's claim to *Portrait of Wally*, which was part of the exhibit:

> The Painting was taken from Lea Bondi's collection — it was hanging in her apartment, where I saw it often as a boy—without her consent by Nazi agents or collaborators. Lea Bondi died at the age of 93 in London, in 1969, having three years earlier attempted to regain this painting. At no time had she or the Bondi family ever consented to any sale or transfer of the Painting. Accordingly, the heirs of Lea Bondi are the true and lawful owners of the Painting.[57]

Kathleen and Rita Reif also wrote seeking the return of a painting, when they wrote to Lowry five days later concerning their claim to *Dead City III*:

> Accordingly, we call upon the Museum to live up fully to its moral responsiblity, as well as its legal commitments, as a leading curator and guardian of works of art by addressing the issue raised by this case. In particular, we call upon the Museum to reach agreement with the Leopold Foundation voluntarily to leave the paintings in New York—with the Museum or with an independent, third-party fiduciary acceptable to all parties that have an ongoing interest in the painting— pending the resolution of this dispute.[58]

The MoMA came under seige. The families had written to them imploring them to do what was right and to withhold the paintings from the planned shipment out of New York on January 4, 1998 to Barcelona, the next stop for the exhibition. The press had picked up on the story, rightly sympathetic to the plight of two families desperately attempting to get back what was theirs. Yet, MoMA held its ground. In a letter to the Bondis, Stephen W. Clark, MoMA's Assistant General Counsel declared "the Museum is clearly not in a position to pass on the factual or legal foundation of your claim…[T]he Museum is under a contractual obligation to return the painting to the lender."[59] The paintings were to be packed up and sent to Spain by January 8.

For the MoMA, this was a painful and embarassing situation. The museum, one of the most prominent in the world, certainly did not need publicity like this, nor did it feel that it deserved it. Located in New York, center to a great art culture and a population already sensitized to the disclosures about the Swiss banks, the MoMA was particularly vulnerable to the bad publicity it received as a result of this scandal which grew worse by the day.

Yet, beyond all of these vulnerabilities, the MoMA's worst one was the fact that Ron Lauder was its Chairman. This was for no other reason than the fact that it was Lauder who helped create and fund the WJC's the Commission for Art Recovery, whose very mission was to work to retrieve looted art. Moreover, Lauder was a collector of works by Schiele and while in Austria in his role as U.S. Ambassador there, encountered a sticky problem that had now come full circle.

Lauder, a collector of some renown, began that collection with his bar mitzvah money to buy a self-portrait by Schiele.[60] He went on to build an impressive collection supplemented by many Austrian artists. While in Austria as Ambassador, Lauder as disclosed by the Austrian magazine *Profil*, was permitted by the Austrian Federal Monument Office to export 120 pieces of "rare art treasures," including works by Schiele, worth at least $3,000,000 over his 18-month term as Ambassador. United Press International, quoting the *Profil* article as having said in the article that he had met with "officials at the highest level" and exporting the art "will be no problem because (an official) will arrange it for me."[61]

Reuters reported that Austrian authorities approved Lauder's purchase of another Schiele painting in 1986, *Winter Trees*, for $2,000,000 without notifying Austrian museums of the sale.[62] Both the Reuters and UPI articles went to great lengths to explain that Lauder's actions, while not necessarily illegal under Austrian law, nevertheless "raised ethical questions."[63]

There were those in the press that took Lauder's history with Austria and the Schieles to its logical conclusion. They surmised Lauder feared his own paintings at one time might have been looted. Others suggested that he had simply passed off the problem to his staff at the museum and the Commission.[64] Either way, Lauder's silence on the matter was deafening.

While angry that January 8 was approaching and their chances to gain some hold on the paintings was diminishing as the hours passed, the Bondis and the Reifs got one of those breaks so rare in life, that saved their cause at the very moment they thought they would lose.

On January 7, Manhattan District Attorney Robert Morgenthau, son of former Treasury Secretary Morgenthau, issued a subpoena for both paintings, asking the MoMA to appear before a grand jury in Manhattan on the following day. Morgenthau's motivation was twofold. First, he wanted to get involved because of all the work his father did. He felt a kinship, that he could finally make a contribution.

Secondly, and of equal importance was the fact that the MoMA had consistently proclaimed to the Bondis and Reifs that they were legally obligated to return all the paintings of the exhibition. This would have been true had they properly filed a registration of the entire exhibition with the United States Information Agency as required for all foreign art exhibits to insure immunity from seizure.[65] Citing this lack of immunity, Morgenthau began his criminal investigation of the ownership of the two paintings.

While the Leopold Foundation had proposed earlier that day to submit the paintings to international arbitration, Klaus Schröder, a member of the board of the Leopold Museum, reacted scornfully by issuing a harsh statement condemning the Bondis and Reifs.

> What is unprecedented, insulting and illegal about the current situation is that the families involved have resorted to a war-like mentality in a peaceable era that warrants, and rewards due process. Rather than pursue the legal system relied upon facts, the Reif and Bondi families waited until the very end of the 3 month exhibition to, in effect, take the paintings hostage by attempting to invoke the criminal process. Thay have unnecessarily forced a situation that breaks the legal contracts that guarantee the return of the paintings between MOMA and the Foundation, cripple MOMA's ability to fulfill its obligations to its benevolent lenders, and perhaps damage the legitimacy of the criminal process.[66]

In its defense, MoMA told Acting New York Supreme Court Justice Laura Drager on the day of the hearing that even under New York law, they were obliged to return the painting. Lawyers for the museum, cited the Exemption from Seizure Law to quash Morgenthau's subpoena, saying that in the thirty years since the law's passage, not one painting had been seized.

While fighting the subpoena in the courts, the MoMA felt it had to do something to counter the rising tide of resentment against the museum and bad press resulting from the case. For publicity control, the museum turned to Kekst & Company, which had already been handling the publicity for the Swiss banks for close to two years. Kekst, though, was in the view of one Jewish leader, no longer held in such great esteem. "If Kekst does for MoMA what they've done for the Swiss banks," said the unidentified leader, "I feel sorry for MoMA."[67]

Kekst might have represented the MoMA and the Swiss banks, but he could not help other museums as well. This would become necessary when it was revealed a week later by the Leopold Foundation that the Klipstein and Kornfeld Gallery in Bern that sold the Foundation the Schieles were part of a group of sixteen sold to museums and private collections throughout the United States. Museums in Oberlin, Ohio; Santa Barbara, California; and the Art Institute in Chicago, were each said to have at least one Schiele's, if not more, in their possession.

Questioning the Origin

The revelations by the Leopold Foundation, along with the general shock of Morganthau's subpoena reverberations throughout the art world. While the Foundation was trying to defend against the accusations directed at it, allegations of other looted works of art exaccerbated the issue causing other museums to refrain from lending paintings from their stocks fearing similar repurcussions.

As the provenance of paintings all over the world became clouded, the question was not helped by a German court ruling on April 17, 1998 revoking the ownership rights of one of the Schiele paintings, *Dead City*, from the Reifs who claimed it. The decision only further complicated the concept of who legally owns a painting and at what point do they own it with clear title.

Three days earlier, Justice Laura Drager ruled in favor of the MoMA in the case of the two paintings, saying New York State's law on immunity from seizure covered this case. With Morgenthau's immediate appeal of the case, the paintings remained in New York pending a decision on their fate.

Yet, the furor caused by the subpoena caused others to not only question the provenance of individual paintings owned by others, but entire nations came to realize that their national collections could well have been built on Nazi seized paintings. Just as France before this found itself in the situation to have been in possession of several thousand paintings, so too did Austria.

The self-proclaimed "first victim of the Nazis," was greatly embarassed by the Schiele controversy and tried to end further questions about looted art in Austria. On March 6, Austrian Minister of Culture Elisabeth Gehrer announced plans to address the issue by forming a commission of Austrian Art Museum directors to examine holdings in the country's museums for their provenance. Having made the preliminary plans a few weeks before, Gehrer declared "I will make every effort in the interest of Austria's reputation as a country with distinguished scientists and researchers to reach an optimal and objective processing of the materials."[68] Although the Commission contained all Austrian experts and no foreign ones, about which D'Amato had inquired of Gehrer, not to mention its mere inclusion of museum directors, it would provide "moral not legal" decisions for Austria on the sixtieth anniversary of the Anschluss.[69] Admirable work, yet Austria has much to examine and with the world watching they will have to pay close attention to the details.

Austria was not alone. Europe, while a rich target for the search for looted artwork, pales in comparison with what researchers could find in the United States. Soon, U.S. museums, including the National Gallery of Art in Washington, the Cleveland Museum of Art, and others throughout the country began to receive inquiries about their collections.[70] Now, stories of looted art would join the lurid stories of Nazi gold and Swiss banks in the headlines across the U.S.

As with the nations that faced questions after all of the revelations about the Swiss, the question immediately came to mind, would the other museums react like the MoMA or would they be more forthcoming? To this question, Robert Bergman, Director of the Cleveland Museum of Art which had three drawings found to have been looted by the Nazis, answered Ted Koppel's question on *Nightline* by saying, "The fair, honorable thing to do with regard to the legitimacy of these claims will be done by our museums."[71]

To do the "honorable thing," Bergman, along with Philippe de Montebello, Director of New York's Metropolitan Museum of Art, Glenn Lowry of the MoMA, and seven other prominent museum directors from around the United States formed the Association of Art Museum Directors' Taskforce to set up guidlines on dealing with Nazi looted artwork. Declaring to research each claim for a looted painting "most seriously," the task force's creation came only a week before Rep. Jim Leach's third hearing in the House of Representatives on looted artwork that took place on February 13, 1998.[72]

For Montebello, the task force's creation, however worthy, was nevertheless an action taken in defense of accusations placed against the museums which he described as "secondary victims rather than part of the problem."[73] Despite Montebello's interpretation of the responsibility of the museums, the jury remains out on how they will react to further claims like those of the Reifs and Bondis. Yet, as District Attorney Morgenthau said in his statement appealing the decision of Justice Drager on the subpoena for the two Schiele paintings, doubt remains as to the museum directors' degree of ultruism. "I am pleased to learn," said Morgenthau, "that 53 years after the end of World War II museum directors have established a task force to address the questions of looted art. Would they have done so if it had not been for our investigation?"[74]

"He demands that his insurance claim be paid"

In one of the most important historical works on the Holocaust, *The Destruction of the European Jews*, Raul Hilberg wrote "[a]n interesting problem, concerning which we have no documentation was the matter of private life insurance."[75] Because of the disclosures about the Swiss banks, Hilberg's lack of documentation is no longer a problem.

"For over fifty years, Jacques has pressed his insurance claim and tried to obtain satisfaction from La Baloise," wrote Kenneth Merlo of his father-in-law Jacques Neuville. "To date the insurance company has 'politely' refused to make payment. Long before the newspapers reported the outrageous behavior of Swiss banks and most recently insurance companies, my father-in-law has tried to obtain a just and fair resolution to this travesty."[76] Many, like Jacques Neuville wrote us seeking relief from their fifty-year fight with European insurance companies seeking payment on policies for their family members murdered by the Nazis. Like the banks, the insurance companies in Europe refused payment to those they insured for frivolous, impossible reasons. For the banks it was the requirement of a birth certificate. For the insurers it was the excuse that the insured missed payments. Fallacious as this excuse was for the banks, it was equally bad for the insurers. There were other reasons as well, but the insurance companies like the banks were complicit with the Nazis as well in that they cooperated with them in turning over policies for the insured.

In January 1997, Bern Radio reported these findings in an interview with Jakob Tanner, a member of the Bergier Commission.[77] We had confirmed this much as well in a document we found in which Helmuth S. Bloch, in declaring his overseas assets in 1943, stated the cash value of $3,087.94 for his two life insurance policies with the Basler Lebensversicherungsgesellschaft in Basel, were surrendered by the company to the Nazis.[78]

The insurance companies first came under the microscope when Assicurazioni Generali of Italy signed an agreement to increase its control of the Israeli insurance company Migdal to 60 percent for $230,000,000 in July 1996. Generali which helped found Migdal in the 1930s and already owned 27 percent of Migdal, was founded by Italian Jews in 1831.[79] Since Generali's founding, the company's agents sold insurance policies in the small towns and shtetls spread across Eastern Europe.

Soon after the announcement of the Generali's purchase, Yad Vashem, Israel's preeminent Holocaust institute and memorial, began to seek information about tens of thousands of files the company, the institute said, held on beneficiaries from the Holocaust. Pressure grew and with Generali's initial denial of the existence of such files, retracted several months later, the Knesset began to examine the issue. With Generali buying an Israeli company, MKs Michael Kleiner and Avraham Hirschson began to question whether Generali would be purchasing Migdal with the assets of Holocaust victims assets never paid out due to their death at the hand of the Nazis.

Soon Generali's denial faded, but Kleiner and Hirschson's interest only increased and they sought to delay the purchase until repayment was made to the growing number of claimants reaching the two. While the purchase of the controlling stake in Midgal later went forward, Generali's troubles were far from over. Generali argued their hands were tied because most of their Eastern European assets along with their offices from which they sold the policies to the eventual victims of the Nazis, fell victim to the post-World War II confiscations by the Communists. This argument, though, failed to persuade those looking for the truth. Now, others began to look into not only Generali, but other insurers as well.

For those using Generali as a first case, others soon came under fire. As with the banks, it did not take long for someone to make a move. In March 1997 in the Southern District of New York, when Ed Fagan struck first when he filed suit on behalf of nine claimants against eight European insurance companies seeking $1,000,000,000 each.[80]

To the charges levied at them, the insurers treaded lightly. Mindful of the harsh and destructive reactions of the Swiss banks, the insurers responded that they would examine all claims against them and try to establish the truth.[81] For those in the Jewish community, in Europe, they too urged caution. Simon Wiesenthal, the legendary Nazi hunter, from Vienna echoed these sentiments when he cautioned the insurance companies to "avoid a loss of brand image which was the case in Switzerland due to the initial attitude of the banks."[82]

When Herbert Hansmeyer, Allianz CEO visited Washington, I met with him in January 1998, almost a year after Fagan's lawsuit was filed, and he was explicit in stating Allianz' commitment to finding the truth. "We are not the Swiss banks," he told me. "We will do what is right."[83] Hansmeyer reiterated the company's preference to settle this case quietly and amicably. Allianz he said, had already searched its archives for answers to the disposition of the policies and found little. Despite that, Allianz, he said, was ready to tackle the issue in a forthright manner.

Like Allianz, Generali also felt compelled to deal rationally with the charges against them. On June 16, in a letter to Rabbi Avraham Ravitz, MKs Michael Kleiner and Avraham Hirschson in Israel, Generali went further than any other company thus far and announced the creation of a $12,000,000 fund in the memory of "the assured of Generali in Central and East European countries who have perished in the Holocaust."[84] Three weeks later, Generali formally admitted to the existence of the warehouse in Trieste and pronounced the files open for inspection.

Within another three weeks, Generali took out full-page ads in newspapers around the world announcing the creation of policy information centers in New York and London and a toll-free number for claimants seeking information on their policies.[85] Soon, Allianz did the same, setting up a twenty-four-hour hotline and claims centers in the U.S., Europe and Israel for claimants as well.

By the beginning of August, it appeared that the European insurers were well on their way to a full-fledged investigation on par with the banks. On August 11, D'Amato helped them along when he wrote to New York State Governor George Pataki seeking an investigation by the State Superintendent of Insurance of the foreign insurance companies operating in New York. "We have reason to believe," wrote D'Amato, "that some of the largest European insurance companies may have withheld payment of insurance claims, assisted in the looting of policies and in some cases may have actually paid policy proceeds to the Nazis."[86] In Pataki's response two days later, the Governor informed D'Amato "I am directing New York Superintendent of Insurance Neil D.Levin, to identify those insurance companies which wrote business throughout Europe from 1933 to 1945 and to meet with their chief executive officers by the beginning of September." Pataki also informed D'Amato that Levin would communicate his sense of urgency in the matter and would ask each company to set up a claims process.[87] Within a week, Levin would leave for Europe to take up the matter with the insurers.

Now the process of investigation of the insurance companies began. While the Swiss banks were an easier problem to investigate, they were more elusive because of a limited, although important exposure in the United States. The insurers, however, could provide more complicated excuses for not paying the policy proceeds, but their exposure in the United States was massive which made them, regardless of the process, much more vulnerable than the banks. While Generali has two subsidiaries in the U.S., Allianz has thirty-one, Winterthur, a Swiss insurer owned coincidently by Credit Suisse has twenty-seven, and Zurich Life has thirty-three.[88]

Sensing a growing problem not unlike the banks, German Jewish leader Ignatz Bubis on August 20, publicly urged the German insurance companies to set up a compensation fund, like the Swiss banks and Generali did.[89] Allianz's response was a wait-and-see approach to reparations, yet when it came to the lawsuit, on the same day as Bubis's call for compensation, Allianz's lawyers filed a motion with Judge Mukasey to have the suit dismissed. The Judge asked Allianz to coordinate its motion with that of the others and to file them in November. Fagan's response to the motion was simple: file an amended complaint with twenty additional plaintiffs suing not only the original insurers, but additional ones as well in Prague and Bulgaria.[90]

By the beginning of September, the National Association of Insurance Commissioners (NAIC), formulated plans to join Levin's investigation with one of their own and as its chair would be Washington State Insurance Commissioner Deborah Senn, appointed at the NAIC Fall National Meeting on September 22. Meeting at the Sheraton Hotel in Washington, D.C, the NAIC Working Group heard testimony from five of Fagan's claimants as well as Richard Williamson, an attorney representing Allianz.

Senn seemed intensely interested about the issue and questioned me afterward about the methods we used to investigate the Swiss banks. She expressed a willingness to jump into the matter and provide a solution. She wasted no time calling hearings or more realistically, forums all over the U.S. After the initial meeting in Washington claimants gave testimony in Chicago on November 10; Miami Beach on November 20; Los Angeles on November 25; Seattle on December 8; Los Angeles again on January 13, 1998 at the Simon Wiesenthal Center; in Philadelphia on February 6; and in New York on February 16.

As the insurance inquiries grew, they seemed, like the banks and artwork cases to draw more and more participants as interest and publicity grew. It seemed to be the nature of the issue in general. With the Swiss banks, D'Amato had the issue fairly well to himself, with the exception of a few hearings by Rep. Leach. On the insurance issue, however, the U.S. Congress was largely silent. This was by no means due to a lack of interest, but largely due to jurisdiction. Life insurance in the U.S. is solely a state-regulated matter with no federal role. This however, provided no obstacle to Rep. Mark Foley of Florida, who offered a sanctions bill in January 1998 to punish the insurers in the U.S. if they failed to cooperate with the NAIC and any others investigating them. Soon he was joined by Rep. Eliot Engel of New York, and Senators Arlen Specter of Pennsylvania and Robert Torricelli of New Jersey with proposals of their own.

Fagan, who increased the pressure on the insurers and really brought the issue to light, was overshadowed by events and the addition of other players in the case. As such, Fagan began to reinsert himself into the fray by offering his expertise and plaintiffs to Neil Levin who honestly did not need him. Fagan wanted to bring his entire entourage in with him whenever he met with anyone, tried to do the same with Levin who refused. Each time rebuffed, Fagan would fax a letter to me for the Senator complaining that he was not getting the proper attention in the matter and sought our help in obtaining a correction to this treatment.

Soon Fagan would also have to deal with another lawsuit. On February 5, Los Angeles insurance attorney William M. Shernoff filed the first of five suits in California courts, this time on behalf of the Sterns, the family of five Holocaust victims sued Generali for $135,000,000.[91] Now, Fagan was not the only one suing the insurance companies. This, along with the expanding role of the NAIC in the matter could only decrease Fagan's influence in the matter.

On February 12, Rep. Leach held a hearing to examine the insurance and art issues. Fagan who Leach's staff had been working with for some time on the planning of the hearing, was left out in favor of Deborah Senn, California Insurance Commissioner Chuck Quackenbush, and the congressional proponents of legislation to punish the insurers, including D'Amato. While the other elected representatives had proposals that were already made known, D'Amato came to the hearing with a new one that grabbed the spotlight away from the others.

What D'Amato had in mind was an international commission for insurance companies to join, patterned after the Volcker Commission. Despite his earlier criticisms of that Commission, the principle was admirable and D'Amato sought to duplicate it to help the insurance claimants.

D'Amato suggested a commission funded by the insurance companies, that would be a fully independent operation, with historians, forensic auditors, lawyers and other experts in the field. The commission would ideally include representatives from the State Insurance Regulatory community in the U.S., the World Jewish Congress, and a Holocaust survivor as well. Moreover, he proposed that the state insurance regulators utilize their enforcement powers to conduct their own reviews and penalize any uncooperative companies. Finally, he proposed the creation of an interim fund for the survivors.

"For their sake, and for the sake of the survivors," declared D'Amato to the Committee, "I think that it would be in the interest of the companies to agree to this proposal. I am quite sure that the individual companies do not want to be in the same situation the Swiss banks have placed themselves in. I would think they care about their good name."[92]

Generali rushed to accept D'Amato's proposal and enthusiastically accepted the call to join the planned commission. The company went so far as to issue a press release saying as much in the morning before the hearing began. "Generali supports Senator Alfonse D'Amato's initiative suggesting the establishment of such a commission," said the company in its release, "and looks forward to working with the Senator and others on this issue."[93] Other insurers, however, were not so forthcoming.

In a reponse to a request by Deborah Senn to allow NAIC investigators to look at Winterthur records William Brodsky, an attorney for the company, was less then willing to cooperate. "Winterthur Life is located in, and incorporated under the laws of Switzerland and is regulated by the Swiss authorities," wrote Brodsky. "It does not conduct business in the United States, and therefore, it is our position that it is not subject to the jurisdiction of federal or state courts or administrative agencies in the United States."[94]

This letter was released at the NAIC hearing in New York on February 16. When Senn released it, D'Amato who testified again on the issue, called the letter "morally bankrupt." D'Amato took Brodsky to task for flatly refusing to allow access to Winterthur's records. D'Amato vowed to pursue the matter. Later, Winterthur officials denied any attempt to block access to information, citing Swiss neutrality and sovereignty as the reasons for barring the NAIC from their records.

Two weeks later, Basler Leben, another Swiss insurance company denied Senn access to their records for the same reasons. This despite a preliminary acceptance from Allianz for the NAIC to examine their records, only added to the total mistrust of the Swiss insurers by the NAIC. Coupled with the Swiss banks' tenuous position in the U.S. at the time, only added to Swiss troubles and brought Thomas Borer back to the scene to calm the mood of U.S. public officials angry at another round of Swiss intransigence.

Generali which had been cooperative from the start, at first objected to NAIC requests to open its records to the U.S. regulators because of the objections of Italian regulators. But by March, Generali agreed to meet with NAIC officials, as did Winterthur, but not before quite a bit of negotiations between the NAIC and the Swiss.

While the two companies finally agreed to Senn's request to examine their records, it would not be Senn or her team that would do the inspections. Levin and Chuck Quackenbush of California, were growing increasingly irritated at Senn's overeagerness and never-ending press campaign on the issue. To them, she was only complicating the process to her own benefit and to the detriment of the others. They were becoming increasingly irritated at her desire to grab the press while referring the work to the other states, such as New York and California. Soon after the acceptance of Generali and Winterthur, Senn was pushed to the side by the NAIC in favor of Levin and Quackenbush to continue the investigation of the European insurers. Quackenbush would lead the team that would go overseas to examine the files. By the middle of March, he would travel to Italy to begin the inspection of Generali's files.

By April 8, Levin and Quackenbush had completely sidestepped Senn and signed a Memorandum of Intent (MOI) with the Chairmen of the Zurich Group, Allianz, Generali, the Equitable Group to form the International Commission D'Amato had proposed at Rep. Leach's hearing back in February. In the MOI, the insurers agreed to formulate a claims process, to seek an exemption from their countries' regulatory actions to allow the Commission access to their records, and an interim fund for Holocaust victims.[95] Participating in these negotiations, along with Levin and Quackenbush, was Israel Singer. This added a greater air of legitimacy to the negotiations for the insurers, who by now had seen the writing on the wall and understood they had to cooperate with Levin and Quackenbush.

To the signing of the MOI without her, Senn expressed anger and concern. According to press reports, Senn did not find out about the meeting to sign the MOI until the night before. She declared that Levin and Quackenbush were acting without authority and that the MOI was not binding on her or forty-seven other NAIC members.[96]

Senn, however angry she might have been, was outmaneuvered. Her actions had piqued her fellow Commissioners. On April 24, in a memo to all Commissioners, Directors, and Superintendents of Insurance, NAIC President Glenn Pomoroy and two other officers of the NAIC informed the membership that they were creating a new task force, the International Holocaust Commission Task Force. The task force would be chaired by Pomoroy himself with Levin as the Vice Chair.[97] Now, Senn was officially out of the picture and Levin, with Quackenbush who also sat on the task force, could pursue the International Commission without Senn's interference. Soon after the creation of the new task force, Senn issued yet another press release, this time to announce in a somewhat concilatory manner, that she would sign the MOI. Two weeks later, on May 7, Fagan, the last of the major parties yet to sign the MOI, announced that he would join the others and sign the MOI.[98]

To back up the creation of the International Commission, legislation was introduced in several states to enhance the powers of the Insurance Commissioners to deal with and punish, if necessary, the insurance companies for noncompliance, just as D'Amato had proposed in February. In April, the California Assembly passed legislation to empower Quackenbush to this end; in May, the Florida Legislature received legislation to do the same; and a few days later the New York State State Senate saw legislation that was signed into law in July by Governor Pataki.

On August 13, one day after the historic agreement to settle the lawsuits against the Swiss banks, Zurich Life became the first company to go further than the MOI and signed a Memorandum of Understanding, committing the company to abide by its April 8 commitment to the principle.[99]

Another Settlement, or so We Thought

Only a week after brokering the historic settlement with the Swiss banks, D'Amato called the Guido Pastori, Vice President of Generali, to his office where, along with Fagan, Swift, and Neil Levin, he brokered a second deal. After hours of sometimes testy negotiation, not without a course of screaming added to the mix, Generali agreed to sign the MOU in order to come into line with the claims process provisions, and agreed to provide $100,000,000 toward claims evolving out of Fagan's class action lawsuit against them. In return, Fagan would drop the suit and the claims process, once certified by Judge Mukasey, would begin. Fagan later denied this pledge to me and promised to press ahead with his lawsuit, despite fighting for a reported 20 percent fee out of the settlement of the Generali case.[100]

Now with Generali on board, the way was clear to align other companies. Once the Swiss banks settled, it was easy for the insurance companies to follow. Following Generali's compitulation, within a week, Allianz, AXA, Basler Leben, and Winterthur signed the MOU.[101]

Yet, all was not well with the Generali deal. Because of Fagan's insistence on "seeking justice for the survivors," Generali's pact with D'Amato and the NAIC would not hold. "I'm sure you will understand," Fagan wrote D'Amato, "you will understand that we must and will do everything in our power to protect survivors against this International Commission which no one can believe is truly what you wanted or how you wanted it set up."[102] Fagan steadfastly denied any role, or that of his partners, in breaking up the Generali deal, but it was unavoidable. On September 20, saying the offer was dead, Generali retracted its offer of $100,000,000.

While he denied any meddling, Fagan felt determined to obtain a higher settlement from Generali. He accused Levin and the NAIC of interferring in the process and begged D'Amato on several occasions to intervene to "save the day."[103] With money no longer on the table, Generali remained committed to the International Commission, albeit in a manner tarnished by its retraction.

With the exception of the Generali case it appreared that all the pieces were falling into line. By this time, there were even rumors that there would be even more settlements by the insurers. The insurers, like the Swiss banks before them, wanted this all behind them. They had learned from the Swiss bankers that the longer went their struggle, the more painful the settlement, morally, materially, and most importantly for them, financially. Indeed, the Swiss had tought the world one thing, quit while you still have some measure of self-respect.

Notes

1. Letter of Emerson Bigelow, OSS, to Harold Glasser, Director of Monetary Research, 21 October 1946, RG 226, Records of the OSS, Entry 183, Box 29, NARA.
2. "Swiss fear forced sterilizations continuing," *Toronto Star*, 29 August 1997, p. 15.
3. Dan Balz, "Sweden Sterilized Thousands of 'Useless' Citizens for Decades," *Washington Post*, 29 August 1997, p. A. 1. See also, "Trauma of involuntary sterilization recalled," *Globe and Mail*, 28 August 1997; and Roger Boyes, "Austria sterilizes mentally handicapped women," *London Times*, 28 August 1997.
4. Stuart Ain, "As if it Were Yesterday, Recent Swiss-Nazi revelations awaken repressed memories and send survivors to special counseling group," *Jewish Week*, 17 April 1998, p. 1; Beth Gardiner, "With Holocaust in the headlines, survivors confront past," Associated Press, 22 April 1998.
5. Avi Becker, "Unmasking National Myths: European Challenge Their History," Institute of the World Jewish Congress, 1997.
6. Oliver August, "Nazi gold controversy comes home to roost," *Times of London*, 10 June 1997.
7. "Jewish community leader calls on German banks to reveal Nazi deals," Deutsche Press-Agentur, 4 August 1997.
8. Andrew Gray, "Jewish leader German banks must probe Nazi past," Reuters, 7 August 1997.
9. Letter of Prof. Dr. Julius H. Schoeps, Director of the Moses Mendelssohn Zentrum, Europäisch-Jüdische Studien, Universität Potsdam, to Senator Alfonse M. D'Amato, 7 August 1997.
10. Fiona Fleck, "Germany Lost Gold Files," Reuters, 22 July 1998. In London, in December 1997, German Historian Hersh Fischler had told me some of Thoms'

papers, in English, did survive and were held by his family and that he had seen some of them.

11. Peter Bild, "Bundesbank inquiry into missing files on Nazi gold," *Daily Telegraph*, 13 March 1997; Telephone Conversation with Peter Bild, 25 April 1997; Letter of Peter Bild to Gregg Rickman, 6 May 1997; Discussion with Peter Bild in London, 3 December 1997. In July 1998, The German Federal Archives issued a report, with a contribution by the Bundesbank, stating that the files were, as a matter of routine, destroyed perhaps as late as 1976. According to Fischler, the post-war German Economics Ministry knew about the files and purposely kept them from view, fearing requests for reparation. See Fiona Feck, "Bonn Kept Nazi gold files from Allies-researcher," Reuters, 23 July 1998.

12. "Conditions in Occupied Territories, The Penetration of German Capital into Europe," The Inter-Allied Information Committee, 1942, RG 260, OMGUS, Finance, Box 41, NARA; "German Banking Penetration in Northern and Western Europe," Ministry of Economic Warfare (Britain), 7 May 1943, RG 260, OMGUS, Finance, Box 41, NARA; "German and Italian Banking Penetration in East and South-East Europe, Ministry of Economic Warfare (Britain), 10 September 1942, RG 260, OMGUS, Finance, Box 41, NARA; "German Banking Penetration in Continental Europe, The Board of Governors of the Federal Reserve, September 1944.

13. Harold Watman, Ruth Abraham, and Michal Schoenberger v. Deutsche Bank and Dresdner Bank, United States District Court for the Southern District of New York, 3 June 1998. In July 1998, Fagan threatened to expand the suit to include a unit of the Bank of Austria, Creditanstalt Bankverein, for its role as a participant in the gold operations of Nazi Germany.

14. Avraham Barakai, Gerald Feldman, Lothar Gall, Jonathan Steinberg, and Harold James, "The Deutsche Bank and Its Gold Transactions during The Second World War," Historical Commission Appointed to Examine the History of Deutsche Bank in the Period of National Socialism, Munich, 31 July 1998.

15. Sven Fredrick Hedin and Göran Elgemyr, "Stolen goods in the Central Bank: Sweden swapped iron for looted gold," 21 January 1997.

16. "Swiss say Sweden received Nazi gold," Reuters, 31 January 1997.

17. Fred Barbash, "Swedes Reassess How Neutrality Assisted Nazis," *Washington Post*, 10 February 1997, p. A13.

18. Conversation with Mike Kinsella, Chief of Staff to United States Senator Alfonse M. D'Amato, 2 March 1997.

19. Letter of United States Senator Alfonse M. D'Amato to President Arnold Koller, 10 January 1997.

20. French Customs Logs, January 21, 1942–May 5, 1944, RG 43, Records of International Conferences, Lot File No. M-88, Council of Foreign Ministers, Conference on German External Assets, Looted Gold, January 1953, Box 203, NARA.

21. "Spanish Connection," *Washington Times*, 27 February 1997.

22. Conversation of Spanish Ambassador to the United States with United States Senator Alfonse M. D'Amato, Washington, D.C. 13 March 1997.

23. Letter of Spanish Ambassador to the United States Antonio Oyarzabal to United States Senator Alfonse M. D'Amato, 3 April 1997, original in Spanish, translation furnished by the Spanish Embassy.

24. Marlise Simons, "Nazi Gold and Portugal's Murky Role," *New York Times*, 10 January 1997.

25. Letter of Portuguese Ambassador to the United States Fernando Andresen Guimarães to United States Senator Alfonse M. D'Amato, 27 February 1997.

26. Marcus Kabel, "Swiss say Portugal was second-biggest Nazi gold buyer," Reuters, 20 March 1997.
27. Margaret Clarke, *The Safehaven Project.*
28. Executive Order, No. 390, creating the Commission on Clarification of Nazi Activities in the Argentine Republic, Carlos Saúl Menem, Letter of the Argentine Ambassador to the United States, Raúl Granillo Ocampo to United States Senator Alfonse M. D'Amato, 21 May 1997.
29. Rabbi Henry I. Sobel, "Looted Nazi Gold," For the conference *The Holocaust, Moral and Legal Issues Unresolved Fifty Years Later*, held at the Benjamin Cardozo School of Law in New York, 8 February 1998.
30. Any Carera, "Panel to investigate whether plundered Jewish wealth entered Brazil," Associated Press, 7 April 1997.
31. Letter of Rabbi Henry I. Sobel to Gregg Rickman, Office of Senator Alfonse M. D'Amato, 15 October 1997.
32. Diana Jean Schemo, "A Nazi's Trail Leads to a Gold Cache in Brazil," *New York Times*, 23 September 1997, p. 1, Section A.
33. Stan Lehman, "No apparent link between fortune left in Brazilian banks and Nazis," Associated Press, 7 January 1998.
34. Address by Alain Juppé Before the Representative Council of Jewish Institutions in France, Paris, 25 January 1997, p. 6.
35. "Museums holding 1955 works of art taken from Jews during the Occupation," *Le Monde*, 28 January 1997, translated by David Skelly. See *Présentation des œvres récupérées après la Seconde Gurerre mondiale et confiées à la garde des musées nationaux* for the comprehensive listing of all artworks presently held by French museums.
36. Letter of French Ambassador to the United States François Bujon de l'Estang to United States Senator Alfonse M. D'Amato, 30 April 1997.
37. Letter of French Ambassador to the United States François Bujon de l'Estang to United States Senator Alfonse M. D'Amato, 11 June 1997.
38. "France, Nazi Plunder Used," *Cleveland Plain Dealer*, 6 December 1997.
39. "Report: French banks still hold funds of deported Jews," Associated Press, 15 March 1997.
40. Fernande Bodner and Anna Zajdenberg v. Banque Paribas, Barclay's Bank, Credit Lyonnais, Societe Generale, Credit Commercial de France, Credit Agricole, Banque Française du Commerce Exterieur, and Banque Worms Capital Corporation, United States District Court, Eastern District of New York, Case No. CV 97-7433, Judge Edward Korman.
41. Telephone discussion with Bill Bowden, attorney for Societé Generale, 18 December 1997.
42. "French daily finds record of wartime Jewish assets," Reuters, 16 January 1998.
43. Interim Report of the Commission for the Study of the Spoilation of Jews in France (Matteoli Report), 31 December 1997.
44. Telephone discussion with Bill Bowden, Societé Generale, 11 June 1998; Discussion with C.S. Duncan, Director of International and Private Banking, Barclays, Washington, D.C., 19 June 1998.
45. "Jewish activists target France in Nazi gold scandal," Agence French-Presse, 22 December 1998.
46. See Http://www.enemyproperty.gov.uk/
47. "Looted Nazi Art Stays in Russia, Court Says," *New York Times*, 7 April 1998, p. 10, Sec. A.
48. Directive of the Reichsmarschall of the Greater German Reich, Hermann Göring, 1 May 1941, RG 200, Abraham Duker/Irving Dwork Papers, OSS Research and Analysis-Jewish Desk, NARA.

49. Lynn H. Nicholas, *The Rape of Europa: The Fate of Europe's Treasures in the Third Reich and the Second World War* (New York: Vintage Books, 1994).

50. Ibid, p. 10; Directive of Reichsleiter Martin Bormann to Reichsleiter Alfred Rosenberg, 21 April 1943, RG 200, Abraham Duker/Irving Dwork Papers, OSS Research and Analysis-Jewish Desk, NARA. As a matter of historical closure, Bormann's remains were positively identified through DNA analysis performed by Munich pathologist Prof. Dr. W. Eisenmenger. See Roger Boyes, "DNA tests on skull end long hunt for Bormann," *London Times*, 4 May 1998 and Letter of Hildegard Becker-Toussaint, Spokewoman, State Prosecutor, Frankurt, Germany to United States Senator Alfonse M. D'Amato, 28 April 1998.

51. Transcript, "Profile: The Search; 50-year family search for stolen painting by Nazis during World War II finally found in United States at the Art Institute in Chicago," *60 Minutes*, CBS News, 19 January 1997. The present-day Goodmans spell their family name differently from that of their father Friedrich Gutman.

52. Typical to Korte's cases, which has prevented many cases from going forward, has been the cost of research and litigation. In the Goodman's case, a public campaign has begun to try to raise funds for them to continue. See the advertisement seeking funds for the Goodman Legal Fund in the *Forward*, 27 February 1998.

53. Discussion with Willi Korte, 13 August 1998; Judith Dobrzynski, "Settlement in Dispute Over a Painting Looted by Nazis," *New York Times*, 14 August 1998.

54. HARP, like so many others involved in this investigation developed a webpage on the Internet. Its address: www.lostart.org/

55. See Judith Dobrzynski, "A Singular Passion for Amassing Art, One Way or Another," *New York Times*, 24 December 1997, p. 1, Sec. B.

56. Ibid.

57. Letter of Henry S. Bondi to Glenn D. Lowry, Director, Museum of Modern Art, 30 December 1997.

58. Letter of Kathleen and Rita Reif to Glenn D. Lowry, Director, Museum of Modern Art, 4 January 1998.

59. Letter of Stephen W. Clark, Assistant General Counsel, Museum of Modern Art to Henry Bondi, 3 January 1998.

60. Laura Jereski and Laura Bird, "Beauty Secrets: Ronald Lauder's Debts and Estee's Old Age Force a Firm Makeover, Cosmetics Giant Sells Stake After Younger Son Sinks Millions Into Art, Deals," *Wall Street Journal*, 9 November 1995.

61. John Holland, "Lauder accused of breaking Austrian export laws," United Press International, 17 January 1988.

62. "Austria to Tighten Art Export Law After Ambassador's Purchases," Reuters, 17 January 1988.

63. Holland, "Lauder accused of breaking Austrian export laws."

64. "Lauder in a Bind That Would Tax Painter's Powers," *Forward*, 9 January 1998.

65. Confirmation of the Museum's failure to register the Schiele exhibition with the USIA, was made to the author by U.S. Customs officials in New York in a telephone discussion of 7 January 1998.

66. Leopold-Museum: Statement on the Claims for Paintings by Egon Schiele by Dr. Klaus Schröder, member of the board of the Leopold Museum, 8 January 1998.

67. Richard Johnson, "Museum puts spin on Nazi dispute," *New York Post*, 5 February 1998, p. 8.

68. Letter of Austrian Minister of Culture Elisabeth Gehrer to United States Senator Alfonse M. D'Amato, 17 March 1998, p.1, translation by the Austrian Embassy to the United States.

69. Jane Perlez, "Austria Is Set to Return Artworks That Nazis Plundered From Jews," *New York Times*, 8 March 1998, p. 27A.

70. See Mike Feinsilber, "Art with a tainted past ound its way into National Gallery," Associated Press, 17 November 1997; Murray White, Executive Director, The Ethics in Art Council, Testimony before the United States Senate Committee on Rules and Administration, 20 February 1998; and Steven Litt, "3rd Drawing Part of Nazi Hoard," *Cleveland Plain Dealer*," 14 April 1998.

71. Transcript from "Nazi Loot in American Museums, What Should be Brian Ross and Ted Koppel, *Nightline*, ABC News, 28 April 1998, p. 9.

72. Judith Dobrzynski, "Museums Call for System To Address Nazi Booty," *New York Times*, 5 February 1998; Press Release of the Association of Art Museum Directors, 4 June 1998. For testimony on the Taskforce's proposed creation, see "The Restitution of Art Objects Seized by the Nazis From Holocaust Victims and Insurance Claims of Certain Holocaust Victims and Their Heirs," Hearing before the Committee on Banking and Financial Services, U.S. House of Representatives, 105th Congress, 2nd Session, 12 February 1998, No. 105-46. For the guidelines, see the "Report of the AAMD Task Force on the Spoilation of Art during the Nazi/World War II Era (1933–1945), Association of Art Museum Directors, 4 June 1998.

73. Transcript of the Address of Philippe de Montebello, Director of the Metropolitan Museum of Art, before the National Press Club, "Art Plundered During the Holocaust," National Press Club, 14 July 1998.

74. Statement by Manhatten District Attorney Robert M. Morgenthau Regarding Court Decision on Subpoenaed Schiele Paintings, 13 May 1998.

75. Raul Hilberg, *The Destruction of the European Jews* (Chicago: Quadrangle Books, Revised and Updated Edition, 1985), p. 302.

76. Letter of Kenneth Merlo to United States Senator Alfonse M. D'Amato, 14 January 1998. On September 3, 1998, Dr. Bruno Dallo, wrote Ken Merlo to inform him that based on Senator D'Amato's request, initially for help in settling the dispute, which was accomplished for $18,000, he would in fact be receiving an additional $7,000, fulfilling D'Amato's second request.

77. "Historian Says Insurance Companies Gave Jewish Money to Nazis," *Bern Swiss Radio International* in English, 10 January 1997, FBIS-WEU-97-008 Daily Report.

78. Form TFR-500: Census of Property in Foreign Countries, Series B: Detailed Property Report of Helmuth S. Bloch of New York, RG 265, Foreign Funds Control, Entry TFR-500, Box 1192, NARA.

79. Galit Lipkis Beck, "Italy's Largest Insurer to buy Migdal," *Jerusalem Post*, 25 March 1996; "Generali ups stake in the Israeli market," *Life Insurance International*, 1 March 1997; Norma Cohen, "Generali Pressed on Holocaust files," *Financial Times*, 26 February 1997.

80. Marta Drucker Cornell, Erna Gans, Samuel Hersly, Igor Kling, Amalia Kranz Burstin, Tibor Vidal, Morris Weinman, Martha Saraffian and Rose Steg v. Assicurazioni Generali S.p.A.-Consolidated, Wiener Allianz Versicherungs Aktiengesellschaft AG aka Phenix Allegemeine Versicherungs Aktiengesellschaft, A.G.F., Assurances Generales De France Vie, Riunione Adriatica Di Sicurta S.p.A.-Consolidated, Allianz Group of Germany, Der Anker Allegemeine Versicherungs AG, Bavarian Reinsurance Company aka Bayerisiche Allegemeine Versicherungs Aktiengesellschaft, Civil Action No. 97Civ.2262, Judge Michael Mukasey, United States District Court, Southern District of New York.

81. See Charles Fleming and Leslie Scism, "Insurers Facing Holocaust Suit Tread Softly, Swiss Banks set Example of How Not to Handle Public Relations Woes," *Wall Street Journal Europe*, 2 April 1997.

82. "Austrian Jews urge 'acceptable solution' to insurance dispute," Agence France-Presse, 3 April 1997.
83. Discussion with Herbert Hansmeyer, North American CEO Allianz Insurance Company, Washington, D.C., 14 January 1998.
84. Letter of Assicurazioni Generali S.p.A. to Rabbi Avraham Ravitz, MKs Michael Kleiner and Avraham Hirschson, 16 June 1997.
85. "An Open Letter to the Families of Holocaust Victims," Generali Assicurazioni S.p.A., an advertisment appearing in the *New York Times*, 25 July 1997; Jenni Frazer, "Generali sets up UK hotline," *London Jewish Chronicle*, 15 August 1997.
86. Letter of United States Senator Alfonse M. D'Amato to Governor George E. Pataki, State of New York, 11 August 1997.
87. Letter of Governor George E. Pataki, State of New York to United States Senator Alfonse M. D'Amato, 13, August 1997.
88. Joseph M. Belth, Editor, *Insurance Forum*, "Special Holocaust Issue," Vol. 25, No. 9, September 1998, p. 83.
89. "German Jewish leader urges insurance fund for Holocaust victims," Agence France-Presse, 20 August 1997.
90. Amended Complaint, Civil Action No. 97 Civ. 2262, United States District Court, Southern District of New York.
91. Adolf Stern; Edith Stern Loewy; the Estate of Rudy Stern and his heirs-at-law Celia Stern, Martin Stern, Alan Stern and Rhona Stern Davis; the Estate of Bart Stern and his heirs-at-law Anne Stern, Johnathon [sic] Stern and Nina Stern Teitlebaum v. Assicurazioni Generali S.p.A., Case No. BC 185376, Superior Court for the State of California, County of Los Angeles, 5 February 1998.
92. "The Restitution of Art Objects Seized by the Nazis From Holocaust Victims and Insurance Claims of Certain Holocaust Victims and Their Heirs,"p. 48; David Cay Johnston, "New Panel is Planned to Press Insurance Firms on Holocaust," *New York Times*, 12 February 1998, p. A 5.
93. "Generali Will Cooperate with Commission Established to Examine Holocaust Insurance Issue," Press Release of Assicurazioni Generali, 12 February 1998.
94. Letter of William Brodsky to Deborah Senn, Washington State Insurance Commissioner, 13 February 1998.
95. Memorandum of Intent between Rolf Huppi, Chairman, Zurich Group; Herbert Hansmeyer of Allianz; Guido Pastori of Generali; and Wendy Cooper of the Equitable Life Insurance Co. and Superintendent of Insurance for the State of New York, Neil D. Levin; Insurance Commissioner of the State of California; Israel Singer representing the World Jewish Congress and the World Jewish Restitution Organization; and Saul Kagan, representing the Conference on Material Claims Against Germany. Signed in New York, 8 April 1998.
96. Stuart Ain, "Insurance Leader Balks at Claims Panel," *New York Jewish Week*, 17 April 1998, p. 31.
97. Memorandum Regarding Holocaust Memorandum of Intent," from Glenn Pomoroy, President of the NAIC, Goerge Reider, NAIC Vice President, and George Nichols III, NAIC Secretary-Treasurer, 24 April 1998.
98. David Cay Johnston, "Accord Signed to Name Tribunal on Holocaust Insurance Claims," *New York Times*, 7 May 1998.
99. Memorandum of Understanding between the Rolf Huppi, Chairman and CEO of the Zurich Group and United States Insurance Regulatory Authorities. Signed at New York, 13 August 1998.
100. "Attorney for survivors says he did not ask for 20% of settlement," *Haaretz*, 31 August 1998.

101. "Four More European Insurers Agreeto Resolve Outstanding Claims of Holocaust Victims," Press Release, New York State Insurance Department, 25 August 1998.
102. Letter of Edward Fagan to United States Senator Alfonse M. D'Amato, 16 October 1998.
103. Ibid.

Epilogue

"Germany and her associates murdered some six million Jews, destroyed all Jewish communal institutions wherever their authority extended, stole all the treasures of Jewish art and learning and seized all Jewish property, public and private, on which they could lay their hands," wrote Louis Lipsky of the American Jewish Conference to Secretary of State James F. Byrnes in 1945. "It has been estimated that the monetary value of the material losses thus inflicted upon the Jewish people may amount of over $8,000,000,000. The mass murders, the human suffering, the annihilations of spiritual, intellectual and creative forces are probably without parallel in the history of mankind."[1]

As the seminal event of the twentieth century, the Holocaust represented a moment when madness went unchecked and millions died. If they were Jews, Gypsies, Slavs, homosexuals, communists, or others, the Nazis determined they had no right to live. While herding them into sealed cattle cars, they took the opportunity to rob them as well.

Wherever German troops went, so did the art appraisers, the gold appraisers, and the common thieves. With the continent laid bare before them, they robbed and killed at will. For individual Nazis, as well as the formal state apparatus of which they were a part, occupied Europe was a playground, an opportunity to enrich themselves. If the people they were murdering were not entitled to life, why should they be entitled to their wealth.

This accumulated looted wealth needed an outlet, a place to make legal the spoils of war. Switzerland, unoccupied during the war had the ability and the willingness to the Nazis' bidding.

If we had learned anything over the past couple of years, it was that the Holocaust, as horrible as it was, came after the wholesale robbery of the Nazis' victims. Those prescient enough to have sensed the coming danger sought refuge for their assets in Swiss banks, at least to ensure their family's future. Most, could not have, and did not imagine they would be swept up by the Nazis and exterminated en masse. But when the war was over, those who had sought financial sanctuary in Switzerland were gone. With them went the secret account names and codes for which Switzerland was legendary. Their survivors, lucky to be alive, tried to obtain the accounts but were told they did not exist, or worse told that it did but that they had to produce the death certificate to claim it which was clearly impossible.

Destitute and homeless, they muddled through, survived and built a life after the war. As the years passed, so did memories of the far-off bank accounts their parents left them. Only after Edgar Bronfman began to ask questions about those far-off bank accounts did people begin to recall them. Memories opened up and so did historical archives. Both unleashed stories and facts, locked up for over half-a-century. Together, memories and archives created more than simple repositories for saddness and long-repressed memories, they formed a "Pandora's box." Once opened, it would be impossible to close. Fifty years ago the world did not care about the looted assets of Holocaust victims. Today, it does.

The Venality of Money

From the beginning, the question had always been asked, "Why did they do it?" Why did the bankers work so close with the Nazis and even after the war actively withhold the deposits of people they knew had to have died during the war. After the review of thousands of documents and the testimony of dozens of claimants, the answer is clear, the venality of money was the motivating factor, with a little self-preservation added into the mix. In reality, the bankers cared little about the source of the money or gold they accepted from the Jews and the Nazis alike. It is not a mistake that over the years the bankers have been fond of the saying "money has no religion."

The fact, however, that the Swiss bankers seemed to go out of their way to accomodate the Germans, adds an evil cynicism to their greed. "Although the great majority of the Swiss people are pro-Allied," summarized Colonel Frederick D. Sharp of U.S. Army Intelligence. "[T]here is an important minority consisting principally of bankers, industrialists, etc., who are pro-Axis," he concluded.[2] For the bankers, making money was a richly motivating factor. If they could help the Germans and make a buck at the same time, they surmised, what was the problem?

Emil Puhl, the Vice President of the German Reichsbank, who at the close of the war travelled to Switzerland to convince the Swiss government to end their brief freeze of German assets insisted upon by Lauchlin Currie, testified as to the fact that he had been "overrun by requests originating with the Swiss bankers," for help in getting the flow of

German money back into Switzerland.³ Regardless of the war's eventual outcome, the Swiss bankers wanted to continue doing business. The Nazis might have been running out of luck, but the Swiss bankers wished to keep theirs going.

When the war concluded, the Swiss had managed to wring all they could from the Nazis. They had also taken undetermined amounts of Jewish wealth, and when the dust cleared, they had survived. They did so by guile, circumstance, and cooperation with the Nazis. As such, while Europe lay in smoldering ruins, Switzerland was swollen with the spoils of war. As Harald Huber had written about the amount of Jewish assets in Swiss banks in 1959, "hundreds of millions [of francs] belonging to missing and presumed dead persons are still in the banks."⁴

We had always guessed, in a figurative sense and half-jokingly, that one day after the war, the Swiss bankers woke up and in unison poked their heads out their front doors, looked both ways, and saw no one coming to claim their accounts. They then decided to keep them for themselves. If anyone would come back later to make a claim, they would stall or simply lie and they would hopefully go away. After all, what could the little survivors do to harm the mighty Swiss banks?

In the interim, the bankers were right in their self-assurance. Fifty years later, the stalling would no longer work. During the course of the July 1998 hearing on the 1946 Washington Accords, this fact would become abundantly clear. At this hearing we featured an intricately complicated, yet fascinating story showing how the heirs of Johannes Rohony, a Holocaust victim, were deceived by the Swiss Government, not the Swiss bankers, who purposely kept them from receiving his assets. The Rohony's case was the most clearly documented case we had ever seen and would go a long way in proving Swiss deceit on this issue.

On September 5, 1938, Johannes Rohony, of Budapest, opened a safety deposit box, No. 137, at Schweizerische Hypothekenbank or HypoSwiss Bank in Zurich, listing his wife Anna Rohony on the box with him. In January 1945, Johannes died at Ohrdruf concentration camp in Germany. Three years later in November 1948, HypoSwiss Bank attempted to notify Mr. Rohony, at an address in Amsterdam, that they have not heard from him since he opened the account ten years earlier. The bank notified him that he would be charged 100 sfr. for this long period of inactivity. Of course no answer was possible or forthcoming. One month later, HypoSwiss again tried to notify him that this fee must be paid or the box would be cancelled.

Following the 1962 Disclosure Decreee, in December 1963, Hypo-Swiss Bank forcibly opened Mr. Rohony's box. In the box, bank officials found six pass books, from different Swiss banks, worth 13,600 francs, 300 sfr., and 150 French francs, as well as two safety deposit box keys. Five of the six pass books were registered in the name of Joseph Rotter, one in the name of Victor Müller. Included as well in the box, were Powers of Attorney from Rotter for Anna Rohony (Mr. Rohony's widow, including her maiden name, Gereben) for two of the accounts. On February 11, 1964, HypoSwiss Bank duly reported to the Swiss Ministry of Justice the existence of Mr. Rohony's safe deposit box, as well as the six pass books and the two keys.

Three days later, a Mr. Weber of the Lost Assets Department of the Ministry of Justice reported in a Memorandum to the File, that he had received the report of the HypoSwiss bank on the assets of Johannes Rohony. Exactly two weeks after Weber recorded receipt of the report, the widow Rohony, remarried and taking the name Anna Magos, inquired in a letter with the Swiss Ministry of Justice about her deceased husband's account. The inquiry was sent to the same Mr. Weber at the Ministry of Justice. Now, Weber had both the bank's report on the Rohony assets and Anna Magos's inquiry on the same assets.

In August, Weber answered Magos's inquiry, sending to her in Vienna, the proper forms to complete providing the information on her husband's assets. On April 28, 1966, in a memorandum to the file, Weber wrote that the names of Müller and Rotter appeared to be fictitious and that the accounts should be turned over to a court-ordered trustee to administer. He also recommended that two specific accounts be merged into one and some of the currency be included as well. On June 10, 1966, HypoSwiss Bank informed Weber this would be done. Three days later, Weber wrote to the Swiss courts to have them appoint a trustee for the Rohony assets and on December 27, 1966, Dr. H. Häberlin was appointed a trustee for those assets.

Despite the fact all this had already been done without telling Magos, on January 23, 1968, Weber write her in Vienna again seeking the completed forms about her husband's assets. On February 1, 1968, Weber's letter was returned as undeliverable and the Magos's case was then considered closed.

On August 30, 1968, in a memorandum to the file, Weber explained the peculiar visit of a Ms. Ilona Varga, widow of Bela Rotter, seeking information on an account he might have had in a Swiss bank. While Ms. Varga was there, she mentioned that her friend Anna Magos, née

Gereben, was also looking for the assets of her husband. Varga supplied Weber with Magos' new address. On the same day, Weber sent out the same information forms to Magos, now at the address in Munich. Two weeks later, Magos returned the completed forms to Weber detailing information about a safety deposit box at another bank in Zurich, the Union Bank of Switzerland, not at the HypoSwiss Bank where her husband had taken out box no. 137. She listed gold items, currency in dollars, stamps, and a cigarette case. She also said her husband and her had always lived in Budapest, not Amsterdam.

Deceitfully, Weber then wrote Magos on September 24, 1968, asking her three questions: Were there any other residences of her husband, other than Budapest? Was there any relationship to people in Switzerland? And finally, did her husband inform him of all of his business relationships?

With the dual role of recipient of the banks' report of the assets of Johannes Rohony, and the interlocutor as well with Anna Magos, Weber was in the unique position to either provide her with leads, or to ask questions she simply could not answer. He chose the latter, asking questions, based on knowledge he had, but she did not and could not know he had obtained. The leading nature of his questions show this clearly. It also seems from viewing the documents, she had no knowledge of the safety deposit box no. 137 at HypoSwiss Bank, hence the question about her knowledge of her husband's business affairs.

On September 10, 1968, Magos responded in a handwritten letter, unable to answer Weber's questions with the limited knowledge she had about her husband's safe deposit boxes. Two months later, Weber in a memorandum to the file, explained that the case was "confusing," and that her answers to his questions did not clarify the case any more. Because she was wrong about the names she listed as having been her husband's friends outside of Switzerland, she was therefore by connection wrong about the bank she listed in Zurich as well. Accordingly, three days later, Weber wrote back to Magos informing her that because she could not provide them with the correct information, including the names of her husband's friends outside of Switzerland and their dates of birth, nothing more could be done.

Five years passed, and on June 13, 1973, 24,659.50 sfr. from the account books were turned over to the Special Fund, established in the Disclosure Decree for distribution by the Swiss Government to charity. This amount represents the principle assets of the accounts as well as some interest, although the proper amount is still in dispute.

From this point, nothing more happened until October 1, 1997, when Susan Ungar, the Rohonny's daughter, spoke with accountants seeking information on her father's assets from Ernst & Young, the accounting firm handling requests for information from claimants. By letter shortly thereafter, she was informed that there was no record of assets for her late father. Less than a month later, however, on October 29, 1997, when the Swiss Bankers' Association published the second of its two lists of dormant accounts, the name of Johannes Rohony appeared.

Mrs. Unger then contacted our office and I spoke to her. I told her we would try to help her. When D'Amato wrote his first letter to Federal Reserve Chairman Alan Greenspan on February 5, 1998, opposing the proposed merger of UBS and SBC, we included the Rohony case to prove the banks participated in an ongoing conspiracy to conceal and prevent the recovery of assets.

When UBS and SBC jointly responded to D'Amato's charges, they made reference to UBS finding an account such as that described in D'Amato's letter, but refused to identify it as being the assets of Mr. Rohony, for reasons of confidentiality. Nevertheless, they said they would turn over the information to the Swiss Federal Banking Commission.

Finally, on April 6, 1998, almost sixty years after her father opened the account at HypoSwiss Bank, UBS, as the successors to the HypoSwiss bank, wrote Mrs. Ungar informing her they were willing to offer her the 24,659.50 sfr. turned over to the Special Fund in 1973, plus interest, bringing the total to 53,377.45 sfr. UBS agreed that if the Volcker Commission's Interest and Fee Panel, chaired by Economist Henry Kaufman, ruled on the addition of more interest to this amount they would of course pay this the agreed upon sum. It was with this letter, that the documents verifying this sordid and unfortunate story came to light for the first time.[5]

"Our country made mistakes..."

"Your accusation against our country, because of our behavior during the second world war," wrote Paul Stalder of Hondrich, Switzerland, "broke in over our nation like waves of the sea."[6] "I know," Stalder wrote in a thoughtful letter, "that our country made mistakes during that time, like many others.... You can be assured that it its painful for me and for many people in Switzerland to have this fact in rememberance and I can understand your accusations against our country."[7] This Swiss citizen was explaining his shock at the disclosures that were made against his country, suddenly he felt, out of the blue. Some Swiss, however, could not understand what was happening to their country.

For some, the accusations caused not "waves," but disgust. "Now, as peace is dawning in the Middle East, fundraising for the Jewish Cause is getting tougher and tougher...Hightime [sic] for picturing a new enemy and for undigging a new gold-mine," wrote T.E. Itin, of Basel, Switzerland.

The Swiss banking scandal, brought out the worst of the Swiss people, in action as well as words. We were accused of encouraging anti-Semitism, of spreading lies, and of unjustly attacking a peaceful nation trying to avoid annihilation by the Nazis. While we did not endear ourselves to the Swiss, we did manage to do what was not done before. We forced open the door to Swiss secrecy, not only bank secrecy, but to that of their entire wartime history. In the beginning we vowed that when we were done, the term "neutral" as it applied to a nation, would never quite mean the same thing again. I think we succeded in accomplishing this.

In what began as an interesting proposal, became a crusade for D'Amato, Bronfman, Singer, Steinberg, our researchers, officials spread throughout the administration, and attorneys and public finance officers across the country. The country itself became swept up in the investigation that produced headlines almost daily. Many of us formed a cottage industry speaking all over the country, in Canada, and even Europe. Sometimes, if one of the ever expanding group could not talk, we passed the offer to another. Interest in the topic was, and remains incredible.

Researchers too, became fascinated by the thought of finding dormant accounts, looted gold, new and undiscovered plots by the "evil Swiss bankers." The National Archives never had such good "business." With lawsuits against over a dozen European banks and companies now making their way through the courts, there are full teams of researchers at the Archives, including those for Barclays Bank and Ford Motor Company.

With the settlement no one believed would ever occur, problems arose and will remain unresolved for some time. The attorneys who brought suit against the Swiss banks and have been left with presenting a plan for disbursement to Judge Korman are at the same time fighting to ensure their clients receive the proper justice, and that they receive the proper attention. Fagan, long upset over Hausfeld and Weiss' entry into the lawsuit game expressed anger to me over his colleagues' seeming interference over his "financial stake" in the settlement.

"I can take care of Hausfeld and Weiss in the press," Fagan boasted. "I'm going to get one of Hausfeld's black clients and put him up there to say he'll take money from niggers but not kikes."[8] Fagan's reference to blacks is to those Hausfeld represented in his racial discrimination case against Texaco, in which Hausfeld did not take on a pro bono basis. Yet, Fagan would fight on in pursuit of fees he denies requesting, but continues to seek.[9]

For D'Amato, the settlement, would seemingly cap a triumphant three year struggle to bring the Swiss banks to justice. While it had started simply as a good idea, the victory in this great battle, we had all thought would by circumstance, translate into victory for Al D'Amato at the polls. This entire process, contrary to what many in Switzerland had declared, was not about winning re-election, it was about justice. Nevertheless, if we could gain a victory in November, no one could blame us.

Yet, as things turned out, this would not come to pass. D'Amato, the consummate underdog and fighter for the forgotten middle class, was unable to stem the tide. In a clear victory for Representative Charles Schumer, D'Amato lost his in fourth bid for the Senate. It was bitter and hard fought, clearly the most watched in the nation.

While we were quite displeased about its outcome, the Swiss, naturally were elated. Based on a faxed letter from Sofia, Bulgaria, to where he was banished by Alfred Defago, David Vogelsanger, the erstwhile member of the Swiss Embassy in Washington, defined Swiss hatred for D'Amato and for that matter, even me, when he wrote:

Dear Ex-Senator D'Amato:

I should like to congratulate you upon your miserably failed reelection to the United States Senate. As a Swiss citizen, I am proud of the New Yorkers who have sent you where you belong, on the dung-heap of cheap and corrupted politics. Your campaign of lies against my country has not saved your political career from oblivion, as planned. I savor the irony that your back was finally broken by your allies in the anti-Swiss smear campaign, the Clintons and the Holocaust exploiters.

Give my regards also to Gregg Rickmann, the little filth-scraper who provided you with the pseudo-historical dirt to throw at us. As for the damage you have undoubtedly done to the over two hundred year old relations between the two oldest democracies in the world, better people than you will work hard to repair it and succeed.

While D'Amato had lost, it was clear that he had made his mark.

In the end Switzerland, individual nations in Europe, not to mention museums, insurance companies and other banks in Europe and the

United States as well, came and will come under investigation. In the coming years, much will be disclosed about what they did and did not do before, during and after World War II. People will want to know if there was another nation which acted like Switzerland during the war or after. People will want to find what we did not examine and they will want to examine what we already looked at to find more.

* * *

It is rare in life that one is fortunate enough to be a participant in a great enterprise. Moreover, it is rarer still to see such an enterprise to a conclusion. I feel honored to have been a part of just such an effort. The campaign to squeeze justice, albeit a measure of justice, was long and tortured, by our standards. Yet, when one considers how long the survivors waited, it was but a blink of the eye. The result has, admittedly not been complete, but it called attention to fact that after more than fifty years, the suffering of the Holocaust will not be forgotten.

While the Swiss banks were brought to justice, the work has not completely been finished, and perhaps it may never be. But as Stuart Eizenstat attested before the Senate Banking Committee in May 1997, "our task, therefore, is to complete the unfinished business of the 20th century's most traumatic and tragic events."[10]

While money cannot solve all the ills of the world, we can only hope that by bringing the Swiss banks to justice, those victimized first by the Nazis and then by the Swiss, can rest a bit easier now. Because justice is never really complete, the dispute will in the end, remain between Swiss banks and Jewish souls.

Notes

1. Letter of Louis Lipsky, American Jewish Conference to Secretary of State James F. Byrnes, 5 February 1946, RG 56, Department of the Treasury, International Statistics Division, Germany 1931–1952, Box 84, NARA.
2. Military Intelligence Division, Current Events # 485 Report, Switzerland, 15 October 1942, RG 59, Records of the State Department, NARA.
3. Letter of Secretary of State James Byrnes to the American Legation in Bern, 23 November 1945, Enclosure of Puhl-Funk Correspondence, 23 March 1945, p. 3, RG 131 Foreign Funds Control, NARA.
4. Letter of Harald Huber to Dr. Fritz Wahlen.
5. Letter of Dr. U. Grete and Dr. D. Heini, Group Executive Board, Union Bank of Switzerland, to Mrs. Susan Ungar, 6 April 1998, with documents enclosed. Translation by Willi Korte.
6. Letter of Paul Stalder to United States Senator Alfonse M. D'Amato, 12 October 1997.
7. Ibid.

8. Telephone discussion with Edward Fagan, 3 September 1998.
9. See "German Jewish leader protests 250 mln [sic] dollar fee for US lawyer," Agence France-Presse, 14 October 1998.
10. Testimony of Under Secretary of Commerce Stuart E. Eizenstat, before the Senate Committee and Banking, Housing and Urban Affairs hearing, "Swiss Banks and Attempts to Recover Assets Belonging to the Victims of the Holocaust," 105th Congress, 1st Sesssion, 15 May 1997, p. 17.

Index